Documents on the Expulsion of the Sudeten Germans

Original German edition: *Dokumente zur Austreibung der Sudetendeutschen.* Selbstverlag der Arbeitsgemeinschaft zur Wahrung Sudetendeutscher Interessen, 1951. Bearbeitet und mit einer Einleitung von Dr. Wilhelm Turnwald.

First English edition: Incomplete, abridged translation of the German original by Gerda Johannsen: *Documents on the Expulsion of the Sudeten Germans.* Study Group for the Preservation of Sudeten German Interests, 1951. With an introduction by Dr. Wilhelm Turnwald.

Scriptorium Reprint: Complete translation of the German original: Gerda Johannsen's selections completed by Victor Diodon and Arnim Johannis under the auspices of The Scriptorium: *Documents on the Expulsion of the Sudeten Germans: Survivors Speak Out.* 1st edition ©2002, 2nd edition ©2022 by The Scriptorium.
wintersonnenwende.com
versandbuchhandelscriptorium.com

A Note to the Reader: please pardon the occasional wrong hyphenation at the end of lines, as well as incorrect formatting of some section titles and between some of the individual reports. The software with which this book is printed inserts these elements automatically, and manual corrections are almost impossible. The actual content is not affected by these flaws.

Our cover design shows ethnic Germans being rounded up under the pretense of being taken to an internment camp for Germans, before being executed in Prague, May 1945. Image source: Wikimedia Commons / Jacksonmcdonald3425, licensed under the Creative Commons Attribution-Share Alike 4.0 International license.

Print edition ISBN 978-1-998785-00-1
ebook ISBN 978-1-998785-01-8

Documents on the Expulsion of the Sudeten Germans

Survivors Speak Out

Dr. Wilhelm Turnwald

translated by Gerda Johannsen, Victor Diodon and Arnim Johannis

8 paws
an army

The Scriptorium

CONTENTS

After the Second World War ended in 1945, one of the most gruesome genocides took place that the history of mankind has ever seen: **the expulsion and destruction of the Sudeten Germans.** The German government has kept knowledge of this extermination and the huge files of documentary evidence quiet, in other words, this chapter of history is supposed to remain tucked away in the hindmost corners of the Federal German archives, there to gather dust and be forgotten. **Its publication is not desired.**

The poor souls who were tortured to a gruesome death can no longer tell their story - but the survivors can. Driven into a truncated Germany of rubble and ruins, where the people had enough to do to get their own lives back under control, the Sudeten Germans soon gave up trying to tell of their suffering; they buried the knowledge deep within themselves - but nevertheless their story has not been lost, as it was summarized (at least in part) in a book titled *Dokumente zur Austreibung der Sudetendeutschen - **Documents on the Expulsion of the Sudeten Germans** -* and it is our moral duty to those who were tormented to death, to tell the world about this death march of a people.

Hushing-up these events has resulted in the fact that many members of even their own ethnic group do not know the truth about the expulsion, much less the younger generation of the nation that expelled them. On the contrary, misinformation from sources with vested interests has left the younger Czech generations with the mistaken belief that they were made to suffer injustices and thus have a claim to restitution. They feel that the Beneš Decrees and the expulsion were warranted. It's hard so see, however, how this can be justified in light of Czechoslovakia's admission to the European Union. The German government, instead of backing its own people, is on the side of the perpetrators' nation and supports its demands. In times of economic hardship even the expellees themselves send "care parcels" to those people whose parents and grandparents robbed them of their home and all they had. Just one case in point is the extensive aid that was sent when the "flood of the century" wrought havoc in parts of Czechoslovakia because the expellers had neglected maintenance on the Oder River. The expellees have ever dispensed with revenge and are satisfied if they can just pay the occasional visit to their old homeland and the present "owners" of what had been their and their forefathers' own possessions.

An ethnic group that has been psychologically browbeaten into cultural illness for half a century is beginning to beg the murderers of its ethnic siblings for forgiveness. For what, may we ask? Perhaps for the things you will read about here? Think about that for a moment.

Everyone has a right to one's homeland, and every people has the right to honor its dead - except for the Sudeten Germans, who evidently have neither.

Scriptorium, December 2022

Foreword, First English Edition

The displacements or expulsions of entire populations of "ethnic groups" from their native soil will surely go down to history as characteristic of our era. It is the expulsions of the eastern, south eastern, and Sudeten Germans which, today, confront Europe with the acutest problem of this nature. The problem created by the expulsion of more than a million Greeks from Anatolia and Eastern Thrace in 1922 was a tragedy which has not been wholly overcome even to the present day. The problem of the "displaced persons" of central, eastern, and southern Europe, the flight of Arabs from Israel, and the vast twofold exodus of Hindoos and Moslems resulting from the partition of India, still confront us. The number of persons affected far exceeds the number of those that made up the great "migrations of the peoples" following upon the breakup of the Roman Empire.

The displacements and expulsions in our own day have been accompanied by barbaric deeds and methods that violate natural law, the teachings of Christianity, and the ethical standards of human-ism. The foundations of international law and of those human rights, in which the last century took such pride, have been shaken by inhumanities which previous generations associated with the barbaric excesses of a distant past.

The first wave of expulsions began during and after the First World War, the second accom-panied and followed the Second World War. It is noteworthy that these expulsions were not all of a unilateral nature. Some of them were ordered or sanctioned at conferences held by the Great Powers - at the Potsdam Conference in 1945, for example. That this should be so would seem to indicate a deep-seated moral defection of an ominous character.

The dissolution of Austria-Hungary did not, in the end, confer upon the original component States the independence they had hoped for. It was followed by an explosive nationalism which operated to the grave detriment of these States by overriding those realities which are determined by geography, numerical strength, and industrial productivity. Excessive nationalism, at times con-cealed beneath doctrines of an ostensible religious or racial character, was amongst the principal forces that engendered the displacements and expulsions.

The creation of a truly organic order in eastern and central Europe was largely thwarted because the right of self-determination was applied in a one-sided manner, to the almost exclusive advantage of the victorious Powers. No "new Switzerland" was established in central Europe, but a region of crises and tensions.

To-day, out of three million Sudeten Germans, two and a half million live as exiles in Germany, most of them in the Federal Republic. The Federal Republic is a friendly land, but it is not their homeland. About one third of the exiles live in the Democratic Republic, amongst a friendly people, it is true, but under Communist domination, the same domination that oppresses their native Czechoslovakia. The Sudeten Germans, therefore, have no true home in Europe to-day, though this fate is not theirs alone - it is shared by millions of Europeans.

This is the essence of the matter. There can be no Europe as an organic whole unless the millions of Europeans in exile can return to their homes. The line known as the Iron Curtain, not only cuts Europe in two, it passes through the heart, cutting that in two. But how shall this division be brought to an end? How is Europe to be restored, to become an organic whole and endure for generations?

These are matters of high policy that will be decided in Washington, London, and Moscow. Upon high policy, the nations of Central Europe can have little influence. But whatever happens (and we do not know, to-day, whether events will move towards a renewed catastrophe or towards a true and general peace) the peoples of Central Europe can promote those conditions which are essential if high policy is not to be rendered abortive. Even if catastrophe comes, those peoples will continue to exist and will surely contribute to the common cause, the European cause. Whether it be peace or war, Western Europe will need the peoples of Central Europe who can prepare in embryo, as it were, their common future and can combine in pursuit of their common purpose - to become the living heart of the European organism.

The following documents provide evidence showing what extreme nationalism can lead to if it is not curbed by sober statesmanship. The present perilous condition of the world makes it seem imperative that the disrupted central European order be restored in the interest not only of the nations immediately concerned, but of all Europe. Memories of a common past, of common aspirations, and of complementary economic interests have revived, in the region, the idea of a federation or of a confederacy. The precise form which any new association of States might assume cannot be determined in advance, but whatever form it may take, it must assuredly be of a kind that will render impossible such deeds and methods as are revealed in these documents.

London, May 1953.
F. A. Voigt

The expulsion of the Sudeten German national group which started in May 1945 is one of those important events which have caused the apparently hopeless situation in Central Europe. As the principal outcome of the expulsion, the Russian sphere of activity and influence has been advanced into the heart of our continent. Unfortunately the expulsion itself, the methods used, the planning and organization of the general excesses (which would seem to contravene the United Nation's Convention relating to genocide) are insufficiently known to the public.

In this fully documented memorandum, the events are described by eyewitnesses or persons directly involved. These reports illustrate only a small part of the dreadful acts perpetrated in the course of expulsion, but they nevertheless try to give some kind of a general view of what happened in the Sudeten German areas since May 1945. The following preface presents a historical and political survey, characterizing the reasons and motives of the expulsion as well as the originators of these excesses. The appendix presents the more important diplomatic, legislative and documentary details.

The publication of these documents is by no means intended to attribute collective guilt to the Czechoslovak nation. It is intended to show how greatly ethical standards and international and natural right were injured by these excesses. Morally and legally the Sudeten Germans have a claim to their homeland which was theirs for almost a thousand years. They have a right, also, to reparation and to the punishment of the culprits. With the expulsion of the Sudeten Germans, Central Europe lost its balance. There is no solution to the Sudeten German and Czechoslovak problems except within the frame of a new European Order.

For the Committee
of the Association for the Protection of Sudeten German Interests:

[sgd.:]

Hans Schütz,
Member of the Bundestag

Dr. Rudolf Lodgman von Auen

Richard Reitzner
Member of the Bundestag

Translation Credits

(Note added by The Scriptorium:)

At this point we would like to add an explanatory note regarding the translations you are about to read.

In 2002, while getting our English translation of the book *Dokumente zur Austreibung der Sudetendeutschen* ready for publication on the Internet, we had the good fortune to come across a partial translation already in existence: a little less than one-third of the reports contained in the original book were translated into English in the early 1950s by Gerda Johannsen, and we have retained these translations here. However, we have supplemented the selection of reports translated by Ms. Johannsen by our own translations of those reports which were left out of the original English publication. The following credits the translator/s of the individual reports:

Reports translated by Gerda Johannsen as published in the aforementioned volume (some *very* slight changes for the sake of "readability" have been made in a few cases by The Scriptorium's translators and/or editor): Preface; Introduction; Reports Aussig 1, 4, 6; Brünn 1, 4, 7; Brux 1; Budweis 2; Gablonz 2; Jägerndorf 5; Kladno 2; Landskron; Mährisch Ostrau 4; Olmütz 2, 3, 5, 7; Pilsen 1, 2; Prague 4, 10, 11, 15; Reichenberg 1, 4, 7; Saaz-Postelberg; Teplitz-Schönau 1, 5; Tetschen-Bodenbach 2; Troppau 1, 3; Arnau; Asch; Barzdorf; Bautsch; Bergesgrün; Bilin; Bischofteinitz 3; Böhmisch Kamnitz 2; Chodau 1, 4, 5; Dittersdorf 2; Dobraken; Duppau 1; Eipel; Eisenstein-Grün; Elbogen 1; Freudenthal 1; Gross-Schönau; Grulich; Haindorf; Heinzendorf; Hermannstadt; Hloubetin; Kaaden; Karlsthal; Karlsstadt; Klattau 2; Klein-Herrlitz; Kleinbocken; Kolin 2; Königshof; Krautenwalde; Kurim 2; Langenlutsch; Liebeznice; Mies 2-4; Münchengrätz; Neurohlau 2, 4; Nikolsburg 2; Ober-Lipka; Parschnitz; Qualisch; Radonitz; Radwanitz 1, 2; Riegersdorf; Römerstadt 1, 2; Sankt Joachimsthal 2; Schlag; Schönhengst; Sörgsdorf; Stecken; Sternberg 2; Tepl 1; Totzau; Tremošna; Tschachwitz; Tschenkowitz; Tschirm; Tuschkau 2; Udritsch; Vollmau; Warnsdorf 1; Weidenau 2; Wekelsdorf 2; Witeschau; Appendices 1, 5, 7-16, 19.

Reports translated by Victor Diodon and/or Arnim Johannis under the auspices of The Scriptorium: Reports Aussig 2, 3, 5, 7; Brünn 2, 3, 5, 6, 8, 9; Brüx 2; Budweis 1; Freiwaldau 1-6; Gablonz 1, 3; Iglau 2-4; Jägerndorf 1-4; Karlsbad 1-8; Kladno 1; Komotau; Mährisch Ostrau 1-3; Mährisch Schönberg 1, 2; Olmütz 1, 4, 6; Pilsen 3, 4; Prague 2, 3, 5-9, 12-14, 16, 17; Reichenberg 2, 3, 5, 6; Teplitz-Schönau 2-4; Tetschen-Bodenbach 1; Theresienstadt 2, 3; Troppau 2, 4-9;

Alt-Bürgersdorf; Althart; Altrohlau; Altrothwasser; Arlsdorf; Arnsdorf; Auherzen-Lihn; Auschine-Raudnai; Bennisch 1-4; Beraun; Berkowitz; Bischofteinitz 1, 2; Blatna; Blauendorf; Bodenbach; Böhmisch Krummau 1, 2; Böhmisch Leipa; Böhmisch Meseritsch; Böhmisch Trübau; Braunau; Bretterschlag; Brüsau; Bürgersdorf; Butschafka 1-3; Chodau 2, 3; Chrastawitz; Chrostau; Datschitz; Deutsch-Beneschau 1, 2; Deutsch-Jassnik; Deutsch-Lodenitz; Dittersdorf 1; Dobris; Dolawitz; Domeschau; Duppau 2, 3; Eisenstein; Elbogen 2-4; Ernstbrunn; Falkenau; Fischern; Frankstadt 1, 2; Freudenthal 2; Friedrichswald; Giesshübl-Sauerbrunn; Graslitz; Gross-Hermersdorf; Gross-Sichdichfür; Haida; Hakelsdorf; Hals; Hannsdorf; Hennersdorf; Hermersdorf; Hinterkotten; Hohenfurth 1-3; Holleischen-Staab; Hostau; Jauernig 1-3; Josefstadt; Jungferndorf; Karwin 1, 2; Klattau 1, 3; Kleinmohrau; Klösterle and Kaaden; Kohling, Schindelwald and Schönlind; Kojetitz; Kolin 1; Komoschau; Königinhof; Kremsier; Kunzendorf; Kurim 1; Liblin; Libochowan; Liebenau; Liebesdorf; Littau; Lyssa; Mährisch Rothwasser; Mährisch Trübau; Malschin; Maschau; Meier-höfen; Melnik; Mies 1, 5; Modrany; Motol; Mühlbach; Neudek; Neuhof; Neurohlau 1, 3, 5; Neu-titschein 1, 2; Nieder-Mohrau and Olmütz; Niemes and Grottau; Nikolsburg 1; Oberpaulowitz; Oderfurt; Pardubitz-Königgrätz 1, 2; Pattersdorf; Pisek and Brünn; Plan; Podmoky; Pohorsch and Karwin; Polepp and Leitmeritz; Pössigkau and Taus; Pribrans and Prague; Radl; Reichenau; Reinowitz; Riesengebirge (the Sudeten Mountains); Rokitnitz; Rosshaupt; Sankt Joachimsthal 1; Schankau; Schildberg; Schlackenwerth, Karlsbad, Kaschlitz and Spickengrün; Schlaggenwald 1, 2; Schönbach; Schönlinde; Schwarzental and Hohenelbe; Schwarzwasser and Freiwaldau 1-3; Setzdorf; Spillendorf; Stefanau; Sternberg 1, 3, 4; Stimmersdorf; Strakonitz and Brünn; Tabor 1, 2; Tachau 1, 2; Tannwald; Tepl 2; Triebendorf; Tüppelsgrün; Tuschkau 1; Unterparsching; Vorderheuraffel; Waldau; Wallern; Warnsdorf 2; Weidenau 1; Weidsiefen; Wekelsdorf 1; Welpet; Willens; Witkowitz; Wockendorf; Zittau; Zlin; Znaim; Zwittau.

Reports translated in abridged form by Gerda Johannsen and completed as necessary by Victor Diodon and/or Arnim Johannis, *OR* reports translated by Gerda Johannsen with more than minor corrections being necessary, and corrected accordingly by Victor Diodon and/or Arnim Johannis: A Note Concerning these Reports, Reports Iglau 1; Prague 1; Theresienstadt 1; Altsattel; Böhmisch Kamnitz 1; Böhmisch Krummau 3; Brunnersdorf; Friedland; Karthaus; Trautenau.

The Scriptorium, 2022

Introduction

I.

Three times since the First World War the Sudeten German national group (which is more numerous than the Norwegian nation and almost as numerous as the Danish and Finnish nations) became an object of international policy, without obtaining a satisfactory solution of the Sudeten German problem. This problem was not invented by Hitler and Henlein. It represents a real problem of space and population. The reasons for this fact are various, but they may be traced back to some fundamental data of Central European history and politics.

Until the 18th century the nations in Central Europe were held together by the dynastic idea as well as by a territorial, as distinct from national, conception of the State. Several wars against the Turks hereby played an essential part as co-operating Western defensive actions. Rationalism and new nationalistic ideas, as transmitted to the European nations by the French Revolution, the replacement of the hierarchic social order by a middle class society, and, in particular, the beginning of a new national consciousness, as formulated by Johann Gottfried Herder and imported to the nations of Central Europe, produced a powerful ferment and movement amongst these nations.[1]

Since the collapse of the Austro-Hungarian monarchy, which offered tolerable political and economic conditions for the various nations and national groups until 1918, this special area of Central Europe has been unable to find a lasting peace. It became one of the neuralgic zones of the continent which demanded the healing art of great and statesmanlike judgement and intelligence. Unfortunately there has not been a cure to this day. Instead of learning something from the different attempts at a solution since 1918, new blunders concerning Central European politics, blunders of great consequences, were made after the Second World War. The Czech-German problem was of special importance. The Czech politicians Thomas Masaryk and Eduard Beneš contributed essentially to the downfall of Austria-Hungary. Referring to President Woodrow Wilson's principles of self-determination and to the historical and constitutional law of Bohemia, they both pursued the foundation of a "Czechoslovak Republic", without succeeding in the creation of a true Czech National State since the non-Czech parts of the population amounted to more than 50% of the entire population. To these national minorities and especially to the 3½ million Sudeten Germans the right of self-determination was refused, even though Austria-Hungary had been destroyed and the Czechoslovak Republic had been established with the help of this right. The creators of the first Czechoslovak Republic were rooted in the nationalism of the 19th century. It was for this reason that they were unable to solve the problem created by the existence of several nations in one body politic. All suggestions for a lasting solution which were made between 1918 and 1938 fell short of expectations, because the Czechs strove for a national state while denying national rights to the nations that composed it.

It was to be foreseen that the expulsion of the Sudeten German group could never definitely settle this Central European question. The idea of the expulsion had its source in the extremely chauvinistic nationalism of which Dr. Beneš was the principal exponent. Nationalism, as an acceptable European ideology, is disproved by this extreme attempt at a solution which shows that it cannot solve the existing problems of space and population, but can only aggravate them greatly. Too many reasons of a historical, political, economical, juridical and ethical nature speak against this kind of solution. But few people could have foreseen that the consequences of the expulsion in 1945 would, after such a short time, recoil on the Czech nation itself.[2]

II.

Of all the Western Slav nations the Czechs extend furthest into Central Europe. In the course of historical developments, the Czechs showed great skill and political adaptability in preserving their national substance in the midst of a German population which surrounded them from north, west and south. The manner of their success is very instructive. In 845 - as reported in the Annals of Fulda - 14 leaders of Bohemian tribes were baptized at Regensburg. Thus they got access to the Western sphere, to its religion and its civilization; and from that time on the living connection between Bohemia, Moravia and the Western German neighbour was never sundered.

During the reign of Charles the Great, the Czechs became tributaries after a short campaign and in the 10th century the Czech Duke Wenzel, later canonized by the Catholic Church, skilfully improved the constitutional tie with Germany by means of his personal connections. In the following years the Bohemian dukes attained the German electoral dignity and received the royal crown from the German Emperor. In the 14th century the Emperor Charles IV, whose grandmother was a princess of the Bohemian Přemyslid nobility, elected Prague as his residence. On account of the diplomatic and politically skilful attitude of its leaders, the Czech nation avoided the fate of the Elbe Slavs, who lost their national independence in constant fights with the Germans. The close political union with the German neighbour brought the Czechs into cultural and economic as well as religious and ecclesiastical association with the Europe of the time.

The part played by the Germans in Bohemia and Moravia was extraordinarily positive. In the capacity of priests and courtiers they worked in the ducal and royal residence at Prague. They built cities, not only in the German colonized border zones but also in the interior of Bohemia. An exception was the Hussite settlement of Tábor. They cultivated land and forests and began mining operations. They brought into the country the juridical systems of the Nuremberg and Magdeburg laws. Their participation in the domain of arts was pre-eminent. The city of Prague with its history and its buildings will remain a permanent symbol of their creative genius.

The specific rights of the Germans in Bohemia were confirmed at an early date, as stated in the Charter[3] of Duke Sobieslaus II (1173-1178). For a thousand years, the two peoples lived together in rarely interrupted, productive co-operation in the region of Bohemia, Moravia and Silesia. If we turn over the leaves of the book of history, we shall observe that the periods of peaceful co-operation engendered an efflorescence of culture and economic prosperity. But periods of strife - e.g. the Hussite wars - were attended by a general decline.

It was the development of the national spirit in the 19th century that caused the severest rupture between Germans and Czechs since the time of the Hussites. But no solution was found either in 1918 or in 1938; and so the end came in the dreadful tragedy of 1945, to which the following documents relate.

The historical development in the region of Bohemia and Moravia shows the disastrous effects of any ideology or historical interpretation which falsifies the true progress of events in this region. We are referring to the interpretation of history as given by the Czech historian of the 19th century, Palacký, who regarded the struggle between Germans and Czechs as the leitmotif of history in the territory of Bohemia, Moravia and Silesia, and the Hussite period as the heroic age of the Czech nation. It is true that the most important Czech historian of our century, Josef Pekař, stressed the positive side of Czech-German relations, so signally personified in the symbolic figure of the statesman Duke Wenzel the Saint. But the Czech political leaders since the First World War, Masaryk and Beneš, were deeply rooted in the historical interpretation of Palacký. This nationalistic application of history visibly bears the origin of the tragic development of the most recent chapter in the history of the Czech nation.

III.

To place the events of the year 1945 in their proper perspective, it is necessary to go back to the periods around 1938 and 1918. The dissolution of the Austro-Hungarian monarchy was accomplished by virtue of the principle of self-determination of peoples. But this same right of self-determination was refused to the Germans in Austria-Hungary. The Sudeten German national group in Bohemia, Moravia and Silesia was incorporated into the Czechoslovak Republic without being consulted. The German delegates from Bohemia, Moravia and Silesia, elected by the Austrian Imperial Council (Reichsrat) in 1911, had decided to establish the Austrian provinces "Deutsch-Böhmen" and "Sudetenland" and to put them under the protection of the new Austrian Republic. But these resolutions were not acknowledged by the Peace Conference. The governments of the Länder (headed first by Rafael Pacher and later by Dr. Rudolf Lodgman von Auen in Bohemia and Dr. Robert Freissler in Moravia-Silesia) were expelled by the Czechs. On March 4th, 1919 the Sudeten German population of all political tendencies demonstrated for their right of self-determination at public meetings in different parts of the country. This political declaratory act of the population was forcibly suppressed by the Czech executive, an action in which many Sudeten Germans lost their lives. As soon as the problem of the German minority in Czechoslovakia came before the Paris Peace Conference (St. Germain) in 1919, the Czechoslovak Peace Delegation, led by the Minister of Foreign Affairs Dr. Beneš, defined their point of view on this problem, especially in Memorandum No. 3,[4] with the intention of dispersing the apprehensions above all of the British delegates. Dr. Beneš must be considered the principal author of the memoranda.

With psychological insight he realised the situation at the Paris Peace Conference and anticipated in his memoranda all the answers to the questions he might have been asked.[5] Memorandum No. 3 contains several crude forgeries of a statistical, economic and historical, as well as a political nature. But above all, Chapter 6 of the aforementioned memorandum is important as describing the future fate of the German minority in the Czechoslovak Republic.[6]

The collection of maps attached to the memoranda gives a partially false idea of the distribution of population, location of settlements, etc. In this respect the map "Les Allemands de Bohême" was an extraordinarily crude attempt, for the compact German settlements are completely torn asunder by false insertions of Czech settlements and are also arbitrarily diminished in size. Thus the impression was created that there were no considerable compact German regions worth mentioning in Bohemia. Between Leitmeritz and Komotau, for example, the Czech region reaches the frontier of Czechoslovakia, so that Teplitz is situated in the midst of a purely Czech region.[7]

Skillfully outlined in Chapter 6 of Memorandum No. 3 was a program concerning the annexation of Sudeten German territories, in which the Swiss Republic was presented as the model for the organization and constitution of the new Czechoslovak Republic. The principal subject was even more precisely expressed in a note, which Dr. Beneš submitted to the committee, elaborating the treaty for the protection of minorities. This step was prompted especially by the concerns of British and American authorities who feared a possible violation of the right of self-determination at the expense of the non-Czech parts of Czechoslovakia's population. The aforementioned note of May 20, 1919 stresses the strict intention of the Czechoslovak Government to accept as basis for the organization of the Czech State the Swiss Constitution, that is, to attempt a sort of new Switzerland at the heart of Europe.[8] With that idea Dr. Beneš believed he had an effective answer to a possible objection that the right of self-determination was not being applied in the special case of the Sudeten Germans. Dr. Beneš, as the actual historical and political development proves, did not intend for one single moment to carry out in Czechoslovakia the principles applied in the Swiss constitution. Memorandum No. 3 only served for the deception of the Peace Conference of St. Germain. An objective and critical examination will reveal that between 1918 and 1938 the Sudeten Germans in Czechoslovakia had no rights comparable with those existing under the Swiss constitution. On the contrary, the Czech authorities intended from the beginning to create an entirely Czech national state, even though the Czechs - as aforesaid - amounted to only 50% of the entire population. The obligations for the protection of national minorities, signed in the Constitutional Agreement of September 16, 1919, were also not observed. The attempts of the Sudeten Germans to secure observance of the obligations for the protection of minorities by submitting 22 Memoranda to the League of Nations at Geneva were in vain, for none of the 22 Memoranda were discussed in the League of Nations on account of Dr. Beneš' counter-measures. The development of the Czecho-Slovak internal situation shows that the Slovaks, too, were not treated as a national group with equal rights as agreed in the Treaty of Pittsburgh.[9]

German political parties of the first Czechoslovak Republic, so-called activist, tried to secure fulfilment of the Sudeten German requests and demands for equal rights for many years without any success.

We must take these facts into consideration if we are to judge the whole situation of 1938 in terms of cause and effect. The success of the Henlein Movement was, on the one hand, due to the unfulfilled promise of St. Germain to carry out the principles of the Swiss Constitution in Czechoslovakia, on the other hand to the belief that since 1933 all economic and political difficulties of the Weimar Republic were being solved by Hitler. The elimination of unemployment could not fail to impress the Sudeten Germans who suffered under the general economic depression, which grew more and more noticeable as a result of certain Czech measures in Sudeten German territories. As in these circumstances they had no hope that their legitimate demands would ever be granted without some assistance from outside, and unaware of the true political intentions of Adolf Hitler, they based all their hopes on German help. Hitler's success in foreign affairs could not fail to create the impression that the Great Powers did not disapprove of the developments in Germany. Furthermore it seemed that, in the beginning, the Henlein Movement was judged sympathetically, above all by British authorities. In home politics Henlein was temporarily favoured by some of the Czech parties, e.g. by the Agrarian Party, in the struggle between the Left and the Right, so that the German parties in the Government were often in difficulties. Events in Austria, especially the enthusiasm of the Austrian population on the occasion of the German occupation with its impressive power of mass-suggestion, had considerable effect on the Sudeten Germans. The one group within the "Sudeten German Party" which in the beginning propagated a Sudeten German autonomy in the Czecho-Slovak Republic lost practically its entire influence after the Austrian annexation.[10] If, after the First World War, the Czechoslovak Republic had been made a sort of Switzerland with full equality for the different national components and with the intention of creating a true neutrality, the whole political development in the areas of Bohemia, Moravia and Silesia would have taken another course. It is evident today that the new Czechoslovak State had the special function of being the Eastern guard against Germany - a function which was planned by the Western Powers, especially by France. But the burden imposed during the years after 1930 grew beyond the new State's control, even within the alliance of the Little Entente. Neutral observers who were in Czechoslovakia in 1938 often portrayed the real situation very clearly. In his report to the British Prime Minister of September 26, 1938, Lord Runciman recapitulated his statements and observations as follows:

"It is a hard thing to be ruled by an alien race; and I have been left with the impression that Czechoslovak rule in the Sudeten areas for the last twenty years, though not actually oppressive and certainly not 'terroristic', has been marked by tactlessness, lack of understanding, petty intolerance and discrimination, to a point where the resentment of the German population was inevitably moving in the direction of revolt. The Sudeten Germans felt, too, that in the past they had been given many promises by the Czechoslovak Government, but that little or no action had followed these promises. This experience had induced an attitude of open mistrust of the leading Czech statesmen. I cannot say how far this mistrust is merited or unmerited; but it certainly exists, with the result that, however conciliatory their statements, they inspire no confidence in the minds of the Sudeten population. Moreover, in the last elections of 1935 the Sudeten German party polled more votes than any other single party; and they actually formed the second largest party in the State

Parliament. They then commanded some 44 votes in a total Parliament of 300. With subsequent accessions, they are now the largest party. But they can always be outvoted; and consequently many of them feel that constitutional action is useless for them.

Local irritations were added to these major grievances. Czech officials and Czech police, speaking little or no German, were appointed in large numbers to purely German districts; Czech agricultural colonists were encouraged to settle on land transferred under the Land Reform in the middle of German populations. For the children of these Czech invaders Czech schools were built on a large scale.

There is a very general belief that Czech firms were favoured as against German firms in the allocation of State contracts and that the State provided work and relief for Czechs more readily than for Germans.

I believe these complaints to be in the main justified. Even as late as the time of my Mission, I could find no readiness on the part of the Czechoslovak Government to remedy them on anything like an adequate scale.

All these, and other, grievances were intensified by the effects of the economic crisis on the Sudeten industries, which form so important a part of the life of the people. Not unnaturally, the Government was blamed for the resulting impoverishment...

This brings me to the political side of the problem, which is concerned with the integrity and security of the Czechoslovak Republic, especially in relation to her immediate neighbours. I believe that here the problem is one of removing a centre of intense political friction from the middle of Europe. For this purpose it is necessary permanently to provide that the Czechoslovak State should live at peace with all her neighbours and that her policy, internal and external, should be directed to that end. Just as it is essential for the international position of Switzerland that her policy should be essentially neutral, so an analogous policy is necessary for Czechoslovakia - not only for her own future existence but for the peace of Europe."

In this last statement of his, Lord Runciman touches one of the fundamental problems, namely the possible existence of small national states in the heart of Europe. We shall briefly return to this problem later on.

From the Czech side the Sudeten Germans were collectively accused of having revolted against the State in September 1938, thereby threatening its security. A witness who certainly is no sympathizer of the Sudeten Germans, the Czech ex-Minister Dr. Hubert Ripka, testifies, in his account of events relating to the Munich Pact, that this accusation is untrue.

He states that Henlein's call to resistance against the supreme power was in no case obeyed by the majority of the Sudeten German population.[11] This fact is the more noteworthy because a strong police-terror was exercised towards the entire Sudeten German group. This terror showed itself in the internment of numerous hostages. In the opinion of Ripka, the main fault of the Czech Government was that it did not try to come to an agreement with the Sudeten German population instead of with Henlein.[12]

This might well have been possible, as Ripka averred, if since 1918 the Czechs had pursued a different policy towards the Sudeten Germans, that is if the latter had been treated as members of a federation like the Swiss, as equal amongst equals. But Ripka as well as Beneš avoided the problem of granting the right of self-determination to the Sudeten Germans. Like Beneš in the Memoranda of the Paris Peace Conference, he conferred this right upon the Czechs, but denied it to the Germans, and for reasons which are in no case clear.[13]

That the Sudeten Germans were merely used as a counter in the European game of politics in 1938 was expressly stated by the subsequent Prime Minster of Great Britain, Clement Attlee, in his speech in the House of Commons on October 3rd, 1938.[14]

The Munich Pact, however, should have made it clear to the Czechs that they, as well as the Sudeten Germans, were only a "counter in the game of politics" of the Great Powers, that they would have no importance as long as they were not united with the rest of the nations of Central Europe in a greater, federative union. The attempt to assimilate the Sudeten Germans was frustrated. Instead of letting the past decades be a warning and an experience, Dr. Beneš, with the assistance of his collaborators in exile, planned a solution of the Sudeten German problem which, after 1945, became a reality. This plan aggravated existing problems to an exorbitant extent, for it was a plan (rejected by Adolf Hitler for the Czech nation!) for the forcible dispossession and transfer of a whole nation in the heart of Central Europe.[15]

IV.

The expulsion of the Sudeten Germans was not the spontaneous reaction of the Czech nation to the German occupation of Czech territories from 1939 to 1945. The plan for an expulsion was carefully prepared by the Czech politicians in exile. Until the revolution of February 1948, there was a passionate dispute in the camp of the "National Front" at Prague regarding the priority of the idea of expelling the Sudeten Germans. The Czech Communist party-newspaper Rudé Právo maintained in February 1946 that the plan was first proposed on the occasion of the ratification of the Czechoslovako-Soviet Pact at Moscow, December 1943.[16]

The Chairman of the Foreign Affairs Committee in those days, Ivo Ducháček, delegate of the "Katholische Volkspartei" (Catholic National Liberal Party), who fled to the West after the February Revolution in 1948, protested against this statement in March 1946 in a parliamentary debate. Ducháček declared: "When in the summer of 1942 the question of transferring the German population reached the stage of private conversation with our three principal allies, Dr. Ripka took advantage of the fact that England and France had already rejected the Munich Pact, and made a public speech in October 1942.[17] Thereafter the question of our German population was more openly discussed from month to month in London. At the end of 1943 all members of the National Front were in agreement. The transfer of the German population was, therefore, the result of the combined efforts of all members and all parties belonging to the National Front. It is a falsification of history when the Communists maintain that the transfer of the Sudeten German population was their work. In a commentary it was pointed out that this transfer was already being discussed in 1939 in the circle around Dr. Ripka whose closest co-operator was Dr. Ducháček. As Dr. Beneš formulated the basic problems of the Czech exile-police exclusively according to his own conception, it can be assumed with certainty that the decisive and final initiator of the transfer idea was Dr. Beneš himself.

There had been rumours in New York since 1941 about a general "Beneš Plan", which was credited with the purpose of solving the problem of minorities by transferring them. These rumours were instigated by two articles by Dr. Beneš in leading periodicals devoted to political and foreign affairs, in which Dr. Beneš propagated the idea of transfer as a means of solving the problem of minorities.[18] As these articles did not state clearly whether the measures planned concerned the Sudeten Germans only, or whether they also applied to non-Czech minorities in the special case of Czechoslovakia, the Director of the Yiddish Scientific Institute in New York applied for particulars to the Minister of Foreign Affairs of the Czech Government in exile, Jan Masaryk, in order to clarify the position of the Jewish minority in Czechoslovakia.[19] In the written answer of Jan Masark it is expressly stated that the transfer of populations refers only to the Sudeten Germans.[20]

Actually, the Jews who claimed the German language as their native tongue in the census of 1930 were in no case treated as Jan Masaryk, with the express approval of Dr. Beneš, had guaranteed. Many of the Jews who had survived the German concentration camps or had returned to Czechoslovakia from exile were not given back their former property. Thus they were forced to emigrate, seeing that Czechoslovakia offered them no living.[21]

The question of transferring the Sudeten Germans was one of the decisive reasons in 1942 which induced the Sudeten German Social Democrats associated with the deputy Wenzel Jaksch to distance themselves from Dr. Beneš (Jaksch went into exile in 1938 and originally tried to achieve constructive co-operation with the Czech Government in London with regard to all Czech and Sudeten German problems). In a letter of June 22, 1942 which he addressed to Dr. Beneš at London, Jaksch said: "The absolute negative attitude towards an agreement, even about temporary political and economic arrangements, deprives our policy of mutual understanding of any basis. The program concerning the transfer of populations is beyond the principle of constitutional continuity, in the name of which the loyalty of the democratic Sudeten Germans abroad was claimed by the Czechoslovak Government."[22]

The consent to a transfer or rather expulsion of the Sudeten Germans was not to be obtained from the Great Powers without certain difficulties. But Dr. Beneš showed himself not very particular about the means he used. In a conference with President Roosevelt on May 12, 1943 he mentioned that the Russians would agree to the "transfer of the Sudeten Germans". 17 days later, May 29, Dr. Ripka explained to the Soviet Ambassador Bogomolow in London that the Americans had already agreed to the transfer and that in these circumstances the Czech Government in exile expected the official Russian consent. On June 6, Dr. Ripka telephoned Dr. Beneš, who was in the United States, that the Russian consent had just arrived - the same consent with which Dr. Beneš had operated in his conversation with President Roosevelt on May 12.[23]

Thus it is made clear that Dr. Beneš was, in the background, one of the initiators of the resolutions of Yalta and Potsdam which dealt with the expulsion of the East Germans.

Since the Munich Pact in September 1938, Beneš felt himself betrayed by the Western Powers. He had to show gratitude for the asylum allowed to him after 1938, but it was intolerable to his ambitious nature that his own construction of Czechoslovakia in 1918 did not take precedence over all other interests. The full recognition of the Czech Government in exile and the juridical continuity of the pre-Munich Czechoslovak state was, in consideration of the obvious legal difficulties, granted by the Western Powers comparatively late and only under the influence of Russia's declaration of war.[24]

After Russia's military successes (Stalingrad), in the absence of a second front in 1943 and under the impression of the strengthened pressure of Moscow upon the Poles in London, Dr. Beneš decided at the end of 1943 to go to Moscow in order not to lose touch with the Czech Communists, and he did so to demonstrate to the Western Powers, especially England, his political independence. He made his trip against the advice of the British Government.[25]

By this trip and by the Soviet-Czechoslovak alliance the further fate of Czechoslovakia was determined. In May 1935, by his first treaty with the Soviet Union, Beneš had proved his intention of binding Czechoslovakia's future closely to Moscow. Returning to London at the beginning of 1944, he expressed his opinion about the future position of the Soviet Union in Europe with great optimism on the occasion of a banquet given in his honour. The subsequent events proved that he was wrong in this respect.[26] To what extent his judgement was influenced by his wounded vanity may be seen from his fourth message to the Czechoslovak Council of State.[27]

Beneš probably had the covert intention of acting as mediator between East and West, relying on his talent for handling difficult conflicts, a talent he had so conspicuously shown in the League of Nations. He by far overestimated his importance.[28]

Today many Czechs are aware that the political development of Czechoslovakia since 1945, especially since the revolution of February 1948, has a certain connection with the expulsion of the Germans (which played an important role in all of Dr. Beneš' deliberations.)[29]

V.

The realization of the plan, directed against the very existence of the Sudeten Germans, was only effected by the occupation of Bohemia, Moravia and Silesia by the Allies. During the war the Czech population neither offered any considerable resistance nor practised any effective sabotage against the German war-industry. The Czechs were exempted from military service. The food was not worse, perhaps even better than in Germany. As a result of the transfer of numerous armament factories and other industries and the establishment of vast depots, Bohemia and Moravia became a sort of store-room for Hitler's war industry. The yield required of these industries as well as of agriculture was, in general, not inferior to the German yield.

As in Germany, the Gestapo in Bohemia and Moravia interned the obvious opponents of the Hitler regime in German concentration camps. A part of the Czechs were called up for service in the German war industries.

No active resistance to the German armies of occupation, as in Poland, was ever observed, not even in the last weeks of war. The attempt on Heydrich's life was planned and organized from abroad. The bloody retaliatory measures for this attempt however, especially the destruction of the village of Lidice and of all its male inhabitants, did raise the Czech spirit of resistance to a certain extent.

These events of course were highly welcome to the Czech propaganda in London. The facts that the Sudeten Germans, as a national group, had no share in the happenings, and that only a small group of National Socialist leaders could be responsible for the retaliatory measures for the attempt on Heydrich's life, were concealed; and as in 1938, the Germans were represented as collectively guilty.

At the end of the war, when during the battles against the remnants of Schörner's army the Sudeten German territories were occupied by Russian and American troops, the same scenes were witnessed as in the German regions. The majority of the Sudeten Germans was ignorant of the post-war intentions of Dr. Beneš and his collaborators in exile. In some places the people hoped that calm would ensue when Czech authorities had taken over the regular police forces and administration. For the Sudeten Germans it was a terrible awakening out of their illusions when the first truck-loads of revolutionary guardsmen, mostly dressed in German uniforms and equipped with German weapons, arrived in Sudeten German areas from Inner Bohemia.

Until that moment local Czech residents, or Czechs formerly in Sudeten German territories and now returned, manifested a comparatively reasonable attitude. In the beginning German anti-fascists were even represented in the local National Committees. But the groups organized and directed by Czech central offices perpetrated a dreadful abundance of murders, atrocities, abuses, rapes, robberies and thefts, as may be seen from the following reports. At some spots, e.g. at Saaz, Brüx, Aussig, Landskron etc, mass executions and massacres were carried out. At Prague these massacres started immediately after the street-fighting on May 5th. But a clear distinction between the conservative middle class and an extreme nationalistic group which worked hand in hand with the Communists was evident. The inflammatory incitements of Radio Prague, which was soon in Czech hands, spread a downright demonic, bloodthirsty mass hysteria through the city and precipitated deeds of horror surpassing those of the Hussite war.[30]

Incidents similar to those in Prague took place at different other towns of inner Bohemia and Moravia-Silesia. At times the atrocities were such that the Russian authorities ordered the Czechs to stop. Under the impact of these mass cruelties, there were epidemics of suicides in Sudeten-Germany, especially among the elderly German population.

VI.

The psychological root of the Czech attitude after May 1945 will be found in the extreme nationalistic conception already referred to, a conception which had been inculcated into the Czech nation for decades with an admixture of Panslav historical ideology. The Czech nationalism was systematically fostered from abroad during the war. Furthermore the German authorities paid little attention to the positive characteristics of the Czech nation during the period of the "Protectorate" Bohemia and Moravia, but wantonly provoked the negative characteristics. In any case, a long occupation was bound to cause resentment. Instead of letting the first wave of resentment decline, the Czech Government, following a carefully prepared scheme, furthered this resentment from the first days of May onwards and encouraged the lowest instinct of some classes of the Czech nation by public incitements to violence and robbery. The same Government, moreover, tried to give the proceedings the guise of legality by the notorious presidential decrees of Dr. Beneš.

The expulsion of considerable portions of the Sudeten German population started long before it was sanctioned by the Potsdam Agreement on August 2nd, 1945. That the expulsion which took place before the resolutions of Potsdam was a centrally directed action may be deduced from the fact that the expulsion orders were issued as public proclamations by the local and district National Committees. The methods were alike in different places, which shows that this important measure was organized in agreement with the central government.[31] These first waves of expulsions were attended by terrible mass cruelties which caused the death of tens of thousands of Sudeten Germans. Among the first victims were chiefly old people, invalids and children. On of the most horrible so-called "Marches of Death" was the march of the expelled Germans of Brünn via Pohrlitz to the Czechoslovak border in the direction of Vienna. In a very short time, sometimes on as little as 10 minutes' notice, the expelled persons had to leave their apartments. They were only allowed to take the most necessary clothes, and were deprived of the best of these during the march and on the border. During the march renewed deeds of robbery and violence were perpetrated. Certain measures that were made to seem those of the local police, but in reality centrally planned and directed, made the situation of the Sudeten Germans intolerable. Even before President Beneš' announcement of the Decrees, the Sudeten Germans were practically outlawed. Their apartments, if they were still in their possession, were open for plundering either on the occasion of officially organized domiciliary visits or by Czech "gold diggers" who entered Sudeten German areas from inner Bohemia and Moravia. Under the pretext of raids for weapons or political persons the RG (Revoluční Garda), the police (SBN - *Sbor Národní Bezpečnosti*) and soldiers, or mere groups of Czech plunderers broke into the apartments and houses, maltreated the inhabitants and took what they wanted. In some places orders were issued that the apartments and houses of the Germans must not be locked. Some orders reduced the lives of the Germans to pure misery. They were only allowed to be on the streets at certain times (curfew), they had to wear white badges as distinguishing mark, they were not permitted to use any public means of transportation (trains, buses, streetcars) or to leave or change their residences. They were forbidden to walk on the sidewalks. They were not allowed to write letters to one another or to visit restaurants, cinemas or theatres. They could only buy at groceries and stores during certain hours of the day. They were forbidden to dispose of their own assets or of any kind of property. Gold, silver, jewelry and other valuables, radios, cameras and optical instruments had to be surrendered. Special ration cards for Germans were issued, without coupons for meat, eggs, milk, cheese and fruit.[32] All German schools and kindergartens were closed. A general labour conscription for Germans was proclaimed; in some places the population capable of work was called together in certain squares by public announcement. Afterwards the assembled people were transported to inner Bohemia as labour slaves on farms, in the mines or in industry. For non-observance of these orders they were threatened with the death penalty.[33] In the beginning, all work had to be done without payment. Later on, low wages were fixed for the German slaves, but as a rule these wages were never paid. Billets and food during the labour conscription in inner Bohemia were often entirely insufficient. There was no sort of social welfare work or insurance for these "free" workers.

One of the first administrative regulations of the Czech Home Office was the establishment of concentration camps for Germans. In many ways they were planned on the model of German concentration camps, judging by the reports of internees who were imprisoned in German as well as in Czech camps. In many cases the food supply and other conditions were considerably worse in these Czech concentration camps, established after the end of the war, than at Dachau or Buchenwald. All imaginable bestialities were committed on the Germans. Even though the treatment of internees frequently depended on the personality of the camp commander, the methods in the different camps were the same. Not only the local, but also the central administrative and governmental circles right up to the President, Dr. Beneš, were well informed about the conditions in the camps. The Czech population, to a large extent, approved of the proceedings in the camps. The name concentration camp *(Koncentrační tábor)* was mostly changed into internment camp *(Internační tábor)* or collecting camp *(Shromážd'ovací středisko)* after a time, but the conditions still remained essentially the same. The inmates of the camps were called up to work like slaves and they were inhumanly tortured and maltreated in the camps and during their work. At night women and girls were frequently handed over to the army of occupation for raping. In the beginning these camps lacked all sanitary arrangements, the barracks swarmed with vermin and the food was less than in German concentration camps. In these camps the majority of Sudeten Germans was driven together and confined, often without any reason, merely because they were Germans or because a Czech wanted to take possession of the house, the dwelling or the factory of a certain German. A very clear report on the conditions of the camps was given by the British member of Parliament, R. R. Stokes, in his article of October 1945 to the *Manchester Guardian*.[34] At that time - according to the statements of Stokes - there were 51 such camps in Czechoslovakia. Stokes describes the way in which the labour slaves were selected and transported each morning at camp Hagibor near Prague; from their description of their diet he found that the amount of calories was less than that of the German concentration camp at Belsen. Even worse than in the various camps were the conditions in the prisons, where besides inhuman ferocities and tortures the prisoners - on account of catastrophically overcrowded cells - had no chance to move around or be in the fresh air, so that contagious diseases and all kinds of sicknesses increased the death rate. A considerable number of inmates also died in consequence of the wholly insufficient rations.

VII.

Only few things were changed after the ratification of the Potsdam Agreement on August 2, 1945, which in article 13 sanctioned the transfer of the German population from Poland, Czechoslovakia and Hungary, strictly ordering "that all transfers should take place in an orderly and humane way."[35] The only result of the Potsdam Agreement was that the Czech Government and the Czech population which participated in the outrages and plunderings of Sudeten Germans acquired the feeling that all these occurrences had a certain international legality. That the ways in which the expulsions were carried out were unaffected by the demand of Potsdam for an orderly and humane fulfilment of the transfer, is made clear by the following reports. The international jurist Hermann Raschhofer rightly deduces from the text of paragraph 13 the duty of the Signatory Powers to see that the terms of the Agreement were being observed.[36] Unfortunately the Signatory Powers did not take the necessary precautions to ensure that the transfer was carried out in the prescribed manner.

The world public scarcely noticed what was going on in the Sudetenland in 1945. At most, some friends of the Czechs-in-exile who still remained in the propaganda organs of the Western nations would comment on these mass crimes from the cynical perspective that "the victim, not the murderer, is to blame". The Czechs themselves either kept the massacres secret or attempted to interweave European interests and necessities with the problem of the expulsions. For example, the former Minister for Export Trade, Dr. Ripka, who is now living in exile, declared on August 20, 1945 over Radio Prague: "...but this necessity (for expulsion) is not only in the interest of all Europe, it is one of the basic acts for the protection of a European peace. It goes without saying that we shall solve the problem in a humane way, as becomes a nation with an old humane tradition, a nation with the humanitarian ideal of Masaryk. And only in this way shall the problem be solved."[37] These statements are similar to those which Dr. Beneš once used at a lecture at Manchester University on December 5, 1942.[38] But how starkly the real expulsion, so full of cruelties, contrasts with the propaganda speeches of these two spiritual originators of the transfer! In order to give the mode of procedure against the Sudeten Germans the guise of legality, Dr. Beneš issued several decrees which show very distinctly how systematically the extermination of a nation (Genocide) was planned and carried out on the Sudeten German national group.[39] In view of these decrees, the expulsions cannot be explained as the spontaneous reaction of the Czech nation against German oppression. Even in the so-called Kaschau Programme of April 5, 1945, in Chapter VIII and IX, the aims of Dr. Beneš' plan are absolutely clear.[40] In further decrees the Sudeten German national group was deprived of citizenship as well as of all civil rights and was declared hostile to the State. By the Decree of Presdent Beneš of May 19, 1945 (Compilation of Statutes and Enactments No. 5), all persons of German or Hungarian nationality were declared politically unreliable. The entire property of these politically unreliable persons was placed under the supervision of a national administration. The national trustees were thereby given the position of public authorities according to the terms of the penal code.[41] By the Decree of June 21st, 1945 (Compilation of Statutes and Enactments No. 12) the confiscation and accelerated partitioning of agricultural properties belonging to persons of German nationality, irrespective of their citizenship, was ordered.[42] The Decree of June 19, 1945 (Compilation of Statutes and Enactments No. 16) demands the punishment of "exorbitant crimes on Czechoslovakia of which the Nazis and their perfidious accomplices have been found guilty".[43] The Constitutional Decree of the President of August 2, 1945 (Compilation of Statutes and Enactments No. 33) regulates the Czechoslovak citizenship of persons of German and Hungarian nationality.[44] The decree ordains that citizens of German nationality who, under German law, had acquired German citizenship, have lost their Czechoslovak citizenship. All other Germans, however, also lose Czechoslovak citizenship on the date of the decree's coming into force. The decree does not pertain to "those Germans who claimed to be Czechs or Slovaks in times of increased danger to the Republic".

According to this decree Czechoslovak citizenship will be kept by those Germans who are able to prove "that they have been true to the Czechoslovak Republic, that they have never offended against the Czech or Slovak people and either actively participated in the fight for liberation or suffered under the National Socialist or Fascist terror."

A further decree of October 25, 1945 (Compilation of Statutes and Enactments No. 108)[45] enacts the confiscation without compensation of personal and real property and of property rights on behalf of the Czechoslovak Republic of the following property-holders:

1.) the German Reich, persons in public law, the German Nazi party and other organizations, formations, undertakings, installations, corporations, funds and property designated for special purposes; and

2) persons of German nationality.[46]

These decrees as well as article 13 of the Potsdam Agreement conflict with the principles of internatioinal law. They represent a complete neglect of human rights, the principles of the Atlantic Charter[47] and the Charter of the United Nations. President Beneš issued these decrees in his capacity as President of the State on the motion of a provisional government, without authority under the Constitution.

The inadequacy of the decrees in relation to international and constitutional law is particularly evident in the Decree of August 2, 1945 (Compilation of Statutes and Enactments No. 33). As a result of the Munich Agreement of September 29, 1938 between Germany, the United Kingdom, France and Italy, the Sudeten German areas were transferred to Germany and the Sudeten Germans became German citizens. The Czechoslovak Government, with Dr. Beneš as President, held a meeting on September 30, 1938, at which the Munich Agreement was accepted. The official report says: "After careful consideration and examination of all recommendations, submitted to the Government, and fully aware of its historical responsibility, the Czechoslovak Government, in agreement with the responsible elements of the political parties, has decided to accept the Munich resolutions of the four great Powers. It has done so in the conviction that the nation must be saved and that there is no other decision possible at this time."[48] During the war the Agreement was declared as not binding upon Great Britain since Germany had already violated it. In spite of this declaration, the conditions juridically established by the Agreement endured till 1945. A revision would have pertained to a treaty of peace with Germany.[49] But even considering the legally and constitutionally refutable thesis of the juridical continuity of the Czechoslovak state, the decrees against the Sudeten German population would still be disputable because they contradict the principles of the Czechoslovak constitution as well as the treaty for the protection of minorities to which Czechoslovakia had agreed.[50]

The expulsion of the Sudeten Germans and the methods applied unquestionably show the characteristics of national extermination or Genocide. The General Assembly of the United Nations declared in its Resolution, dated December 11, 1946, that Genocide is a crime under international law, a crime contrary to the spirit and aims of the United Nations and condemned by the civilized world. In 1950 the United Nations accepted a Convention on Genocide.[51] According to the Convention, Genocide means any of the following acts, committed with intent to destroy, in whole or in part, a national, ethnic, racial or religious group:

a) killing members of the group;

b) causing serious bodily or mental harm to members of the group;

c) deliberately inflicting on the group conditions of life calculated to bring about its physical destruction in whole or in part;

d) imposing measures intended to prevent births within the group;

e) forcibly transferring children of the group to another group.

VIII.

In consideration of a possible peaceful co-existence of all the nations in Central Europe it seems necessary to stress the fact that the reasons for the developments of these last years are much more profound than is apparent in most of the daily political polemics. It is clear that the question of culpability is a matter of importance. After 1945 the Czechs operated with a slogan only too readily accepted by the rest of the world: Hitler originated the policy of inhumanity. On the basis of this claim, and with a daring leap of logic, the collective guilt not only of the German nation but also of the Sudeten Germans as a whole was constructed. Thus, for example, the Sudeten Germans were credited with a share of the guilt for the excesses perpetrated in the concentration camps. In the meantime pertinent objections have been expressed by neutrals as well as by former enemies against the assumption of collective guilt. But that the German people were also the first to suffer under Hitler may be proved by the list of the inmates of German concentration camps. The Sudeten Germans were ill informed as to the true political structure of the Third Reich and its methods. The allegation that the Sudeten Germans were among those collectively responsible for the concentration camps cannot be sustained.[52] There have been signs of a bad conscience on the part of those who are guilty, in whole or in part, for the events of 1945/1946, not only in Czechoslovakia itself but even to some extent among those emigrants who in 1945, directly or indirectly, participated in the cruelties when they held positions of authority in the Government, parliament or in the administration and who, after the revolt of February 1948, went into western exile.[53]

As far as the treatment of the other national group is concerned, the events of 1945 in Bohemia, Moravia and Silesia stand in strong contrast to the events of 1938, for no cruelties were committed on the Czech population after the Munich Agreement, except for some insignificant incidents. To sum up, a general survey of the events of 1945 reveals two aspects:

1. the systematic preparation of the measures and of the cruelties perpetrated, and

2. the extensive participation of the Czech population in these misdeeds.

Both aspects will become clear after reading the following reports. Nevertheless no collective guilt of the Czech nation can be deduced from them; for in the last analysis a certain group is alone responsible for the planning and organization of these acts. Besides, there were Czechs who, conscious of the criminal character of the measures taken, did what they could to help the Sudeten Germans.[54] The demand for punishment of the real culprits is in the interest of the Czech nation itself and is a condition of German-Czech co-existence and understanding in the general framework of a future European new order. The agreement between the "Association for the Protection of Sudeten German Interests" and the Czech National Committee was signed in London on August 4, 1950.[55] In this agreement the Sudetenland is recognized as the homeland of the Sudeten Germans who are regarded as entitled to compensation for injuries done to them. Both parties agreed to uphold democratic principles and - a particularly important point - both parties reject the imputation of collective guilt. Both parties express the will to place the co-existence of the two peoples, the Sudeten Germans and the Czechs, on a new foundation within the framework of a new European order in the spirit of President Wilson's right of self-determination, as laid down in his Fourteen Points. But the great importance of the agreement consists in the opportunity of carrying into effect an ethical idea, namely to overcome hatred and revenge. In this sense the agreement, as a starting point for further developments in Central as well as Eastern Europe, may attain an importance transcending the problem of Sudeten Germans and Czechs.

The course of events in Central Europe since 1918 has certainly proven that the foundation of small national states, constituted according to a belated nationalism, represents no satisfactory solution. By actions like the expulsion, nationalism itself disproved its right to exist.[56] Such an alliance as, for example, the "Little Entente" also proved itself unproductive.

The tragedy of the small nations in Central Europe is evident today. This tragedy cannot be removed until the nations are willing to become part of a new European order. In the special case of the Czech nation such an order cannot be achieved without a constructive solution of the German-Czech question. The assimilation of the Sudeten Germans failed, and as the expulsion did not lead to pacification, new ways have to be found.

Notes:

1. cf. Eugen Lemberg: *Geschichte des Nationalismus in Europa* (History of Nationalism in Europe), Stuttgart 1950.

2. cf. *Democratia militans,* No. 1 p. 65ff. H. Hájek: "Aussiedlung und Putsch" (Transfer and Riot).

3. Amongst other things it said: "I am taking the Germans, living at the borough of Prague, under my protection and favour and it is my wish that they, being nationally different from the Czechs, be also separated from them by their rights and customs. I therefore grant the Germans that they may live according to their German law and rights, of which they have been in possession since the days of my grandfather, King Vratislaw (1071-1092) (vivere secundum legem et justitiam Theutonicorum)."

4. cf.: *Die tschechoslowakischen Denkschriften für die Friedenskonferenz von Paris* ("Czechoslovak Memoranda for the Paris Peace Conference"), edited by Dr. Dr. Hermann Raschhofer, Berlin 1937.

5. cf.: Edvard Beneš: *Revolt of the Nations* (German translation *Der Aufstand der Nationen* by Camill Hoffmann, Berlin 1928), pp. 687/8: "Since I was acquainted with the perils of our situation and did not know which kind of material the Peace Delegation, constituted at Prague, would take to Paris, I started all alone with the preparations for the Peace Conference. I did not want to be surprised by sudden decisions of the Great Powers. Masaryk also asked me in his letters from time to time in the course of 1918 to make preparations for the Conference. I therefore wrote down in the shortest possible time, almost improvising and without support or literature, most of the memoranda, in which I included all our peace conditions. When our Peace Delegation arrived, I submitted them for approbation. Some of the memoranda were supplemented by members of the Delegation, some corrected. When the Peace Conference unexpectedly requested the national Delegations to put their demands in writing, I submitted almost everything that was required right on the next day. This readiness was profitable to the solution of our problems in the different committees of the Conference."

6. See Appendix No. 1.

7. See Appendix No. 2. Compare Appendix No. 3 for the true course of the linguistic borders.

8. The note is printed in: David Hunter Miller, *My Diary, at the Conference of Paris,* vol. 13 (1925) p. 96: "It is the intention of the Czecho-Slovak government to create the organisation of the State by accepting as a basis of national rights the principles applied in the constitution of the Swiss Republic, that is, to make of the Czecho-Slovak Republic a sort of Switzerland, taking into consideration, of course, the special conditions in Bohemia."

9. This treaty was signed on June 30, 1918 between Masaryk and the American Slovaks at Pittsburgh, USA. In it the Slovaks were granted full autonomy in the Czechoslovak Republic, first, in order to secure the co-operation of the Slovaks in the new State and second, to get President Wilson's agreement for a solution in the Czechoslovak way. Later on Masaryk denied this treaty completely.

10. Walter Brand, *Die sudetendeutsche Tragödie* (The Sudeten-German Tragedy), Lauf bei Nürnberg, 1949.

11. cf.: Hubert Ripka, *Munich Before and After,* 1939.

12. Hubert Ripka, op.cit.: "Our capital mistake, in my opinion, was in not attempting to come to terms with the Sudeten German people rather than with Henlein."

13. See: *War and Peace Aims of the UN,* Boston, 1945, vol. I, p. 438.

14. Clement Attlee declared verbatim: "I say that the question of the Sudeten Germans has been used as a counter in the game of politics, and in other conditions, Herr Hitler might just as well have used the people of South Denmark, the people of Trentino or the Germans of South Tyrol."

15. The Prague newspaper *Právo Lidu* reports in its edition of September 3, 1947 about an information which was given by the American Deputy Public Prosecutor, Robert Kempner, in connection with this problem at a press conference in Prague. According to a document, at disposal to the Nuremberg Court, three experiments for a solution of the Czech problem were proposed by Adolf Hitler. **1.** autonomy, **2.** transfer of the Czech population, **3.** attempt at assimilation.

Hitler was in favour of the third possibility and rejected at the same time all other suggestions for a solution.

16. Note from *Rudé Právo* of February 1946: "...the idea of transferring the Germans rose in the minds of our politicians at Moscow. When President Beneš arrived at Moscow in 1943 in order to sign the Czechoslovako-Soviet Pact, Comrade Gottwald started the question concerning the transfer of Germans from our Republic for the first time. Comrade Stalin personally agreed to this proposal. Stalin also used his influence on the assertion of these claims at the Allied Powers' Conference."

17. See note 13.

18. "The New Order in Europe", *The Nineteenth Century and After,* September 1941, No. 774; "The Organization of Postwar Europe", *Foreign Affairs,* vol. 20 No. 2 (Jan. 1942), pp. 226-242.

19. See: Mark Vishniak, *The Transfer of Populations as a Means of Solving the Problem of Minorities,* Yiddish Scientific Institute, New York, 1942. The author of this excellently written book suggests as a possible solution for the problem of minorities the protection of national minorities by international statutes of a global organization. Vishniak quotes parts of President Wilson's speech on February 11, 1918, wherein he attacked the habit of considering nations merely as chess pawns in the political game. On this occasion, the President demanded that every territorial settlement must be carried out with consideration for the interests of the population concerned. The President then said verbatim: "Peoples and provinces must not be bartered about from sovereignty to sovereignty as if they were mere chattels or pawns in a game, even the great game, now forever discredited, of the balance of power... Every territorial settlement... must be made in the interest and for the benefit of the population concerned, and not as a part of any mere adjustment or compromise of claims amongst rival states."

20. See Appendix No. 4.

21. See reports: Reichenberg 7, Eipel, 187, Parschnitz and Qualisch.

22. Wenzel Jaksch, *Benesch war gewarnt,* Munich 1949.

23. Edvard Beneš, *Paméeti,* Prague 1947.

24. cf.: Sir Robert Bruce Lockhart, "The Czechoslovak Revolution," *Foreign Affairs,* 1948, p. 633. "Dr. Beneš was grateful, but not wholly satisfied. He wanted full recognition of the juridical continuity of the Czechoslovak state in the form in which it existed before Munich. In spite of the obvious legal difficulties it was granted."

25. Lockhart, op.cit., p. 633: "In December 1943 against the advice of the British Government he (Beneš) went to Moscow." .

26. See: *War and Peace Aims of the U.N.,* Boston 1945, vol. II, p. 1030.

27. See: *War and Peace Aims of the U.N.,* Boston 1945, vol. II, p. 1024.

28. See: Ferdinand Peroutka, *Byl Beneš vinen?* [Was Beneš Guilty?], Paris 1950: "...He was of the opinion that he might lead some sort of clearing-office of Western and Eastern ideas. He wanted to build a bridge across which everybody would go with delight - and on the first pillar of this bridge his name would be engraved." (Translated from the Czech.)

29. See Note 2.

30. See: Jürgen Thorwald, *Das Ende an der Elbe* (Finale on the Elbe River), Stuttgart 1950, pp. 300ff., and Dr. Emil Franzel, "Prag im Mai 1945" (Prague in May 1945), *Die Welt*, Hamburg 1950, No. 103-105.

31. See Appendix No. 5.

32. See Appendix No. 6.

33. See Appendix No. 7.

34. See Appendix No. 8.

35. Wording of Article XIII of the Potsdam Agreement is as follows: "Orderly Transfers of German Populations. The conference reached the following agreement on the removal of Germans from Poland, Czechoslovakia and Hungary: The three Governments having considered the question in all its aspects, recognize that the transfer to Germany of German populations, or elements thereof, remaining in Poland, Czechoslovakia and Hungary will have to be undertaken. They agree that any transfers that take place should be effected in an orderly and humane manner."

36. Hermann Raschhofer, *Vom Minderheitenrecht zum Unrecht der Vertreibung. Christ Unterwegs* (From Justice to Minorities to the Injustice of Expulsions. Christ on the Road), Munich, 4th yr., No. 11, p. 9: "The Signatory Powers were obliged to take care of the transaction of transfer, which should be undertaken under certain conditions, and to control the States mentioned in the Agreement."

37. See: *War and Peace Aims of the U.N.*, Boston 1945, vol. II, p. 1048.

38. See: *War and Peace Aims of the U.N.*, Boston 1945, vol. I; Eduard Beneš: Lecture at Manchester University, December 1942.

39. See: Definition of Genocide by the General Assembly of the United Nations on December 13, 1946. "Genocide is a denial of the right of existence of entire human groups, as homicide is the denial of the right to live of individual human beings; such denial of the right of existence shocks the conscience of mankind, results in great losses to humanity in the form of cultural and other contributions represented by these human groups, and is contrary to moral law and to the spirit and aims of the United Nations. Many instances of such crimes of genocide have occurred when racial, religious, political or other groups have been destroyed, entirely or in part. The punishment of the crime of genocide is a matter of international concern...."

40. See Appendix No. 9.

41. See Appendix No. 10.

42. See Appendix No. 11.

43. See Appendix No. 12.

44. See Appendix No. 13 and, for sake of comparison, Appendix No. 14.

45. See Appendix No. 15.

46. See Appendix No. 16, in which a summary of the national property of the Germans of the Czechoslovak Republic is given.

47. See Appendix No. 17.

48. *Dokumente der deutschen Politik* (Documents on German Policy), vol. 6, I, p. 362 (Berlin, 1939).

49. See: Dr. Rudolf Lodgman von Auen, *Die völkerrechtliche Grundlage des Sudetenproblems und die politische Entwicklung seit 1945* (The International Basis of the Sudeten Problem and the Political Development Since 1945), Sinsheim 1948, pp. 6ff.

50. See: "A Petition to the Secretary General of the United Nations and the Foreign Secretaries of the Signatory Powers of the Potsdam Agreement from the Parliamentary Delegation of Sudeten Labour in Great Britain", written by Wenzel Jaksch, London 1947, pp. 24ff. It is also indicated there that the special privileges granted to the German anti-fascists in the decrees were not observed in the majority of cases.

51. See Appendix No. 18.

52. Isn't it rather more like the brochure *Tragedy of a People (Racialism in Czecho-Slovakia),* published by prominent American authorities in New York in 1946, states, namely, that the barbarous nature of the expulsion even exceeds Hitler's racist excesses?

53. See: Ivo Ducháček, "Communist Infiltration", *World Politics* 1950, p. 346: "When in 1945 the Sudeten German minority was transferred into the American and Russian zone of Germany, the Czechs - in spite of Germany's total defeat - were more and more afraid of a possible Sudeten German demand for revision, which might bring new fear and insecurity. The fact that some Czechs had taken possession of formerly Sudeten German property in a rather unusual way augmented national anxiety by an economic motive."

54. See: *Dokumente der Menschlichkeit* (Documents of Humanity), edited by the "Göttinger Arbeitskreis", Klitzingen/Main, 1950.

55. See Appendix No. 19.

56. See: Lemberg op.cit., p. 243: "...therefore this fourth stage of attempts to solve the European problems of nationalities reminds one of similar attempts during the period of religious wars. After various cautious attempts there also seemed to be no other way out of the difficulties but the expulsion of those groups which were not of their rulers' religious denominations. As these forcible solutions represented a climax as well as a crisis of the religious concord, so today's inhuman expulsions and massacres of national and racial groups cast a strong and grotesque light upon the crisis of European nationalism, this fundamentally so fertile and productive movement, which may, by such events, be driven to extremity and hence be converted into its own opposite."

A Note Concerning these Reports

The following reports were collected in the years after 1945. The signatures of the authors are legally attested. In cases in which the full name of the author is not given, it has been withheld out of consideration for relatives still living in Czechoslovakia, or for friends to whom publication of their names might be dangerous. The same precautions have been taken with regard to the names of Czechs who are mentioned in the reports and who showed a humane attitude towards the Germans.

The reports published represent only a part of the material available. They are intended to serve first of all as typical examples of the events which took place in the course of the expulsion of the Sudeten Germans. It goes without saying that in view of the limited number of reports which could be published here, not all places and incidents have been covered.

The reports are grouped alphabetically into two sections. Part 1 tells of events in the larger cities and in some smaller towns where particularly detailed reports are available: Aussig, Brünn, Brüx, Budweis, Freiwaldau, Gablonz, Iglau, Jägerndorf, Karlsbad, Kladno, Komotau, Mährisch Ostrau, Mährisch Schönberg, Olmütz, Pilsen, Prague, Reichenberg, Saaz-Postelberg, Tepliz-Schönau, Tetschen-Bodenbach, Theresienstadt and Troppau. Part 2 contains reports in alphabetical order by smaller towns.

PART 1 - Reports on the Events in Larger Cities and Towns

PART 1 - Reports on the Events in Larger Cities and Towns, alphabetically:

Aussig, Brünn, Brüx, Budweis, Freiwaldau, Gablonz, Iglau, Jägerndorf, Karlsbad, Kladno, Komotau, Mährisch Ostrau, Mährisch Schönberg, Olmütz, Pilsen, Prague, Reichenberg, Saaz-Postelberg, Tepliz-Schönau, Tetschen-Bodenbach, Theresienstadt, Troppau.

Aussig, Report No. 1
The explosion on July 30, 1945
Reported by A. U. - Report of February 8, 1951

[Due to various circumstances the author of this report was in the position to give an authoritative and objective account of the explosion and its terrible consequences:]

About 10 o'clock on the day in question I walked into the center of the town. As soon as I entered the busier streets, I discovered both in the former Dresdener Strasse and in the Schmejkal Strasse that the soldiers of the notorious Svoboda-army were attacking the Germans wearing their white armbands, driving them from the sidewalks and even knocking them down. I asked what was going on and learned that during the night the Svoboda-army had arrived at Aussig.

Judging by events in other regions of the Sudetenland I immediately guessed that now rough times would come for the Germans of Aussig and of the whole district.

I arrived at the station just as about 300 persons left the train coming from Prague; they were suspicious-looking people between 18 and 30 years of age and I had the impression that they were convicts released from a prison.

At half past three in the afternoon I sat in my apartment when there was a terrific bang. At that moment I thought that a cupboard had fallen over in the next room. I looked into it, but could find nothing. I then assumed that an explosion must have occurred and went up to the roof. There I noticed a large cloud of smoke rising behind the Marienberg. Several smaller explosions followed. I immediately ran downtown - not wearing my white armband, which proved lucky for me. The hunt after the Germans had begun. Soldiers of the Svoboda-army and individual Russians took part in it. These brutes had equipped themselves with all sorts of makeshift weapons such as fence-posts, crow-bars, shovel-handles and so on. With these they struck down all those who spoke German or wore the white badge. I had the impression that the perpetrators were not Czechs from our own district, but those who had left the train in the forenoon. My impression was strengthened by the fact that they had helped themselves to any instruments at hand to improvise their weapons.

I walked through the streets of the town for about two hours; what I saw during that time was dreadful. Of course, I could not say a word, since that would have exposed me as a German.

The factories closed at 3 o'clock in the afternoon and the Germans who worked in the Schicht-works had to use the bridges over the River Elbe in order to get home. The most savage groups therefore were active near these bridges, in the vicinity of the marketplace and the railway station.

Even women with babies in perambulators were shoved into the river and then used for target practice. The shooting did not stop until none of the women rose to the surface any longer. Other Germans were thrown into the big water-tank on the market-place. Whenever one of them rose to the surface, the Czechs would push him down again and keep him under water with long poles. Only at 5 o'clock in the afternoon a number of Russian officers appeared and tried to clear the streets. Uniformed Czechs helped them in doing so. Loudspeakers announced the curfew in Czech. On July 31st, a printed poster was issued, announcing that the Germans were not allowed to be in the streets after 6 o'clock in the afternoon, the curfew for the Czech population began at 8 o'clock p.m.

In the evening of July 30th the dead were collected at three places and then taken away in trucks. About 400 corpses were counted at all three collection points. How many may have been collected elsewhere and the number of those who floated down the Elbe cannot be established. Not even the most informed members of the National Committee were able to make an estimate.

In the evening of July 30th I obtained knowledge that it was intended to clear all Germans out of the district of Aussig as well as the neighbouring districts of Teplitz and Tetschen-Bodenbach and to send these people to the interior of the country, where they would be used as forced labour.

The Germans were generally accused of sabotage and of the authorship of the explosion.

What had really happened?

In the Schönpriesen section of the town there had been stored the ammunition of the artillery, *Panzerfäuste* - an anti-tank weapon - and similar weapons as well as other ammunition left from the last days of the war in May 1945. According to Czech statements two million articles were in this depot. Prisoners from the concentration camp at Lerchenfeld, among them several prominent Nazis, were occupied with sorting the ammunition, weapons and so on. On July 30th these prisoners had, surprisingly enough, been taken away at a quarter to three p.m., so that for 40 minutes before the explosion no German had been on the grounds. Only Czech guards were there. Several seconds before the explosion an airplane crossed this section of the town - as it turned out later on, the plane was a British one, which had no connection whatsoever with the explosion. In 1947 I talked to one of the passengers who described his observations to me. This airplane played a considerable part in my statements to Czech authorities concerning the causes of the explosion.

The alibi of the Chief of Police of the District National Committee was that he had been consulting a German physician at the time of the explosion and left him only after it was over.

A number of officials, among them the Military Commander, were assembled in the office of the District National Committee. The last-named left the office immediately after the explosion, with the words: "Now we will start the anti-German revolution". Then the slaughter began.

I myself went to Prague on August 31st and visited several prominent Czech functionaries who were known to me and described to them what I had seen. There I also pointed out that the explosion was a sort of "Reichstag-fire" to give occasion for a massacre of the Germans.

In the meantime three Czech ministers had arrived at Aussig, among them General Svoboda. I had the impression that the authorities in Prague had been embarrassed by the incidents at Aussig. It was also rumoured that foreign journalists had filmed the incidents and that the film was already in security. The then Czech Government had still some respect for the opinion of the Western World. The plans for further evacuations were cancelled and further persecution of the Germans prohibited.

It is significant that only one of the main functionaries of the District National Committee in Aussig, who formed the so-called leading group, is still alive. I should like to stress that the Czech mayor of Aussig at that time, one Vondra, attempted by all possible means to check the fury of the newly-arrived horde. Indeed, the mob almost threw the Czech mayor himself into the Elbe.

At the end of November 1945 I went to Prague for a second time. On the train I met a Czech from Schönpriesen and talked with him. He said that he had been ordered to Prague in order to be interrogated as a witness in connection with the explosion at Aussig. He told me that he, like many others, was convinced that the explosion had been carefully prepared and carried out by a camarilla and that the incidents after the explosion also belonged to the pre-arranged scheme. What came of the interrogation I was unable to find out, as I did not meet the man again.

This is the truth about those events. All the other accounts which have been published by the Czechs are not in full correspondence with the truth. The description in Bruno Brehm's new book *Am Rande des Abgrundes* (On the brink of the abyss) is also not accurate.

Aussig, Report No. 2
Eyewitness account of the blood bath of July 30, 1945
Reported by Therese Mager - Report of August 11, 1946

Until the evacuation I lived in Aussig, at Teplitzer Street number 36. On the afternoon of July 30, 1945, around 4:30 p.m., I was walking through Schönpriesener Street to Aussig. Suddenly I heard the sound of detonations from the direction of the Schönpriesen sugar refinery, and soon I also saw clouds of smoke rising up. At the same time the Czechs began to spread the rumor that the Germans had caused the explosions, and began to persecute anyone who wore a white armband. I myself was in the medical corps, and my Red Cross armband clearly identified me as nurse. The Czechs stormed through the streets, beat the Germans down or shot at them when they tried to flee.

I ran to the bridge that crosses the Elbe river, and here I saw hundreds of workers who were coming from the Schicht manufacturing plant, being thrown into the Elbe. The Czechs even shoved women and children and even baby carriages into the river. These Czechs were mostly wearing black uniforms with red armbands (SNB men). They threw women and children who could not defend themselves from the 60-foot-high bridge into the river. I avoided crossing the bridge. Instead, after having seen these terrible sights, I ran through the Töpfergasse [street] back to the Aussig school square. There I went into my boss Dr. N.'s surgery. Four wounded people were already there. At that moment Dr. N. came in. She herself had dragged a badly injured man in from the street. It was 70-year-old Josef Horn of Aussig, who had sustained three severe head injuries and whose throat had been cut. We took Horn to the hospital, where he was refused admission at first, and was accepted only after much begging on our part. The mass persecution of the Germans lasted until late in the evening. We heard screams and crying from every corner and street. Neither an official authority nor the Russian occupation forces took steps to curb this mass murder. Numerous Germans who had initially saved themselves by swimming out of the Elbe were shot at with machine guns. In Aussig the total number of people who lost their lives in this way was estimated at 800 to a thousand.

On July 31 the persecutions slowly abated. The Germans who dared go back into the streets had to get off the sidewalks, and were beaten if they failed to do so right away. From this time on, anyone and everyone who wore the white armband was fair game for abuse, and was treated accordingly.

I reinforce this my statement with my signature and am prepared to repeat it under oath at any time.

Aussig, Report No. 3
Massacre
Reported by Herbert Schernstein - Report of December 9, 1945

I was a member of the Communist Party even before the war, and spent the time from October 18, 1938 until December 12, 1945 in the concentration camps Theresienstadt, Sachsenhausen and Ravensbrück. On July 8 I returned from the concentration camp to Aussig, where the Czechs had just evacuated my mother. Despite my ID cards (Communist Party and concentration camp) I encountered gruff rejection everywhere. I was told that *"Nemec jest nemec!"* (a German is a German) and was denied admission everywhere. Many of my former party comrades were treated the same way despite their ID cards that showed them to be anti-Fascists. For example, my friend Willi Krebs of Leitmeritz, who had been the founder of the Communist Party in Prödlitz, had owned a grocery store, which was taken from him with only five minutes' notice, two months ago. The Czechs and Communists did not in any way stand up for us. I am also certain that there are many Fascist elements in the KPC [Czech Communist Party]. In Aussig, for example, there is one police inspector Dibisch who today pretends to be the biggest Communist possible, but who persecuted me before the war for being a member of the Communist Party.

I am able to give detailed information about the events involved in the great explosion beside the sugar refinery in Schönpriesen, where almost 1,000 Germans lost their lives, because I happened to be passing right by there on a trip from Schreckenstein to Aussig. It was the explosion of a grenade depot located beside the Schönpriesen sugar refinery, which was affiliated with a chemicals factory during the war. The Czechs blamed the Germans for the explosion and proceeded with brutal measures against them. After 4 o'clock in the afternoon members of the *Svoboda garda* drove all the Germans in the surrounding city blocks from their homes and hunted them *en masse* into the Elbe river. I saw women and children vanish under the waves. On the Ferdinand Heights Czech submachine gun positions had been set up, and from there they shot at the Germans floating in the river. I would estimate that some 1,000 Germans were killed in this manner. The Czechs proceeded especially harshly against German anti-Fascists, who were identified with red arm bands.

The Czechs declared that the Germans were chiefly to blame for the events. Many Germans, for example an acquaintance of mine, the daughter of the Klinger family from Prödlitz, are still missing to this day.

Many Germans were herded into the concentration camp in Lerchenfeld, where they had to live under the worst possible conditions. The camp was later transferred to Schöbritz. There one could frequently see the yellow flag that warned outsiders of infectious diseases and meant "Caution, typhus!" In Schöbritz 300-400 Germans died of this epidemic every day. Former concentration camp inmates, among them a certain Vlcek and the Labor Service leader Cuba, proceeded with especial ruthlessness against the German inmates and by far exceeded the concentration camp methods of the Nazis, which I also personally experienced.

Aussig, Report No. 4
Ill-treatment and murder of German workmen
Reported by Max Becher - Report of December 14, 1946

An ammunition dump exploded on July 31st, 1945, in a suburb of Aussig. The Germans were blamed for this and the Czechs used the excuse for an attack on them. Aussig lies on the left bank of the Elbe, and the factory where I worked, Georg Schicht-Schreckenstein, on the right bank. There is one bridge connecting the two sides. After work, at 4:30 that afternoon, we were searched for weapons both on leaving the factory and again at the bridge. Once on the bridge we were not allowed to turn back. On the Aussig end we were received by hundreds of Czechs, armed with clubs and iron bars. I received several serious head injuries, whilst my companion, a 67-year-old foreman, had his skull smashed in. I learned later that his body had been thrown into the river and washed up 10 miles downstream. Then I was told to carry the body of another man whose head had been smashed in, to a dump near by. On my return they said it would be my turn to be killed. I was forced to take off my jacket and to wipe up the pool of blood, while I was struck from all directions. I managed to get away, but a Czech followed and attacked me. He was carrying a heavy club and with it injured me severely. He did not stop until, as I suppose, he thought me dead. When I regained consciousness two Czechs helped me to a house, where the German inhabitants notified the Red Cross. I was taken away on a stretcher and was lucky enough to be admitted to the hospital at ten o'clock that night. This saved my life. The following were my injuries: 3 ribs broken, left arm broken, 6 head injuries, requiring 23 stitches. My left arm, which I had used as a shield against the blows, was so swollen that the fact it had been broken was not discovered until two months later, during the course of an x-ray examination. I stayed in hospital from July 31st to October 20th, 1945, and had to continue treatment at home from October 20th to November 19th, 1945.

As a result of my injuries I still suffer severe attacks of dizziness when I move my head and look upwards, and from pains in the ribs when doing manual labour or during changes of the weather.

Aussig, Report No. 5
The robbing of a blind man
Reported by Franz Habelt - Report of November 6, 1946

On July 5 last year I, like many other "resettled persons", had to vacate my home within ten minutes in order to be evacuated into the Russian zone. In the process I was robbed of numerous violin parts and strings etc., which were very valuable to me, a blind musician. Thanks to the intervention of a German lady physician, Dr. Schiel, I was allowed to return to my home. On September 2 of this year, the consultant in cultural matters, Antonin Tyc, confiscated two classic violins dating from 1700 and 1866 from me. I had acquired these two violins in 1913 at an auction in Vienna. In the course of the resettlement I was deprived of my feather bedding as well as a briefcase full of the tools of my trade, which I desperately need to repair musical instruments in my capacity as piano tuner and music teacher. I have also lost all my sheet music, including manuscripts of my own compositions. These losses are a severe blow to me in my continued professional existence as a blind musician.

Aussig, Report No. 6
Transport of the blind
Reported by Martha Rauscher - Report of November 6, 1946

Since the beginning of the year conferences and discussions had been in progress between the International Red Cross, the Czech authorities concerned, and the Czech hygienist of the University of Prague with regard to the transfer of the blind from Aussig, together with their relatives - both those in employment and those who live in institutions. The International Red Cross intervened with the view to obtaining permission for blind persons to take with them more of their personal belongings and property than usually allowed to expellees. The Czech Ministry of Public Health had already promised to put an ambulance train at our disposal. As a result of a counter-attack by a Czech group in Aussig, however, the transport of the blind was not able to take place in the way originally planned. Notwithstanding this, they allowed us to believe up to the very last moment that the transfer would be carried out under advantageous conditions. But in the end the responsible official at Aussig, Tyc, did not even allow the blind professional musicians to take their instruments with them, although a decree existed which stated that tools and implements professionally necessary might in general be exported. The same thing happened to the blind author Hacker, who was not permitted to take his typewriter, and to a blind professional secretary, who was refused permission to take his Braille shorthand-writer. On account of the different conferences the transfer was delayed into the cold season, but was at last carried out in just the same way as any other transfer of expelled persons, although the members of the transport had to pay the duty on goods as well as other special fees out of their own pockets, as was customary with privileged transports.

During the last months the blind expellees were in great distress - they could often not afford to buy their daily bread ration, since they had lost their jobs as a result of the situation; in spite of numerous requests, no financial assistance could be obtained, even though 20% had been deducted from the wages of German workers for the support of those incapable of working. I myself was repeatedly threatened with arrest for interceding on behalf of the blind. On October 29th, 1945, we were ordered to the camp at Schöbritz, in spite of my request that the blind should not have to pass through a transfer-camp. The conditions in this camp were horrible. We had to sleep on bare boards; in the morning we were driven out of the barracks at 7 o'clock amd had to stand for hours with our luggage in the pouring rain until the transport was loaded up. Instead of the 24 wagons promised, we were crammed into 8, together with our luggage. The greater part of our luggage had been ruined by the rain. 30 persons with their entire baggage were put into each wagon, so that many of them had no room to sit. From Tuesday morning to Wednesday evening all we were given was black coffee and a soup which nobody could eat, and dry bread. In consequence of the fatigues and agitation and of the inhuman manner in which the transfer was carried out, several old people collapsed. At Wiesau two persons with nervous breakdowns and one man suffering from total exhaustion had to be left with the hospital. At the request of the relatives, other cases of serious exhaustion were brought to Augsburg in an ambulance wagon, which was not provided for this purpose until the transport had reached Wiesau. Among these cases was Mrs. Witek, who died at Augsburg, in the hospital of Government Camp B.

Aussig, Report No. 7
Concentration camps Lerchenfeld and Schöbritz
Reported by Heinrich Michel

It was on May 16, 1945 at 5:00 p.m. that I was led off from my house on the orders of the police prefect Douda of Aussig. I was self-employed as master carpenter in Aussig-Prödlitz and was still wearing my working clothes. My wife just managed to slip me some dry bread. Of the men guarding me, I knew the partisan Walter Swoboda of Aussig-Prödlitz, Lange Gasse 116. On our arrival in Aussig, in the coal syndicate where Douda resided, the latter - surrounded by Russians - yelled at me: "You bandit, you crook, you scoundrel, you Gestapo lackey!" Searching me for weapons, he yanked the bread out of my pocket and threw it in my face, with the words: "I'm going to have you shot!" Douda had used to be the head waiter in the Turnhalle. In 1938 he had emigrated to Russia. After all my valuables had been confiscated from me, I was taken to the court prison, into Cell 8. Surmising what kind of Czech terrorism was to come, I had considered taking my life, but I was dissuaded by the other inmate of the cell, the Elbe valley painter Podlebnik from Aussig-Salesel. Podlebnik had been arrested because he had allegedly served people from the Waffen-SS. Podlebnik believed that it was an act of malice by a local Czech, because he had not so much as seen a Waffen-SS man all of 14 days prior to his arrest.

More fellow-sufferers arrived by the hour, so that there were soon nine of us in the cell. There were the weapons dealer Strowik, lawyer Knöspel, Heller and others.

On the second day following my imprisonment, another prisoner came into the cell. More accurately, he stumbled in and collapsed. Soon we noticed a horrible stench. The man lying on the ground before us had excrement running out of his collar and both trouser legs. What had happened here? I got permission from the warden, a Croat, to undress the man and clean him up a bit in the water earmarked for fighting air-raid fires. It had not been changed for weeks, but it was better than nothing. To our horror, there was not even a palm-sized area anywhere from the man's neck to his feet that was not suffused with blood. We didn't believe that he would survive. But he did recover. The abused man's name was Heller, he was from Staditz near Tschochau and was a foreman at the cable factory of Staditz. As Heller told us later, the reason for his arrest was that in his capacity as foreman he had reported a Czech man's act of sabotage to the owner of the factory, one Herr Wild. He had managed to flee, wading twice through the river Biela, but after a downright turkey-shoot conducted by the partisans he was surrounded, taken back to Staditz, and grossly abused here in a cellar.

By the time Whitsun had arrived there were about 180 of us imprisoned here. On Whitsun evening - all the cell doors had just been opened - a partisan appeared (I have forgotten his name, but he was a Czech) and yelled: "I am lieutenant of the partisans. Now I will show you how to deal with an SS-dog!" He emptied a ¾-liter bottle of schnapps. From Cell 15, where the Waffen-SS and other SS members were kept, they dragged out Willi Künstner, the chief of personnel from the Schicht works and honorary member of the General SS. He was beaten, shoved, knocked down, dragged to his feet again, beaten again, and so on without pause. We closed our doors and stuck our fingers in our ears. When we dared open the doors again, we saw how the victim, who had collapsed, was being dragged back into his cell by two SS-men. The cell was so overcrowded already anyway that there was no room for someone lying down. After many entreaties we managed to have Künstner taken to a hospital. The next day we found out, in roundabout ways, that Künstner never regained consciousness at the hospital, and died there. An 18-year-old member of the Waffen-SS in my cell, who was not taken to Cell 15 until later - he was the only child of a widow in Türmitz and had been drafted into the Waffen-SS as late as March 1945 - had been so badly beaten that he got a nervous shock every time someone so much as opened the cell door. I don't know where he was taken to from Cell 15.

The living conditions in this court prison were very bad. Our rations consisted of some black coffee in the morning, two or three potatoes with instant sauce at noon, and 100 grams of bread to last the entire day. Eight to nine people lived in each 9 m² cell. A bucket without a lid had to serve as toilet. And so it was rather a relief for us when work teams were set up. On the other hand, this again provided more opportunity for maltreatment, which was directed particularly at the intellectuals who were not used to hard physical work. At the train station we had to unload supplied that had been intended for the German Wehrmacht - barrels of butter, sardines etc. - and move them into the basement of the former Jepa shopping mart. In view of the bounty we unloaded, the excuse given for our starvation rations, namely that our fellow German pigs had taken all edibles with them, was obviously not true.

At the time, especially the teenaged, 16 to 18-year-old partisans often beat me.

To make room in the court jail, the 50 of us were taken to the former Luftwaffe camp in Lerchenfeld on May 29, 1945. First we had to clean up the chaos left by the Hungarians and the Russian soldiers passing through. We were ordered to run everywhere we had to go in the camp, which was an inhuman anguish for the older ones among us, for example the approximately 74-year-old government official Galle, Mayor Nittner, and others. In this way, we had to lug the Wehrmacht lockers from the camp to the storerooms at the top of the hill, at a run from morning till night. I was fortunate to be appointed Kapo by a Czech locksmith of my acquaintance, who had been apprenticed to Master Locksmith Schiller in Prödlitz. This spared me the worst of the hard labor. In the camp I obtained a push cart, so that four of the older prisoners could ride and walk. The partisan guards forbade this kind of transportation, but I applied to the camp commandant Vrsa and convinced him that in this way four lockers could be moved at a time. New groups constantly arrived from the court jail, and by the end of June our number had grown to 1,000, distributed among the 13 blocks. Four of the blocks housed women. Later, all prisoners - most of them were people who had been arbitrarily arrested - were sent here to Lerchenfeld directly instead of with an intermediate stop at the court jail. From the time the camp had opened, a roughly 20-year-old fellow who had only one arm had been used as messenger. He had to pass on all the orders given by the camp command, and this gave him some degree of freedom. One evening he did not return. Immediately all the surrounding villages, where the partisans serving in the camp were quartered, were informed of his absence. Almost all the camp's partisans, some 80 to 120 guards, participated in this manhunt. Late that night we learned that the escapee had been shot in a forest nearby. The next morning we had to walk single-file past the gurney with the shot man. During the roll call that had preceded this, camp commandant Vrsa had yelled: "This is what will happen to anyone who tries to escape."

Witnesses to all the events which I recount from my time in the Lerchenfeld camp and also in Schöbritz, are: the arms dealer Strowik from Aussig, Hoffmann from Nestomitz, chief engineer Holina from the Solvay Plant, the attorney of the Solvay Plant, the Chairman of the Trade Guild health insurance organization (I don't want to mention his name yet as he is still missing), Hübsch from the Employees' Health Insurance organization, the master shoemaker Heller, Wenzel Behr, an employee of the DAF, the two brothers Mieke from Türmitz, one of which was an attorney with Tuch-Hübel, and all the prisoners of Block 1, of which I was a member and which included all the craftsmen and clerks used in the camp.

It was usually arranged that newly arriving groups of prisoners - generally 30 to 50 but sometimes as many as 100 men - arrived in the evening, when all camp inmates had to be in their cell blocks. From the window of our Block 1 we were able to observe how these receptions took place. The new arrivals had to sing the German national anthem and SA songs, and had to parade along after a portrait of Hitler. They had to run the gauntlet from the barrier to the administrative barracks, which meant a stretch of about 40 to 50 meters lined on either side by partisans who beat mercilessly down on the running prisoners with bullwhips. The women among the partisans were the worst among them, most especially one from Karbitz, whose name is probably known to my fellow prisoner Kohberger from Karbitz. Members of the SA got special treatment. They received 25 blows with a bullwhip or rubber truncheon on their bare buttocks.

In October our numbers had grown to about 3,500. Every day 2,500 went out to work. On July 31, 1945, the Bloody Day of Aussig, one team had not returned from work. As I already mentioned, I was the Kapo (block elder) of Block 1, the cell block where the camp's craftsmen and clerks were imprisoned. This helped me to find out many things that most others didn't know, from the tax advisor Hahnel of Aussig, Hauptmann of Aussig, Stephan, a high-ranking official with the Aussig Main Post Office, the academic painter Ungermann, Mayor of Reichenberg (he was later taken to Reichenberg). Especially Fritz Wolfrum from the Schönpriesen liquor factory must know a lot, since he was the clerk to the political officer in charge and was later also involved in the preliminaries for the People's Court trials. From these clerks, we in Block 1 learned that the account given of the labor team that had not returned stated: "Killed in the catastrophic explosion." According to the accounts of the eyewitnesses to the Aussig massacre, these men most likely fell into the hands of the rabble. The aforementioned clerks also witnessed the shooting of Emil Luprich from Nollendorf. I will never forget this one Saturday in August, I think it was the 22nd, when 22-year-old Emil Luprich from Nollendorf, who had not been drafted into the Waffen-SS until spring 1945, was shot by a firing squad in front of all 3,000 camp inmates. The day before, two men from a labor team had escaped. Saturday evening around 5:30pm, not the usual time, the camp bell was rung. "Everyone line up, without exception," we were ordered. Camp commandant Vrsa appeared, totally drunk, and took his usual speaker's podium. His speech was nothing but cursing from start to finish. In conclusion he screamed that as punishment for the two escaped men, every tenth prisoner would now be shot. The roofs of the surrounding barracks were manned by partisans with submachine guns. The partisans repeated their rifles and got ready to fire. We were prepared for the worst, and only felt sorry for the approximately 1,300 women, who were lined up across from us, calm but deathly pale. And then Vrsa began to curse all over again. The real culprits, he said, were actually the Kapos, and so all the Kapos should be shot. Now all Kapos had to line up side by side, in lines of five. After this was done, Vrsa again changed his mind; now every tenth Kapo was to be shot. I believe I was one of those who would have been shot, because a partisan came up to me and changed my place with another. I guess my carpentry services were simply too useful for the partisan gentlemen to dispense with. - But this order was also not carried out. We figured out later that all this back-and-forth was intended to create panic among us, which would snap at the climax to be expected and provide an excuse to stage a blood bath.

We had been standing on the roll call square for about an hour already. Vrsa began cursing yet again, this time at the women. He said they were German whores, SS-whores, every one of them. A new order was issued: "All members of the SS and Waffen-SS step forward!" The SS-men had been continually sent off to special camps, but unfortunately there were still five Waffen-SS men among us, who had been brought here from the camp at Karbitz. These five were now led off into the former Wehrmacht bunker. As we found out later, they had to draw lots. The young fellow from

Nollendorf drew the short straw. Meanwhile, Vrsa had declared to us that he did not want to be like us, that he would rather show mercy than dispense harsh justice, but that a punishment simply had to be. When the SS-men returned, he called out: "Someone is being executed here in the name of the Republic! The verdict will be carried out immediately!" About 30 feet away, the execution squad took up position in front of the "convicted" man. Hands raised, the young Nollendorfer begged for mercy. Then Vrsa yanked a kerchief off a woman's head. It was tied over the condemned man's eyes. Vrsa repeated the sentence in Czech. Then the sentence was carried out. The tall Czech partisan whose bullet had been the fatal one was never seen in the camp again after that. - We saw Emil Luprich lying in a pool of his own blood. "Dr. Tauber!" Vrsa yelled. Dr. Tauber, the camp physician, examined the young man and found that he was still alive. Now Luprich was shot once more, in the head. It was a few minutes before 8 o'clock pm. A brief order decreed that the square had to be vacated by 8 o'clock. It was thanks to the level-headedness of our camp elder, who immediately saw to our quick withdrawal, and not least of all to the self-control of the women, that the panic which the Czechs probably still longed for did not break out after all.

A time of torment was in store for me as well, namely when Skala, the son of a railwayman from Prödlitz, and Huttig, who lived in the Prödlitz Castle, came to Lerchenfeld as partisans. Huttig beat me with the bullwhip that every partisan carried in his boot until I collapsed unconscious. When I came to, the beating was resumed. One time later on, when I asked Huttig in the presence of another Czech named Vacek why he had beaten me, he declared that it was because when he had been a 12-year-old boy I had ejected him from a fairground for stealing cake. I asked him whether I had also beaten him at the time. "No," he admitted. In Prödlitz Skala then bragged at every opportunity that he had beaten up the master carpenter Michel. During this period my camp comrades had to keep a watch on me to keep me from committing suicide.

One day - I do not recall the date - a father was brought to the camp along with his son who had returned home to his parents' house from the Wehrmacht only the evening before. At the gate to the concentration camp the son tried to flee. He was mowed down with a submachine gun. The father then had to cart his dead son into the camp on a wheelbarrow, and was severely beaten while doing so.

Beatings were the order of the day. The most minor violations of camp rules were punished with 25 to 50 blows. It was such a violation for an inmate to speak to a woman, even if she was his own wife. Then both of them would receive 25 blows. Or if someone was caught smuggling letters. And as I mentioned before, at first everyone was punished if he failed to run through the camp, or stood still for a while. To be punished, it was enough if a partisan said someone had deserved it; nobody checked to see if it was true, and there was no defense. Punishment was meted out every evening at roll call. The prisoner to be punished had to bring a beer barrel and lie across it. Then two partisans beat down on him with their bullwhips. When a woman was to be punished, her head was stuck between a partisan's legs, her mouth was held shut, and then she was beaten mainly on the kidney area. Afterwards the punished prisoners were forced to thank their tormenters. Once the 70-year-old teacher Meiyner from Prödlitz was punished with 50 blows for allegedly having stolen a loaf of bread. Meiyner had actually been given the loaf by the baker who supplied the camp, but he couldn't say so because otherwise the baker would also have ended up in the camp. Meiyner looked horrible. His back and buttocks were suffused with blood and his testicles enormously swollen. We expected that Meiyner would die of this treatment. But he actually survived. Today he lives in the American [occupation] zone [of Germany].

In early October the camp at Lerchenfeld, which was occupied by Russians, was transferred to Schöbritz. But first we had to make the camp livable. For the first time we had to live outdoors, even though the cold nights were already setting in. A time of severe hardship began for everyone except those in Block 1. The dividing walls had to be removed from prefabricated RAD barracks, logs were set up inside at a height of 3 feet and the dividing walls were placed on these, and this process was continued up to the ceiling so that each barrack turned into a three or four-storey shack. Each of these barracks had to house two blocks of inmates, that is 500 men. Altogether we were 13 blocks. There was no straw; we had to sleep on the bare floor, packed like sardines. There was no way to keep the shacks clean; you could cut the air with a knife, the stench was so bad. Whenever someone turned over in his sleep, or had to use the bucket, he invariably woke up all his neighbors. It was astonishing that under these circumstances these people actually still managed to keep the peace amongst themselves. Under the pretext of repairs I often managed to go to the other barracks, and smuggled illegal packages along in my toolbox. Those of us in Block 1 each had our own bed, even if they were stacked two and three storeys high. But this favoritism that was shown to us by the Czechs was not because they liked us, but rather, as mentioned before, because very often they would exploit our labor for their own personal purposes.

Then came November 13, 1945, a horrible day, horrible for those involved and for those who had to watch helplessly how German people whose only crime was that they were Germans, were tortured to death. The day before, two comrades had escaped from a work team. On the 13th, Block 8, which the two men had belonged to, was not allowed to go out to work. At 7:30 am the order was given: "Block 8 line up for morning exercises." Block 8 lined up. From the window I heard how Vrsa said sarcastically to them, since the German people loved gymnastics this was really no punishment at all for them. Then everyone had to march off to the parade square. The lawn there had been removed only a few days before; the loamy ground was still slippery. Then the "gymnastics" began: Up, down, squats, push-ups, and on and on without a break until 11 o'clock. It was undernourished and, in part, elderly frail people who had to do these exercises here. Anyone who could not continue was beaten. Slats were ripped off an old fence and used to ruthlessly beat these people. Hoffmann from Nestomitz and the NSV District Office Chief Stroppe were standing beside me at the window. We had to turn away, and went into our workshop. Gymnastics teacher Langhammer of Prödlitz was one of those who went through this torment. After these agonizing hours it was decreed that Block 8 would have to report again in the afternoon, completely cleaned up. That meant that the overalls had to be washed, and put on again wet since they could not possibly be dry again by the afternoon. From the camp physician Dr. Tauber I learned that this day had cost 9 men their lives and produced 20 injured who had been taken to the infirmary.

In terms of quantity, our rations had increased. They consisted in the main of ground potato starch, which the former Wehrmacht stores were full of. We continued to starve. Those of our comrades who did a lot of work for the Czechs personally, or who received their rations in the Schicht plant or in the Glass Works, fared a little better. The camp's water supply was a disaster. The water was carted in from old wells in the vicinity, in barrels. Typhus raged in the camp from late October until December. One day I saw a line of cars from the Red Cross pull up. The cars had foreign licence plates. Dr. Tauber, who was just crossing the camp square, was called over. The conversation had lasted for about 15 minutes when Vrsa showed up. After the Commission had toured one of the barracks, they left the camp again.

On Christmas Even there was a major roll-call. The entire camp had to line up in front of a Christmas tree decorated with electric lights and was ordered to sing "Silent Night, Holy Night". When our rations suddenly improved, we knew that change was in the air. The ill prisoners received gruel with sugar, and Vrsa showed up in the kitchen and declared that this order was to be strictly adhered to, so that we wouldn't have reason to complain again.

On January 13, 1946 the events of November 13 were repeated. I don't know how many prisoners died; I only saw how dead people were taken on stretchers directly to the morgue, and that many injured went to the infirmary. One day, I and the health practitioner Riedel, the baker Wenndt from Aussig, policeman Hacker from Türmitz, and Schlattner from Königswald observed from the kitchen how an approximately 18-year-old girl was roped to a pear tree from her chest down to her knees and was then beaten in the face by partisans passing by. Then a car pulled up, driven by a man I did not know. It seems that it was on his intervention that the girl was untied a short time afterwards. She had to be taken to the infirmary on a stretcher.

We found out later that beating and abuse was now forbidden in the camp. And on the surface it did seem as though this order was being obeyed, but in actual fact the abuse continued - except that now the victims were taken one at a time into the basements of surrounding houses so that the abuse could no longer be seen or heard. - Now I would like to tell how Dr. Tauber died. In my opinion his conversation with the foreign Commission was the cause of his death. Although Dr. Tauber had to appear to be stern to his fellow prisoners, he took many a chance on our behalf and tried to improve our general lot. I personally was often present when he went up against Vrsa. One evening someone from Block 13 called, "Dr. Tauber!" Block 13 wasn't far from the barbed-wire fence. Dr. Tauber had the right to visit the blocks where he was being called even at night, carrying a lantern. The next morning Dr. Tauber was dead, and no-one got to see him any more. Two inmates had escaped during the night. We were told that Dr. Tauber had tried to escape and had been caught and beaten down by the partisans standing guard. "And that's what will happen to anyone who tries to go over the barbed wire and home into the Reich!" Vrsa announced. Among us prisoners the explanation was that Dr. Tauber had to die because on all the death certificates he had issued he had been forced to give the cause of death as heart failure, weakness due to old age, debilitation etc. Once, when I had been ill and in the infirmary for several days, Dr. Tauber had commented to me: "If this ends well and I get out of here alive, I'll have been lucky. But I don't believe it will happen. I know too much."

In late January we were sent back to Lerchenfeld. The People's Court trials began. Minor offenses, in many cases of an entirely private nature - for example if a Czech and a German had once had a disagreement and they mutually insulted one another - were now dragged into the lime-light and punished with 2 to 3 years' imprisonment. Josef Hergesell of Prödlitz was sentenced to two years for an alleged slap in the face. Hergesell is now living in Germany; I don't know where. Schubert, who had worked in the copper plant in Pömmerle, was sentenced to 10 years for keeping a Czech from committing sabotage. I myself was spared a People's Court trial, as my personal enemy Douda had by then died. He had been removed from all offices and was himself locked up for 8 days; the Czech police inspector Klimesch of Prödlitz had been unable to substantiate his charge that in 1938 I had allegedly stolen his dining room [furniture?], 50 kg of screws and 20 m wood. On September 16,1946 I was informed that I was not allowed to return to my home town, and was deported to Thuringia.

This report represents the truth, to the best of my knowledge and belief.

Brünn, Report No. 1
Death march to Pohrlitz
Reported by M. v. W. - Report of February 22, 1951

I still remember very well the proclamation made by Beneš, broadcast from Kaschau two or three days before the arrival of the Russians in Brünn. I understood all he said, since I speak Czech fluently. I will never forget his solemn vow: "Woe to the Germans, woe to the Germans, thrice woe to the Germans, we will liquidate them!" It was on April 25, 1945, about 4 or 5 o'clock in the afternoon, when scenes of fraternization between the invading Russians and the Czechs took place in the streets. In the evening I returned to my apartment and was able to witness how the public rape of German women, beatings, ill-treatment and abuse brought the entire German population into a state of great agitation and danger.

The next morning all Germans had to report for work in accordance with the notices posted on public advertising pillars. I was assigned to the St. Anna Hospital, the men having found out that I was a Red Cross nurse. First I was given only the most menial tasks. Only through the intervention of a Czech physician who had been active in this hospital for a long time was I reinstated as a Red Cross nurse, but even then I was only supposed to go on duty in the air-raid shelter, a cellar to which all the German patients of this big hospital had been moved. In this cellar they lay on bare palliasses without blankets or pillows, and without any medical care. No medications were available for these patients. The cellar was only scantily illuminated by a little lamp and all I could do for these gravely ill people was to help them by applying wet rags or giving them water.

Already on the second or third day of my activities in this cellar, human beings dreadfully mutilated, beaten half-dead and tortured almost to death were brought in. All I could give them in the way of assistance, however, were consoling words because I had no drugs whatsoever.

The great dying began. All those who had been brought in from the Kaunitz College died almost without exception, and such cases came in without pause. I remember the following cases in particular:

The first to die was a man who had been brought in on the point of death with a horrible injury in the area of the genitals. I could not ascertain his name, as he regained consciousness only for a few moments before he died, and could only briefly reply to my question: "How did you get this terrible injury?" He answered: "I was kicked for having formerly sold vegetables to the Gestapo." With these words he collapsed and I could not elicit any further information before he died.

I also remember another case, that of Mr. Venklarczik, a solicitor, 63 years of age, living at Stiftgasse, Brünn. The man was delivered into the hospital and recounted the following incident: under a threadbare pretext partisans dragged him into the camp in the Kaunitz College and thrashed him there so violently that his back was one gaping wound. He was then forced to thank his torturers for the dreadful ill-treatment. In a semi-conscious state he was taken up to the third floor. In his panic he attempted, during a moment when he was not being watched, to bring his life to an end by jumping through the window. He was saved, however, by a lush tree underneath the window. Instead of being killed, one of his kidneys was torn loose. When he was brought in his excrement and urine were pure blood.

It was not until a second German was delivered with his arteries cut through that I saw a physician for the first time in this cellar-camp full of wounded. The reason was that the man who had tried to commit suicide by cutting the arteries should be brought back to consciousness by a blood-transfusion in order that he might be executed later while conscious.

The physician, a Czech himself, examined Venklarczik, the unfortunate man, and was shocked to see the marks of the atrocious maltreatment and said, "But you didn't get this from your jumping out of the window, did you?" The seriously injured man did not dare to accuse any Czech by answering, as that would have meant the death sentence for him.

There is a further case which I remember: a saleswoman from Brünn, Wiener Strasse, had been brought in. She was about 50 years of age and completely unconscious. She was carried to the darkest corner of the basement, where a group of partisans, including a GPU-commissar, who was a Czech, ill-treated the unconscious woman. I was ordered to undress her, after which the Czech commissar intended to bring her back to consciousness with brutal kicks. I also remember that the Czech commissar then told a nun that the reason for the woman's ill-treatment was that she had stolen a Russian uniform complete with decorations. I myself was forced to give the dying woman a series of Coramin injections in order to get her back to consciousness. But all efforts were in vain, her condition was past all hope. Again and again the commissar returned, cursing her in the most inhuman manner, calling her a pig, a German sow, a German whore, bastard and so on, and giving me the order to bring her to speak by means of artificial respiration. I myself wished her nothing but a quick death, for I imagined what they would have done to her if she had really regained consciousness. It seemed that this woman had refused to allow some man to have his way with her and had defended herself. In revenge she had been dreadfully abused. However, she had had the opportunity to take poison, from which she had sunk into unconsciousness. When she died shortly after midnight, the commissar entered the basement and kicked her from the straw pallet with his boot, furious that she could no longer speak.

Let me also recount the following case of Schlesinger, an innkeeper from Brünn, Neugasse district. He was the owner of a restaurant. Among his guests had been both members of the Nazi Party and also, of course, Czechs. For business reasons he had decided to become an inactive member of the Party. On these grounds this rather weak man 40 years of age was now forced to do hard labour, in particular to carry heavy sacks, accompanied by horrible mishandlings. Since he frequently collapsed under the weight and was forced by blows to continue, he finally contracted a rupture of the wall of the stomach, having formerly suffered from stomach ulcers. After his delivery into the hospital he was operated on without anesthetic and submitted to a stomach resection. I found the man screaming and crying in my ward. He implored me to give him something to relieve his pain.

I decided, although being apprehensive myself, to ask at the Surgical Ward. Upon my arrival there I explained the case to the nun (who was about 60 years of age and the nurse in charge) and received the following answer: "I can hear him screaming but he'll get nothing from me - we don't have anything for Germans, just as you didn't have anything for us." When I remarked that during my eleven years of work as Red Cross nurse at the hospitals in Felsberg and Brünn I had never heard of a single case of a Czech to whom assistance had been refused, the nun yelled back at me: "Don't pontificate here, a German will get nothing - tell him that!" When I answered that I did not dare to tell him that, she replied that she would do so herself. Actually, a few minutes later, the head nurse of the Surgical Ward went to the basement and shouted at the patient as he writhed in agony: "You ought to be ashamed of yourself, you are a superman and roar like an animal! You won't get anything, we don't have anything for you!" The sick man clasped his hands and asked for help for God's sake. When she again refused, he said: "Then give me some poison so I can put an end to this suffering!" The same moment a partisan ran up to the bed and shouted: "It would just suit you, you swine, to take poison and so escape the gallows. The moment your wound is healed you'll be hanged. The gallows are waiting for you!" The man was in actual fact dragged away during the night of the sixth day and from what I heard from Schneider, a partisan, he was hanged in the Kaunitz College.

In order to cloak the fact that they had been murdered, it was customary to deliver persons murdered on the streets to the hospital, in the basement, so that they would be registered as though they had died in hospital.

The Death March.

My experiences of the death march to Pohrlitz on Corpus Christi Day included the following incidents: At 9 o'clock in the evening of May 30th, 1945, the Germans were evicted from their apartments. The whole night long, men, women and children stood crowded together in the monastery garden in Alt-Brünn (a suburb of Brünn). In the early dusk we were driven out of the garden and lined up in three columns in the yard of the monastery. A Staff Captain then arrived, together with a throng of partisans and gendarmes, and shouted: "Hand over all gold, money and savings-bank deposit-books!" Following this order the partisans, gendarmes and he himself rushed up to the defenceless women and elderly people and tore all their jewellery, money and valuables, in a word everything that seemed to be of value, out of their luggage and from the bodies of the assembled. Each of the partisans had boxes full of money, silverware and jewellery. The name of the man in charge was Staff Captain Holatko. While these scenes took place, the National Committee, presided by Matula, Chairman of the National Committee, was holding its meeting in Brünn. (Matula's wife owned a butcher's shop in Brünn; he himself became mayor of Brünn in 1945.)

The following scene took place in front of our very eyes: An old lady wearing beautiful diamonds was relieved of all her jewellery by a partisan. When the partisan tried to take away her wedding-ring, she pleaded with him not to do so, crying: "Sir, please, let me keep just this ring; it is of no value for you and it's almost 55 years since my husband gave it to me before the altar - I wish to be buried together with the ring." He replied: "You old sow, you talk like a book. Now say it all in Czech; we are living in the free Czechoslovak Republic and we speak only Czech!" and thereupon pulled the ring off her finger.

Next Staff Captain Holatko proclaimed in a loud voice that anyone on whom hidden things were found would be shot on the spot. After this a young woman pushing a perambulator with two little babies approached the Staff Captain with two savings-bank deposit-books which she surrendered with trembling hands, saying: "I wanted to keep the two deposit-books for my two small children in memory of their dead father. Since you said you were going to shoot us, I have decided to give them to you." He turned over the pages of the books, then threw them back in her face with the remark: "You mean whore, you sow, you just want to make a fool out of me!" (This is verbatim, as I speak Czech fluently.) The young woman picked up the books and whispered to us: "We are poor, my husband had only 20 crowns in each of them - and that's probably not enough for him!"

The march began. Due to the fact that the assembled Germans had had to stand in the open air all night long on the streets and in the monastery garden, many collapsed after a few kilometers. The road led towards Pohrlitz. It was a heart-rending column and the whole situation was well expressed by a desperate woman who, with her hands raised to heaven, exclaimed: "O my God, such a Corpus Christi procession as this can never have been seen before!" After marching for close on 10 miles, near the village of Raigern, those among us who, tired and exhausted, were unable to walk any further; were driven into the camp at Raigern. Upon their arrival there they were assembled by female partisans, stripped naked, and both men and women searched for jewellery and money. Their garments were literally cut in tatters during the search for hidden valuables. Countless persons were beaten to death and, according to the statements of many of those who reached Pohrlitz, finally shot. Scenes beyond all description took place on the road to Pohrlitz; especially when, in the afternoon, a terrible thunderstorm burst and flooded the ditches. The tired and exhausted marchers slipped on the soaked ground and although whipped and beaten, they were still unable to get up again. The ditches were filled with articles of clothing, bags, food, which the exhausted men and women had dropped, and amidst these lay all those who had collapsed and who finally died of exhaustion.

The majority dragged themselves to Pohrlitz, where, however, thousands died.

The column of Brünn Germans made its way via Pohrlitz towards the Austrian border; I myself reached Pohrlitz, together with thousands of men, women and children, on the evening of Corpus Christi Day. I was so exhausted that I looked for a small spot to lie down. In the darkness I came to a car repair shop, where I crouched exhausted and spent the night. All night long I heard the cries for help of women being raped; early in the morning those able to continue the march were driven back on the road with whips and blows and forced to walk in the direction of Austria. Those unable to go any further - about 6,000 persons - were lodged in the nearby grain elevators, where they camped on the bare concrete floor. Not even the seriously ill patients were given straw to sit on.

I was appointed as nurse to Barrack IV, although there was scarcely anything I could do to aid these exhausted human beings, as neither medications nor any other means were available. I was also seriously ill myself. However, as a nurse I enjoyed more liberty of movement and so came to witness the most incredible atrocities in the elevators. I still remember the first killing - a soldier was chasing a woman. He jumped over the exhausted women on the ground and in the course of the chase landed with both feet on the head of an eight-year-old girl, killing her instantly.

The second death I remember was that of a woman of about 30 years, who was lying on the concrete floor together with her two children, a three-year-old girl and a baby of several weeks. In the early morning we heard the three-year-old child crying for her mother; we then found out that the woman had committed suicide by taking poison. Her face had already turned blue. The baby was dead too, since the woman had clasped it to her breast until it too had died. A Czech gendarme asked me in passing why the woman's face was so blue. I replied that she had probably poisoned herself. He then cursed her, calling her a Nazi whore and a filthy sow for committing suicide after two days in camp; and he ordered me to "throw the sow into the latrine together with her bastard". When I protested, saying that I was a Red Cross nurse and, being bound by my oath, could not carry out such an order, even if he were to shoot me, he hurled insults at me like "German sow" and "German whore". However, he then called for three other women, whom he intimidated more easily as they did not dare to argue against his threats. The names of these women were Agnes Skalitzky from Leskau, widow of a tram-driver, 63 years of age, Franziska Wimetal, about 30 years of age, and a third woman whose name was unknown to me. These women were forced to throw the corpse of the dead mother and the dead baby into the open latrine. Partisans then ordered the inmates of the camp to use the latrine so that "the sow with her dead bastard will disappear from sight as soon as possible". And this was what happened.

Days and even weeks later the little head of the child and the arm of the mother were still to be seen protruding from the filth.

On June 18, 1945 another case of brutality occurred: the order to evacuate the Blaschek Camp in Pohrlitz was supposed to be carried out by a number of gendarmes. A woman far advanced in pregnancy sat in a squatting position on the floor together with her two small children. With her hands raised she implored the gendarme to exclude her from the transport as she was having cramps and was expecting to give birth. The gendarme shouted at her brutally: "You German sow, you'll not give birth here. You can give birth wherever you want, but not here!" And the woman was forced to leave with the transport. As she was in a most pitiable condition, I presume that she died.

I also remember a further case: the mothers of small children and babies attempted to feed their children by cooking half-rotten potatoes, turnips and dry bread to an edible mash in order to save them from dying of hunger. Since there were no cooking facilities, they built themselves a very primitive emergency outdoor stove from tiles and sheet-iron. As there was neither wood nor coal available, they looked for all kinds of things to burn, such as grass, old leather, rags, and so on. They had also secretly torn a piece of tarred felt from the roof of a damaged hut and used it for heating. A gendarme arrived on the spot and was brutal enough to ruin the painfully prepared meal for the almost-starved children by demolishing the stove with a kick. He started cursing in the foulest way, and all his insults ended with "German sow", "Nazi whore", etc.

Night after night all the women, including those who were sick and even the very old ones of 70 years of age or more, were raped. The partisans let the soldiers into the camp and the women were misused twice or more times each night. I was able to witness how a soldier decided to rape an eleven-year-old girl; the terrified mother tried to defend her daughter and finally offered herself to save the child. The soldier beat her until she bled, but she still held the girl tight. I intervened when the soldier threatened the mother with his revolver. Since I speak a little Russian, I was able to reproach the soldier and so he finally left her alone. The desperate woman now did all she could to hide her child against another attack. Shortly afterwards the partisans called out for me and I had to obey and went to the door. There I was turned over to the same man, who dragged me to the sugar refinery, where I was raped by 5 Russians. When I decided to commit suicide and looked for a means of doing so, I became witness of the suicide of an old married couple. Both together hanged themselves in an empty elevator - the same one in which I lay in a state of complete exhaustion. I saw how Czech gendarmes robbed the dead couple of their documents and valuables and then tied a slip of cardboard around their wrists, on which they wrote in Czech: "Unknown, without documents!" This was the custom with all those thousands who died there. 60 or 70 persons died daily in the camp, the bodies being deprived of their shoes and frequently also of their garments; the corpses were piled in a heap and lay in the sun for hours covered with blow-flies. In front of the huts men and women on the point of death or dying from starvation lay on the grass, likewise covered with fly maggots. These unfortunates were given no food at all; they had only what they had brought along or dug out of potato-stacks. The cause of death in most cases was therefore hunger typhus. One of the huts was arranged as a sickroom. The hygienic condition of this room are best illustrated as follows: the patients lay on rotten straw already defiled by those suffering from typhoid fever. Instead of a privy a mason's cement-mixing bucket stood in the middle of the room as a latrine. This was so insufficient that it overflowed every day; the patients were supposed to empty it themselves, but they were unable to do so. An unbearable stench hung heavily over the room which was swarming with flies, lice and fleas. In spite of this no efforts were made to master either the contagious diseases or the vermin. In this sickroom a nurse named Schubert was in charge of everything. She herself boasted in front of witnesses of having dispatched more than 2,000 Germans to the other world and said that she certainly deserved Czech citizenship for her work. It seems that she was a native Czech, but had married a German. She had many Czech relatives to whom she sent jewellery and valuables which she had taken away from the unfortunate German patients or from the dying. The jewellery of less value she gave to the partisans. A principal witness of the sickroom-conditions described above is Mrs. Engelberta Höllriegel from Brünn, wife of an engineer, who confirmed that on June 12, 1945, besides those 60 to 70 persons who died daily, 56 patients had died in the sickroom before noon. She called June 12th "our black day". Mrs. Höllriegel assisted in the sick-room, without being a qualified nurse. Her husband as well as her son had been murdered in the notorious Kaunitz College.

Mass graves had, of course, been established around Pohrlitz. The corpses were buried only a few inches below the surface, so that very soon a smell of decomposition could be noticed everywhere. The newly arrived Czechs now began to protest; they said, "we don't want to have these German swine around here, they infect the entire territory and spread epidemics." It was therefore decided that on June 18 the sick persons and the mothers with children (most of them almost starved) were to be taken away in carts, while the others who were still capable of work were kept in the camp for another day. This transport of patients was led up to the Austrian border, into the so-called no-man's-land. Arriving there, the unfortunate people were left in the woods, in the flood region of the Thaya River, and abandoned to swarms of mosquitoes. Nobody knew of these people's presence there; and almost all of them starved to death and were only found when their corpses were already bloated or eaten up by mosquitoes. These incidents are said to have been filmed and shown in movie theatres in England and the States. At any rate the manager of the estate of Neuhof near Grafendorf, one Antonin Šafář, told me of this several months later. His report culminated in the exclamation: "These Austrian swine have made a fine mess of things for us!"

An individual case remains in my memory. Mrs. Kopřiva from Brünn had died of hunger in the camp at Pohrlitz, her daughter, Hermine Kopřiva, about 38 years old, went insane as a result of starvation and raping. When I reported this to the gendarme, he asked her a few questions which she answered in a confused and wandering manner. Thereupon he remarked that she was good enough for work; and in fact this woman left together with me and many others for Grussbach on June 19th, where we were distributed as labour slaves to the various estates and farms. Notwithstanding her pitiable condition she was forced to do hard labour.

The manager, who had newly been imposed on the estate by force, was a man named Antonin Šafár; the name of his 25-year-old assistant was Miroslav Tvrdík. The latter was a real brute, of whom even the manager was afraid. The following remark was characteristic: "You German swine! You'll have to work here; those unable to work will get starvation rations for 48 hours twice over, so that they'll kick off; those fit for work will have to do hard labour until they'll kiss the ground!" He acted as he had promised. Almost all of the patients died, whereas those able to work did hard labour until they were completely exhausted, as almost none of them were inured to agricultural work and the related fatigue.

Another characteristic remark was that of Dr. Skrašek from Grussbach. When he entered the stable in which our people lay on rotten straw, seriously ill and half-starved men and women, the doctor shouted out from the door: "What am I supposed to do with you? I have nothing but animal charcoal! You are a people who have lost the war and you must not expect to be handled with kid gloves!" That was all he did for the patients or for the exhausted prisoners! It was only when I appealed to him to get us some delousing powder - for we were molested to a terrible degree by lice and fleas, as well as by mice and rats which had gnawed our shoes and garments - did he agree to do so. The menace of the rats increased so much that they ate up our last bits of food before our eyes.

On June 19, 1945 German farmers from Grussbach were ordered to pick us up in the camp in Pohrlitz early in the morning and to take us in their carts to Grussbach. Shortly before Grussbach we passed an alley with cherry trees. The trees were loaded with ripe fruit; it was no wonder that we longed for some of the cherries after the torture of starvation we had endured. The farmer, who drove us, noticed our thirst and promised that he would gather some fruit in an unwatched moment from his own cherry trees which we should have to pass on the road. This indeed he did when we passed his property. But the moment the farmer tried to give the cherries to us a gendarme noticed it, drew his leather whip and lashed the farmer so violently over the face and the head that the weals left by the whip immediately began to bleed. He exclaimed: "You German pig, if you dare to tear down even one more cherry I'll shoot you down like a mangy dog." The farmer replied that he wanted to take the cherries from his own trees, not for himself but for the hungry women and children, and pointed out that the trees and fruit in question were his own property. Thereupon the gendarme cried out: "You German swine, once this belonged to you, now it belongs to us!" Mrs. Skalitzky, Mrs. Wimetal and Miss Hermine Kopřiva and some 15 other persons, whose names I do not remember, were on this transport together with me.

At the Neuhof Estate near Grafendorf.

In consideration of her illness Mrs. Emilie Kurz was appointed by Antonin Šafář, the manager, to work in the kitchen. She suffered from a serious disease of the glands and was inclined to dropsy. She was barely able to stand on her feet, but could still do sedentary work in the kitchen. At the end of June 1945 the new potatoes were harvested. In the course of an inspection by the commandant of the camp, a young man of about 30, the following incident took place: I was called from the fields to accompany the commandant on the inspection. He only visited the quarters of the German forced labourers. On this occasion he saw Mrs. Kurz sitting at the table in the corridor and husking vegetables. He at once yelled at the woman, asking her why she did not work in the fields. "Please," she answered, "I am ill and I have therefore to do this kind of work!" He then shouted like mad, "Get up when you speak to me!" The 63-year-old woman attempted painfully to do so and was shouted at all the more: "You miserable German sow, you dare to tell me that you are ill! I'll tell you what is wrong with you, you have eaten too much meat and butter stolen from our wives and children. Off to the fields with you, on the double!" The ill woman dragged herself to the potato field, but could not pick up the potatoes normally; she crawled on her knees behind the plough, picking up the potatoes and crying with pain. The commandant stood by the manager, gloating over the suffering of this unfortunate woman. When the commandant had left, Šafář, the manager, had pity on her and told her to go back to the kitchen. He realized that she was really incapable of doing this work.

Although we were doing hard labour our food rations consisted only of the following: unsweetened black coffee without bread in the morning, potatoes cooked without salt, fat or spices at noon, and black unsweetened coffee again in the evening. Next day we would be given beans without salt at noon, and as third variant, peas without salt cooked in water. This order of succession repeated itself for three weeks. We never received any bread. Finally we were given ration cards and the meals improved a little bit; we received bread and 70 g of margarine per week, that is 10 g per day (one third of an ounce). Small wonder that almost all of us showed symptoms of hunger typhus, which already had begun to break out in Pohrlitz. During the commandant's inspection I was asked about the disease of which a man lying in the stables was suffering. When I replied that the man was suffering from hunger typhus, he shouted at me: "Don't tell me such nonsense, the haemorrhages are produced by the friction of the intestinal membranes." "Well", I said, "that is hunger typhus; it does not happen if a man has enough to eat"; whereupon he insulted me in the lowest manner.

In my capacity as a former Red Cross nurse I had also to do Samaritan services at the Meierhof, to register the dead and to bury them. I still remember the following persons as having died there:

Theodora Maria Moczinsky from Breslau, 58 years old, a two-year-old girl by the name of Krista Hoffmann, furthermore Raimund Bernatschek, 65 years of age, and his wife Franziska Bernatschek, née Schlosser from Zebrovic near Brünn, Rudolf Nejeschleb, an engineer, born at Stockerau - the wife of the last-named had already died in Pohrlitz - Mr. Karl Kurz, a salesman, born in 1879 at Mährisch-Schönberg, Ludwig Spitzer, retired business representative, born in 1876 at Brünn, Maria Hloucha from Brünn, born in 1885, who died on September 8, 1945, and Anna Douba, widow of a Navy Captain, 58 years of age. All the aforementioned persons died of hunger typhus or exhaustion, however, I was ordered to write down as cause of death: marasmus = weakness of old age, including the two-year-old child. In my memory this girl was as though dried up, her tiny hands resembled the feet of a water bird, for the skin between her fingers was quite transparent and like a web. It seemed that the little child had been given almost no food for weeks or at best only the same food as the grown-ups.

In my capacity as a sort of controller for the hard labourers in the farms of Neuhof, Karlshof and of the factory-yard of the sugar refinery in Grussbach, I experienced the following: I met a young woman who approached me with her arms spread and greeted me with tears. I did not remember her, for I had shared in the fate of thousands of Germans up to that time. The woman, however, reminded me of our being together at Leskau and thus revived my memory. On the occasion of President Beneš' arrival at Brünn all Germans had to leave Brünn and I as well as thousands of others were sent to Leskau. Together with 59 other persons, namely 52 women and 7 children, we were locked up in the lumber room of the badly damaged Military Recreation Home at Leskau. I still remember the manner in which we were inspected by a gendarme in this room. He ordered that any member of the official staff should be greeted by the inmates by standing at attention. A young 15-year-old girl played with a baby and smiled at the child. This enraged the gendarme so much that he commanded the girl to come to him, reviled her terribly and finally led her away, notwithstanding the appeals and protests of her mother. The mother fainted because she could imagine what would happen to the child. The girl did not return until the morning of the next day. She had not only been raped but also most brutally beaten so that she was unable to utter a single word and remained lying on her stomach, trembling and groaning, for several days. Her back and legs were covered with terrible wounds.

I was also ordered to report all new cases of disease to the guards. The very next day a young woman told me that she was seriously ill. She had frequently been raped by Russian soldiers and had contracted gonorrhea. I took the woman to one of the guards and reported the case. The guard referred us to an official of the Sanitary Board, who was expected to visit the camp in the afternoon. We waited, and I then reported the woman's disease to this official. On his question how I had been able to diagnose the disease as being gonorrhea I declared that the woman had been raped and that the symptoms were a sign of gonorrhea. Thereupon I had to listen to the lowest insults, he threatened me with shooting and called me a German whore, bastard, sow and so on, and said that nobody knew where this German whore had picked up her infection. I replied that I would not assert positively that the disease was gonorrhea, since the diagnosis would be the task of a physician. "I'll send this bastard under escort to Brünn. But if your story proves false and it is merely a trick because this German sow wishes to get into Brünn, knowing that our President is there now, I'll have you both shot!" The woman was never sent under escort to Brünn, nor was she attended by a doctor; but, in spite of her condition, she had to do hard labour at the Farm of Karlshof near Grussbach. There I met her in a pitiable condition, for the disease had already reached a dreadful stage. The disease in question was Asiatic gonorrhea.

Before the Germans were locked up there, Russians had been lodged in the camp at Leskau mentioned above. The conditions of the camp were therefore indescribable. There was no corner which had not been used as a privy, the entire implements and dishes, plates etc. were either smashed or filthy. The built-in wardrobes had been used as latrines, whereas the latrines themselves were destroyed. We were only supposed to have been sent to the camp at Leskau for three days, that is, for the time President Beneš stayed at Brünn. Beneš, however, stayed for two more days and our tortures were lengthened by the same period. Since we had only taken food for three days, everybody began to feel hungry. The mothers of children particularly began to look for food in the ruined rooms. Under a heap of fragments they found three 5-liter-glasses filled with marmelade. The contents of these glasses had been spoiled by the Czechs in an exquisitely brutal way for the hungry Germans. The surface of the marmelade had been lifted off, the glass filled with human excrement and then covered again with marmelade. The starving children, in spite of the stench, tried to eat the marmelade and soon reached the disgusting contents.

As to the sanitary conditions, the situation may be shown by the fact that none of the inmates of the camps had taken off their garments, either during their 5-day stay in Leskau when President Beneš had visited Brünn, nor for those 19 days in Pohrlitz, or during the months in the Forced Labour Camp at the Neuhof estate. It is understandable that diseases and vermin were spreading.

When I returned from work the 25-year-old assistant, Miroslav Tvrdíc, ordered me to come and to bring along a thermos bottle as he did not feel well. This was certainly an excuse, for he intended to rape me. Since I defended myself, the assistant tore off the piece of cloth I had wrapped around my head and discovered that I had tied up three pieces of jewellery in the corner of the kerchief. I was then raped several times by this man in the course of the night, the jewellery, however, he left with me, knowing that it would be taken away next day as a result of the search he would order to be carried out by the partisans.

At about 4 o'clock in the morning of the following day Tvrdík entered our room together with a number of partisans and ordered a search of all the inmates of the camp, still lying on their palliasses. Whoever was unwilling to surrender his last possessions of jewellery or valuables was threatened with shooting, while the partisans waved their revolvers in the air. Even those seriously ill were not spared, they were brutally torn from their beds, their garments violently pulled off, and after this, thoroughly searched. On this occasion each one of the inmates lost his very last belongings. A married couple by the name of Zach is still in my memory. There were taken away from them a platinum watch with diamonds, the man's golden watch, and several other pieces of jewellery of less value. The same happened to Mr. and Mrs. Spitzer, another married couple. The woman who had been really badly off was a certain Mrs. Kadera, a poor and crippled woman. All she had in her possession were a few Czech crowns. She lost not only the small amount of money but also the purse. Mrs. Kadera is now residing in Vienna.

At the point of death Mr. Nejeschleb, an engineer, was deprived of his last valuables which he had hidden in a linen-bag hanging around his neck. Two days afterwards he died. The plundering of the dying man was carried out in the most brutal manner; he was thrown out of his bed and the straw upon which he had been lying was searched too.

Since the manager endeavoured to treat the inmates correctly he was especially persecuted by his assistant, who, after the former had given us permission to go to mass in the chapel at the Farm of Emmerhof, exclaimed: "This swine of a manager will certainly end up as a collaborator in a concentration camp." All the inmates had the impression that the manager himself wished to be just, but that he had to carry out inhuman orders from above.

In December I received an order from the manager to register all the inmates of the camp, since they were supposed to be transported to the castle of Grussbach. This castle had a very bad reputation, for no end of people who had starved to death were buried there.

I was finally able to save myself from this miserable situation by escaping to Austria. I owe this rescue to a priest, who not only took care of me but also of all the other refugees and relieved our sufferings. He is now living in Austria after he, too, had been delivered into the concentration camp at Znaim, in spite of his illness, probably on account of the help he gave us.

The escape across the border was exploited profitably by a Czech, who exacted the highest payments for his help in crossing the border. He demanded garments, jewellery, money and split the valuables with the manager of the Trawinghof estate. Both turned the misery into a lucrative business.

Brünn, Report No. 2
Death March and Concentration Camp: an Old Woman's Account
Reported by M. K. - Report of July 4, 1950

On May 30, 1945 at 8:30 in the evening Czech authorities notified us that we would have to leave our house and home within half an hour and would only be allowed to take with us what we could carry by hand. I had two old women, 70 and 75 years of age, living with me in my house and they had already gone to bed. I asked the Czech men to please let the old women sleep. And for that, I was to be beaten up. Five minuted before nine o'clock we were driven with blows from cudgels out into the street, and for starters we then had to walk 25 kilometers by foot. Everyone from the old age homes, hospitals and children's clinics - everyone was thrown on the streets and had to walk with us. Many people collapsed on the way. We were not allowed to help them get up, otherwise we were beaten ourselves. The old women who collapsed were shot on the spot by the representatives of Czech authority, and when old men broke down, Czech boys about 14 years of age were called over and had to trample on the men's heads until they were dead. The bodies were then stripped right away and the clothes put on the accompanying Czech carts, and distributed among Czech gangs.

In the night it rained heavily but we had to march on nonetheless. Many people could not do it. The stretch of about 45 km which we had to walk is virtually paved with dead. At the end of the march we were locked into barrack camps. As camp leader the Czech chose a woman who had once been married to a Jew. Together with this camp leader a Czech doctor made daily visits to the barracks, and the two of them gave the sick and elderly prisoners pills. Every day people died like flies in these barracks. From 7 o'clock in the morning until 6 in the evening two men were kept constantly busy carrying corpses on stretchers to a place about 30 meters away, where the bodies were thrown into a pit. As soon as prisoners died they were stripped and their clothes were distributed among the Czechs. Our rations consisted of a four-pound loaf of bread every five days per 25 persons. That's all we got for the three weeks we spent in this camp. Early in the morning each day the young people were fetched by gendarmes to work on the surrounding farms, and were able to get some extra food there. But the old people starved to death. One thousand and seven hundred dead are officially recorded for these three weeks.

Outside the barracks a pit had been dug and a bar was placed over it, which we had to sit on in order to answer the call of nature. Sick people, approximately 450 of them, were housed in one of the barracks. In this barrack a bathtub was set up in the middle, which the sick had to use as a toilet. The tub was not emptied until it was full to overflowing. It was never cleaned, and so the stench in the barrack was unbearable.

In one barrack a young mother of four children, the youngest of which was three years old, suddenly died. The Czech physician who came to do the post-mortem barked at the dead woman's sobbing mother: "What are you howling for, you German bitch, at least one more German pig has kicked the bucket!" Once a Czech commission of five men came to determine if our rations were adequate. Only the doctor and the camp leader were interviewed, and these two people told the commission that all the camp inmates received milk and butter in huge quantities! Even though all of us unanimously denounced this as a lie, the commission chose to believe the doctor and the camp leader, and it was not until later that we found out how a Czech newspaper had announced how exceedingly well we were being taken care of.

Then we were taken another 45 km away into a different camp, where we were given horse meat from dead horses to eat. The meat was crawling with worms. I myself had to wash the meat out. I washed the meat in 4 buckets of water and was still not able to get them all out. Nonetheless the people ate it, they were so hungry. In this way we held on to our bare existence for all of 8 weeks. Only now was it possible for some people to sneak out of the camp and flee across the border to Austria.

The farmers of the Lower Austrian farmsteads cared for us with touching devotion until we had regained our strength enough to move on to Vienna.

Russians came into the women's camps on a daily basis to rape the women. Even an 80-year-old woman was raped in our camp, as well as a 7-year-old girl. I myself spent three nights sleeping over top of a 15-year-old girl because her mother had begged me to protect the girl. The Russians showed up every day by 7:30 and stayed until 2 o'clock at night.

Every day the Czechs went around to the camp inmates and collected money, with promises to protect us from the Russians in the evening, and to lock the camp so no Russians could get in. Punctually at 7:30 these same Czechs escorted the Russians in and showed them which of us they should rape. And it went on like that every day. From time to time different Czechs went around to collect the money because no-one believed the others any more.

One day it was announced that those of us prisoners who had relatives in Austria might cross the border unmolested. They were given a document to enable them to cross the border. Everyone had to pay a certain fee for it. The people lined up in droves to get a border-crossing permit and to be discharged. In the evening these people returned to the camp and told us that at the border the Czechs had taken away even the very last of their possessions, and that they had had to sign a statement saying that they were leaving Czechoslovakia of their own free will, that they had been taken care of with tender loving care, and that the Czechs had even escorted them to the border. Once they had signed that, they had been whipped and beaten back to the camp.

Brünn, Report No. 3
Death March from Brünn to Pohrlitz
Reported by Ed. Kroboth - Report of August 31, 1946

I am 72 years old. In February of 1945 I had to undergo a prostate operation. My wife is 68 years old, diabetic, and has suffered from ulcerated feet for years. In this condition we had to leave our home with only two hours' notice on May 31, 1945. We were maltreated in the process. Following a night spent under the open sky, we and several thousand others were herded to Pohrlitz near Brünn. It was a death march. People who had died from exhaustion lined the street to either side. Following a night in Pohrlitz, which we had to spend lying on wet concrete, we were driven on further, across the border to Austria, where we had to camp on rain-soaked fields. We were given no food at all. When my wife took a little piece of bread from her pocket, a guard cursed her crudely and knocked it out of her hand with his rubber truncheon. Finally my wife could not go on, and I was not allowed to stay with her. Thanks to the intervention of a Czech priest I was finally permitted to return to Brünn. When President Beneš came to Brünn in July 1945, all the Germans in Brünn were herded into the sand pits and kept there for five days without food and almost entirely without water in the tunnels of the sand pits. About 30 people died there every day. Many lost their sanity.

Brünn, Report No. 4
Kaunitz College
Reported by Katharina Ochs - Report of August 31, 1946

For two months (from May 2nd to June 30th, 1945) I was in the infamous Kaunitz College where I witnessed the most atrocious cases of maltreatment. Several thousand Germans were imprisoned there. It was almost impossible for the Germans to walk downstairs normally, since Czechs were standing on every landing and kicked them down. People were also killed. On one occasion I myself was beaten so severely that I was unable to move for days. I still suffer from pains in the back as a result. As a former Red Cross nurse I was ordered to the German ward of the Anna Hospital for three months. Appalling conditions prevailed there. For those who suffered from diarrhoea there was no diet available, the bed linen was in rags and was only changed once a month. There was no cooking-stove, the water was unfit for drinking. No possibility existed for boiling the water, nor was there any possibility of procuring some tea for the patients from a Russian kitchen. For the most part the sick were brought in too late from the camps, so that the majority of them died. The food was completely insufficient and the patients were forced to pick refuse out of the dustbins. They were chiefly suffering either from malnutrition or from the consequences of tortures, for example, broken jaws, festering wounds and so on.

Brünn, Report No. 5
Kaunitz College
Reported by Josef Brandejsky - Report of August 31, 1946

I spent five months in the Kaunitz College in Brünn (from May 5 to October 5, 1945) and was beaten there several times every day. This maltreatment cost me my teeth. Our rations consisted only of watery soups and raw potatoes. For 17 days we received no bread at all. On our arrival, my comrade, who had an injured foot and yet also had to stand up against a wall for 24 hours, was killed by kicks to the stomach and neck, as punishment for holding on to me in order not to fall over. In the barrack the walls, ceiling, floor and mattresses were soiled with blood, because the inmates were beaten bloody every night. One night five of our number were beaten to death in my barrack. Often we were chased from our pallets at night, forced to crawl on all fours and to bark like dogs. At the same time Czech soldiers beat us. Many of the inmates suffered from dysentery. The facilities were utterly insufficient. Our barracks were always locked up, and we had to use buckets to answer the call of nature.

Brünn, Report No. 6
Internment Camp Klaidovka
Reported by Martha Wölfel - Report of August 31, 1946

I spent 15 months in the internment camp Klaidovka, where many hundreds were housed. The camp was crawling with lice and bugs. Our rations consisted only of water and bread. Many mothers with toddlers were also interned there. All toddlers four years old or younger died of malnutrition, without exception. There were at least 100 such toddlers. My own child also died there on April 12, at 15 months of age. Three or four days earlier my child had been taken to the children's ward, where even the Czechs were horrified by his condition. I was notified in the camp when my child died. But when I asked where he would be buried, a guard hit me over the head so that I collapsed unconscious. To this day I don't know where my child is buried. It was the same for the other women.

I am prepared to take this statement on my oath.

Brünn, Report No. 7
Severe maltreatment of German soldiers returning from Russian captivity
Reported by Emil Hulla - Report of August 21, 1946

On June 23rd, 1946, I arrived at Brünn together with 88 prisoners of war, belonging to a transport which was returning from Russian captivity. At Brünn we were whipped by three Czech soldiers and two railway-men in the most atrocious manner. They beat us severely with wooden clubs. Then we were forced to lie down on the ground, and they trampled on us. One man was maltreated so badly that his bowels evacuated themselves. Two others were ordered to lick up the excrement. We had to box each other's ears and were beaten by the Czechs at the same time. We were all of us in poor physical condition, mostly suffering from scrofula, since we had been released on account of sickness from Russian prison camps. From Brünn we were taken to the Kurim camp.

Brünn, Report No. 8
Luggage allowances for the Brünn transport
Reported by Franz Exler - Report of August 31, 1946

As leader of the transport I am informed about the state of the luggage of the transport members [expellees] in general. Most of the people arrived at the resettlement camp from concentration camps or work camps and had no baggage at all. In the resettlement camp they were given some luggage, so that on average everyone had about 70 kg. But the things that they were given were uniformly unusable. Torn and discarded military pieces were handed out as clothing. One man received a top-hat as head covering. The shoes are without exception full of holes. Many people were given two left or two right shoes, or shoes of different sizes. Pots with holes in them were handed out as cooking equipment. It was not possible for the people to try the clothes or shoes on first to see if they fit. Anyone who refused to take things because they were unusable was threatened that he would be held back. The people's clothes are uniformly in poor condition, and most pieces cannot even be repaired because they are so ragged or brittle that it is not possible to stitch them up. Linen and underwear is in the same condition.

Brünn, Report No. 9

The Kleidovka camp: report about the trial of Jan Kouril before the jury court of Karlsruhe
Excerpt from "Die Brücke", edition of June 10, 1951

Last week the Karlsruhe Jury Court sentenced the Czech citizen Johann Kouril to 15 years in prison for the crimes he committed against German citizens and Sudeten Germans during 1945 and 1946. The 39-year-old accused was found guilty of having killed the Sudeten German Kaleus with a blow from a spade, of having participated in a joint fatal attack on the accountant Beinhauer, and of 28 further counts of inflicting minor or major bodily harm on the internees in the Brünn camps of Kleidovka, Kaunitz-College and Juliefeld. In his Reasons for Sentence the Chairman of the Jury Court emphasized that the Court had acquitted the accused in every one of those cases for which no eyewitnesses were available, but that no mitigating circumstances could be found for his crimes even if it were taken into consideration that he had committed them in a time of [political and social] upheaval.

This Karlsruhe Trial, which was observed with great interest both at home and abroad, was the first to go into the gruesome events that took place in Czechoslovakia and some other countries after the German surrender. Unnoticed by the world public - which at the time was horrified and outraged by the news of the mass murders committed in the German concentration camps - another tragedy took place which rivaled the other in terms of brutality. When the first news and eyewitness accounts of it leaked across the borders, they seemed just as unbelievable and exaggerated as the reports about the German camps had seemed. And just as some of the German people still refuse to believe the extent of the tortures and mass murders reportedly committed in the "Third Reich", a large part of the world public also refused to acknowledge the full extent of the 1945 catastrophe as a fact.

And so the significance of this trial is not so much that one of the guilty was brought to justice, but rather that these events - even though they are only a small sample - was for the first time ever investigated and confirmed by a court.

Probably the trial was possible in the first place only because the accused came to West Germany not for political reasons but for personal motives. In the course of his "activity" in the camps he fell in love with a captive German girl, which he later wanted to marry. But since he was unable to secure residence rights for her in Czechoslovakia, he followed her to West Germany.

In 1949 an inmate of an IRO Camp offered to sell a Munich dentist some loose gold. When the dentist met with the seller, he recognized him as Johann Kouril, the former deputy commandant of the Kleidovka Camp, who was trying to turn a bag of broken-out teeth and [dental] bridges into cash. Later, Kouril, who was living unregistered in the Baden town of Spöck, was seen by Sudeten expellees and reported to the public prosecutor. In the course of the investigation more than 200 people came forward who had been imprisoned in the camps in question. Kouril was unable to claim even one witness for the defense from the list of names shown to him. Under questioning, the witnesses related atrocities such as were committed at all times when sadism and man-hunting were turned into patriotic and religious duty.

Kouril was the terror of the camp. On his orders the prisoners were beaten, trampled and tortured. The prisoners were forced with beatings to drink buckets filled with urine and blood. They had to dance naked for the entertainment of the guards. On one Czech national holiday, prisoners were strung up and pulled up and down on a gallows. Others were branded with a red-hot iron. In the interrogation quarters one witness was shoved face-down into a toilet bowl while having to sing the German national anthem. The former gravedigger of the Kaunitz College camp testified that during his work in that capacity he had had to take away the bodies of approximately 1,800 Germans who had been hanged and beaten to death, among them 250 soldiers who had been handed over to the Czechs.

The accused denied all the crimes he was charged with and merely admitted to first one, then three and finally one-hundred slaps in prisoners' faces. His standard reply was: "The witness is telling tales. He must be insane, I don't even know him." "The witness is undermining himself with his own lies." "The statements of this witness are a disgrace," etc.

It is interesting, but not surprising, that Kouril's defense attorney tried to excuse his client's actions with the same arguments also used by Gestapo people etc. who were charged with crimes. According to him, Kouril should be considered a victim who blindly obeyed his government's orders. The public prosecutor agreed that the attitude of the Czech government at that time had been the cause of the German suffering, but added that the accused was not charged with political acts but rather with crimes for which the legal systems of every nation provide severe penalties.

In the main, the Court agreed with the public prosecutor's view. The trial, said Chairman Dr. Ernst, had revealed the sufferings of an ethnic group that was supposed to be exterminated over night. However, the blame must not be placed on the entire Czech people, for it had been the mob, the rabble, that had descended on the Germans. However, he added, one must also consider that some individual Germans, by virtue of what they had once done to the Czechs, bore some blame for the events in Czechoslovakia after the surrender.

The accused, who by his own admission had not been harmed in any way under the German regime, was no Czech patriot; rather, he had offered his services as slave driver in order to prove his nationalist inclinations after the fact. A person of sadistic and cruel disposition, he got pleasure from the bloody deeds that took place in the Czech internment camps.

Concentration camps are despicable in and of themselves, but when they are additionally turned into sites where brutality is free to run rampant with impunity they can only be described as a disgrace to humanity.

Mankind Must Protect Itself

Mankind continues to stand at the threshold of barbarism. The recent years' events in Europe have proven that. The "Christian West" itself is often little more than a veneer that can quickly flake off; and the face thus revealed can inspire a deadly horror, as we have just recently seen. It is a psychosis that seizes not only the mob and the rabble; in that regard the Court was wrong.

Cruelty and inhumanity can only be eliminated if they are combated everywhere and on principle. One cannot speak out against the brutalities committed by the Czechs while downplaying the inhumanities of the Nazis; but one can also not condemn those of the Nazis while refusing to see those that were committed against the Germans. Unfortunately, both are the case.

The verdict of the Karlsruhe Jury Court punished one culprit, but at the same time many of the originators, such as Mr. Ripka and his friends, are considered to be allies in the "battle against inhumanity", just as in Germany people who bore substantial blame for the crime of the "Third Reich" could be busy preparing another one.

Brüx, Report No. 1
Camp at Maltheuern
Reported by Dr. med. Carl Grimm - Report of December 3, 1950

An Epidemic of Suicides.

In the course of the night between May 6 and 7, 1945 the last retreating German troops marched through Brüx. The same day, that is the first day of the occupation by the Red Army, a wave of plundering, rape and with this an epidemic of suicides set in. Drunken soldiers and civilians forcibly entered the German apartments, broke open the doors, demolished the furniture, raped the women, plundered and shot at random. At the beginning the Germans hoped for a retreat of the Russian troops, but the combat troops were soon followed by the occupying forces. The Russian combat troops themselves declared that they would not meddle with things that did not concern them but were a matter for the occupying forces. There were also several thousands of "East European workmen" - Displaced Persons from Poland, Ukraine, Russia, and so on - who had worked in the hydrogenizing works at Maltheuern and had been freed by the invading Russians. In the outer suburbs of the town the plundering and raping never ceased, night after night the women had no respite, they hid themselves in the attics and spent the nights there like birds sitting on the roof-beams. The voluntary Czech militia was powerless against the riots, although they made some effort to control them. The desperate Germans hoped for the assumption of power by the Czechs and for their protection. But when the majority of the Russian troops had marched off and regular Czech military forces and the state police had taken over in the town, the Czech terror proved to be worse than the Russian and it frequently happened that Germans were protected by Russians against the Czechs. At the beginning of June the Czech military carried out the terroristic measure under which the majority of the German men and a part of the German women were arrested right in their apartments, rounded up like cattle and confined in concentration camps. During the months of July and August the *Národní výbor* (National Committee), together with the military and police forces, carried out the evacuation. The German residents of entire quarters of the town or of whole streets were driven out of their apartments, interned in camps and sent away across the border. During this terror and the evacuation the epidemic of suicides, especially the group suicides, reached its climax.

During those first days of the revolution I was stopped on the street by a drunken member of the Czech militia; the moment he found out that he knew me and that he cherished kind feelings towards me, he sent me to the criminal police for registration. By this accident I became a German subsidiary police doctor of the Czech criminal police, as they were just then looking for a doctor and I lived opposite to the police station. My task as police doctor consisted of the post-mortem examinations of the German suicides, and in this capacity I examined several hundreds of suicides during the months of May, June and July. Thus I became a direct witness of the epidemic of suicides among the German inhabitants of Brüx.

It was a dreadful *danse macabre.* The unusual post-mortem examinations in such numbers affected me so deeply that I was completely exhausted the evenings. The climax of all these post-mortem examinations were the suicides of whole families or of all the residents of a house - the afore-mentioned epidemic of suicides during the months of June and July; one day I saw 16, another day 21 bodies of suicides lying side by side in the mortuary of the municipal cemetery. I was profoundly moved by the suicides of old personal friends, whom I saw again under these terrible circumstances. I found my friend Koupa, with whom I had gone swimming in the bathing establishment on the castle hill for many years, dead of gas-poisoning in his apartment at Goethe Strasse together with his girlfriend. My friend Peil, in whose store I had bought all my books, I discovered hanging in a house on Josefs-Promenade with his arteries severed. I was most of all affected by the suicides of whole families and on each occasion I was struck by the solemnity and care with which they had been carried out. During the first days of the epidemic I discovered a family in Kirchengasse, mother, daughter and little son, all of them dead by gas poisoning. They lay side by side on the floor, covered with a blanket, on which the dead dachshund lay curled up. The daughter had a crucifix and the portrait of her fiance on her breast. Murschitzka, the Provincial Inspector of Schools, I found in a barn on the castle hill, together with his family; father, mother, their three children and the grandmother lay side by side on the floor of the barn, all of them shot in the temple, only the father, as the last one, had shot himself through the mouth. Kletschka, a druggist, and his family I found in their apartment at Seegasse, the two children dressed in black lay on their beds, each of them with a cross and flowers on their breast, the grandmother, too, lay composed on her bed surrounded by a cross, picture and flowers; the father had fallen in a cramped position over the bed, on which the mother was extended, her corpse still warm. The revolver was clenched in her hand, for this mother had shot her children, her mother, her husband and finally herself. I saw three fine old people, an elderly man and two ladies, hanging from the cross-bar of a window; the old man in evening dress, flanked by the two ladies in black silk. As far as the medical aspect of the suicides was concerned, I was interested in the various types of death, about which I thought a great deal. In almost no case was the suicide effected by cutting of the arteries; the severity of the pain and the time taken by this method caused all attempts to end life in such a way to be given up. The suicides committed by shooting were in the minority and occurred only during the first days, for later on the Germans were forced to surrender their weapons. The suicides by gas poisoning, too, remained a minority and were also only possible at the beginning, since the Czechs later cut off the gas supply. The overwhelming majority were suicides committed by hanging. This danse macabre of the hanged was dreadful. They hung from trees, girders, wall-hooks, windows, door-posts; some hung free in the air, some touched the ground with the tips of their toes, some hung with bent knees and one or two were even in a kneeling position. At the beginning it seemed incredible to me; one would think it should be easy for a person standing or kneeling to free his head from the noose. But, in fact, one is unable to do so; the reason being that immediate unconsciousness is caused by the cutting-off of the blood supply to the brain; death from suffocation by the blocking of the windpipe comes about later on.

Since the figures of the suicides had generally been fantastically overestimated, I found it necessary to get objective evidence and asked a German employee of the Czech funeral institution to make an extract of the cases of suicide for the months of May and June. They amounted to 150 each month. Due to the fact that the town of Brüx had 30,000 inhabitants, of which there were 20,000 Germans, this figure of 300 suicides for the two months is equivalent to 1½% of the German population of Brüx. On the basis of this figure I estimated the total number of suicides for the whole period at 600 to 700, i.e. over 3% of all the Germans. This coincides with the figure which I learned later on for the Sudetenland as a whole.

The Military Raid

In the course of the last week of May a proclamation of the Czech Military Commander was issued according to which the state of emergency was proclaimed on the German population in 24 articles. It was then that the Germans for the first time learned of the existence of the Czech military. At the same time, as a result of the proclamation, the Germans were shut up in their apartments and cut off from the outside world. The *Rudá Garda* (Red Guard) also came from Prague to the town of Brüx; they were so-called partisans and fighters on the barricades and were lodged in the vast building on the "First Square", which they turned into a "Red House" by red flags and large black inscriptions. Youths in SA-uniforms and fantastically coloured caps and ribbons strutted proudly on the "First Square", equipped with guns and revolvers; they stopped German passers-by, knocked their hats from the heads, beat and kicked them, lashed them with scourges and finally dragged them into the Red House. The members of the Red Guard pretended that they were responsible for order in the border zone.

The 2nd of June in Brüx

On Saturday, June 2nd, 1945 we were awakened early in the morning by shouting, banging on the house door and ringing of the bell. I opened the window of the kitchen and saw a throng of savage men wearing bizarre uniforms and equipped with submachine guns grouped in front of the main entrance. With threats and insults they demanded to be let in. When I finally opened the door, they immediately attacked me and dragged me into the apartment. Their leader was a Staff Sergeant of the gendarmerie from the village of Hawran, the rest of them were Czech partisans and miners from the neighbouring villages. I recognized two of them. My wife, my little daughter and my mother-in-law had hastily dressed themselves in the meantime, but I myself was still in pyjamas. The Staff Sergeant led me to my bedroom; arriving there, he turned to me with staring eyes and a distorted face and panted: "By all that you hold sacred, on your life tell me, have you any weapons in the house?" First of all I remembered an old revolver which was hidden in the attic, but this would have troubled me less had it not been for my brother-in-law's arms, from which my mother-in-law had not wished to separate herself. I did not even know where these had been hidden. In order to divert his attention, therefore, I told the Sergeant about the old revolver. The men then dragged me to the attic, but they behaved in such a stupid and cowardly way that they could not find it although I indicated the exact place, until I myself took the revolver and placed it on the floor in front of their feet. The moment they were in possession of it, they made a dash at me and blows, kicks and lashes hailed on me from all sides. This was the first beating which I received from the Czechs. After this I was taken back to the apartment, where I was awaited by the Staff Sergeant. He behaved very energetically and acted dangerous towards me, but actually by this means he saved me from the others. He demanded rings, watches, valuables, money and our savings-bank deposit-books. I placed on a table everything which I could find in my haste. Later on I was forced to dress, to take with me a blanket, a tin plate and some food, and was led away. On the "First Square" three columns of arrested Germans were already standing. I had to join their ranks. More and more Germans were driven out of their houses in the vicinity and joined up with us. Russian officers passing by noticed what was happening, turned back and called the Czechs to account with regard to the incident. These dramatic negotiations ended with the release of all the workmen from the hydrogenizing works, to whom the Czechs were compelled to return everything they had taken from them. This is just one example, which I witnessed myself, of Germans being protected by Russians from the terrorism of the Czechs. In the meantime a Czech, who was known to me, passed the column and when he noticed me among the prisoners, he told me to follow him and took me to the criminal police. Nobody there seemed to know me, although I had entered and left the office every day in my capacity as doctor to the police. Even though my Czech acquaintance negotiated with the police officials for a long time, I had to go back and join the ranks again. However, shortly afterwards another Czech passing by took me to the Czech officers who were just arriving at the place. After a brief discussion a Czech Captain decided: all doctors are free so that they can do their duty. On this occasion I discovered for the first time that the whole operation was under the leadership of Czech military forces. Upon my arrival at home I was welcomed like one risen from the dead. The afternoon I was again called to a post-mortem examination.

On one of the following days we received a message as to the whereabouts of the German prisoners and the course of the military raid. The imprisoned men had been brought to the camp at Striemitz, a hut-camp near the village of the same name, about half an hour distant from Brüx, while the women were taken to the Poros-camp, a shut-down glass factory in the Prague Strasse in Brüx. As soon as the men and women had arrived at the camps, a lively trade in human beings, a kind of slave-bazaar, began. First of all those men were released who worked in the hydrogenizing works, in the mines or in other factories of Brüx; however, these major manufacturers continuously asked for further contingents of German workmen and these were subsequently released from the camp. As far as the women were concerned it was particularly the farm of Sarras, then still under German administration, which asked again and again for German women for agricultural work, thus helping them to get released. Owing to the mass demands made by the big companies, it was not difficult - sometimes a telephone call was sufficient - to get dozens or even hundreds of German prisoners released simultaneously. But later on the difficulties increased, the demands had to be addressed directly to the garrison headquarters and the permit picked up personally and presented at the camp, before the prisoners would be released. These formalities had to be settled for the prisoners by their relatives and friends and the headquarters, which was situated in the barracks on Saazer Strasse, was besieged all day by endless lines of Germans trying to get their relatives out of the camp. But the commandant, a Lieutenant Colonel, maintained a very negative attitude and refused any dealings with Germans, whereas his adjutant showed himself more approachable and even more so the commandant of the women's camp, a young Lieutenant, who showed sympathy for the women prisoners. The camps were under the command of the garrison headquarters and the slave trade took place between industry and agriculture on the one side and the headquarters on the other.

Those released received back the keys of their apartment from the National Committee and were allowed to move into their abandoned dwellings again, or alternatively they were lodged in an emergency camp. The National Committee actually had nothing to do with the operation, to which, indeed, it was opposed. I know from a member of the Committee that it made efforts to get the Red Guard out of the city and to keep the Svoboda troops away. As a result of the employment in industry the number of imprisoned Germans sank to a thousand, of which 500 remained in the penal camp at Striemitz and 500 were sent to concentration camp No. 28 near Maltheuern. The number of women prisoners, as a result of employment in agriculture, also sank to a thousand, whom the Czechs pushed over the Saxon border into Germany. I myself witnessed this miserable transport of the women of Brüx on the Prague Strasse, as they came from the Poros-camp. Those unable to march, old women and children, stood on carts, while the able-bodied women and girls marched on both sides and the whole procession was flanked by Czech soldiers with fixed bayonets. From Brüx the column moved via Kopitz, Obergeorgenthal and through Marienthal into the Erzgebirge to Gebirgsneudorf; from there it went on to the Saxon border station Deutschneudorf, where it was supposed to be handed over to the Russians. In Deutschneudorf the women and children remained for several weeks on the street and lived by begging at the house doors. As the Russian finally failed to take over the transport, the Czechs were forced after several weeks to bring it back to Brüx without having achieved anything. This is the story of the transport of the thousand women of Brüx to Deutschneudorf.

Expropriation and Forced Labour

On top of the small daily annoyances and abuses came the great organized lootings and expropriations. They started with objects of value, gold, silver, rings, watches, currency, savings-bank deposit-books, and ended with dismissals from employment, suspension from profession, evictions from business, houses and factories. The intellectual professions were affected first and most seriously: lawyers, university professors, instructors, officials, clerks lost their positions overnight and became manual workers. It was announced that intellectual workers who had thus become unemployed were to report to the labour exchange, where they were ordered to hard labour in the hydrogenizing works or in the mines, which was usually bound up with loss of living quarters and detention in a camp.

In order to avoid forced labour and detention in a camp, the Germans themselves rushed to these concerns, which offered them a sort of protection against terror and looting, and a mass migration of the German intelligentsia to the hydrogenizing works and the mines began. The Sudeten German hydrogenizing works at Maltheuern had immediately been expropriated, transformed into Russian State property and given the name "Stalin Works". After the first directors had escaped, a number of leading German engineers took over the administration under Russian control. These German engineers who were in charge enjoyed a privileged position for a long time, special rights like those of the Czechs; and they also received Czech ration cards. As a result of the backing of the Russian occupying forces they were in a strong position vis-a-vis the Czech authorities and were therefore effectively able to protect their German employees and workmen. Only when the hydrogenizing works were handed over to the Czechoslovak State as a gift from Stalin did these German engineers lose their leading positions and privileges and were brought into Labour Camp No. 27, where I met a few of them. The Sudeten German Mining Company, too, was immediately expropriated, became Czech State property and received a provisional Czech administration. The director-general Mr. Nathow and the director Mr. Matuschka had not escaped; they were now taken to the barracks of Brüx where both were later shot Several other factories in Brüx, the steel works, the power plant and the brewery were also expropriated and put under the charge of provisional Czech managers. Both in mining and in industry, however, these managers preferentially hired German workmen, for the Germans were cheap and diligent labourers whereas the Czechs preferred to give orders rather than to work. Analogous to the experiences of the intelligentsia were those of the German women, who also had to report to the labour exchange and were usually ordered to agricultural work. The German women therefore looked for employment on a voluntary basis, since they were then better treated. The majority of the women found employment at the Sarras-Farm, which was then still under the provisional administration of its former German tenant, named Bertsche. This man supported the German women as far as he could and even covered-up for fictitious employment.

The decisive part in the expropriations was played by the provisional managers mentioned above. Like a swarm of locusts the Czechs from the Protectorate broke into the Sudeten German territory and threw themselves on the German shops. Each Czech selected a German shop for himself, reported it to the National Committee and finally got it; the German owner was detained in a penal camp or ordered to do forced labour. I myself experienced several cases of this: Bittner, my neighbour and owner of the drugstore of Nittner & Bittner, on the First Square, was turned out of his store and died in camp No. 28. The owners of the "Glückauf drug-store" in Weiten Gasse were also expelled from their property; I met the old man later on in the camp at Striemitz, his son-in-law in camp No. 28.

There were two different kinds of provisional managers; the one kind protected the Germans and allowed them to do all the work for them, since they themselves knew nothing about the business and were therefore completely dependent on them. The other kind desired to get the German owner into a concentration camp, thus outlawing him and getting the property into their own possession. The Czech intelligentsia, too, participated in this fleecing of the Germans; physicians, lawyers and even priests were not ashamed to evict their professional or official colleagues and to take possession of other people's property. We German doctors were always told by the Czechs that they were in need of physicians, but this only held good as long as they had nobody with whom to replace us. Whenever a Czech physician arrived in town he looked for a German physician's office, took possession of it and the German physician had to leave his house and his patients within half an hour with 30 kilos of luggage and was then evacuated. The same thing happened to the German engineers and skilled workers, who, in view of their special technical education, were allowed to remain in their positions until the Czechs could find Czech specialists to exchange for them. The moment the Czech worker came, the German had to make him thoroughly acquainted with the work and was thereafter himself sent to a camp.

Expulsion and Abduction

The expropriation of dwellings was another of the sad chapters of the Czech revolution, for this was a deed perpetrated by the Czech nation itself. It began harmlessly, with the Czechs lodging themselves in the abandoned apartments of Germans who had escaped. I frequently met Czech miners and their families in such dwellings with 4 to 6 rooms. But then the Czechs from the Protectorate broke into the Sudeten German territory like swarms of locusts and fell upon the German flats. They went in troops from one house to the other and singled out apartments. The Germans were without any power to prevent this and were forced to let them in. When a Czech had found an apartment which suited his wishes, he reported it to the National Committee and to the housing office. As long as the German in question was still at work, being either a doctor, artisan or miner, he enjoyed a certain protection, otherwise he had to pack up within 30 minutes the thirty kilos of luggage allowed and was taken to a Labour Camp. Moreover the Germans were not only compelled to quit their apartments, they had also to leave behind the whole of their furniture, garments and linen, and the Czechs took over the completely furnished apartment.

Up to this time the dispossessions of whole flats were only individual actions, but once the evacuation began they became well-organized mass operations. The evacuations were carried out during the months of July and August, they took place twice or three times a week and each time whole streets or entire residential quarters were affected. The day before the evacuation was supposed to be carried out the families received the order of evacuation, issued by the Evacuation Commission. On the day that it was to be effectuated the whole street or the whole suburb was isolated by Czech military, then the families with their 30 kilos of luggage were driven out of the houses onto the street and were then escorted by heavily armed Czech soldiers to the transfer camp.

As a result of my post-mortem examinations in the apartments of the German suicides and of my medical attendance in the transfer camp I obtained an insight into these proceedings. The "Negro village", an abandoned anti-aircraft camp on Saazer Strasse, was the transfer camp in 1945. It was very primitively furnished, consisting of plain huts with bare plank-beds without blankets or palliasses; in addition the number of plank-beds was absolutely insufficient, so that many had to lie on the floor.

The medical attendance in the transfer camp was shared out between the German physicians of Brüx, so that altogether we were on duty twelve hours a day. Those evacuated only stayed in camp for a few days; during this time they were not allowed to leave. They were insufficiently supplied with food from a camp kitchen. The luggage was inspected by Czech military and all larger sums of money and all valuables were taken away. Men and women capable of work or single women were evacuated to the labour camps of the district of Brüx. Persons incapable of work, invalids, pensioners, elderly people or mothers with children were expelled across the Saxon border to Germany. I still have some sad cases in my memory: Dr. Rubesch, a 70-year-old retired medical superintendent of the district hospital, was evacuated in spite of the fact that he was suffering from paralysis of both his legs; he died shortly afterwards in Germany. Dr. Roppert, another physician 70 years of age, suffered from diabetes combined with a serious disease of the heart, but he still had to be evacuated; and Mr. Kohlef, the owner of a furniture factory, although he was confined to a wheelchair following a stroke, had to be transported to Germany.

Terrorism and Arrests

The brutal terror continued. The military raid was followed by a wave of arrests of members of the National Socialist Party and its affiliated organizations, as well as of the owners of prosperous retail businesses and of the better houses. Those arrested were locked up in the building of the criminal police, in the barracks, in the building of the district court, in the camp at Striemitz or in the camps No. 27 and No. 28. Dreadful scenes took place among the prisoners. Eyewitnesses reported repeatedly that the German prisoners in the court building had to line up in two rows, facing each other, and were then ordered to box each other's ears, Czech warders watching them so that none would treat the other too gently. On the "First Square" I myself frequently saw German prisoners being slapped, beaten and kicked by Czech warders while working on the fire-extinguishing pool. One day, when I was called to the criminal police in connection with an accident, I discovered four men in a cell as white as chalk with deep blue rings under their eyes. Their faces resembled masks and reminded me of a masquerade - until I discovered the bloody weals an their naked bodies. I had to order one of them to the hospital since he was suffering from a rupture of the ureter and he died there a few days later from urine phlegmon.

But now my own time had come and destiny caught up with me. At that time I had a good deal to do with the medical superintendent of the Czech social insurance company, one Dr. Kumpost, with whom I had been well acquainted since the days of the First Czechoslovak Republic. This man would only have had to say one word to warn me of the danger I was in, but he failed to do so and let me run into disaster.

The Czechs were not satisfied with the one terrorist incident at Aussig, but perpetrated the same in the entire territory of Sudetenland. At Brüx the operation started on August 1st. The same afternoon, while I was out visiting a patient, they broke into my apartment and then searched the whole house. Since they did not find me at home, they forced my wife to lead them to where I was. They found me in the apartment of a young married couple in Bahnhof Strasse, where the young woman lay in bed, suffering from articular rheumatism with a high temperature. There, while I was sitting on the bed of the patient, they arrested me and also the young husband, a dentist by profession. Later on my wife and I were dragged onto the first landing and threatened with a beating if we should exchange so much as a word or a glance. We had to stand side by side like two wax figures. It was then that I saw my wife for the last time in Brüx, and not until 1½ years later did I meet her again, in Germany. Without being able to bid farewell to each other we were separated, and the young dentist and I were hustled along the Bahnhof Strasse, continuously kicked and cuffed. The Czechs whom we met laughed cynically, although we were both wearing the Red Cross band on our left arms. My arrest was carried out personally by the Secretary of the Communist Party, one Mazanek. When he brought us to the local criminal police station, he did not turn us over to the police officials present, but held the interrogation himself so that the policemen had nothing to do and gradually left the room. We stood side by side, the little dentist and I, under an uninterrupted hail of blows to head and face. It was incredible how hard the man could strike, the blows seemed to come rather from a club than from a human fist. Again and again he shouted: "This for what you did to the miners during the war." I began to believe that this must be a confusion of names, for I had had nothing to do with miners during the war. I therefore dared to exclaim: "It must be a mistake, that is not me." This answer, however, proved to be only one more reason to beat me. The little dentist collapsed, and I wondered that I myself was still able to stand. I was bleeding from eyes, nose and mouth and was dragged to the tap to wash off the blood. Later on, when our particulars were being registered, I could not remember the name of my own daughter. I thought: "O my God, if I do not remember my child's name, they'll beat me up again!" Finally I was able to recollect it; but, in fact, I believe I had suffered a slight concussion. After the registration we stood for a long time with our noses pressed against the wall. When we were marched off, we passed a crowd of German prisoners which filled up the entrance of the building. As I heard later on, more than 70 men had been arrested on this day, among them Dr. Nothnagel, a 70-year-old dentist, Mr. Fischer, a master joiner of 70 and Mr. Kny, an architect of the same age. The moment we entered the corridor of the jail, a young Czech policeman let slip the following remark: "My God, the doctor visited us only this afternoon!" We surrendered knives, suspenders, neckties and bootlaces and were locked up in a cell.

Incidents like that described above went on all night long. We heard the shrill voice of the Secretary of the Communist Party in the corridor, the crack of the blows and the cries of those being beaten, then the cell door would open and a newcomer covered with blood would stagger into our cell. At last the number of cell inmates amounted to 23, packed like herrings into the narrow cell. We were standing upright or sitting in a squatting position, and the bucket to relieve the call of nature was passed round. The majority of us were convinced that we were to be shot next morning. So the night passed in apathetic resignation. But we were not to be shot after all. Instead we were driven to the village of Maltheuern, marching for three hours; upon our arrival there we were taken to the notorious camp No. 28.

All terrorist operations ended up in the camps of the district of Brüx. There were, however, not only the labour camps No. 27 and No. 28, but also the camps 17/18 and 31/32 near Maltheuern, the Rösselcamp and camp No. 37 near Brüx. the camps 22/25 near Niedergeorgenthal and 33/34 near Rosenthal. All these camps were in connection with the hydrogenizing works, in addition to these there were also the camps in connection with the mining company, which were not known to me in detail. The total number of camps within the district of Brüx amounted to more than thirty. Their inmates were not only inhabitants of the towns of Brüx, Saaz and Komotau, but also residents of the towns of Aussig, Bodenbach, Bilin, Dux, Kaaden, Weipert, Karlsbad and Marienbad - Germans from half of the Sudetenland and also Reichs Germans and Germans from Hungary, who had been driven into these camps. The terrorism carried out by civilians surpassed that of the military raid by far, but the aims and scenes of the operation remained unchanged.

The coal field between Brüx and Dux, which represents an important economic potential, has again and again become the scene of considerable movements of population and of conflicts of nationalities. The coal field consists of a large seam of lignite at a depth of 100 to 400 meters and represents the center of the North Bohemian brown-coal district which has more than 50 pits and 25,000 miners and extends on one side from Brüx to Komotau, on the other from Dux via Teplitz to Aussig. When coal mining began in the course of the 19th century industrialization, the immense demand for manpower in this area caused the immigration of Czechs, as a result of which the populations of Brüx and Dux became 50% Czech. At the beginning of the Second World War, when Germany built up the hydrogenizing works at Maltheuern, this project called for an additional 35,000 men, and displaced persons and prisoners of war were ordered to work there and labour camps were established. Thus Dutchmen, Frenchmen, Italians, Croats, Bulgarians, Poles, Ukrainians and Russians arrived in the labour camps of the district of Brüx. At the end of the war the displaced persons disappeared and the Germans were put there by the Czechs; in this way the Germans became labourers in the hydrogenizing works and in the mines at Brüx. The use of the Germans for forced labour in the heavy industry of the Brüx coal-mining area was the beginning of the Czech terror. The so-called National Czechs in industry and mining were satisfied by the idea of using the Germans for forced labour and did not agree to their transfer; they preferred to see the Germans remain in the country as labourers, for they were indispensable to the maintenance of industry. The reverse effect of the forced labour was the social degradation, expropriation and proletarianization of the Germans. By turning lawyers, university teachers, instructors, salesmen, artisans, independent farmers and clerks into unskilled or casual labourers in heavy industry, they degraded the Germans from their independent and intellectual positions to manual workers. By depriving the Germans of their shops, houses, factories, their bank deposits, watches and jewellery and by expropriating them and lodging them in hut-camps, they turned them into homeless gipsies and riffraff. Czech newcomers took possession of the property, of stores, buildings, factories, dwellings, furniture and clothing and took over all independent intellectual positions. The money, watches and jewellery which were supposed to be surrendered to the Czech State likewise disappeared into the pockets of Czech patriots.

Concentration Camp Tábor 28

The Czech concentration camp No. 28 near Maltheuern was opened at the beginning of June with two transports consisting of 500 inhabitants of Brüx arrested during the military raid on June 2nd; and furthermore with two transports consisting of 800 inhabitants of Saaz, arrested during the raid on June 3rd, and with a transport consisting of 200 persons from Komotau, arrested during a raid on June 9th. The majority of the prisoners from Komotau went into camp No. 27, situated opposite No. 28. During the months of August, September and October four transports with invalids, altogether 400 men, were transferred to Germany over the Saxon border. In exchange for them, 70 men from Brüx arrested on August 1st, 70 from Aussig formerly interned in the Lerchenfeld camp, 200 from Karlsbad, and another 200 German SS-men from Hungary were brought in. The number of prisoners fluctuated between 500 and 1300 men. The concentration camp was a vast hut-type camp, surrounded by a high fence of barbed wire and divided into two equal halves, each with washing facilities and a latrine in the middle, which we called "the upper and the lower village". Each "village" consisted of the same number of wooden huts, each hut consisted of numerous rooms and each room was full of plank-beds in two tiers; on the average, each room housed more than thirty men. In the beginning there was also a large tent in the "lower village", which resembled a circus tent and which sheltered more than 200 persons. This was, however, removed later on.

The atrocities committed by the Czechs on the German prisoners were terrible. In July, 15 patients with tuberculosis of the lungs, who had been selected for an invalid transport, were shot down by Russian guards at the order of an officer. This was done, it was said, to avoid an epidemic. In August a prisoner was shot by the Czech guard in front of the assembled inmates of the camp because he was alleged to have cut a piece out of a driving belt to make soles for his shoes, an action which was viewed as sabotage. Kadle Vlasak shot his lackey in the head while trying, as a joke, to shoot a hat off his head, and when the shot man was already lying in the coffin Vlasak shot him twice more in the heart because he was not yet completely dead.

The most frightful and degrading thing were the regular beatings. They began at the moment of admission into the camp. Those brought in were deprived of everything, their heads were shaved, they were beaten and then compelled to stand at attention against the wall for hours in the blazing sun. We nicknamed this the "wailing wall". The beatings were carried out with fists, whips and rubber truncheons; they went on day and night. There was never a quiet night, but always blows, screams and the crack of whips and shots. During the night Czechs from outside invaded the camp and the prisoners were dragged from their beds and beaten into insensibility. Then saltwater was poured into the eyes of the unconscious men and their moustache and eyelashes set on fire until they regained consciousness. They were then further abused until the torturers were exhausted or the tortured men had gasped their last. The sadistic orgies were built up on a refined system of torture. The prisoners were first slapped, punched and struck an the face with rubber tubing, then beaten on the head and body and kicked in the stomach, testicles and shins until they collapsed. Afterwards these dehumanized Czechs stood on the prone bodies, jumping and trampling on them with their jackboots. I shall never forget the scene when half-naked men were forced to crawl in the dust and tear up grass, while the Czech slavedrivers in their midst cracked their whips across the naked backs. In the beginning the prisoners were not even given bread and water, but water-soup and black coffee, in reality no more than warm water. There were three mealtimes in the camp, early in the morning black coffee, in the evening, after our return, water-soup and, before going to bed, black coffee again. Later on the prisoners who were working in the hydrogenizing plant were given potato soup with a piece of bread at noon there. This meal seemed so desirable to the starving prisoners that, in spite of their exhaustion, everyone was eager to work there. The prisoners had a working day of 18 hours and 6 hours sleep; they were awakened at four and marched off in two parties at 5 and 6 a.m. The total working time amounted to 12 hours, two hours being taken up by the march there and back. The return to the camp took place again in two parties, at 7 and at 8 p. m.

Day after day the column of the five thousand from the camps No. 27 and No. 28 rolled to Maltheuern and back, those from camp No. 28 in the lead, close-cropped, miserable, emaciated faces and figures with clattering wooden shoes and dressed in rags. In summer and winter alike they were without coats or caps, wearing on their chest their prison-number and on their backs a large white swastika and "KT 28". But the day's work was not finished with the return to the camp, for then the prisoners had to appear in the "lower village" for the roll call, to line up and march in column while singing German songs: "Freier Wildbretschütz", "Westerwald", "Blaue Husaren". At the head of the column marched one prisoner in the character of a clown with an old top-hat, followed by another in an old Prussian helmet. The commandant gave the orders: "Fall in! Fall out! Forward march! Halt!" Then he would begin to shout and to shoot under our feet and over our heads, so that the whole mass of men with their clattering wooden shoes ran hither and thither. Thus the prisoners could not sleep until 10 at night. Their life consisted of blows, hunger and work, work, hunger and blows.

The name of the commandant of the camp was Karel Vlasak, who liked to call himself the "tiger", but the prisoners called him "the beast of No. 28". It was a terrible sight when he stormed through the camp, his revolver in one hand and the cat-o'-nine-tails in the other. One of his favourite sports was to knock down the prisoners one by one, each with a single blow. He used a special trick for this; after the blow giving the prisoner a thrust with his arm. The latter, standing at attention, would lose his balance and fall. Whoever understood what the commandant intended, got off with this one blow; anyone who tried to pull himself together though, would be in for a bad time. The "tiger", growing angry, would kick the prisoner with his jackboots in the stomach and the testicles until he collapsed. After this was accomplished, the "tiger" felt as proud as a boxer in the ring, and the Czechs who surrounded him cheered and applauded him. That was Karel Vlasak, the beast of No. 28.

At the beginning of October the military was replaced by gendarmerie. The young gendarmes were more humane and the number of beatings in the camp gradually grew less. Karel Vlasak was arrested and taken to the district court at Brüx - not because of his atrocities against the German prisoners but because of embezzlement of money and valuables which he had taken from the prisoners, but not handed over.

A new commandant arrived by the name of Řezač, who acted savage but who in reality was a decent man. Unfortunately his accomplices, Rameš and Kulišek, the first an intriguer and the second a real butcher, were by no means so. The barbed wire fence around the camp was doubled and a jail was established within the camp in the former air-raid shelter, in which the prisoners would often be locked up for trivial reasons. In such cases the prisoner would work all day long in the hydrogenizing works and then be obliged to spend the night without food in this underground jail, notwithstanding the cold. Often members of the guard broke into the underground jail and carried out orgies of beating, shooting about at random in the confined space. In January 1946 a prisoner, Kramář by name, was found frozen to death after spending the night there in chains.

In spite of the change of commandant the hours of work remained the same, twelve hours labour and two hours for the march, there and back. Only the exercises were stopped and the prisoners were allowed to sleep during the night. The food was also improved by additional rations of bread and potatoes. Now the prisoners would get black coffee in the morning, potato soup and bread in the plant at noon, and in the evening after returning to the camp, soup, potatoes and bread. Before we went to bed, black coffee again. An increasing number of prisoners were given T 4 ration cards for heavy labourers, containing plenty of additional rations of bread, sausage, bacon, lard, sugar, marmalade, representing quality nourishment high in calories.

Screened by the early night, the series of escapes began. Each week, sometimes even every day, in autumn and winter, a number of prisoners would be found to be missing when the column fell in for the roll-call. Sometimes whole groups disappeared; once 21 men marched off together in a group - even, it was said, taking a flag with them. In order to intimidate the Germans, the Czechs spread the rumour that the refugees would be shot at the border. In fact, those who were caught there were badly beaten and locked up in a dark cell.

Then as a reprisal the Czechs stopped the visits of the relatives, which had been allowed on Sunday and Thursday afternoons. They also held back the parcels with laundry and food. When visitors were admitted, fathers, mothers, brothers and sisters met each other in the big dining-room, where they rushed towards each other, embraced, laughing and crying like children. When visitors were not to be admitted, the women were chased away from the entrance door and struck at with rifle butts; but still they would come back every Sunday and Thursday afternoon, after having travelled or walked a considerable distance, and would wait in wind, cold or rain. In October the transports of invalids were stopped; the last of these was held back and it was not until January and February 1946 that the invalids were sent in groups to their homes, from whence they were expelled together with the regular transports of Sudeten Germans.

During January 1946 the meals continued to improve, 1100 out of 1300 prisoners were given T4 ration cards for heavy labourers, and the general state of health improved in consequence. In exchange for those released during the months of January and February 1946, many men from Brüx and Bilin were brought in, having been seized in the course of a new wave of arrests of members of the SA (affiliated organization of the NSDAP). Up to the last day of the existence of camp No. 28, that is until its dissolution, the newcomers were robbed in the camp office during their registration; they were afterwards placed over a bench and beaten with rubber truncheons on the naked buttocks. Since I had to examine both those released and those coming in under the control of the Czech physician, one Dr. Pivota, I took the opportunity of presenting him with some cases. He did not pass them over, remarking firmly: "I am a good Czech, but I will have nothing to do with things like these." The Czech commandant was furious on hearing of this remark. Since he could not revenge himself on me, he vented his fury by striking Dr. Gmel, the dentist. Shortly afterwards, when some escaping Germans, who had been caught, were brought in half-dead by the Czech guards, the latter slapped me the moment I rendered assistance to the first patient, then kicked me and threatened me with a revolver when I stated that these men had been beaten. I also reported this case to Dr. Pivota, the Czech physician of the hydrogenizing plant. I had the satisfaction of knowing that the cases I reported led to the closing of camp No. 28 at the end of March 1946, the prisoners being taken over by camp No. 27.

The Sick-Bay

The Czech name for the sick-bay was "Marotka"; the "Marotka" of camp No. 28 was opened in June 1945, Dr. Gabler and Dr. Pörner being in charge of it. Both had been arrested at Saaz during the raid on June 3rd. At the beginning the sanitary conditions were shocking, the most elementary medical equipment was lacking. The two physicians had nothing at their disposal but a rusty scalpel and a pair of rusty forceps. On the Czech side there was no presumption of any necessity for medical attention; at the beginning no cases of illness might be acknowledged; the Czech directive read: anyone who is incapable of work is to be shot. Under these conditions the death rate was extremely high. There was no end to series of men shot, beaten or starved to death, no end to the rows of corpses. At the beginning we counted in the sick-bay alone four to five dead men a week. I will never forget the raw, unplaned wooden boxes in which we placed the corpses, as well as the miserable cart which arrived twice or three times a week from Oberleutensdorf to pick up the bodies. It was then that Dr. Gabler rose above himself - I shall always remember the words he repeated to us again and again: We must break with everything that we have known in the past. We must start with nothing as though we had been sent to Alaska or the Congo. He fought for each individual patient. Since he knew how to handle the "tiger" - by behaving like a wild-beast tamer - he finally succeeded in obtaining acceptance of the patients. Assisted by Dr. Pörner he collected one piece of equipment after another - partly from his own property in Saaz and Brüx - and built up the sick-bay of camp No. 28. By the time of its dissolution there was a ward for minor surgery and one for internal medicine together with a laboratory, nurses, sick-lists, diet, bathing facilities and a delousing station.

Our medical knowledge was of little value, however, for the diseases which broke out were completely strange and unknown to us. They were so striking and appeared in such numbers that we called them "camp diseases". These camp diseases were diarrhoea, hunger oedema, phlegmon. Diarrhoea was widely spread and was the cause of most of the deaths. Those seriously ill were terrible in appearance: emaciated skeletons with a paper-thin skin seamed with wrinkles, the body cramped, face twisted into a perpetual grimace, the hands raised uselessly in imploring gestures. Since I observed a connection between the patients' condition and the soup they were given, I was all the more convinced that the disease in question was dyspepsia. I therefore took charge of the sick-room attending the cases of diarrhoea and ordered radical fast-days and quantities of "charcoal", which we had prepared ourselves from malt coffee. There were even more cases of oedema; dropsy was the basis for all the other diseases. The symptoms of those suffering from dropsy were the opposite of those suffering from diarrhoea; the more serious cases were bloated like balloons, their faces were full moons, their bellies swollen sacks of water, their genitals completely disfigured. This disease was absolutely unknown to us and caused considerable divergences of view among us, as to whether we were dealing with heart-, kidney- or some other sort of oedema. We soon discovered what would cure it, namely bed-rest and dry food, which we achieved by omitting the water-soup and the black coffee, distributing only bread and potatoes. By these measures the oedemas were quickly cured and we sometimes experienced water losses of between 20 to 25 liters and a drop in weight of 20 or 25 kilos a week. But the oedemas broke out again and we diagnosed relapses, the same patient sometimes got dropsy twice, three times or even five times. I therefore was of the opinion that the disease was hunger-oedema, which, however, we could diagnose only later on, since the disease was accompanied by various other diseases and the symptoms were not clear. All our medical knowledge and attendance was jeopardized by our own dangerous position, as we were still prisoners despite our somewhat privileged treatment. At the beginning the phlegmon was operated on and in view of its considerable superficial extent there was no limit to the purely surgical possibilities. But the results of this treatment became more and more dubious, the operation wounds healed badly or not at all and scars already healed up burst again if the patient contracted dropsy. Later on diarrhoea, oedema and phlegmon subsided and complications such as tuberculosis of the lungs, heart diseases, inflammation of the kidneys and anaemia came to the fore. In October we received a heavy and unexpected blow: Dr. Gabler was locked up in the camp prison for having admitted too many patients to the sick-bay and for making a few unwise remarks. He was later transferred to camp No. 27. During the months of October, November and December Dr. Pörner was in charge. Under the impression of the unpleasant incident which had happened to Dr. Gabler, he directed a different course and entered into connection with the Czech physician of the plant, one Dr. Pivota, as a result of which we obtained more liberty vis-a-vis the Czech commandant of the camp. In January 1946, when he was released and turned over to camp No. 22, I was appointed as head physician for the period of January to March 1946. Following the example of Dr. Pörner, I maintained the connection with Dr. Pivota and via him obtained access to the Czech medical superintendent of the Stalin Works, one Dr. Fajkus. Through him I obtained permission to share out among the patients, to the best of my medical knowledge, the rations of those of them who held the T 4 hard-labourers card. In this way I finally received the additional food I needed to treat the cases of oedema and phlegmon. It was a great pleasure to watch the result of this treatment: the flabby, swollen-up skin became tight and smooth, the festering wounds and inflammations disappeared and the wounds themselves healed up. During the last months of our stay in the camp the so-called "camp diseases" vanished and I was able to prove statistically the connection between the subsidence of the camp diseases and the improvement of food rations.

Brüx, Report No. 2

Father and brother were murdered

Reported by Anni Wagner, age 14 - Report of December 3, 1946 (transcript of a letter)

Dear Miss Helga!   Hof, December 3, 1946

I found your address among my brother's papers. I must give you the sad news that my brother and father, who returned home one more time, were taken to Brüx by the Czechs on September 30.

They lived for another eight days there. Then they were beaten to death. My mother, who was very ill, succumbed to a heart attack. Now I am entirely alone. I am presently in Hof and will go to the transfer camp so that I can go to the Russian zone to live with my aunt. After all, I'm only 14 years old. My brother often told us about you. He liked you very much. He spoke of you very often, and made plans.

Farewell, all the best for the future, your sad

Anni Wagner.

This news was brought to us by a Czech who ran away from Brüx. He couldn't stand to watch what was happening there any longer.

[Explanation: the original of this letter is in the possession of our fellow-countryman Erich Stangl. The murdered man, Wolfgang Wagner from Marienbad, was engaged to Erich Stangl's daughter.]

Budweis, Report No. 1
Coal pit Lignit-Mylovar, maltreatment
Reported by Karl Stelzig - Report of September 27, 1946

I was released from American captivity on June 10, 1945 but re-arrested by the Czechs four weeks later and detained until early August 1946 in a concentration camp, where I had to work for some time (10 months) in the coal pit Lignit-Mylovar, where conditions were initially very bad. During this time, I was repeatedly severely maltreated, like all the other prisoners there. In June I was interrogated at the District Court in Budweis, and there was nothing they could lay to my charge. A number of Czechs had testified on my behalf. For that reason I was transferred from Budweis to the internment camp on August 6, 1946 to be resettled [expelled]. After 14 days the police got me from the camp and subjected me to another interrogation, which lasted 3½ hours and in the course of which, in the presence of police sergeant Kouba, a Czech police officer severely punched me in the face and about the head, damaging the eardrum of my left ear in the process. In the evening I was taken back to the camp in shackles, but released for resettlement the next day.

Budweis, Report No. 2
Maltreatment, rape, murder
Reported by: A. R.

On Ascension Day 1945 the entire German population of Budweis was ordered to report to the labour exchange. When my parents and I approached the office we were seized by a group of Czechs, who for no reason began to knock us about. They also spat at us and maltreated us in other ways, then they drove us with kicks and blows toward the gate of the labour exchange, where the guards got hold of us once more and beat us with the butts of their rifles until we could no longer get back up.

While we were being mishandled, other German families arrived, among them women with babies in perambulators. The Czechs tore the babies out of the perambulators and threw them into the brook nearby. The women were pushed into the water after them. Whenever a mother with her child reached the other bank, she was again seized, struck and thrown back into the water. This procedure was repeated to the cheers and yells of the Czechs (the majority of whom were women), until the arrival of other Germans diverted their attention. Mrs. Wallisch, a clerk at the labour exchange, was beaten until she was half dead, after which she was forced with blows from rifle butts to lick up the blood off the ground and from the stairs of the labour exchange. The yard looked like a place of execution. Blood was everywhere, men and women were lying on the ground, beaten half to death and horribly disfigured. The rest of the Germans were then ordered to line up, while the sentries stood by with their rifles trained on them; anyone who dared to lean against anything risked a blow. The monk Josef Seidl of the monastery of Budweis was brutally clubbed and whipped for the sole reason that he was German.

The people were divided into different labour gangs and led away by heavily armed guards, while the mob in front of the labour exchange beat them once more. With the gang of labourers to which I had been assigned I arrived at a hospital, where I was told to clear up after the German soldiers who had been there. The sentries kept after us. We had to do the heaviest work and were insulted by being called "German bastards, pigs, whores" etc. In the ward for infectious diseases we had to rip open the old and dirty palliasses and refill them. Unfortunately, while I was working, I stepped on a rusty nail. My foot began to bleed and was extremely painful. Only when the foot got very swollen was I allowed to tie it up, and then only with a dirty old bandage from the refuse heap. Although I was in great pain I had to go on working. They took me to the guard-room, where one of the sentries lanced my foot with a pocket-knife. This operation was repeated the following day. Only when I was at last absolutely unable to walk, the medical officer granted me two days rest.

Once I was detailed, together with other women, to the poor-house and ordered to clear it up. This building was supposed to be turned into a Russian military hospital. There were already Russian soldiers there and, being the only young girl, I was very much molested. An elderly Russian gave cigarettes to the guard assigned to me, after which I received the order to follow him to his room. The Russian was extremely drunk. I refused to drink anything. Then he threw me on his bed and wanted to rape me. I succeeded in pushing him away and jumped out of the window.

When the hospital was taken over by the Czech army, some badly wounded German soldiers were still lying in one room. The Czech doctor entered the room several times without doing any-thing for them. He once said to his escorting officer: "Are those German bastards not going to die soon? I need the room." Then he suggested that they should be given a helping hand; consequently a soldier who was suffering from a bullet wound in the abdomen received an injection that after-noon and was buried in the yard the very next day. The nurse who told me this also reported that several SS-men, 18 to 21 years old, had been dragged into the hospital, killed in the yard, and buried there.

An inspector by the name of Emil Hacker, who was drunk most of the time and who used to drive us with a whip, once ordered me to wash the dishes. Sitting there with his arms folded, he gave me all kinds of orders. All of a sudden he disappeared and returned with a thin rope, which he whipped through the air. He ordered me to follow him to the attic. He threatened the others with severe punishment if they should dare to follow us. Instead of leading me to the attic, he led me into a sick-room on the third floor, which he locked from inside. While he took off his uniform, he threatened what he would do to me if I cried out. He suggested that I should come every day to his room, in return for which I would be exempted from heavy work. He would also give me some ration tickets for bread. When I told him that I hated him and that I would rather be beaten, he brutally raped me. From that moment on I was forced to do the heaviest work under his command and was constantly molested by him.

Canon Jos. Neubauer was first imprisoned and had then to go, together with a labour-gang, to the hospital every day. There he was forced to do the heaviest work and was maltreated and insulted at the same time. Once I smuggled bread into his hand as I passed him. The guard observed the incident and I was punished.

My grandmother, an old woman of 73, was seized in her flat by Czech sentries and dragged to her neighbour, one Mr. Schadt. The latter, who had already been beaten so badly that he was bleeding, was now ordered to beat my grandmother. When he refused to do so, he was struck several more times and was pushed down the stairs. In her desperation my grandmother returned home and severed her arteries with a kitchen knife. Some Russians found her, almost bled to death, bandaged her and ordered that she be taken to a hospital. Lying on a stretcher in the hospital, this old woman was called an old whore and spat upon. She was locked up in a windowless cellar. She received no attendance and her wound was not dressed. My grandmother suffered from excruciating pain. My aunt, who stayed with her, appealed to the doctor for help, but he said laughing, "She's only a German", and left. After many requests my aunt at last succeeded in getting a priest, who administered extreme unction. My grandmother died the next day.

Several German girls were imprisoned in the jail. Each day Russians came to the jail and borrowed women, whom they brought back the next morning.

During the horrible times I spent at the hospital I also saw Czech chaplains, attached to the military unit, who stood over us with a gun in their hands and who yet celebrated communion the next day.

Freiwaldau, Report No. 1
Unlawful confiscation
Reported by Ida Fröhlich - Report of September 7, 1946

My daughter Anna Pische is a trained seamstress and as such she had written permission from the Customs Office of Freiwaldau to take her sewing machine with her [on expulsion]. She also had written confirmation of this permission from the *Národní Výbor* in Zuckmantel. When we left Zuckmantel a gendarme checked our papers and pronounced them in order, and the Economic Commissar put his rubber stamp on the papers and let the sewing machine pass.

In the expulsion camp the Czechs took the papers away from my daughter and confiscated the sewing machine together with the attachments and accessories. When my daughter objected, she was rudely dismissed. My own objections were also without effect, and were vulgarly rejected. The sewing machine was a fold-away Singer machine, bought in 1935, and in any case it appealed to the Czechs very much.

I am ready to take this statement on my oath.

Freiwaldau, Report No. 2
The ordeal of an artist
Reported by G. M. - Report of October 9, 1946

I am a concert pianist by profession, and a state-accredited music teacher. For the last year I have had to earn my living playing in bars just to keep myself, my mother and my two children fed. During this time I was treated by the Czechs in the worst way. In the bar itself I was frequently subjected to the rudeness of the audience. Shouts such as "Play, you German whore!" were the order of the day. On my way home I was repeatedly molested by Czechs, and was also raped several times and injured with kicks. Czechs repeatedly broke into my home at night, and several times they broke window panes to see if I was alone. I lost all my possessions when I was ejected from my 7-room flat. In the resettlement [expulsion] camp I was relieved of another quarter or so of the few things I had been able to save. I was not permitted to take my concert piano, a gold-medal-winning Förster grand Model III, even though I demonstrably need it to practice my profession.

Freiwaldau, Report No. 3

Severe abuse during farm labor

Reported by Else Müller - Report of August 23, 1946

The Freiwaldau Employment Office assigned me to agricultural labor in Brusy, near Prerau, with the farmer Franz Gavenda. That place was hell on earth for me and my 12-year-old son. After I had rejected the farmer's sexual overtures, he beat me and my son daily, and his wife also cursed and harassed us beyond all measure. At the same time, however, we had to do heavy physical labor 16 hours each day, even though the farmer knew that I suffer from heart and thyroid problems. I came away from this work with a severe hernia. After Christmas I complained to the Mayor, but that only resulted in even worse maltreatment. Since I could not get to the gendarmerie to lodge a complaint there, I urged my 12-year-old boy to write a letter to his father, describing our unbearable situation. I hoped that the gendarmerie would take notice of the contents of the letter when they censored it. And indeed a gendarme turned up at the farm soon thereafter and told me that a letter with contents such as this would not be delivered, but at the same time he also reprimanded the farmer for his treatment of us. But after that the farmer maltreated us even worse. I then went to see a physician, who issued me a statement to the effect that I was entirely unfit for work. However, the Employment Office nonetheless sent me back to Gavenda, who now even withheld my small between-meal snacks and gave me even harder work to do, even on Sundays. On May 8, after once again being badly maltreated by him, I ran away from that farm and turned to the Employment Office in Prerau, which assigned me to a different farmer where conditions were more bearable. During the resettlement [expulsion] transport my son and I were dreadfully maltreated by a railway official in the train station Prague-Maleschowitz. He yanked me out of the train compartment and beat me so severely that I fell underneath the train.

In my 10½-month absence from my home almost everything I owned was stolen. My resettlement luggage consists of gifts from my sister.

Freiwaldau, Report No. 4

District Freiwaldau, the Jauernig and Adelsdorf camps

Reported by Alfred Latzel - Report of September 9, 1947

My homeland is the Eastern Sudetenland, which was known earlier as Austrian Silesia and was a crown land of the Austro-Hungarian Monarchy. The District of Freiwaldau is a settlement area of the Diocese of Breslau and, according to the *liber fundationis,* had already been settled by Germans in 1284 "as far back as human memory". My ancestors are documented to have lived in the District of Freiwaldau ever since 1523, as governors, landowners and farmers, and our present-day family estate in Barzdorf was purchased by my great-grandfather Josef Latzel, who pioneered an aspect of Austro-Hungarian agriculture in establishing the Austrian sugar industry. On his freehold property, bought in 1846, he built a grinding mill, a potato distillery, an oil mill, and in 1850 one of the first Austrian sugar factories with a coke and gas refinery. His estate was exemplary and served as model for others. Already 90 years ago the land was drained and was tilled with English steam plows. He founded an agricultural school and set up further sugar refineries in Moravia and Upper Silesia. All subsequent generations continued to improve and enlarge the estate, and in 1945 it covered 225 hectares [556 acres]. Along with some even larger estates in the District it held the lead in production and efficiency. The estate was still in our family under diocesan administration, later under Austrian sovereignty, and also remained in our family in 1919 after we had had to surrender part of our wealth to the Czech state. In 1945 this family property was confiscated with a stroke of the pen, and my family was driven from our estate as beggars. In autumn of 1938, when the "mass flight" began in response to the propaganda from the Reich, I had been the only estate owner not to voluntarily leave his home. When the Russians liberated the Sudetenland and Czechia in 1945 I again remained on the estate. I was persecuted, but I would not voluntarily leave my home and property. Even though most of the means for operating the estate had been taken from us, I continued to cultivate the land as best I could, and on June 20, 1945 a National Administrator was put in charge of the dispossessed property by an office in Ostrau. This administrator is a farmer's son and comes from circles involved in the Czech People's Party, and so in his person my estate has been fortunate to come under the charge of one of the few exceptions to the rule, as shown by the enclosed copy of one of his letters to me. I attach this letter as proof of the views of a middle-class Czech on the conditions in our homeland. It is also to serve as evidence for my own personal, objective attitude towards the current economic conditions, since it shows that my assessment is not clouded by malicious or ignorant Czech destruction of my property.

In July 1945, bourgeois Czech parties warned me that my arrest and transfer into a concentration camp was imminent, and that I should try to get away in order to avoid being tormented by the partisan camp guards. But again I refused to leave my homeland, and expressly stated that I would no more voluntarily leave my home in 1945 than I had in autumn 1938, as I had nothing to fear in political nor in social respects. In mid-August I was arrested by the Czech gendarmerie, allegedly on orders from higher up, and was taken to the nearest town for "a brief questioning in court" on the pretext of allegedly having hidden some valuables. During my questioning a letter that accompanied my committal to the concentration camp Jauernig had been left in the typewriter, but I had ignored it. I was left in the dark until I had passed through the door to the common prison in Jauernig. A German Communist was the prison warden. Conditions here were already indescribable. The tiny cells were crowded with heaps of people who could not even lie on the stone floor, and would not have been permitted to do so even if they had been able.

The next morning I witnessed the first beatings by disgustingly dehumanized Czechs, seconded by German informants. They celebrated their first orgies, which I heard. Other than the wateriest soup imaginable, beatings were all we got. The vermin, and the expectation of even worse to come, kept sleep at bay. I was dressed only in light summer clothes, without a coat or blanket, just as I had come from the field, and my pockets had been totally emptied by the German "anti-Fascist". After four days we had to line up, and our march to the second concentration camp of the district began. It was located at the city outskirts and consisted of former Labor Service barracks. My father-in-law,

Dr. Erich Lundwall, formerly a landholder in Weissbach near Jauernig, was the German camp leader, in charge of and responsible for all the inmates, and he had been one of the first, in June, to help erect the barbed wire fence around the camp. The camp was under the command of staff watchman Anton Pec of the Czech gendarmerie, and the guards were Communist partisans, work-shy elements formerly in Russian service who were now being rewarded. One Czech gendarmerie subordinate who later served as guard of my labor team called them criminals who had murdered countless Czech gendarmes when the latter had tried to bring order to the chaos reigning in those days. He said that where he was concerned, if the elections were decided in favor of the Communists he would take off his uniform and dump it in the ditch and then go straight to the Reich, where he had been well treated. Over time the gendarmerie lost ever more respect and power and came to be quite at the partisans' mercy. Matters of national pride were of secondary importance to the sub-humans that constituted the guard teams. They wore outlandish uniforms, mostly a bizarre mixture of the uniforms of National Socialist organizations, and the "dandies" among them preferred SS uniforms. All of them wore the red enamel Soviet star on their caps and shirts, as well as a red arm band with the letters KTOF (*Koncentracní Tábor Okres Frývaldov*, Freiwaldau District Concentration Camp). The latter proves that real concentration camps had been set up, even though official foreign policy was to deny their existence. Hand guns and whips of all kinds and description completed their outfits. A Commissar in a gray uniform presided over them all. He was a horrible sadist who would trace the contours of the manacled prisoners standing at the door or lying on the floor with thrown knives in order to add a sense of emphasis to their interrogations, and who went around at night in a real SS uniform, goading and terrorizing the civilian population.

Even before being arrested I had heard rumors about the horrors of the camp. I had lost all contact with my father-in-law, and the camp inmates were totally cut off from their relatives and the outside world in general. The inhabitants of the surrounding regions trembled with us in anticipation of our fate. Whenever anyone tried to slip one of the inmates a piece of bread or some decent work clothes, the kind soul was beaten for his troubles. I once saw one of them in the sick-bay; his posterior was totally mangled, and the skin and flesh had burst open in slashes up to 15 cm [6"] long and several cm deep.

July 9 and August 12 - horrible days in the camp - were over. On the first date a shooting had been provoked near the camp fence and the inmates were then accused of trying to escape. It is impossible to describe the beatings that then ensued, all rations were suspended, and tanks that had just arrived at the neighboring Polish border drove up and fired at random into the barracks. The other day two boys, aged 15 and 16, had escaped from the labor team and had been brought back to the camp by their own German Communist father, as it had been made known everywhere that anyone found to be harboring the fugitives would be executed. These two boys were slowly tortured to death, in the truest sense of the term. They were tortured slowly and deliberately before the eyes of the entire camp, and not just for one day. Swastikas were cut into their buttocks with pocket knives - one swastika on each side. Not until the next day were they led to the corner of the woods beyond the camp fence, and shot and buried there in the forced presence of two inmates from each barrack. Calling a priest, or a later exhumation and reburial of their bodies in consecrated soil, was forbidden. On the other hand, the German physician from the hospital who was sometimes permitted to visit the camp for cases of severe illness or the occasional general visit (on which occasions, however, the guards would arbitrarily chase the sick inmates away from the door to the infirmary) reported how the chief guard and deputy camp commandant would sometimes mail C.O.D. parcels with skulls (declared value, Kcs 600 each) to anatomical institutes, since there was never enough ready cash for liquor.

On our committal to the camp we all had to strip down to our pants and were then forced with whip lashes and blows from rifle butts to do hours of squats and push-ups until we were totally exhausted. Some of us, including myself, were then selected for particular "commendation" by the abovementioned commissar, who just shortly before had ripped a medallion of the Virgin Mary from my neck and thrown it on the ground after I had accidentally forgotten to give it up during the preceding inspection. After such strenuous physical overheating we were then chased into the bath room where we had to stand for almost an hour under the shower, which spewed freezing-cold mountain water. With whip lashes our heads were constantly brought back to the position desired by our tormentors, namely one that would allow the water to run into our nose and ears. Then, while a guard armed with a submachine gun stood by, we were doused with hot tea *[tea or tar - original unclear; pub.]* and had to line up in front of three guards. The biggest and strongest thugs had been selected for this purpose. We had to stand a few steps below them, and then, on the mark, they all punched you at the same time in the face and throat so that you flew into a corner like a bundle of rags, and over and over again we had to crawl back for more of the same treatment, to the point of exhaustion. Then we were beaten with long, heavy and also short, seven-lashed whips, until our entire bodies were suffused with blood or simply one huge open wound. The blows administered with a Spanish cane onto our genitals were dreadful - one comrade was still entirely black and blue there even after three weeks and was therefore forbidden to see the doctor, even though in his fear he had vowed to the guard that he did not know why he was black and blue there. Then we were locked into the camp's punishment cell, the dreaded "Basse", which was located beyond the guards' room and where one was at their mercy day and night. We found splashes of blood on the wall, and beneath the bunk there lay a totally blood- and pus-soaked shirt and an identical pair of underpants that had belonged to one of our predecessors. Towards the evening the same procedure resumed again. In the meantime they had found that I had been included with this group of prisoners arbitrarily, and so I was excluded from further maltreatment, at least for this day. The other four had to stand up against the cell wall and were then beaten across their eyes with short whips until all eight eyes were totally swollen shut. They had to keep calling out: "We thank our Führer!" and if they did not shout it they were beaten, and if they did shout it they were beaten all the more. The spectacle was repulsive to the point of being nauseating, and I felt shame at being the only one to be spared this ordeal, especially since it turned out later that these unfortunate victims had also been innocent. The first time I was put into this cell I had to spend three weeks there, sometimes with only one meal a day, without an inkling of what our future fate would be. During the night, after one day of working in the camp, I opened the window of our common barracks as I had to make use of the "facilities", a tin can that stood beside the window in our "bedroom". A guard saw it and leaped in through the window, and after another beating I was sent right back into the punishment cell.

One evening a 67-year-old man was brought in. He had been on the logging team (500 m out of the camp a swath had to be clear-cut to allow targeted firing in the event that someone escaped), and while working on this task he had been accused of harboring plans to escape. He was forced to jump around the small cell with his knees deeply bent in squats. One of the guards jumped on his back and squeezed his throat with his knees, while boxing him about the head with both fists until the old man collapsed. Then another prisoner, a younger, sturdier fellow - an ex-soldier who had been returning home from the war and whom they had simply snatched right off the street and put into the concentration camp - had to endure the same maltreatment, only it took longer for him to collapse. The old man was completely broken, he mumbled prayers day and night and seemed to sense death approaching. And indeed, he was soon accused of having approved a comrade's plans for escape over the double barbed wire fence, even though he was hard of hearing and could therefore not even have followed the conversation in question, which a sentry had overheard in the washroom. As punishment he was slowly trampled to death in the guard room, separated from our room only by a wooden wall. It was dreadful to hear those terrible screams, that grew quieter and quieter and ended in a moan and death rattle. Another elderly man also died in that guard room in a similar way; he was beaten to death and trampled to pulp. All these victims were dumped into a shallow grave in the woods behind the camp, without the benefit of clergy. The German physician was supposed to attest to death by natural causes, but he refused to do so without exhuming the body. That same physician was also supposed, under coercion, to eliminate another inmate by giving him a lethal injection. But it didn't go that far. His father-in-law was a Czech and served the First Republic as legation counselor in Prague, and he told me that he and his circles had envisioned the "liberation" of Czechoslovakia somewhat differently.

In the course of my "examination for admission" during a "treatment" in the washroom on the day I had been committed to this camp, my left ear drum had been punctured, but so far my ear had not festered like those of other prisoners who had been given a similar treatment. I had only lost my hearing. For this reason, three weeks later, a "specialist" gave me a well-aimed hollow-handed slap on that ear, and the sudden air pressure brought about the desired putrefaction. For weeks I then had to go to work with that infected ear, until finally my comrades took me to see the physician who happened to be in the camp. I had to be immediately transported to the hospital to be operated; the pus had already consumed the periosteum and penetrated the bone itself. The very specialized operation was performed by a non-specialist, but ended successfully. Only 48 hours later the pus would have reached my brain, and I would have been lying in the corner of the woods behind the camp. But that wouldn't have mattered, and there was nobody who would have dared object. Not even a Czech. Human lives didn't count for anything. The camp administration did not pay the hospital and doctor bill - instead, it was presented to the forced laborer working on my expropriated estate.

In a 5.5 sq. m. [59 sq. ft.] cell we six men had to lie on the floor without a jacket, coat or blanket, which were forbidden. During cold nights the window under the flimsy roof had to be left open, on hot days it had to be closed. We were let out quite arbitrarily to answer the call of nature, and nobody dared to call the guards for an extra trip due to the beating that could be expected if we had bothered those fine gentlemen. Everyone had to relieve himself only a little at a time into a tooth-brushing glass that served for all of us. This glass was then emptied out the window, clandestinely and fearfully, until this too was forbidden on pain of beatings. Later we were given a bottle, but still everyone could relieve only the worst pressure. It is necessary to have gone through this for a longer period of time to really understand what torture it is. Everything was caked up by the blood and pus from our wounds or the pus running out of our ears, and the air in the cell was enough to knock you out. One of our comrades regularly blacked out when he stood up to go to the window. I happened to have my hat in my cell, and it served as our emergency toilet, but as it was not water-tight we sometimes ended up lying in puddles.

Several inmates managed, at peril of their lives, to escape from the place they had been assigned to work, some managed to climb over the double barbed wire barrier, and some escaped by cutting through this double wire. Every time all the other inmates of the camp were punished with beatings or forced marches through the camp for up to 20 hours, without a break and without the smallest morsel of food. Everyone had to continue this until he dropped, and at first even invalids and amputees had to participate. After we returned from our work details, we were forbidden to hang up wet clothes or shoes to dry in the barracks, else the guards would throw them out the window into the ditch. On countless evenings and often even in the middle of the night we would suddenly be ordered to "line up!", and we had to report in whatever state of dress or undress we happened to be in, at all times of the year and in every weather. Often, after repeatedly lining up and being dismissed again, we then had to stand lined up for hours. Sometimes, "ladies" were also invited to enjoy the spectacle, and these would provoke and rabble-rouse and even make fun of the elderly people who could not keep up any more.

In May of 1946 a battle ensued between the leaders of the two concentration camps in the District. One of the two camps was to be closed and its inmates transferred to the other. Both camps had great stores of misappropriated food that had not been given to the kitchen and that should now have been sent along with the inmates, and each of the leaders worried that he would lose his position and the advantages that came with it. Finally we were loaded onto trucks - most of the hoarded food was not - and we were shipped to Concentration Camp I Adelsdorf near Freiwaldau, a former prisoner-of-war camp. It was crawling with vermin. The first Sunday I was there, I caught 147 bed-bugs in my bed and 94 fleas in the blanket. After we got settled in, we learned of the atrocities that had taken place in this camp. Some of them were even more imaginative than what we had already suffered through, and the most inhumane of them were done in a subsidiary camp farther up in the woods, from where the screams and shots could not be heard down in the village. The inhumanity of this camp was such that even some Czechs had reported it in Prague, whereupon the camp had been liquidated over night. For example, one day every sixth man was shot on the order of the administrator in charge of both of the District's camps, and this was done for no reason at all, with no regard for who the victim was, and with no regard for his "crime", which had not gone to trial for months after the prisoner's arrival anyway. In some cases, even 15 months after their arrival prisoners had not been told why they were even there. Often the only crime was that one had German parents. A doctor who was an inmate in this forest camp was just one huge festering sore, all over his body. He had to crawl painfully across the ground, as he had not been able to walk for a long time. Other inmates had to lick his suppurating wounds, had to eat his excrements, and had to lick each other's genitals. The Communist deputy camp leader Wiesner, who was embroiled in a perpetual power struggle with his boss, camp commandant staff watchman Grenar, had broken his knee in a motorcycle accident while driving drunk, but he insisted on being carried up into the woods on a gurney to attend the executions so that he might watch the blood of the German swine flow. A number of the worst-off in this camp hanged themselves from the barracks beams at night because they could simply not bear the tortures any longer, neither physically nor emotionally.

In early January a cousin of mine had visited me in the Jauernig camp. He had had to leave his home in 1939 for opposing Hitler, had gone via England to the United States, and returned in 1945 as American citizen, officer, and representative of the CIC [Counter Intelligence Corps]. Only after repeated attempts was he admitted, as an officer of the Allies, into the camp that only Russians had been allowed to enter before. Our brief conversation was monitored, and besides, I was too surprised and astounded that there should actually still be someone who dared care about us. We had given up all hope of that long ago. That very same day the gendarmerie, which on the whole had Social Democratic leanings, questioned me without reference to the previous transcript, and then asked me why I was here at all. I had no idea! It was not until further questionings in February and March that I found out from the Czech gendarmerie, through the transcripts i.e. reports of denunciations, that I, like so many others, had been arrested on the basis of denunciations by German Communists. The accusations had meanwhile been disproved by witnesses, but nonetheless I was still detained as work slave, netting the Czech state some 50 Kcs. per day, until my resettlement [expulsion]. In many cases the Czech gendarmerie - whose officials had often been active in our towns and villages prior to 1938 and who therefore knew the inhabitants - told the prisoners during their questioning which of the good German citizens had denounced them, and in every case it was a true-blue "anti-Fascist", in other words, in the Sudeten German case, a Communist or some other kind of subhuman motivated by personal revenge.

Even as late as August 1946 statements were being extorted with beatings to the point of unconsciousness, and when the victim came to again he had to sign the finished transcript without it being read to him, much less translated. These prisoners were then sent in batches from the camp to the Freiwaldau court prison, and from there to the District Court in Troppau, where they were tried by the "People's Court". The results are well known. My 59-year-old father-in-law was sentenced to 18 years forced labor in Mürau near Hohenstadt, which under the old Austrian regime had been the prison for the worst criminal offenders. Many of my comrades were sentenced to many years in prison, or even life terms, and were shipped off to forest camps or coal mines.

As witnesses to corroborate these my experiences in the Czech concentration camps I can name not only a number of my former comrades-in-suffering, who also live as expellees in the Western zones [of Germany] and whose names and addresses I can provide at any time, but also the former private secretary of His Eminence Cardinal Bertram of Breslau Dr. Münch, who visited me repeatedly in the hospital after my aforementioned operation and who was in close contact with the German physician, a former classmate of mine.

Economic Issues

I began my report with a brief overview of the history of my former family estate. Our [the Sudeten Germans'] farms, trades and industries were just as flourishing and productive. As laborer in the concentration camp work teams I witnessed the initially slow decline in all its stages. At first there were still Germans in all towns and cities who were skilled in the work required. Businesses were still on a solid foundation, and reserves were available. Then the decline progressed rapidly, and today our home is literally becoming a wasteland due to ignorance, the people's unwillingness to work, and malice - true to President Beneš's words that it would be better that the thistles take over the German fields than that Germans should continue to work them. I have worked on farms, in the forest and in industry, I had to help loot homes and to dismantle and steal machinery at night so that it would not show up in the inventory before the lawful owners were resettled [expelled]. Locksmiths, street sweepers and mostly pit laborers - all of them honorable occupations in and of themselves, but utterly unsuited to agricultural pursuits - were put in charge of our flourishing farms. They sowed oats in the fall, brought out the tedder to harvest potatoes, and lived on illegal slaughtering and alcohol. The grain was brought in wet, it barely went through the thresher and most of the kernels remained in the straw. When we objected, and fed the sheaves through the machinery more slowly, we were told that it was good enough for a "new farmer".

The Party badge and his political affiliations shielded these newcomers time and again. To give another example: in the lumber industry, water was poured by the bucketful onto the wood wool before pressing it. The lumber was sold not only in the forest but a second time, illegally, on the train ramp, and after repeated sales and resales it was sometimes even stolen before it was to be loaded up. Working on the grinding machine for saw blades, a Czech laborer polishes three or four blades a day, and poorly at that, while his ousted German predecessor had polished some 300 blades. In one linen factory with a branch outlet in the United States, things went downhill just as quickly. When the American representative came over for the first time after the war and wanted to resume business relations and to speak with the owner and directors, he was told sheepishly that they were in the concentration camp and that he could not speak to their wives. The German had to be fetched from the camp to give some estimates. Later on, the shipment had to be canceled for being faulty, the supply quota for 1945 was not filled even by 1947, but 1947 prices were being charged for the remainder. Business relations were broken off by the American side.

In the meantime the resettlements [expulsions] continued, and the shortage of skilled labor increased with each passing week. Estates were put under state control, leased by the state to a Communist association that took over the entire inventory from the state at absurdly low prices. After being released from imprisonment I saw such an inventory for my own estate, and even have a copy of it as proof. A large Hofherr-Schrantz threshing machine (1250 mm drum), that had been purchased in 1944 for about 7,000.- Mark, was declared in 1945 as being worth Kcs 6,000, in other words one tenth of its real value. An old Landauer (closed coach), on the other hand, whose roof had been slashed and windows smashed, was "valued" at Kcs 7,000.

Nowhere was there the slightest indication of any real expertise. Our town had 2,300 German inhabitants, and not a single Czech prior to 1919. In 1938 there were a few Czech financiers, gendarmes and one "minority teacher". From 1938 until 1945 there was not one Czech. Today the town is inhabited by barely 600 Czechs, who are to do all the work in the 2,300 hectare [9 square mile] town.

Many businesses are inoperative, even entire mountain villages are uninhabited, the livestock has been driven off, the houses are falling into disrepair and are looted for parts. In spring 1947 countless hectares of potatoes and turnips had not been harvested, countless grain stores were left empty, and countless potato clamps had been ruined by frostbite due to inadequate winter covering, so that there was a potato shortage in the cities even though the harvest had been unusually good.

My estate has nine draft teams but only five day laborers, and not one reliable stableboy. Both remaining tractors have been wrecked by improper operation. The few workers are only just enough to cart the feed into the stable and the potatoes to the distillery. The administrator, acting on his own initiative, hired and brought in a group of Slovakian minority laborers (my estate has always employed these hard-working piece-workers for its intensive sugar-beet operation ever since 1893), but as per ministerial decree from Prague, these minorities are now no longer permitted to work on the farms in the Sudetengau, and the Labor Office failed to provide any replacement. Instead, however, 6 Bulgarian families were settled on the estate.

Freiwaldau, Report No. 5

District Freiwaldau, the Thomasdorf and Adelsdorf camps, murders and abuse

Reported by Karl Schneider - Report of September 15, 1946

I was imprisoned in the Thomasdorf concentration camp for 14½ months. I had been committed to the camp on June 15, 1945. I was accused of having shot a Czech in 1938. In the camp I was severely and brutally maltreated. In the course of 4 weeks I was beaten 16 times, individually, at various times of the night. My tormentors used rubber truncheons, whips,

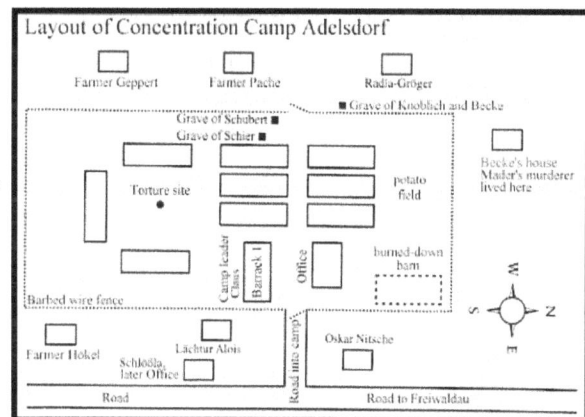

Layout of Concentration Camp Adelsdorf
[Map not in original edition of this book - added by The Scriptorium, taken from: "Zuckmantler Heimatbrief", No. 143, September 2004, p. 98. English captions added by The Scriptorium.]

chains, pieces of squared timber, etc. Each time I was beaten unconscious. I was kicked in the ribs and 3 were broken. They also knocked my teeth in and damaged my shin bone. Whenever I fell to the ground they would fire shots into the ground to either side of my head, set a German shepherd on me, etc.

On August 1, 1945 I was transferred to the Adelsdorf concentration camp, where I was also maltreated. On August 17 Franz Schubert from Niklasdorf was ordered to box me about the head, and since he did not do it hard enough to please the guards he was given a punch in the face that killed him. That same night, comrade Schiebl was also beaten to death, and the 16-year-old lad Knoblich from Hermannstadt was shot after first being horribly tortured all night long. My innocence of the charges against me had already been established by a witness on July 20, but my first questioning was not until August 10, 1946, after which I was released.

In Thomasdorf I also became a witness to the horrific torture of Dr. Pawlowsky from Freiwaldau, who succumbed to his injuries on August 30, 1945. On August 1, 1946, two of my toes were crushed in an accident while I was loading wood. I received no medical attention whatsoever. My foot was neither set nor put in splints. To this day I can't walk normally again.

Freiwaldau Report No. 6
District Freiwaldau, the Thomasdorf camp, description of the camp
Reported b: Karl Froning - Report of January 4, 1949

On July 25 [1945] I was sent on a transport to the concentration camp Thomasdorf. This was a former Russian camp in my administrative district and was located in a forest, in the so-called Vietseifen. It was designated a penal camp. We were to learn soon enough what that meant, but for most of us the reason why we of all people had been sent there remained a mystery, like so many other things in the newly created "Second Republic".

In total the Czechs maintained four such camps in the District: Jauernig, Adelsdorf and Thomasdorf for men, and Biberteich near Freiwaldau for women. The camp in Jauernig was a former camp of the Reich Labor Service, and the camp in Adelsdorf a former English camp maintained by the company Weihönig.

After our arrival we had to line up in the camp square and spread out what we had brought with us, and the contents of our pockets, for inspection. Knives, valuables, matches, cigarettes and anything that caught the Czechs' fancy was taken from us, and without receipt. This inspection already marked the start of the beatings. I heard how the camp commandant Wiesner yelled at a prisoner who stood behind me, who had been badly beaten and was evidently bleeding: "German blood isn't blood, it's swine piss!" The camp was surrounded by a double barbed wire fence, outside of which stood a building for the guard teams, made up of so-called partisans and some younger gendarmes. The camp commandant was the aforementioned Wiesner, his deputy was a certain Opichal, both of them partisans. By our standards the camp had been designed for a maximum capacity of about 100 Russian prisoners-of-war, but the Czechs had crammed more than 200 Germans into it. Among the prisoners there were many that were over 60 years of age, some even were 70 and older. A great many didn't even know on what grounds they had been locked up. There certainly were no war criminals or Party bosses among us, but any random denunciation or even the simple fact that one was German sufficed for an arrest. Even having been detained in a concentration camp in the Third Reich was no protection, and there were a good many among us who got to know both.

The major structures in the camp included a large barrack in which the prisoners slept in double bunk beds on bags of wood shavings. There were no lockers or closets. Then there was also a smaller, somewhat better sleeping barrack - the former dining room - a kitchen barrack, barber room, and infirmary. We had to wash out of doors at a small uncovered water trough, while our laundry was washed in a special laundry barrack. Tailor, cobbler, blacksmith and locksmith shops were located outside the camp fence, but we couldn't get very much made for us there since the workers had only very limited materials, most of which were needed to make goods desired by the guards.

Immediately upon our committal to the camp, we were shaved bald. There was no medical care, and wounds and ulcers - from which we suffered badly - were treated with self-sacrificing care by the hospital assistant Brosig who had used to be a massage therapist at the Priessnitz Sanatorium in Freiwaldau-Gräfenberg. More severe cases, such as phlegmones and blood poisoning, were sent to the Freiwaldau hospital. Every now and then a younger military physician also showed up in the camp, but only in order to certify the death of an inmate.

Our rations were meager, to put it mildly. The main meal at noon consisted mostly of potatoes and old, dried vegetables. Sometimes leftovers from noon were distributed as extras in the evening; but usually all we got in the mornings and evenings was coffee and a wholly insufficient bit of bread.

After we were awakened at about 5 o'clock in the morning, we had to perform morning "exercises", and after some coffee we were sent off to work, which for most of the prisoners consisted of building a new road through the forest. The work, which continued on Sundays as well, was quite hard in and of itself, and the utterly inadequate rations and shelter and the downright sadistic way we were treated only made it worse. Every evening almost without exception, during our Czech "language classes" which were held outdoors, the two aforementioned camp commandants picked individuals for special exercises, such as jogging, crawling, leapfrogging, parade marching etc. Sometimes two prisoners also had to stand facing each other and slap each other about the head, or when it had rained, suck up the filthy water from the ground and spit it into each other's faces. Then the slapping about the head would resume at full force, which cost many of us our hearing; or we were beaten with dog whips, sticks and slats. During the exercises one morning - I think it was August 14 - a larger number of us, including myself, had to line up bare-chested in front of the aforementioned Opichal and were then severely beaten with a bullwhip. An older, 60 to 70-year-old prisoner was especially severely beaten and after every 10 to 15 blows he had to say "dekuji" - thank you. But because in Opichal's opinion he never pronounced "dekuji" correctly, he always received another 10 to 15 blows. This was repeated about 6 times, and you can perhaps imagine what the man looked like after that. Another time Opichal chose me for special attention because I had been a member of the Party and the SA. He demanded that I should curse Hitler, which I refused to do, saying that at any rate Hitler had been the head of state of the German Reich. Opichal then threatened to shoot me in the foot. I replied that it was perfectly clear to me that at present he had the power to do so. He cursed me roundly, but then he left me alone.

For a while Opichal liked to pass out our rations himself, and again every one had to say *"dekuji"* on receiving his allotment. Anyone who Opichal felt did not say it correctly either did not receive any food or was beaten. One time, an older prisoner, rather excited and evidently somewhat hard of hearing, accidentally dumped the hot meal down Opichal's boots. He was beaten half to death over the course of the next few days.

One day the elderly and invalid prisoners had to line up. Allegedly they were to be released. They had to stand and wait for a long time in the camp square, then they were badly beaten and ended up staying in the camp after all. In early August some of the inmates were transferred to the Adelsdorf concentration camp, and others were transferred from there to Thomasdorf in a sort of prisoner exchange. They arrived at night, in the pouring rain, and were very badly beaten during the aforementioned welcoming search.

Slaps and blows were administered very liberally at every line-up whenever we allegedly faced the wrong way or one of the prisoners did not understand, or misunderstood, the orders which were only ever given in Czech. Even if Opichal and his minions felt that our boots were not polished enough, 15 and more blows with a stick was considered fitting punishment.

Every now and then the Czechs got the idea to have us line up in the camp square at night, even several times a night. The partisans and gendarmes would first stand beside the barracks doors and hit randomly and as hard as they could into the crowd of prisoners exiting the barracks. Then the aforementioned exercises were ordered, only in a much more severe form than usual; generally the Czechs were badly drunk while this was going on. It was a popular practice to chase the prisoners around the square with whips and then to suddenly trip them up or shove a rifle barrel between their legs. Anyone who remained on the ground due to exhaustion - and there were many who did so - was beaten until he got up again. If anyone fainted he was alternately doused with hot and cold water until he regained his senses. Bandages were ruthlessly torn off the wounds they covered, even if they were badly infected and dripping with pus. And in conclusion to these night-time drills, which usually lasted for hours, we all had to shout a triple "Sieg Heil" to our Führer Adolf Hitler.

It is beyond me to give a description of these nocturnal scenes in such a way that someone who was not personally involved could truly share the experience. I doubt that anyone could give such an account anyway. Even though I have fairly good nerves, was in good enough physical shape to handle the described exercises, and ultimately survived all this maltreatment without lasting physical damage, I too relived these spectral images in nightmares even later on, with the prisoners being chased about, the crack of the whips, the moans and whimpers of the beaten victims and the hoarse yells of "honem, honem" by the drunk Czechs, all of it only poorly lit by a few stable lanterns. - The physician Dr. Pawlowsky from Freiwaldau was perhaps maltreated worse than anyone else. According to a reliable source, on his admission to the camp he had to walk at the head of his column and carry a sign bearing the words, "We have our Führer to thank for this." In the camp itself he barely ever had a quiet minute, and in the end he was literally beaten to death. His pallet was in my barrack, fairly close to my own, and there was hardly an evening when he did not crawl painfully onto his straw sack totally filthy, soaked to the skin, covered in blood and welts. For some time he was also in my work unit. Aside from angina pectoris he suffered from a very painful ulcer on his behind, which the Czechs clearly knew and therefore made a point of kicking him there. As a reliable source told me, Opichal would grind out burning cigarettes on Pawlowsky's naked body. I myself saw how once he was dragged across the camp square and was supposed to eat some sort of filthy mass off the ground. When he begged that he might be spared that, the mass, which was said to have been his own excrement, was smeared into his mouth. On August 13 I saw him line up outside for the last time, dressed only in black gymnastics shorts; he was covered in wounds and welts, and collapsed from weakness. That night he died in the infirmary.

He bore all these unspeakable tortures silently and with admirable composure, and the Czechs made a martyr out of him - even in the eyes of his political opponents. In a culmination of their actions, as a reliable witness told me, they forced his assistant, a lady imprisoned in the Biberteich concentration camp, to put on mourning clothes after he died.

On August 5, 1945 the farmer Adolf Böhm from Ober-Lindewiese was beaten to death, whereas the lumber merchant Raschke had hanged himself out of despair even before my arrival in the camp. These 3 dead were buried without any ceremony in shallow graves in the woods above the Russian Cemetery. The master stonemason Sohmen from Saubsdorf, a physically small and rather clumsy man, was also abused especially badly, and was ultimately beaten into mental retardation. Aside from a broken eardrum, the physical signs of his abuse included a large festering wound on his neck, where the sinews were already exposed and which was hard enough for the one available orderly to dress with the limited bandages that were available to him. Nonetheless this dressing was also repeatedly and ruthlessly torn off. On July 27 a man named Vater, from Hermannstadt, escaped while on labor duty. That same day, the other 10 members of the labor team were each punished with 200 blows on the bare soles of their feet, which the rest of us had to witness. They were beaten with thick slats, and when they had splintered they were replaced with fresh ones. Naturally the men thus beaten could not walk for weeks, but nonetheless had to attend each line-up, day and night alike. They came crawling to these line-ups like dogs, on all fours, and were often beaten some more on these occasions. The men maltreated like this are:

Brosig, livestock dealer, Oberlindewiese;
Dittrich, locksmith, Böhmischdorf;
Hackenberg, Niederlindewiese;
Hofmann, innkeeper, Weidenau;
Kuchar, Zuckmantel;
Nietsche, forestry supervisor, Böhmischdorf;
Siegel, forestry worker, Obergrund;
Siegel, forestry worker, Obergrund;
Spielvogel, civil servant, Sandhübel;

and a tenth man whose name I was unable to find out. At the end of this beating, which reduced at least one of them, Spielvogel, to a lifelong cripple, commandant Wiesner announced: "If anyone else escapes I'll have you all shot. I'll have 200 new arrivals in the camp the next day anyway." An approximately 17-year-old Czech girl, who was said to have been Opichal's and his buddies' collective affair, watched these beatings with open enjoyment. She seems also to have kept the registers, and read out the names.

Every now and then there were barracks searches in the camp, which were occasions for the Czechs to steal from us whatever they liked. Even the small parcels of food and clothes which our kin were occasionally allowed to bring us were very often stolen. A good sweater was stolen from me in this way. Once, when the accountant Kasper from Zuckmantel reported to Opichal to pick up a small parcel which his wife had walked 60 km [37 miles] to bring him, the parcel was shown him, but not handed over. Instead he received a variety of blows to the head. One day one of the partisans, nicknamed Sherif or something like that, wanted my boots because his were not good enough for him. Luckily for me my boots did not fit him.

On August 15 the camp was supposed to be transferred to Adelsdorf. In the night from the 14th to the 15th a lot of gunfire suddenly began outside, and continued until morning. We had heard the same in earlier nights, but not as severely and not for as long. The following day around 3 o'clock in the afternoon, as work on moving the camp was progressing, six prisoners, including some who had already gone to Adelsdorf with an advance unit, were led off into the forest under heavy partisan and gendarme guard. Shortly thereafter we heard several shots being fired nearby. About half an hour later a team of prisoners were led into the woods with shovels and hoes. Forestry supervisor Emil Locker was one of the members of this work team. The names of the executed men are:

Buschmann, painter, Friedeberg;
Dr. Franke, attorney, Freiwaldau;
Hanke, Rudolf, Mayor, Alt-Rohtwasser;
Klimesch, truck driver, Zuckmantel;
Reinelt, secretary (an invalid), Gross-Krosse;
Seifert, Gustav, foundry worker, Böhmischdorf.

They were buried in shallow graves in the forest a few hundred meters from the camp, to the left above the road right next to the game fence. Captain Novak was said to have issued the execution order per telephone from Freiwaldau, and also to have specified which prisoners to shoot. We were never able to find out what the grounds for their execution were. Commandant Wiesner, who had broken his leg and was therefore not really on duty at that time, nonetheless attended the execution. As various credible witnesses, including some women, told me, Wiesner repeatedly brought up the subject of this execution later, in the Adelsdorf camp, especially when he was drunk, recounted the events and declared that he was not responsible for what had happened and that he had only carried out a written order from Captain Novak, of which he had made copies and bricked up the original in a safe place to establish his innocence.

In addition to the men thus murdered, there are also those who died in the Freiwaldau hospital of the consequences of their maltreatment. They are:

Kintscher, community secretary, Weisswasser, 57 years old;
Ludwig, law official, Freiwaldau, 70 years old;

Seifert, roofer or plumber, Friedeberg;
Watzlawek, retired senior teacher, Schwarzwasser, 70 years old.

Others to die in the hospital were:

Lux, Freiwaldau;
Pelz, farmer, Jungferndorf;
Streit, farmer, Neudorf.

Adding the four more who were beaten to death in Adelsdorf up until August 20, about whom I will speak again later, the number of dead comes to 20. Given the camp population of 200, that makes fully 10 percent, and that was in the space of about 4 weeks.

In the evening of August 15 we were taken to the **Concentration Camp Adelsdorf** where we were initially housed in makeshift emergency shelters. The camp entrance was on the town's main street, and above the gate was a large sign bearing the Czech and Russian inscription: Koncentracní tábor (concentration camp). Later this sign was taken down and the camp was variously described as labor camp, internment camp, internee collection point, and the like. The barracks were not the worst I'd seen, even if they were drafty and damp; occasionally a new one was built. This camp as well was overcrowded, though not as severely as Thomasdorf; two men each shared a small locker. In general everyone received only one blanket, and if anyone wanted a second he had to arrange to have one sent to him from home. During the cold part of the year we were allowed to heat the barracks from about 5 o'clock p.m. until 9 p.m.; unfortunately the fuel was rather scarce. Regarding the tailors, cobblers and other service workers, the situation was the same as in Thomasdorf.

We "Thomasdorfer" prisoners wore a patch with an "A" beside our sewn-on camp number and were forbidden to talk to or get together in any way with the old "Adelsdorfer" prisoners, who wore a "B". We also had to work longer hours and were generally treated differently than they were, in the sense that our night-time "exercises" were repeated even more frequently, so that we practically got no rest at all any more and no longer even dared take off our clothing and boots for the night. Once I could not even recall how I had made it back to my straw sack after the previous night's two such exercise sessions, during which I hadn't even been maltreated beyond the usual degree.

One night I was called away from these exercises and over to a group of Czechs, and a brutal-looking man wearing a Soviet Star asked me for my name and profession. When I stated both, I was hit in the face so severely that two of my incisors were knocked out. Later I found out that this thug was Mader, the Commissar of Buchelsdorf and Adelsdorf; allegedly he had used to be a professional boxer, and had a rap sheet of 16 to 20 previous convictions. Judging from his appearance, demeanor and punching power, I can easily believe it. Another time my tormentors immediately left off beating me when I declared that I was a German national, had been in the Sudetengau only since 1939 and had not been involved in the events of 1938; the following day this same declaration worked one more time.

Prisoners who were beaten to death during and after these "exercises" included:

Knoblich, 15 years old, on August 19 or 20, 1945;
Schniebel, laborer, Niklasdorf, on July 16, 1945;
Schubert, manufacturer, Niklasdorf, on August 16, 1945.

During the night of August 19 to 20 a great deal of shooting once again broke out during the nightly exercises. The lights were turned off, and we had to stand with our hands raised for a long time, until we were chased into the nearest barrack when it was already almost morning. During this to-do the mailman Nitsche from Reihwiesen was shot through the ankle while he lay in a bunk in the emergency barrack. His injury had not fully healed even by the summer of 1946. The next morning Captain Novak appeared, ordered us to line up, walked up and down the rows as though inspecting us, and without saying a word, selected six men, whose names Hansl Velitel had to write down. Evidently another execution was planned, but there was no longer enough time to carry it out because the gendarmerie took over the camp on August 21. But even so it still took several days before the new Commandant - a very civil and proper sergeant of the gendarmerie whose name I think was H..... - arrived in the camp. One night during this interval time my barracks neighbor, the grocer Fial from Freiwaldau, was fetched from his pallet by a partisan wearing a German pilot shirt with a Czech coat-of-arms on the left sleeve. Fial never returned. He had also been an Ortsgruppe leader and had already been badly maltreated with kicks to the abdomen. We never found out with certainty whether he was beaten, shot or choked to death by Commissar Mader, what role the two prisoners-of-war H. from Mannheim and Z. from Berlin had played in Fial's death, and where he was buried; it was said that his corpse is beneath the stacks of wood piled at the end of the camp. The camp leader at that time, Schieche, no doubt knows details. He was dismissed in autumn 1945 after allegedly having passed himself off as a Czech, but was imprisoned again later, served as camp leader in Jauernig for a longer period of time, then was sent to Adelsdorf in May 1946 and then arraigned before the People's Court in Troppau in July or August.

Regarding the night-time shootings, especially the last one, I later heard in Freiwaldau from an older gendarme whom I knew from Jauernig that these had been prompted by werewolf attacks. I had the impression that the gendarme honestly believed this silly tale, which had also been put about by the "Hranicar". The truth is probably that these shootings were triggered by nervous or drunken guards, and most likely that they were deliberately brought about in order to have an excuse to take reprisal measures. It is a revealing fact that following the last of the shootings in Adelsdorf, several farmers from the surrounding area, and their families, were taken and locked up, even though they certainly had nothing to do with any of this. The farms thus vacated then had to be "worked" by prisoners from the camp, for the boon and benefit of the partisans.

When the gendarmerie took over the camp, the differences between the A and the B prisoners gradually disappeared, particularly the beatings stopped, at least for the most part. But even so, mill owner Schroth was still badly beaten about the head as late as January 1946, following one of the evening inspections. However, this incident seemed to be most unwelcome to the camp management, and the perpetrators were even said to have been punished. In spring 1946 the staff leader Schindler from Freiwaldau was badly maltreated by Wiesner and his lackeys during an interrogation in the camp office. Schindler had been caught while smuggling bread into the camp. When the camp Commandant entered the office, the maltreatment stopped immediately.

In March of 1946 Franz Stöhr from Niklasdorf, at that time the batman for labor inspector Kopriva, was beaten almost to death by the latter and two gendarmes. Kopriva accused Stöhr of having stolen a pair of tall boots from him, a charge that later turned out to be totally groundless. And other incidents also still took place every now and then, for example that of the retired Captain Hackenberg from Freiwaldau, who suffered permanent impairment of balance as a result of the beatings he had received.

Every now and then, barracks searches also took place here, and again all sorts of things were confiscated and stolen on these occasions - not only cigarettes etc., which the guards then enjoyed, but also food and valuables such as, in my case, a small can of meat and a gilt cufflink.

Rations improved. Potatoes were now plentiful, vegetables and barley not as much, perhaps once a week we got a bit of meat, and even a bit of margarine or jam every now and then; at Christmas and Easter there were even a few cakes. Bread, unfortunately, was very scarce, and what little there was was often incredibly bad. Sometimes it seemed to have been baked with very dirty flour, and often also with improvised flour made from horse chestnuts. Following a strong complaint by our camp physician Dr. Hajek who, incidentally, stood up for us in every conceivable way, the bread improved again. There was always plenty of coffee - only imitation coffee, of course - but often it was even available outside of mealtimes, and in the mornings and evenings it was always sweetened with sugar. Nonetheless meals were still insufficient, and lacked any variety, especially since much of the rations that were intended for us almost certainly ended up instead in the pockets i.e. in the stomachs of the partisans and gendarmes. Of course it was not possible for us to prove this.

Food shortage in the Czechs' own regions was in no way a plausible excuse for our meager rations, for the Czechs themselves ate and drank quite well indeed, slaughtered livestock illegally whenever they felt like it, fed a great deal of human foodstuffs to the pigs and were quite liberal with food insofar as their own supplies were concerned, as we were able to witness on many an occasion when we were assigned to work outside the camp, especially at some of my own work sites. However, the Czech families for whom prisoners had to work seemed almost consistently to grant their forced laborers adequate to good additional rations, and even the partisans, including Novak and Wiesner, were no exception to that. Incidentally, for the last few months adequate additional rations were not only implicitly expected from our employers, but even demanded outright.

But what deserves special mention in this context is the attitude of the German population, who disregarded strict bans and risked severe punishment to supply us with as much extra food as they could, often enough at the expense of their own, quite meager supplies. Only with these additional provisions, both the allowed and the forbidden, was it even possible for us prisoners to survive our time in the camp without overly severe damage to our health.

In Adelsdorf the health care available to us was much better due to the fact that there was always an imprisoned German physician among us, sometimes even several. But bandages and medications were very scarce here as well. The main health problems from which we suffered were boils, and circulatory disorders accompanied by swelling of the limbs, etc.

Among those to die in the camp were:

Dittmann, innkeeper, Gr. Kunzendorf;
Ehrlich, farmer, Gr. Krosse;
Harwiger, railway official, Zuckmantel;
Harmann, merchant, Niklasdorf;
Mader, senior teacher, Buchelsdorf;
Seidel, innkeeper, Dittershof.

In the course of summer 1946 a dental-care facility was also finally set up, but it served primarily for the free-of-charge treatment of the Czech guards and their family members. We prisoners could at most have a tooth pulled. Washing facilities were rather limited, since the water supply was insufficient for the entire camp population, which at times was as much as 500 men. Once a week we had access to a rather primitive shower, but with warm water. The establishment of a Finnish-style sauna, which we were allowed to use on Sundays, was deemed a luxurious blessing. Fleas and bed bugs tormented us constantly, and it was late summer 1946 before they were brought under control with a white powder, sent from America and supplied by the UNRRA. - As I already mentioned, our treatment became much more humane when the gendarmerie took over the camp, but this too fluctuated; sometimes we were treated better, sometimes quite harshly. As a favorite punitive measure, the Czechs would forbid the delivery of small extra quantities of food by our next-of-kin, which was normally permitted twice a month. This was commonly done as a collective punishment when an inmate had escaped, which did happen every now and then. Strictly speaking, it was not at all difficult to escape, especially from work sites outside the camp, and there was also a good chance that an escapee would actually get away; of about 6 escapees, only one was recaptured. Nonetheless, escape attempts were relatively rare, since most of us prisoners did not want to expose their families to the Czechs' reprisals, and also because the Czechs had told us that this camp was going to be closed down soon. And there was also the fact that the area under Polish occupation - which was the only practical option to escape to - was not a particularly tempting destination.

Smoking, reading, writing, playing cards or chess, visiting in other barracks, bringing food into the camp, speaking with the German population, and many other things were strictly forbidden. Often, however, the Czechs did not bother too much about enforcing their countless regulations - unless they happened to be in a bad mood, or once again drunk.

On October 16, 1945 Captain Novak showed up again and gave a lengthy speech, in the course of which he promised us the establishment of a canteen as well as wages for our work, amounting to three Czech crowns a day, which equals about 30 pfennig. We never saw anything of the canteen or of the wages, even though a pretty sign was painted for the former, and very detailed records were kept of the work done by each prisoner. Incidentally, the employers who benefitted from our work had to pay 70 to 90 Czech crowns per prisoner per day; it would be interesting to investigate where this money went to. We were never able to find out.

In about mid-October 1945 the priest of Thomasdorf was able to hold a Catholic service in the camp; later on he was not allowed to preach any more. At Christmas and Easter and on a few other occasions the prisoners would stage a sort of primitive cabaret entertainment. November 1946 also marked the end of the practice of shaving the prisoners' heads.

Work inside the camp, the division of labor etc., was administered by a sort of German camp service. Engineer Klaus did this rather difficult and also quite thankless job with untiring devotion. Various prisoners who had a command of the Czech language worked in the camp office; this, and the other camp jobs such as cooking, peeling potatoes, repair work, washing, barbering etc., employed about 70 to 80 people each day. The others, insofar as they were not sick or unfit for work, were assigned to a wide variety of tasks outside the camp, in the forest, in factories, on farms, in private households, etc. The most manpower was needed for the various forest labor units, who were used for logging in at times very remote work places. On their way home they often had to bring firewood back with them, and in order to spare the Czechs the expense of using a team of horses they had to haul this firewood themselves, on large wagons which it took 20 or more men to pull. I personally was put to work for about three-quarters of a year at the gendarmerie station and in the gendarmerie school that had been set up in the former Altvater Sanatorium in Freiwaldau. The team that had to work there was generally comprised of 12 to 15 men, most of them tradesmen from various professions; I myself and two of my comrades had to work as a kind of Boy Friday, fetching and chopping wood for the kitchen, operating the central heating, loading and unloading things, as well as cleaning rooms. On the whole the work was not hard, the additional rations were reasonable, our treatment bearable, and we were left almost without supervision while we worked.

Conditions for the other work teams were similar, only the so-called mine-timber commando that brought in and loaded mine timber for a company, and the team working for the company Regenhardt & Raymann in Freiwaldau, were known as "slave-driver commandos"; among the most popular jobs were the (unfortunately always only short-term) postings to private households, because the additional rations the prisoners received there were usually quite good. Another major factor for us was the opportunity presented by almost all commandos outside the camp, namely to contact one's family and the outside world in general. One disadvantage of commandos outside the camp, however - especially the forest commandos - was that these job postings wore out our clothes and shoes much more quickly; since the Czechs did not even provide us with enough material for mending, much less new clothes and shoes, this too was largely to our own expense. Depending on the specific situation, our work output was fairly small, especially since shifts were also relatively short. A typical off-site team (i.e. a team posted to work outside the camp) would march out of the camp at 7 o'clock a.m., work began at my site at about 8 a.m., we got one hour for lunch, two shorter sandwich breaks, and the end of the work day was set for 4 p.m. Whenever we were posted to off-site work we had to wear a yellow armband with a black swastika, specifically those of us from Group A had to wear this on their left sleeve and Group B on their right; ultimately that was the only difference left between the two groups A and B. But there was one advantage after all to being in Group A, since on about September 1, 1946 many of the B prisoners were sent to work in the coal mines, where the work was very hard and rations very poor. Many of those assigned to this work returned some time later, worn out and unfit for work, and had to spend weeks and even months in the infirmary.

To justify and cover up their actions, the Czechs alleged in their propaganda that the Germans had made themselves guilty of incredible atrocities against them, while they themselves just oozed humaneness. Accordingly, even back in the Thomasdorf camp an obituary notice for the Third Reich had been posted, that was evidently intended to be funny or satirical but was really just stupid and in bad taste. Then, in Adelsdorf, propaganda materials about German concentration camps were posted, and in February 1946 we had to submit to a large traveling exhibition, with photographs and documents compiled by a German Communist. However, where the prisoners were concerned these methods completely missed their mark, since the origin of the photos often seemed more than questionable and the presenter already had a pretty bad reputation, and since most of us had seen and lived through enough of these atrocities ourselves, but at the hands of the Czechs; and Wiesner, whom I have already mentioned several times and who reappeared in late February as second camp commandant after having spent a long time being ill and some more time enjoying the hospitality of the prison in Brünn, declared that it would be an easy matter to restore conditions to the way they had been in Thomasdorf. Labor Inspector Kopriva also repeatedly threatened us with this.

At times the partisans also claimed that the treatment we had received was a reprisal and could not compare with what they themselves had gone through in German concentration camps. But since they consistently looked quite well-fed and sported amazingly long hair, it was obvious that the worst that might have happened to them was that they had been put to work in the armaments industry, where by their own admissions they had been very well paid.

What a bad conscience the Czechs, even the partisans, really had and how uncertain they were, deep down, was revealed time and again by their wondering what would happen if the Germans were to return; their declarations that they wanted to emigrate to Germany; and their requests that we should give them something to certify that they had treated the Germans well. In conversation they sometimes expressed pity for the fate of the Germans, but justified it all with the still-ongoing revolutionary conditions which they unfortunately couldn't do anything about. On these occasions they sometimes expressed some surprisingly severe criticism of their government's measures, but it was all only ever said in private. When other Czechs arrived, the subject and especially the tone was immediately changed, since as they themselves admitted, they feared being reported or locked up as collaborators, or for being friendly towards Germans.

Aside from the pictures of Beneš and Masaryk, Stalin's picture and the Soviet flag were also often displayed beside the flags of the Republic. I never saw any pictures of other foreign statesmen, but I did notice the occasional small American and also English paper flags. At least in Freiwaldau and its environs, the number of Soviet flags gradually decreased considerably; where the ratio had initially been about 1:1, it dropped to only about 1:10 later on. However, the Soviet star pinned to the chests of most partisans remained there - often enough happily in conjunction with crosses and medals hung about the neck.

On the whole the partisans enjoyed decking themselves out in a rather odd manner, and availed themselves of the tailor workshops that had been set up for us, to design ever more beautiful uniforms, sometimes based on Russian models, sometimes - evidently even more popularly - in simple black and imitating the cut of the SS. But many of them could hardly handle their weapons properly. Of course they also had an Association of former partisans and politically persecuted people, whose Chairman in Freiwaldau was the infamous Captain Novak. In other respects most of them had accomplished few achievements on behalf of the Second Republic - if one discounts stealing, looting and the maltreatment and killing of defenseless Germans. In any case, after my release a Czech who was in a position to know told me that there was hardly one among these partisans who had ever fought with weapon in hand, or had even committed any sabotage worth mentioning. The Germans, he said, had hanged the few real fighters and saboteurs, and whoever was now still going about in the guise of partisan had at best reached for his gun at the very last moment when there was no more risk involved, after first having worked obediently, earning a good income and dodging service in the real war.

Gablonz, Report No. 1
Robbed in June 1945
Reported by Bruno Hofmann - Report of May 15, 1950

Since January 16, 1939 we had lived in Gablonz on the Neisse. I was transferred there as deputy chief of the currency exchange branch office that had been newly set up in Gablonz; this transfer required my complete relocation from D. to Gablonz.

Since my wife and I had never been followers of the Hitler regime, and my wife had even had to answer to the Gestapo for anti-Fascist activities in 1942, we did not believe that anyone would do anything unpleasant to us.

Many of the Reich Germans who were in a similar situation as we, but most of whom had been members of the Nazi Party, left shortly before or immediately after the Russians marched in, and tried to get back to their old homes. In late May, disaster befell us. We were simply told without much ado that we had to leave Czechoslovakia within 24 hours, that all our possessions including our four-room apartment were being expropriated without compensation, but that we could take along 30 kg of luggage per person. On June 2, 1945 we had to leave Gablonz forever.

Of course we had not weighed the 30 kilos per person exactly, and it may well have been 45 or 50 kilos per person which we tried to take along on our flight. At the Gablonz train station the Czech police intercepted us. We got the impression right away that they thought they had made a good catch with respect to the booty they could take from us. This police gang was made up of about six to eight nasty-looking fellows ranging widely in age. The locals told us that their ringleader was a fat Czech former gendarme. Right away we were relieved of an entire suitcase and several valuables from a knapsacks and other bags. Since naturally I did not give anything up voluntarily, and resisted the robbery in the honest belief that it was my right to do so, the Czech police simply stood me up against a wall and threatened to shoot me if I were to resist these police measures. On my wife's pleading, and as I saw that resistance was futile, I finally submitted to everything. Due to the time that this police action had cost us, our train was already long gone. The next train to Reichenberg did not leave for another six hours, which we had to spend in the train station under guard of several so-called auxiliary policemen. When the train pulled in and we were about to embark with the rest of our luggage, one of the auxiliary policemen still snatched a suitcase with the best of our remaining things from us.

The train took us to Reichenberg. As we got out at the station, the so-called Revolutionary Guard already awaited us, and vented their fury on us. Most of the travelers got off unscathed, but we were assumed to be a good catch and so approximately 12 fearful figures surrounded us, armed with all sorts of weapons and also with heavy bludgeons, and searched us for the very last of anything we had left that was of any value at all. I had to raise my arms sideways, and while two men kept their revolvers trained on me another one searched all my pockets and other gear. They didn't leave me even the simplest things. My wife's reproach, that they should at least leave us the bare essentials for everyday use, was answered only with cudgels raised in a threatening manner. Only with great effort was my wife able to rescue the photos of our son, who had been killed in action. Though we had hardly anything left to lose now, we spent another bad night in the waiting room of the Reichenberg train station, since the many delays had prevented us from making the next connection.

About 6 o'clock the next morning our trip went on, via Bohemian Leipa and on to Bodenbach. In Leipa we had to wait for 7 hours, during which time we and all the other travelers were once again subjected to a thorough ransacking by the so-called Railway Police. But there wasn't much left for them to take from us. During our waiting time we were conscripted to work; some of the jobs we had to perform were very hard. We were forbidden to enter the station tavern and could only get well water to drink. Even though most of our fellow-sufferers were also not treated well, it was not hard to tell that the Czechs had it in for us particularly. Why - we still don't know. In Bodenbach we again had to spend a night waiting, but we were able to spend it in a school that had been set up as a refugee camp; the next morning we were able to escape yet another looting thanks to the friendly help given us by station employees of German nationality, who quickly smuggled us into the arriving train.

Robbed of everything we had, we finally arrived in D. in the evening of June 4. This civilized nation of Czechs seemed unacquainted with even the most basic needs of everyday life, for they left us not so much as a spare pair of socks or handkerchief, never mind any other articles of clothing.

Gablonz, Report No. 2
Fatal maltreatment of an old man
Reported by Adolf Vogel - Report of November 4, 1946

At the end of November 1945 my father-in-law, Anton Weis, a man 81 years of age, residing at Gablonz/Neisse, 18 Alpen Strasse, went to the outskirts of the forest 800 meters distant from his house, in order to fetch moss for the Christmas crib which he built every year for the children of his neighbourhood. While doing so he was stopped by two SNB-soldiers, who knocked him down, trampled him under foot and left him unconscious. The soldiers let him lie there, neither of them doing anything for him. When he finally regained consciousness, he dragged himself home with great difficulty. The doctor, whom we had called, diagnosed a loosening of the kidneys as a result of the blows, as well as other internal injuries. Two days later he died of his injuries. Nobody dared to inform the police. I am prepared to take an oath on these statements.

Gablonz, Report No. 3
Resettlement
Reported by Anton Nitsche - Report of November 4, 1946

On June 15, 1945, Josef-Pfeiffer-Street and the surrounding suburb in Gablonz were totally evacuated within only a few minutes. In this way some 850 people were dispossessed of their homes, and this was done entirely arbitrarily, without regard for party membership or other political activity. The goal was primarily to clear out the better apartments and houses. That same night these 850 people, among them three-week-old babies and old people up to 80 years of age, were taken by car to Harrachsdorf with almost no luggage whatsoever, and herded on foot to Jakobsthal the next day. The Poles on the other side of the border refused to let us in, and so we had to spend three days and three nights camping in the woods by the border, at a chilly elevation of 1,000 m. Many people had no blankets at all. Hoarfrost covered the ground at night. The German Red Cross in Schreiberhau managed to provide us with very meager rations, with Polish assistance. These rations had been procured for us by means of so-called "spoon donations" by going house-to-house. After three days the Czechs allowed us to return to Harrachsdorf.

The next morning we were herded to Grüntal. The afternoon of that same day, we were led along the railroad track on a so-called pascher path, through the railway tunnel and back to the border. The Poles again refused to admit us, but were sufficiently outraged by the Czech resettlement methods to allow us to stay overnight in Hoffnungsthal. These were outdoor accommodations again. The next day, pouring rain made things very hard for us. After negotiating with the Czechs, the Poles led us back across the border again, and the Czechs marched us back to Grüntal, from where we were taken back to Gablonz at night by train and then sent to the Reinowitz concentration camp. We had been a week on the road like this.

The industrial workers were taken out of the camp again and made to work in the factories of Gablonz. In this way I ended up back in my own business. Meanwhile my apartment had been completely looted, and I wasn't able to re-enter it. How the Germans were treated was entirely up to the whims and caprice of the Czechs, who were ever open to bribes. Those Germans who had nothing and could give nothing were in a very bad situation. It was the same whenever our luggage was inspected.

Iglau, Report No. 1
Shooting of women in May and June 1945
Reported by Else Köchel - Report of June 30, 1950

On May 23rd, 1945, we were ordered to clear out of our house within two hours and were taken to a dirty old textile factory in the outskirts of the town. Here the hygienic conditions were terrible: for example, there was only one single water-tap in the yard for about a thousand men. Three latrines, on the ground floor, were in an indescribable condition, and the stairs on all the floors so narrow that only two persons could pass each other.

Young boys and elderly men had to fetch the water for the kitchen in barrels from far away.

We slept on the floor, which was soaked with oil, in four rows, side by side. Every morning at 6 and again at 8 we had to line up for roll call. The moment the *"Velitel"* (commandant) appeared, we had to stand at attention. Our rations consisted of a cup of coffee, a cup of soup and one piece of bread per day.

On June 9th, 1945, they told us: "Tomorrow you will march 30 kilometers [about 20 miles], you may only take with you as much as you can carry!" Our luggage was examined, searched for money and the surplus confiscated. On June 10th, 1945 we started to march to Stannern, another camp, in scorching heat. Naturally, everyone threw away anything he could spare, so that finally we had nothing left. Suddenly we were told that the Austrians among us would be allowed to return to Austria the same day. For that purpose we marched towards Teltsch, but within sight of the towers of the town, we were told that our return was impossible after all and we had to march back to Stannern, another 10 kilometers [6 miles]. On our march we were driven with lashes and rifle shots. There were only two short pauses during this 40-kilometer march. When we arrived in Stannern in heavy rain, tired almost to death, we dropped where we stood.

At Stannern many of us died of malnutrition-related disease.

The camp was located on a hill, surrounded by a fence, and we were heavily guarded; we were not allowed to leave the camp. The women of the village sometimes brought coffee, soup or bread. Since all of us were terribly hungry, especially the children, the mothers would wait at the fence for one of these women to come. One day, seeing a village-woman approaching, three of the women looked out of the camp. Suddenly shots were fired - two women fell dead and the third was wounded; their only crime was that they had looked over the fence. The guard was praised for the deed and even received an award for being such a good shot.

I don't want to talk about all the other things we had to endure, but this crime simply has to be reported!

Unfortunately I do not know the name of this fine *"Velitel"*. I know the name of only one of the three women, Kerpes; the others are unknown to me, but I am prepared to swear to the facts described at any time.

Maybe someone else from Iglau knows this *Velitel's* name and also those of the other women.

Iglau, Report No. 2
Reign of terror
Reported by Franz Kaupil - Report of September 2, 1946

On May 13, 1945 the Czech reign of terror began in Iglau. Approximately 1,200 Germans committed suicide the following night. By Christmas [of last year] the death count had risen to about 2,000. On May 24 and 25 partisans drove the German inhabitants out of their homes within 20 minutes, to be locked up in the camps Helenental and Altenberg. These were officially designated as "concentration camps". 3,700 people were imprisoned in Helenental, in Altenberg there were roughly 3,000. There was not enough water, neither to drink nor for other uses. Toilets and washing facilities were nonexistent. We received no food at all for the first 8 days, and later on, only thin soup and 100 g bread daily. Children received a cup of milk only after the first 8 days. Every day, several older people and small children died. On June 8 the prisoners of Helenental were robbed blind, and then marched 33 km via Teltsch to Stannern the next day. We were hurried along with whips. The older people among us were driven on carts only after they had collapsed. This forced march cost 350 people their lives due to debilitation and starvation.

In Stannern 3,500 people were squeezed into a camp with an intended capacity of 250. Most of them had to sleep outside despite the rain. The next day, families were split up into 5 different camps, segregated into men, women and children. Again there was no food for 8 days, and then, the usual soups. Once, in the Women's Camp, four women were killed with a single bullet, and one was seriously wounded. The victims included Frau Friedl and Frau Kerpes. Corporal punishment was the order of the day for men and women alike. There was also a Beating Cell. The camp administration hired the inmates out to the Czech farmers as day labor. In August conditions improved, but nonetheless some 500 inmates had died in Stannern by Christmas. In January the Stannern camp was dissolved.

I myself was placed in "detention awaiting trial" on January 9, 1946 and released on August 7, 1946. Eyewitnesses told me of horrible cruelties, and I myself experienced my share. On June 10, 1945, 19 inmates from Iglau were taken from their cells and shot in the Ranzenwald [forest]. These inmates included the old city preacher Honsik, Howorka, Augustin, Biskonz, Brunner, Laschka, Martel, Kästler, and others. As late as May 1945 the following were shot in the Court Building without any trial: Krautschneider, Kaliwoda, Müller and Ruffa. One Hoffmann was beaten to death. The overseer who was most feared was Rychtetzky. Factory owner Krebs was scalped. Master builder Lang died of the consequences of maltreatment he suffered. 70-year-old Group Captain Zobel hanged himself in his cell. Many people had been forced by means of dreadful maltreatment to give incriminating testimony and were then detained under arrest for crimes they had not committed. I am prepared to take these statements on my oath and also to bring further witnesses to corroborate them.

Iglau, Report No. 3
Maltreatment, withholding of personal belongings, father was murdered
Reported by Robert Pupeter - Report of September 2, 1946

I was arrested on August 6, 1945 for no reason and without any interrogation, and detained in the Iglau prison for 8 months, where I was badly maltreated several times. Then I had to work in a brickworks, where I lost a finger. I never received any wages. Then I was sent via the concentration camp at Altenberg to work for a Czech farmer. My father and 19 other men were shot in prison without any trial. My mother has been missing ever since she was expelled to Austria. I have lost everything I ever had.

I now have 20 kg of luggage to my name. In the resettlement camp all I received was a pair of overalls. The provisions which my last employer gave me for the journey were taken from me in the resettlement camp by the camp administrator personally, and I even had to carry them into his room for him.

Iglau, Report No. 4
State of the luggage in the Iglau camp
Reported by Alfred Chlad - Report of September 2, 1946

In the resettlement camp in Iglau we were informed that we could take 50 kg luggage with us per person. Prisoners of war and people who had been released from prisons did not have nearly this allowable quantity, in most cases they only had about 15 kg. At the border the American officer who was to admit us objected to this state of affairs, and our transport was supposed to be turned back because of it. Since none of the people to be resettled wanted to remain, and since the Czech transfer officers also urged that we should go on, our transport was finally allowed to cross the border.

Jägerndorf, Report No. 1

Concentration camp Jägerndorf, severe maltreatment of a 71-year-old man

Reported by Josef Kramlovsky - Report of June 29, 1946

In June 1945 partisans took me to the Jägerndorf concentration camp. At the time the entire German population of Jägerndorf was being concentrated in several camps. Everyone was robbed blind on his or her arrival. Every evening, starting several days later, everyone was ordered to line up and then we had to march around in a circle. Suddenly we were ordered to run. Since I have had a bullet lodged in my hip joint ever since the first world war, and am 71 years old, I was unable to run. And so a partisan took a flying leap at me and kicked me in the stomach with both his boots, so that I collapsed in convulsions. Then he kicked me repeatedly in the leg and screamed: "You German bastard, if you report sick tomorrow you'll be shot."

The next morning my leg was so swollen that I could not walk. But I did not dare to go see the doctor, and dragged myself painfully on. To escape the constant harassment and abuse, I volunteered myself and my wife, who was 66 years old at that time, for labor duty in an industrial camp, where we then worked. But we were constantly tormented there too. We had to provide our own food, and received no pay for the work we did.

On December 7, 1945 my wife and I were discharged from the camp due to our advanced age. By that time our home and all our furnishings, linen and clothes had been confiscated. We were not allowed to enter our home again, and got none of our things either. We had to go to some acquaintances to even have a place to sleep. We had to beg for some supplies for our resettlement.

In the resettlement camp as well, the people were intimidated with harsh punishments and verbal abuse. The authorities in charge took anything they liked from the people being expelled.

Jägerndorf, Report No. 2

Abuse during transport and in the camp

Reported by Johann Korsitzke - Report of July 4, 1946

I was arrested in my home on June 13, 1945 and detained for three weeks in the District Court of Jägerndorf. Nobody ever interrogated me. On my committal to the court I was beaten unconscious. Then I and about 250 other men were squeezed into 2 wagons and taken to Moravian Ostrau. During the transport a guard walked up and down and randomly beat us over the head with his whip. Then he ordered some of us to open our mouths, and spat into them. During the entire transport, at each of the train's more than 20 stops, we had to sing the German national anthem and the Horst-Wessel song. In Ostrau, despite totally insufficient rations, we had to do the hardest manual labor in the coke refinery, so that everyone was soon quite debilitated. In July I was once again beaten, because I had exchanged a few insignificant words with a comrade - in German. The Germans were forbidden to speak German amongst themselves in the camp outside the barracks. In December I was discharged for health reasons, and went to work for a Czech acquaintance of mine in Jägerndorf.

Jägerndorf, Report No. 3
Attempted rapes
Reported by Erika Kunisch - Report of December 13, 1945

In early June my mother and I returned to Jägerndorf, which had been evacuated during the battles that had taken place there, and later we lived in Braunsdorf near Jägerndorf. Whereas the Germans in Jägerndorf were put into camps right away, we who lived in Braunsdorf were able to remain in our homes for the time being. But the Czechs kept the town under close guard. They had set up a machine gun in the Church tower, for example, and shot at anyone who tried to leave the town without permission.

In late July my parents and I were sent to a camp in Jägerndorf after all, where all of us were treated very badly. Rations were extraordinarily poor. The men were gradually sent off into the mines, and many were shot for no reason at all. The wife of Mayor Kieslich of Braunsdorf was beaten up, had cold water dumped on her, and was then shot by Czech partisan guards. All of us were forced to watch this execution.

In the evening the Czechs often let Russian soldiers into the camp, and these would look for German girls and women and rape them. Once, a Czech lieutenant had already taken me and my mother to a Russian officer's car. But my mother pretended to faint, and so we got free again.

In mid-July my aunt had returned to Braunsdorf. When she left the town, her entire 30 kg of luggage was taken from her. The Czechs fired from the Church tower at any German who tried to escape into the hills and mountains.

In the Jägerndorf camp I was put to work washing locomotives. The rations I got consisted of 100 grams of bread, and two cups of soup in the morning and at noon. In Jägerndorf the Czech guards also tried to rape us. I managed to escape into the Altvater Mountains, where I was able to find a temporary place to stay with my aunt. Later I went to Germany.

Jägerndorf, Report No. 4
Burgberg concentration camp, maltreatment resulting in death
Reported by Olga Arndt - Report of June 19, 1946

In late May, I and several hundred women and children were driven and whipped out of our homes at gunpoint and chased through the streets of Jägerndorf into the Burgberg concentration camp. There we were herded into mostly empty barracks and had to stay there for three days without getting anything to eat. Men were housed in the same camp as well, and for 14 days, several times each day, they had to strip to the waist and then the bue-uniformed Czech militia would beat them. Two men, one of them by the name of Sieber, were beaten to death. Sieber was buried in the camp square. A latrine was set up over top of his grave.

After about four days a uniformed woman appeared. We had to line up, and this woman relieved us of all money, jewelry and savings bank books. At the same time the barracks were searched. After I had already handed everything over, this women called me up with the words: "You black bitch, come here!" She body-searched me in the lowest manner, without finding anything. Then she hit me in the face three times, yanked me by the hair and chased me away with a curse. After 14 days I was sent to a factory camp, where conditions were quite a bit better.

Jägerndorf, Report No. 5
Cases of severe maltreatment in the court prison
Reported by Otto Langer, veterinarian - Report of September 30, 1946

Although I have never been a member of any political party organization, I was arrested on June 15th, 1945, at Braunsdorf and taken to the court jail at Jägerndorf. There I was repeatedly maltreated for several days without any cause. Since I am a veterinary-surgeon, the Czechs considered me capable of giving medical attention to my German fellow prisoners, whom they designated as animals, even in the notices on the cell doors. I was thus in a position to note the results of the horrible maltreatment; I also witnessed the abuse of prisoners. The beatings were carried out with rubber tubing, lengths of steel cable, whips, chair-legs, clubs etc. Each one received from 80 to 160 blows from several people. I saw with my own eyes how two persons were beaten so severely that they died within two days. One of them was the gardener Schmalz from Olbersdorf. I also attended a man who suffered from fractures of the collarbone and the upper arm, both caused by blows. I requested his transfer to the hospital, which was refused with the words: "There is no hospital for Germans."

When I attempted to bandage a German woman, who had a purulent wound on her foot, I was prevented from doing so: "Germans are only animals, it is a pity to waste bandages on them."

I saw the bodies of many tortured people, literally covered with bruises; three prisoners, among them a young woman, were driven to desperation by the maltreatment they had endured, and hanged themselves. In spite of the extreme heat of June the corpse of the woman was left in the cell for three days. When a transport of 160 men left the jail for Witkowitz, many of them were sent along half-naked, their garments and shoes having been taken away from them. The diet in the camp consisted mainly of watery soup. For the first week we received 100 g of bread, later on we had the same quantity twice a week. As a result of malnutrition, dangerous cases of diarrhoea occurred. There was a shortage of medicines and a lack of adequate sanitary arrangements. From 17 to 32 prisoners would be crowded together in cells 14.3 meters square (about 17 yards square). The doors of the cells were always kept locked, and the bucket we used to relieve ourselves was much too small for the purpose. Each cell received only 3 liters of water (5.2 pints) a day both for drinking and cleaning. On August 7, 1945, I was released and received employment from the district committee at Olbersdorf as a veterinary surgeon. In the meantime my wife had been sent to agricultural labour where she suffered severe injury to her health. As a result of her condition she was released in March. We have seen nothing more of our property or personal belongings. The luggage, which we finally took with us on our transfer, consisted for the most part of articles which had been given to us.

Karlsbad

Karlsbad, Report No. 1
Arbitrary arrest
Reported by F. Danzer - Report of July 22, 1946

On September 5, 1945, just as I was doing the inventory prior to transferring my business to a Czech administrator, I was arrested and committed to the Karlsbad Police jail. My fiancee who had been helping me with the inventory was also arrested. During her arrest she was slapped in the face for no reason at all. I myself was beaten with rifle butts, and kicked. On arriving at the jail I was again severely maltreated. Two ribs in my left side were broken in the process. My face and head were swollen beyond recognition, and several of my teeth had been knocked in. I also suffered contusions on my tailbone and right leg. I was thrown unconscious into the cellar. I was not interrogated until late June of this year. I was not charged with anything. In mid-July this year I was discharged, to be resettled.

Karlsbad, Report No. 2
Severe maltreatment in the camp
Reported by Josef Mörtl - Report of September 29, 1946

I had been an officer at the police headquarters in Karlsbad since 1939, and in May 1945 the Czechs left me in office because no-one had brought any charges against me. In late July 1945 the Czechs dismissed me. In the meantime I had repeatedly witnessed the maltreatment and execution of Germans. Several times Germans had been taken from their cells and gunned down in the yard. On the 13th [of August?] last year I was arrested myself, and committed to the Auschowitz camp in Marienbad. There I saw many people who had been beaten beyond recognition. An 86-year-old man by the name of Zeiler, from Einsiedl, told me that he too had been badly maltreated. I also had to spend 8 months in Neurohlau. 13 and 14-year-old boys were imprisoned there, and were also badly abused. In the meantime my family was repeatedly thrown out of our home and robbed blind. I have nothing at all left of my belongings. My resettlement luggage consisted only of what some good-hearted people gave me.

Karlsbad, Report No. 3
Karlsbad Court prison, Neurohlau
Reported by Hedwig Nao - Report of September 13, 1946

On July 21, 1945 my 80-year-old husband Marko Nao was arrested right off the street and sent to the Karlsbad Court prison. Despite his age and his weak constitution he was put to performing clearing operations. The very first day he collapsed at work and had to be carried back to the prison. The men who carried him were beaten, and my husband also was hit over the head. A week later he was sent from the Karlsbad prison to the concentration camp Neurohlau, where he arrived in such a weakened state that he could not even give his name. On August 4, 1945 he died of debilitation. He was not given a religious burial and therefore his death was not registered and I have also not been officially notified to this day. I had to learn it all from other men who were imprisoned along with my husband, and from Dr. Kudlich, the camp physician of Neurohlau, as well as from the German camp administrator Korb.

Karlsbad, Report No. 4
Severe harassment by an administrator
Reported by Wilhelm Meindl - Report of September 13, 1946

I owned a mill-construction business in Karlsbad. On October 1, 1945 the Czech Jan Verner was appointed as trustee to my business. He saw to it that I was not present when inventory was taken, and consequently the inventory ended up being too low by 250,000 Kčs, as was discovered later on. By means of slander and defamation he made it impossible for me to report his misdeeds to the police, and he covered up his own irregularities by constantly accusing me of sabotage. In this way he tried to intimidate me. Nonetheless he tried his best to prevent me from being expelled because he wanted my expertise in mill construction. When it was time for me to be resettled, he saw to it that my luggage was looted. All my bags were searched and mostly my winter clothes and linen were taken from me. I was prevented from taking any tools with me, even though the District Resettlement Commission had given me a permit allowing me to do so.

Karlsbad, Report No. 5
Maltreatment of a 65-year-old woman by Czech youths in the street
Reported by Leopoldine Schneider - Report of September 13, 1946

In mid-August 1946, at 6 o'clock one afternoon, I was walking home through Panorama Street in Karlsbad. I was wearing my white armband. About halfway down Panorama Street, near the milk bar, a 12-year-old boy holding a whip barred my way and cursed me in Czech. I tried to go around him, not saying anything. He hit me over the head with his whip. Then four or five other boys of the same age came running up and also hit me with their whips. I began to run, and they pursued me with whip lashes, heckling and cursing me, for about 15 minutes all the way home, where I arrived sobbing and exhausted. On the way, Czech adults looking out of windows and doorways as well as Czech passers-by in the street watched the spectacle, laughing and shouting encouragement to the boys.

Karlsbad, Report No. 6
Severe abuse of a police constable
Reported by Alfred Müller - Report of September 13, 1946

I was police chief in Karlsbad and was allowed to remain in office when the Czechs marched in in early May 1945, as there were no charges against me and as I was commonly known to be loyal and kind. I continued to serve as deputy chief of the police jail. There, I saw how from the very first day on all the men being brought in were grossly maltreated until they collapsed, covered in blood. I was horrified at these happenings, and commented accordingly to the Czech N., who himself disapproved of the abuse and stressed that not a single blow had been dealt out here during the time of German administration. Someone else must have heard this comment as well, for only half an hour later I was dismissed from office.

That was on May 28, 1945. In early July I was summoned by the police, detained in the jail, and badly maltreated there myself. I received about 100 blows to the head, and just as many punches to my back and stomach and, as I fell to the ground, kicks to my head and face. With his boot heel one of them knocked out three of my teeth and injured my left eye. I was then handed over to the court without any interrogation whatsoever, and four weeks later the court sent me to the Neurohlau concentration camp. In Neurohlau I was again maltreated very badly and repeatedly. Being a former police officer did not help my situation. Once I was beaten unconscious. It was not until September that my personal data was registered and I was interrogated. Dr. N., who conducted the questioning, suggested that I would be released in as little as 14 days. But as it turned out I had to spend 13½ months in the camp, and was then discharged without even a trial.

Karlsbad, Report No. 7
Karlsbad, execution of the sexton
Reported by Marie Scherzer - Report of January 23, 1951

(**Publisher [Scriptorium] notes:** in a special reprint of this book issued in 1951 by the Europa-Buchhandlung in Munich, pages 294+ contain the following report which is not included in the original edition. This supplementary report is introduced as follows: "This report, which is a significant contribution to the accounts of the events that took place in Karlsbad in 1945, was included here instead of Reports 171-176 of the previous edition." The original reports 171-176 in question are the accounts that have been reproduced above as Reports 1-6.)

After the Russian troops marched into Karlsbad,* a Russian division, among others, set up camp on the car and carriage parking lot beside the cemetery, about 50 steps from the cemetery administration building where my parents (Franz Weis and Julie Weis) and my sister (Gertrud Weis) lived. On October 17, 1945* around 11 o'clock p.m., some 30 Russian stormed the house, broke down the house door, invaded my parents' apartment and the office rooms and engaged in a frenzy of senseless destruction. Due to the danger of looting, my parents and sister had not stayed the night in the apartment, but rather with acquaintances living in the closed settlement region. We learned of the incident the next morning, and when we were able to get back to the house and apartment after three days, what awaited us was a dreadful scene of destruction. In the office, the closets, desks, safe etc. were broken open, the money, files, books, documents etc. were torn up and strewn all over the floor, even the typewriter had been thrown on the floor. The apartment was in an even worse state; linen, clothing, bedding and cook pots were gone, and some items were found in the nearby woods, torn and dirty. Some of the things that were left, such as furniture etc., were smashed, food was dumped on the floor, and the entire apartment was disgustingly filthy. It was a shocking, devastating sight. My parents and sister had to stay with me now. *[*Scriptorium notes: the date seems to be an error and should probably read **May 17, 1945**. The Russians marched into Karlsbad on May 6, 1945 and the rest of this report deals with events in June 1945; October would be outside the relevant chronology.]*

After the wave of lootings subsided, my father resumed his job in the cemetery administration, and my mother attempted to restore the apartment to order and cleanliness. But during these days they were constantly harassed and bothered by Russian soldiers as well as by partisans and Czech civilians claiming to be Commissars. While working on the Jewish cemetery on June 1, 1945, my father was attacked by two Czech gendarmes, who beat him to the ground with bludgeons and knuckle dusters. Then these two gendarmes went into the cemetery administration building, where they found my mother. They dragged her into the kitchen and began to beat her too. After adding this misdeed to their accomplishments, they locked her into the kitchen. Then they went into the office and vented their fury on the employee, Alexander Neumeyer. He sat unsuspectingly at the typewriter, typing. He too was beaten. It is said that he died of the consequences of this beating. In the meantime, my mother in her fear and pain had opened the window and cried for help. My father, who was just dragging himself into the house, heard my mother's cries for help, and tried in the depths of his despair to put an end to the martyrdom by slashing his wrists and carotid artery. A woman visiting the cemetery found my father in the new section of the Catholic cemetery, where he had dragged himself, lying on a grave in a pool of blood. The woman hurried to the cemetery office and told Mr. Neumeyer, who meanwhile had freed my mother from her kitchen imprisonment, and she also told my mother. Mr. Neumeyer immediately telephoned the rescue service, who came and took my father to the hospital.

On June 3,1945 my sister Gertrud Weis, my brother-in-law Ernst Scherzer, and I visited my father in the hospital. My brother-in-law left the hospital shortly before 5 o'clock p.m., while my sister and I stayed with our father a bit longer. Suddenly the sounds of howling and yelling penetrated the ward, and a short time later four Czech civilians appeared, led by the alleged "Commissar" Crha, and asked who we were. After we answered, they yanked my father out of the bed, took away his pocket-watch, and declared that the three of us were under arrest. When I asked on what grounds, they roared at me: "More Germans must meet their maker!" With crude curses, they herded and shoved us down the steps - my father was only wearing a thin shirt and pants - and forced us into a waiting car. The four civilians sat on the wings, and off we went to the *"Národní výbor"*, which was housed in the former Jewish retirement home, now a government building. Two of the civilians went into the building and returned a short time later with several bottles of liquor. They distributed these among themselves and wasted no time drinking to each other's health. To constant curses, and threats such as "Take one more good look at everything, this is your last ride, you Nazi swine," "Your final hour has struck," etc., the ride went on to the "Golden Cross" in Waldzeile [Street], the headquarters of the Czech police, commissars, partisans etc. When we had arrived there, we were pushed into a ground-level room at the left and inundated with the crudest kind of curses. The term "German Nazi swine" was the mildest. My father had to take a seat, and my sister and I stood to either side of him. The four civilians were joined in this room by more and ever more "Commissars", some 8 of them, armed with rifles, rubber truncheons, leather straps, knuckle dusters etc. Then "Commissar" Crha turned to my father and began in broken German, "Well, you German Nazi swine, how many men did you hide at mobilization when Adolf came," and right away all the "Commissars" began raining blows on my father with whatever they had in hand, so the blood gushed to all sides. When my sister and I began to cry, we too were given a hefty share of blows. The they dragged my father into an adjoining room and threw him onto a plank bench, and the beating began anew. After these tortures he was brought back into the first room. Meanwhile some of the Germans being held prisoner at the "Golden Cross" had been fetched. They had clearly undergone beatings of their own, and were disfigured almost beyond recognition by bloody bruises, cuts and swellings all over their faces and hands. Each of these men was now asked, "Do you know this German Nazi swine?" With a single exception they replied "no", and we too did not know the men in question. Only one, the former senior groundskeeper of the cemetery garden, Alfred Lippert, who was also disfigured by blood-suffused bruises and swellings, said "yes". At that, Commissar Crha said to Lippert: "Here, take Puška and shoot all three." But Lippert replied: "Commissar, I can't do that. Shoot me if you must, but these three have done nothing." Then the prisoners were hustled out of the room again. While they had been there, the "Commissars" had gone to work again on my father. One of them was constantly yanking on his ear and even cut into his right ear, another poured gasoline over him and wanted to set him on fire, which a third, however, prevented him from doing by knocking the lighter out of his hand. Yet another kept shoving sharp cartridges into my father's back and sides, and others hit him with their rifle butts or kicked him. Then father was pushed back into the adjoining room.

Then "Commissar" Crha asked me: "You have last wish?" At that, I knew what was to be done with us. I told him that I would at least like to see my mother and my three little children (3½ months, 4 and 6 years old) one more time and to say farewell to them. He demanded proof that I had children, and I happened to have a photo of them with me. Then he said: "You want to say goodbye to father and sister, or not?" I thought of my mother, my three little children, and my husband, of whom I had had no news for over a year, and replied: "If it has to be so, yes!"

I was herded into the adjoining room, and under guard I had to say farewell to my dear father. He spoke softly and said, "give my love to your mother." He was bleeding from his mouth, nose and ears, and one eye was swollen shut. I squeezed his hand and kissed him on the forehead. I was unable to speak for agitation and sorrow. And already the guards roared, "out!" I returned to the other room where my sister stood, to say my farewells to her too. She was as pale as a sheet, and hugged my neck and would not let go. This took too long for the thugs' liking, and they began to beat on us with rubber truncheons until my sister collapsed. They yanked her back on her feet and roared, "quick, quick, we don't have all day." Some of them were already leading my father from the room, and others dragged my sister along behind. I had to join the procession. It goes without saying that we were surrounded by a horde of "commissars" at all times.

When I reached the gate and had a view of the square - my father and my sister had already had to enter the square - I had to stop, and "Commissar" Crha, standing in the gateway, counted "jeden, dva, tři." Shots rang through the square, the shirt on my father's chest turned red and bulged, and he sank over backwards. His head hit the pavement. Before the sound of the shots had even faded away, another two shots fell, and my sister collapsed. All this took place within just a few seconds. With blows from rubber truncheons I was driven back into the room, where Commissar Crha said only: "I am dismissing you for today, but you must promise me that you will not say anything about what happened here. [If you promise] I have a heart for your children." To rude curses I was then chased out of the "Golden Cross".

All the events I have described took place between our arrival in the "Golden Cross" and my release from this house without any grounds or interrogation, in barely 30 minutes - we were not there longer than that.

Karlsbad, Report No. 8

Karlsbad-Lesnitz, severe abuse on the grounds of a false accusation on July 4, 1945
Reported by Anton Riedl - Report of June 22, 1946

I was arrested in Lesnitz on July 4, 1945 and taken to the Karlsbad District Court. I was accused of having led transports of people into concentration camps. I denied it, and named the Czech engineer N., Chief of the company Pittel & Brausewetter in Karlsbad, as witness who could confirm that I had been employed in the Egerland ore mines in Schönfeld, District Elbogen, and had not left the facilities even temporarily. At that, the Czech who was interrogating me roared at me: "What, you German pig, you're even trying to justify yourself!" He then hit me twice in the face, hard enough to make me stagger. Right afterwards I was beaten in the corridor by three men with rubber truncheons and bullwhips. I suffered about 60 blows. One hour later I was beaten bloody again the same way. I then spent 36 hours crowded into a 20x20' cell with 14 other men. This was followed by another interrogation, during which I was again beaten up. For the next two days I then had to stay in a laundry room with approximately 80 men of all ages, all of whom had been beaten in the same way as I. On July 11 I was called out yet again. The Czech engineer N. was there and told me that I had been arrested on the basis of false charges and would now be released. He drove me home in his car. The consequences of all the abuse laid me up for 4 weeks. After that I worked for this engineer until I was resettled [expelled].

Kladno, Report No. 1

Kladno concentration camp, the march to the border, and rapes

Reported by: Dipl.-Ing. Eugen Scholz - Report of June 28, 1950

My family and I left Brünn on April 21, 1945, and after a 12-day train ride we ended up near Kladno. Our refugee group, which by then had grown to about 2,000 people, was distributed over several towns, most of which also already housed Silesian refugees. My family was quartered in the Katschitz town school.

Due to a severe lung injury accompanied by pneumonia, I had to be transferred to the District Hospital of Kladno on May 4, 1945, the second day after our arrival in Katschitz.

One afternoon all the male German patients of the hospital were brought into our room. Several German members of the Wehrmacht, who had also been here as patients, were separated from us, and after that there were about 30 of us left - mostly children and several teenagers, and the only adults left were an old man and I. Czech partisans which had been hidden in the hospital up until now appeared in our room. Accompanied by much yelling, they beat the children crying for their parents, then ordered two older boys to stand close to the wall and proceeded to punch them so hard in the backs of their heads that their faces were repeatedly knocked hard into the wall. It goes without saying that on this occasion we were also relieved of all our valuables. I myself had the honor of surrendering my things to a Czech "police inspector" who resided here as patient and had even shown up holding a pistol, with which he tried to impress primarily the children. We weren't left in peace even at night. Among other practices, the lights were turned on and off at brief intervals all night long, with the intent that the recurrent harsh light would keep us from our badly needed sleep.

The next morning we were loaded under police guard onto a truck and taken to a sports field in Kladno. On the way we also stopped at a Czech clinic, in front of which stood a young Silesian refugee woman with her baby and six other refugee children aged 2 to 7 years, whose parents were somewhere in the surrounding towns. These children, who were suffering from inflammation of the middle ear and still had thick bandages around their heads, had been driven out of the clinic. Instead of returning them to their parents, they were simply abandoned to an uncertain fate. Already the very next day their bandages were soaked through with pus and we had no way of changing the dressings. With a great deal of trouble we finally managed to bring in a captured German military doctor, but he could not help either because he had no medicines or supplies. Thanks to his energetic intervention the children were at least transferred to a sort of minor infirmary on the Kladno airfield. Before they left I had hung a little sign around each child's neck, stating his or her name and other information, insofar as I was even able to find this out from them. On one of these signs I could only write the first name of the child in question, as it was barely old enough to speak.

So, after this refugee woman and the children had joined our group, our trip went on to the aforementioned sports field. When our pathetic group arrived there, we saw the following. Huddling in the middle of the square under strict Czech guard *(Národní Výbor)* were some 150 German civilian men, including some war-disabled ex-servicemen from the first World War, who had been rounded up in Kladno and its environs. I was able to briefly speak with some of them during the next hours. They assured me that they had committed no crimes and had only done their duty as employees in various offices etc., since they were unfit for military duty.

We were admitted by the Czech guard commandant, an older NCO, whom I informed of our place of origin and specifically pointed out the sad shape we were in. To be fair, I must mention here that this Czech was an exception among the others who worked here. He really felt sorry for us, and also assured me with reference to his own family that he abhorred everything that was being done to the innocent people here. But being a Czech ex-soldier, he had had to comply with doing duty here. Even if this man couldn't help us very much, we did nonetheless feel his clandestine efforts and I personally know that he went as far as he could without endangering himself. In any case I owe him my life as he let me stay with the women and children; probably the very bad state I was in contributed to persuading him to this decision. I would not have survived this terrible day if I had had to share the fate that was visited on my fellow-countrymen here. We were ordered go to the edge of the sports field to join a larger number of women and children who had been brought here before we were. It is probably not necessary to mention that we were deprived of even our last valuables here. Several of the women told me that on their way here they had first been taken to a barrack square where they were forced to watch young members of the Waffen-SS being beaten to death. These young men were stripped to the waist, tied up with their arms pulled up, first beaten unconscious, then doused with water and beaten again after they had regained consciousness. This process was repeated until these unfortunates had breathed their last.

In the afternoon of this excessively hot day we and our comrades on the square got black coffee to drink. On the occasion of this distribution of coffee some comrades passed by near us, and from their blood-encrusted faces we could tell that they must have endured terrible things already. This was our only opportunity to exchange a few words with them.

During the day things were relatively calm, and the only disturbance was the appearance of one Czech partisan who acted like a madman and was respectfully called "Ivan" by his buddies. But in the late afternoon an ominous disquiet began. All sorts of Czech rabble congregated behind the wall surrounding the sports field. The German men were ordered to line up in rows of three and then to lie down on their stomachs, and then there began a spectacle that is no doubt unique. Under terrible blows from about 20 Czechs, these unfortunates had to crawl once around the entire sports field. They were beaten with rubber truncheons, wooden clubs, bullwhips and rifle butts. Anyone who did not keep to the crawling pace or tried to find some relief by raising himself up was beaten mercilessly, and it was primarily the back and the kidney area that these Czechs targeted. There were only few who got through this procedure without being hit. The Czech people behind the wall, who were inciting and agitating more and ever more viciously, tried time and again to get inside the sports square to participate first-hand in these atrocities, but the guards prevented them from entering. Any of the beaten men who stayed on the ground exhausted or unconscious were dragged into a corner of the sports field by two of their comrades specially appointed to this task - and these were not permitted to treat the victims half-way gently, but had to simply drag them by the legs across the square, where they and the other victims were left to lie until night. This procedure took about an hour and escalated into an ever more vicious frenzy.

Then the already totally exhausted men had to line up close by us in rows of two and to punch each other in the face, taking big swings at each other without holding back, alternately left and right. Anyone who did not beat his opposite hard enough was treated to punches in his own face from the Czech guards. Additionally the Czechs constantly ran up and down the lines and beat the victims from behind. This ensured that no-one could go the slightest bit easier on his opposite. These men could hardly keep on their feet, staggered, fell down, were forced with kicks and blows to get back up and to continue beating their opposites, and those who could not get back up were dragged away in the manner described above.

The last part of this performance went off similarly; for about 15 minutes the victims had to kick each other in the rear.

We, as spectators, were not allowed to avert our eyes even for a second from this scene. Among us there also were women and children whose husbands and fathers were among those being tortured.

Then the men were herded back to the middle of the square, where they were left in peace but under spotlights and heavy guard for the night. The rest of us were locked into a room that was so small that most of us could only spend the night standing, crowded closely together. I happened to stand near one of the two open windows, from where we could see clearly that the victims who had been beaten unconscious or to death that evening were taken away on a truck. It took the truck several trips.

The next morning a car with several Russian officers showed up. We saw that they were talking to our fellow-countrymen, and from their gestures we could tell that the Russians were asking them about what had taken place. As a result the Czechs were given a strong dressing-down by the Russians, and further maltreatment was forbidden. The valuables that had been stolen from us also had to be returned, insofar as they were still around and had not been taken away yet. I was not able to see to what extent the ban on maltreatment was actually observed, since the rest of us left the sports field that same afternoon and the German men remained behind alone. I don't know what happened to them after that.

In the afternoon the rest of us were herded onto a nearby airfield, where there already were many other refugees, divided into several groups. Here I saw a German woman who had allegedly worked for the Kladno Unemployment Office and whom the Czechs had beaten so badly that she was no longer able to get up from the ground. She tried several times, but she could not manage more than to crawl a little way on all fours before collapsing again, groaning. We received a bit of bread here, our first rations since leaving the hospital. And here we also heard that each of us would have to return to where he had last lived in 1939. Since I was eager to get out of this hell as quickly as possible, and as I also assumed that my wife would wish to do the same, I joined a group of others who were to return to Germany proper.

At intervals the various groups of refugees left the airfield under guard. Our group had to depart in the late afternoon, and we were taken to Karlsbad. There were 68 of us, mostly women and children. One man from Troppau - who would be shot by Russians the following day before the eyes of his wife and two children, on the request of a Czech partisan woman - and I were the only two men in the group. With constant blows we were herded from town to town. Often we also had to cover long stretches at a run. In the towns the Czech inhabitants were already waiting for us and literally made us run the gauntlet. The guards herding us along relieved each other in every new town we reached. Our way also led past Lidice, among other places, where we were received with particularly vicious hatred and were treated accordingly. On the way we also picked up a white-haired old woman whose head was basically only a bloody lump. Her face had turned every imaginable color and was totally disfigured. We took her in our midst and tried to help her along. But since she could not keep up the forced pace for very long, we soon had to leave her behind again.

Since everyone was afraid of collapsing and being shot, it was already during the first leg of the trip that people began discarding one piece of luggage after another, to have enough strength to drag themselves and the children along. Later on we were not even allowed to drop our things of our own accord; if someone wanted to discard a burden, he was forced to still bring it to the next town, where it was then easy for the Czech inhabitants already lying in wait, to carry it off. And especially the first day we were deliberately prodded along at such a speed that there was hardly anyone among us who was not forced to throw away heavy bags just to be able to keep up. It is known that the weather was unusually hot during those days, and this caused us great suffering especially since we were forbidden to stop anywhere where there was water. The first day we were herded along almost without any pause, until finally near midnight we stopped in a town where we could stay the night in a school. It was here that the first baby in our group died of hunger and thirst, and others soon followed. We had a kind soul to thank for our first real meal here, which had been prepared in a Russian field kitchen.

The next morning had hardly dawned before we had to move on again. On the whole, this day passed like the day before. The only change was that on the way Russian soldiers dragged women and children out of our lines and into the bushes where they were raped, often up to 15 times. Sometimes they were brought back to the group on a truck. The younger girls in particular showed the effects of this treatment. Along the way I met a Silesian refugee who was on the road with a horse and cart. His 14-year-old daughter had been so severely raped by Russians that he had to leave her behind, dying, in a hospital. His two older daughters, about 18 to 22 years old, had gone through the same ordeal and went into convulsions whenever Russians even came near. This family spent the following night with us in a barn in a Sudeten village. It was the day we had reached the Sudeten German region. Here the Czech guards who had accompanied us thus far began to grow afraid, and finally let us go on alone.

To protect the women and girls from being raped any more, we spent the following two nights in the outdoors, and on the fourth day following our expulsion from Kladno we reached Karlsbad. But we were kept from entering this city, as it was already very overcrowded with refugees.

Our group, which had grown very much in number by this time, split into smaller groups here and I myself went on with such a smaller band, via Joachimsthal to Saxony, where I first spent several weeks searching in vain for my family and then moved farther west. It was not until Christmas 1945 that I got back in touch with my family again. My wife had traveled the same route from Kladno to Karlsbad with our 3½-year-old daughter and 6-year-old son. She had then managed to take the train from Karlsbad to Brünn. At that time the Germans were forbidden at grave penalty to use the trains, and my wife had to take great pains throughout the trip to keep the two children from talking, since that would have given away their German ethnicity. She managed to keep them silent only by threatening them repeatedly that she would throw them from the moving train if they so much as said one word. And indeed they succeeded in reaching Brünn, but had to leave the city again in the evening of the same day and, along with many other fellow-sufferers, had to endure the infamous Death March of Brünn, which cost so many of our countryfolk their lives.

Kladno, Report No. 2
Persecution of Germans from the Protectorate
Reported by Erika Griessmann - Report of January 29, 1946

I was born on October 4, 1927 at Masshaupt and I have always lived with my parents at Kladno. On May 5, 1945, the revolt of the Czech underground movement started at Kladno. Armed members of the *Národní Garda* [National Guard] blocked all the streets, cleared the billets of the German army and the military hospitals and turned the wounded out into the streets. I saw how these wounded soldiers were stoned by the mob. On May 6, 1945, the so-called house-searches, in the course of which all German apartments were looted, began. My father, an official of the "Poldihütte" (iron works), was arrested on the evening of the same day and we never saw him again. I myself got a box on the ears from a Czech soldier during the first search of our house, allegedly for not having told him where we had buried our jewelry.

Next Monday the wave of persecutions of Germans ran particularly high. We watched from the first floor of our house how innumerable German men fled across the fields, endeavoring to escape from their persecutors and how they were machine-gunned like rabbits. This was the fate of every German, without distinction whether he were a civilian or a soldier, a party-member or not.

The Russians marched into Kladno on Wednesday and within the hour all German dwellings had to be evacuated. I heard our Czech neighbor weeping in the street. She said that soon it would be our (the Griessmann's) turn and nobody would be able to help us. 15 minutes later, members of the *Revoluční Garda* [Revolutionary Guard] entered our house. The leader, a tall fellow covered with blood, threw a hand-grenade through the window. When he found my mother, my 15-year-old brother and me alone in the house, he pushed me onto the ottoman and said: "I won't rape you, the Russians will do that!" The Czechs plundered our house, threatening us awhile; my mother and my brother escaped through the front door, whilst I jumped through the window. We had to run the gauntlet through our own street, the Wras-Gasse. Crowds of Czechs rushed at us, striking us violently. I saw only a few of our neighbors, who were looking out of their windows in tears.

Without any possessions, in the same condition in which we had fled from our home, we joined up with a number of other refugees, who came from the surroundings of Unhožd. Most of them were bleeding, for the Czechs had thrown hand-grenades at them. We were driven into the yard of a factory where we had to stand against the wall with our hands above our heads. First of all my 15-year-old brother was lashed; after that several Czech women seized me and my mother. My mother's head was already bleeding. They took off my earrings and my hair ribbons, for they intended to cut off my pigtails. While all this took place, a Czech appeared and shouted over the heads of the crowd: "The attractive ones are for the Russian officers!" We were then driven off and repeatedly struck on the way. One man finally caught me by my hair and dragged me into a car. I fainted. When I regained consciousness, I was lying on a sofa with bandages on my head and hands. About five Russian officers of high rank stood around me. One asked me if I were hungry, and where I wanted to go. I told him that I would like to go to my mother. He then ordered me to be driven by car to the football field, where I met my mother and brother right at the entrance. When my mother saw the condition I was in, she fell on her knees and screamed out that the tortures should be stopped and that they should just shoot us. After that she broke down, unconscious. All this took place at Kladno during the morning of May 9, 1945.

Shortly after noontime we were driven up to the edge of a pit and told that we were now to be shot. However, a Czech officer appeared and said that it was too soon yet. We were loaded on a truck together with many other Germans and taken to the market-place of Masshaupt. After the mob had stoned us and spit upon us, we were taken back again to the football field of Kladno. Many German soldiers were lying on the ground, suffering from bullet wounds in the head and the abdomen. Nobody took the slightest care of these seriously wounded men. Here my mother fainted for the second time. A German doctor, whom I had asked to help her, was knocked about by Czech guards. Later on we had to undress on the open square until we were wearing nothing but a chemise, and were searched by the Czechs. Afterwards we were again loaded on cars and taken to the military barracks in Kladno. There we saw a terrible sight: Civilians and soldiers lying in their own blood, to whom no one was allowed to render assistance. Many escaped from their tortures by committing suicide. I saw several small children whose throats had been cut by their parents, in order to spare them further tortures by a quick death. A Czech surgeon, who arrived with a nurse, bandaged up some of these. During all the time we received nothing to eat.

In the afternoon of May 10th the seriously wounded were put into ambulance cars. Those less seriously wounded prepared to march. In the meantime a howling mob gathered in front of the barracks and began to throw stones at us. A Czech read a proclamation from a large piece of paper, in which all Germans were accused of being criminals. He shouted that we should have to atone for everything now when we left the barracks. Suddenly hand-grenades were again thrown into the crowd of German prisoners, causing terrible carnage. A Czech priest appeared and administered extreme unction. But many of the wounded men and women rejected his services. My mother succeeded in getting us into the ambulance car. A nurse gave me a DRK-cap [German Red-Cross cap], which afforded me some protection. On the way out of Kladno we were stopped by Russian guards. A soldier of the Red Army opened our ambulance car and ordered me to follow him, since I was not a nurse. But the wounded interceded for me. The Russian then declared that they should either give him all their watches or surrender me. The seriously wounded German soldiers delivered up all their watches and rings and I was set free.

Our column then drove to the western part of Bohemia. Very soon we had to leave the ambulance cars and to join crowds of refugees, walking in the direction of the American occupied zone. We received nothing to eat during all the time. We mostly slept in the open field and were often molested by Czech and Russian soldiers during the night. Several of the DRK-nurses, who escorted us, were raped by Russian guards outside Petschau. Together with my mother and my brother I finally arrived at my grandparents' house at Hermannshütte near Mies, where I succeeded in getting employment on a Czech farm. In November 1945, when the Americans withdrew to Bavaria, they took me with them.

The concentration camp
Reported by Ottokar Kremen - Report of June 25, 1950

I returned home from the Wehrmacht on May 7, 1945 and was unable to enter my apartment because it was occupied by Russian officers. Therefore I went instead to my sister-in-law in Gersdorf, District Komotau, to stay there with my wife until my apartment was vacated. I went to my apartment to get some linen and clothing. While I was there, the officers apologized and did not keep me from taking my clothes and linen with me. I had arrived on a bicycle, but while I was in my apartment the bike was stolen. When the officers noticed what had happened, one of them, a Major, went out into the street with me and flagged down a Russian soldier who was driving by on a Sachs motorcycle. He levied the motorcycle from him and gave it to me as replacement for my stolen bike. He gave me a paper in Russian so that I would be able to pass the Russian sentries without trouble. And indeed none of these sentries gave me any trouble, and I arrived safely in Gersdorf with the motorcycle. The officers had mentioned that they would be moving out in three weeks at the latest and that I would be able to move back into my flat then. But that's not how things turned out:

On June 3, 1945 nine Czechs came to my temporary lodgings at my sister-in-laws's place in Gersdorf. Except for one, the Czechs wore civilian clothes, but you could tell at first glance that they had stolen them as there was not one among them whose jacket or pants fit properly. Only one of them wore a uniform (Staff Captain of the gendarmes), which appeared to belong to him, since it fit. They searched my quarters, and others from the same unit searched the entire house. They took all the clothes and linen which the Russians had let me keep, as well all of my sister-in-law's clothing and all the food there was. They shot the rabbits that were in the hutch, and left them lying there. I had to undress and was examined for evidence of having been in the SS. When no such evidence was found they asked me if I was a member of the NSDAP or the SA, and when I said no, I was hit in the face to the point where the blood ran from my nose and mouth. When they had collected everything that they intended to take, including the motorcycle that the Russian Major had given me, my sister-in-law's son had to harness the oxen and cart the booty to the road. I myself also had to go along. I was taken to an inn in the town. Other men were immediately brought in, and we were forced to beat each other up - each had to punch or slap the other. From there I was taken to the police jail in Komotau (formerly the Hotel Weimar).

June 3 was a Sunday. I was put into a cell meant for two. There were 16 of us in this cell, among us an 11-year-old boy whose parents were in a different cell. I don't remember the names of all the prisoners, but one of them, whom I knew well personally, was the teacher Kny from Sporitz. The

11-year-old boy was the son of engineer Merden from the bell-foundry Herold in Komotau. Both father and son were later shot in the camp and are buried somewhere in a field in Trauschkowitz. The mother had to remain in the camp. We had to stay in this police jail until Thursday, without food or water. Finally, on Thursday afternoon, our situation changed. We were lined up in the jail yard and made to face the wall. It was lucky that I understood Czech and could therefore understand what the Czechs were planning and saying to each other, and I was able to let my fellow-sufferers know what was being planned. One by one we were interrogated by a lieutenant of the gendarmes. When it was my turn I asked the lieutenant why I had been locked up here. He replied: "I didn't bring you here and so I can't discharge you either." When we had all been interrogated, we had to line up in the yard in fours to be transported off. One of the Czechs held a bust of Hitler and demanded that everyone marching past had to give the Hitler salute, and another one of these Czechs took up position on the other side with a submachine gun. I understood when the Czech holding the bust called to the other guard: when one of the raises his paw, shoot immediately! By 'paw' he meant 'hand'. I was just able to inform the others of this so that they would not salute, and we marched out the gate without even a glance at the Czech with the bust. Naturally the guards leading us were angry that they had not managed to get one of us to raise his hand, so as to be able to shoot at him. En route we were maltreated with kicks and with whip lashes for allegedly not marching properly.

We were put into a camp, it was the old Glass Works near the Municipal Estate of Komotau. Once there, we had to line up single-file at a distance of three paces from each other. First we had to empty our pockets and place everything on the ground before us, and then to strip naked. When we had stripped, the camp guards rifled through our pockets. Woe to anyone who still had anything at all in his pockets, even if it was just a tiny scrap of old paper; he was immediately whipped, or punched in the face so that he could hardly find his way back to his place in the line. Those who had good clothes or underwear or shoes were relieved of these things and got clothes instead that had belonged to fellow-sufferers who had already been beaten or tortured to death. These clothes were either torn or covered in blood. Then we were taken into a large room where there was a total of 78 men, among them Herr Rafler-Müller from Neudorf/Biela, weapons dealer Böhm, and others whose names I do not recall. The room was paved with bricks and covered with a roof of roofing felt. It had a single window, where a guard stood all day, watching us in the room. It was as hot as an oven in this room. None of us had any bedding or even a blanket, much less a straw pallet. We had to sleep on the bricks. All day long, from 6 o'clock in the morning until 10 in the evening, we had to parade to Czech orders. There were old men 70 to 80 years of age among us, and even they had to drill along with us. One day the guard did not like how we performed the drill, and he said: "Well, what's wrong? If you can't do any better than that I'll teach you." No sooner said than done - he took groups of nine men at a time out into the square to parade, but God help anyone who turned to the wrong side, then he was pointed in the right direction with the guard's leather whip. Then we were urged into a jog, again with lashes from the leather whip. On their return many of the men collapsed and begged to be killed, put out of their misery, but nonetheless the torture went on. In the evening the camp commandant entered our room and asked if there wasn't anyone among us who was familiar with Czech command. When nobody spoke up, I raised my hand. The commandant asked me if I spoke Czech well, I said yes, and he put me in charge. I asked him if it might be permitted to give the prisoners classes in Czech. The commandant agreed to it, and in this way we got out of the parading for a while, since it was permitted to sit during the classes, albeit only on the brick floor.

During this time our daily rations consisted of 100 g bread and a cup of coffee, nothing for breakfast and at noon, and another 100 g of bread and a cup of coffee in the evening. Often we were harshly awakened at night, forced to stand at attention and to endure any and all harassment and torments that Czech civilians chose to inflict on us. One night a group of Czechs came in, among them a gendarme, and we had to line up in rows of three and at three paces' distance, and then the Czechs went from one to the other and asked each if he had been with the Party or the SS or SA. Woe to any unfortunate who had been! These had to run into the yard, under blows from the whips; once all had run out, the Czechs left the room and we could lie down again, but there was no question of sleep, for we were all too agitated and didn't know what would happen the next moment. Shortly afterwards we heard the rattle of submachine guns. It was already dawn. A truck drove past our window and was loaded up with the bodies of the shot men. There were 78 of them. That same morning right after reveille I and three others had to fetch a wheelbarrow and to cart sand into the yard to cover up the pools of blood left by the unfortunate men. It took us 18 wheelbarrow loads of sand, they had to be filled right up and even so it was only enough for a sprinkle over the blood. Later the truck returned and I had to wash it, since it was all covered with blood. As I heard from a guard, the men were dumped into a shallow pit in a field in Trauschkowitz. The dead included the aforementioned engineer Merden from the bell-foundry Herold and his 11-year-old son, whereas their wife and mother was still in the camp.

One day the order was issued to vacate the camp, as the inmates would all be taken across the border to the Russians. A transport was put together, and off we went. In the evening I found out from the camp commandant, who was a Staff Captain with the gendarmes, that everyone had been taken to the infamous concentration camp of Maltheuern. Those who had to remain behind in the Glass Works camp included: a doctor named Lockwenz from the Komotau District Hospital; an engineer; an Austrian who had done the Czech laborers many good deeds during the Hitler years - this was well known in the camp, and such former Czech beneficiaries actually visited him and brought him cigarettes as thank-you, but nonetheless this man was not released; a former Staff Captain from the Czech army; a Yugoslav; a postal worker named Havel from Görkau; and I. We asked a guard who was a little more approachable what was to be done with us, and he replied: "You weren't with any Nazi organization and you will be released." But the release didn't happen. The Austrian and the Serb were sent under guard to their native countries, and the rest of us continued to remain in the camp. Hardly 8 days had passed before the number of inmates had increased to 360, 78 of them women. Of the new arrivals I remember the following names: Herr Mader, Director of the Mannesmann pipe manufactory of Komotau; engineer Vierlinger from the same factory; one Herr Dr. Meier, the largest merchant in Komotau; Herr Taud, the Administrative Director of the royal demesne of Rothenhaus-Görkau; the sausage manufacturer Herr Mittelbach of Komotau (he was tortured to death in the camp), Herr Müller, gravel pit owner from Komotau-Oberdorf; the priest of Eidlitz near Komotau; one Herr Heger from Natschung (he too was beaten to death); and many other people whose names I do not recall. Together with the new arrivals we were divided into labor gangs for the CSD (Czech railroad) in Komotau and had to clear away the rubble from the bombed-out boiler house. An engineer Sturm from Komotau was also there. I had to go along on these work details to serve as translator, to convey the railroad foreman's or team leaders' orders to the prisoners. There were many among them who had never done this sort of work before in their life, and they were speeded up in their efforts by the whips of the Railway Police guards who oversaw the work gangs. This hard labor was accompanied with rations consisting of unsalted soy-meal soup, and nothing else at all except 100 g bread a cup of coffee in the morning and evening. If a prisoner escaped, the team leader, who was also an inmate, was treated to a session "on the teeter-totter" (torture room). I will return to this torture method a little later. Many inmates were no longer able to return home after that - for example Herr Mittelbach of Komotau. He had been beaten so badly that his face was steel blue and he did not recognize anyone nor even know where he was. He was quite out of his mind. His own daughter did not recognize him when he passed her during the march-out from the railway station, and anyone else who knew him and didn't know that it was him also did not recognize him, that's how badly this man had been disfigured.

At the railway station I met a young foreman who had been assigned a 3-room flat in Komotau, Klingergärten, but who refused to move into it. He often said to me: "Where is all this going to end? I won't take a flat here, because everything here has been stolen." But this man was the only one of this mind-set whom I ever met. Later he gave us two cartloads of potatoes for the camp, so that the inmates could cook them. He also brought many an inmate some bread, and gave away his own lunch rations.

Whenever someone collapsed at work, the Railway Police found it amusing to throw him into a water-filled bomb crater, and would laugh when the victim surfaced, all covered in mud. We were often glad when we could go to work, and feared Sundays, as torture by the camp guards and civilian Czechs from the city were the order of the day on Sundays. Even at night inmates were often called out in order to be tormented. One example of Sunday in the camp: in the forenoon civilian Czechs, including women, came to the camp and selected their victims, whom they abused by beating them in the face with their shoe heels, or had them beaten by other prisoners. If the one in question did not beat his fellow-sufferer as he was expected to, he himself would be beaten by the Czechs, sometimes with knuckle-busters. Everyone man or woman who had been a member in any NSDAP organ, or whose sons or husbands had been members, were taken straight to the torture chamber right after being body-searched. This torture chamber was a room where the people had to strip naked and were then beaten by eight guards armed with clubs. Then he or she was taken to another room and made to stand at the wall and to hold a piece of paper to the wall with his or her nose. God help you if the paper dropped, then you were punished with punches and blows to the head. One day the officers of the former municipal police were brought to the camp. It goes without saying that, like all the other torture victims, these men were also beaten every third day. One of the policemen, quite a big, strong man, responded to the first blow he received by reaching for the throat of one of the guards. The other guard standing nearby shot him down. Then the tortures were stopped for a few days.

Then came a new invention. A gear wheel was installed, across which a rope was drawn. On one end the rope had a loop, through which the unfortunate souls had to put their hands. The loop was then pulled tight, and after the victim had been hoisted up the other end of the rope was tied to a post to ensure that the beaten man could not retaliate against his tormentor. Often these unfortunates were left hanging, or lying on the ground. Those who had already been beaten twice or even three times had festering wounds. The pus soaked through their shirts and jackets. The poor people's backs were covered with flies and stank horribly. They were put into a separate little room, the so-called "marodka", but there could be no suggestion of recovery or healing. Once 8 to 10 prisoners were in this "marodka", these beaten people who could hardly move had to dig a pit 2 meters deep and about 60 cm wide. In the evening, when the pit was finished, they were stood beside it and the first of them had to lie down in the hole (grave). Only after he was in it was he shot, from above. The second had to lie down on the corpse and was also shot from above, and so on until the grave was full. Once there was enough room left for one more, and so they fetched a 67-year-old woman. Her hair was cut off. She was beaten for refusing to reveal where her son was, and had to lie down on the previously murdered inmates. Then she was shot just as they had been.

Words fail me to describe how those people looked who had been beaten twice. I saw one man from the Waffen-SS who had already been beaten twice. Aside from his body, which was basically pulped, his manhood was swollen to an average of 8-9 cm [approx. 3 inches] in diameter, entirely suffused with blood, and his testicles were beginning to suppurate; the entire area right to his anus was full of pus, and he stank horribly. And all this had been done to him only because he was a German and a member of the SS. More and more people arrived every day. The "Stráz bezpecnosti" brought the people in already half-dead. Once they brought in a badly injured Latvian who had been in the infirmary to recover. They brought him on a stretcher, dressed only in a shirt and underpants. He did not speak German well. When I had to question him, he told me that he regretted not having known what the SS meant when he had volunteered for battle. He had ended up with the SS without knowing it. This poor man was shot that very evening. Later on, officers from the Czech army came and chose some victims from among the prisoners. They found an old, formerly retired German Colonel who had served in the Czech military from 1918 to 1924 and had been pensioned off from there; he was literally beaten to death. The photographer Schuster from Komotau and piano-maker Lutz were also beaten to death in this camp, as was the municipal surveyor with a Polish-sounding name. Once a number of Czech officers came to the camp and criticized the camp commandant because the former members of the municipal police were still alive in the camp, and one of them said: "Get rid of that rabble!" He said it in Czech, but I understood it.

For a time I also had to serve in the kitchen. There was nothing but unsalted soy-meal soup on the menu and, as already mentioned, some bread and coffee in the evenings. But meanwhile the butter, margarine, noodles, barley and other foodstuffs were going bad in the store houses. Every guard, even the commandant, would drive away in stolen cars packed with full suitcases, taking food, clothing, linen and other things home. The inmates' family members brought clothes for their fathers and sons, as well as bread and other food. The guard at the gate would take these things, and in the guard room they were examined and if there were good articles of clothing among them the guards would divide them up amongst themselves. The food was eaten by the guards or left to go to waste. It was not until close to the end that the women got some margarine on their evening bread and the soup was salted, and it was even longer before the commandant could be persuaded to cook some horsemeat in the soup once a week. And so it went until we were transferred to the former Ciprian camp in Oberdorf. In this camp I had to undergo an operation and was then permitted to stay there. After I had recovered, I planned my escape, which I carried out.

And that's what the civilized world - that dares call itself democratic - sanctioned and deliberately hushed up, and praised as "liberation"!

Mährisch Ostrau, Report No. 1
Arrest, expulsion, death march
Reported by Rudolf Schneider - Report of June 14, 1950

My family and I lived in Moravian Ostrau for many years. My children, and I too to some extent, attended the Czech school there. I was not a member of the Nazi Party or any of its formations or organizations (except for the NSV [National Socialist Welfare Organization]). In late March 1945 my wife and 14-year-old daughter were ordered to leave Moravian Ostrau, and they went to Aussig on the Elbe, to stay with some relatives. As railwayman (I was a conductor) I was not allowed to leave my position, and did not want to either, as I always got along well with the Czechs and never discussed politics and only lived for my work. Besides, I speak Czech perfectly and served in the Czech army, and I may say I served well, for I made it to the rank of NCO in the "Hranicársky prapor c. 3" in only two years.

But things turned out differently. On April 30, 1945 the Russians came. I was arrested by the Czechs and turned over to the Russians. After a week (and it was a difficult week) the Russians released me, as no charges could be proved against me. I was not able to return to my home, as by that time it had already been occupied by one of the sons of my best Czech colleague (Josef Nowak). His wife had immediately notified the Czech bandits, the so-called partisans, that I had been released, so that they were at the ready to arrest me again right off the street and put me into the concentration camp in Moravian Ostrau-Oderfurt (City Hall). While in this camp I wrote a petition to the *Národní výbor*. In this camp I was robbed of everything the Russians had left me, including my clothes and underwear, and I was given an old shirt and trousers instead. That was all. We had to work very hard in this camp, even at night. For the first time we got no food at all; I lived on what I found in a garbage can while working. It's unbelievable, but true. Later we got a cup of fish soup once a day, but neither bread nor potatoes. Consequently many people died in this camp, and neither a doctor nor a priest was allowed to visit us. We had to cart the dead away to the Oderfurt cemetery and bury them like dogs in one corner. After work we had to join the guards in the yard to sing and parade-drill, and were beaten bloody while doing so. The Czech police (Commandant Sergeant Prokop) watched these atrocities with evident pleasure.

Then my wife and daughter returned from Aussig in late May 1945 and I was told by some Czech acquaintances that they were in the concentration camp "Mexico". I was not allowed to go see them. On June 12 we were "invited" to volunteer for field work, and we were assured that we could take our families with us. And so I volunteered myself and my wife and daughter. My wife was brought to our camp that very evening, but unfortunately without our daughter who was ill and feverish and staying with some Czech relatives. We were allowed to go to town for two hours to procure some food and clothing. But in the evening, once we had cooked the food, it was all taken away from us and the Czech police had a good time with it until next morning. On June 13 we were herded to Silesian Ostrau, onto a sports field, where we were searched. Many were dragged aside and beaten, and stripped of their clothing and shoes. And after that the march began, on foot through Hultschin, Troppau, Jägerndorf. We were marched for three days, hunted along by Czech soldiers, without any rest. Most of us were women, children and old men. We got no rations whatsoever on the way. Anyone who collapsed was shoved into the ditch, regardless whether it was a woman or child. *"Chcípni, nemecká kurvo!"*, that's all we ever heard. ["Shut up, you German whore!"] On June 16, 1945 we were chased into the forests outside Neustadt (Upper Silesia) and robbed of even our last meager possessions by our Czech escorts. But the area was already under Polish occupation. We had no identity papers and could not even prove that we had been expelled by the Czechs, and so we could only sneak on at night. Later the Poles did not pay much attention to us any more. Since we had no papers or money, we worked our way on the various demesnes.

Aside from many people whom I did not know, my following acquaintances lost their lives on this death march: Fröhlich, senior Reich Railroad inspector from Oderfurt, buried in Bärndorf (District Frankenstein), and engineer Schiffner from Witkowitz, who lies buried in Libenau (District Frankenstein).

Mährisch Ostrau, Report No. 2

Inhuman brutalities in the Hanke concentration camp in 1945

Reported by Ernst Schorz - Report of June 24, 1946

On August 27, 1945 I was taken to the concentration camp in Peterswald near Moravian Ostrau, probably on the instigation of the Czech administrator of my estate. In the camp a medical exam found me unfit for work in the mines, and I was sent instead to the brickworks camp in Moravian Ostrau. On our way there we were all beaten and kicked. In the camp I was assigned to a burial detail, and had to do this work for three weeks. During this time we had to take the prisoners who had died in the camp to Palatzky Cemetery and bury them there. In the course of those three weeks I had to take approximately 200 bodies to the cemetery, where I also saw the dead that had been brought from other camps. Most bodies came from the Hanke camp in Moravian Ostrau. Usually these bodies had also been mutilated. There were many bodies of women among them. These were buried at the cemetery, but dug up again three weeks later and burned in the crematorium. On his deathbed my friend Krischka from Klantendorf near Fulnek told me the following, which he himself had witnessed: in the Hanke camp his wife, 8 months pregnant, had to stand naked against the wall and was bludgeoned on the stomach until the fetus aborted and she herself died. Krischka, who had spent a long time in the Hanke camp, also told me that he had witnessed how a woman, with her hands and feet tied behind her back, had been hoisted up a wall and how both her breasts were then cut off with a knife.

I myself was grossly maltreated in the brickworks camp, like all the inmates there. All the teeth on my right side were knocked out, and my hands and arms were sprained. The camp leader urged that the two guards who had maltreated me should be punished, but at the hearing the judge declared: "He's a German, they should have beaten him even more."

Mährisch Ostrau, Report No. 3
The Hanke concentration camp
Reported by Alfred Kutschker - Report of August 3, 1946

I had to spend from early June until August 16, 1945 in the infamous Hanke camp in Moravian Ostrau, where I and all the other inmates were stripped on our arrival of everything we had, even clothing, underwear and shoes, so that we were completely naked. We were then thrown some rags to dress in. Like everyone else there, I was beaten daily - 120 blows. Every day we were choked until we passed out. Six people were beaten to death before my very eyes, among them Langer, Miesner, Konetschny and Kron. Then I had to spend a month in the District Court of Moravian Ostrau, where we were ordered to dig up the bodies of German soldiers and to throw them into the garbage pit of the cemetery of Silesian Ostrau. From Ostrau I was then transferred to the Troppau prison, where I was discharged on July 12th of this year without ever having been given a trial. I have nothing left at all any more to call my own, beyond the clothes on my back and what some acquaintances gave me. My deportation luggage weighed all of 20 kilos.

Mährisch Ostrau, Report No. 4
Severe ill-treatment and murder of prisoners of war
Reported by Heinz Lapczyna - Report of January 10, 1947

I was released from Russian captivity on the day after Christmas, and against the advice of the Russian doctor I went to Czechoslovakia, since my wife and my child were living there. I finally arrived at Mährisch-Ostrau via Petrowitz-Pomil. At Mährisch-Ostrau I made inquiries as to whether my relatives were still at Budweis. I and my three comrades were thereupon arrested by two Czech policemen, who put us into the police jail at 2 o'clock in the morning after we had waited for three hours. There were 60 men of us there pressed together in a cell 10 x 20 ft. As there was no ventilation, the air was exhausted within a few hours, so that we had to fight suffocation. The prisoners included the former Landrat [head of the administration of a district] of Mährisch-Ostrau, various engineers, and schoolboys 14 to 16 years of age. The last-named had to work in the mines, in pits with 8% gas. In the prison we received two thin slices of bread and half a liter (1 pint) water-gruel per day.

In the camp people were often called for trial and returned afterwards badly maltreated. In order to extort confessions the interrogators thrust red-hot needles under the nails of the persons being interrogated, until the victims collapsed from the pain. They then attempted to bring the victims back to consciousness by hitting them with rifle butts or by other abuses. When this failed, they were simply thrown back into the cell, where they remained without nursing or food only to go through the same torture the following day.

Another method of extorting confessions was to beat the victims on the bare sole of the foot until the skin burst. In order to make them suffer a little more the men would have to kneel for several days until they fell unconscious. The daily greeting was: "Has any German swine kicked the bucket?" and if such was not the case: "Then we'll have to lend a hand!" Witnesses to the afore-mentioned cruelties are: Stanislav Kaminonka, also Jan Blaha and Walter Schmidt.

I was finally released after some weeks, but in spite of my serious injuries I was sent to the internment camp near Mährisch-Ostrau. At that place it was the commandant's custom to chase the women internees through the yard in their nightgowns every night.

Everything which we had still in our possession was taken away. Terrible cruelties also took place in a camp (Hanke-Lager) at Mährisch-Ostrau. 20 men would be shut up in a little room and ordered to sing Fascist songs, and afterwards they were clubbed to death with fence-posts or hanged. At the daily orgies of the sentries women and girls had to serve at table completely naked and were afterwards raped. The elder women were killed. Witnesses to these obscenities and cruelties were: Rudolf David and Albert Liebner.

On March 12, 1946, I reached Kutiny near Brünn, where I was interned for the second time. There were other camps at Dolní Lotška and at Kuřim. I myself remained at Kutiny. All these camps also had cellars in which the more unpopular Germans had been shut up and slaughtered.

We were allowed to write only a postcard of 15 lines once a month; this almost never reached its destination. I therefore wrote a letter, and was locked in a cell for 20 days for this offence. Every second day we received 1 pint of water-gruel. The bread intended for us was sold by the guards among themselves. We never received any of it.

We were lashed with short lengths of steel cable until we could scarcely stand on our feet. Al-though I was weakened by many operations on my foot and had to walk on crutches, nobody took this into account.

Another form of abuse was that we were ordered to strike each other with wooden boards, in which there were rusty nails; if this was not done to the full satisfaction of the guards, they showed us how to do it, but in such a brutal way that nobody was able to stand on his feet afterwards; they practised their boxing techniques on us and also knocked us down with their carbines.

I suffered all this for twenty days. Only when we were already covered with blood and lying on the floor would they stop for some hours, but only to start again after this interval. Our cell resembled a torture chamber. The floor was a pool of blood and the walls were splashed with it up to the ceiling.

There were other methods of extorting confessions: a tube would be forced into the victim's mouth and the other end fixed to the water-tap. Or: we internees had daily to run the gauntlet between lines of the guards; these were armed with whips and scourges, with which they struck us - the best runners were the lucky ones. Going on crutches, I was so badly knocked about that I always ended up unconscious on the ground.

Even the churches at Mährisch-Ostrau and Kutiny were barred to Germans. The German relatives of a deceased person were only allowed to go as far as the gate of the graveyard. They were not allowed to visit the grave. According to my wife, the graves of the Germans were also broken into and robbed, the objects of desire being gold teeth, jewellery and so on.

Mährisch Schönberg, Report No. 1

Severe maltreatment in the prison of Moravian Schönberg, February-March 1946

Reported by Hans Wisur - Report of June 21, 1946

I was arrested in Stubenseifen, District Moravian Schönberg, on January 28, 1946 and taken to the court prison where I stayed until March 7, 1946. There, like all the other prisoners - some 700 of them - I was severely beaten every day, with lashes, fire pokers and rifle butts. One gendarme had a special technique which he liked to use on us. The inmates had to take their shoes off and were then pounded on their toes from above with the rifle butt until blood shot out from under the toenails.

In the yard there was the so-called "Separation", a small building where the gendarmes on guard duty would take arbitrarily selected inmates for maltreatment, as night-time entertainment. In the morning you could see the trails of blood left in the snow where the badly injured inmates had been carried out.

On March 7 I was transferred to the Troppau prison. The first week I was beaten so badly there that I lost consciousness. Beatings were the order of the day there as well. On June 8, 1946 I was released for deportation without any preceding trial, since there were no charges against me. During the expulsion I was relieved of my nickel-plated watch.

Mährisch Schönberg, Report No. 2

Elderly people maltreated while withdrawing savings at City Hall

Reported by Moritz Hilscher - Report of June 23, 194[6?]

Like many other people, I had to report to City Hall in Moravian Schönberg every month to request the release of a monthly sum from my savings account. On this occasion the Stráz would abuse and maltreat the people requesting their money. I myself, aged 71, was slapped about the head twice. That was in March and May 1946. In May of this year I witnessed an 82-year-old man being hit on the head so badly that he lost consciousness. The women were cursed as German whores, and the old people were threatened that they would be burned in the gas works.

Olmütz, Report No. 1

Concentration camp Hodolein: maltreatment, robbery

Reported by K. S. - Report of February 12, 1951

During the occupation of Olmütz hundreds of Germans of all ages and both sexes were locked into the barracks basements, crowded in so tightly that they could hardly move. They were left like that for three days and even longer, without a drop of water or a morsel of bread. As a result of the bad air and the dirt and filth (no-one was allowed to go outside) there were several deaths. I. G. was among those locked into these cellars. He told me that he knows as a fact that more than a hundred, or even several hundred, Germans were herded into the subterranean tunnels in the Michaeler Ausfall, where they were bricked in alive and died horribly. I. G. also spent several months in Barrack 7 of the Hodolein camp, where he had to suffer through the almost-daily beatings that everyone was subjected to. He was so badly injured in the process that he excreted clotted blood and it was like a miracle that he even survived. Karl Prachtl suffered several broken ribs during the beatings.

Olmütz, Report No. 2

Camp Hodolein: Cases of maltreatment and murders

Reported by K. S. - Report of January 23, 1951

I lived together with my family (five persons) in our own house in the neighbourhood of Olmütz. At the beginning of May 1945 I took both my children, 10 and 14 years old, to Pohorsch in the mountains in order to protect them from possible danger in the course of the occupation. Only my daughter, who was 20 years of age, stayed with us. Later on my wife decided to bring the children back home again and we set off in the morning hours of May 5th, 1945. It was a Saturday. We heard that the Russians were only a few kilometers away, and several airplanes already flew over the area. The German Wehrmacht was retreating and was in process of disintegration. We packed our baggage and decided to return at 4 o'clock in the afternoon. But it was already too late, as Russian motorized units had cut off our way back and partisans were concealed in the woods.

That very evening Russian patrols drove up the hill to the village and several men entered the house; we were immediately searched and interrogated. For the moment I was able to protect my family and a number of other persons through my knowledge of the language. The mayor of the village had ordered that all weapons were to be collected and with this believed himself safe. But he too disappeared on one of the following days along with many other men, all of whom were most probably kidnapped.

More and more Russians arrived in the village during the following days and finally they drove up in empty trucks, looting almost all the houses of the Germans and driving away the cattle. Many of the men, who were capable of work, were taken off for forced labour, others maltreated or shot down and many women were raped. We were threatened with severe punishment if we left our apartment. An inn-keeper was shot together with his wife, because he could no longer serve alcohol. A number of persons committed suicide. The Tannenberger family of five persons attempted to hang themselves. The mother and the three grown-up children were cut down in time, but the father was already dead. Mrs. Tannenberger and her two daughters, in search of protection, joined up with us; both the daughters, 18 and 20 years of age, had been molested by Russians. Our neighbour, Mrs. Jahn, who was 65 years old and paralyzed and who was therefore confined to bed, was beaten black and blue by the Russians and finally raped. Her husband who came to blows with a drunken Russian, was maltreated and had to fly for his life. She told me that herself, crying, when I one day entered her house.

One night heavily armed Russians broke in the doors and windows of our little apartment, threatened us with their weapons and looted the cellar, where our landlady had hidden her valuables. A woman from Brünn who also slept in our apartment, was dragged outside and raped. She disappeared and we never saw her again. Mrs. Tannenberger's two daughters lay under the beds and were not seen. I myself was only able to save my family by pretending that we were Czech citizens. A Russian staff-sergeant had told me of Stalin's orders that anyone harming a Czech citizen should be court-martialed, whereas the troops were allowed to do whatever they liked with the Germans, since these were considered as outlaws.

The owner of the house we lived in, one Mrs. Kimmel, had to flee from her apartment to escape from 16 and 17-year-old members of the Red Guard, in order not to be raped. Her further fate is unknown to me. Many others had similar experiences. My wife had to do the laundry for the Russians and to cook the poultry which they had stolen, in order not to incur their displeasure. After a week had passed and after making many requests, we received from the commissar a permit and were allowed to return to our home with the few articles we had been able to keep. Our own house had also been looted in the meantime. All that was left were the empty cupboards. Two Russians were still "working" when I arrived. My elder daughter succeeded in escaping to one of her relatives, otherwise she would scarcely have survived the events. In the cellar, where we had stored the greater part of our belongings, there was only a chaos of demolished articles.

Almost everything in our house as well as in other houses of the village had been looted at the instigation of our neighbour, one Josef Dostal. This 45-year-old Czech had been to German schools, and he had a German wife and children who could only speak German. During the period of the Third Reich he had had a well paid job with the German construction firm of Schneider. All of a sudden, after Germany's collapse, he discovered himself to be a fervent Communist and a hater of the Germans. As a member of the "National Committee" he became housing control officer. As such he directed in the most brutal manner many expulsions and lootings. He was responsible for the loss of several lives, among them that of his own brother-in-law, a certain Panak, who as a German had been interned in a camp at Brünn. The latter's wife, who had 10 underaged children, was transferred and it is said that she died in Bavaria. The 75-year-old father of Mr. Hartmann, a teacher, was put into the poor-house by this Dostal, where the old man died from hunger and cold the following winter. His wife, who was 70 years of age, hanged herself in her house before she could be expelled. Another Hartmann as well as one J. Pallik and several others were killed in the camp at Ratibor. The same Dostal sent my own relatives to the local camp, allowing them to take only a spoon and a blanket with them. Being familiar with the neighbourhood there is no doubt that he had a finger in most of the crimes and lootings as well as playing the role of informer. The feeble-minded Herentin and the one-eyed Rudolf Raab were brutally butchered. A former staff-sergeant by the name of Kunz, a man of 60 years of age, was beaten to death on a table-top, the partisans' favourite method. Zednik, a pensioner, was shot. Many women and even schoolchildren were raped. Mr. Steiger, the old grave-digger, told me that he had to bury 12 corpses in the first few days after the end of the war. Some of them had been murdered, others had committed suicide, among them a former ship's captain, Tobias, from Nimlau.

The Chairman of the National Committee was a teacher by the name of Hecl, another important Committee-member was Očenášek, the names of the rest of them are unknown to me. Other atrocities of which I had heard in the neighbourhood were the following:

A relative of mine had been raped by the Russians or partisans and her four-year-old son shot. She afterwards jumped into the well and drowned herself. When her mother heard of this, she and her second daughter also drowned themselves and the father set fire to the house and hanged himself in the flames. Tragedies like the one just described happened very often. Schwarz, an innkeeper, committed suicide, the old locomotive-stoker was shot, also a farmer by the name of Eduard Sach. The one-legged Glier and Franz Sauer, a clerk, were maltreated so badly that they died. Sander, a salesman, and another clerk by the name of Sach were ill-treated and then executed. H. Kwapil, who was a schoolfellow of mine, was severely ill-used and died of hunger in a camp.

I reported to the Committee, as every German had to do if he did not wish to lose his property. This was a trick to get hold of everyone. On the following days bills were posted with the inscription *"Národní majetek"* (National Property) on every German house. Other placards with inflammatory slogans and threats were also posted up at the street comers. They were signed by the National Committee and by either the mayor of the town or Dr. Zenkl or Dr. Blaha and other members. One night there appeared an armed gang in front of our house, who threw a heavy stone through the window. They demanded to be let in. The men went through everything. Finally they attempted to rape my wife. I was only able to prevent this by a vigorous intervention made possible by my knowledge of the language.

The following day I went to the National Committee (Heel) and protested about the incident. They promised me satisfaction, but nothing followed. Later on I reported back to my former place of work and was ordered to take part in the cleaning-up of the railway-station together with Franz Müller, an official, and ten other colleagues. We were supervised by partisans, 17 or 18 years old, who spared us no threats or abuse.

In the middle of May 1945 we were told to report to the Russian Headquarters for registration. The secretary of the Communist party, one Slansky, ordered the station-police to take us there, but we were delivered instead to the camp at Hodolein. There were already about 2000 persons assembled, men, women and children. They had been fetched out of their apartments or had been seized in the train or on the street, in order to be robbed and maltreated at the camp.

The moment we arrived at the gate, our pockets were emptied by the guards who took away even our matches. Then the corporal of the guard unit laughed cynically and asked us: "Take your choice, do you want to be hanged or to be shot?"

After this they put us in little cells, intended for solitary confinements, into which 10 men had already been squeezed. Some of them had been dreadfully maltreated and showed black and blue weals on their faces and bodies. We had hardly room to breathe in the little cell. The heat, too, was unbearable. Outside, in the gangway, the partisans were looking for a certain Weiser from Sternberg. When they finally found him an hour later, he was terribly knocked about. Several days afterwards I met this man, who was about 60 years of age, in the courtyard. Whenever the partisans caught sight of him, they gave him a beating. At last he disappeared and only his green hat remained as a memento in our barrack. That first evening Müller and I were taken to barrack No 3, opposite the main guard house. There was much coming and going, for most people were searched and "interrogated" there - the cries of the tortured men were to be heard constantly.

After interrogation the men were jammed into the cells. In the single rooms of the barracks a person had on the average 1.2 square yards of space at his disposal. It was only possible to sleep lying close by one another, packed like herrings, or sometimes only squatting or even standing. Everything was locked during the night. Nobody could leave. Sometimes indescribable scenes took place. Naturally we had nothing but the bare floor to sleep on and most of us had no blanket, not even an overcoat at our disposal. We were woken at 4 o'clock in the morning and then cleaned the cells. After "breakfast" the Czechs formed working squads for the removal of barricades, or refuse and so on. Our diet consisted of a cup of unsweetened black coffee and a piece of bread morning and evening, at noon a thin potato or cabbage soup with 40 to 50 g bread. All the meals taken together amounted to no more than 300 to 400 calories per day, although we had to do heavy work. The number of deaths would have increased considerably if relatives and acquaintances outside the camp, or our employers, had not given us food secretly. Several inmates collapsed - after they had spent 14 days in the camp - from exhaustion and hunger. In addition they were maltreated by the partisans. At night, especially in the barracks situated at the rear, the most atrocious cases of ill-treatment occurred regularly. The torturers used for their beatings heavy metal-studded whips or steel rods. Whenever the maltreated men collapsed bleeding, cold water was poured over them. The next morning they were driven again to their work. The corpses of those who had been beaten to death were buried without ceremony somewhere behind the barracks. Hearses often drove up.

Some of the inmates committed suicide when their torments became unbearable, as for instance Hvabcik, the soap-boiler of our village. When the tired and half-starved working columns returned to the camp in the evening and failed to march in smartly enough, they had to have extra drill until some of them collapsed - notwithstanding which they received further kicks and blows. German boys of school age were also forced to parade and to sing inflammatory Czech songs on penalty of beating and the withholding of food. The prisoners were maltreated by having their beards pulled out, they received kicks or blows and were placed by a wall, against which their heads were thrust with violence. For quite trivial reasons people were put into the damp and dark cellar on bread and water. Many were tortured to death in these cells. After staying down there for only a few days the men looked as shabby and run-down as tramps. Among them were some acquaintances of mine, as for instance Eduard Biebel, a farmer, and a retired railroad employee by the name of Matzner. I often saw German boys of 15 or 16 years, dragged to the cellar by policemen or partisans. Arriving there, they were clubbed and otherwise maltreated. Many never left the cellar alive. On Czech national holidays an extra beating was regularly added to the normal quota.

Among the policemen there were many familiar faces, whose names unfortunately I did not know. Only a certain Labounek was known to me by name. It was said that several professional killers boasted of 50 to 60 homicides. They prophesied "mountains of coffins" and I believe that this prophecy was realized. Nobody's life was safe. A Silesian engineer from Schweidnitz of some such name as Keitke was hanged without previous trial or interrogation, allegedly because he had made an unexpected attack on the guards! In actual fact he had only defended himself against the usual maltreatment and he had now to atone for it. He marched to the gallows apathetically, his head bruised and swollen. The corpse was left hanging in the courtyard for several days. A Czech cloth-merchant named Hunka, another man and later on a number of Germans were ordered to kneel in front of the corpse. The Germans were forced to call out in the courtyard: "We thank our Führer!"

On May 29th, all "internees" were commanded to fall in. Orders were read out and the artisans were picked out from among the prisoners. Later on the roll was called in front of the barracks and the men were reassigned to different barracks. I now slept in barrack No 11, where glazier's work had to be done, together with my comrade Müller. The reassignment went with a hail of insults and blows from the brutal guards. The final amusement was to make the inmates turn somersaults in the gangway, beating them while they did so. Müller got off quite lightly, while I myself sneaked round the barrack and crept in through the window. We both lay down on the floor in the dark. Suddenly Müller, who was already half asleep, imagined that the partisans had called his name in the gangway. All my objections were in vain, he stood up and went outside to report. The brutes received him with abusive words, drove him back to the cell and told him that they would come for him later on. After an hour had passed, some of the men entered. They did not see me in the dark. They dragged Müller across the gangway to the guard-room, where others were assembled; there the howling mob tore his clothes off and lashed the naked victim almost to death. I was stiff with terror as I listened to the screams of pain and cries for help of my tortured comrade, but I was unable to assist him, for the same would only have happened to me. When the blood splashed around too much, the guards dragged him across the gangway to another room, in order not to make a mess of the guard-room. They then completed their infernal work.

The commandant of the barrack was one Vítavský and to him Müller had surrendered his money, amounting to 1000 Kčs; the receipt, however, showed only 850 Kčs; a matter actually of no importance, but Müller hoped that because he had not protested he might receive better treatment in the camp. At the beginning he seemed to be right. I should mention here that Müller was no Nazi, on the contrary, he had been, like myself, a member of the Trade Union for many years. Following a sudden inspiration, I packed my few belongings, jumped again through the window and went across the courtyard to my former lodging, barrack No 2. When I arrived there at 11 o'clock p. m., I ran into the arms of the partisans, who were making one of their usual searches, during which they took from the prisoners whatever they wished. I was struck a number of times and was ordered to place myself with my face against the wall.

After a very minute interrogation, during which I used some excuses, I was allowed to go to sleep. Of course, I did not sleep very much and my first steps in the morning after the reveille led me back to barrack No 11, in order to get information about Müller. Since the entrance to the barrack was watched, I crawled through the window as on the day before. Poor Müller, who was rather stout, lay naked on his cloak on the floor, a glass of water next to him. His back was one black and bleeding wound, the skin burst open from the lashes. At some spots the torn flesh stuck out. But strong as he was, he was still breathing. I attempted to get a few drops of water into his mouth, but it was in vain, he was evidently dying. With great care I crawled out of the room again and joined up with a working column. When I returned in the evening, Dr. Himmel, who was just then in barrack No 2, told me that Müller had died early in the morning and had been buried somewhere or other. Deeds like the one just described happened unnumbered times. I worked for several days at the section of the railway line near Stefanau. One of the Czech railroadmen, whom I did not know, abused me whereupon the partisans gave me several blows with their rifle butts. The railroadman then said: "I like Germans best four meters under ground!"

In the middle of June 1945 a former Czech colleague from my office helped me to get out of the camp, in order to work for a Czech farmer at Nedweis. Seven other workers, all of whom I knew, came with me. S., the farmer, at least gave us enough food to appease our hunger, even though we were still treated like prisoners. We slept in a small room in the basement, pressed against one another. The room was filled with vermin. Here too we suffered some chicaneries, although not to the same extent as in the camp. The farmer, who spoke German fluently, proved himself to be humane. When the Russians entered the farm he hid himself and let his relatives negotiate with them. There were also some other Czechs who behaved like human beings and helped us in other ways.

In general, nobody was allowed to walk on the streets without a permit, even if he were only fetching laundry from his relatives. The badge with the "N" [for the Czech word *Nemec* = German] had always to be worn, otherwise we were subject to annoyances. We could go into the town only at our own risk. There we were forbidden to walk on the pavement or to use the streetcar; it was easy to get into fights or to get sent back to a camp. In spite of all this I succeeded in getting into town a few times, since my wife was employed there. I noticed that actual murderers were now publicly lauded as "heros" in newspapers and on posters, as for instance a certain Jan Smurda who at Pirk had shot two German border policemen and injured a third and who had escaped. This man was nicknamed admiringly "Jan-who-could-not-be-caught". There was also a certain Šafář from Nimlau who boasted of having stabbed at Olmütz, in the Romhofgasse, a man called Svoboda (or a similar name), who had been a member of the SA. A young fellow also from Nimlau by the name of

König, who worked with us, told me about Šafář. On the other hand the names of many Germans were also publicly pilloried, although they had never touched a hair on the head of any Czech; they were denounced as monsters and the scum of humanity merely because they had held a public office. There were also many fanatics who distinguished themselves in the persecution of Germans. Among these were especially the following: a youth by the name of Walter Kořalka (who by the way had German relatives), one Andrysek and his son, both teachers, the Czechs Barta, Čuka, Polonský, Kolman and others. All these were outstanding in the persecution of defenceless Germans, instigating beatings and arrests. These people once faked a case of arson, which they laid at the door of the Germans. As a result of this B. Hausner, a man who had had his leg amputated, was severely maltreated. Albertine Kollmann, a German girl, hanged herself several days after Germany's collapse in order to avoid rape and ill-use. A cattle-dealer by the name of Dostal beat the dead girl's body with a pole. Her mother, a woman of 60 years of age, was sentenced to ten years penal servitude because she had once slapped a Czech. In this region many German men were severely ill-treated by the partisans and the women raped. Just as everywhere else, almost all Germans of both sexes from ten years upwards were sent to the camps. Coufal, a teacher of 60 years of age, was tortured to death in a camp after he had spent a week there. The local National Committee, presided over by Andrysek senior, gave the order for Kleiber, Müller and Skacel, all of them farmers, to be put in jail, where they were executed. These men were accused of having been responsible for getting a Czech into a concentration camp during the period of the Third Reich. The notorious judges of the People's Court were one Matura and one Svoboda.

The unchristian activities of part of the Czech clergy should also be mentioned here. They claimed the major credit for the expulsion and extermination of the Germans by reason of their underground activities during the war.

The priest of our own village prohibited Germans from visiting the church and refused to consecrate the corpses of Germans, who were then buried in some corner without ceremony.

Olmütz, Report No. 3
Camp Hodolein: Shooting of elderly people
Reported by Hermine Pytlik - Report of July 5, 1946

I was an inmate of the camp at Olmütz-Hodolein from June 4, 1945 to June 10, 1945 and I was an eyewitness when some 15 inmates of the old people's home of Olmütz, who had been taken to the camp in the beginning of July, were divided into two groups by the National Guards and shot with pistols at point-blank range. The shooting took place in the evening right in front of the windows of my barrack. The victims were all old and ill and from 65 to 80 years of age.

Olmütz, Report No. 4
The concentration camp, maltreatment
Reported by Dr. Hein - Report of July 5, 1946

I was arrested in Olmütz on May 28, 1945 by members of the Revolutionary Guard, taken to the concentration camp and beaten severely with rifle butts on the way, and flung with kicks into the bunker where I had to remain until June 21 of last year, lying on the damp earth with no blanket and not enough food to keep body and soul together. Every day, both morning and night, about eight Czechs came to beat me with cudgels, steel rods etc. I was locked into this bunker with several other Germans, three of whom died miserably without anyone bothering to care for them. Every second or third night I was dragged from the bunker, several times in each case, and taken to a barrack where I was dreadfully maltreated. I have come away from this abuse with a number of permanent physical injuries. I am deaf on my right ear, have only partial control over my right foot, I suffer from kidney trouble and constant back pain and can hardly stand up straight. I suffer from daily headaches and sometimes my hands shake uncontrollably.

Olmütz, Report No. 5
Camp Hodolein: Withholding mail from England
Reported by Walburga Lindenthal - Report of October 6, 1946

I was engaged to a former British prisoner of war, who returned to England in June 1945 and sent me a certificate through the British Embassy in Prague, requiring the Czech authorities to give me preferential treatment. In spite of the certificate I was conscripted for labour in the iron-works without payment and for this reason was detained in the camp of Olmütz-Hodolein for four months. Letters from my fiancé were frequently held up. I received no mail at all since May 1946, although I know that my fiancé has regularly written to me once a week.

Olmütz, Report No. 6
Concentration camps Olmütz and Stefanau, harassment of old people
Reported by Hermann Komarek - Report of August 1, 1946

My wife and were imprisoned in the Olmütz and Stefanau concentration camps from July 11 until October 6, 1945. Despite our age (we are both 63 years old) we were treated very badly there. I was often beaten, for no other reason than because the guards felt like it. We were given so little food that we were constantly starving. In early October we were released for health reasons, to return home. My wife was in such bad shape and covered with festering wounds that she did not recover, and died in early November. Meanwhile my house had been confiscated, and looted to the bare walls. All my better suits and shoes were taken from me. All I have left now is torn clothes and one pair of shoes that are falling apart.

Olmütz, Report No. 7
The Hodolein camp, maltreatment
Reported by Kurt Domes, engineer - Report of January 17, 1951

On May 5th, 1945, my wife and I drove to Hombock near Olmütz. On May 7th the Russians marched into the village without resistance. This was the long expected signal for the Czechs to start robbing and looting. Radio Prague broadcasted day and night the announcement: "Exterminate the Germans wherever you find them". President Beneš personally issued this invitation to murder at the beginning of May in a speech he held over the Czech radio.

On May 13th, at quarter to 12 a. m., Blaha, a lieutenant of the police came for me. When I hesitated and pointed out that today was Sunday and promised to report the next day, he replied harshly: "No, that is impossible, you have to come with me at once, it is an order!" These words were the beginning of a time full of suffering for me. Partisans took me over at the police-station. These youths were the most feared of all and, indeed, we were all welcomed with 25 blows from rubber-belting and the butts of submachine guns. Bleeding from the nose and mouth, I was marched to the shooting-range near Olmütz together with nine fellow-sufferers. On our way, in the neighbourhood of the monastery of Hradisch, we were received by about 30 persons, mostly women, who lined both sides of the road. These women were armed with clubs, with which they struck at us violently. Their sadism is only explicable as a result of incitement by the Czech radio to the organized murder of Germans, for which exemption from punishment was promised. The Americans, who marched up to the line between Prague and Pilsen, passively watched the horrible crimes of the Czechs. Arriving at the range, we had to strip to the waist and to take pick-axes and shovels. While the men of the guard-unit as well as spectators struck us constantly, we had to dig up the corpses of 22 men and women. We were then told that we, too, should be shot and buried, after we had got out the corpses. More and more Czechs arrived, who participated in the general beatings. All of a sudden a Russian appeared who was accompanied by a Czech. He chose one man out of our lines, took him behind the [shooting range]. After some minutes had passed we heard the sound of a shot. We were never to see our comrade again.

When the corpses were dug up, we were ordered to wash them, to lay them in coffins and to load them on trucks, while a Czech filmed the whole event. During all this time we suffered from constant maltreatment. At 9 o'clock in the evening, notwithstanding the previous threats that we should be killed, we were taken to the jail at Olmütz, where we had to stand in a small gangway with our faces to the wall. Again the ill-treatment began. The blows fell mainly on our heads and backs until blood dripped from our mouths and noses. Then we were thrust into a narrow cell, where seven of us were confined in a space of about 10 square meters (11.9 square yards). There we had to sleep on a cold concrete floor without a blanket and with only our shoes as a pillow. An uncovered bucket served as toilet and only once within 24 hours was the window opened for 15 minutes. The first two days of our imprisonment we received nothing at all to eat. On the third day we received the thin soup which remained our principal dish thereafter. Two months later, by which time I was only able to hold myself upright by leaning against the cell-wall, I was informed that I could go home as there was nothing against me. A warder then took me to the office of the prison, where my release was made out. It was handed over not to me, but to the policeman, who ordered me to follow him. When I said that I had been released and could now go home, he replied: "You'll go home via the concentration camp at Hodolein!" Anyone who knew this notorious camp, in which it was estimated that more than 3,500 Germans had been beaten to death from May to November 1945, would understand that I was terror-stricken. The policeman took me to the camp and handed me over to the office of the camp. I was ordered to barrack No. 2 and met there an old acquaintance of mine. He warned me to conceal my title and rank, since the Czechs took special measures against the German intelligentsia. This friend was Mr. Cepe, an Austrian engineer and commissioner of forests, about 60 years of age. He prepared me for the suffering which awaited me. The "protector" of the camp was one Dr. Rehulka from Olmütz, a member of the Czech Christian Socialist party and a fanatical chauvinist. I spent eleven full months in this camp.

The camp at Hodolein was a so-called barrack-camp, housing [3,000] to 4,000 internees. As fast as prisoners died or were released, the numbers were made up again by newcomers so that in this camp alone about 17,000 Germans had been interned in the course of a year, between May 1945 and May 1946. The warders, mostly youths of the worst type, were born sadists. Especially when they were under the influence of liquor the prisoners were brutally abused. Every night deafening noises and terrible screams made us tremble. One comrade was dragged out of our lines, driven from one corner to the other of the long corridor and then lashed with length of copper cables, belts and sticks until he lay insensible on the ground. If anyone survived the torture and dared to file a complaint, he was certain not to live through the next night. These beatings to death were always carried out during the night, mostly about midnight. First of all the kidneys of the unfortunate men were loosened with blows and then the maltreatment went on until he lay dead on the floor. One of the most notorious of our slaughterers was a certain Smetana from Olmütz, who was also personally known to me.

On October 27th, 1945, I was ordered to the guard-room of barrack No. 12 and there ill-used in the most frightful way by three youths under the command of the notorious Smetana. They all took part in the beating. A lucky chance saved me in this terrible situation. Two policemen arrived with a new transport of 30 men from Sudetenland. I received such a kick that I flew against the door like a piece of paper, while the slaughterer yelled at me: "You will report to-morrow at midnight, then we will finish you off!" I returned to my barrack, beaten and trembling. But I could not sleep for pain and terror. In the morning I immediately reported for work outside the camp, in order to go and see a friend of mine, a professor, during the lunch-hour. The Czech professor immediately went to the police-station, where he talked to the chief of police, saying that he would not tolerate the way in which I was being treated; if I had done something wrong, it would be in the competence of the People's Court to punish me. After these words the chief of police yelled at the professor that he would arrest him if he attempted to use his influence on behalf of a German. The professor answered that he could arrest him if he liked, but he would not accept the mistreatment of a decent and honest man whom he knew and for whom he would stand guarantee at any time. This conference was successful in the end and when I returned from my work in the evening and delivered my work-certificate, a policeman told me to fetch my belongings and to follow him. He took me to the police-barrack No. 6 and said that no one would molest me in there. But at midnight a sentry opened the doors of all cells and asked for the names of the inmates. I gave him a wrong name. The sentry slammed the door and yelled that the swine was nowhere to be found. In front of the barrack I heard Smetana, the slaughterer, scream: "We will search for that bastard until we find him and then we will finish him off; this time he won't get away." The guards had obviously got knowledge of the intervention on my behalf and they were seeking revenge.

Next morning I left again for work and went to the professor at noon. This time he succeeded in getting me employed as servant in a convent. I was sent for immediately. Thus I escaped from a sure death at Hodolein. Later on I learned how lucky I had been from my brother-in-law, Stephan Wallaschek, a locksmith from Olmütz, who had been interned in the camp at the same time as myself. During the first weeks he was ordered to dig up unexploded shells and was also forced to sleep at night together with other fellow-sufferers, in a squatting position. They were forbidden to lie down. During the daily parades he was beaten with belts and sticks. At night he was taken out of his cell, tied over four chairs and beaten into insensibility. After this he was burnt with cigarettes and if he then still showed any sign of life, the beating was continued. This procedure [had to] be endured four times. When my brother-in-law was so weak that he could only get along by resting his hands against the wall, he was released by the camp-judge with the following words: "Nothing has been found against you, see to it that you get home." With his kidneys loosened, his teeth smashed in and deaf in one ear he returned home. Even after a year he was still unable to walk a few hundred meters without pain.

When I was assigned to the convent as servant, the mother superior explained to me that I could not leave the house, since I should be in great danger. The Czech professor visited me every day, as did my wife, and I was able to tell them for the first time of my experiences in the camp. As a result of malnutrition I became ill in the convent and suffered from a carbuncle, as big as a fist, on the buttocks, so that I soon was unable to move. The doctors gave orders that I should be operated on, but no hospital would admit me as I was a German. A Czech doctor wrote on the back of the certificate of illness: Germans not admitted! My former doctor then attended me free of charge. After six weeks of illness I was turned out of the convent. Again I was ordered to the camp at Hodolein. In my fear I applied to a priest who succeeded in getting me a job as a workman at the municipal timber-yard. I was still in custody and had to work in all weathers; as a former town-councillor the Czechs liked best to have me sweep the streets in front of the town-hall, but we were no longer maltreated as in the camp at Hodolein. One day I was re-arrested by an agent of the secret police and taken to the police-station. After three days had passed I was put in jail for the second time and kept in suspense. A relative informed my wife, who went to the police in order to find out what I had been accused [of]. On her arrival she was told that there was no accusation at all and that

I would be released the next day. Months of imprisonment went by and on the urging of my wife a well-known lawyer took up the case. Obtaining sight of the court-records he saw that, in fact, there was no accusation against me and obtained my release after six months of imprisonment. On the date of my release I had been in detention for more than two years, in prison cells or in internment camps, without a concrete accusation, simply because of my German nationality.

The description above concerning my experiences in my homeland is in accordance with truth. I have endeavoured to be objective, and if anything seems exaggerated, my fellow-sufferers can confirm the correctness of my statements.

Pilsen, Report No. 1

Experiences in the district prison of Pilsen

Reported by Oskar Gellrich and Franz Reich - Report of November 23, 1945

Shortly after he had been brought in, Mr. Altherr from Wenussen near Pilsen was placed in the "correction cell" No. 23; he died there after three days from the torments inflicted on him. This happened between the 15th and the 20th of May [1945]. The prisoners here worked outside the building under the surveillance of the Red Guards, removing air-raid shelters. This job of clearing away the shelters and removing the bricks was speeded up by the guards, who wielded rubber-truncheons and shouted: "Get a move on". The bricks had to be carried away on the double, while the men were kicked in the region of the genitals and of the kidneys, apparently by order.

The diet consisted of 120 to 150 g of bread per day, in the morning a cup of black coffee, at noon either a thin soup or three or four small potatoes with a repulsive sauce, and in the evening a thin soup. The cooking was miserable and without salt.

After the prohibition of corporal punishment came into force in June 1945 the treatment improved. But as far as the diet was concerned there was no change. This may be seen from the fact that a typhoid fever epidemic broke out in the convict prison at Bory, to which some warders also fell victim. How many German prisoners were among the victims was not revealed.

Pilsen, Report No. 2

Convict prison at Bory, May 1945 to March 1946

Reported by Karl Oberdörfer Report of June 3, 1946

I was arrested on May 6, 1945 in Pilsen and was held in the district-prison until May 24th and afterwards in Bory until March 19th, 1946. I never knew the reason for my arrest. I was interrogated for the first time in April in the internment camp of Tremoschna, whence I had been taken from Bory. Even Dr. Krofta, who interrogated me, could not tell me the reason for my arrest.

I and the other inmates were seriously maltreated every day in the district prison of Pilsen and in the convict-prison of Bory. Only during the few days when American commissions visited us, was there no ill-treatment. In the cells at Bory we were knocked about every morning and then taken down to the cellar, one by one, where we had to lie down on a bench equipped with two boards. Our heads were pressed between the boards and then we were beaten with sticks and rubber-truncheons by the warders and also by Czech convicts until each of us lost consciousness. Then they threw us into a corner and poured cold water over us. Corporal punishment was at its worst on Saturdays and Sundays. My left leg was so badly damaged that the wounds are still open.

The food was absolutely insufficient. In Bory I lost about 34 kilos [75 pounds] between May 24, 1945 and March 19, 1946. The washing facilities were also insufficient. There was only one hand-basin and about 8 liters of water [2 gallons] for 30 men. During the whole time we only twice had a possibility of taking a bath. Spotted typhus broke out in August and lasted for about three months. Up to 15 men died every day and one day we counted 49. There was no medical attention at all. The prison doctor, Dr. Nemecek, took no notice of the Germans. Only at the instigation of the American commission were interned German surgeons employed.

The conditions in the internment camp of Tremoschna were a little better, but members of the Czech militia there also maltreated many of the internees. I myself was once knocked down in the latrine. I can confirm these statements on oath.

Pilsen, Report No. 3
A German family's account
Reported by Maria Schöber

On May 7, 1945 my husband and I were taken from our flat; at 9:30pm four Czech men with whips showed up and ordered us to come along with them at once. I was in my housecoat and was only allowed to quickly change into a dress, but I had to do so in front of a soldier. My husband took his air-raid suitcase along. Together with many other Germans we were herded into the Bory Prison. There, the women and men were separated. I sever saw my husband again.

Two days later I was given my husband's dirty collar and two blood-soaked handkerchiefs, and 300 Kronen of about 18,000 he had had.

In Bory we 35 women, with children and infants, were crowded into a cell meant for 4 people. We got food only once a day, and there was very little of it, and very bad.

Each night we heard the screams of people who were being beaten, and the shots from countless executions.

After three weeks I was sent away from there, and was taken instead in succession to the following camps: Pilsen-Karlov, Eisenach in Thuringia, and from there the Americans sent me back to Bohemia, specifically to Pilsenetz, Dobran and Staab.

The lodging and rations in the camps were mostly unfit for human beings. Often the men and women were quartered haphazardly together, with no washing facilities, the toilets in unimaginable condition, sheds and barracks so overcrowded with people that they could only lie squeezed tightly together. There were straw sacks and other pallets for only a few of us.

Children and adults alike died every day.

Rations consisted unvaryingly of small quantities of dry bread, black coffee and watery soups.

The treatment we got at the hands of the guards was uniformly very bad, downright subhuman. I only had to work in Bory - the younger women were herded to a work site two hours away by foot, had to walk on the gravel and were beaten with whips if they tried to avoid the gravel or could not do the work they had been assigned.

In September 1945 my daughter managed to have me released from the camps and sent to live with her.

To her repeated inquiries in Bory my daughter was always told that her father was well. In October 1945 I was permitted to send him a parcel, and did so. But this parcel was returned to me in November, with the notice: "Died on September 19." My daughter then asked again to at least be told the cause of death. She was given a printed form stating "stomach cancer". That's all we ever heard.

Pilsen, Report No. 4
Severe maltreatment, death, dysentery, typhus, dropsy
Reported by Franz Pilfusek - Report of August 7, 1946

I am 55 years old, was employed with the Railroad since 1913 and have never been politically active. I did my duty until May 18, 1945. Since May 6, 1945 American soldiers were quartered in my house, and we got along well with each other.

In the late afternoon of May 18, as my family and I sat unsuspectingly in our garden, three younger Czechs, among them a gendarme, suddenly burst into my yard and arrested me for no reason whatsoever. My wife fainted right then and there, and I was escorted to City Hall.

When I arrived, some other comrades were already there, with faces bloody and clothes dirty. Suddenly a younger Czech, Karl Petrikovic from Kosolup, lunged at me and punched me in the face. Some other comrades were also brought in, 11 in all. Then a large truck pulled up and we were forced to get in as fast as we could. In downtown Tuschkau four more comrades joined us, and then we were taken to Pilsen to the District Court. When we arrived there at about 8 o'clock p.m., a large crowd awaited us, and beat us as we got off the truck.

In the corridor of the District Court we had to stand facing the wall and to strip totally naked. We were not allowed to turn around or to say a word. Many a one of us was shoved with his face into the wall, and we were kicked, and hit from behind with rubber truncheons, rifle butts and the like.

After our personal data was briefly recorded in two offices, we were crowded into single cells in groups of 8, 10 or even more, without being given anything to eat. We were locked in, and the next day we were distributed amongst the common cells. The maltreatment and beatings continued. Rations were very scant and bad. For cooking they used stale, stinking water, and the unpalatable end results were prepared without any salt or spices and with dried vegetables and the like.

After a week, we several hundred men were herded back to Bory, and from there we were taken to the prison of Pilsen-Bory. Maltreatment and beatings by the staff were the order of the day there.

Many people died of the consequences of this inhuman, brutal treatment. There was no medical care for them.

For weeks on end we only got very small rations twice a day. Later on we got some spoonfuls of black coffee in the afternoons, and we were also assigned to various work details. It was impossible to sleep at night without being tormented by all kinds of vermin. Not until we were only skin and bones were we allowed to receive food parcels of up to 3 kg from our relatives.

Suddenly, various diseases such as dropsy, dysentery, and several form of typhus broke out. Then the doctors among the prisoners were told to treat us, but it was too late, and besides, there were no medications. In some divisions the death toll was said to be more than 70%. I myself spent almost two weeks laid up with raging fever and typhus.

In this way I and several comrades spent until March 1946, some of us even longer, in the horrible prison of Bory. From there we were transferred to the internment camp in Tremosna near Pilsen, where I was released on July 16, 1946, for health reasons, after having been ill for 14 months already. My son, who had also been interned in Tremosna after returning from American captivity, was released from there a week before I was, even though he had appealed to the Pilsen District Court to have me released for joint resettlement [expulsion] with him. At the court he was repeatedly told that my name was not on any prison list and that therefore I had not been reported for arrest.

Shortly after my arrest, my family was expelled from our own home, and the house was totally looted by Czechs. On my arrest a Czech gendarme had relieved me of my pocket-watch and pocket-knife, with the comment that I would get them back on my return.

In conclusion I want to mention that, in the district resettlement camp shortly before being transported off, my son was beaten by a Czech gendarme and robbed of his rubber raincoat, leather gloves and boots. After making a complaint to the Staff Captain stationed there, his things were returned to him.

Prague, Report No. 1
Prague, Events in May and June 1945
Reported by K. F., physicist - Report of December 27, 1946

May 5th 1945. Shortly after Prof. Gudden had telephoned us not to defend the Physics Institute under any circumstances (we had no arms anyhow, with the exception of three pistols), armed civilians entered the house and searched for weapons. There was just enough time to hide the pistols. After they had gone again, we hid the weapons with more care, since we were most unwilling to surrender them. All uniforms were also hidden. From the confusing news broadcasts of 'Radio Prague' it was impossible to gain a clear picture of the situation.

One hour later we were taken to the Police post in the Karlshof Church and interrogated. A low level air attack with bombs and gunfire started while the interrogation was going on. During this time we were left to our fate in the church. Afterwards members of the regular Police ordered us to go to Czernin Palace, where German Government offices were supposed to be. We were, however, to go one by one.

We went to collect our most important belongings. As I left the Institute with my assistant, Miss Tiedke, night was just beginning to fall. The shooting had almost ceased. We had hardly got as far as Appolinarius Str. - 12 yards away - when we were arrested by the nearest "partisan" and taken to the Psychiatric Hospital which seemed to have been turned into some kind of Headquarters. We were searched and our most valuable things were taken from us. Then we were sent to a room in sick quarters. The company was not very pleasant, but one was more or less undisturbed.

There was no change in our situation for the next two days, May 6th and 7th. Dr. Sturm, an acquaintance, visited us occasionally and told us what was going on.

Fighting was taking place about 12 yards from where we were, but the liberation we were longing for did not come.

On May 8th the fighting almost ceased, but the house was still under fire. This day I and four other men were put into a cellar. Food and treatment were still good.

On May 9th the guards were talking of the Russians being already in the City and there were some disappointed faces amongst them. Zero hour came at about 11 o'clock - a turning point for us. The mask fell, the individual disappeared and the mass only ruled.

Partisans crowded in from the street and drove some 30 men to Weinberg Avenue in front of the Mathematical Institute to clear away the barricades. The first one was cleared away quickly. Then there was the second, at the corner of Weinberg and Linden Avenue. This second barricade was built more solidly, with stones, earth, iron bars and so on. An inquisitive crowd had gathered and there were many agitators. The doings there on the afternoon of May 9th went beyond anything one could imagine.

After the first hour we were all covered with blood, as a result of kicks and blows upon the head and neck. Everything from shovels, iron bars and lead pipes up to poles was used on us.

The intoxication of the crowd was increased by the sight of blood. We were forced to go on with our work and dared not to rest for a second if we did not want to be beaten to death. There was a 70-year-old woman whose head had been shaven clean, the one-armed doorman of the Institute and a number of nurses in our group. Our shoes were taken away from us and we had to walk bare-footed over the glass shards on the ground.

Two shots fell near us, and we were driven along the street to serve as living firewall. I think there was none amongst us who did not hope for a sudden death. The snipers could not be found, I suppose they were from the same gang and did not know how to handle weapons properly. We were forced to parade then on glass shards and afterwards were driven to work again, where everything started once more.

What could demonstrate the general sadism better than the following incident: A partisan pointed his gun at my chest and I told him to press the trigger and get it over. He just grinned and forced me to go back to work, saying: *"To by šlo moc rychle"* ("That would be much too quick")!

When dusk came we could hardly stand. We were bent almost double, without the strength to stand up straight. When the crowd had dispersed, three policemen told us to stop work, and we dropped down like sacks. When I looked round I found that only 4 of the original 30 men remained. The others had been killed or taken away.

The policemen then took us behind the garden wall of the Institute and gave us a bit of rice and water. They kept looking around in fear of being seen by the partisans. Although we were starving we were too worn out to eat.

A few minutes later we were loaded into a lorry and driven to a former German College at Stefansgasse 22. All our belongings were left behind in the Institute and we never saw any of them again. So there we stood, barefoot, dirty, beaten up and near to collapse. It was impossible to sit down, because the mob was in charge again. The episode with the policemen had merely been a breather.

In one of the wings of the College we were forced to stand against the wall with our hands raised, until one after another collapsed. But then it really started. We were taken to another room, where what they called the *"Gestapáci"* were being kept. There we were chased about by a man, already hoarse with shouting orders. There were about 50 of us. We were ordered to hit each other in the face and when that was not done to the full satisfaction of our jailers, we were shown how to do it properly. When I collapsed again, a burning match was held to my toes until I came to. Then I had to get up again. The second time I was permitted to lie there a little longer. Then they trampled on my face, but since there was still no reaction on my part, I was left lying there. Anyone who put up the slightest resistance was shot dead.

During the night and on the following morning Miss Tiedke and several other women were led twice through the room; I have not seen her since. The morning of May 10th went by quietly. I tried to remove a glass splinter from my right toe, but it stuck in too deep; it was not removed until 2 months later. Until then I felt it with every step I took.

The afternoon of May 10th brought what was probably the most horrible incident of these days. A group of armed men came in and selected the 6 youngest and strongest men, I being one of them. After promising our guards that they would, if possible, bring us back alive, they took us to Wenceslas Square. The Square was packed with a yelling crowd and a path had to be cleared for us. I would have never believed that the human face could be degraded to such a grimace, the people looked like snarling dogs, showing their teeth, spitting and screaming at us. It took all the force available and the pistols of our guards to keep these creatures - one could no longer call them human beings - away from us. We reached the corner of Wassergasse and there we were confronted with our task: Three naked bodies, burned with petrol, were hanging by their feet from a large advertising board. The faces were mutilated beyond recognition with all the teeth knocked out, the mouths no longer anything but an opening full of blood. The roasted skin stuck to our hands as we half-carried and half-dragged the bodies to the Stefansgasse.

One of the passers-by tried to photograph our procession, but he was seen and beaten half to death.

After having put the dead bodies down we were ordered to kiss them on the mouth: "To jsou přece vaší bratří, ted' je políbejte!", they said. (These are your brothers, now kiss them!) I can still hear those words as though it had happened today. The will to live conquered all disgust and we pressed our lips into that pool of blood where the mouth should have been. I can still feel the icy-cold heads in my hands.

I had hardly washed the blood off my face and crawled instinctively into the furthest corner of our room when our guards entered, looking for the six of us; somehow I suddenly realized what was bound to happen now. We had seen far too much to be allowed to live. Only the dead would be silent.

With kicks and blows from rifle butts we were driven together in the centre of the room. While still being knocked about, we were asked our names and professions and then given the order: *"Do sklepa smrti!"* (To the death cellar!) Soon afterwards we found ourselves in a cellar, evidently the one with that ominous name. Since there was no doubt in our minds as to the final outcome of the affair, we had only one wish, that it might happen quickly. This, however, was not our "judges'" intention.

Apparently the guards in the house were already fed up with shows of this sort, so they brought in one of the "partisans" from the street, whose desires in this direction had not yet been satiated. Then began something which we had already witnessed repeatedly and had feared for ourselves. It was slow, sadistic torture to death, reaching a climax of blood lust bordering on insanity. These people wanted to see blood and more blood and to rip the life out of the wincing bodies of their victims piece by piece...!

The first of us was done with and lying on the floor in his own blood. Then the second had his turn. I should have been fourth. But as the second victim was lying on the floor the door opened and a Czech, who looked somewhat more intelligent and who, judging by the guards' manner, had a certain amount of authority, entered the cellar. Later I learned that he was a nephew of Minister Stránský. He asked who we were and after a good deal of hesitation, he had me and a boy of 17, a former member of the Hitler Youth, brought out of the room, because we were the only ones who could speak Czech and were therefore best suited to explain the situation.

When we passed the guard, he grinned and remarked that we were the first ones to leave the cellar alive. The others were left behind. We do not know what happened to them, for we have never seen them since.

In the meantime dusk had come. We were taken upstairs and told we could collect our belongings from the cupboard in the *"Gestapáci"*. In my case that was only a blanket which did not seem to belong to anyone and which I took possession of. I did not want to enter that room again and I was glad when I could no longer hear the screams of those being beaten there. A number of partisans had been "enjoying" themselves in that room again.

We were taken first of all to interrogation and following that to a classroom on the 4th floor. Roughly 60 people had been pressed into that narrow room, so that there was not sufficient space for everyone to lie down. I found a narrow strip of floor between one of the benches and the wall and there I rolled myself into the blanket. After the strain of the last hours I cared nothing about my surroundings. All I wanted was to rest. This state of mind lasted a week. - Slowly I began to wonder whether and where one could have a wash; but only after being urged by the women present did I look round for a possibility to have a shave. It all seemed to senseless and unimportant to me, after what had happened. After a few days had passed, without any more people being killed like vermin, hopes began to rise that one might be able to survive this hell after all. - But what did our surroundings look like! All the classrooms were packed with people: women, children, old and young men, all mixed together, and with hardly any sanitary arrangements. A great number of the inmates had lice and were consequently treated by the others like lepers. The food defied description. In the morning we received 1 or 2 slices of bread and a cup of coffee, at lunch-time a cup of water-soup and in the evening again coffee. So it went on for weeks and soon we were completely debilitated.

Everything was arbitrary and apt to sudden changes. All of us were at the mercy of our "rulers", especially the women. They were taken to interrogations during the course of which. they were forced to undress.

After a fortnight a colleague of mine from the Physics Institute was brought in, who, not suspecting anything, had just arrived in Prague on his way from Brüx. We remained together until I escaped. As a result of my experiences I avoided being selected for forced labour as far as I could. Only once I could not escape it. Luckily we were ordered to work in a quiet street. On this occasion I added a bread-basket to my belongings. I also inherited a pair of sandals from a dead man, but I still had no socks.

Three weeks later about 100 of us were brought to another school in Leihamt St. The food and treatment became much worse again. Our welcome was a dead body, shown to us with the explanation that this would happen to anyone trying to hide valuables. Following that, everything of value, including wedding rings, was taken from us.

Our general exhaustion soon reached a stage at which we had to lie down a great deal and where it took us several minutes to get up, owing to lack of blood in the head. But even this would have been bearable, had it not been for the intolerable uncertainty as to whether one would not serve as an object for the satisfaction of some partisan's blood lust.

It had become an unwritten law that anyone wishing to torture or kill a prisoner could come in from the street and select a victim for himself. One of these individuals came into our room every day, always ill-treating the same person in the most horrible way. There were no limits to his sadism. After lengthy ill-treatment he would hand his victim a gun with the safety catch on and tell him to shoot himself. The victim took it seriously, the more so as he considered this to be the only way out for himself. He put the gun to his head and pressed the trigger. Since the safety catch had not been released, the gun did not go off. The owner then released the catch, explaining apologetically that he had forgotten about it. The act was repeated, but again the gun did not fire, because it had not been loaded at all. The whole act had been staged in order to torture the victim. - One such victim jumped into the yard from the third floor and was killed instantaneously. This went on for a whole week. On the last day we were given nothing at all to eat. That night so many persons were pressed into the one room that most of them had to spend it standing up, with all the doors and windows closed.

The following morning - it must have been May 29th - about 800 of us were gathered in the back yard and searched again, though there was nothing more that could be taken from us. In the scorching sun, and still without any food, we were taken to the Moldau Railway Station. No incidents occurred on our way there; but entering the Station, the last man in the line, who was leading an old lady, was shot dead by a policeman on the demands of the mob. We were loaded onto coal wagons, about 60-70 persons in each, and were left standing there in the burning sun without food or drink until dusk. During that time Russians came and took from us whatever they thought desirable.

In the evening our wagons were coupled to a passenger train and we were relieved to discover that we were northbound, not travelling east. At Melnik we spent the night on the wagons. On the following morning, the third day without food, we were taken to the ramp were we had to line up neatly, and then the slave auction began. Farmers had arrived from the nearby villages and selected suitable "goods".

Together with my friend I was allotted to a group of 8 men and 11 women, designated for the village of Lhotka about 5 miles southeast of Melnik, close by the radio station. There all of us slept in the hayloft of a farm. To begin, we had a wash, and noticed for the first time how our bones were sticking out. The first food I took I could not digest, I was sick and had to lie down the whole day. Slowly, and by taking small amounts at a time, my stomach finally got used to receiving food again.

Every night Russians came and raped the women. So each of us was billetted with the farmer for whom we had to work. The food was good and I had no complaints as far as treatment was concerned. I had a palliasse and the farmer gave me a pair of boots for work.

Meanwhile I had reached an understanding with my friend that we would escape one day. Once I had escaped it would certainly be impossible for others to get away, so I crept through the village to my friend's billet only after I had left that farm. Everything went well and I woke him up. But he decided that it was too dangerous for him and he would not risk an escape. He gave me a pound of bread and I stole away again by the same route. I collected my bread basket, which I had hidden in a ditch, and as I left the village in the direction of the Melnik radio tower, a strip of light could already be seen on the horizon in the east.

Prague, Report No. 2
Prague-Theresienstadt, maltreatment of old women
Reported by Anna Seidel - Report of July 4, 1947

I am 67 years old, the widow of an engineer, and have lived in one and the same house in Prague XVI-Smichow, at Hollergasse 16, for 40 years. In all those years I never once had the slightest quarrel or difference of opinion with anyone, neither in everyday matters nor in terms of politics, which is something I was never active in, in any way. Nonetheless four civilians (partisans) armed with fixed bayonets dragged me from my home at 3 o'clock on May 9. In the corridor four elderly women stood with their faces to the wall, "hands up", with a man armed with a rifle standing behind each. They included Frau Kogert, 67 years old, the widow of a senior engineer, Frau Arbes, 70 years old, the widow of a professor, and her daughter, all of whom lived in the surrounding houses. We were led to the suburb of Radlitz, into a factory where we were deprived of everything, truly everything we had on us: money, papers, jewelry etc. We were maltreated, kicked in the back and beaten so badly that for weeks afterwards we were black and blue all over. Our hair was brutally chopped off, then they painted black swastikas on our foreheads, poured several buckets of cold water over us, loaded us onto a truck, where we had to remain in a kneeling position, and drove us like that slowly through the streets while still continually beating us. At the same time we had to shout: *"My jsme Hitler-kurvy"* = "We are Hitler-whores," and if we didn't shout this loudly or convincingly enough they landed further blows, ever harder, on us - on helpless and defenseless old women! In this way we finally arrived at the police headquarters, where we had to spend all night in the yard in our wet clothes. The next morning we were taken to the prison in Pankratz, where we had to stay for four weeks. After that they carted us in open coal wagons to the "Small Fortress Theresienstadt", where we spent an entire year locked up behind barred windows and forced to do heavy physical labor: entraining coal on the railroad, also lumber, furniture, clearing barracks, cleaning overflowing toilets whose doors could hardly even be opened any more, and doing duty without any protection or sanitary measures in undescribable conditions in typhus barracks. All of this was done in striped prison garb, which we had been given immediately upon arrival after we had had to strip totally naked and to throw our clothes onto a big pile, of course never to see any of them ever again!

The martyrdom inflicted on the men was horrifying (they had to roll around and crawl in sharp gravel and if they did not do it vigorously enough they were tormented with kicks). And it was horrible to see how the people died left, right and center! Our rations consisted of two cups of watery soup per day, usually none or only very few potatoes, 200 g bread, and bitter black coffee. Only at the very end did we receive a little sugar and margarine, which made us conclude that our release was imminent, which was the correct conclusion since our deliverance came in mid-May.

I am ready and willing to take this my report on my oath at any time before the appropriate authorities.

Prague, Report No. 3
Inhuman atrocities in Prague
Reported by Marianne Klaus Report of June 26, 1946

On May 9, 1945 my husband Gotthard Klaus, 66 years old, was beaten to death in the police headquarters in Prague. I saw him for the last time on May 10, at 4 o'clock in the morning. He had fist-sized lumps on his face, his nose and mouth were a bloody mass, and his hands were hugely swollen. I also saw how two SS-men were beaten in the face with whips until they collapsed, covered in blood, then they were kicked in the stomach until blood burst out, and then they were dragged down some stairs by the feet. I saw how a Wehrmacht assistant was stoned until she collapsed, and how she was then hanged from a store awning. On the Day of Revolution I saw an SS-man hanging from a candelabra, hung by one foot and burning from the head up. That was May 9, 1945 in Prague.

Prague, Report No. 4
The fate of German women in 1945
Reported by Helene Bugner - Report of June 7, 1946

From the 5th of May, 1945 onwards, the Germans in Prague were not allowed to leave their apartments. On May 9th I was knocked about by the janitor in my apartment, then, without luggage, led away in order to take part in the work of removing the barricades in the streets of Prague. My labour group consisted of 20 women, among them some 60 to 70 years old. We were in the charge of Professor Zelenka. When we stepped out of the house, Professor Zelenka handed us over to the mob with the following words: "Here are the German bitches for you." Calling us German whores, the mob forced us to kneel down and then our hair was cut with bayonets. Our shoes and stockings were taken off, so that we had to walk barefoot. With each step and at every moment we were inhumanly beaten with sticks, rubber truncheons etc. Whenever a woman sank to the ground, she was kicked, rolled in the mud and stoned. I myself fainted several times; water was poured over me and I was forced to continue working. When I was quite unable to do any more work, I received a kick in the left side which broke two of my ribs. During one of my fainting fits they cut a piece of about 4 square cm (about 0.6 square inches) out of the sole of my foot. These tortures lasted the whole afternoon. Among us were women far advanced in pregnancy and nursing mothers, who were ill-treated in the same way. In the course of 3 or 4 days one of the women had a miscarriage.

In the evening we went home. I was so disfigured from the maltreatment and tortures which I had suffered that my children no longer recognised me. My face was crusted with blood and my dress reduced to blood-stained rags; two women living in our house committed suicide in despair, another woman became insane. Our bodies were swollen and covered with black and blue marks, and all of us had open head wounds. Since none of us was able to move, we were kept in custody in a small apartment in our house for three weeks. During this time we were subjected to unendurable mental tortures by threats that our children would be taken away from us and that we should be deported to Siberia.

Three weeks later we were sent to the camp at Hagibor. There were 1200 persons lodged there in four barracks. All fell sick with hunger dysentery, for the diet consisted of a cup of thin water-gruel twice a day for children and for the grown-ups a cup of black coffee with a thin slice of bread morning and evening and a watery soup at noontime. The privies could be used only three times a day at certain hours, although everybody was suffering from dysentery. There was forced labour for everybody. Each evening the labour groups returned to the camp badly beaten up. Medical care was completely lacking. A German doctor, who was also a prisoner, did what was possible, but he had nothing, neither medicaments, bandages nor the most common instruments, as for instance a clinical thermometer; thus women who arrived at the camp with bullet wounds or other injuries had to remain virtually without medical attention. Epidemics of measles, scarlet fever, whooping-cough and diphtheria broke out, which could not be dealt with.

One day we were ordered to line up for roll call. We had to stand in the open air for seven hours, while a terrific thunderstorm with hail and a high wind, which unroofed two barracks, burst right over our heads. The very same day we were transported from the station in open coal wagons, which were in a bad state of repair. The space between us was so small that there was hardly room for us to stand. At 3 o'clock in the morning we arrived at Kolin while it was pouring rain. At Kolin we were lodged in the heavily damaged school. Two women died of exhaustion while marching from the station to this school. During the march we were struck repeatedly with rubber truncheons until almost everybody was bleeding. Next day we were taken from the school to the building of the Czech Red Cross. The Czech Red Cross nurse admitted groups of Russian soldiers to the camps each night and called their attention to several attractive women and girls, who were raped, sometimes up to 45 times a night, in the most inhuman and barbarous way. One could hear their desperate cries for help during the whole night. Next morning some of them showed the marks of bites on their faces, their noses were bitten off and they were lying there without any medical care, for in this camp also no professional medical attention was available.

After several days I was sent together with 45 other women, among them a woman with 6 small children, to a Czech estate, in order to work there. Here we stayed for 3½ months until all of us, including myself, broke down from exhaustion and debilitation. Receiving the same kind and the same amount of food as at Hagibor, we had to do the hardest agricultural work, even on Sundays.

The children received the same food as the adults, without one drop of milk, so that three out of four died. All the children under a year old had already died in the camp in Prague.

While we were working we were watched by armed guards, who abused and tormented us every day. Became of my fractured ribs I was unable to do any work where I had to bend forward, therefore I hoed the turnips in a kneeling position. While I was working the guards would insult me and strike me. When my child, like the others, got scarlet fever and I implored the foreman to get the doctor, he simply told me, "The *Národní výbor* has ordered that Germans should not get medical attendance."

Every night the villagers sent groups of Russian soldiers to our lodgings, who raped the women. For 3½ months we lived in this way, working hard from sunrise to sunset, constantly mistreated and insulted, with no food worth mentioning, the children without control or care, scabby and full of lice, we ourselves delivered over to Russian soldiers during the night. Cleaning facilities were non-existent, since we were not even allowed to have a pail. Besides vermin we all suffered from all sorts of open, festering wounds. I had one festering boil next to another on my right hand, the hand with which I had to work.

A doctor, who was one of our fellow prisoners, explained to me that he was not allowed to accept exhaustion as grounds for incapacity for work, otherwise he himself would get into very serious trouble. As a consequence of my fractured ribs I contracted pleurisy and was sent to Prague, in order to be transferred to Germany. When I arrived in Prague, the transfers had already been suspended and I stayed in a camp there until Christmas. The camp was so crowded that none of the inmates had enough room to lie down.

We and our children had to sleep in a squatting position on the bare floor, without straw, while the Czechs who had been interned were lodged in two barracks furnished with beds. Whenever foreign observers visited the camp, they were only taken into these two barracks.

The sanitary arrangements beggared description. Often there was no water for three days. Children and adults contracted scurvy of the mouth and festering abscesses. Oozing exanthemas, tuberculosis, spotted typhus, smallpox and children's diseases broke out. Every child had rickets. Women gave birth to children while wearing the same dresses and underwear they had been wearing for months. Most of the infants died. Only a few mothers were able to feed their babies.

In the camp at Prague there was a dark cell. Inmates of the camp were confined there for quite minor offences for as long as three days, without food.

As a result of an intervention by the British Embassy, by whom I had been employed as secretary for 12 years, I was released and sent to the town of Asch at Christmas 1945.

I am prepared to swear to the truth of these statements.

Prague, Report No. 5

The ordeal of an inventor

Reported by Johann Schöniger Report of October 14, 1946

Until 1939 I was in London, where I owned a store. At the same time I maintained an experimental laboratory in Prague, where I worked on various inventions. In May 1945 I was arrested by the Czechs and imprisoned in Prague Public School XIII , where I was literally tortured, as they wanted to extort details about my inventions. They knocked nails into the soles of my feet and pounded on them with iron bars, and generally beat me up on a daily basis. My colleague Schubert was beaten to death. Then I was taken to the penal camp Ratisko near Stechovice, where like all the other inmates I was beaten daily for 14 months. We were robbed of everything we had, even the clothes we wore were literally taken off our backs by the guards. In the winter we had to do heavy manual labor, barefoot. After the camp was disbanded in June of this year, I was sent to the Hagibor camp near Prague, where conditions were a little better.

My wife and our children, aged 4 months and 5½ years, spent this time in the concentration camp Melnik-Pechovka, where she and the children had to do day-labor for a farmer in the area. Our clothes are totally ragged and tattered.

Prague, Report No. 6

Blood bath in the Scharnhorst School concentration camp

Reported by Hildegard Hurtinger - Report of November 6, 1946

I have lived in Prague since 1923, with the exception of a five-year period from 1938 to 1942, dring which time I lived in Teplitz. On May 5, 1945 a Czech mob took me from my home and, beating and clubbing me all the while, dragged me by the hair some 500 meters into the Scharnhorst School, where I was robbed of everything so that all I had left were my stockings and the dress I wore. I was immediately interrogated by a Czech commissar, a woman, and accused of having sent 16 Czechs to die in a concentration camp - in 1942, at a time when I was not even in Prague. Every time I denied an allegation I was slapped about the head. Then I was taken into so-called Separation, where I and my fellow prisoners, men and women, were brutally maltreated. At night all inmates were repeatedly called out into the yard, and groups of 10 men, women and children were counted out - among them my two brothers and their families - and shot before the eyes of the other inmates. My brother's youngest child was only 5 months old. Then the rest of us had to dig graves, strip the bodies, and bury them. At other times as well, day or night, the guards would take random shots at the prisoners. Thousands died in this way. One such time a bullet grazed my neck. I stayed where I lay under the corpses for a whole day and night because I did not dare get up. Then Revolutionary Guardsmen stepped over the bodies and blindly stabbed any who still lived with their bayonets. My left hand was impaled in the process.

In Separation we got nothing at all to eat. Children were given spittoons as 'meals'. Those children who refused them were beaten. Armed Czech women dragged pregnant prisoners from the cells and out into the yard, where they stripped and beat them, then stuffed them into latrines and beat them until their bellies burst. I myself had to help carry off the bodies of the women who had died that way. For many days at least ten women died in this way every day. During the day groups of six to eight women were taken to work in St. Gotthard Church. There we had to kiss the dead bodies that were already rotting, pile them up, and clean the church floor of the blood that ran there by getting down on our knees and licking it up. A Czech mob supervised this work and beat us. This went on for days. I also saw how candle flames were used to burn swastikas into the palms of German men, among them engineer Färber from the German-Czech Technical College.

On May 20 we were led to Wenzel Square where German boys and girls, and soldiers too, were hung alive by their feet from lamp posts and trees and, in front of our very eyes, were doused with petroleum and set on fire. I myself had to stay at the Scharnhorst School until September 20 of last year. The brutalities went on the entire time, without respite. Then I was transferred to Pankratz, from where I was sent to work at the Philipps Factory in Prague. On November 6 of last year I was brutally beaten with a rubber truncheon by the camp leader there because I had expressed a wish to go to church, as it was my wedding anniversary. - Later, our treatment improved considerably, as did our rations.

Prague, Report No. 7
Inhuman atrocities
Reported by Alfred Gebauer Report of June 21, 1946

On May 6, 1945 I was arrested in Prague for the crime of being a German, and was interned successively in the concentration camps set up in the Ministry of Education, the Scharnhorst School, the Wehrmacht prison, Riding School, Stadium and Work House until late September, when I was committed to the court prison of Troppau.

From there I was released for resettlement [expulsion] on June 12, 1946. I am a seriously disabled ex-serviceman, and on my arrest Vlasov soldiers slapped me about the head and robbed me of everything I had. I became an eyewitness to the following events:

In the Scharnhorst School female employees of the SS had to roll around in a shallow pond, entirely naked as the clothes had been torn off their bodies. Then they were maltreated with kicks and blows from rifle butts until they lost consciousness. In the Stadium, before 5,000 inmates, SS-soldiers were hunted with submachine guns like in a turkey-shoot. 20 SS soldiers were shot in the process. Some were forced to jump into the latrine, where they were shot with submachine guns. Their bodies were left in the latrine, and the other inmates had to keep using it. On one transport some women were so badly beaten with rubber truncheons that they collapsed, covered in blood. In the Riding School some inmates were randomly selected and beaten so badly, before the eyes of all the others, that they collapsed in bloody heaps. Then they were dragged out, and we heard several shots ring out. Many Czech collaborators were also beaten to death there.

For the first five days after my arrest, we got no rations other than one bucket of water for 600 of us. On the sixth day we got a sugar cube and one biscuit. From the 7th day on all we got was watery soup, and consequently from 15 to 20 people died of debilitation each day.

On my committal to Troppau prison I was badly beaten. For eight weeks the food parcels which my sister sent me in prison there were misappropriated by the guards.

I am prepared to take this statement on my oath.

Prague, Report No. 8
Prague-Wokowitz, penal camp Kladno
Reported by engineer Franz Rösch Report of June 26, 1946

From June 12 until 15, 1945 I was assigned to the burial detail in Prague-Wokowitz. In Prague-Wokowitz I saw thousands of German soldiers and civilians, men and women and even boys 10 years and up, being brutally murdered. Most of them were bludgeoned to death by the Revolutionary Guard; a smaller number were shot. Most were shot only to torture them with flesh wounds, and then beaten to death. Often the dreadfully beaten bodies were rubbed with hydrochloric acid to heighten their agony. One Frau Blume from Berlin had to record the deaths. In some cases people with tight-fitting rings had their fingers torn off while still alive. The bodies were buried in mass graves in Wokowitz near the cemetery.

I then worked on a farm until May 2, 1946, even though I had lost my right arm in the war. I had to load manure and do other hard farmwork with my left arm. When I could no longer do these jobs, I was sent to the penal camp of Kladno on May 2, 1946. There I saw how prisoners were basted with hot tar on their bare skin and on their backs and buttocks, and were beaten terribly. I myself was beaten every day during the two weeks I was there. My right kidney was knocked loose, so that I had to be sent to the hospital in Schlan.

Prague, Report No. 9
Concentration camp Prosetschnitz
Reported by Dr. Pohlner - Report of June 26, 1946

From January 10 until May 3, 1946 I served as physician in the concentration camp Prosetschnitz near Prague. The camp was surrounded with barbed wire, decorated with the Soviet Star and guarded by 100 SNB armed with submachine guns. When I left there were still more than 8,000 prisoners there. The quarters were bearable, and we were able to move around the camp somewhat. On the other hand, the slightest violation of the orders, which the camp administration issued daily and which can easily be described as harassment, was immediately punished by withholding rations from the entire camp, including the children, for one day. In view of the already insufficient rations this had disastrous effects. Normal rations consisted only of black, barely sweetened coffee twice daily, two cups watery potato soup and 250 g bread. That comes to 400-500 calories at most. Yet everyone in the camp had to work. Without exception, if a prisoner did not receive extra food from relatives outside the camp, the men would die within 3 to 4 months, the women within 4 to 5, from *instritio universalis* marked by total emaciation, swelling of the limbs and face, and sudden heart failure. Mortality due to starvation accounted for 5 to 10 deaths every day. Added to that were just as many deaths from typhus, paratyphus, dysentery, scarlet fever, diphtheria, tuberculosis and normal internal diseases which could not be treated or cured due to the lack of a reasonable selection of medications and dietary treatment. The camp leader, Mahol, only ever responded to appeals and requests with a shrug of refusal. In April the camp was inspected by a committee from the International Red Cross, with whom I spoke personally and who also promised assistance. From the following day on rations got even worse, and remained so. The treatment of the inmates also grew harsher, for example, even the children were beaten. Children and teenagers got the same rations, and if they were under 6 years of age they might get a bit of milk every now and then. Infant mortality was very high, and nursing mothers got no extra food other than a double helping of soup at noon.

Prague, Report No. 10

The camp at Rusin, the march to Dresden

Reported by Hans Freund - Report of March 9, 1950

I was captured by partisans in Prague on May 5th, 1945, and taken to Rusin, where we stayed four weeks. The treatment was bad, we were thrashed with clubs and rifle-butts, then forced to stand with our faces to the wall and our hands up; anyone who moved was knocked down. I saw a Sudeten German private, 23 or 24 years old, being shot down for answering in Czech.

Our daily food ration consisted of 40 g of bread, a cup of soup, sauerkraut and coffee. Four weeks later we were taken over by the Russian army and sent to Dresden.

I myself witnessed the following scene at the Sparta Square in Prague: we were marched to the well-known sports ground and after being commended to "halt" we were asked for our German military papers. About 50 men handed over the pay-books while some 300 - and I was among these - did not deliver them. The 50 men were rounded up on the sports ground and had to stand facing the wall. Afterwards the gates were shut and the 50 men were mowed down from two sides with old German machine guns, which were served by two women.

Three Czech civilians, wearing red badges, mistreated us severely at the jail in Rusin during those four weeks. Their names were Josef Navrátil, Miloslav Kopecký, Pokorný.

When the Russian army took over the prisoners, a Czech lieutenant named Jara Procházka was shot by an adjutant because he attempted to torture us, which the Russian Colonel would not allow.

While marching to the Sparta sports ground I saw a group of Czech women take a German woman of 20 or 21 years of age, who was just getting into a truck, tie her up together with her child and throw both into the river Moldau.

On our march from Rusin to Dresden, elderly people who were unable to walk any further were simply shot by the escorting partisans.

We had to march in terrible heat (June 1945) and we received no water, so that it was no wonder that elderly people collapsed.

I am prepared to take an oath on these statements.

Prague, Report No. 11
My experiencs in Czechoslovakia 1945-46
Reported by W. L. - Report of June 21, 1947

Since November 1944 I had been lying in the military hospital VII (Prague-Kleinseite, formerly the Tyrs House) with a shattered forearm. In April I was already allowed to go out with my arm in a sling. Everything in Prague was quiet and peaceful at that time. It was perfectly safe for me to move around. The Czechs showed themselves friendly and obliging.

On May 4, 1945 all was quiet, even the three-days public mourning for Hitler's death, which had been ordered by Frank, the Minister of State, was carried out without incident. No one would have thought that the Czechs, who during the whole of the war had dared to make very little resistance to the German Military Authorities, would after the capitulation give way to a paroxysm of cruelty against defenceless people. Still less that they would not even spare wounded soldiers, women, children and other helpless persons.

The following is a rough sketch of my own experiences and observations:

During the evening hours of May 4th the Czechs in Prague began to take down the German sign-boards and posters and refused to answer any questions asked in German. The attitude of the police remained passive.

On the morning of the 5th of May things were still quiet. I had had to leave the hospital, which was very overcrowded, and was convalescing at home. On this day I saw no danger in going in my Lieutenant's uniform from my flat to the hospital, in order to have my bandages changed. About 11 o'clock great tumult was to be heard on the streets. The houses were suddenly decorated with Czech flags. People were embracing one another everywhere and waving Czech flags or throwing flowers.

I left the hospital with my arm in the sling, pushed my way through the crowd, jumped in a passing streetcar and travelled across the city to my house. Apart from a few insults and curses I experienced no further signs of hostility. During this time, as I heard later on, weapons were being distributed to the Czechs in the area around the Bubner Station and shots were fired at a German ambulance train. In the meantime the Czechs had taken the Prague radio station in a surprise attack. They broadcast incessant appeals to the population, inciting them to revolt and repeating the savage slogan: *"Smrt němcum!"* (Death to the Germans!)

After my return I saw from the window of my parents' flat a German soldier covered with blood, who was lying near the station in the blazing sun. He was being brutally maltreated by the Czech who was guarding him. Meanwhile I had changed into civilian clothes and pretended to be a university student. Nothing was done to the inmates of our house, and save for small-arms and cigarettes nothing was taken away. That night and the following Sunday, May 6th, brought no special events, except that we were called up to build barricades and received orders to leave our flat and to take refuge in the air-raid shelter. It was not until the late evening of the 6th of May that a number of men came into the cellar and called out: "All men out to come with us!" I was the only one of my family living at home and my mother clung to me and wanted to come with me. She was torn from my side and thrust back again. We were not even able to take leave of one another. I was not to see my mother again for the next two years.

We were taken to the Oko (Orion) movie theatre and shut up there together with men, women and children from other districts. Our treatment was not bad at first; the guards did not take much notice of us and we were given a bit of bread and soup to eat.

On May 8th we had reason to hope for an early release, for the shooting increased nearby and the guards showed growing nervousness and anxiety. A few even began to talk to the Germans and sought reassurance that the latter had been well treated so that the advancing German soldiers would deal gently with them when they came. But night fell without any change in our situation. That was the night which brought the end of the war and with it the end of the battle for Prague, the arrival of the first Russians, and the time of murder and atrocities.

At noon of May 9th armed louts with red badges stormed yelling into the theatre. With kicks and blows from their rifle butts they drove groups of 10 to 15 men (and later women) together and herded them out to tear down barricades. I was standing with a group of Austrians and called out that we were Austrians. But even that did not help much. We were nevertheless driven out together with the others. However the "guard" did tell us that he would take note of the fact that we were Austrians. We all had to run through the streets with our hands up. We felt the first blows of the crowd. A few streets further on stood a big barricade which we were to clear away. It was 2 to 3 meters high and consisted chiefly of paving-stones, iron bars and barbed wire. We pulled it down and replaced the paving-stones.

A big crowd of spectators gathered. Swastikas were chalked on our backs and marked on our foreheads with hot tar, and in some cases shoes and new articles of clothing were taken from us. The whole afternoon I had only been able to work with my right hand, since my arm had been in a cast until recently; the wound was not yet completely healed and was festering. My constant reminder that I was an Austrian, and my knowledge of Czech, saved me from the fate of the many who were killed on that day.

We were forced to greet passing Russian cars by kneeling down and bending our heads to the ground. Sweat and blood stuck to our bodies, our tongues were swollen so that we could hardly speak. The sun burned down. It was impossible to straighten up, let alone to rest or to get a drink of water. During all this time we were being driven by kicks and blows. Towards evening our work was finished. On the way back we were forced to run, to lie down momentarily and to hop in a squatting position. On the way I received a blow on my wounded arm from a Czech woman with a fence-post; it paralysed my arm. Only a part of the work group returned. Most people were wounded and the women had had their heads shaved.

Even at night we were deprived of the rest we longed for. Russians and Czechs came for the German women and girls. Desperate shrieks could be heard from the entrance hall. Men who attempted to protect their wives were struck down. Children, clinging to their mothers, were taken along to witness their violation. As a result of being raped my former dancing-teacher went out of her mind. In desperation a number of people tried to commit suicide by cutting their wrists, hanging themselves or throwing themselves down from the balcony of the movie theatre. I myself protected a 16-year-old girl by hiding her under the seats and lying down above.

During the next few days all our personal possessions down to pocket-knife, nail-file and comb (and of course our money) were taken from us under threat of death. Every day men and women were fetched for some kind of work and often very few of them returned. 14 days later came Whitsuntide. On this day, as I was told later on by a fellow-prisoner, one Dr. Küttner from Halberstadt, a numberof Germans were tortured to death in the riding-school on Hybernerplatz. The death-cries mingled with the solemn sound of the organ from the nearby church, where these same people were "devoutly" praying to the God of Charity and Mercy!

There was nothing to be done but to submit oneself to the will of God and to suffer with patience, if one wished to avoid an agonizing death. I have often wondered what it was that suddenly awakened such an abysmal hatred in the hearts of these people. After all, they had come through the war better than any other nation in Europe. The Czechs had been treated by the Germans as equals and were better nourished than many Germans. One had sat next to the Czechs in railroads, movies or cafés; no difference was made - except that the Czechs did not have to enlist and had no losses to lament.

During the week after Whitsuntide we were all driven out of the movie theatre and into the former Scharnhorst-School in Prague-Dejwitz. At the entrance we saw the welcoming inscription *"Koncentracní tábor"* (concentration camp). And, indeed, they did their best there to surpass every-thing that they had heard of the Nazi concentration camps. We lay there on the floors of the empty classrooms. There was no soap to wash ourselves with, but instead there were 25 lashes for each louse found, and a warning to that effect was posted in the corridor.

Every day at the roll-call shootings and beatings took place. If one sank to the ground with a bullet in his stomach, his neighbour had to remain standing motionless. The bodies would be several days in the yard before they were buried somewhere without ceremony. Children and old people died off, for the rations were bad and ridiculously small.

I was glad when one day they began to ship us off for agricultural work. On my reminder that I was a wounded officer I was assured that I should be put in a PoW-camp. On the other hand the camp commandant, a Czech Staff Captain, shouted at me that my war-injury was a disgrace to me and no honor.

On June 2nd 1945 I marched off with new hope, together with several German soldiers who had worked for the Russian army for a considerable time as drivers and had been sent home, but whom the Czechs had arrested. We were being sent under guard to the PoW-camp at Prag-Motol.

There, I thought, the rules of the Geneva Convention would obtain and I should be treated as a human being again and not as a thing below the level of an animal. This opinion was first shaken when I saw a man with a red arm-band and a rubber truncheon standing at the entrance of the camp.

We were drawn up in the courtyard and thoroughly searched. They could not find much on me, but they deprived the Russians' former drivers of all their tobacco, canned food, bread and money. Then, as was often the case in other camps, we had to strip to the waist and were examined to see if we had the SS tattoo-mark. There was one of those among the soldiers and he was at once beaten up by the camp commandant, Staff Captain Masanka - a Czech staff officer -, personally. When he raised his hand and swore to God that he had never been in the SS, but had received the same mark as a returning settler from Eastern Europe, the Staff Captain struck him in the face and said: "You swear to God? But the Germans have no God!" The poor man disappeared into the SS-cellar, from which no one escaped alive.

The was no improvement here in treatment or in rations. In the morning we would find men, who had gone to the latrine during the night, lying shot and bled to death in front of it. The only difference from the other camp was that here there were only men who had been accustomed by the war to exhaustion and danger and that to our own suffering there was not added that of seeing the torments of desperate women and innocent and once-happy children.

I myself together with most of the other officers was commanded to the most strenuous tasks, as for instance carrying cupboards through the town, etc. More than once I was struck in the face with a leather strap by one Sergeant Kuzbach.

The prisoners were so undernourished that many of them lost all self-control and during working times they fell on every dust bin and grubbed in it for mouldy crusts of bread or potato peels whenever the guards did not prevent them.

While at work I got to know a 21-year-old guard who was unexpectedly friendly and with whom I would talk in Czech about various things. He said among other things that the present rulers of Czechoslovakia should not get the idea that they could set up the same regime as before 1939. "During our being in Germany", he said, "we saw and received what we workers should demand and what they will have to give us! So I do not belong to any of the old parties, I am a Communist!" This man was perhaps the first Czech who worked in German factories during the war and was well paid and looked after, who did not afterwards claim that he had been in a concentration camp, like all the others did.

He also told me about a horrifying murder in May 1945. According to his story a Czech girl in Prague-Weinberge, who had been the mistress of an SS-man and was now pregnant, had been dragged into the streets by the Czechs and bestially murdered. She lay there with her breasts cut off and her stomach slashed open. Journalists, including foreign correspondents, were called; and finding out from her papers that she was a Czech, they concluded that the atrocity could only have been perpetrated by the Germans. In that way, the stories of German bestialities during the Czech revolution originated.

This same guard, under whose supervision we were working in the suburb of Wrschowitz, escorted me to a Czech family whom I knew well and who lived in the neighbourhood. The father of the family, a childhood friend of my father's, whom my father had helped to a good position during the occupation, was not at home. All I wanted was to give a sign of life, so that at least one being on earth should know that I was still alive and was in the camp at Motol, for in those days one still had to expect to be killed any day.

The woman got such a shock at the sight of me that she would have liked to throw me out of the house at once, if the guard had not been standing there. Her daughter began to call down curses upon the Germans and said that if she had got her hands on one during the revolution, she would have finished him off herself.

The guard took the woman aside and said to her in a low voice that she should give me something to eat, since we suffered so much from hunger. He admitted to me afterwards that he had done so because he was sure that I should find it beneath my dignity, especially in this situation, to beg for anything. So at least I got a piece of bread and marmalade, which the woman wrapped up and gave to the guard with an anxious look, saying: "I give it to you, do what you like with it. I don't want to have anything to do with it."

Unfortunately we had this guard only for three days. He was the only humane Czech whom I met during my imprisonment.

As a result of hard work and bad food the condition of my injury became worse. The scar had opened along its whole length, 12 by 6 cm, and was festering badly. Other small wounds on my body were also festering and would not heal. At last I could work no longer and was put into the so-called hospital-camp of Motol. It consisted of several stone buildings around the court-yard. We slept in the former hay loft above the empty stables with nothing under us and I, like most of the others, also without a blanket. There the sick and wounded lay crowded closely together. The doctors, who were also prisoners, could do practically nothing, for they had no medicaments, not even enough paper bandages.

The distinction between officers and men consisted only in the fact that the ill and wounded officers were ordered to coal-shovelling and street-cleaning almost every day. For the amusement of the Czechs we had to parade and drill with our brooms. (*Slowe arms!* Order arms!)

In the opposite building was the notorious SS-cellar. There in a little coal cellar 80 to 100 men were jammed. Day after day they were dragged out and tortured. As soon as the guards were fired with giving beatings, the prisoners were made to face each other and to box each other's ears. Now and then they stripped them naked and then beat them. The men looked like skeletons, for they were also being slowly starved. Sometimes on the return to the cellar they stood each man in turn in the doorway and kicked him down the steps. If anyone was skilful and agile enough to make a good landing below, he was fetched up again and the same thing was repeated, or else they made him kneel down in the threshold, facing outwards, and bend his head. Then he received such a kick in the face that he plunged down the steps backwards.

While this was going on we were driven up to our loft, but we could observe what was happening through cracks in the door and gaps in the roof, so far as our horror did not prevent us from doing so.

The number of inmates of the cell increased constantly. There were even 14-year-old boys from the Hitler-Youth Home Guard. When a second room was also overfilled, they started "to make room". To prevent the guards becoming infected by the diseases, which were rapidly getting the upper hand in the cellar, chloride of lime was often sprinkled in through the barred windows. They also shot blindly into the windows with automatic pistols.

At night regular mass-executions were carried out. First in line were all the wounded with their casts and bandages. All the inmates faced certain death. Small wonder that two youths, who had to carry out the excrement bucket, dropped it suddenly and, calling to us: "Love to the Homeland! Love to Germany!", ran off as quickly as their feeble legs would carry them. They ran to their death, for there was no way out of the camp. Soon shots rang out and their sufferings were over.

Those executed were mostly shot - not in the neck or head, but through the stomach, so that they would linger for hours in agony. During these times, mostly at night, we were not allowed to leave the loft; we were all ill with kidney trouble as a result of sleeping on the cold tile floor and needed urgently to get out. But whenever anyone tried to do so, the guards fired from below. Nor were we allowed to have an excrement bucket up there. Later on, a group of ten men was usually fetched to cart the corpses away and bury them and to sprinkle the great pools of blood with sand.

For a long time a work group was busy every day digging out mass graves.

In the meantime our bad and insufficient diet had "improved" to 400 g of bread a day, a pint of water-soup and, twice a day, so-called coffee. As a result, my condition, like that of many other of the wounded, had grown so much worse that I lay there for a long time apathetically. Many of us remained lying there for ever.

I had managed to send word to my relations in the Sudetenland. Now, in the middle of August, I heard secretly through them that my mother and father were still living. This revived my will to live and made it my duty as the last surviving son to survive. I searched desperately for an opportunity of changing my condition and to escape this slow death. Finally I took the only chance there was: I volunteered for farm work.

The big Czech farmers in inner Bohemia regularly employed a large number of farm labourers. But all these people had now gone to the Sudetenland, where they received German farm land. The harvest was overdue and had to be brought in. So the farmers asked for Germans as help.

On the 2nd of July 1946 we finally left this country in which we had experienced so much.

I had escaped with my bare life, even if I did not know where to turn or what to do now.

Prague, Report No. 12
The Motol camp
Reported by Mr. Schreiber - Report of December 3, 1946

I was Chief of the police office in Neudeck until 1938, and after the Sudetenland rejoined the German Reich I was arrested in Lubenz on October 5, 1938 and detained in the concentration camps Dachau and Flossenbürg until November 13, 1942. After that I served as truck driver in Norway, where I fell into British captivity after the German surrender. In October 1945 I was put on a transport of repatriates and sent back to Czechoslovakia, but once we arrived there, I and all the others on my transport were arrested and put into the concentration camp Motol. The plentiful and good clothing and rations which the British had issued us on our departure were taken from us, with one thin blanket as the only exception. We were housed in bare, unheated rooms with stone floors, without so much as a straw sack to sit on. For 4 weeks many of the camp inmates were beaten almost every day. Labor teams were sent from the camp to work for area farmers, in factories and on street construction in Prague. Many of the laborers on these work details were also beaten while they were at work. I myself saw how a pregnant woman who had to carry cement bags and who was almost exhausted and who collapsed repeatedly, was prodded by the Czech overseer to work faster. When one of the prisoners objected to this, the overseer declared that she was just a German and it wouldn't matter if she croaked. - On New Year's Eve my nephew was in Prague, on his way home from work, when he was stopped by a Russian soldier and beaten so badly with a submachine gun that he sustained severe injuries and later died of them.

In early March [1946] I was released from the Motol camp, to return to Neudeck, where I held a position on the Antifascist Committee. In granting the status of antifascist, the Czech authorities differentiated greatly between the Germans who were in Social Democratic organizations and Germans who were Communists. In 1938 only about 10% of the Social Democratic Germans were acknowledged as antifascists, as compared to twice as many Communist Germans. It seemed as though the granting or refusal of antifascist status was influenced by how wealthy the Germans in question were. As a rule, the Germans to be resettled were deprived of all their papers and valuables. When I was released from the camp I literally had nothing left to call my own. Since I was an acknowledged antifascist the *Národní výbor* did issue me the bare necessities of clothing and items for everyday life, but these things were consistently of poor quality, so that I was dependent on the aid and support of friends and acquaintances.

Prague, Report No. 13
Execution of 18 prisoners of war on August 9, 1945
Reported by Eduard Flach, lieutenant colonel (ret'd.) - Report of March 6, 1950

I am a former Lieutenant Colonel and was Chief of a Pay and Allowance Office of the Luftwaffe. I was 58 years old when I fell into Czech captivity in Prague on May 6, 1945. Together with some

600 other German soldiers, also prisoners-of-war, I spent the time of my captivity in the labor camp Roudnice on the Elbe River, in the "Benzina Plant", a large industrial facility formerly belonging to the Organisation Todt. I wish to state the following facts for the record:

In the evening of August 9, 1945 we had to line up in the parade square outside the barracks and take off our shirts. An investigative commission had arrived from Prague in order to examine the POWs to see if they had been members of the SS. 18 men were discovered, among them several prisoners who had been drafted into the Waffen-SS without their own doing. The tattooed "a", the sign of membership in the General Waffen-SS, was only found on a few, and some of these had already left the SS.

These 18 POWs now had to stand side-by-side facing a wooden barracks. And now, before our very eyes, the Czechs committed what I can only describe as a very brutal crime against those defenseless prisoners. The Czech guards and soldiers beat the pitiable victims on their bare backs with iron bars and rifle butts until they collapsed in bloody heaps. When the prisoners lay on the ground moaning, the Czechs stood them up again and dumped cold water on them. To this day I recall vividly how the fingers of some of the prisoners were smashed with rifle butts; this maltreatment, unparalleled in my experience, lasted for about 2 hours, until the onset of dark. Then we were allowed to withdraw, and the unconscious prisoners were dragged away to the soldiers' camp, which was separated from the prison camp itself by a barbed-wire fence, and there they were abused some more and finally shot. Still that same night, the stripped-naked bodies were thrown into a drained former reservoir and buried in shallow pits. The next day we had to begin to fill in the pit. When this task was finished several days later, we were able to observe how the Czech guard teams used the filled pit as a football field. I am convinced that the families of these 18 POWs, who were tortured to death without any sort of trial, are still totally in the dark about the tragic fate of their husbands, sons etc., since we and the camp administration were strictly prohibited from making any notes about what we experienced during our captivity.

The fact that during our stay in the Roudnice camp we former German POWs not only had to do hard physical labor for utterly inadequate rations but were also looted of everything we owned and received no POW pay or any other compensation for the work we did - unlike the policy practiced by the Americans and British - is something I just want to mention on the side.

On February 12, 1946 I was to be released, and was sent, severely ill, to the transfer camp Prague-Motol. But my release still took until June 8, 1946. After I was finally released I had to spend several years in medical care, to undo some of the damage to my health caused by the inhuman treatment I had suffered at the hands of the Czechs. I am prepared at any time to take this report on my oath.

Prague, Report No. 14
Prague-Raudnitz
Reported by A. W.

Wednesday, May 9th [1945] was the most horrible day of my life. In the early afternoon that day, my flat was suddenly opened from the outside, and a man wearing the [Czech] tricolor ordered me to follow him. I wasn't allowed to take anything at all with me. I was only just able to put on my coat, but aside from that I was not permitted to take even my handbag, not even a handkerchief. Like that, totally empty-handed, I was expelled. I've never seen my flat again since. On the street, cursing women searched me for weapons, then forced me into a house and shoved me into the cellar there. The cellar door was locked behind me. Once my eyes had adjusted to the dark, I saw that there were already quite a few other unfortunate people huddling in the corners. We were sure that we would be shot. Over and over again the door opened and new delinquents were pushed in. Finally, after perhaps an hour, we were brought out again. The howling crowd greeted us with curses and threw rocks at us, and it was only a few minutes before blood flowed. In the middle of the street stood a big bucket full of white paint. We had to stand facing the wall, and one of the worst agitators - it was the caretaker of house no. 11 in our street - painted huge swastikas on our backs, to the roaring laughter of the spectators. A number of Red Guardsmen then took charge of us - they all wore an armband with the letters R.G., which meant either *"Rudá Garda"* - Red Guard, or *"Revolucní Garda"* - Revolutionary Guard - they were choice samples of brutality, apparently convicts released from prison specially for this purpose, and they threw themselves at us with rifle butts and rubber truncheons and urged us to greater speed at the work we were put to. We had to tear down barricades consisting of huge, heavy stones, thick wooden beams and even entire garden gates and wagon wheels. I had eaten almost nothing for four days, hardly slept at all, and felt ghastly. Besides, I was not used to heavy physical labor, and this hard work was simply impossible for me. Therefore I was beaten dreadfully by these dehumanized creatures, with rifle butts, rubber truncheons and whips. We were completely at the mercy of our yelling, shooting tormentors, who rained blows down on us without restraint wherever they could. It was an unimaginable pandemonium. With a superhuman effort of will I remained standing despite all the maltreatment, because God help anyone who fell. The crows howled with glee every time it happened, and clapped their hands in joy. The fallen victim was urged back on his feet with rifle butts. We were spoken to - or more precisely, roared at - in a uniformly rude manner, as "German pig", "German sow", "German whore". Right at the beginning I had already noticed the many glass shards that covered the street, and now we were suddenly ordered to take off our shoes and stockings and to finish our work barefoot. That's why they had scattered glass shards in the street. We had to continue working on dreadfully painful, bleeding feet. In an unsupervised moment I had quickly slipped out of my warm coat and hung it over a garden fence, as I had begun to sweat very much, given the warm May day and how weak I was to begin with. Then, when we were herded on, I was violently prevented from taking my coat with me.

Finally the barricades had been cleared. We were herded together and made to line up in twos. A large picture of Hitler lay on the ground, and everyone had to trample and spit on it. Then we had to kneel down and pray for the souls of the fallen Czechs. But then we were not allowed to get up again, instead we were ordered "hands up", and like that, in this humiliating and impossible position, on our knees and with arms raised, we had to move on. The entire path was strewn with glass shards. The inhabitants lined the street to both sides, clapped their hands and screamed ironically: "Sieg Heil". Many photographed and some even filmed our sad procession. Our escorts with the RG-armbands seemed to have fallen into a veritable ecstasy of sadism. They now beat us quite arbitrarily. In front of me, behind me, the people dropped like flies. I don't know how many of them didn't get up again. "Faster, faster, faster," the guards roared, and beat us and beat us. Only once I heard one say to another, "you mustn't hit them on the head, because then they're dead right away. We want them to suffer a lot, and for a long time still."

Now, it is almost impossible to move forward in the position described above, on one's knees and with arms raised. Soon all one could see was a mass of tumbling human bodies, a wide, long trail of blood along the entire street, and bestial creatures beating wildly at their victims. The screams of the tortured mingled with the yelling of the guards and the cheering of the crowd. Someone began to pray loudly. Once, a married couple beside me lost their balance. The man seized what he believed to be an unobserved moment to jump to his feet and take a few quick steps. A terrible blow showed him the error of his ways. He collapsed, but his wife had to scramble on. She never found out if he survived. One old man implored them to have mercy on him, being 83 years old. He too fell under a violent blow, accompanied by a terrible curse.

In the beginning, when we had had to line up, we had graciously been allowed to take our shoes again, but not to put them on. So we had to hold them in our raised hands, and suddenly I dropped one. I wanted to quickly pick it up again, when a terrible blow crashed onto the back of my head. Things grew dark before my eyes. I did not lose consciousness, but from that point on I suffered from a constant hissing in my ears, day and night, that almost drove me crazy. Also, as soon as I tried to speak, my hearing faded. I was almost deaf. Speaking was very difficult. This distressing condition only gradually faded after I was already in Germany. Needless to say, I also lost my second shoe.

Suddenly we were ordered to stop. Now a number of women appeared, each of them armed with a pair of scissors, grabbed us women by the hair and cut off the hair on one side of our heads. The cut hair was forcibly stuffed into our mouths. Then the cry rang out, "water!" Interestingly, the spectators immediately understood what was meant by this. Women and men with buckets came out of all the houses and dumped freezing-cold tap water or disgusting filthy water on us.

During this stop, a long column of motorcycles came towards us from the opposite direction. Since we were on our knees and I did not raise my eyes, I only saw a lot of feet, perhaps twenty pairs of men's feet in strong, tough shoes. The column drove past us very slowly, evidently to savor the spectacle we offered. They took the convenient opportunity to treat us kneeling people to powerful kicks in the face.

And finally another group of harridans came to relieve us of our jewelry.

Finally we had reached our destination, the Cinema Slavia in Reif Street (Rípská ulice), which had been designated as concentration camp. Outside the cinema itself a large obstacle was set up which we had to leap over - we, with our throbbing, bloody feet and our tormented, beaten bodies, soaked to the skin. The Cinema Slavia is one of the few ground-level movie houses, not underground like the other Prague cinemas. On one side of the hall there are three large gates that lead into a yard, where in normal times the moviegoers could go during intermission. We were herded into this yard and had to line up with arms raised. We were left to stand like that for a long time. Then we were sent into the movie hall and had to sit down in the rows of seats. Several Red Cross nurses and two doctors, Dr. Günther und Dr. Lacher, and one woman doctor, Dr. Lang, received us. They too were Germans, and prisoners like us. Our mangled knees and soles of our feet were washed and some kind of antiseptic was applied, and drinking water was also handed around, but that was all they could do for us, for they had almost no medications or other aids, and further, they themselves were kept under very close guard and were only allowed to treat the very worst cases.

There was one thing we were very worried about, and that was that we did not want to be sent home before dark because we feared the Czech population. With our beaten limbs, our bloody feet, our badly cut hair and our filthy, sopping wet clothes we would have been immediately recognized as Germans, and the entire horror would have begun all over again. But this concern was quite unnecessary. When no motion was made to send us home, we thought that we were to be shown a propaganda film or something. But evening came, night fell, we shivered in our wet clothes, barefoot in this dank, cold movie theater. Now we understood: we were prisoners, we were in a concentration camp. We got nothing to eat that day, just some more water.

On the stage, in front of the movie screen, sat a Red Guardsman who constantly kept the barrel of his revolver aimed threateningly at us. We were not allowed to look to the left or the right, only straight ahead at the movie screen. Suddenly this sinister fellow began, in a subdued hissing monotonous voice which was all the more dreadful for it, to expound the most horrific threats against us. There is no conceivable crime he did not lay to our charge, no torment that he did not announce as being in store for us. He only interrupted himself once, to leap down from the stage to yank one unfortunate out of his seat and to curse and abuse him for having dared to turn to his neighbor. Then the gruesome sermon went on, until a new tormentor showed up to relieve the first; he went on exactly like his predecessor, and soon the intent and method became quite clear. This went on for half the night. I got goosebumps in horror. This could not help but result in madness! And indeed, after only two days of this treatment, combined with the constant nagging hunger, the first cases of insanity began. My next-door neighbor, whom I saw again here, a weak slightly hysterical woman, was the first. Six or seven others soon followed suit. They stood up and began giving irrational speeches, threatening the guards that they would not be tormenting us much longer, that the Americans would be coming to our assistance and then just wait and see, and the like. One of them jumped up onto her seat and looked around her insanely. General panic broke out, many screamed, others threw themselves to the floor as the guards seemed about to start firing. Then two of the more level-headed among them leaped at the two women, dragged them into the anteroom and threw the still talking and screaming women from one corner into another until they both fell silent. Nobody ever saw the two again.

To return to that first night. Finally they left us in peace, but we looked around in vain for someplace to sleep. We had to spend the rest of the night on the folding chairs, or underneath them, for we were so exhausted that we slid off the seats and were then allowed to remain lying there, in the dirt and garbage that was still there from the last movie showing, insofar as one can even speak of lying among the barred chair legs and the feet of those still sitting.

Naturally it was out of the question to undress for the night. I did not get out of my dress for five weeks.

The next day, and the following days, we were given some bitter black coffee and a few slices of bread, and nothing more. Some time later we also got a little soup, a small coffee cup full with a slice of bread. And these rations never increased. Other than the bit of bread we never got anything solid to eat. The soup seemed to have been made of the scraps scraped off the plates of the soldiers and guards, for it contained the most bizarre combinations of ingredients. Nonetheless we tried with every trick we knew to sneak ourselves a second cup. The soup cup was passed around - there were about 5 or 6 altogether, so that at least 100 people had to drink from the same cup, which of course was not washed.

There were at least 500 of us, possibly more, definitely no fewer. But the movie theater had only one washroom, 2 stalls for men and 2 for women, outside of which there were always long line-ups, all the more since many people soon suffered from severe diarrhea, which went untreated. Every day people committed suicide there. Even though nobody had any weapons any more, many still had a razor blade or a small pair of scissors, with which they cut their wrists. Soon this got so out of hand that the guards saw themselves forced to unhinge the doors, as this kind of self-help was not what the camp administration wanted. And so now there was not a single spot left where we could be alone for even a minute or two.

The terrible maltreatment, the constant hunger, the surfeit of horrible impressions in quick succession, my aforementioned painful condition as a result of the blow I had received to the back of my head, all this had produced a strange sort of condition in me. I never really slept and was also never really awake. I registered everything as though from a great distance, and yet very clearly. It seemed to me like a dream from hell. I fainted frequently, something that had never happened to me before in all my life. I recall how once I must have fallen down while sweeping the hall together with the others. Evidently someone had called one of our Red Cross nurses, and what brought me back to consciousness were her efforts to open my convulsively closed hand, in which I clutched a bread crust that I had found in the garbage and which I would not give up under any circumstances. Another time I was particularly fortunate. I found a piece of a bacon rind, which I cleaned off on my dress - as I had no handkerchief or the like - and which I then kept in my mouth for hours. It gave me the illusion of having eaten something.

Every morning we were called out to go to work. We women had to pave streets and cart off the rubble from bombed-out houses, while being constantly beaten and cursed by the guards if the work didn't progress fast enough for them, mocked by the citizenry, and woe to anyone who dared set foot on the sidewalk on her way to work. I too became guilty of that monstrous transgression once. I was yanked down by a brutal hand and flung into the middle of the street. "German sow, you dare step on the sidewalk like a normal human being!" Each and every Czech who needed a worker for some or other job could fetch himself some Germans in the camp for the purpose. During those

Days of Revolution, Prague never ceased to celebrate, and the next morning the evidence had to be cleaned up again. Some of these celebrations must have been indescribable orgies, to judge by what was expected of us women in the line of disgusting clean-up jobs.

The most horrible thing was always when the order came for 15, 20, 25 men to go and dig graves. In those days in Prague there were in fact still a large number of unburied dead from the last battles. But when the men who were to dig the graves for them came back, some of them would always be missing, sometimes half of them, sometimes even more. They had been buried right along with the corpses, in some cases even before they were quite dead. So we were told by those returning, half-mad from the horror.

Every evening some men were taken into the anteroom, then the doors were closed, and during this time nobody was allowed to go to the washroom. Shortly afterwards we heard horrible screams and the dull sounds of blows. Soon the unfortunates were brought back. Most of them were younger men, good-looking and of fine stature. But what came back were images of misery, aged 20 years in just fifteen minutes, dragging themselves painfully along on sprained limbs, their muscles literally beaten off their bones. I don't know how many survived this treatment. It couldn't have been very many.

With time, the utterly rigid discipline relaxed a little, and sometimes we were allowed to spend some time in the yard. But one can imagine how much relief that really was, when one considers that we were between 500 and 700 persons and that the yard in question was a small city compound surrounded on all sides by tall houses. At night this yard was the scene of tragedies of which nobody will probably ever learn. Then it was forbidden, on pain of death, to enter the yard. Every night there was shooting in the yard. Each morning, some of our people were missing. But new victims arrived daily, and so numerically it wasn't noticeable. Given the incredible crowding and the never-ending milling-around, only the respective seat neighbors could tell when yet another one was gone.

In the row in front of me there sat a woman who had a pair of rubber boots standing underneath her seat. Not everyone had arrived as totally stripped of everything as the group with which I had come in. Some had been able to bring a few things along. They were relieved of them easily enough later. Since I was barefoot, as I've already mentioned, this woman lent me her rubber boots some-times when I had to go to work. One night she too was among those who were fetched outside - most of them were taken at night - and as it was one of those nights where there was much shooting in the yard, we were certain that she too had had to make her way across the yard. I still have the rubber boots today.

Since the guards were almost always drunk, we were constantly in danger of our lives, as they played like children with their loaded weapons. They laughed like crazy and wanted extra entertain-ment. For that reason, in the evenings they would fetch our exhausted men, who were almost dead on their feet from the hard labor and lack of food, and made them perform squats in the yard. They had a wonderful time whenever another one of the unfortunates collapsed.

A number of women sitting near me were ordered every day to report to the former SS barracks on Lobkowitz Square, where Russian soldiers were quartered now. Despite the quite incredible work loads that were foisted on these women, nonetheless we all envied them, as they were not subjected to additional torment and humiliation there, and most of all because they got something to eat there. They usually brought something they had saved for us back with them in the evening, and we impatiently awaited their return. Since there were many of us who sat in the immediate vicinity of these much-envied few, there wasn't more than a spoonful for each of us, but even that was already a significant improvement for us. Unfortunately the guards soon grew wise to this matter, and so the women were now searched on their return each evening, and were relieved of whatever they had brought with them.

One time a group of men had to do some work on a construction site behind a big fence. Some onlookers stood outside and made fun of them. That gave the guard the idea to put on a show for the crowd. The German men had to spit at each other, box each other's ears, finally they had to eat filth from the street, and more of the like. This was repeated for several days, with some variations, and there was not a single Czech there who could be bothered to protest against this shameful exhibition.

Once, some of our women returned from work in terrible agitation. Horror was still written on their faces, and they were racked by sobs. They had been put to work in a depot of the German Wehrmacht, bundling dozens of sweaters and the like that the Czechs had appropriated, and had also had to sort a great many blood-soaked uniform pieces that were lying around there. In some places they had literally had to wade through blood, and had had to stomp on hundreds of Iron Crosses and other medals that lay in the blood there. Probably this was where one of those last battles took place, one of those incredible tragedies that no-one will ever hear about. The unhappy vanquished were stripped of their uniforms and thrown naked into the mass graves, often while they were still alive. This is not just my own supposition, it has been generally alleged and no doubt really happened. How many people who are now missing may have suffocated in a Prague mass grave!

Every day we were threatened with being shot. These threats abruptly ceased when we begged time and again that they would follow through and release us from this martyrdom. One day it was announced that anyone who was Austrian should speak up, as they were to be released immediately. This included a young woman, who reported right away and couldn't contain her joy. When she was driven from her home, her six-year-old daughter had happened not to be at home, and the poor woman had spent the entire time fretting in worry about her child. Her husband had fallen in the war, so this woman had more than her share of hardship and we were glad for her that she was to be freed. But a few documents were still needed for her discharge, and of course she didn't have them with her. So she was sent to fetch them from home, accompanied by a guard. Unfortunately the man found more than he was looking for, namely proof that she had been employed as typist in a Gestapo office. From that point on her fate was sealed. Naturally her dream of being released was over. But what that unfortunate woman had to endure from that day on is simply unimaginable. She had to clean dreadfully filthy latrines with her bare hands, without any tool and without water, she was locked into a dark basement for days and nights on end without food, she was flung head-first against the wall. Several weeks later, when we finally started out on our death march (which I will mention later) to the train station to be sent to Raudnitz to the slave auction, we tried to save her by keeping her, who could barely still walk, as far as possible in the middle of our group.

Someone had lent her a large kind of shawl so that she could disguise herself. Nonetheless one of the henchmen recognized her, and she was beaten to death right before our eyes.

I have already mentioned my strange half-awake state. Almost like a dream image, I recall a corner by the gate that we called the suicide corner. I see again a large tub of water and quite a number of pitiful figures huddling around it, waxy pale in the face, with mad looks and expressions of pain, holding their hands immersed in the water. These were the prisoners who had cut their wrists. Really, every effort was made to prevent suicides. For example, I know of a man who had swallowed some poison. He was in terrible condition and it was no small feat to get him back on his feet again. When he had finally recovered, he was shot.

Every night there was some new kind of excitement. I don't recall a single quiet night. After midnight some "delegates" usually showed up in order to fetch young women and girls for the officers. We tried our best to hide them, but it didn't help much. I find it difficult to recount what all happened in this regard. Just imagine the worst you can, and no doubt it will still be a pale shadow of what really took place.

Another favorite kind of entertainment were the nightly lootings. I and those who had arrived with me had nothing to fear in this regard, as we had nothing left to steal, but the others had to be constantly prepared for being deprived of what little they still possessed. The first thing to be taken from everyone, without exception, were their timepieces. Watches were the most popular. One Asiatic fellow wore about 20 of them on his arm. With a bestial grin he would yank them off the arms of the victims lying helplessly before him.

It was terrible to witness the suffering of the ill prisoners who had been under medical care and now had to die here miserably without their medications and diet. After all, even most German patients had been chased out of their hospital beds.

Our sadistic tormentors took special pleasure in making us line up for hours on end, whether it be to take us to work or to simply chase us back into the hall hours later. Whether it was raining or scorching hot outside, while we were lined up we were not allowed to move, to turn around or to speak. Aside from my own distress, at times like that it sometimes took me all my common sense and self-control to keep from lunging at the throat of one of these monsters when we had to watch how he would beat a poor sick old man and yank him by the hair or force him into some ridiculous position as punishment for looking to the right instead of the left, for example.

One day the news spread that we were to be sent to a different concentration camp. A paralyzing dread took hold of us, for as wretched as our existence was in this camp, at least we knew what our torment entailed and knew more or less what degree of abuse to expect from each new day. Elsewhere it might possibly be even worse, and perhaps it meant certain death. Why didn't they just let us starve right here? For we did not doubt that we would be slowly starved to death.

The name Theresienstadt was put about. Then there was talk of a GPU camp in the Reich, but nobody knew anything definite. Finally, one day, things began in earnest. It began as always, namely with an hours-long line-up, this time on the stairs, then we were marched one story down, then two stories back up, and finally we were back in the large yard where we had to line up four to six rows deep and facing the wall so that we couldn't see what was happening behind us. At times we had to stand like that with our arms raised as well. Finally, after several painful hours, it was my turn and that of those standing nearest to me. We were allowed to turn around, and then we saw several tables that had been set up in the yard, behind which sat some young girls. Several open boxes and cartons stood on the tables, some of them filled with money, others with wedding rings, others again contained papers. Evidently our guards had learned that the Mark currency had not been discontinued and had retained its value, and so they had decided to relieve again us of the Marks we had been allotted. During the aforementioned lootings, wedding rings had still been respected, at least in some cases. This oversight was now being remedied. Any personal documents anyone still had were also collected. Now most of the others had nothing left at all anymore, like I had had nothing left from the start.

In the course of all these revolting happenings, evening had come. We had not received anything to eat that day, since actually we should have been marched off long ago. Allegedly no more supplies had been brought in for this day. Now it was too late to march off, and they made do with herding us back into the theater after this supposedly last looting. The upper rooms had already been locked in the meantime, and we had to squeeze together even more closely on the first floor. Suddenly one of the guards appeared. It was the one we all feared most. I have never seen him in any state other than screaming, enraged and drunk. For some reason he had missed the looting, he had come too late, which made him even angrier than he usually was. Nonetheless he clearly hoped that some rings might have been missed here and there, roared at us, "Show your paws," and beat us over our fingers with a cane he had brought especially for the purpose. It hurt hellishly. Since he failed to find anything, he roared and yelled more and more. The children began to wail in fear, which enraged him even more and he screamed at them like I have never heard a human being scream. I thought my eardrums would burst under the infernal noise.

Finally, when he had left, we were given a bit of crispbread, two slices for each of us, with the comment that we should not eat it all at once as we would not get any more tomorrow and would have to be on the road all day.

Finally, when we were about to get some sleep as far as that was even possible under these over-crowded conditions, we suddenly heard a very strange, frightening noise that got louder and louder and came ever closer. Sounds of yelling and running were to be heard in the house, commands rang out, and a very unusual excitement lay in the air. Suddenly someone who had been standing by the window cried out, "for Heaven's sake!" We rushed over, and in the early dusk we saw a seemingly endless crowd of people coming closer and closer, gesticulating wildly with sticks and cudgels and screaming threats. Those were aimed at us. The people had learned that we were supposed to leave Prague the next morning and would thus be removed from their sphere of power, and so they had come in order to quickly vent their spleen on us one more time. They simply wanted to lynch us. I thought my heart was going to stop, I was so horrified. An indescribable panic broke out. Some cried out like wild animals, some clung to each other as though to protect each other, others again stood silently, frozen like pillars, pale as plaster and trembling violently. It was one of the most dreadful scenes I have ever seen. We understood perfectly that we were doomed. How could we unhappy people, fatally weakened by starvation and maltreatment, have defended ourselves without weapons against this raging, incited mob?

Apparently there was some negotiation going on between the guards and the ringleaders, which took valuable time and it was during that time that a miracle happened, a real, true miracle. Nobody had noticed that a storm had been brewing, and yet, suddenly there it was. Like a bolt out of the blue a cloudburst began, accompanied by strong winds and hail, and thunder and lightning followed in quick succession. The mob beat a hasty, screaming retreat; one of the more sensible ones among our guards had quickly closed all the doors, and we were saved.

The next morning, or more exactly around noon, after more hours-long line-ups on stairs and in hallways, when we were already faint from hunger, for of course everyone had already eaten his second slice of crispbread - around noon, then, our march-out began, the start of that horrible "Death March". The Red Guardsmen, our guards, also knew that this was the last chance for them to exercise their sadistic inclinations on us, and evidently they had agreed to make the fullest possible use of this last opportunity.

We had to line up in rows of three. As soon as we had done so, the guards claimed that they had ordered rows of four, and they beat us and beat us. Then they called for rows of five or even six, then rows of three again, and so it went on. An indescribable confusion ensued, all the more so as every guard gave different orders for the area under his command. No progress was made at all, and the guards roared and cursed and hit and beat us blindly. I received a terrible blow from a rifle butt to my ribs, and a blow on the shoulder because in all the madness I suddenly no longer stood neatly in line. Finally they had had enough of this game, and to make up the time that had been wasted we now had to run, faster and ever faster. I recall sending a quick prayer to Heaven that I might have the good fortune to drop dead, to be released from this torture that was simply no longer to be borne. Others probably did the same. This was also the last day for the poor Austrian lady whom I've mentioned earlier. Many others also did not survive that day. Every step we took put us in some new mortal danger.

I believe that an entire deportation group from another concentration camp had joined ours, for there were many who drained their energy by dragging suitcases and the like with them. Now, when this terrible running began, these poor people had no other choice than to throw their heavy encumbrances away, just so they would not be beaten to death. And all the while, along our entire path, the spectators cursed us and rained their terrible threats down on us. Everyone tried to move to the middle of the rows, as the danger was greatest at the fringes. Many people fell, and of course I don't know what happened to them as we had to keep moving, faster and ever faster right over those who had fallen. If we had tried to help them, we would have been beaten to death ourselves.

Finally we arrived at the Hyberner train station (known as Masaryk Station again now). We were led onto the station grounds from behind, from Florenzer Street, when suddenly we were ordered to stop. A guard called out in a strangely friendly tone: "We are looking for a woman with a good education, who can speak foreign languages and knows how to do double-entry bookkeeping. Any volunteers?" A few unfortunate women who still hadn't clued in to the game spoke up. Perhaps they thought they would be able to improve their lot and remain in Prague, maybe even work in an office. But then the guard grabbed one of them by her collar, yanked her out of the row and roared: "All right, come on, you sow, you will now clean all the toilets in the station." The poor woman had to follow him, to the yelling, laughter and applause of the people that stood crowded together outside the gate that closed off the station grounds. We were ordered to lower our heads, not to look right or left and not to move. It is useless to try to describe what took place here, it simply can't be described. Turning one's head even a hair's breadth sideways could mean death, and meant exactly that for probably a great many people. Peering out from under my brows I nonetheless saw how a group of people in horrible condition passed us in the opposite direction. All of them were covered in blood, and among them was our Dr. Günther. I don't know what had been done to them or where they came from. Between the people was the occasional cart, on which dying or mortally injured people lay, as well as some which I assume had suffered a heart attack. The howling crowd outside watched the display with growing interest, and at every particularly entertaining incident they broke out in loud cheers, for example when someone fell and could no longer get up. Under the circumstances described, the view I got was naturally very limited, and I sensed more than saw all the atrocities that took place there. I myself was closer to death than to life at that point. I recall hellishly loud noise, a mixture of laughter, howling cheers, applause, the tormented people's screams of pain, the whimpering of the dying, and the stomping of countless feet.

Finally we were herded, always with blows from cudgels, across many tracks and towards a railway car that was intended for us. It looked as though the guards were mowing hay with their rifle butts, for this time they were aiming at the legs of the running people in order to make them fall. I was "lucky" enough that a woman fell onto the tracks right in front of me, and before the guard could swing back for the next blow I had slipped through. The railway car was of course a coal car, and we had to squat on the floor in a layer of coal dust several centimeters thick. Naturally the car was far too small, that is, there were several of them but no doubt it was the same everywhere. I was still wearing the dress I had not been able to change for weeks, and huddled in a dirty corner, happy for the moment to have escaped imminent death. We were packed into the car like cattle or some inanimate cargo. But we had hardly been entrained before the Red Guardsmen showed up once more, this time in the company of their girlfriends, whom they urged to help themselves to whatever they liked that we still wore. "Don't be shy, take what you like. Look, this sweater is really quite nice," etc. Most of the girls made disparaging faces and declared that there was nothing they liked. However, I believe that they were ashamed to take the clothes off our very bodies and only said that they did not like anything. Some of them were less sensitive, and many a woolen vest, many a sweater was taken off its owner. One young woman was wearing a par of men's trousers which tempted one of the guards. She had to take them off on the spot, and was left wearing only her underwear. There was really nothing left that could have been taken from us if we were not to be stripped totally naked, and so the train finally set off. A guard with fixed bayonet sat on an elevated seat. We were strictly forbidden to get up, and so we squatted as well as possible in the thick coal dust. Whenever anyone even tried to straighten up to at least recover a bit from the uncomfortable position, a shot always rang out in close proximity, without us ever being able to locate the marksman. The train stopped at several stations, and then a number of Asiatic faces always appeared over top of the sides of the car and asked, grinning, "Where are you taking that?" "Where they belong, into slavery" *(do roboty)*, was the unvarying reply.

In my possession were a dirty, ragged dress, a set of underwear in similar condition, and a pair of rubber boots which I had inherited from the woman who had been shot. Nothing else!

I affirm in lieu of oath that this my report tells the truth in every respect.

Prague, Report No. 15
Prague 1945 - 1947
Reported by Dr. Hans Wagner - Report of September 27, 1950

In a sudden attack of the Revolutionary Guards on the radio-station in the Schwerin Strasse, now known as Stalinova, the Germans lost one of their most important positions, the radio-station. The Czechs immediately began broadcasting their slogans of hatred, calling for the extermination of the Germans: *"Smrt všem Němcum! Smrt všem okupantum!* Death to all Germans! Death to all forces of occupation!"

"Kill the Germans wherever you meet them! Women, children, Germans of all ages - every German is our mortal enemy! Now is the chance to exterminate our enemies! Let us make an end of them!"

A few hours after these slogans had been broadcast, numerous reports came streaming in of murders and dreadful atrocities committed against German soldiers and civilians, as well as accounts by terrified eye-witnesses of the first human torches.

It was primarily SS-men who were committed to this kind of fiery death, but since the Communists generously considered any wearer of a uniform to be an SS-man, numerous soldiers of other Wehrmacht formations and members of various units were among the victims.

On May 7th, 1945 the battle of Prague reached its climax. The fury of the Revolutionary Guards against the German civilians continued and the smell of burnt human flesh lay heavy over the town. We received reports concerning the evacuation of German clinics and civilian hospitals according to which seriously ill patients were torn out of their beds and driven into the hands of the mob.

Witnesses gave an authentic report of the death of the last rector of the German university in Prague, Professor Albrecht, Director of the German Neuralgical and Psychiatric Clinic, who was attacked by the mob in his clinic, knocked down and finally hanged in the attic of the lunatic asylum. At the same time the death of Professor Dr. Rudolf Greipel-Bezecny, the Director of the German Dermatological Clinic, became known.

On Tuesday, May 8th 1945, the constant fighting increased, but later on began to subside, since there were rumours of an impending cease-fire, and in fact at 12 o'clock the general cease-fire was announced.

The military surgeon and I immediately paid a visit to Military Hospital VIII, Thierschhaus. We found that its name had been changed to *Náhradní nemocnice*, emergency hospital. As medical superintendent the Czechs had appointed one Dr. N., whom I had known for a long time. He was a good-hearted man and as medical superintendent during the First World War had displayed a proper understanding of the needs of the wounded. He gave a free hand to the German military surgeon in attending the patients. While we were talking to Dr. N., the police-station at Prague-Kleinseite (a Prague suburb) called and asked the hospital to take in some 100 wounded. Ambulances immediately left and brought in 100 corpses, mostly of young and healthy people, with dreadfully mutilated limbs and faces disfigured past recognition. Each one of them had received a shot through the neck at the end of their torture. The idea of delivering these victims to the hospital was nothing but a clever method of camouflaging the crime. I also paid a visit to a section of the hospital in which a number of my former patients were lying. It was in this room that I myself witnessed how the Revolutionary Guards broke in. When I pointed out to their leader that an armistice had already been declared, he merely threatened me with arrest. Under the pretext of looking for weapons the partisans robbed the wounded soldiers.

The withdrawal of the German Wehrmacht was supposed to be accomplished by evening. We therefore went back to Dejwitz - in order to get instructions for the invalids and population to be withdrawn together with the Wehrmacht. The offices of the commanding officer were, however, in full dissolution and neither he nor his deputy, one General Ziervogel, or any of the officers of the Staff were to be seen. The colleagues of the military surgeon took leave of him, his personal adjutants choosing freedom. I myself elected to do my duty and remained behind with my wounded comrades. We then instructed all hospitals in contact with us that all patients able to walk, as well as all nonessential medical personnel, should join up with the withdrawing Wehrmacht. Unfortunately we had no possibility of informing the already occupied hospitals and the inmates of camps, which - according to the agreement with the Czechs - should have been done by the Czechs themselves. In the course of the discussions the withdrawal of all Germans had been expressly mentioned and a special clause included. As a result of the fact that the Czech National Council broke its word, some 80,000 Germans were made prisoners or internees.

Whereas the Wehrmacht and a few groups of civilians moved towards the West in the direction of Pilsen, where American troops were stationed, we moved to Hospital XVI, which had been set up in the building of the Rumanian Embassy, in order to be close to the International Red Cross. About the same time the so-called "death marches" of the Prague Germans to Theresienstadt began, in the course of which scarcely one in ten of those who had marched from Prague arrived alive.

On Wednesday, May 9th, a group of Revolutionary Guards, led by a police inspector, burst into the hospital, maintaining that shots had been fired from the building. Unfortunately we were still in possession of our revolvers since we had had no opportunity to surrender them. We officers of the Medical Corps were on the point of being lined up against a wall to be shot, when by a lucky chance a Czech doctor of the International Red Cross arrived to prevent it.

Shortly afterwards police entered the hospital for the second time and ordered us to close the front door and the front windows. The German patients were forbidden, under pain of death, to look out of the windows while Russian troops marched through the town. A few hours later heavy tanks drove down the street. The Red Army had entered the town. The large building next to the Rumanian Embassy, which had been used as a Military Headquarters during the time of the

Austro-Hungarian monarchy and the Czechoslovak Republic, as well as during the Third Reich, was now also chosen by the Russians as their Military Headquarters for the District of Prague.

On Tuesday, May 10th, 1945, when I left for the Thierschhaus to see Dr. Dobbek, I met a long column of refugees, consisting only of women, children and elderly people. I learned that they had come from Ohlau, in Silesia, and had been surprised by the Revolution on their way through Prague; they hoped to get assistance from the International Red Cross, but had not even received milk for the babies. I returned to the hospital and picked up two bottles of milk, but when I tried to give these to them, the bottles were knocked out of my hand by Revolutionary Guards and smashed. Children dropped down from the carts and attempted to lick up the milk from the street, but the partisans prevented them and threatened to shoot me. The column remained halted for several days, both horses and people dying of hunger and thirst. One morning the carts had disappeared.

Dr. N. helped us to find General Srunek, the chief of the Czech Army Medical Service, residing in Bartholomäusgasse, opposite to Police Headquarters. In this building shots and cries were to be heard. General Srunek received us correctly and accepted our requests with understanding. Our requests were as follows:

Appointment of Czech medical officers as commandants of the hospitals instead of the Revolutionary Guards; provision of requisite food rations for the wounded and space for the inmates of Military Hospital I, whom the Russians had threatened to throw out the window if the hospital were not evacuated without delay; aid to the Germans in camps and prisons. Srunek promised to accede to our requests as far as possible. As to the transport of whole Military Hospitals, however, he could only endorse our requests as the Government would have to negotiate with the Americans. He could not, however, do anything for imprisoned civilians, since these were under the jurisdiction of the police.

On Friday, May 11th, we went to see Srunek again. The appointment of the Czech medical officers seemed already to have been carried out, since one, First Lieutenant Dr. Haas, reported to our Hospital XIV. He spoke German fluently and confirmed the medical superintendent as head of the hospital; he also took steps to see that rations were delivered.

In the course of a discussion with the International Red Cross we presented a petition concerning the dreadful death-rate in the concentration camps, especially in the Strahov Stadium, where there were 25,000 persons crowded into a confined space and camping out in the open air. They were receiving no food whatever; even drinking-water had been reduced to a minimum. We also described from our own experiences the brutalities that had been committed against Germans while they were forced to tear down the barricades; as a result a number of dead and injured people had been left lying on the ground. We furthermore urgently requested that the evacuation of hospitals and clinics be halted and that death marches like the one to Theresienstadt should not occur again in the future. These men certainly attempted to do everything within their restricted competence, but they were unable to accomplish anything, since their actions were too much determined by their fear of the Russians.

One day I drove to the Czech children's hospital with a child suspected of having diphtheria. Arriving there the nurse threatened to set the dogs on us if we did not disappear immediately; the

Czechs even considered our expectation of their admitting a German child into a Czech hospital to be an unheard-of provocation which only German swine would dare to commit.

The same day I received the order to immediately report to Dr. N. He told me that the police was very much interested in my person, but that he had stood up for me, so that they had refrained from arresting me.

On Saturday, May 12th, 1945 I obtained a lift to my former apartment at the Wenzelsplatz. Upon arrival I found a slip of paper on the door indicating that one Dr. Tichý, gynaecologist, had occupied my flat. The door had been broken open and I entered. The individual rooms as well as the consultation room were in complete chaos; in the wardrobe I happened to find a dark suit which I exchanged for my uniform.

On Sunday, May 13th, 1945 President Beneš arrived at Prague, and rows of Germans were set on fire as human torches in his honour.

During the following days many conferences were held with the International Red Cross and as a result of our talks with the Czech commandant of the hospital we frequently succeeded in getting better rations for the wounded. In Military Hospital VII we discovered Surgeon-General Dr. Otto Muntsch and his wife both dying as a result of violence done to them.

Due to the measures of the Russians, who were waiting to take over all the still remaining hospitals, and through having to take in Germans who had collapsed from mistreatment and exhaustion at their place of work or on the streets but had been given shelter by Czechs who had taken pity on them, and also through having to take in the evicted clinic patients, an incredible shortage of beds and space had set in, so that any proper supervision of the hospital was out of the question. Dr. Dobbek and I therefore decided to call on and see General Gordow, the Russian governor of the city, in order to find a solution. General Gordow, however, told us; "If you haven't enough room for your wounded, throw them into the Moldau River, there's enough room for them!"

In the afternoon I succeeded in taking another walk through the town, where I saw the charred ruins of the burnt-out town hall and other buildings against the sky-line. Hanging from the wrought-iron sign-board of a well-known restaurant opposite the theatre, I noticed the charred remains of a German soldier upside-down. The right arm was missing; probably he had been an amputee. All of the larger stores bore the inscription *"Národní podnik"*. In the Graben-Strasse flags were displayed and every second building had a board with the inscription: *"Majetek komunistické strany československé"* (property of the Czechoslovak Communist party). The "Deutsche Haus" was now called *Slovanský dum* (Slav House) and also belonged to the Communists. The building of the Bohemian Escompte Bank had become the Headquarters of the Social Democratic Party. The most important Czech bank, the Živno Bank, bore the inscription *Národní podnik*. Although he had not been a collaborator, its President, old Jaroslav Preis, had been interned in Pankratz. Petschek Palace in the Bredauer Strasse, which had been used as the Gestapo Headquarters since 1939, now lodged the GPU. The building was surrounded by a cordon of guards and no loitering was allowed in the vicinity. The German theatre bore the inscription *"Divadlo pátého května"* - Theatre of May 5th.

I entered the Elektra-café, owned by Wagner & Co., of which I was a partner. The waiter now in charge complained of the present trend of business. He gave me a good meal and also a written statement, signed by the 35 employees present, confirming that I had always treated them well.

Screams were heard coming from the main entrance of the Wilson Railway Station. I noticed that a blonde woman was being attacked by the crowd, although she defended herself in Czech, which she spoke without an accent. She was quickly surrounded, her dress torn to shreds, and although she was soon lying on the ground covered with blood, the mob continued beating her. At the same time a heavy beer wagon arrived at the spot; the two horses were unharnessed during the commotion and each was tied to one of the woman's legs and then driven in opposite directions.

On Thursday, May 17th, 1945, I paid a visit to the International Red Cross early in the morning. The usual bustle in this building had ceased. The Russians and the Revolutionary Guards had searched the house. All visitors had been frightened away. The International Red Cross had failed to obtain recognition by Czechoslovakia, although according to information from Geneva Yugoslavia had recognised this Institution.

When I returned to the hospital I found two men waiting for me, one in uniform and the other in civilian clothes. "Leave everything at the hospital", they told me, "you are to be taken for a brief interrogation."

I bade farewell to Professor v. Susani, the advisory surgeon to the military surgeon of the army district, and to Dr. Hanebuth, the former surgeon in charge of Military Hospital I.

At the Police Headquarters, in the corridor, I saw a woman whose head was wrapped in a swastika flag; save for this she was naked. Her skin was covered with black and blue marks and abrasions. Police and members of the Revolutionary Guard lined up along each side of the corridor were driving her back and forth with blows of fists and rifle butts. She was hardly able to walk.

I was led to one Dr. Weiss, an official of the criminal police, on the fourth floor. He picked up a photograph from his desk and asked if it were of me. I answered in the affirmative. He then said to my escort, "red sheet". I asked what this meant and he answered that I was arrested. I then showed my credentials as delegate of the International Red Cross, but he merely made a disparaging gesture and said, "You had better repeat that when you are interrogated." - The escort ordered me to follow them; we entered a large room, in the middle of which was a table at which a number of officials were seated; in the right-hand corner of the room were several crying women who had no doubt been arrested. As before, the interrogation began with questions printed on a questionnaire. I once more protested against my imprisonment by showing my International Red Cross credentials. The official's only answer, however, was: "You had better repeat that when you are interrogated!" Part of the money I had in my pocket disappeared into the drawer of his desk; the man obviously collected it for his privy purse. Soon afterwards all the men were taken to a cell in the basement. The prisoners sat jammed like herrings on a plank-bed and there was no room even to lie down on the floor. The air was unbearably stuffy. Men crawled along under the planks. I was nearly suffocating, but succeeded in getting close to the small window, where I was able to breathe. All of a sudden the door was opened and names were read out. Mine was among them. We were marched to a dingy yard, where we had to stand facing the wall with our hands up. The Revolutionary Guard marched up; the triggers of their automatic pistols clicked, but no shots were fired. Women joined up with us as fellow-sufferers. A wild mob came in through the gate, took our last possessions away from us and dealt out blows. Suddenly we were commanded to run to the bus parked in the road opposite. It was difficult to get through the howling mob to reach the bus and some of our number remained lying on the pavement, beaten up or dead. Even when we were inside the bus, the crowd threw stones at us and threatened us with knives.

We were taken to the prison at Pankratz. Another mob received us at the gate of the prison with stones and revolver shots. The bus remained halted for some time. Finally we drove into the prison-yard. The warders there welcomed us with blows of rubber-truncheons, or *"pendreks"* as they were generally called. We were then led into the building of the prison and registered, our very last belongings were taken away and we were finally assigned to the various cells. Two of us were put together with eight other prisoners in a cell which had formerly been destined for a single inmate. In spite of the summer-like heat, only the upper half of the small grated window was open, the palliasses were old and damp and the bugs almost unbearable.

The group commandant was a supervisor named Koberle, who understood well how to make our daily exercise of half an hour into an additional martyrdom. The meals we received were just pig-slop, consisting of dried vegetables, old cabbage, turnips and black, half-rotten potatoes. In the evening we received soup, that is, warm water with some bran in it. The bread and black coffee were also unfit for human consumption. In addition to this the rations were very small. After a few days had passed the majority of us already suffered from gastric or intestinal catarrh. The privy in our cell was occupied day and night; toilet-paper, soap, brush, towel and comb were luxury articles. Suddenly Koberle became a clean-fanatic and we were issued soap and cleaning materials, the reason being that typhus had broken out in the prison at Karlsplatz, with a supervisor as one of the victims.

At Whitsuntide the trials began and I was among those called up. A Russian captain and a female commissar interrogated us, she interpreting my evidence, as none of them was able to understand Czech. I was asked about the authorities in the Wehrmacht and German administration, as well as about medical installations of the Wehrmacht, and similar questions. I was very reticent and gave them to understand that I did not wish to act as an informer.

It became customary for the "heroes of the nation", after carousing, to visit us in the prison as a climax to their amusement. The guards allowed them to enter without any ado. One of the prisoners was seized at random and driven out of the cell with blows and shoves. His cries of pain were to be heard for a long time until he was finally tortured to death. A special sort of sport was at that time very popular at Pankratz. This consisted of throwing the badly beaten victims over the balustrade of the third floor and using them for shooting practice as living targets during their fall.

On Sunday afternoon a group of members of the Revolutionary Guard entered one of the double cells of our section, in which about 25 boys, 14 to 16 years of age, were lodged. These boys were from the Reichenberg region and were supposed to have been "Werwolves". We heard from the orders given how the boys were made to stand in front of our door in two files. First of all they were forced to take part in "cock-fights", to shout "Heil Hitler" and to beat each other. Spectators, men and women, forced them on, sometimes lending a helping hand with rubber-truncheons. This spectacle degenerated into bloodshed. The boys had to lick up the blood from the tiled floor. Whoever refused to do so was half beaten to death. A number of children vomited and the others were ordered to eat the vomit. At last the tortured youths were unable to endure this any longer and were thereupon beaten further until their blood ran over the whole floor. The boys had to clean the floor themselves. Later on the "delinquents" were forced to undress and to lie on a table, on which they were whipped until their flesh was torn to ribbons. The torturers could not restrain themselves from vile jokes and obscenities. After all the young people had been mistreated in this way, they were dragged to the basement and those who still showed signs of life were hanged from hooks on the wall until they were dead.

In spite of extreme hunger and constant pains in the stomach, I was forced to carry 187-lbs flour bags from the truck downstairs to a store-room. After I had carried the eleventh bag I felt sick and dropped it. I myself sank to the ground. Shortly afterwards the warder forced me to go back to my cell. A group of men were exercising in the yard. I discovered among the imprisoned men Professor Dr. Maximilian Watzka, the last Dean of the German Medical Faculty. I cautiously nodded to him. The warden noticed this and kicked me so violently that my right knee hit the stone steps and I injured myself considerably.

As a result of the accident during my work, haemorrhage was added to my gastric complaints, as I was able to diagnose from my tar-coloured excrement.

The sick-room had a bad reputation and it was therefore with reluctance that I decided to apply there for aid. Koberle had no objections. The man in charge of the sick-room was named Černý. When I was there he grabbed the first patient, who complained of angina, by the neck, professed to be able to see nothing, and threw him out. The second patient complained of pains in the chest - a violent punch was aimed at the aching spot, and the consultation was over. The third pointed to the bandage on his leg; Černý immediately tore off the bandages so that the wound started to bleed again. He thereupon assisted the patient out of the room with a kick. Both doctors, also inmates of the camp, stood helplessly by, unable to help. Černý asked me: "What's wrong with you?" "A haemorrhage in the stomach." "What? Tell that to the doctor, but if it is untrue you will be beaten as never before in your life!" A spoon of "Karlsbader Salz" (a laxative) was put into my mouth. The coarse grains stuck in my throat, so I went to the water tap and took a mouthful of water. At the same moment Černý screamed out and when I turned round I was hit on the right and left cheek so violently that blood came from my mouth and nose. I also lost two molars.

The first of our group to be interrogated was the head of our cell. He did not do too badly, as his sister had been a Communist for many years and had marched into Prague together with the army of General Svoboda, a Czechoslovak formation within the Red Army. She had the rank of staff-sergeant and had been decorated with the medal for bravery.

The next from our cell to be interrogated was an architect and it seemed that the GPU had forgotten him. He did not appear for a long time. It was not until after supper that he was thrown back into our cell. We could hardly recognise him. His whole body showed signs of the most dreadful ill-treatment. He lay unconscious on his straw-bed for several hours and was ill for many days.

Victim No 3 was Mr. Reiss, an engineer, who was also dragged back dreadfully disfigured, beaten half-dead and unconscious. When he regained consciousness he told us that the Czechs had kicked him in the stomach.

The continuous loss of blood finally made itself felt. I was able to crawl only on all fours. Buzzing in the ears, fainting fits and unconsciousness for four days finally induced Koberle on July 20, 1945 to deliver me to the prison hospital. Thanks to the care of two German doctors, who, although it was strictly forbidden, smuggled in mashed potatoes, I slowly recovered. The diet of the German patients consisted of the same food as that distributed in the cells, only the quality was even worse. Minister Machník, formerly Minister for National Defence and leader of the Czech Peasants Riding Union, was interned together with me. Another fellow-sufferer was Mr. Bubeniček, a German head clerk in the wholesale timber-firm of Lechner. Together with many other Germans Bubeniček had been forced to run barefoot over glass splinters in front of the church at Holleschowitz. In doing so he had cut his foot and now suffered from a malignant inflammation of the tissues which necessitated several operations, during which the surgeons were not allowed to use narcotics or local anesthetic.

Bubeniček had been a witness of the happenings which caused the death of Dr. Lang, head of the tuberculosis ward of the Bulowka-Hospital, the largest modem hospital. The then-Director Professor Dr. Walter Dick is today the Director of the Surgical Clinic II in Cologne.

Immediately after the revolution began, on Saturday, May 5th, Bubeniček had been imprisoned together with many other Germans in the basement of the Hotel "Schwarzer Adler", a former brothel of the Wehrmacht. The prostitutes and their procurers celebrated orgies of sadism and perversion with men and women stripped naked. Dr. Lang was particularly severely ill-treated. Covered all over with wounds he was driven insane with pain and hanged himself from a pulley for beer-barrels, under which his torturers had forced him to stand.

Notwithstanding the fact that Bubeniček's wound was still festering, he was released from the hospital by order of the Czech surgeon in charge, one Dr. Rein (from Postelberg, of German descent), and was returned to a Forced Labour Camp.

Another cell-inmate of mine was one Dr. Chrobok, an Austrian, who had been transferred to the Ministry of Postal Services in Prague during the period of the Protectorate. (Protectorate = Czechoslovakia between 1939 and 1945, excluding the Sudeten areas.) His son was said to live in Linz. He was moved to the prison hospital with an acute gastric and intestinal catarrh, probably of infectious origin. The patient received only several powders, which had no effect at all. Animal charcoal, too, was without effect. Instead he was given a tin plate of pudding, which he eagerly swallowed down although he had been forbidden to do so as he suffered from unappeasable thirst. The consequences set in at once. He died at night after enduring great pain. I crawled to the door and knocked, since there was no bell. The night-watchman came at last, and when I told him that Chrobok had died, he said: "And that's why you are bothering me? Thank God there's now one German swine less."

Every morning the first work was that of the *Gonkaři,* as the men were called who had to carry the five to seven corpses of those who had died at night to the room where the corpses were deposited.

I stayed in the hospital till August 20, 1945, and, although I was hardly able to stand on my feet, I was turned over to Section IIa of the so-called People's Court. Almost all of those prominent persons were held here who, according to the recently issued Retribution Edict of President Beneš, were to be brought before the People's Courts. Owing to the elasticity of its articles, any Sudeten German, and even more so any member of the Wehrmacht, could be charged under this Edict with high treason. My gastric complaint became considerably worse, furthermore there were such swellings on my limbs that I was unable to remove my trousers in the evening. In addition I contracted an acute articular rheumatism, which especially affected the right side of my body. The right knee which had been injured by my fall on the stone steps was swollen up like a balloon and very painful.

There I met Dr. Viktor Kindermann, the medical officer of Prague, who had been disfigured past recognition when he was arrested by the Revolutionary Guard at Aussig on May 27th. He had been delivered to Pankratz from the police headquarters in Prague.

My stomach pains became intolerable and I reported to the sick-room where conditions had improved since Černý had been appointed commandant of the hospital. Among the patients I met Dr. Hans Neuwirth, former delegate of the Sudeten German party. While I waited for the doctor in charge, I was able to exchange a few words with one Professor Dr. Josef Pfitzner who suffered from a serious angina and was also supposed to see the doctor in charge.

On September 5th, 1945 I was transported to the prison-hospital for the second time; cell 13 became my quarters.

It was here that I learned that Bubeniček, whom the Czechs had sent on hard labour in spite of his still un-healed leg, had been returned to the hospital. A malignant inflammation of the tissues required repeated surgical operations. As before, no narcotics were allowed to be used. But all the operations had not the slightest effect and a general blood-poisoning finally freed him from his sufferings.

Colonel Walena from Bilin, a cellmate of mine, contracted an inflammation of the lungs aggravated by a heart disease and died three days afterwards - his debilitated body, enfeebled by hunger, no longer had any power of resistance.

Another member of my cell was one Cink, a Czech watchman from the Walter Automobile and Aeroplane Motor Works in Jinonitz near Prague, who suffered from a high temperature; the doctors diagnosed disease of the kidneys. In his delirium one night he fell out of bed and remained lying on the ground unconscious. When I drew the blanket from his bed in order to cover him up, the unbearable stench coming out of his bed almost caused me to faint. He had never been given a urinal or any chamber-pot. On the point of death he was transferred to the General Hospital. When the so-called "sheet" - a rotten rag full of excrement - was taken off, I noticed that the entire palliasse was grey-white. Looking closer, I discovered it to be crawling with flea larvae and maggots.

One fine evening in September there was an immense tumult on the square in front of the court-building at Pankratz. That part of the square which I was able - though forbidden - to see from my window was crowded with cars and pedestrians. Mothers pushed their perambulators and children of school age climbed on the tops of the cars. All of a sudden continuous applause was to be heard. Professor Dr. Josef Pfitzner was being hanged from the middle one of three gallows, built up on a base covered with black. About 50,000 spectators were present at the execution.

Pfitzner was followed by an SS-officer of high rank from Berlin by the name of Schmidt, an inspector of the labour groups of PoW-camps. He was succeeded by Dr. Fritz Schicketanz, a lawyer, who had been accused of high treason because he had drawn up a legal opinion for the Sudeten German Party which was presented to Runciman in 1938. Number 4 was Dr. Blaschtowitschka from the German Special Court at Prague. Shortly afterwards his father, President of the Senate in Prague, died of hunger.

Among the next victims was Dr. Franz Wabra, head of the ward for Internal Medicine and Director of the hospital at Bernina; together with him, a certain Stanek, a Czech official of an insurance company, had to ascend the gallows.

The treatment and medical attention in the ward were still very bad. The brother of Moravec, who had been Minister during the period of the protectorate government (see above), was admitted. Both his legs were paralyzed after his bout with typhus and he had been transferred to this hospital from the German hospital in the Salmovka Strasse. Another prominent man was General Blaha, who was delivered into this hospital after an attempt to commit suicide.

At Christmas 1945 the central-heating apparatus ceased to function after feeble attempts had been made to start it a few days before.

The trial of Blaha, Richtrmoc and Major Mohapl was fixed for the middle of January. This was the first trial to be carried out by the newly established National Court *(Národní soud)* before which such Czechs could defend themselves who had transgressed against the national honour.

General Blaha was the founder of the Society of the Friends of Germany, the presidency of which he had passed on to Richtrmoc. Later on Blaha founded the League of Czech Veterans, Major Mohapl performing the duties of a Secretary-General in both organizations. Blaha and Richtrmoc were sentenced to death, Mohapl to twenty years imprisonment.

In January 1946 Dr. Jaroslav Preis, director of the Žinvo Bank, died in an adjoining cell.

From the beginning of my second stay in the hospital I was also able to watch Karl Hermann Frank (Reichskommissar of the Protectorate) take his daily walk between 1 and 2 o'clock in the afternoon.

On February 20, 1946 I was discharged from the prison-hospital and moved to a cell in the basement of the main building. On February 21st I was sent to work, without a hat, stockings, or even a coat. I was assigned to a labour column at Holleschowitz, where I met the children of Dr. Egon Ritter von Weinzierl, a university lecturer who had been killed by the Czechs. As a member of the work group I sometimes had the opportunity to go to town to visit Czech acquaintances who supplied me with money and food. At the end of March I was taken to the transfer-camp at Moderschan-Modřany. Here I met Professor Dr. Riehl, head of the Institute for Experimental Pathology, Dr. Hoffmann from the Ministry of Commerce at Prague, Mr. Manzer, an engineer, Baron Korb v. Weidenheim and many others. It was here that I received knowledge from an eyewitness of the death of one of my closest friends, Dr. Viktor Kindermann, who had died in the prison-hospital at Pankratz. Shortly before our transport group was marched off to the station, I was told that I would be kept back because of important evidence. I was thus brought back to Pankratz on April 5, 1946, where I met the following persons known to me: Dr. Polk, doctor from Smichow, Farnik, an engineer, head of the Pensioner's Institution of the Mines and Metal Foundries Association in Prague, Mr. Ferg, another engineer, and so on. The former State President Beran was held imprisoned at the same time. The doctors in charge of the sick-room were Dr. Kleveta, a Czech, and Professor Hohlbaum, head physician of the Clinic, as well as Dr. Erich Brandstätter.

At the end of August I was transferred to the prison on the Karlsplatz.

At the beginning of 1947 the executions of Ernst Kundt, Hans Krebs, Hans Westen, Schreiber, Böhm and Werner took place. Dr. Karl Feitenhansl, the leader of the physicians during the period of the Third Reich, was sentenced to penal servitude for life. The accusations against Rudolf Jung and Dr. Rosche were dropped, since both had starved to death at Pankratz.

On April 8, 1947 I came to Pankratz for the last time, where I met one Thomson, deputy-head of the Gestapo at Kladno, and Dr. Fritz Köllner.

My trial before the People's Court was fixed for April 15, 1947. The main witness for the prosecution, Mrs. Černiková-Fischlová, failed to appear. The other witness, a Czech officer of higher rank, stated that I had given medical attention to him and his Jewish wife long after the time that this had been made illegal; and that I had protected him in autumn 1944 from being assigned to a labour camp.

After the trial had lasted for four hours the court announced my acquittal. On April 24, 1947 I was released from Pankratz together with Mr. Anton Kiesewetter, director of the German Kredit-Bank in Pankratz, who was later transferred to Reichenberg.

I was transported by truck to the camp in Rusin, where I again had to do hard work, which I was barely able to accomplish owing to my gastritis. Kant, the inspector, ignored my protests, however. Together with me in the same labour group was Dr. Wilhelm Pleyer, the well-known author. From Rusin I was sent to the transfer-camp at Leschan, and after All Saints Day to that at Taus, the small amount of luggage left to us being pilfered on the way. On November 27, 1947 an ordinary passenger-train took me across the border to Furth i. W. My luggage consisted of a bundle of old linen and a few moth-eaten garments.

I hereby declare under oath that the foregoing deposition is true in all of its details.

Prague, Report No. 16
Pankratz, mass graves, mutilations
Reported by Sebastian Herr - Report of October 14, 1946

I am an ethnic German from Romania and worked as tailor in the SS Newscasting School in Leitmeritz. In May of last year I wanted to return to Romania, but I was arrested in Prague and incarcerated in Pankratz prison. There, on May 22 last year, I and other prisoners had to dig up the bodies of SS men who had died during the Revolution and had been buried in mass graves. In the process I saw from the dug-up corpses that their ears and noses had ben cut off, their eyes were gouged out and their hands had been scalded. There were 60 of us who had to do this exhumation work, and while working we were beaten so dreadfully that many of us lost consciousness. When we washed up after our work excavating the bodies, we were shoved head-first into the dirty wash water. I have only just been released from Pankratz.

Prague, Report No. 17
The transport of Modrany
Reported by the border superindentent of Wiesau - Report of May 21, 1946

This report is prompted by the countless complaints of Sudeten German refugees passing through the border train station of Wiesau on May 17, 1946 on their way from Prague. These are not the allegations of individuals, but rather the unanimous complaint of a total of 1,200 persons. I wish to give a general account of life in the concentration camp, which is typical for camps such as Modrany or Theresienstadt.

The camp inmates are not allowed to walk. Their normal speed of motion is running. One woman, a singer from Prague, describes life there as follows: "60 percent of the German women have at one time or another been handed over to the Russians to be raped. Every day the Czechs let Russians into the camp to rape me and the other women, whomever they chose. Many women are still being raped to this day. My legs are now paralyzed.

One pregnant woman who had to share with us the terrible life in the concentration camp was forced, whenever a Czech soldier entered the room and spat on the floor there, to kneel down and lick up his spittle. If she refused she was beaten and kicked. But that was not enough. One of the soldiers beat her until she threw up blood, and then forced her to eat her own vomit. Not until then did the soldier deem that she had adequately obeyed his orders."

Czech priests, who openly declared that they had no pity for Germans, refused to perform the last rites or to give spiritual aid to dying Germans.

Czech doctors refuse to treat sexually transmitted diseases resulting from rape even though the German women beg them for help. Syphilis is not treated at all. Gonorrhea is treated with a few tablets, which is considered sufficient. The refugees are refused all other medications. Wounded soldiers who are covered in open sores crawling with worms are simply left to their fate. They have to treat each other and are given neither bandages nor ointments. People who do not yet suffer from dysentery are forced to lick the dirty underwear of dysentery patients, at the whim of the soldiers who throw the infectious garments in their faces. If they refuse to lick on command, they are beaten senseless.

One fifteen-year-old boy whose father escaped from the camp was beaten every day until his father was found again. He (the father) was then tied up and doused with boiling water. The screams of the man thus tortured to death prompted nervous breakdowns in many camp inmates.

Convulsions and nervous breakdowns are the order of the day anyhow, and the Czechs consider them quite a natural state of affairs. It is impossible to describe all that has happened. I have only given a few examples here.

I stress again that these are not individual allegations, but rather the unanimous testimony of the Germans of Prague. The Germans have no rights at all in Czechoslovakia.

This transport from Prague was called a transport of the sick. By far the most of the refugees had to be unloaded immediately and taken to hospital. 90% of the diagnoses were for general weakness and debilitation. "Catastrophic" is how the doctors describe the state of health of the Germans from Prague.

All refugees are malnourished and totally emaciated. The overabundance of complaints and suffering prompted me to send the transport directly to the destination train station Schwabach, where the people can make their depositions. The chief physician of Schwabach was alerted by telephone to the incoming patients so that preventive measures could be taken to deal with the infectious and sexually transmitted diseases.

Reichenberg, Report No. 1
Report about the events of 1945-46
Reported by Emil Breuer Report of July 1948

On May 9th, 1945 the Russians marched into Reichenberg. About noontime, without any reason, Russian aeroplanes bombed the town and machine-gunned the columns of refugees and others on the roads. Russian soldiers forced their way into the houses and looted stores and apartments.

The Czechs, who in the meantime had arrived at Reichenberg, participated in the lootings. They drove up to the solitary villas at night, in their trucks, they threatened the residents with pistols and carried off whatever seemed to them of value. At the same time the Czech Revolutionary Guards (RG) started their pernicious activities. Germans were stopped in the streets, on their way to and from work and their watches and jewellery taken away; they were assaulted and locked up in cellars. In some cases they were even shipped off for forced labour. Sometimes they were obliged to take off their shoes and stockings and to walk barefoot to work. One day towards the end of May, at 7 o'clock in the morning, everyone was stopped at the Tuchplatz in Reichenberg; they were driven out of the street-cars and then deprived of their shoes and stockings. Many of the men were placed against the wall and two of them were shot. The others owed their lives to a Russian officer who intervened and stopped this Czech "justice". Germans had to dig mass-graves and to fill them up again. More than a thousand men had to make a so-called hunger-march, starting from Gablonz/ Neisse, for several days, during which many of them collapsed from exhaustion or hunger and died in the ditch. A Russian officer had been shot in the town and the Germans were being punished collectively. Later on a Ukrainian was identified as the culprit. On May 24, at noontime, two Russian soldiers and an interpreter seized me at my apartment. Together with other Germans I was put into the Russian section of the local jail at Reichenberg. Next morning we had to march to Ratschendorf. There we were all briefly interrogated by a Russian major; about noontime we were allowed to return home. Our treatment was absolutely correct.

On the afternoon of June 7th, 1945, after my apartment had been searched, I was taken to the office of the Revolutionary Guard. From there I was driven by car to house No. 22 in Gablonzer Str., where I was led to the second floor. The door was scarcely shut behind me, when I received violent blows in the face; my glasses were knocked off and a part of my false teeth was broken. Notwithstanding my age of 60 years, two men struck me with rubber-truncheons and [bullwhips] on my head, chest and back. In tearing off my tie they almost choked me to death. Each question by

Dr. Rokos, who interrogated me, was accompanied by a blow. A typist watched this maltreatment, smiling. I was ordered to give him the names of members of the "Werwolf-organization", but first I had to take off my jacket and my shoes and lay myself on the table; in order to extort a confession they used instruments of torture on my back and the soles of my feet. Since I was unable to name members of this organization, the ill-treatment was brought to an end with the threat that my whole family would be shot before my eyes at 8 o'clock next morning, unless I gave the names required. I was then flung down the steps into a cellar, where I landed on a heap of straw. I was lacerated and exhausted. I found myself in the company of fellow-sufferers who had preceded me.

Many severely maltreated persons lay there in the cellar. Thereafter, day after day, inmates were taken out into the cellar-passage and abused in such a way that they returned half-dead and covered with blood. Even those among us who were war-invalids were not spared. The number of the imprisoned persons in the cellar soon exceeded 50, among them 2 women. There was not enough room for all of us to lie down at the same time, we had to sleep in turns.

On June 10 Dr. Fritz Werner, a physician from Reichenberg, Johannesthal, was brought in. Through the cellar-door we could hear every single word of his interrogation, which took place in the passage outside. He was being confronted with some of the other prisoners. We heard his cries of pain and his prayers for mercy, but the maltreatment continued. Whenever he collapsed cold water was poured over him and as soon as he came to the torturing began again. Finally his cries ceased - for ever.

Following is a translation of the record of an examination, as made in the police department of the Revolutionary Guard at Jung-Bunzlau, to determine the cause of death of Dr. Fritz Werner:

Reichenberg, June 10th, 1945

Record of examination:

On June 10th, 1945, at 7 p.m. I examined the corpse of a man, 164 cm. (5' 5"] tall, about 60 years of age, a little stout. It was Dr. Fritz Werner, physician at Reichenberg, in whose possession a document was found, dated August 1st, 1944, recording that as an officer he had received from Adolf Hitler the cross for distinguished services to the German nation (Verdienstkreuz II. Kl.)

I noticed blue marks on the chest and the face, the results of a contusion, as well as a gaping wound on the left side close to the spine. The chest was undamaged. [Pupils dilated, pulse not palpable], no breath reaction on mirror.

[Cause of] death: *Commotio cerebi propter apoplexiam cerebi ac. Vulnus contusioni lacerum regionis occip. lat. sin.*

Signed Dr. Rocus m.p.

Policejní oddělení R. G.

Velitelství Ml. Boleslav.

On June 10, 1945, after being brought in for confrontation, Dr. Fritz Werner, physician at Reichenberg, died of apoplexy of the brain. The cremation took place at the crematorium at Reichenberg on June 11th, 1945. The record of examination is attached.

Reichenberg, June 21st, 1945.
Local judicial commission at Reichenberg

July 12, 1945.

To Mrs. Liese Werner, Reichenberg.

Your demand of June 26th, 1945, for delivery of the urn containing the ashes of your husband, who was cremated in the local crematorium on June 20, 1945, will be met, provided that the urn be interred in the family vault at the local cemetery.

The director of the office
Čapek
The Chairman
(stamp and signature)

On June 13 almost all of the imprisoned persons were briefly interrogated and divided into groups. About 11 o'clock in the evening I was taken to the district court building at Reichenberg together with 21 other prisoners. We were forced to kiss a defaced Hitler-picture and then, completely naked, to kneel for hours in the cold and draughty gangway with our hands above our heads, while the [thugs] who had brought us in beat us with steel rods, rubber-truncheons and [bullwhips]. All this happened in the presence and with the co-operation of the wardens of the district-prison. The marks of the ill-treatment were visible on us for weeks. I myself had an effusion of blood in the left eye as a result.

Night after night Germans were brought to the prison and abused in the same manner.

Our cell No. 59 was intended to house five men, but at the beginning of our imprisonment there were nine of us and soon afterwards twenty. We slept for weeks in our light summer-clothing on the rough boards. Finally we received a few blankets and palliasses which we used as pillows. Our daily diet consisted of a thin soup, coffee and 150 g of bread. It was absolutely insufficient and we became enfeebled within a short time. Inside a few weeks we lost up to 30 kilos (66 pounds) in weight. The only thing of which we had an abundance was maltreatment. Especially during the so-called "walks" in the prison-yard, which were combined with gymnastics requiring great muscular strength, we were regularly beaten. Whenever, as a result of the enfeeblement, anyone failed in the exercises, the wardens had a welcome reason for abusing him. On Sundays, in addition to the wardens, men of the Revolutionary Guard participated in the atrocities.

At the end of August the soup became a little bit better and the daily bread ration increased. Furthermore the relatives of the prisoners were allowed to deliver every week a parcel of food, weighing not more than 2 kilos (4.4 pounds). Those German women cannot be sufficiently praised who, in spite of the small rations for Germans, were able to save their husbands and sons from starvation by these additional food-supplies. Some of the women had to carry their parcel as much as 30 kilometers (20 miles), since no Germans were allowed to use the railways. But in many cases this help was already too late. Cases of death in consequence of starvation or enfeeblement or of insufficient medical attendance are reported not only from the district-prison at Reichenberg but from all other camps and jails.

Even before I was arrested at the end of May, it had been announced that all Germans, who had arrived in Sudeten German territories after the 1st of October 1938, would have to leave Reichenberg and could take only 30 kilos (66 pounds) with them. Anyone not observing the order promptly would then be allowed no more than 20 and later on no more than 10 kilos (22 pounds). The local authorities confirmed by word of mouth to those Sudeten Germans who had moved to Reichenberg that this order would only concern the so-called Reichs-Germans who had not lived in the Czechoslovak Republic before 1938.

My second daughter, who had been sent for four weeks to an absolutely Czech region for agricultural labour, had just returned when she was forced to leave her homeland without having the opportunity of bidding farewell to her 60-year-old father in prison. All she was allowed to take was a rucksack containing underwear. The same thing also happened to other relatives of ours. Before they had even reached the border they were deprived by the Czechs of a number of their personal possessions; their savings-bank books and personal documents were destroyed; they had also to take off their shoes and stockings and to continue the march across the border barefoot. Sheets and mattresses were torn out of perambulators and the milk for the babies was poured out on the ground.

My imprisonment at the district-prison at Reichenberg left me in a state of complete exhaustion. Probably as a result of my condition I was transferred to the camp at Reichenberg. I was so enfeebled that even the short march from the prison to the camp cost me a great deal. At the camp I received more food. The larger rations - food which was given to me by fellow-prisoners working outside the camp, and also supplies which my family had smuggled into the camp - quickly strengthened me. The out-of-door activities in sun and open air did the rest. A few days later I, too, had to start working. At some of our places of work we received additional meals. The only exceptions were the local administrative authorities who either gave nothing or distributed to the Germans the leavings scraped together from the plates of the municipal employees. The pilots sometimes gave us only a thin soup and other times so much food that we were able to take a great deal of it back to the camp for our comrades.

At the aerodrome there were dust-bins near the billets. These dust-bins had to be emptied from time to time. We always looked forward to this moment, since we often found pounds of bread and pastry as well as cheese, still wrapped up in tin-foil. On these days we were able to carry home additional food for ourselves and, more important, to bring our fellow-sufferers, who were [unable to] work, the necessary food. Those who were able to work, were for the most part forced without distinction to do heavier and heavier work, shovelling coal, digging out foundations, felling trees and loading trucks. The women were sent to restaurants and to private households for cleaning or laundry work. Besides this, many were ordered to farms, to quarries, mines and to unhealthy occupations in the interior of Czechoslovakia. Germans were sent to the mountains, to saw-mills and for felling timber. Only during the summer of 1945 ill-treatment took place generally. Thereafter only infrequent cases of maltreatment were reported from camps and work places.

In spite of my age I was also among those who were sent to heavy work. I fell ill twice. The first time I contracted an inflammation of the throat as a result of being compelled to trail logs in the hilly woods, even though I was suffering from fever. The second time I contracted articular rheumatism through digging drains during a long period of rain. I was incapable of work for several weeks. I wish to express my appreciation of the medical treatment I received from the camp-physician Dr. Pott, a fellow-prisoner.

After 13½ months of imprisonment I was correctly interrogated for the first and last time. This was finally brought about by the representations of my wife and took place at the police-station at Reichenberg on July 24th, 1946. I was promised a quick decision and an early transfer. But things turned out differently. A supplement to the law regulating the infliction of punishment, which was issued at the beginning of August 1946, established that in the case of "Foreigners" sentence could be commuted in favour of transfer, if the State were more interested in the transfer than in punishment. But at the same time the power to initiate a prosecution before the People's Courts was withdrawn from the police authorities and entrusted to the district attorney.

The district attorney based his case against me on Article 3 of the Edict of Retribution, issued by the State President. On October 30th, 1946 I received the bill of indictment. Again I was told that the trial would take place within 8 days. But in fact I was not summoned before the Special People's Court until November 21st, 1946. The ex-offo-counsel for the defence did not get in touch with me and - as far as I know - was not present at the trial. After the day and the hour of my arrest had been established, the court withdrew and then pronounced judgement. I was sentenced to 17 months imprisonment in consideration of the extenuating circumstances as laid down in Article 16 and especially of the fact that I had never made any National Socialist propaganda. The sentence was considered as already served in view of my 17½ months of imprisonment on remand. The whole trial lasted no longer than 10 minutes. Since I had been brought before the court from the camp, I was taken back there. I was still detained and not released to my family, although my sentence was already terminated.

Shortly before my sentencing, that is on November 14th, 1946, the last large transport from Reichenberg left for the American zone of Germany. Soon afterwards the Czech Government had the effrontery to declare publicly, even though they knew that more than 200,000 Sudeten Germans were waiting for their transfer and their reunion with their relatives in Germany, that the transfer of the Sudeten Germans was [complete]. My wife was living together with our two younger daughters and a grandson in a humble little apartment at Reichenberg-Rosenthal. The entire furniture of our apartment had been taken away from her, they had removed my considerable library and she herself had been forced to clear out of the apartment. Hoping that I would soon be released, she had waited for me in 1945 in spite of the chicaneries of the various authorities. In 1946 she was no longer able to leave, since as a result of an American protest families could not now be transferred without their bread-winner.

In 1947 the conditions in the camp improved considerably. The number of inmates was diminished. Each one of us had his own bed. After the People's Courts had been dissolved we were no longer prisoners, we were only Germans to be transferred. But the barbed wire around the camp still remained; only that round the individual huts was removed. One was allowed to visit acquaintances in other huts. We had more liberty to move within the camp and sometimes we were permitted to go out on Sundays. The diet, too, improved. Working clothes were distributed in cases of necessity; in the workshops which we set up ourselves shoes and clothing were repaired free of charge. The percentage of our wages, which all factories, undertakings and households employing camp-inmates had to pay to the camp-administration, was increased from 2 to 10 Kčs per working day. Cigarettes and sweets could be bought in the camp.

Since in view of my articular rheumatism the doctor had certified me not fully capable of work, I was sent only to light work after I had been before the court. In March 1947 I was called for as a specialist on liquidations, in connection with the liquidation of the German banks. I remained in this job until my transfer. But even as a specialist I received no more than 10 Kčs for each working day as salary besides the food in the camp, although the camp-administration demanded higher wages for my services than before. In March 1947 we accidentally heard about an order which had been issued by the Minister of the Interior on December 1946 and according to which during the temporary suspension of transfers transports could take place via Taus and Furth i. Walde for the purpose of reuniting divided families. Since my elder daughter had found shelter in the neighbourhood of Detmold-Lippe since November 1945, I made efforts to be transferred via Taus. But even when I could show offers of work in Germany, my application was always put back with a reference to the fact that my wife and four members of my family were still living in Czechoslovakia and we were therefore not considered as separated. Families only came into question, when wife and husband were separated or children divided from their parents. So 1947 passed.

By December 1947 the conditions in the camp became worse. We were only rarely allowed to leave the camp on Sundays. Even at Christmas families might only be visited on a single day for a few hours. It was not advisable to speak German on the streets. At the end of February 1948 it became even worse when the Communists usurped the Governmental Power. Those Germans who were still employed in individual undertakings as irreplaceable specialists had to be fired. It became dangerous to speak German at all. We were scarcely ever allowed to leave the camp except for work. An English course, which inmates of the camp held among themselves and only during the evening hours, was now forbidden.

The People's Courts were re-established and were ordered to review all the previous cases which had come before them. Germans who in 1947 had been released after being in prison on remand for 1½ and 2 years without ever having been tried, were re-arrested and were sentenced to at least 5 years imprisonment. The extenuating circumstances of Article 16 were now never applied to Germans. Even those Germans who had formerly been acquitted were re-arrested and new prosecutions ended with heavy sentences. Those, too, who had been already sentenced were brought back before the Communist People's Court, which always raised the penalty. I myself, before I was transferred, had knowledge not only of the case of a German who had never been prosecuted and who was now sentenced to five years, but also of two similar cases. In one the punishment of 18 months, served long ago, was increased to 15 years, in the other case the former sentence of 10 years was changed into 20 years. These three sentences were passed by the renewed People's Court at Reichenberg on May 19th, 1948. The sentences were published in *"Stráž severu"*.

But not only Germans were threatened by new perils, the Czechs and especially the partners in mixed marriages were endangered too. Lawyers who had successfully defended Germans in the proceedings before the People's Courts were suspended from the legal profession as [being] unreliable; Czech witnesses for the defence were to undergo an investigation.

At this time first of all the inmates of the camps and then all Sudeten Germans were informed of the possibility of being transferred at our own expense. For transport-charges to the border the inmates of the camps were required to pay 1,000 Kčs and all other Sudeten Germans had to pay 1,500 Kčs per head. After the first sentences had been passed by the new People's Courts, everybody attempted to escape as soon as possible. I had now to pay 6,500 Kčs for my own, my wife's, my two daughters' and my grandson's transport to the border (one of my daughters was also a camp inmate, but worked for a farmer). Friends of mine helped, as I alone would have been unable to meet the cost. But again I was set back from the first transport and we were assigned only to the second one. Our luggage was cleared by the customs and on May 26th, 1948 we climbed onto the truck, together with 51 other Sudeten Germans. Our luggage was put on a second truck and its trailer. We drove via Prague, Karlsbad and Asch to the border, which we crossed in the morning hours of May 27th, after our small luggage had been passed by the customs.

Reichenberg, Report No. 2
Massacre on Tuch Square, May 3, 1945
Reported by T. M.

I lived in Reichenberg in the high-rise apartment building of the "Reunione adriatica sicurta". On May 13, 1945 I was in bed suffering from a high fever and angina. At 5:30 in the morning someone pounded on our door with rifle butts. Outside stood two young fellows in Africa uniforms, who drove all inhabitants of the house, including me, out of our homes without even giving us time to dress. My wife asked the two to please let me get dressed, to which they replied: "You German whore, you don't need to get dressed, you'll both be cold in an hour anyway." We had to walk down the nine stories of our building on foot. This was accompanied by a great commotion, yelling, shots, cries for help, and screams.

All the inhabitants of the house had to line up to the right and left of the house gateway in the Färbergasse, opposite the District Court. Almost all of us were only scantily clad.

Czechs ran up and down the Färbergasse, eyes and rifles pointed at the windows. A group of Czechs went up to the Health Insurance office, went in and came back out grinning. When they closed the door I saw them shove a corpse lying in the anteroom aside with their feet.

A man who was walking along the Färbergasse towards Tuch Square was stopped and forced at gunpoint to take off his shoes, socks and coat and to place them on the ground along with his full briefcase, and then he was chased away back in the direction whence he had come.

After some time all the inhabitants of the house in which I also lived had to march to Tuch Square. There were about 60 of us. The crowd of Czechs had grown larger. One who was particularly noticeable was a man with a wild shock of black hair who beat wildly into the crowd of Germans with his nagaika. This was the starting sign for maltreatment by the Revolutionary Guard. People, especially men, who got off the street cars or were just walking along were beaten, robbed, and many of them had to join our group. We were segregated according to sex, and I stood on the one side towards the Donauhof. The Revolutionary Guardsmen who maltreated us were mostly younger fellows about 18 to 22 years old. Suddenly the order was given that all men had to line up along the wall of the row of houses between Körber and the German Labor Bank. I had already seen a young man lying there dead, face down in a pool of blood. Then more RG men appeared with automatic weapons and ordered those standing along the wall to take off their shoes, to put them on the ground beside them and remain standing there barefoot. Meanwhile they worked us over with rifle butts, punches and kicks and even an alpenstock.

One boy about 16 years old was beaten beyond recognition. He remained on the ground as a convulsed, bloody lump. I myself had taken my shoes off immediately and was not maltreated. Then the RG demanded that we take off our shirts, and we had to stand facing the wall with arms raised. Behind every German standing there like that stood a young RG man who held his weapon aimed at the ready. All those lined up before me had vanished, I don't know where they got to.

When the Czech Commandant and four higher-ranking officers arrived at my position, he was suddenly called away. When he returned he wanted to see my papers. I handed him my green ID with the large letter "P" (Pracujíci) and asked him quite insolently whether I should also fetch my other papers from my flat, which he permitted. The RG standing in front of me ordered me to dress.

I picked up my shoes and finally reached the house entrance. We went up 10 stories by foot, which was very difficult for me in my feverish condition. In my flat I took the papers, and we went back down. The RG handed my papers to the Plukovník, who pronounced them in order. I was allowed to leave. My wife, who was fluent in Czech, had already returned home earlier. Shortly after that, the sound of four detonations came over from Tuch Square, and when I looked down I saw four dead bodies. Calm was soon restored, as one woman informed a Russian Commandant in the Hotel Imperial of the events and the executions were then stopped.

700 men from the RG were quartered in our high-rise for about six weeks. An RG man sat outside each apartment and accompanied every resident wherever he or she went, even to the toilet. Downstairs in the watchman's room sat guards, and whenever anyone left the house they would issue them a pass specifying a time by which they had to be back, and these times had to be strictly obeyed. All the apartments were looted. The cellars of the house served as RG prison.

Reichenberg, Report No. 3

Expulsion of Reich Germans on May 30, 1945

Reported by Heinrich Ackerhans and 8 other Germans from the Reich
Reports of July 11, 1950 and May 31, 1945

Lichtenberg, May 31, 1945

City Hall, the Mayor's Office
Appearing in City Hall:

1. Ackerhans Heinrich, born Sept. 16, 1886, Senior Government Construction Counsel with the Reich Government Representative in the Sudetengau in Reichenberg, resident in Reichenberg, Pestalozzi St. 9

2. his wife Anna, née Eidtmann, born March 21, 1891

3. Holberg Wilfried, born Nov. 23, 1930, resident as for 1.

4. Kohlmeyer Sophie, née Benkert, born July 15, 1902, resident in Reichenberg, Aloisienhöhe 7, wife of Karl Kohlmeyer, born June 8, 1901, Chief Inspector of the Reichenberg Office of Weights and Measures

5. their daughter Christa, born Dec. 21, 1928

6. Leonhardt Walter, born Jan. 26, 1893, senior civil servant with the Reich Government Representative in Reichenberg, resident at Joh.-Strauss St. 37

7. his wife Frida, née Walther, born June 13, 1897

8. his daughter Gerda, born Sept. 13, 1927

9. Spiegel Erich, born Nov. 14, 1895, gov't. inspector with the Reich Government Representative in Reichenberg, resident at Johann-Strauss St. 35

The persons listed under 1. through 9. state:

As per radio broadcast and newspaper announcement by the *Český národní výbor* in Reichenberg, all Germans from the Reich had to leave Reichenberg *immediately*. 10 kilos of hand luggage was all they were allowed to take with them. Consequently we had to leave Reichenberg on May 30, 1945, leaving behind our entire movable and immovable property, including stocks and shares, savings and bank books. We had to leave on foot, with only some hand luggage. The food stamps for Stamp Period 76 had not been handed out at that time, and we also did not receive them later.

On May 31, 1945 at 2 o'clock in the afternoon, after having been looted repeatedly and robbed of our hand luggage and cash by members of the Czech Revolutionary Guard (RG), we arrived at the first Reich-German town, Lichtenberg, in the District of Zittau in Saxony.

The aforementioned Reich civil servants state further:

The permanent deputy of the Reich Government Representative, President Dr. Vogeler in Reichenberg, has informed the Division Heads that as a result of the offices having been transferred to the *Ceský národní výbor v Liberci,* employees of these offices have been relieved of their duties as Reich officials in the Sudetengau, and that the succeeding Czech authorities would not be taking them on as employees of the new system. A written confirmation of this decision was not issued despite requests to that effect.

Read, approved and signed:
[sgd.] Heinrich Ackerhans, signing also on behalf of his wife
and the minor Wilfried Holberg
[sgd.] Walter Leonhardt, also on behalf of his wife and daughter
[sgd.] Sophie Kohlmeyer and daughter
[sgd.] Erich Spiegel

As per the local conditions of which I am aware,
these statements are factual and true.
Concluded: the Mayor, [sgd.] Adolf Trenkler

Report about our expulsion from the Sudetenland in May 1945.

I, Heinrich Ackerhans, born on September 16, 1886, was first transferred to Karlsbad as official of the German Reich in 1939. When the office was closed I was transferred to the office of the Reich Government Representative in Reichenberg in 1940. My family therefore moved from Berlin to Reichenberg.

After the surrender and the end of the war, most Reich officials, employees and workers continued to do their duty until the end of May 1945 in the former Reich Government Representative's office, now known as *Ceský národní výbor.* Then they were forbidden to enter these premises again.

On Tuesday, May 29, 1945 the National Committee of the new Czech government announced via radio and newspaper notices that all Germans from the Reich who had been locally resident since 1938 were to leave Reichenberg immediately with a maximum of 30 kg of hand luggage (later reduced to 10 kg) and to assemble behind the train station by midnight to be transported. Many Reich Germans, including us, did not obey these instructions, but fled on our own instead. On Wednesday, May 30, 1945, around 4 o'clock p.m., we, that is my wife, myself and our 14-year-old nephew who was living with us, left Reichenberg with a hand cart filled with suitcases. We left together with two civil servants and their families (9 persons altogether). We had to leave all our property and possessions behind, with the exception of the minor values contained in the suitcases which were later looted anyway. Near the municipal woodland by the People's Gardens in Reichenberg, four members of the Czech Revolutionary Guard (wearing armbands marked with RG) attacked us. We were threatened with submachine guns and dog whips and were first body-searched and deprived of our valuables, then they rifled our suitcases and helped themselves to any valuable contents such as watches, silverware, linen, a pair of binoculars, tobacco, briefcase, the suitcases themselves etc. One civil servant was relieved of all his money. All this had to proceed very quickly, probably because the Czech looters were afraid of the Russian garrison. On Thursday, May 31, 1945, after traveling via Schönborn and Nenndorf, we reached Lichtenberg in the District of Zittau, the first Reich German town, where we instituted proceedings as outlined in the transcript enclosed.

Reichenberg, Report No. 4
Treatment of sick people
Reported by Justine Pilz - Report of October 15, 1946

In May 1945 I was working at the military hospital in Reichenberg. After the capitulation, the German wounded soldiers were turned out of doors and were maltreated in such a way that many of them lost their lives; I myself saw wounded men, with amputated legs or arms, in a terribly bruised condition. Civilian hospitals also turned out all Germans, irrespective of their physical state.

Doctor Posselt, who worked at the hospital, told me himself that one woman was put out of the hospital although she was actually in the process of giving birth to her child. A subsidiary hospital for Germans was established in a school, I myself was employed there as a nurse. All the Germans who had been mistreated and tortured in prison or in the camps were sent there. Among them were many who died of their injuries shortly after being admitted. There were also many who, after a short time, died of exhaustion or malnutrition.

People had often to be discharged from the hospitals who were by no means fit to be released. After two or three days they were often sent in again almost at the point of death. We had 6 or 7 deaths every day. The bodies had to be placed in a shed, where they were often gnawed by rats. All my efforts to remedy the abuses and to improve the situation of the sick were fruitless.

There was no improvement until July 1946.

Reichenberg, Report No. 5
Imprisoned one year for no reason
Reported by Franz Fiedler - Report of November 8, 1946

I was the proprietor of two hotels in Reichenberg. On June 12, 1945 I was arrested for no reason whatsoever and detained in the District Court in Reichenberg. As late as October 10 no grounds for my arrest had been determined, as I myself was able to see by chance when I happened to catch a glimpse of my arrest record. On October 25 it was noted in this record that I had allegedly been rough to my employees and that a German apprentice boy with a Czech name had been punished in my business. Czech witnesses who had been called in my case testified in my defense. Nonetheless the People's Court did not release me until July 25, 1946, and I was dismissed without any documentation. During my detention I was repeatedly maltreated, like the other prisoners as well.

Reichenberg, Report No. 6
Maltreatment of women
Reported by Marianne Chytil - Report of July 5, 1946

I was arrested on May 31, 1945 in Langenbruck near Reichenberg and committed to the District Court prison in Reichenberg. On committal, the 20 men in our line were brutally maltreated, naked. Meanwhile I myself was guarded by two Revolutionary Guardsmen, and whenever I so much as shed a tear at the men's screams of pain they boxed me about the ears. Afterwards they tore the clothes off my body as well and threw me naked onto a writing desk, and then four others beat me with leather straps until I fainted. One guard had squeezed my throat so that I could not scream. When I regained consciousness I found myself in a cell together with another woman who had been terribly beaten up. She died three days later of the consequences of the maltreatment she had suffered. After about 7 weeks I was to be interrogated. In the anteroom of the examining magistrate the inmates awaiting interrogation were tormented and abused by the SBN in a variety of ways. I myself was given 50 blows with a cane, on my hands. 15 weeks later I was transferred to the internment camp of Reichenberg, and sent on into the Czech region for farm labor the very same day. The work I was expected to do there was very hard, and I got almost nothing to eat.

Reichenberg, Report No. 7
Treatment of Jews
Reported by Dr. Rudolf Fernegg - Report of June 21, 1951

The son of the liqueur destiller Soyka at Reichenberg, who was well-known to me and who had fought in the French army during the war, came to Reichenberg after the political change-over. He told me that he planned to get back his father's villa as well as the factory from the Czechs. First of all he was only allowed to use a room in the attic of his house, but was not allowed to enter the living-room, bed-room etc. Some weeks later he declared that the negotiations concerning house and factory had turned out to be so difficult that he would probably not go on with them. I am not informed as to the final result of his negotiations, since I myself had in the meantime been arrested and was later transferred [expelled].

Czech reign of terror
Reported by Dr. jur. Franz Freyer, district judge - Report of March 3, 1951

In the morning hours of May 9th, 1945 Russian tanks drove into Saaz. Uncertainty as to what the near future would bring lay heavily upon the inhabitants. Women were raped, a number of persons were shot and some disappeared, of whom no one ever heard again. Many lost their nerve and hanged themselves or opened their veins.

At the end of May it became known that an edict had been issued by President Beneš, putting all German property under "National Administration". Many Germans expected that the Anglo-Saxon Powers would intervene and that, after some time, a bearable co-existence between Sudeten Germans and Czechs might be achieved. On June 2nd, the Russians left and the troops of the Czech General Svoboda occupied the town. On June 3rd, a Sunday, disaster overwhelmed Saaz. This was the day on which the male Germans of Saaz were expelled. Czech gendarmes and soldiers forced their way into the houses and drove men and boys to the market-place. The streets echoed with screams and shots; soldiers on horses and bicycles hunted the people into the centre of the town. Many were obliged to run for their lives. The men of Saaz were herded together there: some were elderly and ill and had been examined and rejected ten times over by the Wehrmacht, the Reich Labour Service and the Todt Organization; at their side stood boys scarcely out of childhood. Some 5000 were assembled there. Many of them were knocked about by the soldiers there and then; any who were particularly noticeable or who, as a result of clumsiness or weakness, did not stay properly in line or who provoked the Czechs by wearing German national costume, were severely maltreated. A straggler was shot down. The treatment was so inhuman that three Germans who watched the incidents from their apartments committed suicide in order to escape a similar fate. In the course of the forenoon men and boys were then driven in three columns to the little town of Postelberg, 15 kilometers distant from Saaz. On their way they were knocked about further.

Postelberg seemed quite deserted - later on the forlorn condition of the place was explained: the inhabitants had already been driven out of the town before the men from Saaz arrived. In Postelberg are situated the cavalry barracks, a rectangular building about 100 years old. The men and boys of Saaz were led into the court-yard of the barracks, were ordered to sit down and not allowed to move.

In the meantime, but hidden from the eyes of the public, another tragic scene took place in the district court building at Saaz. Czech personnel had been on duty there for several days. The prisoners were illtreated, Czechs entered the cells at night and vented their fury on the defenceless inmates.

The Czechs maintained that a number of them committed suicide. Now the 150 prisoners were examined and divided into those who were about to die and the others who were minor offenders. The treatment of the former was such that it made it easy for them to die. They stood in the court-yard of the prison in scorching heat, their heads bare, their hands raised, until one after another collapsed. Czech police and soldiers walked down the lines and chose their victims. These would receive a jab in the stomach from a club a meter long, and when they doubled up they got several blows on the head. Many of the men so maltreated vomited blood and were hardly able to stand.

In the evening soldiers entered the yard; they had whips in their hands and hand-grenades at their belts. They laughed and jeered at the prisoners. Marek, the captain of the police, gave the order to march. A prisoner stepped forward and reported that he had a serious disease of the heart. A punch in the face drove the man back to his line-up and soon afterwards the prisoners marched in rows of eight out the gate. The market place was deserted. The column passed the town hall, reached the Priestertor (gate of Saaz). Here the soldiers lifted their whips and lashed the prisoners until the column arrived at the outskirts of the town. At midnight these prisoners, too, reached the little town of Postelberg, while at Saaz thousands of frightened women waited in vain for the return of their husbands or children.

June 4th was the day of lootings. The prisoners had spent the night lying in the dirt of the barrack-yard. No one was allowed to leave. The Czechs threatened anyone who moved with death, even if he only wished to relieve himself. Then the order was given to come to attention. Some of the prisoners got up, while others remained sitting. Immediately afterwards shots rang out. Dead and wounded men lay on the ground, the wounded were dragged towards the ditch, one of them lifted his hand and said: "Farewell, comrades, it will soon be over." The prisoners were forced to throw dead and wounded into the ditch, several shots with automatic pistols followed, and all of them were out of their misery. The ditch had served as a latrine for thousands. Now the latrine became the grave of many men of Saaz.

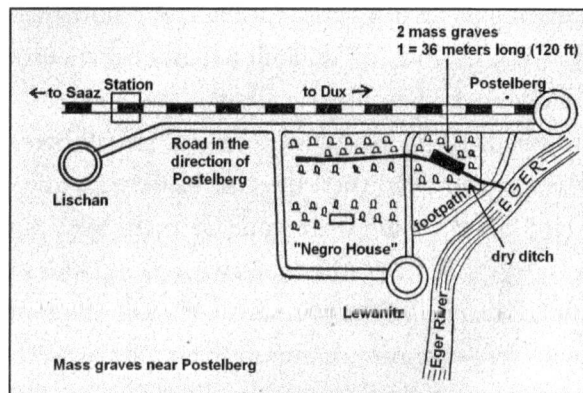

New commands were given. All had to surrender their money and valuables. "Anyone who attempts to hide anything will be punished with death," said the Czechs. Nobody doubted the reality of this threat. Watches, money, rings and other articles were surrendered at once. The money stolen filled whole boxes. Afterwards the prisoners were thoroughly searched, shoes had to be taken off, articles which were of no value to the Czechs, such as letters, documents and medications, were destroyed. Meanwhile Czech soldiers went up and down the lines and the insults and blows went on without a stop.

In the evening of the same day certain classes of persons were allowed to leave the courtyard of the barracks. These included: physicians, apothecaries, priests, men with important professions, indispensable artisans, half-Jews, husbands of Jewish or half-Jewish women as well as former German inmates of concentration camps; but not all of them were long able to enjoy their freedom: on his way home one of the Capuchin monks, who was a poor walker, was simply shot down, the majority of them were taken to the camp at Saaz. The prisoners at Postelberg spent the night from June 4th to June 5th in the stables. They were naturally unable to sleep, the confinement was oppressive in itself and they could hear shots all night long in the yard, in the town and from the surrounding country.

On June 5th the killing began. The doors of the stables were opened and the order was given: *"rychle, rychle!"* (quickly, quickly). Anyone who moved too slowly was shot down. No assistance was given; in essence, any injury was fatal. Many of those who bled to death in the course of the day could have been saved by proper attention. The dead and the wounded were again thrown into the latrine and the customary shots, which Captain Marek called "mercy shots", were fired with automatic pistols.

Later on Captain Marek examined the prisoners. Members of the SS, SA, NSKK (affiliated organizations of the NSDAP), of the Wehrmacht, and also the functionaries of the NSDAP and former members of the SdP (Sudeten German Party) had to report. The chaos and the misunderstandings were immense. Should one report that one had been in the Party if one had also been in the Wehrmacht? It is difficult to describe what took place in the yard of the barracks on this and the following day. In order to obtain a clear and trustworthy picture, it would be necessary to investigate hundreds of people. While one was struck here, another one was shot down there, here a corpse was dragged away, there the Czechs were examining Germans for their capability as workers, finally marching them off; there some Germans were put behind barbed wire, others were locked up in the stables, the whole yard echoed with commands, screams, insults, violent blows and shots. By sunset probably most of the prisoners - who on this as on the previous days had received no food at all and who were now rounded up in the stables or were forced to lie down in the barrack-yard - had given up all hope of their lives and were ready to die bravely. The victims of this day were not counted up. At night the constant fire of automatic weapons could be heard from near and far.

June 6th was the day of child-murder.

At first there was again the endless dividing and forming up of labour groups. Close to the gate, as on previous days, there sat 120 boys between 13 and 18 years old. They, too, had received no food for three days. Five of them unobtrusively joined up with a labour group in order to escape from their confinement. But when they got to Postelberg, they were seized and brought before Captain Marek. The other men and boys, shaking with horror, witnessed the dreadful scene, which was introduced by the following threats: "Any objections and we will shoot at once!" The five boys were led to the riding-school, where they had to take off their trousers and then the corporal punishment began. It was revolting to see how the Czechs crowded round eagerly in order to land their blows. The merciless beating with sticks and whips wrung from the boys heart-rending moans. Blood ran down their thighs. Afterwards the Czech "soldiers" dispersed. The boys remained standing with their faces towards the wall, a sentry placed himself besides them. After a while the distraught spectators calmed down. Everybody believed that the boys' ordeal had come to an end. But after half an hour a number of Czechs armed with guns placed themselves behind the boys. One of the guards called out: "Anyone who attempts to escape will be shot as these boys are going to be shot!" But this man himself could not have believed that the threat concerning the shooting was meant literally. The boys looked round fearfully and then turned. Two Czechs trained their guns on the first boy at point-blank range, shots cracked and the boy sank to the ground. His blood reddened the wall. The other boys screamed: "Captain, we won't do it again!" The second boy ran towards his executioners, intending to push up the muzzles of their guns. But the murderers had already reloaded and the second boy also fell. Plaster flew into dust and again the wall was reddened with blood. The rest of the boys bravely submitted themselves to their fate. The third one cried for his mother before he collapsed. The fourth remained standing after the first salvo, looked silently at the lifted rifles and only sank to the ground after the second salvo. The fifth was also shot down. The boys were perhaps 15 years of age. The grown-ups watched the murders, unable to do anything. Resistance would have caused a real massacre, since machine-guns were posted near the gate.

But the mental tortures had not yet come to an end. Those who were about to die were lodged in the stables at the other end of the yard. Every hour, punctually as the clock struck, a group of Czechs armed with sticks and whips would enter the stables and then for the next ten minutes the sound of blows and the cries of the tortured men was to be heard. This lasted until evening. Even the shootings were not such a strain on the nerves as the sounds of this maltreatment.

Then there was another spectacle. About twenty of the prisoners were led out of the back gate. They carried spades and hatchets. They were followed by a troop of gendarmes and soldiers armed with submachine guns. We all expected executions. But we waited in vain for the salvos to follow. After an hour had passed the prisoners and the soldiers returned.

At noontime on the fourth day we received food for the first time - one loaf of bread to 10 prisoners. In the afternoon the fury of the Czechs increased. Again no single observer could fully comprehend what was going on in the vast yard. Here one was cuffed, there another one was trampled under foot, here a savage dog was being set on the prisoners, there a number of prisoners were being thrashed on the naked buttocks with rubber truncheons; next to these, prisoners were being forced to crack each other over the head with sticks, while guards saw to it that the blows were not too light. Now and then Czech women would walk across the yard and gloat over the spectacle.

In the evening hundreds of prisoners were rescued from their mental and bodily pains - at least for a short period. Buses drove up in front of the barracks and fetched "material", that is to say forced labourers, for the hydration plant at Brüx.

At dusk as many people were thrust in the small and low-roofed stable as could stand there. The doors were closed and a guard was posted in front of the stables. The men who had been locked in - 275 of them, as a later count revealed - found themselves in a room, the ceiling of which they could almost reach with their hands. The only window, that above the door, was closed. They were almost unable to move, let alone lie down. Soon the lack of oxygen became noticeable, everybody began to drip with sweat and those suffering from heart disease collapsed one after another. All of a sudden yelling began, which reached a pitch of madness. The sentries threatened to use their hand-grenades and finally several of the cooler-headed men succeeded in calming their frenzied comrades, so that they could parley with the sentries. They asked for permission to open the door, which was at first refused; but later the guards relented and one left in order to consult their superiors as to whether the door could be opened. The request was again refused. The raving and screaming started again and the soldiers threatened the men once more. Soon some of the tortured men showed signs of mental disorder. One was of the opinion that he were at home, he searched for his keys and invited the men around him into his apartment. Another one began to talk to Americans over the telephone and then calmly announced that American tanks were in the vicinity and that the hour of our liberation would soon strike. At midnight the sentry opened the door for a short time. The fresh air of the night revived the tormented men. Soon afterwards the door was closed again and the tortures began anew. Again the raving, again the threats, again men sank to the floor or went out of their minds. At 7 o'clock the hour of salvation had struck for the men in this torture chamber.

The victims of this night were never counted. As the survivors ran out, their eyes were immediately drawn by new incidents. The first one, who rushed out of the stable, threw himself upon the sentry and attempted to tear away his automatic pistol. He was shot down immediately. Many of the men cast themselves on the ground, their eyes starting from their sockets, their faces twisted; some shouted insults, others attempted to speak but were unable to do so. One came out, completely naked, dancing on the tips of his toes like a ballet-dancer, swaying his hips. How on earth did he manage to get undressed in that crowded stable? A German Wehrmacht Captain asked Captain Marek if he might die like a German officer. Marek drew his pistol, asking: "You want a shot of mercy?" Then he led him to the ditch, told him to kneel down and shot him through the neck. But the German Captain turned round: "Shoot better!" he said. A second bullet sent him to the ground, but only the third brought relief. This was the introduction to day 5 at Postelberg.

The following day was the day of mass-murder. The day on which the place was cleared out. Larger groups of up to 80 men were assembled and led outside the barracks. The men knew what was coming next. They marched, holding their heads high, and with stony faces passed those who remained behind. Not one begged for his life. They marched in the direction of the Lewanitzer Busch. There has been no report of witnesses to the executions, but new mass graves were found later on, in the neighbourhood of which hats and caps were lying about.

The incidents in the jail of the court building at Saaz and those of June 4th, 5th and 6th I witnessed myself. The descriptions of the other events have been made based on reports by reliable witnesses.

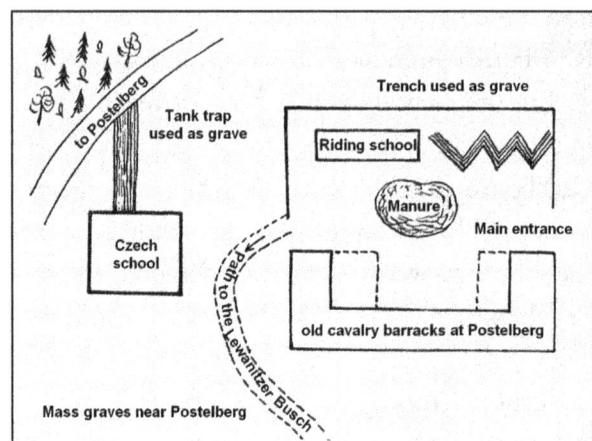

Teplitz-Schönau, Report No. 1
Woman brutally abused
Reported by Julia Käthe Tseng - Report of September 25, 1949

The undersigned, Julia Käthe Tseng, née Patsch, born on April 19, 1897 at Teplitz-Schönau, residing at Teplitz-Schönau, 459/19 Hamburger Street, Chinese citizen by marriage with the late Mr. Tseng Dean Yi, declares herewith under oath as follows:

On June 9, 1945 at 3 o'clock in the afternoon I was arrested by a member of the *"Národní výbor"* (National Committee) and two Czech partisans. They threatened me that I should be shot for espionage. One of the soldiers, supposed to be a corporal, examined my handbag, took all the jewellery and money out of it and furthermore two wedding-rings from my hand as well as my ear-rings and a small chain with a cross from my neck. The man of the "National Committee" searched the whole apartment. About 14 days later the aforementioned corporal was the owner of the "Rathaus-Hotel" on the market-place.

After this search I was taken in a car to the "Hotel Sachsen" in the Bahnhof Strasse. There I was locked in a room and after three to four hours a soldier took me to the local jail on the market-place. There I found Mrs. Frank from Teplitz, Goetheplan, with her daughter and a young girl from Auperschin. With our hands lifted and our faces towards the wall we had to stand absolutely motionless for a long time. Even the slightest movement provoked a lash with a whip. One of those who lashed us was a soldier, who later took over the forwarding agency of Schuster and Nettel. All this took place in the yard of the jail; afterwards we had to go up to the 2nd floor and the Czechs took this opportunity to beat us again. On the 2nd floor the warder by the name of Franta Landa waited for us and locked us up in our cells. 28 to 32 persons were imprisoned in cell No. 7 and there were also between 28 and 30 women in cell No. 6. In No. 6 I had to stay 3 or 4 days while the other inmates were allowed to go to work. In the morning of the fifth day they took me in a car to the villa Sieh at Goetheplan, where - as a first greeting - I had my ears boxed by a woman, who was some kind of a secretary there. After I had been locked up first in the hay-barn and then in the coal-shed, the interrogation finally began. A tall, stout man, wearing a khaki uniform and calling himself a colonel, asked me if I knew why I was on trial. I answered him that I did not. Thereupon I had my ears boxed again, twice on the right side and twice on the left. I was then told to sit down at the table; the soldier played constantly with his pistol. He took up a longish object, a steel spiral, and struck me with it on the head and on the chin, he then did the same with his pistol. Several times he or the girl shouted: *"Zatracená špionka"* (damn spy). Later on the girl pulled me up, turned me around and kicked me in the back. When I sat down at the table again, the man slapped me once more. After some time had passed I was taken in a car back to the local jail.

I remained in the local jail till July 21, 1945, but this time I was allowed to work.

On July 22 we were divided into three columns in the prison-yard; one group was transported to the internment camp (Internační tábor) at Hansa Strasse, another troop to the court-building, the last group to the camp in the Lasten Str. The rest remained in the local jail. I myself was taken to the camp at Hansa Strasse. My number was 87 on the list. In the camps we were permitted neither to sit down nor to lean against anything and we had to watch how those persons, whose numbers on the list were from 1 to 86, were clubbed, punched and kicked until they were bleeding. Among them were old people of 70 or 80 [years of age]. There were also younger persons who underwent the same treatment. I was also ordered to go to the office, where I was whipped, even receiving a lash in the face. In the office we received our prison-numbers, my number was 325. As long as I remained in the camp I went to work and was no longer beaten.

On the evening of August 27, 1945 at half past seven, one Horst Sonn of the Czech police arrived together with other soldiers. Sonn was in civilian clothes. It was a short interrogation. I was asked what Germans were known as having been in the party or otherwise for their bad treatment of Czechs. The interview took place in a billard-room and I was beaten by a soldier with the nick-name of "Prügel-Tondo" (Tondo the beater) with a billiard cue. Horst Sonn continually urged on the soldiers to further blows. Afterwards, I had to stand with my face pressed against the wall, a piece of paper was drawn along between my nose and the wall and whenever the paper stuck for a moment I at once received further blows on my back and legs. This lasted for almost three hours. Then I was permitted to go to the storeroom. "Tondo the beater" came back about 10 o'clock in the evening and led me to the gate. There was a car parked there. Dead mice were lying around. Tondo forced me to put one in my mouth which he [held] shut, meanwhile hitting me in the face. Outside the door I had to spit out the mouse, put another one in my mouth and spit it out and then again for a third time. After that I was put into the car and was driven to the Czech police-station at the Hahn-Villa in Masaryk Str.

In the office there I was punched and lashed with a whip for almost two and a half hours without interruption. Whenever one of the policemen grew tired of hitting me, another one started. This was carried out by "Tondo the beater" and a certain Wandierek. Sonn himself merely encouraged them.

I remained at the Hahn-Villa from August 27 to September 25, 1945. We had to work there and were struck at every opportunity.

From the Hahn-Villa I was taken back to the camp at Hansa Strasse. I remained there from September 20 to October 2, 1945, working outside the camp. From October 2 to October 26 I was in a hospital with a German [lady] doctor, who spared no pains in taking care of the prisoners. Mrs. Görg, another [lady] doctor at the hospital, also took care of the prisoners. On October 26 I came again to the camp at Hansa Str. On November 6, 1945, at half past eight in the morning, I [escaped] from the camp and met my mother at the cemetery. I had told her of my intention when she had visited me in the camp; she brought food and an overcoat with her. We succeeded in crossing the border by secret paths and arrived at Altenberg on November 6, 1945.

The following persons were struck until they were bleeding in the jail and in the camp:

Mrs. Hanni Fingerhut and her daughter Margit from Turn as well as her sister; Mrs. Marek, clerk at the local administration; Franz Öser, employee of the Wenzel-pit; Mr. Zibelius, apothecary and his wife from Schönau; Mr. Wagner, salesman, Duxer Str.; Pohl, salesman, and his wife from Weisskirchlitz; Mrs. Absalom, Josefinenbar, Edmund Str.; Mrs. Wild, Prague Str.; Mr. Müller, priest, from Schönau; Mr. Wittenbrink, dean, from Teplitz; Mr. Kutschera from the gas works at Schönau; Mr. Michel and his wife from the power plant at Teplitz; Mrs. Tomann, Goetheplan (her husband was shot); the whole family of Meissner, the pastry-cook from Königs Str.; Dr. Hiebsch, dentist, with his son and maid from Königstrasse; Mr. Illemann, butcher, and his mother, Waldtorplatz; Mr. Arwed Grohmann and his wife; Mrs. Nikodym.

Teplitz-Schönau, Report No. 2
Maltreatment in prison
Reported by A. B.

I am a Sudeten German and was born on July 25, 1885 in Gross-Chmeleschen, District of Podersam, Bohemia. Together with my wife and son Gerd I was expelled from Teplitz-Schönau on August 4, 1945. My son and I spent two months in prison in Teplitz-Schönau. Beatings from morning till night were the order of the day. My son and I were incarcerated right off the street, on June 29, 1945 at 8 o'clock in the evening. The first welcome we were given there were punches in the face. We had to spend several hours standing facing the wall, and the blows to the back of the head were almost unbearable. I fended off one punch to my face, and for that I was dragged into an adjoining room, where they tore the clothes from my upper body and threw me onto a wooden plank, to which I was tied. Then two men (one of them was called Josef Landa) beat me with rubber whips and then also with a rubber hose until I lost consciousness. Then they dragged me into a solitary-confinement cell. It was twelve hours before I regained consciousness. Then I was given a mouthful of bitter, cold black coffee. Our daily rations [in the Teplitz-Schönau prison] consisted of a little soup, a few potatoes and a morsel of dry bread. 22 prisoners had to spend the night[s] in a 4½-square-meter room.

Teplitz-Schönau, Report No. 3
Deportees robbed on June 1, 1945
Reported by Walter Weichert - Report of November 9, 1947

Until May 31, 1945 my wife and I lived in our own home in Teplitz-Schönau. On May 31 we were expelled from Czechoslovakia by the *Csl. Národní výbor, bytový úrad, pododdelení úrad evakuacní, Teplice Sanov*. This office appointed me as transport leader for a transport of expellees to southern Germany. This transport consisted of 8 men, 62 women, 5 children and 4 infants, all of them Germans from the Reich.

Thanks to the kindness of the station master in Teplitz-Schönau two covered freight cars were provided for the transport, so that around 6 o'clock in the evening of May 31, 1945 - the day that had been fixed for our expulsion - we left on time on a train bound for Komotau, Karlsbad, Eger. I had distributed the expellees among the two freight cars in such a way that the same number of people were in each car. I myself was identified as transport leader with a "Red Cross" armband and a Russian stamp.

On June 1, 1945, at about 5:45 am, we arrived at Neudau station. Most expellees were still sleeping. I myself sat by the open door of Wagon No. 2. While the train was yet pulling in, I saw two men dressed in eccentric uniforms standing on the platform. They were armed with revolvers and riding crops, and one also had a rubber truncheon hanging from his belt. The two men came walking along the train, directly towards our two cars. They spoke Czech and cursed at us in broken German. I tried to negotiate with them, but only received a crack with a whip in reply and was shoved aside. First the male prisoners had to leave the train. They were chased out with kicks and whip lashes and the words, "you German dogs don't need to ride". These two Czechs cursed us left, right and center. The expressions "dogs, swine, bastards, German crooks, hang you, stand you up against the wall" etc. were the most restrained of their repertoire. At the same time they wildly beat and whipped the women and children. The men were herded across the tracks to the other side of the train. I did not see them again for the rest of the trip. Then the women and children were thrown from the cars. It didn't matter how old the women were; and it also didn't matter if they had brought all their luggage out or not. I saw later that much luggage had been left in the train. Referring to my "Red Cross" designation, I tried again to convey to these people that we had been given permission by the *Národní výbor* in Teplitz-Schönau to use the train, but I was not allowed to say my piece. The two Czechs indifferent flung luggage and baby carriages with the babies still inside from the train onto the embankment, while maltreating the women and children with kicks and whip lashes. Even as the train was starting off again, they threw a baby carriage with a female infant out in a big double somersault. It was almost a miracle that the baby was unharmed. When the train had left the station, the Czechs herded us back along the tracks towards Komotau, constantly beating us with their riding crops. Anyone who couldn't walk fast enough for them was forbidden to go further, and had to remain behind. I found a spot on the otherwise steep embankment where we could climb up. We did so, and found ourselves on a road, from where we had to watch how the Czechs ruthlessly beat the women and children, who were laden down with their luggage and quite helpless. Then, on the street, when I gathered together the transport that had been entrusted to me, I found that no more than 25 people were left from the initial 79. We waited for about half an hour, but nobody else turned up. Since the grounds surrounding the tracks were level, I would have seen it if some frightened people had headed off in a different direction. So I had to conclude that these two Czech partisans had forcibly detained the missing people. I also noticed that a large amount of luggage fell into the hands of these two partisans.

I then continued our journey on foot with the remainder of my transport group, via Altrohlau to Johanngeorgenstadt.

The following persons can confirm these events: Mrs. Frieda Weichert, Mrs. Alice Hoffmann, Mrs. Elsa Günther.

I can name further witnesses on request.

Teplitz-Schönau, Report No. 4
Mental patient murdered
Reported by Theresia Wiegand - Report of August 9, 1950

Together with my husband, Paul Wiegand, the retired City Resort and Theater Musician, I lived in my home town of Teplitz-Schönau, at Schlossplatz 1, until we were expelled.

Mrs. Dick lived next door to us in the "Kreuz" Inn. Her husband had been in a psychiatric hospital, but had been released to be cared for at home.

During the days of the persecution of Germans in 1945 Mrs. Dick came to me, crying, and told me that her husband had gone out the night before to walk the dog and had not come back. The little dog had returned alone at 3 o'clock at night, and had been let in by a servant at the inn.

I advised her to check at the cemetery morgue to see if he was among the dead. The next day the poor woman really went there, and found her husband - he had been murdered. Mr. Dick had sat down on a bench in the park grounds (which Germans were forbidden to do), and as punishment some partisans had dragged him to the police station where he was savagely murdered.

All Germans were buried in mass graves. When her husband had already been buried, Mrs. Dick went to the Czech police one more time to ask for details, and the Czechs told her that the Russians had abducted her husband. His watch, money and rings had also been taken off his body.

Teplitz-Schönau, Report No. 5
A typical woman's fate
Reported by Käte Leitenberger

I lived at Teplitz-Schönau together with my four sons. All of them had joined the army. On May 10th, 1945 two Czechs in uniform with riding whips came to my apartment, of which they made a thorough search. Later on they took me to a sawmill, where I had to pick up stones.

In the course of the night of June 2nd, 1945, six armed partisans forcibly entered my apartment, threatened me, opened with their bajonets wardrobe and doors, got drunk and left after two hours, loaded with plunder. In the course of the summer I was taken to the *Národní Výbor* (National Committee) several times and interrogated concerning the whereabouts of my sons.

On August 28th, 1945, I was arrested and sent to the local jail and later to the *Internační tábor* (internment camp), where there was plenty of hard work and conditions approaching famine. The Czechs received 55 Czech crowns per day from our employers, but we got nothing. Only one more piece of bread in the evening than those who did not work. Some time later the Russians requisitioned us for work in various camps. They took away from us the small amount of money which we had been able to hide.

At the beginning of January 1946 I collapsed as a result of exhaustion; the camp physician declared me incapable of work and I was released on February 1st, 1946, but in view of the fact that I had no longer a home, I was expelled from Teplitz. I therefore went to the *Národní Výbor* (National Committee), in order to get back a part of my property, the 50 or 60 kilos (110-125 lbs) which one was permitted to take along; unfortunately, I fell there into the power of a former partisan. His wife, a member of the Czech Communist party, had formerly been the maidservant of a hairdresser, who lived in the same house as ourselves. I had not known the husband before. His name was Stepanek. This man now arranged that all I was allowed to take with me should be old shoes and an old coat - no underwear and no dresses - as well as a blanket and a pillow out of my apartment. The latter had been requisitioned by a Czech family. Thus my whole property amounted to only a few kilos. Since I was born at Graz in Austria, I had already got in touch with the Austrian "Geschäftsstelle" - a kind of emergency Consulate - for the purpose of obtaining transfer to my old home country and had also deposited there my money and my valuables. A person, supposedly a Roumanian, who posed as Consul, embezzled the money and delivered up some of the valuables only under pressure from abroad. In this swindle a Czech lawyer, his friend, played quite an important part. Shortly before my transfer to Linz on September 9, 1946, which this "Consul" tried to have cancelled, he was arrested as a previously convicted swindler by reason of considerable new swindles and embezzlements. He was led away in fetters. His previous sentence had been seven years hard labour. Now my way to Austria was free.

It should be mentioned here that I was neither tried nor accused during my imprisonment of five months. They only told me: "We believe it is because of your sons." Actually, on August 26, 1945, Czech police came for my eldest son during the night, but did not find him - two days later they came for me.

I was not permitted to take any money on the transfer [expulsion].

Tetschen-Bodenbach, Report No. 1
Severe maltreatment
Reported by Max Griehsel - Report of September 7, 1950

On June 3 [1945] I was called to the Community Office in Johnsdorf. Once there, I was told to wait outside the door. After about half an hour two SNB-men and that Chairman of the *Národní výbor* accompanied me back to my parents' home, where I was staying at the time. I was told to surrender what weapons I still had. Since I didn't have any, I was unable to oblige. After they searched all the rooms, they took me by car to the court prison in Tetschen. Here I had to stand facing the wall, and everything I had in my pockets was taken from me. Then I was shoved into a cell already holding about 15 men. I was greeted there by my comrade Karl Wischolit, about whom I had heard that he had been taken and shot by the Russians. More new victims were constantly brought in, some of whom showed signs of severe maltreatment.

The next day one Helmut Kuhn was brought in. He claimed to have been in the concentration camp Buchenwald. He introduced special new methods of maltreatment. One popular sport was to face two inmates off against each other, making them "go at each other" until one of them sank to the ground and could not go on. And then the Czechs would still brutally beat these unfortunates. Our rations consisted of a little watery soup and one loaf of bread per ten men. This went on for three days.

On June 6, 1945 we were lined up in the yard, loaded onto a bus and taken to Bodenbach, where we - some 60 persons - were squeezed into a cattle car and later unloaded in the train station of Rabstein. From there we had to march on foot to the concentration camp in Rabstein. We were escorted there by soldiers of the Svoboda army. Other Czech soldiers or partisan groups already awaited us in the camp.

We had to march into the camp in pairs. The soldiers took up position in such a way that we had to pass right by them, and then they beat us with rubber hoses. I avoided a blow aimed at my throat by ducking my head. Angry at not having landed a proper blow, the soldier ran after me and hit me over the head so badly that I staggered. Once we had arrived in the square, we had to strip totally naked and place our clothes on a pile. Then we were issued old and unspeakably filthy prison clothing. We were squirted with water and then chased into the barracks. Gross maltreatment was the order of the day.

We got so little to eat that people collapsed from hunger. Any opportunities we might have had to snatch a bit of bread or a few potatoes on the side were prohibited, and anyone who tried it anyway and got caught received 25 blows across his buttocks with the rubber hose.

Beyond that, individuals were also singled out to be victimized. They were led into the basement and beaten so brutally that many of them did not make it back out alive. Many chose suicide (for example the master builder Appelt from Bohemian Kamnitz). One man by the name of Przkal had served as a guard soldier in the Mattausch Plant and had been attacked by a Cypriot. He had fended him off. For this act of self-defense Przkal was beaten and tortured for days and then, one day, literally trampled to death in one of the barracks. Since he had tried to justify himself by saying that he had acted in self-defense, his beatings were accompanied by constant brutal shouts of, "Ja ti dám notwehr".

Many another German who had been framed or denounced shared the same fate as Przkal. For example, the case of Dr. Anton Kreisel from Bodenbach. He was left unmolested for one or two weeks. Then, repeated "treatments" in the basement inflicted physical damage to such an extent that he died of the consequences. The last time he was so inhumanly maltreated in the basement, he lost consciousness and was revived with cold water. He then contracted pneumonia, and died of it. His brother Lutz Kreisel, who was imprisoned in Rabstein at the same time, can confirm it.

Women were also brought to Rabstein, and treated just as inhumanly as the men. They were also forced to do the Czech soldiers' bidding sexually. Rapes were the order of the day.

Every now and then, someone escaped. Then we all had to line up outside. Dr. M. from B. was the camp physician. One day, when he had escaped, we were made to stand lined up from 6 o'clock in the evening until 5 the following morning. We also had to do all sorts of exercises: squats, running with knees bent, etc. Many of the old and sick prisoners collapsed; they were carried off and left to lie where they were dumped. During roll-call it often happened that someone mis-counted. Then the barrack elders were punched and beaten for it. One time someone was missing again. After much searching he was found: he had hanged himself in a corner of the basement. Now all the men who shared the same barrack room with him were beaten.

Of course people were also denounced in the Rabstein camp. A Czech by the name of Teltscher snooped around everywhere. Having been born locally, he spoke German as well as Czech. Many were sent to the basement on his instigation.

The actual commandant of the camp was a Captain who lived in Bohemian Kamnitz. Whenever he came for inspection in the evenings, everyone in the camp trembled. Another Czech staff captain resided in Tetschen Castle. In the time I was in the camp, he came three times to conduct night inspections. A Czech named Kucera had been committed to the camp because he had served with the German Wehrmacht. The staff captain beat him brutally and screamed at him: "You served with the German army and now you claim to be a Czech!" Crude curses against the German Wehrmacht then followed. This man Kucera was repeatedly "treated" in the basement.

One time, more Germans - men and women alike - were again being brought in by car. Every time when newcomers arrived, we had to go into the barracks and close the wooden shutters. But these shutters were cracked, and we could peek out. I witnessed one reception of new arrivals. The people were crammed into the car like herrings. Then they had to jump out. A Czech stood there with his leg out, so that they all fell over it. Several brutal thugs were also there and cruelly beat the Germans regardless whether they were men or women, young or old.

Starvation and maltreatment were the Czechs' "educational techniques". The aforementioned Helmut Kuhn ultimately became camp elder, and as such he has the deaths of many Germans on his conscience.

Among the Czech soldiers was one who spoke to me several times. I never learned his name. Once he asked me what sort of relationship we had with our camp elder, Helmut Kuhn. I told him that there were many here who could not understand Kuhn's actions against the rest of us.

All medications in the camp were destroyed. Barracks searches were carried out for the Czechs' amusement. The smallest trifles they found - a pencil stub, paper or even a knife - prompted furious outbursts. The culprit could count himself lucky if he received his beating in the barrack. For more serious offenses, he was taken to the basement. - In the evenings we had to stand guard to ensure that none of the despairing prisoners sneaked into the basement to hang himself. When we begged the Czechs not to take prisoners to the basement any more, because then many were so afraid that they preferred to commit suicide, they promised that we would not be beaten any more. But the next day the beatings went on, perhaps even worse than before. We were forced to do pointless work in order to torment us and to provide occasion to beat us. One man was beaten so badly that his eye burst and drained. There was no medical care for him, and so he was left to go blind.

On August 20, 1945 I and 30 other comrades were sent away from Rabstein and posted to a labor team. We had to work for the entrepreneur Frantisek Ruzek on a small repair shipyard for Elbe and Moldau barges in Staré Ouholice. Ruzek's main objective was to get the most he could out of us. His son was a crude fellow who also beat some of us. The civilian guard was decent to us; his wife slipped many of us some extras, but it always had to be done in utmost secrecy.

On March 7, 1946 my right hand got caught in the circular saw. There was no safety guard on the saw. I was taken by motorcycle to a doctor by the name of Weltrus, who looked at the wound and put some drops of hydrogen peroxide and a loose gauze bandage on it. At 4:30 pm I was admitted to the Raudnitz hospital to be operated. I was put into a room where there were almost exclusively Czech patients. While the Czechs received their prescribed diet, the Germans had their early-morning coffee supplemented only with potatoes, with or without some sauce, and rarely with a few dumplings with a bit of sauce. We were constantly mocked. The nurse (all the nurses belonged to the Norbertine Order) only ever gave me the sleeping powder that the doctor had prescribed for me, after I begged her for it repeatedly. For 14 days I had a fever and was always very thirsty. In the evening I asked her for some tea. She told me, "drink water, that's good for thirst too." A Czech partisan, a Communist by the name of Fryda, from Raudnitz, had been there since May 1945, being treated for an injury. He repeatedly bragged that he had blown the German soldiers away like rabbits.

When I was half-way recovered again, I was transferred to another part of the hospital where only Germans were quartered. Rations were even worse there. We usually did not even receive what little was earmarked for us. After three months I was discharged. First I was sent to Lobkowitz Castle in Raudnitz. A kind of temporary camp had been set up there. We were not treated too harshly. I spent about three weeks there.

Then young Ruzek from Staré Ouholice came to pick me up, and took me to Tetschen. However, I was not admitted in Tetschen, and sent to Aussig instead, into the concentration camp Lerchenfeld. Approximately 4,000 Germans (roughly 3,000 men and about 1,000 women) were detained there. The administrator of this camp had used to operate a merry-go-round, and he treated us very decently, in his opinion. He addressed the women as swine and whores and us men as "lazy Hitler-swine".

From there I was sent to the resettlement [expulsion] camp of Altstadt near Tetschen. I had to stay there until November 23, 1946. Then I was committed to the court prison in Bohemian Leipa. The guards and inspectors there treated us very roughly and brutally. Our Czech fellow-prisoners, most of whom were criminal convicts, exercised a regular reign of terror over us. They were our room commandants; none of us were allowed to sit down.

On November 29, 1946 the People's Court in Bohemian Leipa sentenced me, a former employee of the German Labor Front, to 5 years' imprisonment, which was commuted to forced labor. The trial lasted all of 8 to 10 minutes: the Court rose, withdrew behind a curtain, came out the other side, and read the verdict. There was no defense.

In the course of the next few days, we, that is the convicted prisoners, were issued prison clothing, and then we were sent off to work. Due to my crippled hand I was unable to do many tasks at all or to the satisfaction of the civilian or state overseers, and was therefore a favorite target for harassment. *"Ty svine germanský! Hitlerový bandit!"* were the guards' usual terms for us. I spent many weeks working in the former Bohemia Wagon Works in Bohemian Leipa. The work there was especially hard. We received enough potatoes to eat, but very little fat. Then I was sent for a time to work in the former Jahnel Scrap Iron and Second-Hand Goods business, where we were assigned only hard labor. Women were also put to work in this establishment.

In August 1947 I and five others were sent to the Bory Prison, near Pilsen. The SNB that escorted us were decent fellows and allowed us to use our money, insofar as we had any, to buy soup, bread, sausage and even cigarettes. But when we arrived in the train station of Pilsen they urged us to hurry up and finish smoking our cigarettes so that they would not get into trouble for it.

After admission to the prison, we were put into the so-called correction cells. More than 2,500 inmates, mostly political prisoners, were housed here. For two days I was sent to work in the Skoda Works, then a transport was put together and we were sent to Libkowitz near Maria Ratschitz, where we were assigned to work in the coal pits Kohinoor I and II.

Some 140 fellow-sufferers were already there.

We had to work 10-12 hours each day. Our rations here included sufficient fat, but only 400 g bread per day.

Our camp doctor was Dr. Gaag, a physician from Eger, who had also been sent here as political prisoner. He did his level best for us and helped wherever he could. In January 1949 I heard that he had died of tuberculosis in the Bory hospital.

After some time I was sent back to Bory. I had to stay there for about a week and then I and another fellow-sufferer were sent to work on a state farm in Sedlecko near Klattau. 16 prisoners were already working there. Our rations were good, but meager; there was little bread. But at harvest time we received 3 cups of whole milk and a little more bread daily.

On October 1, 1948 I was recalled from there, back to Bory. I hoped that I was to be released, since after all two-thirds of my sentence were already over. But that was a vain hope. On October 4 I and several comrades were sent to Kaznejov (Gassnau near Pilsen). It was a chemical factory, and we again had to do hard labor there. The civilian militia was a crude bunch and constantly drove us to work harder. There was enough to eat, but the rations were quite devoid of fat.

Then our work team was disbanded, and I was sent back to Bory along with the others. We spent 4 days there before being sent out with another work team, this time to Horní Briza, a kaolin plant near Pilsen. We were treated pretty decently there.

On March 19, 1949 we were again sent back to Bory. For the first time ever, I now heard German being spoken here, and some individual guards even condescended enough to speak German to us now.

On March 23, 1949 we were sent to the resettlement [expulsion] camp Alt-Habendorf near Reichenberg. Those of us who had money could buy whatever they wanted now. For my more than 2 years of hard labor in the prison I had received 192 Czech crowns. Whatever else we should have received for our work was kept back by the Czech state.

On April 6, 1949, after 14 days in Alt-Habendorf, we were put on a transport and shipped off to Germany.

Tetschen-Bodenbach, Report No. 2
Maltreatment
Reported by Karl Pless, engineer - Report of September 15, 1946

I was born on July 16, 1881 at Graupen near Teplitz-Schönau, Sudetenland. As an architect I taught at the school of architecture in Tetschen, from September 1st 1913 to May 8th, 1945 (33 years). On July 8, 1945 at quarter past 2 in the morning I was arrested by the Czechs, together with my family, consisting of my wife, my daughter-in-law and my 2½-year-old grandson, and then interned in the military prison at the castle of Tetschen. Over a period of 14 days a Czech commissar would lash me at any hour of day or night with a steel whip in such a manner that my whole body was encrusted with blood. Many times I became unconscious as a result of blows on the head and was left lying on the floor. Being considered as a major offender, I was kept in solitary confinement. At the time of our arrest my wife had not even been allowed to dress herself. She had been forced to accompany us in her night-gown and she remained without other clothing for four weeks. She was also beaten and dragged round by her hair in the cell.

The [secondary school teacher] Victor Kerbler, who resided in the same house, was arrested to-gether with me. My colleague Mr. Kerbler suffered a concussion of the brain as a result of blows on the head so that for several days he talked in a confused way. He was released as not guilty after three weeks. Four weeks later I and my wife were taken to Böhmisch-Kamnitz. There we were minutely cross-examined and afterwards brought back to the prison at the castle of Tetschen where we were released the next day. On our arrival at our apartment we discovered that it had been requisitioned by a Czech teacher. We were not allowed to take anything out of the apartment. Nothing remained in our possession except what we were wearing. A friend gave me a suit and some underwear. On December 17, 1945 we left our home-country.

My report is in accord with the truth.

Theresienstadt, Report No. 1
Internment camp "Little Fortress"
Reported by Dr. med. E. Siegel

I spent eight months in Theresienstadt and as physician had the opportunity to see more than most others, and so I shall give an account of the events in the so-called "Little Fortress" in Theresienstadt (Czechoslovakia); this account holds true with only minor variations for any other internment camp or prison in Czechoslovakia as well.

The first inmates to be imprisoned there were the soldiers from the German Wehrmacht who were marching through or were on their way home and whom the Czech "Revolutionary Guard" (known as RG) arrested. At that time the RG were the main of the occupying forces.

The "Little Fortress"

During the war the whole population of Theresienstadt was evacuated and the town was set up as a ghetto, in which some 40,000 Jews were housed. On the opposite bank of the river Eger, about a kilometer away from the town, lies the "Little Fortress" which was used as a concentration camp. It consists of four buildings, adjoining a little park with mansion, barracks, store-buildings, stables and a cinema, a large swimming pool and a rock garden.

The first three buildings included offices, store-rooms, carpenters' and locksmiths' workshops. The casemates served as lodging for the internees. These lay within the thickness of the ramparts, which like the whole of the fortress dated from the time of Maria Theresia. In the first few months only the fourth building was occupied by prisoners. This lay between the inner and outer rampart and was reached by a sort of tunnel, 15 to 20 meters long. The courtyard of this building is about 80 meters long, the longer sides of which were occupied by newly built cells, the single (solitary confinement) cells being on the right, lined up in groups of 10. Each solitary confinement cell is of bare, smooth concrete, about 4½ feet wide and 8 feet long. In the corner there is a porcelain bowl with flush system and a small, thick reinforced-glass window looking out onto a small yard. The door opens into another yard and has a roughly 1 x 1 ft opening, closed off with a wire screen. The small yards are approximately 8 ft wide and 45 ft long. Each of these yards opens onto the main yard via a door which is also locked at night. Three or four of these small yards were roofed under glass, the others were completely open to the elements.

Along the left side of the main yard are five large cells housing 200 prisoners each. These cells contain three stories of wooden bunks, as beds. The bunks are of unplaned wood (straight from the sawmill). Each cell has two toilets and a few sinks. To either side of the end of the yard there are three cells, or more accurately, dark, fenced-off tunnels, formerly casemates in the outer wall.

Reception of the Victims

A typical reception of prisoners took place on May 24, 1945. A transport arrived consisting of some 600 people of both sexes and of all ages. Among them were many Red Cross nurses from the Prague clinics.

Red Cross flags waved on the ramparts. Many of those present to receive the prisoners also had Red Cross bands on their arms, which went badly with the iron-tipped staves which they held. In the dark passage, some 4 yards from the end, the paving-stones had been torn up. The hole lay right across the path and was almost invisible in the darkness. First of all the newly arrived men were driven through the dark passage with shouts, threats and blows. The first to reach the hole fell and the next stumbled over them. The guards, who had stationed themselves along the passage, struck violently and uninterruptedly with their iron-tipped staves into the struggling pile of men. Hardly anyone reached the court uninjured. The guards kept strictly to the rule that anyone who could not get up unaided should be beaten to death (or as they said: "finished off"). Once in the yard, the unfortunates were driven along again; it was a sort of running the gauntlet. When anyone fell and was unable to rise, the commandant Pruša stalked up to him and struck him to the point that first the left and then the right kidney was knocked loose. Those who had been "finished off" in this way were dragged into the concrete cells and left to perish. The commandant's way of counting the prisoners was to hit each of them on the head with an iron bar. Then everyone had to stand against the wall for eight hours with raised hands. Anyone who let his arms drop was pitilessly beaten. This reception alone cost 70 men their lives. 500 men were driven into a large cell, in which they could only lie down packed together like herrings. The stillness of the night was broken by shots and the shrieks of those being beaten. The heat was terrible and the air suffocating. Such nights were to be repeated for months.

Next day all our clothing was taken away and ragged convict uniforms were distributed. Each man had a strip of hair shaved off from the forehead to the nape of the neck. The supervisors were mostly criminals and sadists. Both to keep their positions and for their personal pleasure, they tormented the internees in every possible way. Everything was done by shouting. The prisoners had to wait for their meals for half an hour in a squatting position with outstretched arm. If anyone lost his balance and fell, it was an excuse to beat him anew. In the cell the men had to stand close together. Sitting or lying down during the day were strictly forbidden. The men had thus to be on their feet from 5 in the morning until 9 in the evening, often with a roll-call in the yard which lasted for hours and included insults, beatings and every kind of abuse. Pruša and the deputy-commandant, Tomeš, constantly repeated that nobody who had come to the camp would leave it alive. Nobody, however, was accorded the mercy of a quick death. Everybody had to "atone"; in other words, one could only be gradually beaten or tortured to death. Almost every day piles of personal documents, souvenirs, photographs etc., belonging to the prisoners, were burnt, for as the commandant maliciously explained, no one would need souvenirs or identity papers any more.

The proposed gassing of the prisoners could not be carried out for technical reasons and so there remained only the method of slow death. The inhuman packing of more than 500 men into cell No. 43 lasted for weeks. The other cells were probably also very overfilled, if not to this unimaginable extent.

My own Experiences

I shall describe my own arrest and imprisonment in detail only in order to provide a first-hand account.

I should mention to begin with that I was never politically active. I was Deputy District Representative of the German Red Cross. I could not be the head, since this position was reserved for a representative of the Party. During the war many Czechs, Slovaks and other Slavs came to me for consultation. I always spoke Czech with them. I had therefore no reason to believe that anything would happen to me from the side of the Czechs. On May 30, 1945, about noontime, there was a sudden banging on my door. Two cars full of heavily armed men stood outside. I heard a shout: "Police! Open up!" I opened the door and was at once thrust backwards and compelled to let the horde in. I was frightfully knocked about. They shouted at me, asking where I had hidden my SA-uniform and my weapons. When I answered that I had never been in the SA and that I had already surrendered my arms, I was struck again. My wife and I were constantly threatened with a pistol at the breast and the flat was systematically plundered. Objects of value, shoes, linen, clothing, watches, money etc. were packed in my own leather suitcases and carried off. They found no gold, jewellery or valuable watches, since my wife had hidden them all in the attic. I had no idea where they had been concealed. Before I could explain this, I was choked into insensibility. I was shown to my wife in this condition and she was told that she, too, would be choked and the children would have their eyes put out, if the gold and jewels were not handed over. Trembling with fear, my wife ran for the valuables. The thoroughness with which the apartment was stripped showed considerable practice on the part of the police. As they found no SA-uniform, they tried to force me to admit that I had hidden it. I, however, could admit nothing of the sort, since I had never possessed such a uniform. In consequence I was struck repeatedly with a poker. Then I had to take off my shoes, lie on the stomach and lift my feet to receive a bastonade. After many blows and much ill-treatment, without having seen my family again, I was shoved down the stairs and taken by car to Theresienstadt. On the way they described to me how painfully I should be beaten to death.

Once arrived at the fortress of Theresienstadt, I had first of all to stand with raised hands against the wall, occasionally receiving a violent box on the ears. Then the interrogation began. I was asked: "Were you in the SS? Were you in the SA?" and so on. And on each answer I was struck and punched with full force. Then I was stood up against the table and was struck so violently in the stomach that I fell each time. As I lay on the floor, I was viciously trampled on and kicked, particularly in the chest, head and sexual organs. One of them kept on to dislocate my arm. Later on I saw many with arms pulled out of joint. As soon as I was on my feet, I was knocked down again with blows to the stomach. This went on for some time. Afterwards I was put on a plank-bed and a dirty towel was stuffed in my mouth. Then they showed me an iron-tipped stave more than a meter long and told me that they were going to knock out my teeth. An internee had to hold my head and they struck me with the greatest violence in the mouth. My teeth withstood the blows, since the material covered them, but my lips were completely disfigured. The internee, Karl Erben, told me afterwards that the sight had made him sick as he held my head and that he had had to leave. I was later placed on my stomach on the bed and beaten with the stave, which was swung with both hands on the buttocks, the back and the nape of the neck. They also hit me deliberately on every joint as well as in the ribs. I suffered a fracture of the forefinger of the right hand and two further fractures of the bones of the same hand. I still have a scar on my forehead from hair to eyebrows; my right ear was lacerated and crushed and I was covered with gashes and abrasions. My whole body was black and blue. In this condition I was dragged to an ice-cold cell in the ramparts. They left me lying in my blood on the bare concrete for three days and three nights. I wore only trousers and a shirt so torn that the upper part of my body was practically naked.

As a result of the blows on the spine and the joints my body was practically paralyzed and I lay almost unable to move in terrible pain and trembling with cold. I prayed to be freed from my torment and to be allowed to die at once. On the third day a Czech doctor came into the cell and shouted at me to stand up. Since I could not move, he pulled me up by the hair and threw me down again. This was my first medical treatment by one of my Czech colleagues. I was insanely thirsty. Nor did I get anything to eat; but with my injured mouth I could in any case have eaten nothing. When I was at last given a cup of coffee, a soldier, who on the third night had been locked in with me, had to introduce the liquid gradually by one corner of my mouth. The warders looked in every now and then to see if I was still alive, remarking: "He'll soon kick the bucket...."

Appointment as Camp Doctor

On the fourth day a fellow-prisoner came in to see if I was still alive. He advised me to report myself fit for work, otherwise I should be left there to die. I therefore reported myself for work, but more because I thought that when they found out the deception they would finish me off quickly. I was lucky, however, and was appointed as camp doctor. The prisoner came back in an hour to tell me the news. He helped me onto my feet and after several attempts I slowly staggered out. The usual strip was cropped through my hair. I received another pair of trousers, a shirt, a jacket and shoes and was then ready to begin with my duties. "Begin my duties", though, is somewhat of an exaggeration. I could not even sit down without help, much less get up. I constantly had to hold up my head with my left hand, for the neck muscles had been terribly injured. I could not see properly with my left eye, but only vaguely distinguish light; and as a result of the blows on my ears, I could scarcely hear. In the sickbay I was first bandaged and with a certain amount of help I was able to quench my thirst. There was a woman doctor there who knew me. She had worked in the German clinic in Prague, had been arrested and was also interned here at Theresienstadt. She sent me a palliasse to sleep on, for the internees had nothing but planks on the bare floor. One can hardly imagine the agony of those who had been beaten all over. In many cases the pulped flesh turned gangrenous and often fist-sized chunks of flesh separated from the body. As a consequence many internees succumbed, after weeks of suffering, to the beatings they had received long before.

My colleagues laid me on the palliasse and I slept like one dead. Two hours later the Czechs asked if I were at work. They were told that I had been working up to that moment and was taking a short rest. Following my ill-treatment I suffered from a serious heart defect and my life was only saved by injections of a combination of glucose. These were given to me by Dr. Benna, who had been arrested and came here via the concentration camp at Pankratz. He was still suffering from festering wounds on the head from the clubbing at the time of the reception in Theresienstadt on May 24th. Dr. Benna had equipped himself with these injections, among other things, from the piles of medications in the former ghetto in Theresienstadt.

Murder by Order

I gradually began my duties; but very soon I was ordered to kill the internees of cell No. 50 by means of injections. A refusal would have only meant being beaten to death. I pointed to my injured right hand and explained that I could not yet give injections. Two or three days later the order was repeated. They simply said that it was not worth the expense of feeding these elderly people since they could do no equivalent work. My injured hand was no longer taken as excuse. Anyone with any sensibilities can imagine what pain this order gave me. Since a direct refusal would have meant death, I agreed, but hid the ampules for the injections under my palliasse. A further postponement was hardly possible. It was only a question of days, and new ampules were ordered. Then something else came to my help. Since spotted typhus had broken out in the camp, Dr. Patočka, the head of the Hygienic Institute in Prague, came to Theresienstadt and examined the internees for cases of infection. He diagnosed 16 cases and therefore ordered the establishment of a typhus station in the isolated rooms of the movie theater. On the 6th of June I was appointed as doctor in charge.

As a result I was released from giving the injections. In my new capacity it was my duty to examine all the cells, so that I can give an eyewitness account of conditions in this cell No. 50. It was an annex to cell No. 49, the sick-room. Even in these cells there were no palliasses, but only unplaned boards on the floor, on which the patients were packed so close together that they could not lie on their backs, but only on their sides. Among them were many with recent amputations. They were almost all boys between 16 and 18 years of age, allegedly from the SS. They could not prevent their amputated limbs from striking against one another, the bandages were soaked with pus, stank terribly and were crawling with maggots. I shall never in my life forget the agonized faces, marked by terrible pain and despair. These poor unfortunates were the pride of the commandant Pruša and his accomplices. The cells were not generally shown to the commissions coming from Prague; the commandant would only show them now and then to amuse his personal friends. I was not allowed to bandage or even speak to the boys. On my visits I was taken by the arm and warned that if I spoke a single word, I should have to stay there with them. This martyrdom lasted several weeks. I saw the victims one time more - as corpses bruised with blows, especially on their stumps. Whether they had been beaten to death or strangled according to "Theresienstadt custom", or had received a merciful injection, I do not know.

The Typhus Station

When I set up the typhus station on June 6th, 1945, I was given a staff of two nurses. On the first day we had 16 typhus cases (men) and on the second day 15 more men came. All had high temperatures and as a result of their illness could barely hear, and most of them were delirious, restless and suffering from diarrhoea. There was no linen for the patients. The place was jumping with fleas. In their delirium the patients moved about incessantly and responded to no directions, and soon the entire room and toilet was befouled with runny stool, as were the palliasses and the patients themselves. In addition we were overrun with fleas and lice and tormented by swarms of flies coming from the morgue opposite. Since we were given nothing for the patients to drink, they constantly attempted to use the water from the toilet. I was still in such a condition that I could not get up from a chair alone and a nurse had to put me to bed, wash me and get me up in the morning.

I was so desperate that my only hope of freedom from my cares and sufferings was, that I myself would catch the typhus infection.

On the third day the situation changed suddenly. An inspection from Prague was expected. I was now given five nurses, plenty of linen, enough coffee for the patients, and D.D.T., with which the whole sickroom was dusted over. The result was fantastic. In a couple of hours the swarms of fleas were completely destroyed, the floor was black with dead flies, after two days the bugs began to dry up and also the lice, our greatest problem, were wiped out. It was the first ray of sunshine in my hopeless situation. Soon the typhus station became a little model, in the sharpest contrast to the rest of the camp and the treatment of the internees. Prof. Dr. Patočka inspected us often. I obtained the necessary linen, medications and D.D.T.

The following incident is indicative of the attitude of the camp administrators themselves:

Beasts in Human Form

I had diagnosed a new case of typhus and had the patient brought on a stretcher from the courtyard out to the isolation-station. As I came out of the dark passage I was stopped by deputy-commandant Tomeš: "What swine have you got there on the stretcher?" he demanded. "A typhus patient," I answered, to which he replied: "Why make so much fuss over the swine. Kill the bastards off right away. Why should they get fed, everyone in the camp has got to be finished off!" He shouted to the nearest of the gendarmes to get rid of them all. At a later date the commandant, Tomeš and others were arrested and brought before the district court at Leitmeritz, not for their many murders but because they had embezzled valuables belonging to the internees which should have been turned over to the state.

The commandant had a daughter, Sonja Prušova, whose jewel-case was stuffed with diamonds, gold, watches, jewellery and other objects of value, all taken from the internees from Prague. This girl, although barely 20 years old, was an extraordinary sadist and I was told that she had helped in the beating to death of not less than 28 people. Women told me from their own experience that she had torn out their hair, punched them in the face or the stomach and thrashed them with a whip.

Whenever she ran through No. 4 court with gleaming eyes and greedy mouth, I knew that people were to be tortured again and that blood would flow.

Several times a week, especially in the evening or at night, drunken Russians would come into the fortress. The women had to assemble and the Russians picked out those they wanted. In return the supervisors were given spirits, tobacco, bacon and so on. The then-supervisor of the 4th building, a Pole named Alfred Kling, had a venereal disease, which did not prevent him from constantly picking himself girls from those recently interned.

"Alfred" regarded the killings from a scientific point of view. He asserted that he could calculate the beatings which he gave exactly and know whether the victim would die in two hours or in two days, or even after as long as a week; or on the other hand that he would be well again in a fortnight. He gave us practical examples of his science. For example, an internee had stolen bread three times running; the Kapo, an old criminal, decided that he must be finished off. First of all he was beaten bloody. In this condition he was brought to "Alfred" who announced: "Fifty strokes - two hours!" In front of the women internees, who were forced to watch, one by one he smashed the prisoner's arms, legs, ribs and left him lying on the floor. Two hours later he died and "Alfred" was obviously proud.

Our two commandants were also really proud that the internees looked as wretched and ill after two or three months as the concentration camp inmates did after three or four years. They boasted: "We have messed you up as much in two months as the Gestapo could have done in five years!"

The Commandants

Towards the end of June and the beginning of July a new commandant was appointed to the camp, a certain Staff Captain Kálal. He was no friend to the Germans, but still he was correct and a real officer, which in such a camp means a great deal. But he was completely isolated and all his subordinates were united against him.

I believe that it was thanks to him and perhaps also partly to Prof. Dr. Patočka that not all the prisoners were killed as Pruša, Tomeš and Co. had intended. The camp doctor Dr. Schramm as well as one or two employees of the camp proved to be decent people who did their duty, but had retained some feelings of humanity.

Alois Pruša, the first commandant of "Little Fortress", who called himself "Captain" and mostly went about in a uniform decorated with the Soviet star, hammer and sickle, was a fat, brutal man and had formerly been in the German concentration camp in Theresienstadt. His greatest pleasure was torture, but he also enjoyed beatings to death, provided that they were done as brutally as possible. He used to gloat especially over the amputees who had been jammed together in two cells and whom he often visited, jumping up and down with glee like a clown at the sight of them.

Orgies were celebrated almost every day. These took place in the rooms which adjoined Pruša's apartment, where his wife and his two daughters would be sleeping. The girls among the internees were "invited" and the orgy usually ended with his favourite game: playing brothel. The girls had to undress and what followed is impossible to describe. I received this account from two girls, one of whom had her knee slashed open by Pruša with a bottle in a fit of drunkenness. She sustained a long, deep wound that took months to heal. A second girl also confirmed the same. She too had been "invited" by Pruša and I shall refrain from giving details here.

600 Calories - but Millions Looted every Day

To begin with the food was plentiful, although the meat was often spoiled and the bread mouldy. But soon the diet became very insufficient. By order of the Ministry of the Interior the bread ration was halved and the soup, which had previously been nourishing, came to resemble dishwater, in which a few grains of barley and some bits of potatoes floated. For months no salt was put in anything. We estimated that we received from 600 to 800 calories a day without any extra in winter, although, working in the open, we were constantly half-frozen. It may be objected that rations of 250 g bread and 70 g cereal are not sufficient for survival. This is true, and such was the intention. If some of the internees survived, it was due to the fact that the Russians, who showed themselves in many ways more humane than the Czechs, very often fed the groups which were allotted to them for work so well that prisoners were able to bring food back to their comrades in the camp. The Czech farmers also often showed themselves good-hearted. In addition the general chaos allowed frequent stealing, often on a large scale.

The Russians also showed themselves in other ways to be far more decent. For example, they often intervened when our people were too badly beaten. Every morning the Russian doctor would bandage the heads of those who came for work, and in the evening he would remove the bandages again so that they should not be torn off by the Czechs. The Russians even helped many internees to escape, simply by driving them in their cars across the border. I counselled many girls, who came to me in desperation after having been raped repeatedly, rather to pick a Russian and to escape with him; and I know that in many cases this proved to have been good advice.

In our leisure time we estimated, on the basis of a thorough inquiry, the extent of the personal property stolen in Theresienstadt. On a conservative estimate this amounted to 500 million Czech crowns. I do not believe that more than 50% was turned over to the Czech state.

The Czech Ministry of the Interior attempted to carry out an extermination of all non-Czechs, outside as well as inside the camps, by withholding all supplies of protein (save for ½ a pint of milk for children and a pint for babies, the ration cards for Germans made no provision for any distribution of protein). If this extermination was not as complete as planned, this was in part due to a certain carelessness in carrying it out. This enabled the German population to obtain foodstuffs illegally, all the more so as there was plenty available. Moreover a few Czechs and also the Russians had remained good-hearted. In addition many of the officials never grasped the actual meaning and purpose of these directives. So it happened twice, for example, that a horse which had had to be destroyed was distributed to the internees and several times animal blood was given out with the food. The distribution of several tons of dried cheese provided by the Swiss Red Cross in December 1945 was also an unconscious contravention of the official directives by subordinate officials who did not know the real state of affairs. The receipt of monthly food parcels of up to 3 kilograms (about 6½ pounds) was allowed during the late autumn and winter: another measure which frustrated the 100% success of the plan of the Ministry of the Interior. An absolute deficiency of protein in the diet will cause the death of any human being, not rapidly but with complete certainty. Those who succumbed were either emaciated skeletons as a result of inadequate food, or monstrously swollen up; in the latter cases death was more often consequent on terminal diarrhoea. The German PoWs also returned from Russian captivity in a bloated state owing to a deficiency of protein.

We had plenty of both types at Theresienstadt, the emaciated as well as the bloated victims. But consider what a person must suffer through to starve to a skeletal state, spending the nights lying on unplaned boards or on a concrete floor, tormented at night by the impossible need to relieve himself, plagued by the cold or the heat and by air almost too thick to breathe, driven to work time and again with beatings or equally vicious tongue-lashings - it is gruesome, and a graphic reflection of the intentions held by the Ministry of the Interior at Prague. The beatings and tortures meted out to the prisoners whenever inspectors went through the institution were probably also a uniform aspect in all camps, regulated by a central directive.

"Hitler Did a Poor Job"

The anti-Semitism of the Czechs can be seen from the following story. A Slovak Jew named Müller, who had already spent five years in a German concentration camp, was brought to the "Little Fortress" at Theresienstadt at the beginning of June. He had in the meantime recovered from his experiences and looked well. He repeatedly claimed, "They won't get me to work." The Czechs regarded him as a comic figure. They used deliberately to order him to various kinds of work, which they knew in advance he would not do, such as putting him in a line of men who were passing tiles from hand to hand, knowing that on principle he would drop every tile, although he was well aware of what would follow. "Don't beat me too hard, Mr. Commandant", he used to say, ducking his head. His work always ended with slaps and blows to the amusement of the guards. Another time they put a railroadman's cap on his head and a red scarf around his neck and ordered him to push a wheelbarrow on the double. The Kapo ran with him, tripping him up unexpectedly. Beatings again followed. Later on he was sent to the ghetto at Theresienstadt for several days. When I met him there, I was hardly able to recognise him, so wretched and haggard did he appear. The Czech GPU interrogated me on the subject of this man. During my interrogation I pointed out that Müller had been in a German concentration camp for five years and asked that he be released, since he was certainly neither a Nazi nor even a German. But Müller remained in the camp, where he died after 5 or 6 months as a result of too much ill-treatment and not enough rations.

There were also other Jews interned at Theresienstadt. Among them were Schück, Glässner, Spieker, Herbert, Geitler, and others whose names I do not remember.

The Czechs often remarked that Adolf Hitler had done a poor job, since there were still plenty of Jews alive.

Death Rate Over 50%!

In May 1945 72 soldiers of the German Wehrmacht, none of them SS-men, were taken to Theresienstadt. In September 1945 only 34 of them were still alive. During the months of May and June 200 men and 6 women are shown as having died as well as those whose deaths were not recorded. The extremely high death rate of men in relation to the almost equal numbers of men and women in the camp can be easily explained by the fact that men were most subject to ill-treatment and blows.

The death rate among those suffering from typhus was low owing to the medical attention they received and to the use of the medications found in the ghetto at Theresienstadt as well as to the relatively good accommodation and the mild type of the disease itself. Out of 74 cases only 11 died. 50% of the deaths were caused by bedsores, the result of previous mistreatment, because the victims had been so grossly beaten that fist-sized chunks of flesh separated from their buttocks and back. No special diet was available for the patients, but an epidemic of dysentery could to a great extent be controlled by bacteriophage provided by the laboratory of Prof. Dr. Patočka.

Pathological Lying

The men comprising the camp leadership were pathological liars.

Whenever a commission arrived at the camp, Pruša would lead them past the prisoners in their cells, remarking that all were SS or Gestapo men. When a member of the Russian commission doubted the truth of this, seeing that there were several boys of 12 or 14, who could hardly have been members of the SS, Pruša lied, declaring that these were sons of SS or Gestapo-men and that one of them alone had killed eleven Czechs.

As many who listened to the official Czech broadcasts can confirm, the Ministry of the Interior repeatedly asserted to the foreign countries that only members of the SS, Gestapo and other major offenders were at Theresienstadt, although in fact half of the inmates were women up to the age of 92 years, and small children. The men were mostly Germans from Prague and among the civilians were a number of blind men. Blind soldiers had also been taken out of the hospital at Aussig or seized in the course of the Czech lootings. There were also prisoners who had been turned over to Theresienstadt because the prisons were overfull and they were not charged with any serious crime.

As previously mentioned, the commandant Pruša used to count the prisoners by hitting the men on the forehead with a club. Since some of the boys were small, the club struck the skull instead of the forehead. The wounds were not allowed to be bandaged, but were left to be infested by maggots and smelled terribly. The dates for release which were fixed monthly led the prisoners to hope for a discharge, but the recurring disappointments brought deep depression. For the camp administration the release dates, which were constantly set fictitiously for the next month, and the next, and the next, had another advantage - namely that many prisoners postponed their attempts at escape, thinking time and again that they had a chance to be discharged properly.

Victims from Aussig "Brought in Dead"

At the end of July 1945 an ammunition depot exploded at Schönpriesen near Aussig/Elbe. This explosion was followed by a general persecution of the Germans, mainly carried out by the members of the Svoboda Army. Many of the Germans, including those of the Schicht works, were driven into the river Elbe, shot or killed by hand-grenades. On July 31, 1945 21 men were brought to Theresienstadt in a closed car, wearing white bands on their arms with the inscription "Závody

Schicht". They were said to be "Werewolves" and were stood against the wall the whole afternoon. Shortly before midnight we heard the well-known sounds of blows and screams, of clubs striking on skulls. An acquaintance of mine later told me that he and other internees had that night had to clear away blood, brains, teeth and hair and to strew fresh sand in the entrance to the courtyard. I never saw the 21 men again. I made inquiries in the office: there the men were booked as having arrived dead.

Miss M. W. reports on her internment from May 13, 1945 to October 10, 1946 at Theresienstadt as follows:

Account of my Internment in Theresienstadt, Czechoslovakia from May 13 to October 10, 1946 (by M. W.)

"On May 13, 1945 I was arrested by a party of 20 armed Czechs in Zwettnitz near Teplitz-Schönau and from there I was taken to the internment camp at Theresienstadt. My father and an agricultural apprentice were brought in at the same time as I. Upon our arrival we were separated and put into cells which were dark and cold. Our apprentice, a war-invalid, is said to have been killed soon after his arrival; in any case we have not heard of him since. My father occupied the cell adjoining mine. All twenty cells in that corridor were intended for solitary confinement; none of them was empty. I was the only woman there, but I too was shut in by an iron door with three locks. During the day and even at night I heard the sounds of ill-treatment. My father was punched so violently by a Czech with a knuckle-duster that I could hear him moaning the whole night. The next day a nurse visited him. The same afternoon we were supposed to be interrogated and on this occasion I met my father again, but did not recognise him, since his garments were tattered and torn and he himself beaten black and blue. Three days later he was taken away by a Russian officer; he was released by the Russians in February 1946, but on his return to Czechoslovakia was again interned until May 1946. I myself remained in solitary confinement for twelve further days. I, too, was ill-treated and the small amount of water-soup I was allowed was sometimes thrown in my face. After these 12 days I was taken by a guard to another building of the fortress. While being registered, I was badly knocked about and even lost one of my teeth. Together with the wife of an SS-man I was ordered to hold up a flag and to sing the German national anthem. Then we had to spit on a bust of Adolf Hitler, saying: "Hitler, you swine, what have you got us into?"; and then to kiss it with the words: "Thank you for all you have done for us throughout the years!" After this I was led away, but the SS-woman was forced to sit upon an SA-dagger. I heard her screams as a group of men took me back to my cell, where I had to undress and was again beaten. Since I was covered with blood, they brought me water to clean myself and then I was locked up naked in one of the cells. All I got was a flag to put my feet on. I had to stand like that in the cell all night long. Next morning I was given the usual convict's garb and was taken to a cell, where 200 women were already lodged. That same day I was immediately sent to work, even though I was so beaten up that I could hardly move. Together with other women I had to clean the ghetto and to nurse Jews suffering from typhus. The Russians stationed there molested us constantly during the four days we worked in the ghetto at Theresienstadt. The next thing I had to do was agricultural work, since I was used to it; although it was heavy work, we were given nothing but a pint of thin soup and a small piece of bread to eat, which had to suffice for the whole day. At night the Russians gave our Czech guards spirits or cigarettes and then entered our cells and took away several girls.

I stayed with this labour group until August 12, 1945. That day I was accused of having murdered Czechs during the revolution. I was given no opportunity to say a word in my defence and was sent back to solitary confinement, classified as a mass murderess. I kept demanding to be confronted with witnesses, but nobody paid any attention to me. From the very first day, for four weeks, I was chased around the entire yard twenty times each day by a guard of the Women's Camp, then I had to go to the shower where I was doused with cold water; then, wet as I was, I had to lie down on a bench, where I received 25 blows each day with a rubber truncheon, cane, belt or whatever else the guard could find. He was a very young fellow and kept trying to rape me; but since I resisted he beat me even more, until I collapsed. Then my head was shaved, and as I only had a blanket that was what I had to sleep on in my cell, on the concrete floor. It was hoped that one day I would succumb to these torments. A woman guard would watch all this with a smile on her face. A towel was stuffed into my mouth so that the other women in the yard would not hear me scream. Nonetheless they all heard it and they also saw how beaten and bloody I always was when I returned from the shower and was hunted like an animal into my solitary confinement cell. Often I got nothing to eat all day. The women later told me that I looked like death warmed over. When I could no longer bear it all, I tried to commit suicide, but I never succeeded because the guards came by too often. After these four weeks I was assigned as the only woman in a group of SS-men to carry corpses of prisoners, most of whom had died of typhus. While working the SS-men were often beaten with such violence that they were left lying dead on the ground. Whenever I fainted from the smell of the corpses, a bucket with cold water would be poured over me and I had to continue my work. I often fell on top of the corpses lying in the mass graves. Sometimes we had to dig up corpses previously buried with our bare hands and without any safeguard against infection and had to put them in coffins. When a wound on my foot became inflamed, I was simply given a shoe and had to continue with the digging. But six days later this came to an end. I was left in solitary confinement in an unheated cell and with insufficient rations. When the weather grew colder I was given a second blanket, but that was all. We shivered in our unheated cells; later on other women were also locked into solitary confinement. Rations were small and the food was mostly unsalted. We received only two cups of watery soup, so-called potato soup but the potato pieces were few and very far between, and this soup was unsalted too. Our daily ration of bread was a two-kilo loaf for ten women; and two cups of black, mostly cold coffee. In this way, Christmas passed. On February 15 I had the first opportunity to take a bath, for the next morning I was to be interrogated in the office, where a number of Czech lawyers had assembled. After two hours I was told that there were no witnesses against me and that I had been cleared and would be released very soon. I was sent again to the large cell and found myself among other human beings for the first time after 20 weeks of solitary confinement. I had grown very shy and afraid of people, and many doubted my sanity, but thanks to the good comradeship among us I recovered my health and spirits in a very short time. In April the first of us were already released. I hoped for my own release every day. When I came out of solitary confinement I was allowed for the first time to send my mother a message. Many inmates, male and female alike, had died of starvation during the cold months. Many of the girls were raped terribly by the Russians. In the evenings they were simply dragged from their cells, or did not even return from their work. The guards sold us - what could we do? If one of the girls resisted, she was beaten and locked into a solitary cell. During my period of solitary confinement the Russians had been allowed to enter my cell and I, too, had been raped. For a great many girls this abuse ruined their entire lives. Many girls were in sickbay with venereal diseases. I was put to work in the camp bakery and when the woman Kapo was discharged, I became Kapo and had to supervise all the women and to do the bookkeeping. In that position I recovered a bit of my health. Also, my supervisor was good to me and gave me the occasional bit of bread when I cleaned up her room. The transports were leaving one after another, only I was never among those released but was put off from week to week. Finally, on October 10, 1946, I was turned over to the transfer-camp at Leitmeritz, from whence my transport left for Bavaria. My parents and my sister still live in Czechoslovakia, my father is working there and my sister is attending a Czech school.

When I was interned, I was almost 20 years old, having been born in 1925. Those who were interned with me can testify that my report is in accordance with the truth. I shall never be able to forget what was done to me. Many innocent people had to die."

The Significance of International Commissions

The behaviour of the camp authorities when a commission arrived was almost comical. For instance, at the beginning a Russian would ask for what purpose the bloody club was used which lay on the table in the cell: "Has anybody here been beaten?" All 500 inmates would shout in unison: "Nobody!" It is impossible to imagine what would have happened to anyone answering in the affirmative. Later on, when a British commission (mostly journalists) was announced, the whole camp was in a state of excitement. The cells were hermetically closed, no internee was allowed to leave and the British journalists were led through the fortress surrounded by the commandant and his officials. The commission missed everything worth seeing, but was bombarded with information about the atrocities the Germans had perpetrated. Some of the stories were ridiculous, for instance thousands of Czech women (and it was never less than thousands) had been raped by SS-men in a steep rock garden and had afterwards been drowned in the swimming pool. The steepness of the rock garden would have made such exploits difficult indeed for even the most experienced womanizer.

The brutality which was customary at the beginning, the constant and unrestrained beatings, were later forbidden. The new commandant himself backed up the prohibition and saw to it that order was kept. Owing to the poor discipline and the hostile attitude of his subordinates towards him, however, he was only able to limit the maltreatment; behind his back many abuses still occurred.

Help from Switzerland

In December 1945 there came at last a shipment of food from the Swiss Red Cross for which we had long been waiting. It consisted of noodles, canned vegetables, dried cheese, preserved milk and powdered milk etc., about 4 tons in all. The effect was that the death rate dropped 50%. I want to take this opportunity to thank the Red Cross that really showed great good will and helped us as much as it could, and I only regret that we had to wait seven months for this help. Probably wisened by experience, the Swiss Red Cross handed over the consignment to me for the internees, against receipt, and inquired whether my fellow prisoners would benefit from it. I answered: "I hope so." This was, indeed, the only way in which a proper use of the material could be assured. I had a constant fight to prevent the camp rations being discontinued on the ground that the Swiss gift could be used instead. In fact over 80% of the articles sent were used for the purpose intended, whereas, if this care had not been taken, not more than 10% would have reached the prisoners.

In retrospect I must correct one thing. After I was released in late January 1946 a considerable amount of these Red Cross supplies were still left. Inmates who were released later informed me that these supplies were largely misappropriated after all, and the inmates received little of them.

Babies, Small Children and Adolescents

It is significant that babies and children up to 12 years of age were also interned. We had about a hundred of them. Children over 12 were considered to be grown-ups and were treated and mistreated in the same way. Although milk was fed to the pigs which were kept in the fortress, not a drop of milk was available for the babies. For that, permission had to be obtained from the authorities, a process which took 2 or 3 weeks. I had to face the desperate problem of nourishing some 20 babies with gruel and a little sugar, without a drop of milk. I succeeded in obtaining and bringing secretly into the camp an adequate supply of preserved milk. Later this was discovered and the internee who had provided the money for the milk was put in solitary confinement.

The children were housed in a wooden hut and had a big yard to play in, where diapers and laundry could also be hung up to dry. This children's section, which was headed by a woman doctor under my supervision, became a small model. It was used by the Czechs to show to visiting journalists, some of whom even took films of it. A remark which was made to me - "We Czechs died here, but you are allowed to survive" - shows the real attitude of the officials. The wooden shed, however, became more and more unsuitable as the weather grew colder, for the gaps between the planks were such that one could see through. I was promised every week that the children would either be released or better housed. The commander of the fortress and even more so the District Medical Officer took a great deal of trouble in the matter, but the competent authorities remained immovable. There was no room for the children. A great number of large rooms stood empty in Leitmeritz, as did more than 600 apartments, but there was no room for these children. October came and the children suffered terribly from cold. With November the first frosts began, the water was frozen in the morning and it was impossible to keep the children warm, even by bedding them close together and well covered up. There was very little fuel and in any case the temperature only became bearable quite near the stove; in the rest of the hut it remained below freezing. Some children suffered from frostbite on the hands, others could not hold their water in the cold and remained lying in wet clothes on the wet palliasses. At the end of November or beginning of December, thanks to the efforts of the commandant, Major Kálal, I was successful in getting the children transferred to a large cell in the 4th building, where two big stoves were installed and the temperature became bearable. The nurses slept in the aforementioned wooden barracks, six to a room, which did not stop the yard commandant, a young fellow names Benes, from entering the room several nights a week, throwing himself boots and all into the bed of one of the internees, and having sex with her in front of all the others.

Trade with Spirits, Tobacco and Women

It is significant that in all conflicts between the superior and the subordinate officials, the latter were successful. The position of the commandant was therefore extremely difficult. Certain sadists such as Truka, a supervisor and deputy commandant of the 4th building, were able to terrorize the whole fortress. Everyone was afraid of these brutes. Valchař, the commandant of the 2nd building, was a man of the same type; he was on hand for every murder or other atrocity. Some of these subordinates made a great deal of money. One Ortl had the internees make leather flowers to the number of 45,000 in two months. One can imagine what he earned from their sale.

After the transport of the Jews from Theresienstadt hundreds of horsehair mattresses were collected and brought into the fortress. They were pulled to pieces by the internees, the hair packed in bales and sold for the profit of the officials. Furniture and other items were manufactured in the large woodworking shop in the 2nd yard. In addition Ortl traded women to the Russians in return for spirits, bacon and tobacco. Once, as a special delicacy, he handed over nine women in their last month of pregnancy. The fact that as a result one or two children were born dead could not have disturbed him. One of these women attempted to resist. I saw her a few days later and she had been so ill-treated - her upper body and especially her breasts and arms were scratched and black with bruises - that I was surprised a premature birth had not resulted.

Women were also officially assigned to the Russians for work, when they were also used for sexual purposes. Anyone who attempted to resist was returned to the camp as lazy, and punished.

The Old People's Home

A series of small cells in the 4th building were set apart as a home for old people and invalids. The cells opened onto the smaller court and when it rained the water ran over the floor and caused the palliasses to moulder. In September it was bearable, but in October, when the cold nights came, these people suffered terribly. In one row of cells of 27 inmates, after two months, only 7 survived. At the beginning of winter I was finally able to get about 50 of the survivors into a casemate, where at least they suffered less from the cold.

Conditions in Cell 44 of the 4th building were far worse. No heating was allowed, water dripped from the ceiling and plaster became loose and fell. Everything was wet, including the blankets, and few possessed winter overcoats. The poor devils were never allowed to leave the cell, even to go to the sick-bay. They had to die where they were. As long as they had strength they kept moving half the night to keep themselves warm and then had to creep under the wet blankets again.

Part of the time the floor was icy. It was inevitable that prisoners died *en masse*. Although Major Kálal had forbidden beatings, they still occurred; often, during the night, we would hear the smashing of clubs on skulls, the whack of slaps and rubber truncheons making contact, the screams of the tortured and the roars of the guards.

Another Individual Case

In the first months of his detention Count Ledebur, a former member of Parliament for the Christian Social Party, a quiet, distinguished and likeable old man, was kept continuously in solitary confinement. He was forbidden contact with everyone, save the doctor. He was an idealist and believed firmly that he would be given a hearing. He told me that he had been imprisoned in connection with an archeological piece of jewelry, the property of his wife, which it had proved impossible to find. He would gladly have revealed its whereabouts to secure his release, but he had never inquired where his wife had kept it. For this reason, he assumed, he was being closely watched.

In spite of his 72 years he held out for months. After some months, however, he had to take to bed, as a result of an abscess on his foot which I treated. I myself was sent to the Leitmeritz hospital for eight days, for x-rays and treatment of my hand which had been fractured in the course of my abuses (and the purpose of my stay in Leitmeritz was also to see my wife and children). When I returned to the camp I noticed a worsening of his condition and incipient gangrene. I therefore attempted to secure his removal to the hospital in Leitmeritz, saying that the foot would need to be amputated, otherwise the Count would die. I was told, *"At chcipne!"* - he might just as well die where he was. I was thrown out.

Since I felt very sorry for the old gentleman, I still tried repeatedly to get him into the Leitmeritz hospital, but it was always in vain. His wife, who was also interrogated about the missing jewelry (she was still at liberty and lived in a small cottage in Milleschau), took advantage of the opportunity to send him several baskets of fruit. I don't know if he ever saw so much as two apples from all this fruit.

After another 10 to 14 days the old man's condition was very poor. A commission arrived from Prague and I was sharply censured for not having transferred him earlier, and he was admitted to the hospital the same day. I told the catholic nuns that the Count had been the leader of the Christian Social Party and begged them to do all they could for him. The catholic nuns, who always had a good heart towards the internees and whom the internees rightly described as "angels", did their best. But the Count died, just on the day when the British ambassador and the Prince of Liechtenstein were to have visited him. The Countess was dragged before the Leitmeritz district court sometime in the winter months.

Criminals

I must give a short account of one Kurt Landrock, a Kapo of the notorious cell No. 50. He was a beast in human form, a specialist in strangling, who curiously enough could be very nice to his favourites. Thanks to him the sick-bay became a hell for the patients. In my capacity as head doctor of the fortress I attempted to have him removed, on the grounds that he was unsuitable and that he could also speak no Czech. But the man enjoyed such credit for his misdeeds that his position could not be shaken. It was not until after the fact that I noticed that he preferentially accepted patients with gold teeth. It turned out that he collected these, which he wrenched out of the mouth of the patients. This, however, proved his downfall; since he had not handed the gold over to the state, he was brought before the district court in Leitmeritz.

The following example demonstrates the low opinion the Czechs had of the international public's intelligence: In order to be able to say that the abuses were not the work of Czechs, such a man as the Pole Alfred Kling, who had carried out many murders with his own hands, was declared to be German. Landrock was a German, a criminal whom the Czechs had selected as Kapo for his record of cruelty and who had already spent several years in German concentration camps. Therefore: all the numerous murders were not committed by the Czechs, but by the Germans. This ruse had a two-fold purpose: first, it washed the Czechs clean of the charges of mass murder, and second, it cast the Germans in a dreadful light once again. The fact that Captain Pruša or Tomeš could have prevented the ill-treatment, and could have prevented any murders at all from taking place, were things that the dumb foreigners won't realize - or so the assumption went, and I would not be surprised to see trials of these "Germans" being staged to pull the wool over the public eye. Where the many smashed jaws are concerned, none of the victims will speak up - for someone who has a broken jaw and is given nothing but hard bread and a bit of soup to eat, does not live to tell his story.

The Pole, Alfred Kling, was also a "sports champion": he was able to kill someone with a single blow to the neck with a small club. Despite many tries, none of the Czechs were able to duplicate this feat, and Alfred enjoyed considerable prestige as a result.

Remarks by Way of Comparison

From the many inmates who had formerly been imprisoned in German concentration camps and who had to continue their detention in Theresienstadt, I am fairly thoroughly informed first-hand about the methods used by the Gestapo and the brutalities in the camps, by people who themselves were inmates and had no reason to praise these camps but who unaninmously stated that the Theresienstadt camp was worse. I won't go into detail and will just mention two monsters in human form: one Valchar, who was cruelty and brutality incarnate, and one Truka, his equal in every way. It would take many pages to describe how these two yelled, beat, slapped, kicked, and tortured their victims in every conceivable fashion. One of Truka's little pleasures was to order the SS men to lie on the ground and then to take a walk on them, choosing the most sensitive places to step, jumping with both feet on the kidney areas, and the like. It is easy to imagine what cold, constant starvation, yelling, abuse, being stood up against a wall, being rolled on the ground etc. can do to people both mentally and physically. But to describe how the internees had to spend Sundays and holidays permanently locked up in the dark grave-like vaults to allow their overseers some time off, and more of the like, would go beyond the scope of this report. I should only like to add that Theresienstadt was no exception. I have talked to inmates of other camps and prisons and the system was everywhere the same. It was decreed and controlled by the Ministry of the Interior, although nobody now wishes to take the blame.

One may believe this account or not. But all who were in Theresienstadt can confirm that what I have said above is neither exaggerated nor untrue. Whereas the practice of beating prisoners to death more or less stopped later on, other factors took its place. The cold, and inadequate clothing; the lack of heating fuel and the months-long starvation. The torments involved in these are by no means less than they were in being beaten to death, for it is possible to let a great many people die without using violence on them.

Thousands of people are suffering under medieval-like slavery to this very day [1951]. I only have one wish: that my truthful account, which I am ready and willing to take on my oath, may help to prompt international authorities to take all possible steps against these inhuman conditions!

Theresienstadt, Report No. 2
Severe abuse in the camp
Reported by Hans Strobl - Report of June 26, 1946

Complying with the official instructions, my family and I reported to the Prague Police on May 9, 1945, and were detained for 14 days in Pankraz, where all of us inmates were grossly maltreated. On May 26 I was sent from there to Theresienstadt with a transport of 600 prisoners - men, women and children alike. On our arrival we were all brutally beaten, quite arbitrarily, with cudgels, axe handles, rifle butts etc. 59 men were beaten to death in the process; most of them were older men who couldn't run fast enough. In the time following, about 200 people died of the consequences of maltreatment.

Where I myself am concerned, my elbow joint was smashed and my ulna and radius bones were broken during the abuse I suffered. There was no medical aid. It was not until August 25, three months later, that I was admitted to the Leitmeritz Hospital to be operated. I then had to spend five months in the hospital.

Theresienstadt, Report No. 3
A prisoner's eyewitness account
Reported by Eduard Fritsch

The May 24, 1945 transport from Prague brought nearly 600 people of various ages and political orientations to Theresienstadt. All of them expected to be released to go home again after just a brief stay. At the gate to the fortress, the transport was segregated into men and youths, women and children, ill people and war-disabled. After a Czech wearing a Red Cross armband addressed us and treated us to a litany of all the evils the SS had committed in Theresienstadt, we were herded into the fortress. Many of us were already beaten during this procession. The path to Square 4 consists in part of a fairly long gate entrance sloping down to the square, and former inmates of the Theresienstadt concentration camp waited for us there to either side of the path. They were armed with iron-reinforced hoe handles, and it is difficult to describe what took place here. The approximately 10 meter (30 ft.) long gate entrance was lined with writhing, convulsing human bodies, who were screaming and whom we could not help, for none of us got through without a beating. The Czechs deliberately beat us on the kidney area and the back of the head. In the square itself, the remaining arrivals had to line up in rows of five and conduct their own head count. Since this took too long for the commandant of the fortress, Prusa, he took over the head count himself, by hitting each of us on the head with his iron-reinforced handle and counting as he went. It is not hard to understand why not many of us were left afterwards in the row that had been counted by Prusa. I chanced a glimpse towards the gate entrance, and a glimpse backwards. It was a gruesome sight. The ground was littered with people moaning in agony, and those who were silent were already dead. One of my cell-mates from Prankraz prison in Prague lay there with his skull smashed. Another man from Munich stood alone and quite helpless by the garbage pit. He was covered in bood from head to toe, forgot to join the line-up, and was driven to our line with constant blows. He walked with difficulty, dragging his feet, and the blows just rained down on his body. It was amazing that he managed to bear up under this treatment. We noticed that those who were beaten to the ground did not get up again. They were then beaten entirely to death. Those of us who managed to survive this procedure then had to stand facing the wall, hands raised, from about 9 o'clock until 5 o'clock p.m. Around noon it began to rain, and the water ran in our sleeves and out the bottom. Whenever anyone lowered his arms that was taken as a cause for the henchmen to knock our heads against the wall. During this time no doubt each of us decided that if we were not beaten to death or shot soon, we would commit suicide.

Evening came, and we were distributed among the cells. 480 men were crowded like sardines into our cell. Night fell, we heard shots outside, and screams, and we waited until it was to be our turn. Many were taken out and never returned. The next day we were disinfected and deloused. A strip of hair was shorn off from the forehead to the nape with a shaving machine. The Czechs called this shorn strip "Hitler Street". Then we had to run across the square naked to be issued our prison uniforms, which were dirty and often blood-stained. The next day, labor teams were sent out to various places to work. Together with some other men, I was ordered to clean up the solitary-confinement cells where those who had been beaten to death still lay. The floor was covered inches deep with coagulated blood, cut-off ears, knocked-out teeth, chunks of scalp with hair still on them, dentures, and the like. The stench from the blood etc. soon made it impossible for us to wash the cells and hallways. After two to three days many of the men on our cleaning team began to show growths and swellings on their back, neck, head and arms. Their heads looked like masks, all swollen up, eyes bulging out, lips thick, ears sticking out, the entire head swollen far beyond normal size, they were a heartbreaking sight. After two days I was ordered to report to the sick-bay. This facility consisted of five one-man cells. Each was occupied by up to five men, some lying down, some squatting or sitting on the floor. It was there that I saw something that utterly horrified me:

patients from these cells were stripped naked and laid on a gurney, and then the doctor gave them an injection of some fast-acting poison. These people died within a minute. I admit that this injection was a release for many, but there were also people among them who could easily have been cured. It was the commandant of the fortress who had ordered that the sick people were to be disposed of in this manner. Many of my acquaintances ended like that.

For the first while, the rations we received consisted of coffee and soup containing potato and some rotten meat, some of which was riddled with clumps of maggots. This rotten meat, which was sold by shops specializing in substandard goods, was fed to us for three months. After the German salt stores had been used up, salt shortage began. In August 1945 a day's rations consisted of a half-liter of soup (read: unsalted water), with a few little pieces of potato if you were lucky. Also 6.3 ounces of bread. Despite these meager rations the internees had to do very hard work, such as digging graves etc. - and some barely had the strength to lift their hoe. Typhus raged among the prisoners. Great hunger was our constant companion. We had to dig up mass graves, retrieve the corpses and put them in coffins with our bare hands - all this accompanied by intense August heat and the penetrating stench of the decomposing bodies, constant hunger, and we were even beaten while we worked, some of us were even beaten to death. Due to the danger of cholera our overseers urged us to work faster and faster, and these conditions soon drove us to despair.

One execution method favored by the Czechs involved one Czech stepping into a rope loop and holding it down with his foot. The rope was then placed around the prisoner's neck, and at the other end of the rope was a second loop into which a truncheon was put. This truncheon was used to gradually tighten the rope, and in this way the victim was slowly asphyxiated.

It was not until the Russian camp command learned of these conditions that investigative commissions were dispatched, who actually took energetic action. The iron-reinforced truncheons were burned. The lethal injections stopped, and we began to be treated somewhat more humanely.

I came away from this prison camp with a pelvic injury, a broken nasal bone, an injured arm, and I lost all my teeth in my upper right jaw - and I consider myself fortunate not to have suffered even worse injuries.

Troppau, Report No. 1
Severe maltreatment of a woman in 1945
Reported by Elfriede Hanke - Report of June 21, 1946

On June 2, 1945 I was sent to the camp at Troppau. There I was beaten, half-strangled and threatened with being shot, because I said that I [was not] a member of the party and that I know nothing of any ammunition, neither of which they were willing to believe. I was taken to the camp-prison on July 6, 1945, where I was severely maltreated. Immediately on my arrival I was punched, trampled under foot and thrashed with rubber-truncheons.

This treatment was repeated day after day for a period of 13 days. On the 13th day one Fitzek came, together with several other Czechs. They threw me on the [pallet] of my cell, took my pants off and lashed me with rubber-truncheons from the hips to the calves of both legs, so that I had to be taken to the sick-room in the evening, where I had to lie flat on my face for four weeks, since I had big festering wounds on my buttocks and on both calves. My sores also had to be lanced several times.

I was ill for four months. After this I was no longer beaten, but, like the others, was pushed about, ill-used and yelled at. On February 8, 1946 I was released.

Troppau, Report No. 2
Collection camp, torture of a sick man in autumn 1945
Reported by V. Skolaut - Report of June 21, 1946

In early July 1945 I and the rest of the city's German population were taken to the collection camp Troppau. From there I was sent every day to perform heavy physical labor in the electricity plant, and my health was not up to this work as I was 52 years old and suffering from severe angina pectoris, and had only recently had a severe inflammation of the gall bladder.

In the afternoon of August 3 I had a heart attack. When I returned from work in the evening with the rest of the inmates, I went to see the physician and before I could even consult him I was assigned to more physical labor in the camp. I obeyed this order without objection, and only asked permission to fetch my evening soup first as it was being distributed just then. The militiaman agreed to that. When I went into my barrack to get my dish, another militiaman came along and maltreated me. He knocked me to the ground with a wooden slat and kicked me all over my body, to the point where I had open wounds in my sides and lay unconscious for hours. Nonetheless I had to report for work as usual the next day, and the militiaman who had maltreated me jeered and made fun of me for my weakness and pain.

In the course of the forenoon, when I was carrying some office equipment up some steep stone steps, I was suddenly seized with weakness and fell down unconscious, breaking my kneecap in the process. First I was not even acknowledged as being ill, and was forced to continue working. It was not until two days later, when my swollen knee looked ominous and the pain got steadily worse, that I was transferred to the hospital, where I had to remain for four weeks. Towards the end of this time I was asked to donate blood for a Czech, which I did.

Troppau, Report No. 3
Cases of severe maltreatment in the camp
Reported by Emma Bittner Report of June 21, 1946

On May 31, 1945, I was sent to the labour camp at Troppau and remained there until June 5, 1946. I worked in this camp for three weeks and took part in all the parades with their accompanying maltreatment and humiliations.

When I collapsed during a roll-call as a result of the constant terror, the doctor certified me unable to work and [unfit] for further detention in the camp; thus I came to the sick-room on [June] 20, 1946, where I stayed for several months. During this time drunken members of the militia, led by one Grossmann, known as the "tiger of the camp", broke into the cells which were nearest to our barrack. Female members of the militia were also involved. The inmates of these cells were beaten so terribly that their cries of pain could be heard for hours. A wholesale merchant named Habel from Troppau was killed on this occasion. Such beatings went on for months. I myself saw the bruises of the victims. The diet consisted of only 100 g of bread and a thin soup without [nutritional value].

When the camp was moved to Eichendorff Platz, Troppau, at the end of August, the food improved thanks to the influence of a German partisan by the name of Gebauer. But we suffered from vermin, as the washing facilities were entirely insufficient. Three months later a shower-bath was built. There were, however, still beatings of men, women and girls as well as base insults. When I was brought to the camp, my last shirt was stolen.

I am prepared to swear to the foregoing statements.

Troppau, Report No. 4
Severe maltreatment in the camp
Reported by Rundt - Report of June 21, 1946

On June 4, 1945, arriving with travel permission at the Troppau train station from Böhmisch-Leipa, I was arrested for being a German, with no official reason given, and was taken to the police prison, where I was beaten and robbed of all my valuables. After three days I was transferred to the Troppau labor camp and immediately put into solitary confinement where, for two weeks, like all other inmates in solitary, I was beaten every day. The militia beat us all over our bodies with belts, rubber truncheons and sticks. Many of us passed out, and had open bleeding wounds. I myself had several open wounds on my back, and since I was nonetheless still beaten every day they eventually suppurated. The worst of the Czechs were Grossmann, Fitzek, Noss and Hoza. The German partisan Gebauer frequently stood up for the inmates, and saved many a life by doing so. When he was on duty I was not beaten. After bearing these tortures for 14 days, I volunteered for farm labor in the country. It took another two months before my wounds had healed.

Troppau, Report No. 5
Woman fatally injured on or about November 20,1945
Reported by Alois Leckl - Report of June 21, 1946

On or about November 20, 1945 my aged mother, Irene Leckl of Troppau, was walking along Ginschwitzer Street, and used the sidewalk to cut across a corner. A Czech woman shoved her off the sidewalk. She fell and hit the back of her head, and remained lying in the street, unconscious. She was taken to the Nursing Hospital of Troppau, where she died of brain hemorrhage without ever regaining consciousness. She was buried in the Troppau municipal cemetery, but church consecration was denied. At the cemetery itself I managed with much effort to persuade a Czech clergyman who happened to be there, to consecrate her grave. Charges were brought against the Czech woman who had pushed my mother. She was acquitted. I was not allowed to attend the trial, as I was in the labor camp.

Troppau, Report No. 6
Abuse and rape
Reported by M. T. Report of June 19, 1946

On June 19, 1945 four partisans beat me up in my home. I had to lie across a chair, and one held my head between his legs while another beat me with his leather belt. My 66-year-old father was beaten up in the same way after they finished with me. After that I had to lead the partisans through the entire house, from the basement to the attic. In the attic they attacked me and raped me. My father and I were then taken to the Troppau camp without being allowed to take anything at all with us from our home.

Troppau, Report No. 7

Confiscation of a family tomb

Reported by Wilhelm Loy Report of August 3, 1945

I spent 13 months in the Troppau concentration camp and was severely maltreated after my arrest and my committal to the camp. In the Troppau cemetery I owned a family tomb, in which my first wife had been buried for the last 10 years. In September 1945 - as I found out in October - my wife was exhumed and reburied elsewhere at an unmarked location. A Czech master-turner, a member of the Vrablik family, was buried instead in my family tomb. The German inscription on the grave stone was removed.

Troppau, Report No. 8

Eye injury as result of abuse

Reported by Dr. Karl Prokop Report of August 21, 1946

Because I am an Austrian I received Czech food-ration cards *[which were much better than the ration cards issued to Germans; pub.]* from June until October 1945. Due to an informant's denunciation I was summoned to the police office in Teichgasse [Street], Troppau on November 2, 1945 for a follow-up questioning, and there I was told that I am not Austrian. When I objected and said that I certainly am Austrian, I was boxed about the head three times so severely that I was quite dazed for the rest of the day and experienced impaired vision. At the same time I was dragged off to the concentration camp, where I was detained for eight months until at long last it was found that the denunciation had been groundless. From the camp I was sent to a Czech ophthalmologist by the name of Dr. Steffek, who diagnosed retinitis and clouding of the vitreous body. He accepted me as patient, but seven weeks later, when he asked me when I had first noticed these problems and I answered him honestly that "on November 2nd I was slapped about the head and the defects in my vision began after that," he refused to treat me further.

Troppau, Report No. 9

Concentration camp Schimrowitz, woman maltreated after giving birth

Reported by Maria Weisshuhn - Report of September 21, 1946

On May 15, 1945 I and my three children, of which the youngest was two weeks old, were committed to the concentration camp Schimrowitz near Troppau, where I was forced to work in the paper mill and to do the dirtiest and hardest jobs usually reserved for men, even though I had just given birth shortly before. Time and again I heard: let's hope she croaks, she and her German children. I was forbidden to nurse the baby. I had to give it water and black coffee.

After 8 weeks I was released from that camp. While there, I had been robbed of everything I had brought along for myself and the children. My home had also been looted. Even my resettlement [expulsion] luggage was looted, including a bag of clothes and linen, the baby buggy and diapers, the night pot and other things for the children, and all cutlery and dishes for four people. I immediately protested to the gendarmerie and the Resettlement Commissar in Bautsch, later to the district captain in Bärn, and finally to the Czech border official in Wiesau, but nothing helped.

The Resettlement Commissar was drunk when I spoke to him. When I applied to him again the next day, when he was sober again, he stated that I could not have my things back because he needed them for himself. I know that his wife was expecting a baby in the next few days.

My husband, engineer Karl Weisshuhn, born in Innsbruck on March 13, 1902, was arrested on May 12, 1945 and sent via Troppau and Ratibor to Auschwitz. All my efforts to find out what happened to him were in vain.

PART 2 - Smaller Towns and Villages

PART 2 - Smaller Towns and Villages, alphabetically:

Alt-Bürgersdorf, Althart, Altrohlau, Altrothwasser, Altsattel, Arlsdorf, Arnau, Arnsdorf, Asch, Auherzen-Lihn, Auschine-Raudnai, Barzdorf, Bautsch, Bennisch, Beraun, Bergesgrün, Berkowitz, Bilin, Bischofteinitz, Blatna, Blauendorf, Bodenbach, Böhmisch Kamnitz, Böhmisch Krummau, Böhmisch Trübau, Böhmisch Krummau, Böhmisch Leipa, Böhmisch Meseritsch, Braunau, Bretterschlag, Brunnersdorf, Brüsau, Bürgersdorf, Butschafka, Chodau, Chrastawitz, Chrostau, Datschitz, Deutsch-Beneschau, Deutsch-Jassnik, Deutsch-Lodenitz, Dittersdorf, Dobraken, Dobris, Dolawitz, Domeschau, Duppau, Duppau, Eipel, Eisenstein-Grün, Eisenstein, Elbogen, Ernstbrunn, Falkenau, Fischern, Frankstadt, Freudenthal, Friedland, Friedrichswald, Giesshübl-Sauerbrunn, Graslitz, Gross-Hermersdorf, Gross-Schönau, Grosssichdichfür, Grulich, Haida, Haindorf, Hakelsdorf, Hals, Hannsdorf, Heinzendorf, Hennersdorf, Hermannstadt, Hermersdorf, Hinterkotten, Hloubetin, Hohenfurth, Holleischen-Staab, Hostau, Jauernig, Josefstadt, Jungferndorf, Kaaden, Karlsstadt, Karlsthal, Karthaus, Karwin, Klattau, Klein-Herrlitz, Kleinbocken, Kleinmohrau, Klösterle and Kaaden, Kohling, Schindelwald and Schönlind, Kojetitz, Kolin, Kolin, Komoschau, Königinhof, Königshof, Krautenwalde, Kremsier, Kunzendorf, Kurim, Langenlutsch, Liblin, Libochowan, Liebenau, Liebesdorf, Liebeznice, Littau, Lyssa, Mährisch Trübau, Mährisch Rothwasser, Malschin, Maschau, Meierhöfen, Melnik, Mies, Modrany, Motol, Mühlbach, Münchengrätz, Neudek, Neuhof, Neurohlau, Neutitschein, Nieder-Mohrau and Olmütz, Niemes and Grottau, Nikolsburg, Nikolsburg, Ober-Lipka, Oberpaulowitz, Oderfurt, Pardubitz-Königgrätz, Parschnitz, Pattersdorf, Pisek and Brünn, Plan, Podmoky, Pohorsch and Karwin, Polepp and Leitmeritz, Pössigkau and Taus, Pribrans and Prague, Qualisch, Radl, Radonitz, Radwanitz, Reichenau, Reinowitz, Riegersdorf, Riesengebirge (the Sudeten Mountains), Rokitnitz, Römerstadt, Rosshaupt, Sankt Joachimsthal, Schankau, Schildberg, Schlackenwerth, Karlsbad, Kaschlitz and Spickengrün, Schlag, Schlaggenwald, Schönbach, Schönhengst, Schönlinde, Schwarzental and Hohenelbe, Schwarzwasser and Freiwaldau, Setzdorf, Sörgsdorf, Spillendorf, Stecken, Stefanau, Sternberg, Stimmersdorf, Strakonitz and Brünn, Tabor, Tachau, Tannwald, Tepl, Totzau, Trautenau, Tremošna, Triebendorf, Tschachwitz, Tschenkowitz, Tschirm, Tüppelsgrün, Tuschkau, Udritsch, Unterparsching, Vollmau, Vorderheuraffel, Waldau, Wallern, Warnsdorf, Weidenau, Weidsiefen, Wekelsdorf, Welpet, Willens, Witeschau, Witkowitz, Wockendorf, Zittau, Zlin, Znaim, Zwittau.

Reports on the Events in Smaller Towns and Villages

Severe maltreatment in the course of house searches
Reported by Adolf Lux - Report of September 30, 1946

On July 2 of last year partisans searched all the houses in Alt-Bürgersdorf. My house was searched as well, and they helped themselves to two violins and other things they liked, especially linen, clothing and shoes. They took off their own clothes and changed into mine. I was not personally attacked during all this. Then they went to my neighbor's, where they allegedly found a revolver. Thereupon they returned to my house, turned everything upside down and demanded a revolver from me too. I had none. This prompted them to maltreat me badly. I was punched in the face to the point where I lost 4 teeth, and another 3 were knocked loose. They threatened to shoot me, and did indeed fire shots in my home, hitting me in the foot. Then they ordered me to carry one of my blankets to the collection point in the local school. I hobbled painfully to the school. On the way back I went to a local creek, took off my shoe and washed out the bullet wound. When I returned to my home another partisan was waiting for me, and led me off to the Commissar, where he maltreated me again and then kicked me out of the house.

Slave labor, inspection of personal belongings
Reported by Reinhold Meiniger - Report of October 15, 1946

I was an orderly in a field hospital and was discharged from my duties there by the Russians on June 24 of last year. In Althart, near Slabings, the Czech gendarmes detained me, beat me up and robbed me blind (they even took the boots off my feet), and then I was put to agricultural labor on the Hejnitz farm near Slabings. For 4 weeks we got no bread at all there. We literally lived on dry potatoes. We got no salt for half a year. There were 32 of us there - discharged soldiers, all of us sick or injured since the Russians had not discharged any healthy ones. We had to work from 4 o'clock in the morning until 10 at night, with a one-hour break at noon. Anyone who was not up to the work load due to his poor health, or who did not know how to do the farm work (some of us were students), was beaten mercilessly. I was put to work on the chaffcutter, which I had never operated before, and in the foreman's opinion I was not productive enough the first day, and so, that evening, he boxed me about the head and beat me with a stick. I complained to the administrator, but all that got me was another beating the same night from the gendarmes who were called in. The foreman's name was Josef Brychta. Beatings like that took place every day. I had to work on the farm under these circumstances until August 8th of this year. My wife had already been expelled from our home the previous summer, with our two children and only a bare minimum of hand luggage. In this way we lost all of our possessions. Our resettlement [expulsion] luggage consists only of old things that were given to us by others, and on our expulsion the *Národní výbor* of Christofsgrund near Reichenberg looted even this meager luggage and took everything that was remotely usable, for example all our dishes, all the children's clothes, etc. After we complained about this in the resettlement [expulsion] camp in Alt-Habendorf, the *Národní výbor* of Christofsgrund was ordered to return the stolen things to me. Instead, I was given a few other items that were much worse than what we had had, for example a mismatched pair of shoes, and no dishes.

Altrohlau

Sick old woman robbed

Reported by Anna Drösler - Report of August 19, 1946

I am 62 years old and suffer from heart disease. For 4 years I have been widowed. On September 1, 1945 five Czech civilians, among them the postman Brechal, came to my home and conducted a wild house search, confiscating everything of value in the process. On September 2 some gendarmes came and did the same, even more destructively. On September 25 a gendarme arrived with several civilians, among them the new owner [of my house], kicked me out of bed - the doctor had given me an injection just shortly before - and gave me only 20 minutes to vacate my home. They threatened to beat me with a bludgeon. Being a sick woman, I was hardly able to pack anything to take with me in such a short time. I was driven from my home and found a place to stay in one of the cellar rooms, where I have lived without any furnishings until now. My request, to at least let me have a sofa from my home, was refused. I had to lie on boards and straw. The new owner Jakob declared that Germans must not be allowed to keep anything. All my linen and clothes remained in my home. The only luggage I had at the time of my expulsion belonged to my sister-in-law, and I even had to surrender three sets of underwear and a dress from this hand luggage.

Altrothwasser

Maltreatment of a farmer's family
Reported by Emilie Reinhold - Report of August 23, 1946

On September 8, 1945 a Czech administrator was posted to our farm. He treated us very badly. My family of five were the only laborers on the 96-acre estate. The administrator himself didn't do any work at all, but constantly accused us of sabotage even though we worked like mules 15 hours a day just to manage everything that needed to be done. For 7 months we were each paid only 1,000 Kcs. in wages, and only 1,500 Kcs. for 2 months. We had to buy our own food on so-called German ration cards. In the morning of January 13 two horses were suddenly missing, and the administrator accused us of having secretly sold them. We were led away, and my son and I were dreadfully maltreated. We were released to go home again the very same day, since probably nobody seriously believed that we had stolen the horses. But from that day on the administrator's harassment became unbearable. When my daughter fell ill on June 3 of this year, he was so enraged and threatened us with maltreatment that I suffered a nervous breakdown and was unconscious for hours and couldn't walk for three weeks afterwards.

Altsattel

Tormenting of an invalid
Reported by Anton Stockner - Report of August 22, 1946

I was arrested on July 4th, 1945, at Altsattel and taken to the camp at Elbogen. Although - immediately on my arrival at Elbogen - I had reported that I have a pneumothorax, I was not separated from the other persons, but was forced to participate, together with the others, both morning and evening in compulsory sport. We had, for example, to run a hundred times around the chalet, which I was quite unable to do. When I reported this, I was struck several times and was forced to continue the exercise. On another occasion when I could not run any longer I was forced to lie on the ground and do push-ups until the others had finished their hundred rounds. Whenever my arms collapsed, I was kicked. The other strenuous gymnastic exercises were often too much for me and in consequence I was always receiving blows. I was not to see permitted a doctor until July 10th. He then sent me to the hospital where they diagnosed an exudate as a consequence of overexertion. Subsequent to my discharge from the hospital, at the end of August, the pneumothorax was filled once more on September 24th, but when I returned in October, in order to get another filling, it was refused to me.

In November I was transported to Třemošna where, while going to fetch a parcel for a comrade, I was struck three times with a whip. At the beginning of December I came back to Elbogen as an invalid. There, when I failed to appear for the roll call, from which sick persons were usually exempted, I was slapped so violently that my spectacles broke.

Arlsdorf

72-year-old man harassed
Reported by Albert Geppert - Report of October 9, 1946

On September 22, 1945 I was stopped on the street and asked for my identification. I showed my ID card. It was taken from me; no reason was given. I was committed to the concentration camp Arlsdorf, where I was detained until May 24 of this year despite my advanced age (I am 72 years old). The rations we received were totally inadequate. Once, when I brought a bit of bread back into the camp from work - bread that an acquaintance had given me on the way - the guard boxed me about the head to the point that I have lost my hearing in my right ear. Parcels were regularly looted. When I was released, the watch that had been taken from me on my committal was not returned to me. Two other watches which I had sent out for repair were confiscated from the watchmaker by the gendarmerie.

Arnau

Murder of a husband and wife
Reported by Marie Rumler - Report of January 14, 1948

I lived in the Gebirgs-Strasse at Arnau in the Sudeten Mountains. At the same address there also resided my son, Josef Rumler and his wife Marie, née Petrik. My son was a master locksmith and my daughter-in-law a teacher of English at the High School in Arnau.

On June 18, 1945, my son and his wife were due for transfer. When the people were assembled in the market-place of Arnau, my son must have stood in the wrong place. He was terribly beaten and when his wife tried to protect him, she was also struck and dragged around by her hair. Then they were both driven into the court of the town-hall, beaten once more and finally shot.

I can swear to the correctness of this information; moreover almost the entire population of Arnau witnessed the incident.

Confession extorted by means of maltreatment
Reported by Karl Ehrlich - Report of June 19, 1946

On December 19, 1945 my wife and I were taken to the community office of Arnsdorf near Hennersdorf. I was asked whether I could speak Czech and whether I owned weapons. I replied no to both questions. Consequently I was severely maltreated. The Czechs repeatedly threw me against the wall, and punched me in the face at least ten times, knocking out two of my teeth. They interspersed it all with persistent questions about where I had hidden my weapons and ammunition. Then I was forced to sign a Czech police statement, the contents of which I did not know. This abuse lasted all night.

In the meantime my wife was maltreated as well. She had to raise her arms and was then punched in the side. Then she was locked into the cellar, where she was boxed about the head until she fainted. The partisans came to me several times during the night and said that my wife had just confessed where my weapons were hidden. They had also gone to my wife and said that I had confessed. The next day I was sent to Jägerndorf and then, from there, to Witkowitz for forced labor. As a result of the abuse my wife was so ill the next day that she could not be moved, and therefore she was not sent to the labor camp until February 1.

In Witkowitz the people were beaten up and harassed as well. If anyone went missing, the entire group was locked into the cellar overnight without food, to be sent back to work without rations the next day. That happened to me too, repeatedly.

Maltreatment for the purpose of intimidation
Reported by Anna Koch - Report of June 7, 1946

At the beginning of May a transport left the transfer-camp at Asch for the province Hesse. At the time the transport of expellees left the camp, I was standing in my sister-in-law's garden together with several women, among them a woman well known as an anti-fascist; the garden was right opposite the camp, separated from it only by a road. Suddenly a man of the SNB and one of the NB appeared in the garden and ordered us to go into the house. When we got into the house, each woman had to stand with her face to the wall. The anti-fascist woman was told to slap the faces of the others. Since she did not carry out the order to the satisfaction of the NB- or the SNB-man, she received a blow on her legs with a stick. Then the man demonstrated to her how she should strike us. I received from him two blows on each cheek and so did the others. Then the anti-fascist woman had to repeat the blows. Laughing, the two Czechs left.

Such events happened quite often in those days, sometimes the people were beaten till they bled. I am prepared to repeat these statements under oath.

Auherzen-Lihn

Abuse of Germans in May 1945
Reported by Anton Woeschka - Report of June 3, 1946

On May 8 last year I was arrested, along with 24 other inhabitants of my town Auherzen. There were three women among us. With our hands raised, we had to line up beside the village pond, and had to stand there until all 25 of us had been rounded up. If anyone lowered his hands due to exhaustion, he was immediately clubbed about the head. This went on for about 4 hours. Then we were loaded onto a truck. While boarding, everyone was beaten with sticks. We were carted off to Lihn. During the ride a man in the truck beat us terribly, so that everyone bled from wounds on their head and face. When we disembarked in Lihn we were also beaten until we reached the Town Hall. In the Town Hall we were beaten even more, until none of us could still stand upright. Then we were looted of our possessions. We all had to undress completely for this procedure, and then we were robbed not only of any and all watches and rings but even of our clothes. Then former Russian prisoners of war were ordered to beat us, which they did. Then the Czechs took over and beat us all over again. By this time everyone was bleeding from many wounds. Then we were ordered to beat each other with a heavy strap. A bucket of cold water was dumped on each of us, and then we were herded into a room where we were locked up. The next day we were interrogated. I was dismissed as being innocent. The Czech commission was made up of young people aged 18 to 20.

I can take this statement on my oath, and Josef Heckenthaler, Josef Lappat, Josef Peller, Wenzel Cibulka, Josef Holley and Josef Jaklin can corroborate it.

Auschine-Raudnai

Blind woman robbed
Reported by Marie Schlechte - Report of November 6, 1946

On June 11, 1946 my husband and I were admitted to the hospital. Ever since 1938 my husband has suffered from a severe psychosis and arteriosclerosis, and on that day he had attempted to take his and my life. The *Národní výbor* in Auschine-Raudnai, Aussig District, the community where I lived, assured me repeatedly that my home had been sealed and would be left as was until I returned from the hospital. In late September the hospital gave me leave to fetch clothing, linen, shoes and bedding from my home, to take with me for my impending resettlement [expulsion]. But my home had been occupied by the Czech Vyskocil. I was forbidden to enter it, and only got a very small portion of my things, which he selected. I was given someone else's linen, of poor quality, and no underwear at all. So I had to ask acquaintances for these necessities to supplement my expulsion luggage. My wedding ring was withheld from me, on the grounds that as a German I allegedly have no right to own gold. Being blind, I was resettled [expelled] via the blind people's transport. My husband had already passed away in the hospital in Aussig on June 16, 1946.

Barzdorf

Juveniles in the coal mines
Reported by Rudolf Koppe - Report of October 9, 1946

On October 18th, 1945, I was called up by the gendarmerie for five weeks' service in the sugar-refinery of Olmütz, together with 9 other juveniles from Barzdorf. On the next day our employment was changed into 3 months' service in the mines of Ostrau, as voluntary workers with full Czech rations. In fact we ended up working there for 11 months, down in the pit; the food was very bad, we received almost no salary and we were exposed to constant terror and maltreatment. The daily working-time was 8 hours below ground and 4 hours above ground. The food there consisted of nothing but water-gruel for the first months, later on we got 30 grams meat daily and 400 grams bread. Anyone who cooked potatoes in addition was punished. On arrival at Ostrau our pockets were completely emptied and the contents were not returned to us when we were released. After our discharge we had to pay the fare home ourselves. The treatment was bad. Every day we were called names and boxed on the ears; this occurred in the camp as well as in the pit. In addition to the 12 hours working time we also had to do some work for Czechs from outside the camp.

Bautsch

After release from Russian imprisonment, forced internment in the Czech camp Gurein
Reported by Erich Granzer - Report of September 13, 1946

On June 26th, 1945, I was taken prisoner by the Russians and sent to Saratow. On October 1st I became seriously ill, was released, and arrived in Brünn on November 4th, 1945, together with a transport of about 2,000 released prisoners of war. We were completely ignorant of what had happened in the meantime in the German areas of Czechoslovakia. From Brünn we were moved to the camp at Gurein. There the Czechs took away our Russian discharge papers, telling us that we should get Czech discharge papers the following day in order to be released to our homes, since these were situated in Czech territory. But in fact there was no question of any discharge. Although seriously ill, everyone was forced to work. The treatment was inhuman. We were crowded into barracks, packed together and we had to sleep on a bare earth floor; we received no blankets and suffered severely from the cold. There was no fuel. The food consisted of soup and 200 g bread once a day, black coffee twice a day. 12 to 16 men died daily from exposure, maltreatment and weakness caused by malnutrition. The dead were stripped and then thrown into a common grave. At every opportunity we were severely beaten. There were 300 men in a barrack 15 by 6 meters (50 x 20 ft) in size. One night during the winter, when 6 men failed to take off their shoes because of the terrible cold and were caught by the nightly inspection, all of the prisoners in the barrack were forced to parade barefoot in the snow; the 6 men themselves had to kneel on chairs and were beaten with rods on the soles of their feet until these were covered with blood. One month later I arrived at the prison-camp in Brünn where conditions were a little better, although we were also beaten. Since my health was not the best, I was ordered to the soap-works Krassel in January 1946, where I was given lighter work and was able to recover. There I remained in internment until July 1946. When I ascertained, accidentally, that my family had been transferred to Hesse, I used the opportunity to escape and I succeeded in crossing the Austrian border on foot. In the vicinity of Brünn are vast camps in which there are still thousands of Germans, civilians, women and children and also prisoners of war. All these people are forced to do the hardest and most dirty work. As a result of the cruel mistreatment and the bad food the death-rate is extremely high. The people are reduced to skeletons and die en masse, the bodies are stripped, taken out of the camp on rack-wagons and hand-carts and buried outside the cemeteries, in the fields or at the edge of the woods, in mass graves. From the Czechs one hears only the slogan: the Germans must die. And they do everything to carry it into effect.

I am willing to testify to my statements upon oath at any time.

Bennisch

Bennisch, Report No. 1
Concentration camps Hodolein and Stefanau, Severe harassment of old people.
Reported by Valerie Klos - Report of August 2, 1946

On July 19th of last year, some 750 people from Bennisch, including very many old and sick people and women with young children, were herded together with almost no advance notice and with a bare minimum of luggage, to be sent into the Czech regions for three weeks to serve as laborers for the harvest season. The next day, in Olmütz, the old people and the women with small children were culled from the rest and sent to the concentration camp Hodolein. Among these people were my parents, my father aged 74 and my mother aged 54. After 10 months, my sister and I were sent to a farmer, where we were treated very hatefully and were often cursed and even spat at. My father fell ill in Hodolein as a result of the maltreatment and poor rations, and according to an order of the chief police physician of Olmütz he was supposed to be released for health reasons, but instead he and my mother were sent to the concentration camp Stefanau, where the poor care and housing aggravated my father's condition to the point where he died on September 24. He had ulcers on his head and sides, the result of beatings. In only this short time he had lost so much weight that he was just skin and bones. My sister and I were only about 30 km away, on labor detail, but we were not allowed to go see our father one more time before he died.

When we were released and went home, none of our things were still there, and we were forbidden to enter our home. The luggage we have for our expulsion consists only of things that acquaintances gave us, and these items are mostly old and partly already worn out. We have no winter clothes at all.

Bennisch, Report No. 2
Girl severely maltreated by employer
Reported by Hildegard Maschke - Report of August 2, 1946

The Employment Office in Bennisch sent my 16-year-old daughter to work for the Czech farmer Uhlír, where she had to work every day from 5 o'clock in the morning until 10:30 at night. The farm is about 100 acres in size and my daughter was the only farmhand. And so in time the work got to be too much for the child. In early April my daughter came to see me one day, early in the morning, and asked me to accompany her to the Employment Office, since she could no longer manage all the hard work. But even before we could set off to the Employment Office, Mrs. Uhlír arrived with Túma, the Head of the Employment Office, to fetch my daughter. Túma beat her until she agreed to return to the farm. I too was beaten twice by Túma. In early July my daughter was again badly maltreated by Mrs. Uhlír and accused of having stolen some new things from her. I have a Czech gendarme to thank for the fact that my daughter was even released for resettlement at all, and has now been expelled together with me.

Bennisch, Report No. 3
Abuse in the coal pits of Ostrau
Reported by Johann Januschke - Report of August 2, 1946

On September 24 of last year the Employment Office of Bennisch sent me off to Moravian Ostrau to work in the Ida mine. Both the treatment and the rations we received there were very bad. In early December one of the guards gave me a beating when I reported to him, as per regulations, that while I was working one of my fingers had been caught in a cogwheel, which had crushed the first tip of the ring finger on my left hand. I had to continue working despite this injury. The second time I was severely maltreated was on Christmas Day. When I arrived for my shift in the morning I was smoking a cigarette. One of the guards came up to me and slapped me. When I turned away, he followed me and beat me with his rubber truncheon and rifle butt across my back and chest and on my head and hands until I lost consciousness. Afterwards, the physician diagnosed pulmonary bleeding, cardiac insufficiency, and bruising all over my body. I had to remain in bed for several months. For two months I couldn't even eat on my own. The physician attested that as a result of the maltreatment I had suffered, I would be unfit for physical labor for several years. Consequently I was dismissed from working in the mine on April 4 of this year.

While I had worked in the mine I had not been paid any wages, and my wife and our four-month-old child had not received any support whatsoever.

Bennisch, Report No. 4
Abuse in the camp's cold store room
Reported by Erwin Plisch - Report of September 9, 1946

The terror of all inhabitants of Bennisch is the Ice Cellar, in which 15 men were constantly kept imprisoned until October 1945. The prisoners were always changing, some being sent in, some out. I myself was imprisoned there for three weeks. In the Ice Cellar a team of thugs was constantly on duty to beat us, and the inmates were severely maltreated by them every day. I was beaten there twice myself. I also witnessed how some people were so badly maltreated that they had to be taken the infirmary, where many of them died of their terrible injuries.

I was released on August 7 of last year, as being totally innocent of any political wrongdoings. Even at the time of my arrest I was told that I would be released again immediately if I agreed to join the Communist Party. Since I refused, I was maltreated.

The teacher Anlauf of Zossen was released on August 7, along with me. He had been beaten bloody in the Ice Cellar. When he found out in early September that he was to be arrested again, he committed suicide.

Beraun

Murder of German soldiers
Reported by Franz Tengler

In 1942, as I still had my Czech citizenship, I was called to Kladno where I was told, since my parents were Germans: "You've got a choice, either you enlist or you'll be sent to a concentration camp." I chose the first option, and after an army medical exam I became a GvH [gendarme?]. I went through the training course, and fell ill. I spent a year in the army hospital and was then sent back to my regiment in Tábor. I stayed there for a short time and was then sent to Prague; after a brief time in Prague I was posted to a bridge guard detail in Dobrichovic. Following the surrender, the bridge guards were arrested by the Czechs and quartered in a school. 358 men and 9 women were quartered there. We stayed in Dobrichovic for two days and were then moved on to Beraun. As I speak Czech perfectly, I was used as interpreter for the transport, which was led by the Czech gendarmerie. Before moving out of Dobrichovic, I got a Czech major to issue us a paper stating that our group was a labor gang, had not been in combat, and was unarmed; I believed that with the aid of this paper the transport would proceed smoothly.

Each Czech Communist carried a gun, and considered every [German] soldier to be a member of the Waffen-SS. We moved out of Dobrichovic without any difficulty or harassment. But outside Tetín we were stopped by Vlasov troops; the leader of these troops ordered the women thrown into the water. Since the Beraun River was not deep at that point, we managed to pull them out again. Then the leader of the Vlasov troops ordered a sergeant major from our unit to undress, took his clothes away and gave him his own louse-ridden clothing instead. Then he said that he would take one of our lives in retribution for his mother, who had allegedly been shot by the Germans. I went to him and spoke to him in Czech, and in Russian as best I could, to dissuade him from his purpose. I managed it; and he let us move on.

Near Beraun we were greeted by Communists with guns at the ready. But there was no major incident. They took charge of our group and locked us into a garage. The first two days went by quietly, but on the third day the Communists stormed in and body-searched everyone to see if anyone from the Waffen-SS was among us; I honestly didn't know, but I showed them the paper that the Czech major had given me. As I found out later, there were in fact 14 SS-men in our group, but they had been drafted into that unit only at the very end of the war. Four men who were found to have the SS tattoo were taken out of the group and trampled to a pulp before our very eyes; and when they lay on the ground all covered in blood, they were doused with water and yanked back onto their feet, forced to hold photographs of Hitler against their chest, and put on display for the crowd in the barrack square. Some Communists pressed a pistol against my chest and told the others, "Watch this fellow, he's one of them too." I never found out how the four men who had been led off ended up.

On the fifth day we were handed over to the American forces who took us to the concentration camp in Rokycan. I fell ill in that camp and was taken to the hospital in Pilsen. But as the hospital was overfull, the new arrivals had to spend the night in the garden. After a few days I felt better and therefore I was sent to Tepl, near Marienbad. After half a year I was discharged to stay with my aunt in Hermannshütte. I spent almost three months there; I planned to wait until things quieted down, and then I wanted to return to Beraun, to my wife. I did so. But the very night I arrived in Beraun I was arrested by the Czech criminal police and locked into the barracks where I, like the other inmates, was beaten on my naked upper body by four men armed with rubber truncheons, until I lost consciousness. When I had to answer the call of nature, which was allowed only under guard, I saw a dead soldier in the cubicle next to mine. His silver cross still lay beside his body. I do not know how many soldiers lost their lives in these barracks.

My health deteriorated more each day, and my nerves suffered most of all. After five months I was sent to a concentration camp, where I was immediately assigned to a work detail. We were quartered 120 men in one room. There was no way at all to wash, and it was not long before the lice got out of hand. Almost every day we were searched for weapons and cigarettes. The treatment and rations in this concentration camp were beneath all human dignity, and so it was no wonder that half the inmates died of starvation and the other half were mere skin and bones. Just one example, the fate of my friend Andreas Rott: he was in the Sick Room, as he had tuberculosis. His mother was imprisoned in the women's section of the same concentration camp; but she was not allowed to visit her son as he lay fighting for his life, to exchange a few kind and consoling words with him. I visited this gravely ill man every day after work to change his bedding. A merciful fate soon released him from his suffering.

Critically ill inmates were housed in an attic room, whereas the deceased were taken into the cellar. One day, as I was again carrying a corpse from the attic to the cellar, I saw how a woman who was still showing signs of life was also being taken into the dark cellar.

Depending on where workers were needed, I worked in a quarry, an iron foundry and on a farm. Despite the very hard labor the rations were totally insufficient, and very bad: barley groats without salt, peas without salt. For those in the Sick Room there was a small piece of bread in the morning, a bit of soup with four pieces of potato at noon, and some cabbage soup in the evenings. Sometimes there were a few boiled potatoes in their jackets. The potatoes were salted only on holidays.

But despite the inadequate rations, maximum work performance was demanded. When I was working on the large farm, I was expected to unload 28 wagon loads of grain into the machine [thresher?] within 9 hours. During the fieldwork I observed how one woman - she is said to be the wife of a professor - could not bind the grain sheaves as quickly as was expected, since this kind of work was totally unfamiliar to her. The guard on duty also observed this, leaped at the woman in a rage and dealt her such a blow that she fell. In his inhumanity he then even kicked her in the stomach, so that she screamed in pain. But it was impossible to help the woman, as doing so entailed the risk of being shot down by the guard. I do not know what happened to this woman after that.

On this large farm there were also evacuated German women from the Reich, who were also conscripted into labor. Whenever Russian soldiers came to this farm these women were mercilessly raped by them.

In this concentration camp there was also a student who was beaten until he had become totally feebleminded; we were never able to find out just why he was being beaten.

After some time the concentration camp was moved from Skurov to Karlstein. Once again I became gravely ill, and was transferred to a hospital in Beraun. The food was better there. Even though I was not yet fully recovered, I was put to work in the hospital. In 18-hour shifts I had to cart 140 Zentner [14 metric tons] of coal into the boiler room and to stoke one and sometimes even two boilers to keep the hospital supplied with steam and hot water. To save some time I set up my pallet in the boiler room.

During this time my wife was admitted to the same hospital, as she lived in Beraun. She had to have an operation. According to my wife she had been raped by a Czech, and was pregnant; due to sepsis the operation had to be performed without delay. I was forbidden to go see my wife. When I had managed to obtain permission, I only saw that my wife was dying, as the operation had been performed too late. At midnight I left the hospital and returned to the boiler room. At 5 o'clock in the morning I was awakened by the telephone; the nurse who had been attending my wife informed me that my wife had passed away. She was taken to the morgue, 10 steps from my place of work. My wife was Czech by birth, but she had automatically become German because I am a German. A Czech living in the same house as I - politically he was Communist - had requested that my wife should be buried in a mine shaft. My brother-in-law managed to prevent this, and so my wife was buried in her mother's grave.

Several weeks after the funeral I was assigned to a transport and shipped off to the Harz Mountains (Russian Occupation Zone). From there I went to the American Zone. I no longer recall the exact dates, since the repeated maltreatment in the various camps has left me with brain, gall bladder and spleen injuries.

Bergesgrün

Murder of women and children, amputee killed with his own crutches
Reported by Eduard Kaltofen

I, Eduard Kaltofen, was born on March 15th, 1921 at Bergesgrün, in the district of Brux, Sudetenland, my parents having been born at the same place. In 1941 I was called up for the Luftwaffe; in 1942 I was ordered to the Russian Front on reconnaissance. At the same time my father was enlisted in the gendarmerie and ordered to Yugoslavia. I was twice wounded, the last time at Kitzingen by American low-flying airplanes. Because I was no longer fit for military service, I was given my soldier's pay book and advised to try and reach my home as soon as possible. I left the hospital on April 28th, 1945, and walked in the direction of Salzburg and Linz. From Linz I went to Budweis and Prague by goods-train. I reached Prague on May 4th, and on May 5th I arrived at home without any difficulty. I stayed with my family and my mother for three days; we did not know where my father was stationed. On May 8th the Russians arrived, but they only stayed for two days. Ukrainians visited our house and looted it. Whatever they liked they took along, underwear, dresses, watches, chains, even the small amount of food we had. Most of the flour and sugar was spread about the streets and wasted. Murders, homicide and rape were common. The Russians were followed by the Czechs but nothing changed. The first Czech military group called themselves partisans; some of them were dressed in the German uniform of the Africa Corps, but the majority wore civilian clothes. They were equipped with machine guns, carbines and pistols. 8 to 10 partisans would enter German dwellings, loot them and rape women and girls. During the night this Czech elite troop - as they called themselves - shot women and men of all ages; men were cruelly tortured and killed, while women and children were forced to watch. At the neighbouring village of Bruch all men and boys were driven together and beaten with whips and rubber tubing lined with copper wire, until all were wounded and their wounds bleeding; afterwards they threw salt and pepper on the wounds. On May 10th it was my turn. Civilians seized me on the street and took me to the so-called *Národní výbor* (National Committee). Without being accused of anything, I was imprisoned for 8 days. There were 8 men in a cell. 3 men were shot the first night and replaced by others in order to fill the narrow space of our room. The windowless room was so small that we could not get enough oxygen to breathe properly. We lay on the ground, almost unconscious and next door to suffocation. Latrines were not available, we had to use a corner of the same little room. Only the following day were we allowed to relieve ourselves in private. The cell was never cleaned. Every fourth day we received some water and 100 g of bread with the remark: "You German bastards should die like rats, a bullet or a rope is much too good for you." After 8 days of imprisonment I was released, but 6 days later I was again put in jail. I was destined to see again the same cell. They ordered me to undress and to stand against the wall, then I was whipped by two men until my back bled. Afterwards I was struck so heavily on my head with a wooden club that I lost consciousness. When I came to, I found myself lying on the ground in a pool of blood, together with four other comrades who were in the same condition as I. Soon after the sentry entered the room and asked us if we were well and if we had any wishes. We replied that we would like to get washed and bandaged up, but we did not dare to ask for some food. He then started laughing and said that he would be right back and that he himself would wash and bandage us. It was not more than five minutes before two partisans and two civilians entered the room and thrashed us till we fainted. On the third day 20 of us were taken to the jail of Oberleutensdorf by the criminal police, where we were told after the first corporal punishments with whips and copper cables that none of us Germans would ever leave the jail alive. All Germans, they said, ought to die. We had not the slightest doubt that these words would come true; our only desire, which we also expressed to them, was that they should hang us. The answer to our request was more laughter.

I spent four weeks in this jail. Day and night we were knocked about every hour or two; we no longer had any feeling in our bodies. In this condition we were forced day after day to dig the mass graves. Even at the cross-roads we had to bury those who had been tortured to death. German men and women were buried in fields and woods so that the mass graves should not become too large. The second week a 16-year-old boy was thrown into our cell; he was beaten by the partisans until he scrambled to his feet, unable to endure the pain. With that his fate was sealed; he was shot down in front of us, there in our cell. In the course of the very same night we heard shots five times, each time in a different cell. Next morning we had to bury five of our comrades in the mass grave; they had been beaten and then shot with automatic pistols.

These things went on for four weeks, day and night. We only looked forward to release from our tortures. In the fourth week those of us who had survived, beaten up beyond all recognition, were rounded up in the yard of the jail. We were lined up in rows of five. There were 20 men, among them workers, salesmen, doctors etc.; leading officials of the NSDAP or the military forces were not among them, since these had already fled before the revolution or had been shot by the Czechs shortly afterwards. Not one of the 200 men assembled was conscious of any guilt, but they had to suffer for being Germans. We had to run at top speed for nine kilometers (5 miles) to the jail in the county town of Brüx. There everything was a little better; we were still struck occasionally, but not to the same extent. We were employed in the hydrogenizing works at Maltheuern, which were lacking in skilled workmen. Our diet consisted of one cup of coffee daily, 100 g of bread and a watery soup at noontime. I spent two weeks in this jail. But we were soon to find out that something even better was in store for the Germans. Camp 28 was established, the Czechs called it concentration-tábor 28. We were transferred from the jail at Brüx to this concentration camp. The inmates numbered 1400 men. In this camp we were again mistreated in the most inhuman way, each Czech who wished to vent his fury on a defenceless German was permitted to enter the camp and use the lash for as long as it pleased him. The more he tortured us the greater was the satisfaction of the guards. Indeed, the guards themselves were continuously going up and down our ranks and striking us in the face with rubber truncheons; we were often kicked so violently that we lost our balance and fell.

One day a group of a 100 Germans was brought into the camp; first of all, all their possessions were taken from them (tobacco, wedding rings, money, watches, bread), they were deprived of absolutely everything and the guards fell on the booty like wild animals. One of the group was a veteran on crutches, who had lost one leg in the war. This man was beaten with his own crutches until he was left lying dead on the ground. Several days later all prisoners had to line up behind the barracks. Thirty meters [about 98 ft] distant there was a sand pit. By this sand pit stood the commander of the camp, addressed as *"Velitel"* (commandant) by the Czechs. To his right there were 4 Germans holding their coffins in their hands. First two of them were shot in the neck and then the other two. We were forced to witness these executions. During this time hundreds of Germans were murdered, being shot in the neck; each night we heard the sound of shots at the sand pit. There was no end to the transporting of corpses out of the camp. We were outlawed and treated as slaves. Any Czech could do anything he wanted to us.

Via a German comrade, who was still at liberty, I received a word that my father too was in the hands of the Czechs. Eight more days passed and I was released; the Czech criminal police certified that I had been a member neither of the Party nor of any of its affiliates, but had only served in the German army. I was therefore permitted to be reunited with my family after nine weeks of imprisonment. I collected information about my father. He had been in American-occupied territory behind Karlsbad, where the gendarmerie was being demobilized. Through refugees from our village he learned that I had been taken prisoner by the Czechs, he therefore returned home. At the small town of Einsiedel, situated in the Erzgebirge, he was captured by partisans. They struck him with clubs and rifle butts, then they tied him to two poles, forming a kind of ladder. One Wenzl Bervid, who was the son of a German mother, then fastened this contraption to a motorcycle in such a way that my father's head and shoulders touched the road, after which he drove for 2½ hours to Bergesgrün at a speed of 10 kilometers per hour. When they arrived there, in spite of his pitiful condition, my father was beaten again, his teeth were knocked out and his face was disfigured to such an extent that he was unrecognizable. Afterwards they took him to the jail of Oberleutensdorf. Beaten, dirty and suffering from wound-fever, they left the unfortunate man alone in a cell. The following day he was ordered to help in the demolition of tank barriers. Since this work was too much for him and he was quite unable to do it, the guards knocked him down with the butts of their rifles. Only after this was the Red Cross informed and asked to pick him up. A Red Cross nurse recognized my father and sent me the following report: "Your father was beaten and disfigured in the most dreadful manner, not a single part of him but was bruised all over, his teeth were knocked in, his eyes bloodshot, his skull fractured by the blows of rifle-butts. Half an hour later he was cleaned and bandaged and with great difficulty was brought back to consciousness. Unfortunately he was not in a condition to answer questions and relapsed again into unconsciousness. Only when he came to for the second time was he able to collect himself. His first words were: 'They've knocked me silly', then he asked for something to eat, but he could take no food, for his mouth was too badly bruised. His next question was, if his son were still in prison?" Since the nurse wanted to spare his feelings, she told him that I was already reunited with my wife. Although his features were twisted with pain, a happy smile crossed his face on hearing this answer and his words were just audible: "Now I can die in peace."

On June 8th we received the written notice from the *Národní výbor* (National Committee) that my father died on June 7th about 7 o'clock in the evening in the jail and that we should have to pay RM 159.-- for the coffin and the transport of the corpse. Through the German coroner, who was still living there, we found out in which mass grave my father had been buried. We left some flowers on the grave, but the Czechs threw them away the next day. Sentries were constantly in the cemetery, watching the Germans at their work. To pass the time the sentries fired at tombstones and graves. Anyone who approached the mass graves was struck and driven away.

Berkowitz

Harassment of a farmer's family
Reported by Anna Schneider - Report of June 15, 1946

In June 1945 a Czech administrator named Anton Gorec came from Berkowitz to take over our farm. On July 20 he brought his family as well. When he arrived with his family and 8 partisans on July 20, he tried to beat me. I dodged, so then he caught hold of my 15-year-old son and maltreated him badly. For two hours he punched, slapped and kicked him and pulled him by the hair. Finally my son managed to get away. Since then we have no idea where he is.

Following that, he treated my 17-year-old son like a prisoner. During the day he had to work hard, without food, and was locked up at night. On September 23 he too ran away.

On August 26 my husband was taken to the *Národní Výbor,* where he was beaten so badly that he tried to commit suicide, but a neighbor prevented him from doing so.

As early as July 26 Gorec had taken all food, clothing, linen, bedding etc. from us and locked all the rooms in the house. We lived in a tiny hut, 6 people in one small room, and at night we had to sleep on the bare bed boards, 3 people per bed. At Christmas and Easter he turned our water off. Every day around dinnertime he came into our room to check what we were eating. When I carried water in buckets because he had turned the water off, the Gorec family made fun of me. He harvested everything in the garden. We did not receive so much as one green leaf or even a single potato, even though we had to do all the gardening work.

Gorec had no inkling of agricultural work. He could not hitch up a cow, neither could his wife milk one. I had to milk for her. The milk was taken from me before I ever left the stable. I am prepared to repeat this statement under oath.

Bilin

Invalids shot during the expulsion
Reported by Anton Watzke Report of January 15, 1950

On June 15th, 1945 at 6 o'clock in the morning about 10 heavily armed Czech soldiers of the so-called Svoboda-army appeared at my flat at 18 Teplitzer St., Bilin (the dwelling and business premises belonged to me and my wife) and ordered us to clear out of the house within five minutes. An officer present counted the minutes with the watch in his hand. Since my wife was in bad health and confined to bed, we were able to snatch up only a few articles of clothing and some linen in the hurry of dressing and getting ready within the five minutes. We exceeded the time limit by two minutes and the officer refused our request for permission to fetch a hat for my wife. Our money, watches, jewellery etc. were taken from us. We were allowed to keep only 20 Marks each. We were also repeatedly threatened with the words: "If money is found on anybody he will be shot immediately." The residents of Teplitz St. were gathered in the guest room of the Gaudnek Inn. A machine gun was set up in the restaurant, ready to fire. While we waited there for what might come next, I saw Germans being beaten up with police truncheons. On our forced march to the border - although it was extremely hot - the soldiers struck women, children and elderly people, who were unable to keep up, with the butts of their rifles. I myself saw three dead bodies at the left hand side of the road; all of them had been shot in the neck because they were unable to move fast enough. Thy were: Fiebach, his daughter, and a certain Swoboda. I knew them all personally. I myself was lucky enough to escape from this hell. Although I was not present, I know that my brother Hans and his wife were barbarously mistreated at the town hall of Bilin, that my brother Julius was killed, and that the clergyman Köckert, the forester Tost and many, many others whose names I do not recall, were shot.

Bischofteinitz, Report No. 1
Concentration camp Taus: Robbery and maltreatment
Reported by Robert Hartl - Report of July 20, 1946

On November 22, 1945 my wife and I drove in a rental car from Karlsbad to Hostau, District Bischofteinitz, to my mother-in-law, who is 72 years old and disabled, in order to be resettled [expelled] with her. On our arrival in Hostau we were arrested by the gendarmerie. My wife and I were both beaten by them. All our things - clothing and suits, underwear, linen and tablecloths, shoes, my watch and that of my wife, cash in the amount of 1,900 and 4,500 Kc respectively, and even our wedding rings - all was taken from us. They also took our personal papers and documents. Then my wife and I were detained for 8 months in the Taus camp, for unpaid slave labor. We were not even interrogated until mid-June, on my appeal. Nobody knew why we had been imprisoned. There were no charges against us at all. On June 22 we were discharged. The things that had been taken from me and my wife were not to be found. As replacement we received 45 kg of poor-quality and in part entirely unusable clothes, linen and shoes. The stolen money and papers could not be replaced.

Bischofteinitz, Report No. 2
Concentration camp Taus: 35 Germans vanished without a trace
Reported by Maria Büchse - Report of July 20, 1946

My husband Emil Büchse was arrested on June 16, 1945 in Bischofteinitz by the two Czech officers Karasek and Schlais and led off to Taus after a ruthless 3½-hour house search, in the course of which all our cash, our savings bank books, my husband's supply of gold which he needed for his profession (he was a dentist), all our family jewelry and even my wedding ring were confiscated. My husband had already been excluded from the Party and the medical corps of the SS in 1939 and had not been publicly active in any way at all. All my inquiries at the appropriate offices, regarding my husband's fate, were scornfully dismissed. Another 35 men from Bischofteinitz also vanished without a trace, all of them after having been committed to the concentration camp of Taus. The wives of these men were not given any information about what had happened to their husbands even though they appealed to the authorities many times. Before we were resettled [expelled], I and all the other women tried to find out where our husbands were being held, so that we could either be resettled together with them or at least get an official death certificate. All our efforts were in vain. Based on the reports of released prisoners, we must assume that our men are dead.

Bischofteinitz, Report No. 3
Massacre of 35 Sudeten Germans on July 11th, 1945
Reported by Ludwig Schötterl - Report of March 3, 1948

After the American troops marched into Bischofteinitz, Sudetenland, on May 5th, 1945, Czech gendarmes made mass arrests. They delivered about 70 Sudeten Germans to the court jail of Bischofteinitz on May 11th and May 12th, 1945; most of the Germans were in a pitiable condition after having been thrashed and humiliated by armed Czech civilians.

Day after day we had to do compulsory labour under guard; our wives or relatives were permitted to deliver food for us to the guard twice per day.

At the beginning of July we were transported by truck and under heavy gendarmerie guard to Chrastwitz near Taus; we were told that we should be interrogated and afterwards released. On our arrival there we were received by a crowd of Czech soldiers armed to the teeth, equipped with cables, lengths of wire etc., and then a terrible and inhuman beating began during which many of us lost consciousness. This beating was repeated day after day and during this time we were kept without food. There was always aimless firing in front of the barrack, single individuals were taken out of the camp and never returned, others received as many as three beatings a day as a result of which they died.

During the late hours between June 11th and June 12th, 1945, all hell broke loose. We were forced to line up, surrounded by sentries and gendarmes with rifles, ready to fire; a gendarme unfolded a piece of paper and started reading names. The men called up were brutally beaten as they were driven out of the room, terrible cries and wailing filled the place. Each one was beaten into unconsciousness in front of the barrack, his garments being torn to shreds in the process; afterwards the sentries threw the unconscious bodies into a truck. That was the fate of 35 of my comrades, among them my best friend, Max Netopill from Bischofteinitz, and his son.

Thanks to the circumstance that a driver yelled, "the truck is full", I as well as five other comrades who were standing in line are still alive. As I learned later on, the 35 unconscious men were transported during the night to a sand pit between Taus and Trasenau, where they were literally slaughtered by two drunken Czech butchers. The corpses are said to have been buried without ceremony in the sand pit. The wives of the murdered men repeatedly applied to various Czech offices for particulars of their husbands' fate. The answers they received from the diverse offices and authorities, the Czech Red Cross, the gendarmerie and the *Národní výbor* (National Committee) differed totally from each other and all evaded the truth as to the cruel fate of their husbands. Shortly afterwards, German women in prison at Taus-Milotow received blood-stained male garments with orders to clean them. In one of the coats a woman found a tobacco ration card, issued in the name of Alois Schlögl, Bischofteinitz, who was one of the 35 men killed. None of the 35 men has ever been heard of again.

Blatna

Maltreatment of Germans

Reported by Alois Meissner - Report of June 3, 1946

On December 21 of last year the Employment Office of Tuschkau sent me to Blatna to work, and while I was there I witnessed the maltreatment of Germans.

I saw how 12 German men and women, with their heads stuck through the rungs of a ladder and their hands tied to the ladder, were forced to run through the city streets, being beaten all the while with cudgels and switches. I saw how in the cemetery German men and women had to dig the bodies of Germans and such that had been murdered by Czechs out of their graves with their bare hands and dump them outside the cemetery wall instead, into a ditch-like pit.

I saw how, after the Americans had left, German girls who had gone out with American soldiers during the time of American occupation were shorn bald and then locked up.

I also saw how a German girl defended herself against being raped by a Czech farmer, and how he then chased after her with a pitchfork.

Blauendorf

Farmer's wife abused

Reported by Amalie Gödrich Report of June 10, 1946

In June 1945 I was taken to the police, where I was accused of having forced my farmhand, a Pole, to work the fields in the snow, of having had a sack of shoes on the trek without giving him any, and of having reported a deserter to the field gendarmerie. It wasn't even possible to justify myself; I was not allowed to say a word. I had to lie down on a bench and lift my dress, and then two men beat me with rubber truncheons, 25 blows for the alleged working in the snow, then 25 blows for the shoes and another 25 blows for the deserter. The chief of police then forbade me to tell anyone about the beating, otherwise, he said, I would get another instalment. Then he slapped me so hard that I fell down.

I had pain in my left ear for a long time after that. My body was entirely covered with black bruises, from my shoulders down to the back of my knees.

Beatings, women and girls raped

Reported by N. N. - Report of May 23, 1946

Together with my wife and two sons, I lived in a three-room flat in Bodenbach. Until September 5, 1945 we were spared any persecution - aside from comparatively minor harassment. I had already lost my job earlier, since the firm with which I had been employed for many years had been dissolved. I had found temporary employment as construction assistant, as had my younger son.

On the aforementioned date - none of us happened to be at home - an Investigative Commission of the "Svoboda Army", led by a Captain, broke into our home. Their house search was still in progress when I happened to arrive home with my wife. Beds, closets and chests were turned upside down, their contents in an unholy mess, trampled, crumpled, dirtied and scattered all over the floor. Immediately they began interrogating us. I was accused of being in cahoots with a Captain J. (I'd never even heard the name before) and of having hidden jewelry, gold and Persian rugs for him. I tried to demonstrate the groundlessness of these accusations - in vain! They searched night tables and sewing kits for the hidden Persian rugs, which were their main concern. They spat on me, hit, punched and shoved me to try to coerce me into revealing the hiding place of the rugs. How could I have! I had no idea who might have hidden rugs where. The Captain himself, in other words a higher-ranking officer, spat in my face, cursed me crudely, kicked me with his boots and even demeaned himself so far as to stick his tongue out at me. Since all torments still led to nothing, they arrested me and my wife. But first my old mother-in-law also had to succumb to a wild house-search in her home in K., which ended just as unproductively as the one at our place had. Since I and my wife were dragged along on this search, it was only natural that I was subjected to renewed maltreatment. The Captain's chauffeur particularly distinguished himself this time. No Persian rugs were to be found at my mother-in-law's either. Now my wife and I were put into the Captain's car. Neither of us were dressed warmly enough to stand the chill of the drafty drive to Böhmisch Kamnitz, a town about 20 km from Bodenbach in the District of Tetschen. That's where the Svodoba troops were headquartered. We were taken to the Villa Hübel (property of a textile manufacturer). I found out later that this villa had gained notoriety as a GPU dungeon.

Meanwhile evening had come. There was much bustling activity in the villa. The officers dined in the sumptuously appointed rooms. NCOs caroused in adjoining rooms. After about an hour the Captain handed me over to two inebriated NCOs, both of them of colossal stature. While my wife had to continue to wait, these two ordered me to go down into the cellar. What took place down there is almost impossible to describe. When I replied "yes" to the first question, whether I was a German, one of the NCOs punched me in the face. Punches and blows hailed down on my nose and mouth. I lost almost all my teeth in my lower jaw during this treatment. Several times I collapsed, was jerked back on my feet and beaten some more. Blood was running from my nose and mouth. Blows with a rubber truncheon all over the back of my head, neck and back knocked me unconscious for several minutes. Kicks, punches and thumps brought me back to consciousness. Now I had to undress. The two NCOs then went at my back, loins, thighs and calves with leather belts, rubber truncheons and whips. I could hardly speak any more, but I kept trying to tell them that I could not possibly know what they wanted to know from me because I had never seen and never owned the Persian rugs. Finally, after I was beaten half-unconscious again and my body was covered from top to bottom with welts suffused with blood (as my wife observed later), the two monsters left me alone. A few minutes later they shoved my wife into the cellar with me. She had been forced to stand on the cellar stairs and listen to me being tortured. Now we had to spend the night in the dark, dank, cold cellar, without a pallet to sleep on, without light, without a bite to eat (we had not eaten since noon), and without blankets. I was so badly beaten that I could hardly move. My wife was not warmly dressed, and got very cold in that cellar. Further, we were tormented by the uncertainty of what had become of our son. Possibly my persistent claims that I did not know anything of the rugs had been convincing; for the next morning we were taken out of the cellar, put back into a car and driven back to Bodenbach, albeit not to our home but to the police prison. I had to spend seven weeks there, my wife three. Even the police repeatedly stated that there had been neither any charges brought against us, nor even a statement taken down. We were never questioned. Also, no trial had been instituted, and therefore there was no conviction. Under the circumstances, the treatment and food we were given in the police prison can be described as good.

The police themselves confirmed to me that I had neither committed any crime nor become guilty of any kind of political activity. To free some space in the prisons (in B. there were more than 70 prisoners crowded into 3 cells that had been designed for 2 prisoners each!), the police sent those against whom no crime could be proved into the inner regions of Czechoslovakia to serve as harvest laborers. That included me. Before we were transported off we were told that we would not need any food stamps, blankets or dishes - we would find plenty of all we needed where we were going, and besides, we would only be there for 10 to 14 days and then we would be free and could go wherever we liked. We were also promised that we would be quartered in vacant houses, and that for the duration of our assignment our families would enjoy safe quarter at home.

Once we arrived at our destination, a sugar factory in V., we realized right away how hollow these promises had been. Pistols and rubber truncheons were the accessories of choice that our "supervisors" had put on for our reception. We were assigned quarters beneath all human dignity in a damp cellar room. Straw sacks without blankets had been thrown onto iron sugar transport cars. Water dripped from the ceiling, ran down the walls and collected in puddles on the stone floor. The door was locked behind us, so that once again we were confined like prisoners. Our protests were dismissed with the scornful comment that we were Germans and so anything was good enough for us. In the morning we were herded to work at pistol-point and urged along with rubber truncheons. For 10 to 12 hours every day we now had to dig sugar beets. For most of us it was unfamiliar work, and too hard. The food we received, while good, was enough for a three-year-old child at best. Later on, our treatment, housing and rations improved a bit, and by the time our assignment there ended they could almost be described as adequate. After three weeks our work at the sugar factory was finished. Now we were supposed to be released to go home. We were already packed and ready to go, when suddenly we were told that we would have to do one more job, a special case. Allegedly it was a matter of only eight days. We had to help out on two dairy farms that were behind in their beet harvest. Without much ado we found ourselves loaded onto the usual trucks, and off we went. Together with five other fellow-sufferers I was taken to Vlacice. Already on the way there, we heard from Germans returning from field work that Vlacice was hell on earth. But we thought that it couldn't be any worse than V. had been.

In Vlacice there was a concentration camp for German internees that was under the charge of a partisan. The six of us were assigned to this camp. The accommodations defied description. The pallets were crawling with bed bugs and lice. There were armies of fleas! Our pallets were located in former stable buildings. Doors and windows were missing, and stoves and lamps would have been luxury items. Almost no-one had a blanket, and my coat was my only cover when I slept on the half-rotted straw. Water was a precious commodity; its only supply was a puddle in the yard, which served as open-air bath for the geese and ducks. Nonetheless the people also used it for cooking and washing. Women and men had to answer the call of nature side-by-side in the open fields. Our rations consisted of 200 g bread a day, at noon some potato soup or dry potato without any condiment, and some very questionable excuse for black coffee in the evenings and mornings. We had to work 12 to 15 hours every day, regardless of the weather. After three weeks my weight had dropped to 46 kg [101 lb] - my normal weight was 66 kg [145 lb]. What was most shocking about this camp was the fate of the German women that had been banished here. It is impossible within the scope of this brief report to describe what had taken place in the concentration camp of Vlacice before our arrival, and what consequences we were able to observe. Without proper clothing of any kind, dressed only in rags and odd uniform pieces they had found here and there, stripped of their rights, defenseless and at the mercy of anyone's whims, fair game for physical and psychological cravings - that's how these poor women lived here, always hoping that even their time of suffering might come to an end.

Our stay in Vlacice lasted three weeks. Today I am safe among the hospitable Hessian people and am slowly beginning to regain my humanity.

Böhmisch Kamnitz

Böhmisch Kamnitz, Report No. 1
Maltreatment and killing of prisoners of war
Reported by Rudolf Schütz - Report of August 29, 1946

In September 1945 I and other Sudeten German prisoners of war came on a special transport from Russian captivity to the Sudetenland. At Tetschen-Bodenbach the transport was stopped by the Czechs and we were immediately incarcerated in the camp at Böhmisch-Kamnitz, which may be described as an extermination camp. Every day several people were beaten to death, among them many war-invalids with amputated arms or legs or other disabilities, who had not the endurance for the brutal exercises to which we were submitted, and sank to the ground, where they remained. Six weeks later everybody was in such a bad condition that they could hardly stand. Nevertheless we had to walk to Tetschen; on the way there anyone who collapsed was shot by the guards. I myself was completely undernourished and as a result I had dropsy, up my legs and right up to the hips. The others, approximately 120 men, were in just as bad a physical condition. In this state of health we were sent to the mines at Dux for forced labour, where they found that we were incapable of doing the work. Not until February were we able to start work. Regular maltreatment in the camp was the norm. The maltreatment lasted till July 1946 and only in the last few weeks did food and treatment improve. There were efforts to prevent us from being transferred and to persuade us to accept voluntary work.

Böhmisch Kamnitz, Report No. 2

Prison at Böhmisch-Kamnitz and concentration camp Rabenstein, mistreatment and murder

Reported by Albin Mübisch - Report of June 28, 1946

I was arrested at my apartment on August 16th, 1945 on the pretext that I had buried tins of gasoline, and was badly maltreated. I was repeatedly struck with a club in the face, on the head and on my bare feet; blood was running all over me and my toenails were beaten off my feet. Afterwards a Czech drove me into a corner with the machine gun and kicked me in chest and stomach. I was then handed over to the prison at Böhmisch-Kamnitz, where I was to be ill-treated in the most dreadful and inhuman manner. My son, who had already been there for three weeks, had now to witness my tortures. From there I was sent together with my son to the concentration camp at Rabenstein near Böhm.-Kamnitz. There about 800 prisoners were gathered. I witnessed several times how these prisoners were maltreated in the most dreadful way by special beating-commandos. During the three months I spent in the concentration camp, 8 men were beaten to death. It was said that 74 had been killed in the same way shortly before.

At the end of October 64 Rumanians, 16 Hungarians and 16 Austrians, who were released from Russian captivity, arrived at the camp. A square for the newcomers was outlined on the yard, in which they had to spend almost four weeks, day and night. With the start of winter, they were locked into a small, dark cellar. The food ration was so insufficient that many died from debilitation. On December 1st, 1945, we were transported to the prisoner-of-war camp at Tetschen, where the conditions were slightly better. On May 30th, 1946 we were discharged for expulsion.

Böhmisch Krummau

Böhmisch Krummau, Report No. 1

Looting

Reported by Klara Kretschmer Report of September 19, 1946

During luggage inspection in the resettlement [expulsion] camp in Bohemian Krummau the inspectors opened one of my trunks, threw everything onto the ground, and helped themselves to anything of value, including a suit, a piece of linen, 6 bedspread covers, 2 sheets, 6 shirts, 5 hand towels, 1 kitchen clock, 2 skeins of cotton yarn, 2 skeins of thread, darning yarn, 2 pairs of suspenders, and cutlery. The dishes that were still in the trunk were smashed.

My husband is a factory worker. There was hardly anyone on the transport who had less luggage than we did. When I objected to the confiscation, I was threatened with a beating. I was resettled [expelled] with our three children, my husband is still in captivity in Italy.

Böhmisch Krummau, Report No. 2

Concentration camp Welleschin camp, maltreatment

Reported by Hedwig Feyerer - Report of September 27, 1946

On August 15, 1945 I was arrested and badly maltreated because I could not say where my employer had hidden a rifle. I was beaten to the floor and then hit until I passed out. Then I was sent into the concentration camp Welleschin near Bohemian Krummau, where the maltreatment continued. I also saw many other inmates being brutally abused there. Once we were awakened at 1:30 at night. 20 men were called by name to report to the camp office. 10 of these men had to lie down on the floor and the other 10 had to walk on their faces with nailed boots. The faces of those lying down were slashed and mangled. Then they had to switch, and those on the floor had to get up and walk on the other men's faces. The women in the camp were forced to watch. Many of them fainted. These and similar brutalities continued until November, when a new commandant was appointed, who had been in a concentration camp in Germany himself and therefore put a stop to these cruelties. I had to remain in the Welleschin concentration camp until February 12, 1946, when the camp was closed down. Then I was transferred to the camp in Bohemian Krummau, where conditions were better.

Böhmisch Krummau, Report No. 3
Expulsion, looting, conditions of hygiene
Reported by Franz Janovsky Report of September 27, 1946

I had been in the United States for twelve years and from there I took home numerous joiner's and other tools, as I intended to establish a little factory in my homeland. These tools as well as all the machinery were taken away from me by the Czechs. Furthermore, notwithstanding my age of 71 years, I was imprisoned in a camp for twelve months and was maltreated at the time of my arrest. The conditions of the transfer-camp at Böhmisch Krummau were beneath human dignity, the camp was unbelievably filthy, the latrines overflowing so that they flooded the pathways of the camp. The food was inedible.

Böhmisch Leipa

The concentration camp
Reported by F. Fiedler - Report of July 10, 1950

In the vicinity of our town, soldiers who had returned home from the war, disabled ex-servicemen, and also Germans who had belonged to the NSDAP, were taken away and imprisoned in the new Czech concentration camp in Bohemian Leipa (40 victims from Sandau are known to me by name). 96 soldiers who had returned home from the war and who had previously been detained in the District Court prison of Bohemian Leipa were transferred into this concentration camp on June 6, 1945. Now the tormenting and torturing began. These people were thrown fully clothed into the reservoir that had been set up there for firefighting purposes. Their every attempt to leave the basin was punished with whip lashes and blows with rifle butts. Then, furniture and bed frames that were lying around were thrown onto the victims in the water in order to injure them.

Each week 100 people from the District Court prison were transferred into this torture camp. Half of the inmates had to undress and lie down on the floor, and the other half, wearing shoes and boots, had to jump from back to back of their prostrate comrades. Every attempt to land on the floor rather than on one of the backs was punished with brutal maltreatment. After this procedure there were always a few comrades who remained on the floor, dead, with broken ribs (for example the comrade Tille from Leipa, lessee of the "Breite" Inn).

In mid-June the following concentration camp inmates: District administrator Thume, price control commissar Richter, and wine tavern owner Pihan, were ordered to report to the Czech police in Sonnengasse [Street], to work there (street sweeping). Pihan was beaten to death there by that police team. Richter was left unconscious, and in order to avoid further tortures he commited suicide that same evening in the concentration camp, by hanging himself. Administrator Thume fell gravely ill as a result of the abuse he had suffered, but was nonetheless imprisoned in a solitary-confinement cell. He was not given a container to use for answering the call of nature, and the Czechs repeatedly shoved his face into his own excrement and maltreated him unspeakably in the process. In November 1945 Administrator Thume died of the consequences of this abuse. The same day he died, comrade Schreiber of Wolkersdorf was also beaten to death by these bandits. Others to die in the District Court prison were Herr Hiebsch from Hirschberg am See, who died of dysentery, and innkeeper Böhme of the Inn "Stadt Graz" in Bohemian Leipa; the cause of his death was never satisfactorily determined.

On October 9, 1945 the railwayman Franz Mai of Körnerstrasse, Bohemian Leipa, was beaten to death by Czech partisans in the District Court prison. At that time the concentration camp population had risen to 1,200 souls. In December 1945 approximately 300 Czech partisans (of the Svoboda hordes) carried out raids among the German camp inmates and stole all watches, cutlery and electric razors they could get hold of. The only dishes anyone had after that were old food tins they had dug out of the trash heap.

Raids in the Women's Section: the female prisoners' clothes were searched and looted on the occasion of these raids. During the raids, which were carried out by about 100 Czech bandits, the 100 women and girls, aged 16 years and older, had to strip stark naked and perform squats in front of the entire guard team for the whole duration of the search, which took almost 2 hours.

Alarm: repeated alarms were sounded in the concentration camp, and every German, regardless whether he was an invalid or otherwise ill, had to report instantly to the parade square. Barefoot, the people had to"stand still!" from 7 o'clock p.m. until 2 o'clock at night. This was repeated again in the morning, from 7 o'clock until 2 in the afternoon. This was during December 1945. People who collapsed were severely whipped. Every evening three Germans were dragged to the guard room, stripped, thrown across the table and whipped into unconsciousness. Then cold water was poured over the victims, and when they came to again these bestialities were repeated (the occupants of the houses near the concentration camp closed their windows so they would no longer hear the moans and screams of the tortured. These nearby residents were the first to be evacuated so that the tortures could be carried out unimpeded). Many comrades committed suicide to escape these agonies. This prompted the new camp commandant, Wepper, to discontinue the beatings. Shortly thereafter, Wepper was replaced by a new commandant who was in charge of all concentration camps. This was the feared thug Vancura, who got particular pleasure from atrocities and brutality. Under his rule many comrades were beaten to death, and Dr. Steinitz, physician from Leipa, was forced to state "heart attack" as the cause of death on the death certificates; there were 251 such victims in just one year. The young pharmacist Hollitzer from Sandau, as well as senior teacher Hiecke from Wolfersdorf, among others, also died suddenly of questionable causes. The German prison supervisor Püschel from Bohemian Leipa was hanged on the District Court square, to the howls and cheers of Czech immigrants to the town who also participated in the execution to the fullest extent of their ability.

The rations we received were bad and insufficient. Medications were not available to us, and sick inmates were left to their fate. Our treatment was brutal and inhuman. Czechs wearing black uniforms (German military trousers and SA shirts) and "SNB" armbands were especially feared.

This horde, which frequently carried out night-time raids, took even the slightest opportunity to knock their victims' teeth out as savagely and violently as they could.

Investigative commissions which showed up in order to inspect the camp and ensure humane treatment for us never even saw the camp. They were shown into the camp office and sent off again from there.

As of July 1945 the German population began to be evacuated, and most of them were expelled from their own homes and farms, dragged through this camp and either detained there or parceled out into expulsion transports. These many unfortunate people were crowded into this concentration camp under the worst imaginable conditions. They had to sleep without any straw for bedding, on the hard floor and in filthy horse stables.

Day in, day out, this concentration camp was jammed with hundreds of families that were to be expelled from their homeland. 24 mothers and their children had to vegetate in small, 24'x15' rooms, sleeping on the hard floor without straw or the like, for weeks and even months pending their expulsion.

Hunger and privation was great. A single dry potato was enough of a luxury to make the children stop crying. Every day, many toddlers and elderly people died. And to top it all off, these overcrowded rooms were frequently invaded at night by armed partisans who would select their victims by candlelight, choosing from among the young girls and women. Then the candles were extinguished, and the chosen victims were raped, repeatedly and by several of the marauding savages, regardless whether their mothers, fathers or brothers lay on the floor beside them.

When the groups for expulsion were being assembled, the family fathers were forced to march through the camp grounds at a run so that they could not say their farewells to their wives and children. Any food which relatives tried to bring the starving inmates was confiscated by the Czechs at the camp entrance, and either kept for their own enjoyment or else broken and trampled into dirt before the eyes of those who had brought it. The booted Czechs then kicked these couriers (mostly women) in their private parts and drove them away with whips.

Böhmisch Meseritsch

Maltreatment during slave labor
Reported by Adolf Mader Report of August 30, 1946

From October 9, 1945 until Christmas 1945 my son and I had to work in the sugar factory in Bohemian Meseritsch. Even though it was hard labor, we were not paid anything for our work. The living conditions there were inhuman. There were no major incidents of beating, however. After a mass examination, I was sent from there to work in the coal mine "Luzna" in Luzna, Rakovník District, where I did slave labor from December 24, 1945 until June 25, 1946 and had to submit to dreadful beatings. Only one supervisor indulged in the beatings, during the night shift. I had the bad luck of being assigned to the night shift shortly after I arrived at this work site. Here I and my fellow laborers were beaten every night, for half a year.

The procedure went off as follows. First everyone had to report for duty in the mine. There were 17 of us German laborers. Some hateful article was read aloud from a newspaper, and then we were systematically beaten with fists and sticks. Most blows were aimed at the head. Due to my age and the debilitating consequences of inadequate rations I was not always able to do the hardest jobs by myself, and as punishment I and other sick or weak comrades who were in the same boat as I were treated to extra installments of blows to the head, administered with heavy cudgels, so that I repeatedly collapsed. These inhuman beatings have left me with a severe hearing defect, and to this day I still have open wounds on my feet. The treatment was so bad that we had resigned ourselves to meeting our Maker, especially since many could not endure the hardships.

I can take this statement on my oath and bring witnesses to corroborate it.

Böhmisch Trübau

Railroad camp
Reported by: Karl Schilling Report of June 27, 1946

I was released from Russian captivity in October, and on my way home I was arrested by the railway police in Bohemian Trübau and taken to the railroad camp in Bohemian Trübau, operated by the Liticka company. There were about 250 men in that camp. We had to work very hard there, even on Sundays. Rations were very meager. The Germans were used for the hardest jobs, and 50% greater work output was demanded of them than of the Czechs who worked there. For example, if it took 15 Czechs to carry a rail, only 10 Germans were assigned to do the same. The Czechs received additional rations for heavy labor, whereas the Germans were given only the insufficient camp rations. Among the German prisoners there were old and sick people as well, but they had to work just as hard and were often beaten if they could not do everything that was demanded of them. Younger people were beaten even more, even though they sometimes collapsed from hunger. The physician refused to certify sick inmates as unfit for work. In all the seven months that I worked there, we received no wages. Our clothes were very ragged and were neither supplemented nor replaced. In winter many had to work without a coat. Due to the poor conditions, several prisoners attempted to escape. When they were caught they were horribly beaten. We were allowed to write only one postcard each month, and these had to be written in Czech even though most of us did not know Czech. Mail that arrived for us was not handed out if it was written in German. After the first escape attempts we had to surrender our civilian clothes and were issued prison uniforms instead. On our release, many of our civilian clothes were not returned. I was released to be resettled [expelled] in early July, but the Reich Germans and the Sudeten Germans whose families had already been expelled were detained further.

Maltreatment and robbery in May 1945
Reported by Josef Lausch

On May 17, 1945 two Czech gendarmes came to the Braunau Post Office and asked the deputy where postal assistant Lausch was. The deputy pointed to me at Counter I. I had to accompany the two gendarmes, who handcuffed me, to the District Court. In an anteroom I was relieved of all papers, 1,765 Mark in cash, one postal savings book with more than 3,000 Mark, my suspenders, shoe laces, in a word: everything.

While stripping me like this, they beat me almost unconscious with revolver, knucklebuster and rubber truncheon. Then, covered in blood as I was, I was taken to interrogation. I was accused of having been a Troop Commander of the SA and a Lieutenant General of the SS, and when I said that I had never been with either the SA or the SS I was again beaten half to death. I named our mayor as witness that I had never been with either formation, but the mayor himself sat under arrest in the room next door.

All covered in blood, I was then thrown into a dark cell onto the stone floor. For two days I got nothing to eat, all I got was constant interrogations and beatings. Then I was put into a three-man cell, in which 9 people were housed. At almost all hours, day and night, the door was yanked open and one or several Czech youths 16 to 18 years of age came in, beat us brutally and left again, laughing.

The court provided us with no rations at all. Family members had to bring us food from home, and I will leave it up to the reader's imagination what state the food was in when we got it in the cell. This torture lasted for 10 days and was repeated in brutal variations on a daily basis.

After 10 days I was taken by car to the factory of the Pollak company and handed over to the GPU. From there the trip went by car to Waldenburg, in Silesia, on by foot to Oppeln, Upper Silesia, then to the fortress of Graudenz and later to the concentration camp of Fünfeichen near Neubrandenburg in Mecklenburg. In July 1948 I was released, and after much searching I found my wife living here in bitter poverty. She too had been abducted to the interior [of Czechoslovakia] by the Czechs.

After a year of hard labor she returned home in rags and tatters. She wanted to get some things from our home to take along on the expulsion, but by then everything had been looted and stolen. And so she was thrown out with only the rags on her back. As for myself, I returned from the concentration camp wearing only rags as well, and suffering from dropsy.

Groundless arrest of all the men in a village
Reported by Wenzel Parth, sacristan Report of August 14, 1946

On April 14, 1946 all the male inhabitants of the village of Bretterschlag who were between the ages of 16 and 60 were arrested by the community authorities and committed to the concentration camp Kaplitz. To provide an excuse for these arrests, customs officials, soldiers and gendarmes had come to the town and alleged that the Germans had shot at the customs officers. In fact the town had been surrounded by soldiers who had fired shots themselves. What is more, not a single weapon had been found when the German were arrested. Clearly that too had only been an excuse to arrest the Germans. I was also arrested even though I wasn't even a resident of Bretterschlag but had only happened to be there that day. During the arrests we were all grossly maltreated. Some were seriously injured. We were detained for 6 months, but nobody saw fit even to question us during this time.

Shootings and maltreatment
Reported by Wenzel Parth, sacristan - Report of August 14, 1946

At the church of Wistritz, where I was residing, the following happened on July 24 or 25 - I no longer remember the exact date. In the evening, about half past eleven, the Czechs came. I had personally delivered the monstrance and communion cup to one Mr. Scheffler, a Czech, who was known to me as a catholic. I had no opportunity to inform a man of the cloth because our priest Hanus of Brunnersdorf had already been sent to the camp the day before; I also could not go anywhere further away because of the curfew. Early in the morning, at 6 o'clock I had to report to the camp. On the street, before we started marching, the commissar asked me if I had the golden church vessels with me. I explained to him that I had given the monstrance and communion cup to Scheffler. He then asked me about the rest of the church vessels. I told him that they were still in the tabernacle and that I could not touch it. I was forced to hand over the keys, and to accompany him to the church and the tabernacle. "Open it!" the Czech yelled. I refused to do so: "I am not allowed to." He threatened me but I said no to him a second time. Then the man said, *"To je fuk"*, he himself grabbed at the tabernacle, took the ciborium together with the consecrated Hosts, stuffed everything into his portfolio and went away. To what place everything was taken, I do not know. I came to the camp and immediately reported the incident to the priest, Mr. Hanus. I could do no more from inside the camp. On April 30th, we were moved.

The aforegoing statements I can testify to under oath.

At Brunnersdorf seven men were severely beaten; afterwards they were led to the cemetery, where they were ordered to dig graves behind the wall. When they had dug deep enough each one received a shot in the neck, then they were thrown into the graves and the earth shoveled over them. At Kaaden three farmers from Karkau, one by the name of Guba, were shot one morning. In the afternoon 7 men, among them Proschka, Bard and a salesman from Radonitz, were rounded up at the market place, where the citizens were forced to watch while they were shot. I myself was present together with my daughter. I cannot describe the panic which broke out among the people present. The men were shot first in the legs, then in the abdomen and finally in the head. Is that human? At Prösteritz two men were shot on a turnip field and buried there; 7 men were killed and buried at Dehlau and at Kaaden 40 more in the court-yard of the prison. If necessary, I am ready to take witnesses right to the place in question, in order to give them the opportunity of verifying what happened there. I was sacristan at Brunnersdorf and Wistritz for twenty years; there are still many things to be told, but that would be up to our priest.

Brüsau

Looting, maltreatment
Reported by Franz Langer Report of September 26, 1946

My entire family and I were detained in the concentration camp Brüsau from December 9, 1945 until March 30, 1946, for no reason whatsoever. I was robbed of all my possessions.

The rations we received in the camp were very bad, even though we all had to do hard physical labor. Everyone depended on getting extra food from outside the camp, else they would have starved even if they had not had to work - that's how insufficient the rations were. All valuable foodstuffs, such as butter, jam, sugar, baked goods etc., were confiscated by the guards. In early February, while I was working, I was given a piece of bread. I ate part of it at once, and put the rest in my pocket in order to take it back to my wife in the camp. The camp leader found out about it. He called me over and maltreated me severely for it. First I was slapped about the head so hard that I fell down, then he beat me with a dog whip - 10 blows on each sole of my bare feet - and then I received 5 lashes with a bull whip. Then several guards kicked me.

Bürgersdorf

Severe abuse
Reported by Adolf Aust - Report of September 30, 1946

On June 30 all 6 SA men in the community of Bürgersdorf - men who had never worn an uniform and only ever paid the membership dues - were arrested and taken to the Würbenthal concentration camp. The next day, 102 people were marched 36 kilometers from there to Jägern-dorf. On the way, a butcher from Karlsthal was shot when he moved about three steps out of line to relieve himself during a rest period. In Jägerndorf, SA and SS men were put behind bars and maltreated horribly, repeatedly, for three days. Gesierich from Heinzendorf, who had been given a medical check prior to joining the SS but had not yet been drafted, was worked over with rubber truncheons for more than a quarter of an hour until he could no longer get up. One Klement from Karsthal got the same treatment. I myself suffered two blows to my right eye, which was then totally swollen shut for a month. There was no medical care for the injured. As a special form of torture we were forced to crawl over scattered glass shards, during which we were also beaten and kicked. All of us had cuts on our elbows and knees. After three days, 100 men were transported off to Wittkowitz to work in the firebrick factory, the blast furnace, etc. There, the maltreatment was continued every day, before, during and after work. One Mr. Ott from Ludwigsthal was forced to go to work there even though he was ill, and when he collapsed, he was forced back on his feet and beaten so badly with rubber truncheons that he died the next day.

Our rations consisted only of watery soup. All of us had swollen feet. In the first 14 days in Wittkowitz, 12 people died of exhaustion. After 9 months there, I myself was so exhausted that I could no longer stand. I was sent back to Jägerndorf, where the physician called me a walking corpse. After another 11 weeks I was released as totally unfit for work.

Butschafka

Butschafka, Report No. 1
Harassment of a farmer's family
Reported by Marie Breier - Report of June 19, 1946

Since November 22, 1945 a Slovak administrator named Petr oversaw my farm. In the afternoon of December 19, 1945 I went to Liebental to buy some groceries with my food stamps. When I returned in the evening the administrator accused me of not working, and claimed that I had stolen a hundredweight of grain from him. I said I had done no such thing. Then he went to the *Národní výbor* to fetch the Commissar, who beat me and knocked me to the ground. The next day I could not get up for the pain. So the administrator fetched the gendarmerie, who took me by cart to Jägerndorf to the court. The judge pronounced me not guilty. But when I attempted to leave the courthouse with my release paper, it was taken from me and I was detained in a cell for 8 weeks.

Meanwhile no-one cared for my two children. In January the administrator threw them out of the house as well. My 13-year-old son was also locked up for three days, and twice he was beaten so badly by the gendarmerie and the Commissar that he could not get out of bed with fever for 14 days, and lost his hearing. All my clothing and linen were taken from me, and I got none of it back later. On February 20 the court in Jägerndorf decided that I was allowed to live with my children in my house in Butschafka.

Butschafka, Report No. 2
The Pardubitz-Königgrätz concentration camp, looting of luggage
Reported by: Heinrich Furch - Report of July 4, 1946

As transport leader of Transport 96 I was in a position to determine that 30-40% of the members of the transport did not have the permitted 60 kg of luggage. Most of them were people who had spent months in labor camps, where they had been forbidden to bring many of their possessions and where they wore out many of what clothes they did have. I personally tried to see to it that the luggage of an old man who didn't even have 10 kg would be increased. Even though mountains of confiscated goods were in storage, this man did not receive a single thing. One Mr. Fuchs, who was in the same situation, was given a much-mended, barely usable suit and a pair of old shoes. His own things had been confiscated by the *Národní Výbor* in Butschafka while he was in the Pardubitz and Königgrätz concentration camps.

Furthermore, I witnessed how during the luggage inspections the chests and suitcases of the resettlers [expellees] were drilled into, chopped to pieces or otherwise made unusable for the transport. Anything and everything that the inspectors liked was simply taken. In particular, documents and various papers that had been issued by former Czech offices were confiscated, including especially such papers issued by Czech authorities attesting to assets that had been surrendered or left behind in Czechoslovakia. Also, there were many cases of feather bedding being slashed open and searched, so that most of the feathers were scattered and lost.

Butschafka, Report No. 3
Maltreatment
Reported by Hilda Breier Report of July 4, 1946

In early October [1945] the farming families from Butschafka, whose farms were in the charge of Czech administrators, were all taken to Jägerndorf and put into the concentration camp. At that time I and my four children - the youngest was two years old - went to Ober-Paulowitz to stay with my grandmother. In November I heard that a letter from my husband had arrived in Butschafka. I went to Butschafka to fetch the letter. When the administrator of our farm saw me in the street in Butschafka, he came up to me, took my husband's letter from me - I hadn't even had the chance to open it yet - and punched me with his fists until I fell. Then he kicked me in the side. I managed to get away from him when he finally left off and began to read my husband's letter. He summoned the commissar and followed me to Ober-Paulowitz. By the time I arrived there myself, I was so exhausted that I fainted.

Chodau, Report No. 1
Husband murdered
Reported by Fanny Karner

I declare herewith in lieu of oath that my husband, Matthias Karner, born on June 20th, 1901 at Chodau near Karlsbad, was murdered by the Czechs under the following circumstances:

My husband was called up for active service with the German army in 1941 as Red Cross orderly. I myself have six children, and I have already lost two sons in the war. My husband returned from Russian captivity on May 22nd, 1945. But our joy that the children's father and our sole supporter had come back was not granted us for long. After he had been home for a fortnight, the Czechs came one night in order to plunder the houses. When the owner of the house, Mr. Stangel, did not open the house door at once, the Czechs immediately started shooting. Besides my husband there were three other men present and when the door was finally opened, we were forced to leave the house and were taken to the school, that is to say the gendamerie station. We women were separated from the men and made to stand with our faces to the wall; the same was done with my three little children, aged 3, 5 and 10 years. We had to raise our arms above our heads and to remain in the same posture the whole night. We were released the next day, but we heard nothing of my husband nor of the other men.

Later we learned that my husband and the other three men had been forced to dig their own graves at a place quite close to our house, after which they had been beaten to death. Several days later the corpses had been dug up again and buried in the cemetery.

Several days afterwards, severed limbs of the murdered men were found at the spot.

I am prepared to take the aforesaid on my oath.

Chodau, Report No. 2
Baggage inspection and looting in May 1946
Reported by Marie Weiss - Report of June 1, 1946

On or about May 20 [1946] I petitioned the Control Commission in Elbogen for permission to take extra clothing, underwear and shoes for my son Rudolf Weiss, who had been in English captivity until April 30, 1946 and was waiting for me in Bavaria. The Control Commission gave me written permission to take the items for my son. Nonetheless, when my luggage was inspected in Chodau, all luggage intended for my son was taken from me. They also kept back part of my own luggage, so that I now have barely 40 kg for both of us, my son and myself. I am ready take this statement on my oath.

Chodau, Report No. 3
Baggage inspection and looting
Reported by Josef Zillich - Report of July 17, 1946

During the luggage inspection in Chodau, my sister had to endure that her dress was violently torn off her body. I and my two sons, aged 13 and 16, had to take off the suits, shoes and coats we wore, and instead put on some old clothes we still had in our luggage. Even our feather bedding was taken from us, except for one. Even our hand luggage was confiscated, so that I am now missing cutlery, my pajamas, my wife's night gown, and other things that would be badly needed by my family on the trip. The Czech gendarme who was present during the inspection said to me later that I had been downright looted and that he would like to help me, but couldn't.

From my main luggage, all my new clothes were confiscated, as well as much more that I haven't been able to itemize yet. The next day, when I complained about the looting, the camp administration ordered that I should receive 5 coats and 2 pairs of shoes back. None of the suits and other clothes were left in the luggage room - they had all been carted off already.

Chodau, Report No. 4
Baggage inspection
Reported by Emilie Dotzauer - Report of July 17, 1946

The baggage inspection office at Chodau confiscated all the shoes which I had packed for my husband, my daughter and myself. I was also ordered to take off the shoes I had on and instead of them they threw me a pair of old sandals, which I am still wearing. In addition they took all the underclothing and bedclothes as well as my own and my daughter's pyjamas and a dressing gown. In exchange for the bedclothes they gave me some old, worn-out dresses. The white lace collar was ripped off the dress I was wearing. My cutlery and kitchen utensils were also taken away from me. In the transfer camp at Neusattel I received a few odd plates and dishes in exchange for the items mentioned.

Chodau, Report No. 5
Severe maltreatment
Reported by Karl Kempf - Report of June 22, 1946

I was arrested at Chodau on May 27th, 1945, because I had once - in my capacity as gendarme of the reserve - arrested a German from Poland, who had been convicted of theft. When the American troops entered our area, this man, claiming to be Polish, denounced me and maintained that I had stolen his property. I was not tried until March 1946 in the camp at Neurohlau. I was then able to clear myself and was released as a result of the trial. In the time between my arrest and trial, or rather release, I was maltreated in the most cruel manner. At Chodau I was kicked and punched until I was covered with blood and lost consciousness. It was also at Chodau that I witnessed the maltreatment of an SS-man, who was then shot and buried in the cemetery during the night. From May 31st, 1945 to the evening of June 2nd we received no food at all, not even water, and were jammed together in one cell at Elbogen. From there we were moved to Karlsbad. On our arrival there we were beaten by a squad of 10 men until we were bleeding and in a fainting condition. 24 of us were crowded into a cell of about 11 square meters (about 122 square ft.); after a day or two our number was increased to 35. Morning and evening we got a cup of coffee, at noontime a cup of cabbage soup without bread. There, too, we were beaten frequently. On July 19th we marched to Neurohlau. Many collapsed from weakness on their way. Mistreatment and tortures were also a part of the programme. I myself was twice beaten while I was there. Whenever a prisoner escaped another was shot in his place, without consideration. A certain Lippert from Elbogen was shot in this way. An elderly man from Jedlitz was also shot because, when he was hungry, he ate potato peels out of the dustbin. The same tortures and mistreatment to which I was subjected were also the lot of my fellow-gendarme Lehrl, who had been arrested together with me.

Chrastawitz

35 SA-men murdered on July 11, 1945
Reported by Eduard Polz

Truthfully and in full awareness of the significance of such a declaration, I attest objectively in lieu of oath to the statements made by a Czech, before several witnesses, about the treatment and execution of approximately 35 imprisoned SA men from Bischofteinitz District, Sudetenland, who were imprisoned in the Chrastawitz concentration camp near Taus.

During haymaking in 1946, at the Feast of Corpus Christi, the Czech N. N. who was at that time employed as coachman by N. N. in Taus stated that in the evening of July 11, 1945 the SA men from Bischofteinitz had been driven by truck from Chrastawitz to the sand pit located on the right-hand side of the road from Taus to Trasenau, where they were slaughtered and then buried in the area surrounding the sand pit. To my question, whether he knew for certain that these men were from Bischofteinitz, he stated that he had personally known a good many of them since he had been imprisoned along with them for several weeks. He also reported that the truck was supposed to make a second trip but that the truck driver refused, saying that he could not watch any more such bestialities. The atrocities were committed by officials from the gendarmerie, officers, and the S.N.B., most of whom were drunk. N. also described the brutal maltreatment of these men on the evening of their transport from Chrastawitz, where most of them were loaded onto the truck unconscious and already half beaten to death.

Since I myself was imprisoned in the same camp from August 30, 1945 until July 27, 1946 and am aware of other, similar monstrosities that were committed there, and since none of these men were heard of again, N.'s statement appears to me perfectly credible and in accord with the facts.

Chrostau (Concentration camp in District Zwittau)

Maltreatment of young people
Reported by Herbert Heinz - Report of June 15, 1946

On May 10, 1945 all young people between the ages of 14 and 20, and even some 12- and 13-year-olds, were rounded up and put into the Chrostau concentration camp in Zwittau District. In total there were about 350 of us. On May 30 we were transferred from there into the political camp in Zwittau. We were dreadfully maltreated in the camp. The Commandant of Chrostau, Janecek, was so brutal that we only ever called him the Butcher. When he walked through the camp he would beat any boy who came near him over the head with his riding whip. Often he beat boys over the head with his riding whip for no reason at all until they collapsed. Then he would say, "that'll do you for a while."

Every day we had to do "morning sports". First, a quarter of an hour of exercises, then another quarter of an hour of games, then at least half an hour of constant up and down. Push-ups, stoops, deep squats, etc. Anyone whose strength failed him had to repeat these exercises in front of the camp commandant, and was beaten while doing them. Many had to work in a plant nursery, and were beaten while at work. The rest of us had to remain in their rooms, but were forbidden to look out the windows. Anyone who was seen at a window was also beaten.

Our rations consisted only of black coffee and thin soup with stinging-nettles, and 2 pounds of black bread and 1 pound white bread per week. There was one gendarme whom we called "the tiger", because every word he said to us was a curse word. In Zwittau the treatment was the same, the only difference being that not only were there "morning sports", there were "evening sports" as well. In Chrostau two of the three wash rooms were closed before the first week was over. The remaining wash room had running water only at certain times of the day. There were only 8 sinks for 300 prisoners. Several boys got scabies. Several others had been brought to the camp with heart and lung conditions. Scarlet fever and diphtheria also broke out in Zwittau. The sick were sent to Zwittau to the hospital, where treatment was good. I was resettled [expelled] together with my parents. One day prior to my resettlement a partisan beat me with his fists and a stick for wearing a military cap.

I am ready to take these statements on my oath.

Datschitz

Murder of German forestry commissioners
Reported by forestry official Herrmann Hübner - Report of May 28, 1950

In May 1945, forestry commissioner Ernst Pittinger from Schaschowitz (Sasovice) and senior forestry administrator Robert Fritzen from Reilsberg were murdered by Czech partisans in Datschitz (Dacice) in Moravia.

I learned of this tragic incident in the District Court in Iglau, where the local People's Tribunal sentenced me to 6 years in prison.

Senior forest administrator Fritzen had two school-aged sons, and it is possible that these two boys were left in Budischkowitz (Budiskovice), District Datschitz (Dacice).

In Krasonitz (Krasonice), District Datschitz, the gravely ill retired forester Franz Schulla was beaten to death in his own bed.

Deutsch-Beneschau

Deutsch-Beneschau, Report No. 1
71-year-old man abused
Reported by Johann Schmoz - Report of July 24, 1946

I was a woodcutter in the Bürgerwald of Deutsch-Beneschau, District Kaplitz. Gamekeeper Pils instructed me on February 8 to go pick up my wages from the forestry official Kolar in Deutsch-Beneschau. When I got there, the Czech farmer's leader Kucera, whom I had not met before, spoke to me in Czech. When I apologized and said that I do not understand Czech, he boxed me twice about the head and kicked me twice in the leg so that I could not bend my knee for 8 days. I am 71 years old.

Deutsch-Beneschau, Report No. 2

Maltreatment in the Women's Camp

Reported by M. Swoboda-Frantzen - Report of Nov. 2, 1946

On September 15 of last year I arrived in Deutsch-Beneschau. All my papers were in order, and I also reported my presence to the police immediately, as required. The purpose of my visit was to see my sick mother and to obtain copies of some lost documents. I was refused the documents, and on September 22 I was arrested even though I had never been a Party member.

No reason for my arrest was given. During the subsequent interrogation I was also not told why I was under arrest; instead, the protocol stated that I refused to make a confession. I was kept under arrest for 13 months, first in the District Court in Kaplitz and then in the concentration camps Gmünd and Kaplitz.

During this time I was repeatedly beaten, for the last time on July 27, 1946. Other kinds of maltreatment continued until October 16 of this year.

Like the other [German] women here, I was only ever addressed as "swine" and "whore". The guards and overseers repeatedly tried to rape me and the other women. I sustained bruises and bite wounds in the process. My last attempted rape was by the Mayor of Kaplitz, Vítek, on October 20 this year.

In the court prison in Kaplitz Frau Schuhmeier was wounded by a guard's negligent use of a firearm, and was denied access to medical care even though the wound suppurated. In October 1945 a young mother and her toddler were abducted into the Czech interior.

Sanitary facilities were totally inadequate. There was no way to take a bath, and we did not even have wash bowls, brooms or rags for cleaning.

In February 1946 my mother requested permission to visit me, and was rewarded for her troubles with a day of imprisonment. Another women was imprisoned for 7 weeks for the same reason. I have barely 50 kg of resettlement [expulsion] luggage, and even these are primarily my mother's things. My documents were never returned to me.

Deutsch-Jassnik

Severe maltreatment

Reported by Josef Schneider Report of October 13, 1946

I was arrested on the orders of the *Národní výbor* at 1:30 pm on June 6, 1945, at my place of work in the community of Deutsch-Jassnik, in the district of Neutitschein in the eastern Sudetenland. I was taken to the Raiffeisen bank branch, where I was maltreated by the two gendarme guards Hranicky and Skoumal and by two partisans from our neighboring community (their names were Bork und Hurka). I was beaten on my back with a 5-foot-long rubber hose so that I turned black and blue from my neck down to my buttocks. I was also shoved up against a wall my face until blood ran from my nose, and I was spat on, and much more.

This went on for one and a half hours, and all of it was intended to force me to betray some comrades who belonged to a particular unit - but I did not do so. Then I was locked into a basement room, without anything in the way of an evening meal. Later in the evening I was joined in my cell by my comrade Josef Kahlig, prisoner number 8, who was also from Deutsch-Jassnik and who was also beaten horribly, as I was able to tell from his screams which I heard from our cell.

The next day we were taken to the district town of Neutitschein, together with a third comrade who had been maltreated back in the basement. First we were dressed up as a sort of jester, draped with swastikas and German ribbons, and SA-caps were placed on our heads. We were forced to sing the song "Deutschland über alles" [the German national anthem; trans.] and paraded along the street under guard from two men armed with submachine guns. We were threatened that if we refused to sing we would be beaten.

Once we arrived in the district town we were taken to the court prison, where we were robbed of our last possessions, such as money, watch and pen-knife, and then thrown into a cell. I was held in this prison for two months, and had to work every day for poor rations (70 grams of bread and some black coffee in the morning, at noon some soup made from cabbage and turnip leaves, without any fat or salt, and in the evening some more black coffee, and potatoes, some of which were also black).

On August 7, 1945 I was put on a transport of 70 men and sent to Göding, to a labor camp where I was sent out to work in a brown-coal pit, without pay of course. Since I was 50 years old and became very run-down from this kind of work (I lost 22 pounds), I was sent back to the labor camp six weeks later where I had to help with clearing and construction work.

On January 18, 1946 I and six other comrades were sent back to our home-base camp Blauendorf, in the district of Neutitschein, where we were assigned to cottage-type work for the hat factories located there, since they suffered from a labor shortage. On April 4, 1946 I had to report to an examining magistrate to be interrogated about my party membership, and was to be arraigned before a People's Court, but on April 27, 1946 the public prosecutor dismissed me, with permission to emigrate, since there had been no grounds for my arrest in the first place. On April 28, 1946 I arrived at the resettlement camp, where my family was also ordered to report for emigration. On the whole, the treatment we were given, as well as the rations, left a great deal to be desired, and it was usually the younger Czechs who were the most violent. I have not seen my homeland again since my arrest. Now I want to recount my wife's tribulations, which I only learned of after she also arrived at the resettlement camp. She had had to endure several house-searches, and everything that was not nailed down was stolen and carted off (clothing, linen, bedding, food and many other things) and when my wife objected, she was beaten on her back with a rifle-butt, and threatened with submachine guns.

I am ready and willing to repeat this my report under oath at any time.

Farmer maltreated on September 16, 1945
Reported by Richard Sirsch Report of November 18, 1947

I, the undersigned, Richard Sirsch, wish to make the following report about my experiences during the time of the Czechs' barbaric activities against the Sudeten Germans following the German surrender:

On May 10, 1945 the first Czechs came onto my property in Deutsch-Lodenitz. From that point on, violent Czechs armed with rubber truncheons and rifles descended upon my home every day, and ransacked it from the attic to the basement. - On July 24, 74 Germans from my town were taken to the concentration camp in Sternberg, including my 52-year-old wife and our two daughters, so that our 11-year-old son was left without a mother from that time on. I myself had to remain on our estate, to help the Czech who had taken over it to bring in the harvest and the hay.

On September 16, 1945 at 9:30 p.m. several ferocious Czechs came into the house, beat me and punched me in the face and led me off to the camp office in charge of labor details to see to the harvest in Deutsch-Lodenitz. There I was body-searched, and everything I had was taken from me, the sole exception being the clothes on my back. Then they pulled my pants down to my knees, laid me across two chairs and began to thrash my buttocks with their truncheons, in triple time to accompany their taunting chorus of "SdP, SdP...." (Sudeten-German Party).

When I had almost passed out from this abuse and these vengeful savages were at a momentary loss for anything else, one of these brutish Czechs took two belts, slung one of them around my neck, buckled it to the second and pulled me up over the door. When I had almost lost my senses he dropped me, dumped a bucket of cold water over me, dragged me outside by the legs and then even asked me, derisively, whether I wouldn't like to hang myself now. About half an hour later they led me into a cold basement, without even giving me a blanket. -

The second day after this, 6 people from our community, including me, were taken to the concentration camp in Sternberg. I had to stay there for nine months. Once I received 25 blows with a rubber truncheon because my axe handle had broken while I had been chopping wood. - Finally, on June 5, 1946, I was sent home from this camp, to be expelled. When my wife was released from the camp after having had to stay 7 months there, she found nothing left but an empty house. We had neither clothes nor bedding, nor linen, and were expelled from our homeland half-naked.

Written and signed on November 18, 1947.

Dittersdorf, Report No. 1

Freudenthal, maltreatment, expulsion with insufficient luggage allowance

Reported by: Max Schindler - Report of August 21, 1946

In Dittersdorf, Bärn District, in June of 1945, three Czech National Guardsmen arrested me - without justification, as Czech officers admitted - and took me to the police prison in Freudenthal, where I was severely maltreated twice. The beatings left me deaf on my left ear. My fellow prisoner Sezulka was beaten into a lump of unrecognizable pulp. On the seventh day I was released. I never got to return to my home in Troppau, as I was detained in a labor camp until I was resettled [expelled]. I have lost everything I owned. My expulsion luggage consists only of two backpacks, a total of 25 kg. On my attempts to have my luggage supplemented in the resettlement [expulsion] camp, all I received was 1 pair of pants, 1 jacket and 1 pair of shoes.

Dittersdorf, Report No. 2

Looting of the parsonage and church, shootings and maltreatment

Reported by: Rev. Johann Hofmann - Report of January 3, 1947

I should state to begin with that I have always been against Hitler and against Fascism. For this reason I was imprisoned by the Gestapo for six months which I spent at Zwittau and Moravian Schönberg in autumn 1938; after my arrest I was under police supervision for 6 years, was not allowed to teach in the schools, and moreover had to post a bond of 500 Marks as a political guarantee over a period of three years.

In spite of these facts Russian soldateska looted my property and broke open the tabernacle. Czechs, too, looted the parsonage and the church and finally arrested me and my housekeeper. The arrest was carried out in the following way: poor persons from my parish and a tailor by the name of Hirnich from Dittersdorf had also been robbed when the Russians marched into the village; in order to save at least something, they brought the few articles they had been able to secure to the parsonage and to the church. One Pistella, the *Oberwachtmeister* of the gendarmerie in Breitenau, who was also a Communist, must have had word of it. One day he arrived at the church together with the local commissar Hampel and N. N., the secretary of the Community Council. The latter, in order to cover his past as a former employee of the German aerial defence organization in Freudenthal, was now serving as a police spy for the Czechs in Dittersdorf; both men demanded entrance to the church and the parsonage, where they, together with Pistella, made an extremely thorough house search. Afterwards my housekeeper and I were arrested, held in the school until dusk and then driven on a cart to the next gendarmerie-station at Breitenau, where we stayed over night.

Next morning we were taken under escort to the district town of Freudenthal and finally put in jail there. Representations had been made to the district commission of the gendarmerie to secure our release, but these were unsuccessful. The priest Hofmann and his housekeeper Elfriede Alfa had therefore to remain in the jail, Hofmann for eight days and the housekeeper for 14!

No German, even if he were an anti-fascist and a friend of the Czechs, was allowed to listen to the radio, nor was he permitted to use the railroad, the bus, or his bicycle. If he did so, he ran the risk that the bicycle would be taken away from him or that he would be thrown out of the train. Anyone who wore the badge with the "N" [N = *Němec*, Czech word for German] had to get permission from the local gendarmerie if he wanted to go from one village to another.

There were no meat rations for the Germans.

The German farmer had no right to protest if some day a Czech arrived at his farm and requisitioned the property, together with the whole inventory and all his personal possessions. The farmer had then either to clear out or, if he was allowed to stay in a little room, had to work hard for his new Czech master, without payment and with almost no food. As a rule the Czech did not work, he only drove about, slaughtered the cattle and was very rarely sober.

In May, at the time of the revolution, the majority of the farmers, who had joined the SA in order to avoid being called up for active service, were driven together, beaten with rifle butts and then locked up in a cellar; from there they were taken to the notorious prisons in the castle or in the town hall of the district town of Freudenthal.

In these prisons they were beaten almost to death with rubber truncheons and loaded canes. Confessions were extorted from them in the most atrocious manner, in order to send them, after long imprisonment, to the mines or to other places for forced labour. Many of them died before they arrived at their destinations; many were shot after they had been forced to dig their own graves with bare hands. It is reported that 20 such victims were shot down in the yard of the military barracks at Freudenthal.

Many, however, who had been able to survive the terrible conditions in the mines at Ostrau or elsewhere, did not find their families when they returned; for these had been independently transferred and were waiting in vain for a reunion with their father or husband.

The worst of the officials at Freudenthal was Dr. Josef Rybař of the district administration. He simply threw German petitioners out of his office; and it was all the same to him if the petitioner was a priest, a nun or a layman. In his capacity as a district commissar this official had put many Germans in jail, or sent them to the camps; applications of petitioners who asked for the acknowledgment of their Czech citizenship were simply sent back without decision, and the enclosures were withheld.

Ill-treatment of a former concentration camp inmate
Reported by Franz Wagner Report of July 11, 1946

As a member of the former Communist Party I was imprisoned at Dachau for three and a half months from 1938 to 1939. On March 6, 1946 I was arrested for the second time by the Czech gendarmerie of Dobraken and I remained under arrest till June 15, 1946 in the district court building of Pilsen. During the time of my arrest I was slapped and struck a number of times. In the meanwhile garments and underclothing were confiscated from my apartment. Only a few things were returned when I was ready to be transferred. At the time of my transfer I only had 180 kilos of luggage, for four persons. In order to increase this to the full amount allowed, it was suggested that I should go back to Mies; but I did not take up the suggestion, since I had been threatened with renewed arrest.

Women body-searched
Reported by Elisabeth Lomitschka Report of August 25, 1946

I owned a 13-hectare [32-acre] farm in Cwinomas, District Mies. On July 4, 1945 Czech partisans looted our estate, and on August 27 we were assigned a Czech administrator.

On October 28, 1945, at 2 o'clock at night, I was abducted to Pribram District for agricultural labor, together with my 8-year-old son and my parents-in-law. In Pribram we were constantly being cursed and spat at by the Czech locals, and my son was often beaten.

On July 17, 1946 we were transferred to the concentration camp of Dobris near Pribram. About 400 women and girls and 200 men were imprisoned there.

The second day all women had to assemble in a loft. Then 10 uniformed and armed young Czech women came in and examined the vagina and uterus of every woman and girl for jewelry, as they said. They pushed down on the stomach with one hand, and inserted the other into the vagina and rooted around inside. They proceeded like that from one woman to the next without washing. Even 12-year-old girls were examined like that. Many women had pain afterwards. Mrs. Wenisch from Otrocin developed fever and such severe pain in her belly and lower back that she had to be sent to the hospital in Prosecnice. I too have had abdominal pain ever since then, and need medical care. I was just having my period at the time of that examination. On my brother-in-law's request I was then sent to the resettlement camp in Mies. I do not have nearly as much luggage as is officially allowed.

Dolawitz

Looting
Reported by Karl Ullsperger - Report of July 3, 1946

In the community office of Dolawitz we were relieved of a suitcase of clothing. Also, my wife was robbed of her horn-rimmed glasses, dish towels and all hand towels, her and our daughter's underwear, a pair of leather shoes and a pair of slippers. Of her seven dresses our daughter had to give up five, as well as two nightgowns. It was Anna Odlas, the wife of the administrator of my farm, who took these things from us. In conclusion Mrs. Odlas also punched my wife and daughter in the head and back. She even helped herself to the toothbrushes that my wife and daughter were using, as well as the soap and laundry detergent that had been bought with our last ration stamps.

Domeschau

Severe maltreatment and torture
Reported by Johann Rösner - Report of October 17, 1946

On November 16, 1945 my family and I were sent to the Czech regions to work, and were sent back home on August 15, 1946 to be resettled [expelled]. That same night 3 Czechs wearing civilian clothes - one of them also had a gun - dragged me out of my bed, took me to my former house which is currently under a Czech administrator, and there I was literally tortured. One of the 3 Czechs, Lenert Vojtek, punched me in the face until I bled. In the process he damaged my nasal bone, which is still visible today, and smashed my dentures. Then he choked me until I fell to the floor. Then I was given some water to wash up, and had to use my hands to dry myself. Then, sharpened matches were driven ½ to 1 cm deep underneath all ten fingernails and then lit, so that my fingernails caught fire. During this I was forced to hold my hands up. I almost fainted from the agony. I was supposed to sign a statement to the effect that on November 16, 1945 I had threatened to murder my administrator's family and set the whole town on fire. I did not sign the statement despite the torture. Then I was sent home. Half an hour later Lenert came by again and forbade me to tell anyone about what had been done to me. The next day the gendarmerie took up the case, and I was ordered to see a doctor. Lenert was not to be seen for 3 days after that, but then he did return and is still in Domeschau today.

Duppau, Report No. 1

Shootings and murders

Reported by Eduard Grimm Report of January 19, 1947

I served in the Czechoslovak gendarmerie and was ordered 1945 to take over the position of the mayor of Duppau near Karlsbad, who had fled.

The first to be shot in Duppau by the Czechs was the German soldier Franz Weis, who was on a visit to his poor mother and his little sisters and brothers. The corpse was thrown in the market place and left lying there.

Shortly afterwards two war invalids, Josef Wagner and Franz Mahr, both from Duppau, who had been enlisted in the SS without their agreement and who lay at home seriously wounded, were arrested by the Czechs and shot.

The following members of the teaching staff of the High School at Duppau were murdered: the principal of the school, Andreas Draht, and three teachers, Damian Hotek, Franz Wenisch, Rudolf Neudörfl, all of them entirely innocent.

Karl Schuh, the postmaster, was first bestially tortured and then killed. All those named above were shot or killed in other ways by the Czech military; the Czech commanders were at that time Captain Baxa and Lieutenant Tichý.

At the small village of Totzau near Kaaden the mayor Schmidt, the forester Bartl and his two sons, as well as other Germans, altogether supposedly 34 German men, were killed, though innocent of any crime, because they were in possession of a few arms for the protection of their homes, notwithstanding the fact that they had obtained the necessary permits from the American occupation forces at Karlsbad.

In October 1945, the wife of one Holzknecht, a knacker from Dörfles near Duppau, heard a suspicious noise one night and therefore looked out of the window; she was then shot by a Czech gendarme.

At Puschwitz, in the district of Podersam, the German farmer Stengl was barbarously tortured and shot. He was accused of having hidden a gun in his manure heap; this was untrue. Close to the county town of Podersam, in the vicinity of the Jewish cemetery, more than 80 defenceless German men were shot by Czech military in August 1945. Most of the shot men had nothing to do with Nazism or politics, they were ordinary German farmers, artisans and salesmen, among them the mayor Groschup, from Gross-Otschehau, and Pfaff, a bookbinder from Podersam, an old man with white hair.

German women were horribly maltreated and died from the effects: the wife of a certain Knic in Radnitz, a dairy owner, and the wife of one Marek, a salesman from Mekl in the district of Kaaden.

German women and girls from Duppau had to fell trees, even in winter, in deep snow; 18-year-old Anna Grund, daughter and only supporter of her aged, ill parents, was killed by a falling tree.

Alois Guth, a confectioner from Duppau, in the district of Kaaden, was also murdered by the Czechs, although entirely innocent, on June 26th, 1945 in the garden of the High School at Duppau. This was reported by his brother Julius Guth. Alois Guth had intended to remove from this garden a wooden cross, which had been erected in honour of his son, who fell in the war; he was caught and, together with 21 other innocent Sudeten Germans, was shot in the garden of the former archepiscopal boys' seminary, after they all had had to dig their own graves.

The aged Mrs. Jansky from Duppau was threatened with hanging by the Czechs of the *Sbor Národní Bezpečnosti* (National Security Corps), in order to extort from her information about other Germans. They put a rope around her neck, pulled her off the ground, so that she almost suffocated, set her free again and repeated the torture until she fainted.

Josef Glatz, aged 13, was put in the court jail at Duppau for 6 weeks, together with other innocent boys. Glatz and the other boys were beaten by Czech gendarmerie with police truncheons on the back, evening after evening.

Duppau, Report No. 2
Severe abuse of a woman, deportation into the coal mines
Reported by Friedrich Liebner - Report of January 12, 1946

A closed transport of 400 Germans left the little town of Duppau for Saxony as early as July 25, 1945. In the course of the following six months the majority of the remaining German population of Duppau was deported to the Bohemian interior for forced labor.

These deportations were accompanied by numerous brutalities. For example, Mrs. Knie of Rednitz near Duppau had been found to have sewed some bank notes, which were after all her property, into her girdle. As punishment she was stripped naked at the Czech gendarmerie office in Duppau, and beaten so badly that two days later, after she had already been abducted to Bernau, she died of a spinal cord injury.

Due to their inaccessible location, the towns in the Duppau mountains are largely still inhabited by Germans. Only in Duppau itself were the farmsteads taken over by Czechs.

Recently all men between the ages of 16 and 45 were arrested and taken away for forced labor in the Brüx coal-mining region.

Duppau, Report No. 3
Severe maltreatment in the course of house searches
Reported by Alois Zörkler - Report of December 31, 1946

In September 1945 the gendarmerie performed a house-search one afternoon in my home at Duppau No. 7, District Kaaden. In the process they beat me unconscious for no reason at all. Ever since then I suffer from a buzzing in my left ear. Various items were stolen from me during the house-search.

Eipel

Treatment of Jews: excluded from the family business
Reported by Dr. Rudolf Fernegg - Report of June 21, 1951

The son of the owner of Buxbaum Brothers linen spinning and weaving mill at Eipel left for the United States even before the German annexation of the Sudeten territories and the establishment of the Protectorate. During the period of the Third Reich the whole family followed him to America. Mr. Buxbaum jun., who had in the meantime become an American citizen, established contact with the personnel of the factory, in order to ascertain their opinion as to whether he would be able to take over his factories in Eipel again. He received the answer that nothing could be done.

Eisenstein

Maltreatment of an invalid
Reported by Alois Sperl - Report of June 28, 1946

I was arrested in Eisenstein on May 18, 1945 and taken to the court prison in Klattau, where I was repeatedly severely maltreated. I sustained an injury to one of my kidneys, and the stump of my arm was beaten bloody at the amputation point. In both cases I was denied treatment by the prison doctor. I had to bandage my arm stump with my dirty handkerchief. Even though I was an invalid I nonetheless had to crawl on the ground and submit to other harassments. I was not given any reason for my arrest. Later I was always told that it was because I had allegedly tried to defend Eisenstein.

Eisenstein-Grün

Ill-treatment of a little boy
Reported by Klara Obermaier - Report of June 28, 1946

At the end of May 1946 my son, who was not yet 10 years old, was so badly beaten by a gendarme at Grün in the district of Eisenstein that he bled for hours. Since that time the child's hearing has been impaired. The circumstances were as follows: The policeman found my boy still on the street at 5 minutes past the curfew hour of nine o'clock. First he booked him for a fine, but then he crossed this out, took the child into the gendarmerie station and beat him up.

Elbogen

Elbogen, Report No. 1

Cases of severe maltreatment

Reported by Franz Weinhard Report of June 22, 1946

I was arrested on July 20th, 1945 at Gfell and was moved to the camp in the castle of Elbogen. There I was dreadfully maltreated, as were the other inmates. Twice and sometimes three or four times a day we were thrashed with a horse-whip until we bled. While we were tortured we screamed so loudly that the American guard could hear us through closed windows at a distance of about a hundred meters. Finally - it was in the evening of about the 6th of August - an American sentry fired several rounds with the machine-gun towards our windows. Two days later an American committee arrived at the camp; they inspected us and discovered the marks of ill-treatment on our naked bodies; photographs were taken of our backs and faces. We did not dare to tell the Americans anything of our treatment for fear of further beatings. Four weeks later the political prisoners were sent by the Americans from Elbogen to Landshut, where everything was better. On September 15th, 1945 we were released by the Americans and taken back to Czechoslovakia. There the Czechs took away our American discharge papers and we were transported to the labour-camp at Plan. During the time of my arrest my flat was searched and looted a several times. Even my daughter's wedding trousseau (she had married a French prisoner of war in May 1945) was stolen. Of the few things which were left in my possession, blankets, linen and tableware were, however, taken away from me at the luggage inspection at Gfell. My cell-companions at Elbogen were: Heinrich Gräf, Ernst Frisch, Fechter, Franz Kolb and Rudolf Jessel. They were just as badly mistreated as I.

Elbogen, Report No. 2

Fortress Elbogen, treatment in Czech prisons on April 11, 1946

Reported by Heinrich Meier - Report of June 1, 1946

On April 10, 1946 I was arrested on the allegation that in late April 1945 I had said that dead Jews should be buried where animal cadavers are dumped.

On April 11, 1946 I was severely maltreated in the Fortress of Elbogen, on the orders of the commandant. I was led into a closed room and had to lie across a bench. A guard who was there for the purpose then gave me five blows on my buttocks and upper thighs with a cudgel as thick as an arm that took both hands to handle, and then ten blows from the commandant himself, with a riding whip or rubber truncheon. This maltreatment remained visible for 4 weeks in the form of bruises on my buttocks and thighs. Finally the gendarme Frante from Schönfeld punched me in the face with a gloved hand. There was a hard object hidden in his glove, and my jaw was dislocated, which is visible to this day.

After a month I was released from the prison without any trial. On my release, Dr. Jäger, Justice at the Elbogen District Court, informed me - but only verbally - that an investigation had shown that I was innocent. I am prepared to take this statement on my oath.

Elbogen, Report No. 3
Concentration camp (Neurohlau, Kladno), maltreatment
Reported by Karl Haberzettel

On June 17, 1945 I was arrested in Altsattel together with 19 other men and one woman, and we were taken to the fortress in Elbogen, where we were all brutally beaten unconscious. In the three weeks I had to spend there, we were beaten several times each day. In the morning we had to do exercises until we collapsed. Several times during the day, and at night as well, partisans invaded our cells and arbitrarily beat the inmates. Whenever a guard approached the window of the cell, the inmates had to call out, with fists raised: Long live Dr. Eduard Beneš, President of the Czechoslovak Republic, and Marshal Stalin!

From Elbogen we were taken to the concentration camp in Neurohlau. Our welcome there consisted of a beating. In this camp we were put to work in the quarry or on the railroad. Our rations were grossly inadequate, consisting only of 100 g [3½ oz.] bread and a watery soup. In the evening we had to stand outside for 2 hours, even when it rained, while the guards intimidated the people with shots fired in the air, slaps, curses etc.

In late July I and 120 other men were sent to Kladno to work in the mine. The rations there were also so insufficient that many collapsed at work. On November 1st the mine began to issue us somewhat better rations, but it was still much less than the Czech miners received. We were not paid at all. On October 15 the Ministry at Prague ordered that the German miners were to receive a daily ration of cigarettes, depending on the work they did. And indeed the laborers in the surrounding mines received them, but not those in the Prague pit in Kladno-Dubi. Our quarters were crawling with lice and bedbugs.

In late January a cold resulted in my falling ill with glandular suppuration. Despite my illness I was forced to continue working in the mine underground. Only when my condition grew worse and ever worse was I discharged, on March 27. In Elbogen I had to spend 7 weeks in the hospital, where I underwent 5 operations. I am ready to take this statement on my oath.

Postscript: Soon after my arrival, other prisoners from Elbogen were brought to Neurohlau as well. All of them without exception were in an entirely battered and beaten-up condition. Among them was an acquaintance of mine from Altsattel, Peterl, whose wounds were dripping with pus. He was unable to walk. I helped him clean his totally mangled and crusted face. Peterl was taken to the sick-room, and I never saw him again. The physician said that he had been taken to Karlsbad to the hospital. But according to a memo from the internment camp, dated January 12, 1946, Peterl died of blood poisoning in the Neurohlau camp on July 11, 1945.

I am ready to take this statement on my oath as well.

Elbogen, Report No. 4
Concentration camp, maltreatment
Reported by Karl Jessel

I was arrested for no reason on February 27, 1946. I was accused of having been with the volunteer SS of the SdP. I had never even heard of this organization. While it goes without saying that my accusers were unable to provide proof that I had been with this group, I was expected to bring proof that I hadn't.

I was detained in the Elbogen concentration camp until June 1, 1946, and my wife and 8 children spent this time without their breadwinner. During my imprisonment my wife was allowed the monthly sum of Kc 1,500 from the funds we had on deposit with postal savings, but only 1,000 Kc were actually handed over to her, so that she had to spend the second half of each month entirely without money.

As in all the camps, the rations in Elbogen were totally inadequate, and the prisoners depended on receiving extra food from their families. Beatings were common in the camp. No prisoner was allowed to have anything at all in his pockets. If anyone carried even so much as a button that had fallen off his pants, or some cotton that he needed for an ear infection, he was beaten for it. Once every prisoner in the camp was beaten because it had been rumored that one of the guards was having an affair with a women who worked in the kitchen. I can take this statement on my oath.

Ernstbrunn

Looting and abuse
Reported by Rudolf Baier - Report of August 7, 1946

After the German surrender in May 1945 our town was occupied by American troops. Ernstbrunn was a purely German community, only the owner of the glassworks was a Czech. For as long as the area was under American occupation, life went on as usual.

In June the Czechs took over the civil administration. From that moment on, Czech partisans and the gendarmerie began a looting spree. Both day and night they went through our homes (we were forbidden to lock the doors) and helped themselves to anything and everything they liked.

We Germans had to wear identifying armbands, and whenever a Czech encountered a German in the street and liked anything this German had, the Czech simply took it. Shoes were taken off right in the street, pockets were searched, money, watches, jewelry, even wedding rings were taken from us by teenaged Czechs armed to the teeth. My brother, who was relieved of an old silver watch and who begged that he might be allowed to keep this memento from his father, was punched in the face. They took the watch and locked him into a shed. Later three Czechs returned and maltreated him terribly.

Livestock and horses were also driven away by the Czechs. The farms in the area were mostly settled by Slovaks, people the Czechs brought in from as far away as the Carpathian Mountains. They were consistently poor Slovaks from the mountainous areas who were forced to take over the German regions and who complained to the Germans, often in tears, that they had been forced to leave their own homes.

Even though the Slovaks arrived without any luggage and had been promised that they would take over finished and furnished homes and businesses which the Germans had voluntarily abandoned, the Czechs had nonetheless first carried off whatever they could, in other words clothing, linen, grain, tools etc. The Slovaks were aghast that they were supposed to help expel the Germans, and swore to the Germans time and again that it was not their doing and that they would rather have remained at home.

The glassworks in our town had employed more than 300 workers, all of them Germans. The factory is now idle. On the formerly German farming estates the former German owners have had to cultivate the fields for the Slovaks, who know little of such things. However, many houses and even entire villages are still totally empty - ghost towns that have yet to be resettled.

On June 26, 1946 we were ordered to report to the collection camp Christiansberg on June 28. We were allowed to take only the items specifically listed in this deportation order. Once we had arrived in the camp, the men had to line up hands raised beside a table and were searched by the gendarmerie (body check).

The women were searched the same way, by women but in the presence of men, and their skirts were lifted and even their underwear was felt.

Whichever of the permitted items we had with us that were relatively new and not badly worn were mercilessly taken from us. Our savings bank books, all jewelry (including wedding rings), watches and valuable documents, especially those attesting to property holdings (deeds of sale etc.), had to be surrendered. We did not receive any receipts for them.

We had to stay 12 days in the camp. The camp consisted of 9 barracks, housing 2,600 people. There was little space. We slept tightly crowded together on the bare ground or on our few remaining possessions. Our rations consisted of black coffee in the morning, turnip or pea soup at noon, and black coffee in the evening. After 12 days we were loaded into railroad cars and shipped under military guard to Furth im Walde.

Robbery and theft
Reported by Adalbert Sturm - Report of September 4, [1946?]

Ladislav Prokop, an inspector at the Graslitz-Falkenau/Eger dairies, was a frequent visitor to our house at Schram Street No. 5 in Falkenau/Eger, where he visited his friend Kotrc and also got to know us. My daughter Margarete Wagner was employed in the dairy in Falkenau on the Eger. He asked my daughter about details of our financial situation. Unsuspectingly, she told him about our very valuable family jewelry and after he threatened her she also told him where it was. This fine gentleman, who had wormed his way into our home so cunningly, then robbed my wife of this jewelry, including highest-carat gold set with many diamonds, gold watches, necklaces, and other gold and silver objects to the total value of half a million Czech crowns. Then he also stole our linen, two radios, shoes, clothing, suitcases and purses etc. He loaded everything onto a truck owned by the dairy and had it taken away, destination unknown. After this great raid he reported to work as being sick, and was allegedly transferred to the dairy in Starý Kostelec n/Orl. He wrote us repeatedly that he would return all our property to us. Then one day we no longer heard from him - the fine fellow had disappeared without a trace. Several times in Falkenau/Eger he brought us some butter and rotten meat, things he no doubt had also stolen. I didn't become aware of this fine gentleman's thefts until later, but there was nothing I could do about him because at that time, until July 1946, robbery, murder and looting were the order of the day in Czechoslovakia and if we had reported him we would have risked being arrested ourselves. And so this crook easily managed to take his loot, worth at least half a million Czech crowns, to safety and to disappear into Eastern Bohemia to Starý Kostelec/Orl.

Luggage inspection
Reported by Raimund v. Wolf - Report of September 13, 1946

During the inspection of my expulsion luggage in Fischern the control officers confiscated a suitcase with dishes and food, and a suitcase containing carpentry tools for which the resettlement [expulsion] commission had issued me written permission to take them with me. When I objected to the confiscation I was threatened that they would also take my suitcase with weaving supplies.

After this looting I was left with less than 70 kg of luggage per person. I filed a complaint in the resettlement [expulsion] camp in Meierhöfen, and was given some chipped dishes that are almost unusable. In the resettlement [expulsion] camp I found out that the inspection officers in Fischern had been drunk and that the only expellees to get away without being looted were those that had given them alcohol.

Frankstadt

Frankstadt, Report No. 1
Maltreatment in Frankstadt and during labor in the mines in June 1945
Reported by Rudolf Dobias - Report of June 10, 1946

On June 6 I was arrested for no reason and detained in the prison in Frankstadt, where I was brutally maltreated. Aside from dreadful beatings that disfigured us beyond recognition, we also had to kneel down and put our head on the cobblestones, and then a partisan would trample us on the head. In my despair I attempted to commit suicide. As I lay there all covered in blood, one of them even wanted to finish me off by beating me to death, but one of the others stopped him. Then I was taken to the Friedeck hospital. While there, I saw men and women being admitted, totally battered beyond any hope of recovery. Prontosil tablets were all that was available for our treatment.

A few days later I was sent to work in the mine. The hard labor and lousy rations there were accompanied by constant maltreatment. We had to work underground from 5 to14 o'clock and above ground from 14 to 18 o'clock, and only then did we receive anything to eat. Our pay amounted to 5-10 Czech crowns per day. I had to work in this mine from August 16, 1945 until March 16, 1946. Then I was sent to Freistadt to be interrogated. I was accused of having been awarded the Medal of Distinguished Service. From there I was transferred to the Neutitschein District Court. When I entered the court I was greeted with a blow to the head. From there I was sent to the resettlement [expulsion] camp. Rations were insufficient all year long.

Frankstadt, Report No. 2
Conditions in the prisoner-of-war camp Frankstadt
Reported by Adolf Hauk - Report of June 23, 1946

I was released from American captivity in Tepl on July 31, 1945. For 5 months I worked for a farmer near Furth im Walde. On November 10 I returned to my home town of Heizendorf, near Hansdorf, and since November 15 I again worked in the brewery in Hansdorf, where I had already worked for 18 years before the war. On November 11 I had reported my presence as required to the Hansdorf police, and presented my American discharge papers. In the time that followed I was repeatedly summoned by the gendarmerie and interrogated about my military service. I had served in the Wehrmacht's medical corps.

On March 2, 1946 I was arrested and taken into the POW camp Frankstadt near Moravian Schönberg. I was immediately beaten for having been a German soldier. Corporal punishment was the norm in the camp. The people were beaten for the most trivial things, and locked into a barbed-wire cage set up in the yard. This cage had no roof, and the prisoners were exposed to wind and weather and had to go without any rations at all every other day.

Rations consisted only of barley soup and bread. As many as 160 men had to sleep in a single room. Everything was crawling with lice and bedbugs. A single pump in the yard was the only washing facility, and not until the last few days was a distributor pipe with 6 outlets affixed to it. Beatings were always done with wooden canes. Every day we were cursed in the vilest way imaginable, by the civilian population as well whenever we worked outside the camp. On our way to and from work we always had to sing Czech songs. On May 25 I was released, to be resettled [expelled]. Wounded and sick people were also imprisoned in this camp. There was no medical care for anyone, and no bandages to be had either.

Freudenthal

Freudenthal, Report No. 1
Report on events at Freudenthal in 1945
Reported by Dr. Carl Gregor, physician - Report of November 25, 1947

I was arrested three times by the Czech police. The first time was at Grulich in May 1945, the second time at Freudenthal in June 1945, when I was taken to the concentration camp together with my wife and my mother-in-law; and the third time again with my wife at Freudenthal, shortly before Christmas.

My third imprisonment was preceded by three house searches. I no longer lived in my house at that time, but had found shelter in the catholic parsonage. I was arrested because the censors had objected to a letter which my wife had sent to her sister, who had been ordered to forced labour.

My first arrest took place on my flight to Grulich. It was the day on which all German men were rounded up on the market-place of the town. They had to empty their pockets and their rings, including wedding rings, were taken from them by the Czechs. About 9 o'clock in the morning the whole crowd of men with their hands above their heads were driven on the double through the streets of the little town towards the district administration building. Then we had to stand in front of the building, our hands still raised. We were led in small groups before a tribunal, which consisted of Russian officers, partisans, the Czech mayor and other Czech functionaries. This tribunal sentenced everyone to a certain amount of corporal punishment. There was also a group of German boys of school age in front of the building, who were constantly being beaten and knocked about. Whenever one of the boys collapsed, he was kicked and cold water was poured over him until he came to. A group of men were treated in the same manner after having been forced to hold up the insignia of the district administration building, a heavy eagle weighing several zentners [1 zentner = 220 lbs], with arms fully outstretched. I still remember a 70-year-old man who was severely affected by the tortures to which he was subjected and often collapsed from exhaustion. It should be stressed that the intelligentsia was especially singled out by the Czechs as an object for their sadism. A citizen of the town, who presumably had hidden himself but had been discovered, was wrapped in a swastika flag and driven through the streets with blows. His face was a mass of blood. When he finally collapsed, the Czechs trampled on him with their boots. He did not regain consciousness and was then dragged behind the building of the district administration. The sound of a shot made us assume that he had been shot there.

Since I was not an inhabitant of the town, the tribunal acquitted me, but strictly ordered me to return to Freudenthal without delay.

My car had been taken away from me, and I walked back to Freudenthal together with my wife, our three children, my mother-in-law, my sister-in-law and our maid. Freudenthal was still occupied by the Russians. As I was the only doctor in town, the Czech local administration ordered me to take up my medical practice again. My house had been wrecked and most of my possessions looted, but after provisional repairs I moved in and began my medical work again. When the Russians left the town, a tank regiment composed of partisans entered it. With this, the period of suffering began for the German population. I will not describe individual cases but only my own experiences.

On June 14th, in the forenoon, two Czech military surgeons appeared during my consultation-hours, checking my licence and informing themselves very thoroughly as to conditions in my house. I had particularly to show them the stock of my medical instruments. On June 15th, 1945 my house was surrounded by partisans and, under the leadership of a Lieutenant Colonel, it was searched, while I was threatened that I would be shot if a weapon should be found in the house. After the search ended without result they all left, taking with them both my typewriters. It seemed that the officer was pleased with my house and decided to move into the apartment in the ground floor, which had formerly belonged to a Major in the Wehrmacht. The apartment had quickly to be put in order by German women, and within two days it became a repository of stolen German property. Among other things there were precious antique pendulum-clocks from the German Castle of the Order, six radios, Persian carpets and many other articles. On June 17th, 1945, at one o'clock p. m., my house was again surrounded by partisans, who were now the executive power. They forcibly entered my house, took all the jewellery, all money and my documents and led me, my wife and my mother-in-law through the town under escort. I wore only light house-clothes and was not allowed to put on my shoes. My three children and the maid were driven out of the house and into the street.

We were taken to the former prisoner-of-war camp in the outskirts of the town, right opposite of the military barracks. First of all we had to remove the dirt and the refuse and were subjected to a short interrogation. During the latter I learned that I was accused of having killed 150 foreigners. We were the first prisoners there, but soon after our arrival more than 80 inhabitants were brought to the camp. Because of the fact that I spoke Czech fluently I had to interpret when the particulars of a prisoner were to be taken down. At dusk I, together with other prisoners, had to fetch straw from a barn at the other end of the town for our night's quarters. The carts of straw were not drawn by horses, we had to pull them ourselves. The camp inmates were divided into men and women and were lodged in two rooms, each about 40 square meters [about 48 square yards].

About 7 o'clock in the evening two partisans escorted me to the military barracks. I was led to a room in which, beside the two military surgeons already mentioned, there were also present officers, soldiers and partisans. The accusation that I had killed 150 foreigners was repeated. I repudiated this baseless accusation with the remark that I was accustomed to help people and to preserve life, not to kill anyone: I should like to be confronted with the person who was able to produce evidence for such an accusation. A cadet, completely unknown to me, then declared that he knew me and maintained that I, like the other German surgeons, had murdered foreigners by means of injections. After making thorough inquiries, he had allegedly learned that the accusation was well-founded. I replied that I did not know the accuser and protested sharply against such an accusation. The reply to my protest was scornful laughter and a kick in the stomach. They then said that I must be shot, but that first I should have a few things to put up with.

I was taken to a room in which a large table was set up. As a result of the kick in my stomach and the blows on my head and my shoulders I was now quite dazed. A feeling of tiredness and indifference seized me. I was ordered to lie on the table, face downwards. Two partisans held me firmly by the arms, a third one cocked his pistol and pressed it against my neck. Any utterance of pain was forbidden. They beat me indiscriminately. I estimate that about 18 men, including the officers and the military surgeons, beat me with lead pipes, sabres, bullwhips and sticks. When, probably as a result of a blow with a lead pipe, the skin of my buttocks burst open, which caused unbearable pain, I groaned aloud. The result was that I was gagged, with a gag defiled with human excrement. The beating continued. When I was very near to collapsing, I was put back on my feet and since it seemed that I would sink down, I was again kicked in the belly and struck on the head. I was unable to hold my head up, which actually prevented me from being hit in the face.

After all this was over I had to drag myself back to the camp. I was told that I was to be shot the next day. At the camp I was handed over to the commandant, who was to keep me in close confinement. In view of my knowledge of the Czech and Slovak language he installed me as camp leader and declared me responsible for everything going on in the camp; attempts to escape or suicides of inmates would be followed by my immediate execution. Thereafter I was present at all trials and interrogations and had to watch the torture and ill-treatment of my fellow-citizens.

A young boy, accused of having hidden weapons, was especially ill-used. Another boy, not quite 17, who had escaped from his place of work, was also beaten half to death.

It became customary to take men and women from the camp for clearing work. When the above-mentioned boy did not return to the camp, all the other members of the working group, since they could give no information as to the boy's whereabouts, were punished by caning on the naked soles of their feet. Later on the boy was brought back and all the men of the group, who had just been punished, were forced by the camp commander to knock the boy about. In addition he too was accused of possessing weapons and was taken to the military barracks together with another youth. We did not see them again until they were brought back to the camp for execution. Both were beaten beyond recognition.

All of the camp inmates had to line up to witness the execution. In the meantime we had been moved from the PoW camp to a military barracks opposite the brewery. A deep hole had been dug behind the camp; in front of this hole the two boys were placed, while four soldiers, who were supposed to carry out the execution, stood at a distance of three paces. I was now ordered to stand next to a Czech officer, about 5 paces distant from the hole. This officer read out the sentence of death in Czech and I had to translate it into German. It was signed by two officers, which shows that the sentence had not been passed by a regular court. Another similar sentence on the innkeeper of a neighbouring village, which was carried out in the camp, was also signed only by two officers. In both cases the possession of weapons was the reason for the sentence, which was executed by shooting. The names of the boys shot were Leo Kübast and Helmut Muhr. The innkeeper was Thiel from Vogelseifen.

As I learned after my release, the parents of the youths had not been informed of the shooting.

During my stay in the camp a number of inmates were killed. I can only remember the name of one Karl Kunze, a brewery-wagoner who, like myself, was accused of having killed more than a hundred foreigners. I was also ordered to examine the corpse of a murdered woman by the name of Kloss or Klohse. In a few cases I had to give death certificates and I was forced to give "heart failure" as the cause of death.

Even women were not spared from maltreatment. I may mention here the case of Herta Klein from Altstadt near Freudenthal. She was maltreated by the camp commander himself and was later ordered to strip and to exhibit the marks before the eyes of the assembled prisoners.

I should mention here that juveniles and preferably war-invalids were used for the necessary grave-digging work. They had to dig out the graves with their bare hands.

Our diet consisted mainly of rotten food and of meat from road-kill.

After I left the concentration camp I heard that a mass-execution of 20 men had taken place.

On my release from the concentration camp I was forced to sign a declaration that, on pain of death, I would reveal nothing about conditions in the camp.

I should not fail to mention that all medical attention for the camp inmates was left to me. No medications or other remedies were put at my disposal. When I attempted to exempt ill persons, elderly people and those who were injured by constant beatings from forced labour, the distribution was withdrawn from my control and I myself had to go to work. Among other tasks I had to clean latrines and to help as an assistant in a mechanic shop. Since I was unable to bend forward as a result of the tortures I had endured, I was beaten and scoffed at.

Freudenthal, Report No. 2

Executions in the Freudenthal camp in 1945

Reported by Johann Partsch - Report of June 24, 1946

On June 24, 1945 the so-called German Revolutionary Guard randomly rounded up 8 men in Engelsberg, including me, and took us to the concentration camp in Freudenthal. We were left 10 days in isolation there, and during this time we were beaten every night and several times during the day as well. The beatings were repeated at half-hour intervals each night. We were all disfigured beyond recognition. The worst day was July 4. That day, the beatings already began in the morning. Then 25 inmates had to dig a pit. They were constantly beaten while digging. Then all the prisoners were assembled around the pit. At the same time, the members of the German Revolutionary Guard were locked up. A Czech verdict was read out, but most of us didn't understand it. Then 20 half-dressed men were brought out from a barrack. 10 of them had to kneel before the pit. 10 Czechs with submachine guns shot them and threw them into the pit. Then the second group of 10 followed. This group included Wilhelm Baum from Engelsberg as well as 6 other men, including senior teacher Hermann Just from Engelsberg, who had been discredited as civil servant for being a former Social Democrat, radio expert Fochler from Freudenthal, who had been an anti-Fascist with the German Revolutionary Guard, and the farmer Zimmermann from Dürrseifen, who had been found to favor ethnically foreign employees. Grave digger Gustav Riedl from the first group had not been mortally hit. After three minutes he staggered to his feet in the pit and begged for a mercy bullet. A Czech fired his submachine gun at him again. After another few minutes Riedl again got up. He was shot once more. Gustav Alraun and Alfred Nickmann, both from Engelsberg, had to fill in the pit. They saw that Riedl and several of the others were still living, and those unfortunates were then finally beaten to death with rifle butts.

The background to this execution was as follows: two Czechs from the municipal guard had been injured while handling a Russian hand grenade. One of them was killed, the other badly injured. These were the findings of the Russian city headquarters. But the Czechs claimed that a time fuse had exploded in a radio shop, and that the Germans had placed this time fuse there. The Czechs demanded permission from the Russian office to execute, first 100, then 50 Germans, which the Russians refused. The 20 men were then shot without the Russians' permission.

Youths aged 11 years and up were also imprisoned in the Freudenthal concentration camp. Helmut Muhr, 16 years old, was shot on June 26 because he had gone to visit his mother. It was then proclaimed that anyone who escaped the camp and was caught would be shot along with 10 other inmates of the camp, and if he were not caught, his family and 10 inmates would be shot. I know of at least 10 other executions. I personally had to bury the innkeeper Adolf Thiel from Neuvogelseifen, digging his grave with my hands because I was forbidden to use the shovels, of which there were several in the camp.

Friedland

Treatment of Jews: Prevented from recovering own law office
Reported by Dr. Rudolf Fernegg - Report of June 21, 1951

A fellow-member of our alumni society, Dr. Bermann, a lawyer from Friedland, was detained in the Little Fortress at Theresienstadt during the Third Reich. After May 9th, 1945 he paid me a visit and told me that he was trying to get back his house and law office at Friedland. His wife had had to sell the house during the past years and had gone to Prague. Several days later he returned and told me that he would have to go to Prague too, as all his attempts had proved to be in vain.

Friedrichswald

Arrest, concentration camp, farm labor
Reported by Franz Simon - Report of July 4, 1950

To start, I want to point out that in 1945 I was 67 years old and was never a member of the National Socialist Party. During the war I had been an air-raid warden.

On June 12, 1945 at 5 o'clock in the morning there was a knocking on our door, and we were told to open up. I opened the door and immediately found myself surrounded by a gang of partisans, who ordered me to get dressed and to come with them. While some of them, I don't know exactly how many, rummaged through closets and cupboards and threw everything into a mess, another one never let me out of his sight and urged me with cynical remarks to hurry up. When my wife tried to give me something to eat, to take with me, she was shoved aside with the comment, "he won't need anything". Outside on the street there stood a bus at the ready to take us in; some fellow-sufferers were already in it, and several others were still picked up. Some of the partisans were drunk. They threw pictures of Hitler around the bus, and then claimed that they were ours and we had tried to get rid of them. Our first stop was the secondary school in Reichenberg, where we had to stand facing the wall in a room on the third floor. After a while someone walked along our row with a whip and beat into us. We had to say "Heil Hitler". Then we were taken one by one into a room where we were supposed to make a statement. When I said that I had not been with the NSDAP my interrogator gave me a powerful slap about the head, followed by many whip lashes. With satanic cunning someone had slipped a knuckleduster into my ID book. Following this "interrogation" we had to stand in the hall for half an hour, holding our arms out front, i.e. extended and raised to chest-level. Anyone whose arms drooped was beaten. Then I and one fellow-sufferer had to wash a room and a hallway, after which we were locked into a dark hole which seemed at one time to have been a tool shed or the like. Victims from the previous day were already there. In the afternoon we were taken to Laufergasse Street (the police prison), but it was already overcrowded and so we were brought back to the barracks on Langen Weg [Street]. Coarse laughter, curses and kicks into our backs were our constant companions. The kicks to our backs worked especially well on the steps leading into the police prison, as anyone who was not expecting them and holding on to the handrail fell down the steps. In the barrack on Langen Weg we had to stand facing the wall and keep our hands raised, for an entire hour. If anyone lowered his arms even the slightest bit, or turned his head a little, got special attention - slaps, and blows to the back with rifle butts - from the partisans marching up and down the hallway. This was again followed by individual interrogations, during which everything except our eyeglasses was taken from us, every morsel of bread and every cigarette we might have had in our pockets. The interrogator first asked me where I was from. "From Friedrichswald", I replied. With the words, "don't you know that's Bedrichov now," he boxed me about the head so that lights flickered before my eyes like fire. The camp administrator beat me from behind. After all of us fellow-sufferers had been relieved of our possessions in this humane manner, we had to line up and, knees deeply bent, hop once around the barrack, and then crawl around on all fours. And in this way the first day concluded. So far we had not been given anything to eat at all, but now we were divided among the barracks and received a bowl of bitter, black coffee and half a slice each from an average-sized loaf. This amounted to about 20 to 30 grams [2/3 to 1 ounce] but that was the entire day's ration for us. We continued to get this amount in the mornings and evenings, and a bowl of watery soup with no nutritional value at all at noon. One day a week our relatives could come to pick up our laundry, and on this occasion food parcels were also brought in, but when we received them after inspection they had usually been raided. We had to transport cabinets, wash floors and do similar work. The camp administrator, a Czech who was said to own an inn (a German estate) between Reichenberg and Gablonz and who had been an inn-keeper in Reichenberg during the war, seemed to have made it his self-imposed duty to ensure that his camp inmates were always kept moving. Anyone who could drag his emaciated body only slowly to "dinner" was hurried along with the whip, as the administrator was all for "speed". One man from my home town found an opportunity to escape; that was on a Wednesday. As punishment all the bread that our women brought on Friday was confiscated. The escapee was captured, and I will spare myself an account of how he was tortured.

Towards the end of July we were put on a transport into the Czech interior. We had to make the trip standing in cattle cars, and anyone who sat down was beaten up for it by the guard. In Jungbunzlau we had to get out. In order to avoid "meetings" we had to stand facing the wall while waiting for the other train. My journey ended in Schumbor, a dairy farm in the District of Nymburk. Utterly emaciated, weak and covered with bruises, we were now expected to assume the roles of strong farmhands. My hope, that here we would at least be able to eat our fill, had been in vain. The very first day we were told that there was very little food here, and only peas for us. The first day I had to chop wood, while my companions in misfortune had to clean toilets. From the second day on I was to drive a team of two horses, but I couldn't because I had never before in my life driven horses. And so I had to take care of the horses for the driver, and work on the fields during the day. The morning feeding was at 4 o'clock. One horse had kicked me so badly in the leg, on my varicose veins, that I could hardly walk. As I could not comply with the overseer's order to move faster, he beat my back black and blue with his cane. His complaint to the partisans who came by to inspect us every day prompted them to thoroughly box my ears.

In late September I got my first chance to write, and it was not until then that I could inform my wife that I was still alive, and where I was. There was no opportunity ever to take a bath. The only bathtub there was, was constantly in use by the women, who had much to suffer from the Russians. There were veritable scenes of despair. We were louse-bitten, starving and ragged. That was how my daughter found me when she suddenly stood before me one fine Sunday morning. I found out that both my daughters had also been forced to do labor in the Czech interior, one of them in Nymburk District, and also that my wife was ill. She suffered from great depression and was getting weaker and weaker. My ulcerated varicose veins had gotten worse, to the point that I could not always go to work in the morning. The administrator threatened to whip me, and did so several times. In my despair I wrote a postcard to the concentration camp in Nymburk, stating that due to my ulcerated leg I could not work. Then the administrator was instructed to take me to the Nymburk camp, where I was sent to the hospital. The treatment was humane there. One of the patients to share my hospital room was a German (64 years old) who had to have one leg amputated after it was excessively frostbitten. On February 3, 1946 we were sent back to the camp in Reichenberg, that is, to the resettlement [expulsion] camp in Habendorf.

I do want to mention that after my two daughters found out where I was, they were able to send me some food. I say this in order to acknowledge that even here there were people whose heart had not turned to stone. My family did their best to obtain permission from the local *Národní Výbor* that I could come home even for a single day; I would have liked to see my home one more time, especially as I was only two hours away by foot. But all pleading was in vain. When my wife joined me in the [expulsion] camp she was physically and psychologically destroyed. She was unable to recover, and on July 7, 1947 she died in Kaufbeuren.

Giesshübl-Sauerbrunn

Expropriation, robbery
Reported by Maria Pichl - Report of June 22, 1950

During the expulsion of the Germans from Czechoslovakia, even Germans who (according to Beneš's Decrees) would have had the right to remain in the country were also expelled. I would like to give some examples of how these Germans were treated. I will start with my own experiences:

I was born in old Austria, trained at a Catholic institute to become a teacher, taught for a time in Austria and then in Czechoslovakia, and in 1923 I emigrated to the United States (Chicago, Illinois). On my American citizenship papers I declared: "It is my bona fide intention to renounce forever all allegiance and fidelity to any foreign prince, potentate, state or sovereignty and particularly to the

Czechoslovak Republic of whom I am now subject; and it is my intention in good faith to become a citizen of the United States of America and to permanently reside therein: So help me God." Proof attached: citizenship paper dated October 13, 1923.

Since the American labor market was affected by a great depression in 1932 and I had to keep changing jobs, I returned to Czechoslovakia and worked again as German teacher in the German region of the country. In other words, I had not even been in the country during the 1929 Census and could not have declared myself to be a German, but rather I had at that time declared allegiance to the American state. I still have my original citizenship paper today, and in 1945 after the Revolution I also showed this paper to the Swedish Consul Harden in Karlsbad, who represented the American interests. He told me that this document protected me and my family and property against the effects of the Revolution, and that I should report this to the Czech Commissars, which I did.

At that time a certain Sokol came to my house and told me that I need not fear, since Czechoslovakia was going to be restored to the way it had been before the war. Since the American document lapsed after 7 years, I had actually remained a citizen of Czechoslovakia, and could not return to the United States.

Now the partisans came and urged me to reapply for Czech citizenship. I was to work as English teacher. But this was made conditional on my joining the Communist Party. I asked: "Can I keep my property?" (My family owned 2 very nice houses.) I was told that I would have to give up this property and go where I was posted to work. I asked: "What is to become of my 84-year-old mother, my helpless invalid brother and my retired sister?" (Up until then I had taken care of my mother and brother.) The partisans (gendarmes) told me: "They're all going to be resettled to Germany!"

I found that all this was very inhumane, and applied to the Ministry of the Interior in Prague with the request to arbitrate my case. I was told that it would be investigated. But very soon hereafter the partisans returned, searched my house, helped themselves to anything they wanted, and said: "Get a move-on across the border, so that we can finally be rid of you."

When I realized then, in 1946, that the country was going to be restructured along entirely Communist lines, I finally told the partisans that I was prepared to share the lot of all the other Germans and that they might resettle [expel] me as a German. In late August my mother, brother, sister and I were all resettled [expelled] to Bavaria.

The baroness Nina Riedl-Riedenstein, of the Dallwitz-Karlsbad Castle, went through similar experiences. She had been born in Greece and her husband was Austrian. They had great land holdings and were considered to be very wealthy. Her mother-in-law was an American. Russian officers billeted themselves in her castle, stole whatever they liked, and smashed anything they could get their hands on when they were drunk.

Since they knew that the Baroness wanted to keep her properties (her husband was already deceased), they stole all the documents that would have proved her ownership, and took off with them.

One time I appealed to the Swedish Consul in Karlsbad. He was the director of a bank in Karlsbad. At that time he told me: "Now the Czechs have taken over my bank, fired me, and confiscated the houses belonging to my wife, who was born in Germany. In this way I have been deprived of my livelihood, and I will have to go to some other country and start all over from scratch."

A Slovak lady of my acquaintance, whose husband had been a German physician, worked at the Commissariat in Giesshübl-Sauerbrunn. I often discussed the various cases with her, as well as my personal affairs. One morning she told me: "It's sad, we are governed only by Communists, and they decide who is to be dispossessed. They don't ask if the people are foreigners or Germans, they just want their property, that's all!"

Everything I have said is the truth, and can be substantiated in part with original documents.

Graslitz

Luggage inspection
Reported by Margarete Poppa - Report of July 7, 1946

During the luggage inspection in Graslitz in the resettlement [expulsion] camp I was robbed of my entire hand luggage, two blankets and a pillow. When I objected to this, the inspecting official threatened that I would be sent into the Czech interior for hard labor. I am 73 years old and now I have to undergo the several days of transport without even a blanket to cover up with.

Gross-Hermersdorf

Maltreatment, abduction into coal pits
Reported by Hugo Ehler - Report of November 24, 1946

On May 17, 1945 a Czech by the name of Klement Biskup dragged me out of my house and locked me overnight into an empty cattle barn belonging to a different house. He shoved and hit me. Two days later the same fellow, Biskup, came back to my house again accompanied by Josef Hilscher from Sponau and three other Czechs from Laudner, District Moravian Weisskirchen. That town is also where Biskup is from. All of them were young people between the ages of 17 and 25. Biskup ordered me to stand outside my house door, where he stood with his revolver drawn and yelled at me: "Hands up!" The three fellows aimed their rifles, and then he said to Hilscher, "now give it to him," whereupon Hilscher took a rubber truncheon out of his coat and hit me with it on my hands until they were black with bruises. Then I had to lie down, and Hilscher beat me black and blue from my shoulders to my ankles. Afterwards they forced me to kneel by the door while they beat my 74-year-old father, screamed at my wife and then searched through my entire home, stealing even the last of our food.

On August 17, 1945 I was taken to the gendarmerie office and sent from there to the court prison in Odrau. It is simply impossible to describe all the beatings and abuse we were subjected to by the militia there. There was maltreatment without end, and the rations were unfit for human consumption.

On October 15, 1945 I was transferred from the court prison to the Odrau labor camp. The treatment we got there was the same as in the prison. On October 17 the militiaman Anton Wenzlik kicked me in the shins to the point where the sores became infected and did not heal up until April 1946. Her also repeatedly boxed me about the head.

On January 28, 1946 I was sent from the Odrau labor camp to the camp at Poruba near Orlau, to the coal mine, where I had to stay until May 11, 1946. The militia there treated us just as badly as that in Odrau.

Gross-Schönau

Murder of a 13-year-old schoolboy
Reported by Franz Josef Hille and Emilie Hille - Report of November 24, 1946

In February 1946 a 13-year-old schoolboy, Herbert Neumann, while on his way to visit his grandmother, was treacherously shot by a Czech at Gross-Schönau. The bullet penetrated the abdomen and the child was left lying in his own blood without any help until he died after three hours of terrible suffering.

A worker by the name of Konrad, living at Gross-Schönau, was shot in the same way by a Czech in May 1946 at a place close to his house; he died a few hours later.

I, Franz Josef Hille, witnessed this incident with my own eyes in June 1945, when near the town hall Mr. Franz Grohmann of Gross-Schönau was thrown down the stone steps and remained lying unconscious on the pavement. Mr. Grohmann was 72 years old. Close by stood three Czech customs officers, who watched this act of violence and expressed their satisfaction with loud laughter.

I, Emilie Hille, saw with my own eyes how Walter Helth, an innkeeper from Gross-Schönau, a man 60 years of age, had his face slapped and received such a severe blow on the jaw that he fell backwards and remained lying unconscious until some German men carried him away. This occurred while German inhabitants were being expelled.

Gross-Sichdichfür

70-year-old woman maltreated

Reported by Marie Adler - Report of June 14, 1946

I was ordered out of my house and home on September 21, 1945. 8 days later a gendarme and a Czech administrator gave me permission to remain in my house. I spent one night there again. The next day the police chief from Gross-Sichdichfür came by, boxed me - a 70-year-old woman - twice about the head, shoved me to the ground and kicked me.

Grulich

Severe maltreatment and shootings of Germans

Reported by Alfred Schubert - Report of October 9, 1946

On Tuesday after Whitsun 1945 seven workmen between 16 and 60 years of age were taken from the joiner's workshop - where I was an apprentice - to the market place of Grulich, where they were tortured and maltreated in the most inhuman manner. At the same time other Germans were savagely ill-treated. Three of them were shot immediately afterwards; one of them was shot by a woman. Another man died next day as a result of his injuries. They were beaten with heavy clubs, chains and whips. The surviving employees of the joiner's workshop were all ill for some time after this experience, one of them had to remain in bed for three weeks, another for four months. I personally was a witness to the events and I am prepared to take an oath on my statement at any time.

Haida

Murders in May 1945

Reported by F. Fiedler Report of July 10, 1950

In Haida the following Germans were shot by the Czech soldateska after first being brutally tortured:

The brothers Heinz and Albert **Rachman**n, owners of the glass and metal goods factory;
engineer **Richter** from the glass and metal goods factory;
Frau **Werner,** movie house cashier;
Fräulein **Werner,** employee of Pistor's glass manufactory;
Herr J. **Langer,** shoemaker;
Herr Eduard **Podbira,** 83 years old, glass refiner;
(Herr E. **Schowald** got away by good luck).

In late May 1945, when the first Czech partisans and their Svoboda soldateska descended upon the glass manufacturing center Haida, that horde carried out raids on the town's inhabitants (allegedly they were searching for weapons). In the attic of 83-year-old Eduard Podbira's glass refinery, an old bayonet was discovered which Podbira's brother, a combatant in the Prussian War of 1866, had kept as a souvenir, without Podbira's knowledge. For this reason 20 Germans were arrested, and 6 of these were selected and brutally maltreated while the remaining 14 had to watch. The 6 victims, including Frau and Fräulein Werner, had to strip naked to the waist and take their shoes off. These people had to kneel on the pavement of the market square and were then beaten by the Czech gangsters with rubber truncheons on their naked upper bodies and on the soles of their feet until the poor victims collapsed unconscious. Cold water was then poured over their heads to revive them, and the torture was continued.

Albert Rachmann, who could not bear to continue watching his younger brother Heinz being tortured like that, tried to flee in the direction of the Czirnich pharmacy, but was caught by the Czechs and forced to undergo the same torture. This maltreatment went on until daybreak, when the half-dead victims were shot by these Czech savages on the market square of Haida. The other 13 scapegoats were then abducted to the vicinity of Rumburg.

Eyewitness: the brother-in-law of the murdered Rachmann brothers, language teacher Lehmann from Haida.

Haindorf

Murder of two young girls at Easter 1946
Reported by Ernst Jesensky - Report of May 15, 1950

My name is Ernst Jesensky and I was born on September 4th, 1908 at Haindorf, district Friedland, where I owned a transport business. When the Czechs moved in, there commenced a reign of terror: daily arrests, house searches, lootings, the taking of hostages and harassment of all kinds. Many people committed suicide. It would involve a much too detailed description if I were to report all the cases of those who were taken to the woods, beaten to death, shot and buried without ceremony. The mayor of the town, Dir. Hornischer, was one among many who - in order to avoid torture - threw himself from the third floor and died of his injuries.

I myself had to work with a firm preparing wood for generators. Later on I became ill and was afterwards employed as a chauffeur until I was transferred to Germany.

At Easter 1946 my daughter and her cousin took a walk with two of their schoolmates; on their way they were suddenly attacked by armed Czechs and shot down without cause. The girls took bullets in the head, neck and chest and died immediately, the boys received slight chest- and head-wounds and were able to flee and report the matter, otherwise this crime - like many others - would never have come out.

When we arrived at the camp (Neustadt a. d. Tafelfichte) in order to be transferred, we were not allowed to use the transport bound for Bavaria, but had to wait seven weeks in the camp until the first transport left for the Russian zone. It was also intended to intern us and for this reason we were taken to the internment camp at Friedland; it was, however, overcrowded and we were not admitted.

During an inspection of our luggage and a search of our personal belongings, the clothes and the coat of my murdered daughter were taken away from me, among other things.

Hakelsdorf

Daughter was raped
Reported by Anna Stanek - Report of August 18, 1950

On July 5 [1945] my daughter was thrown out of her home with only 10 minutes' notice. Then she was taken to the Russian camp.

During the night a young Mongol came with a flashlight and wanted a blonde woman. But his potential victim had her brother-in-law there to protect her. So then he went to my daughter; she resisted. He tore everything she wore off her body, kneeled on her and choked her until she turned blue. Her child was screaming, so he grabbed it and threw it against the wall.

Six men watched everything he did to my daughter. On July 8 they left again. The same [Mongol] confiscated all my daughter's possessions in Reichenberg. Ever since then both my daughter and her child are ill. They are now in the Eastern Zone [East Germany]. The child is in a tuberculosis sanatorium and my daughter suffers from heart trouble.

Maltreatment on the grounds of false information
Reported by Dr. Hampel - Report of July 3, 1946

I was arrested by the local gendarmerie on February 13 of this year at my father-in-law's home in Hals near Tachau. A protocol was written up as I watched, and in it I was accused of the most monstrous crimes, allegedly on the basis of some denunciation. Even the simplest investigation would have shown the falsehood of these claims within only a few hours. I was asked about each of the several points of the protocol, and my every "No" was countered by a blow with a dog whip. When I finally said that all these accusations had to have been prompted by an error or a denunciation, this resulted in my interrogators yanking me into an adjoining room, where I was beaten with a stick and the dog whip until I blacked out. Then I was imprisoned in the Tachau camp, in a small unfurnished room. The food rations were totally insufficient, and food parcels from the outside world were forbidden. After 5 weeks I was so weak that I could hardly remain on my feet. With the help of repeated interventions by my family doctor and the official Czech physician who knew that I was suffering from a tropical disease, I finally managed to persuade the camp administration to grant me a proper questioning, which quickly established my innocence. On April 7, 1946 I was released to go home. On my arrest I had been relieved of approximately 3,000 RM and 10,000 Czech crowns. Some of this money were business funds belonging to my father-in-law, who was still working as an architect. I was not given a receipt. When I was released, I got only a few hundred crowns back.

Maltreatment in the Hannsdorf concentration camp
Reported by Emil Tegel - Report of June 23, 1946

On May 30 of last year I was arrested in Hannsdorf and detained in the prison there until October 28. On my committal I was punched so badly that I collapsed. Then I was also kicked. The guards were very often drunk, and then they would beat the inmates with bullwhips. I myself was beaten up at least 2 to 3 times weekly. Six times the totally drunk guards came into our sleeping-hall shortly before midnight, tore down all the bed frames and threw our clothes all over the place. They smashed the dishes against the wall. Then they gave us an hour to reconstruct the bedsteads, without tools, and to restore order to the room while constantly urging us to greater speed with their bullwhips. We had no opportunity to complain about these excesses by the guards. One time the crew from the Blanik Armored Train came to the camp and raged among the inmates, many of whom were covered in blood afterwards. After I had been in the camp for three months, the gendarmerie interrogated me about my political activities. They were unable to give me a reason for my arrest. Another two months later I was released.

Heinzendorf

Barbarous treatment of an old man
Reported by Marie Menzel - Report of September 30, 1946

On August 14th, 1945, the majority of the farmers at Heinzendorf near Olbersdorf were removed to the camp at Jägerndorf. We had to leave the house within 15 minutes and could take almost nothing with us. At the same time my 77-year-old husband was beaten badly about the head by four Czechs, so that he bled from an open wound. In addition they struck him in the side with the butt of a rifle. In the camp at Jägerndorf the men had to lie on the bare concrete floor. I tried very hard to get my husband into the infirmary, but the doctor rejected him. It was not until August 21st that they admitted him into the ward. The following day he died of his injuries.

Hennersdorf

Rapes, extortion of false confessions
Reported by Rudolf Knauer - Report of February 1, 1947

I was an eyewitness to and victim of barbaric methods used in my hometown community of Hennersdorf and in the resettlement [expulsion] camp in Jägerndorf, Troppau Street, in which I was interned from August 13, 1945 until February 15, 1946, and as such I wish to make the following report, which is based on my own experiences and on the statements of my fellow-sufferers.

Returning from the Wehrmacht, I arrived in my home town Hennersdorf at Whitsun 1945. Our home had been broken into and drawers and closets rummaged through. Russian troops were quartered in the community as occupation forces and were supposed to ensure peace and order.

The inhabitants of our wholly German community were going about their business as usual when the first Czech gendarmes, so-called financial fiduciaries, moved in in early June 1945. They established a *Národní Výbor* which also took over official community duties. This take-over inaugurated our time of suffering, a veritable hunt for the industrious native German population after they had complied with the regulations and turned over all their weapons (hunting rifles, air guns, stabbing weapons etc.).

Regardless what political party the Sudeten Germans belonged to, they had to wear an "N" (Nemec), meaning "German", sewn onto their jacket, were forbidden to use the sidewalks or trains or to enter restaurants, and were allowed to enter shops and stores only at specific times. After 8 o'clock p.m. we were not allowed to be out in the streets any more.

A time of terror began for the women and girls, as the soldiers from the occupation forces hounded and raped them at any time of the day or night. The men were unable to protect their wives and daughters and in fact were even forced to watch as the victims were violated. Czech laborers from the region of Friedek-Mistek were brought in by car; they took over and moved into the farmsteads first, and in the following days they also took over the remaining houses, claimed to be administrators, confiscated the entire possessions including food, clothing, linen and furniture, and assigned the true owners, who were thus turned into beggars overnight, to the tiniest available room in the house or in other buildings.

The most horrific maltreatment often accompanied this. I myself witnessed two farmers (Josef Andres and Adolf Stefan) being so badly beaten by Czech partisans that they were left lying with blood-covered faces and their bodies entirely suffused with blood. To extort a confession from them, they were threatened with being shot, and were forced to dig their own grave. Since the farmers were innocent, they bore the injustice being done to them with an admirable calm, but they and their kin (wives and children) had terrible tortures to endure. That was just one of the methods these brutes often used.

In the Kuhberg colony, a group of 10 houses that were part of the community, all the inhabitants (loggers) were robbed of their food (meat, flour, grain etc.) and forest ranger Schnaubelt was tortured by a different method of choice. He too was supposed to make a false confession. He was hung upside-down, beaten on the soles of his feet, and drawn up. When he was unconscious they dumped water on him, repeated this treatment several times, and then left him lying unconscious. The tortured man told me this himself, and the inhabitants of Kuhberg, who presently live as expellees in Münnerstadt, District Bad Kissingen, can testify to it as well.

During the house searches, which were done door-to-door during the confiscations, all the inhabitants of the community were more or less frequently beaten and robbed until the very day of their expulsion.

The farmers were busy bringing in the main harvest when unrest seized the community in the night of August 12-13, 1945. Around 4 o'clock in the morning there was suddenly a banging on our door, and a bellowing voice ordered us to report to the estate inn within one hour, with 30 kilos of luggage and rations for four days. We had no idea what they were planning to do with us.

And so we were herded - shoved along with rifle butts - to the assembly point, where we had to stand around until 2 o'clock p.m. Older men and women who could not move along quickly enough with their baggage were slapped and punched. Children screamed out of fear and hunger, and their mothers sobbed because the guards escorting us roared at us like animals.

At 3 o'clock we set off on our foot-march into the unknown. People were driven like animals from their native home, which their ancestors had made arable 700 years before. We unfortunates, about 1,200 inhabitants, mostly women and children and old people, had to march 25 km on the hard county road to Jägerndorf, where we arrived dead tired at 11:30 at night. We were taken to the concentration camp in Troppauer Street. Behind us closed the gates of a camp fenced in on all sides, from which many hundreds never emerged alive again. But still there was to be no rest for us yet. Families were separated, and the men had to line up for registration. After questioning we were shoved into pitch-dark sheds, where we had to spend the night sitting on the floor. The women and children were put into barracks crawling with bed-bugs.

The next morning we had to line up to be body-searched. Czech guards (men ranging from 20 to 50 years of age) searched us. They took all our cash, any usable items of clothing, other necessities such as razors, cutlery, even our travel rations, while shoving almost all of us around with their rifle butts, and punching many in the face. After this first encounter with the representatives of the Czech camp, to whom we had to take off our hats when standing before them, we were assigned a badly damaged tank garage as sleeping hall, to house 2,000 people. The straw bedding was full of bugs. From 10 o'clock in the evening until 5:00 a.m. we were forbidden to leave the garage, and had to answer the call of nature into barrels set up for the purpose. The only way we were ever addressed was "you German pigs". Whenever a guard appeared, which happened almost every half hour, we had to call "Attention!" and freeze in "halt" position. If anyone failed to hear the call to attention - which happened especially to the older men - they received a punch to the face that knocked them to the floor.

One Sunday in September 1945 we were taken to the Burgberg concentration camp to visit with our families. The trip was led by the head guard, a monster named Hudec who called himself Commissar. Together with a few other guards, this man managed on the way back to the camp to accuse about 300 of us of not having properly greeted three Czech officers passing by, and once back in the camp, he punished us as follows:

He ordered us to *"pozor"* (stand still), and we had to remain like that for half an hour. Other guards with sticks saw to it that we remained in the desired position. But then the real torture began. We got alternating commands: seesaw, down on the ground, crawl across the big square and back on our elbows without using our feet, then we had to alternately march and run. The weak old men received kicks if they could not keep up - and after all they were not young recruits, more than half of them were over 60 and about 50 of them even over 70 years of age. Daughters and wives could only weep as they had to watch this torture without being able to help. For two full hours these innocent men, of whom I was one too, had to suffer, until they collapsed.

There was no end to the sadism. For example, other transports (women, children and old men) who came to the camp after us had to spend three to four of the cold autumn nights sleeping on a concrete floor under a tent-like ceiling and surrounded only by a fence, before even being assigned barracks. In the late fall, so many men were crowded together in a barrack that two men each had to share one bedstead, after we had been sleeping on the bare floor for weeks. Sick patients, who mostly suffered from starvation-related typhus, could only be taken to the hospital by fellow prisoners and on small hand carts (children's carts).

The concentration camp also served as slave auction. The transports destined for the coal pits of Moravian Ostrau, and for the Czech interior for agricultural labor, were put together here. The trips to our destinations went via open cattle cars. The victims were given barbaric treatment, not only while they were alive but even once they were dead. No clergy saw to their spiritual aid, even though three months after our arrival two well-fed Czech clergymen held Holy Mass in the open air in front of a latrine in the camp every Sunday and therefore knew very well how badly we were being treated. But there was not so much as a word of sympathy or criticism to be heard.

Our rations: breakfast: boiled brown water, so-called coffee or tea without sugar; lunch: unsalted potato soup (made mostly with frozen potatoes) mixed with potato starch, all of which together made for an inedible sort of slime; supper: see breakfast; plus 200 g [7 oz] bread to last the entire day.

For this diet, for which we were forced to line up for hours on end even in rain and snow, the men and women had to work hard all day long, without pay, and were often harassed and tormented for up to two hours during the roll-calls that took place at 7:00 p.m. each evening, to which the men had to report without their hats even in the cold and the rain. The result was that even a few weeks later the camp inmates were only skin and bones and especially the older people died of starvation.

That we got no fuel to heat with in the winter is something I just want to mention briefly. It was part of the inhuman treatment we got, as is the fact that the resettlement [expulsion] transports began in the cold of January 1946.

That's what the resettlement, that was proclaimed to the world as a humane procedure, was really like - and it is remarkable that the rest of the civilized world keeps silent about all these atrocities. Our settlement area where we lived had never been Czech.

Hermannstadt

Shooting of a German girl
Reported by J. Schöppel - Report of October 6, 1946

On July 8th of this year, my daughter Hildegard, born on June 3rd, 1928, was shot by the Czech commissar Anton Konecny at Hermannstadt. She was working for a Czech farmer; on the third day of her employment, while she was spreading manure, the commissar, who lived in the same house, stepped out and shot at her with his 9 mm Flaubert rifle. She was hit in the right breast and died the next morning. The ambulance had been sent for, but had arrived only five hours later. Konecny attempted to clear himself by asserting that he had shot her by accident. The Czech farmer in whose service my daughter was employed told me that he had heard of Konecny having shot another girl at Römerstadt. A week earlier he had also endangered the lives of the German farmer Kröner and his son.

Looting, maltreatment
Reported by Franz Kreissl - Report of September 26, 1946

I worked as a miner in the Lichtenstein coal and clay works. On September 2, 1945 my home was totally looted by Czechs. They stole clothes and linen, bedding, dishes and food, as well as several musical instruments. On September 9, 1945 the Czechs returned and maltreated me and my wife, who was seven months pregnant. They beat us with cudgels, pistols and rifle butts, and kicked us. They shoved pins under my wife's and my fingernails. Then I was led off, bleeding from my mouth and nose and two head wounds, but was released again to return home after a few hours. The next day the Czechs returned yet again and forced my wife, despite her pregnancy, to get on the motorcycle with which they fetched me from my place of work. Now I was imprisoned. In November my wife and our children were driven out of our house with nothing but a few old rags, two days before my wife delivered. On January 19, 1946 I was released from the camp at my employer's request.

The Kuttenplan camp, expulsion from own farm
Reported by Engelbert Watzka

In late July 1945 a Czech mayor came to our community with his secretary, took over the Town Hall, ordered the public school to be cleared out, and set himself up there. News from the cities revealed that transports of expellees were already being resettled in September. As of August 15 the first Communist Czechs arrived in our village. We called them Commissars. They looked like vagabond, poorly dressed, dirty, with torn shoes, and each of them always carried a briefcase under his arm, in which they carried documents to prove that the Communist Czech government had granted them the right to take possession of and "administer" any farming estate, inn or business they cared to take over. Several times groups of 10 to 15 Czechs arrived, strolled through our town, looked at the nicest of the farms and all the newly built houses, and wrote down the house numbers. The following day they would return with the Chief Commissar to appropriate these farms and businesses. Entire families also arrived, and the Germans had to leave their homes instantly, without notice, and were assigned a spare room somewhere where they then had to live. They had to leave all their goods and possessions for the Czechs, with the sole exception of a few pieces of furniture, bedding and feather ticks, clothing and linen. By September our town, consisting of 130 numbered houses, was occupied by 76 Czech families.

We had to work all day long. Every morning at 5 o'clock Czech guards blockaded the streets, and no Germans were allowed on the streets after 7 o'clock p.m. If more than two people were seen standing together during the day, they were dispersed. There were at most 4 or 5 experienced farmers among the Czech invaders. All the others were circus folk, street performers, actors, dairy farmhands, and to a very great extent they were work-shy vagabonds. The first transport from Hinterkotten, of 5 Germans families being sent as forced laborers into the Bohemian interior, left in early October and these returned before Christmas the same year. They told us that they had had to work all day outdoors in the fields even in bitterly cold weather, with insufficient rations, and had to spend the nights in unheated emergency shelters where the wind whistled in. When these families returned and wanted their property back, it had already been confiscated by Czechs and they were no longer allowed to enter, but given some empty rooms to stay in.

In late September 1945 a Czech administrator came to us and wanted our farm estate. He could hardly understand German. Later he returned with the Chief Commissar. Both of them were young fellows, about 19 or 20 years of age. He informed me that our estate now belonged to him, and that everything in the house, stable and yard belonged to his colleague Josef Rojsek. He demanded our savings bank books and cash. Then these two fellows went from room to room, into the yard and the stable and the granary, noted everything down, locked everything and informed us that if we needed anything we would have to ask him for it. Josef Rojsek immediately made himself at home in our best room and with our best things. He had been a butcher's apprentice, and had not the slightest knowledge of farming. A lady interpreter had to come every morning and tell us what he wanted that day. He was only interested in eating and drinking, never in working. We had to continue to work the farm, and he would only check on us occasionally. So at least we didn't go hungry, and we got whatever we needed.

The first transport from Hinterkotten left in late January 1946. The expulsion luggage, limited to 50 kg, was inspected at the Town Hall and anything that was new was confiscated. Poor people were first sent to the Kuttenplan concentration camp, where they had to stay 10 to 14 days. In the camp they were left to go hungry if they had no relatives or friends in our town who could secretly bring them some food. The transport took place in very cold weather; sometimes the train would just stand on the tracks idle all day long, and the entire trip took 6 to 8 days. The wind whistled through the dilapidated cattle cars, and most of the people on the transport fell ill and some even died.

In late April 1946 there was a fire in Kuttenplan. It was in the evening. A house burned down, approximately 1 hour's distance from us. Still that same evening the Czech gendarmerie came, drove all the men of the community together and out of our town. They were taken to the customs office in Promenhof, where the gendarmerie was quartered, and there they were all beaten with rubber truncheons, boots and bludgeons. The next day they were herded to Plan. They had to march through our town, more than 100 men. In Plan half of them were locked into the concentration camp, and the others, mostly younger men, were sent to do forced labor - on a diet of bread and water. Many of them were also abducted into the Bohemian interior, where they had to do forced labor.

On June 26, in the evening as we were returning from making hay, the town constable Mann showed up unexpectedly and informed us: "Watzka family, ready for transport at 7 o'clock tomorrow morning." Our Czech administrator wanted us to stay. We had to report to the Town Hall, where our luggage was inspected one more time, and all objects of value were taken from us. We arrived in the Kuttenplan concentration camp at 11 o'clock. Every arriving family had to put their possessions in a little pile, and then the Czech gendarmerie arrived, did a head count and re-evaluated the piles of luggage once more. If a family was small, it was not unusual for the luggage pile to be reduced by another suitcase or something else. We were quartered in the third story of the Kuttenplan Castle, where 4 families were squeezed into one room. We only had to stay there 4 days. On the second day we were examined by a physician and disinfected, and on the third day each of us was issued 500 RM by the camp administrator. On July 30 our luggage was retrieved from the basement and loaded up, after which we had to guard the wagons, while being ourselves guarded by Czechs. On July 1 [1946], a Monday afternoon, an altar was set up in the anteroom of the camp square, where a clergyman read the Sacrifice of the Mass, then gave a sermon and blessed us. After that the Czech commandants ordered us expellees to assemble, and a higher-ranking official in uniform addressed us and told us how we were expected to behave during the transport. Then we 1,200 persons were lined up in rows of four and herded to the train station. Everyone was issued a car number. Groups of 30 were entrained in each wagon. We had to spend the night in these wagons, until the transport moved out at 4:15 a.m. of July 2. It took hours before we reached Eger. In the afternoon we arrived on German soil and could rid ourselves of our white armbands.

Hloubetin

Rescue of a German soldier by the commandant of a camp in 1945
Reported by Erwin Rebel Report of June 16, 1950

In spite of the many grave charges which I could bring, I consider it my duty rather to report the case of a Czech who saved my life.

On May 8th, 1945, by order of my unit, I was sent together with two other soldiers to Badnovice near Eipel (Ipolice) in the northwestern part of Czechoslovakia, in order to secure quarters. As a result of the capitulation my troop probably marched in another direction; in any case it did not arrive at the place previously designated. I had, however, got in touch with the mayor or other residents of Badnovice and was given a perfectly correct reception.

Attempting to reach the German border by bicycle and later on foot, I was taken prisoner together with other soldiers. We arrived at last by a circuitous route at the internment camp of Prague-Hloubětin. The then camp commander was a certain N. N. from Hloubětin. Since all my documents as well as my outer clothing and shoes had been taken from me at the time of my capture, I was unable to prove my identity. I was recommended to obtain a certificate from some-where to the effect that as a soldier I had never been involved in military activities in Czechoslovakia and was also not a member of the SS, Gestapo or other party organizations.

With the consent of the camp commander N. N., I wrote to the mayor of Badnovice and asked for such a certificate, as I had made there very precise statements about my person; in my conversation with the municipal council I had given them some details of my life. Several weeks later a letter arrived at the camp, in which it was stated that I had stayed at Badnovice on the day of the capitulation and had behaved correctly, but according to the evidence, given by some inhabitants of the village, I had come back with an artillery regiment several days later and had probably participated in the shooting of two Czechs.

N. N. was supposed to submit this letter to the judicial investigation board present in the camp. This would have meant my being handed over to the camp guard, who were not under the control of the camp commander and who had already beaten to death two inmates of the camp on the grounds of unproved denunciations. I myself had helped to put the bloody corpses on a truck. N. N., who knew me as the senior of the barracks, asked me to see him, interrogated me, going into all details, and then personally gave me the letter to destroy, as he had convinced himself from my interrogation that the statements from Badnovice could not be true. I immediately burnt the letter.

By acting in this way, N. N., assisted by his interpreter, who up to 1947 was still living and working in Prague, saved my life.

Hohenfurth

Hohenfurth, Report No. 1
Sudeten Germans arrested by Czech gendarmes in Austria
Reported by Johann Staudinger - Report of November 2, 1946

On August 17 of this year I was stopped between Leonfelden and Zwettl by uniformed Czech gendarmes and an Austrian gendarme and asked to produce my ID papers. I am a Sudeten German and had been released in April of this year from French captivity, to go to Austria. The Czech gendarmes confiscated my French discharge paper, and then they took me and two friends by car to Czechoslovakia. They beat us throughout the 20 km long trip. Our hands had been tied. On our arrival in the prison in Hohenfurth we were beaten so badly that we passed out. I had to spend a week in medical care. The District Court of Kaplitz eventually discharged me into the resettlement [expulsion] camp.

Hohenfurth, Report No. 2
Arrested for no reason at all
Reported by Dr. Josef März - Report of November 2, 1946

I was Chief of the Hohenfurth brewery. On July 13 of last year I was suddenly arrested at my place of work, and accused that in 1938 I had allegedly "climbed up the brewery smokestack with a machine gun" and, from there, shot a Czech soldier. For months I was detained in prison like a murderer, forced to wear convict clothes, and repeatedly severely maltreated. I was not interrogated until February 18, 1946, and the actual reason for my arrest was barely mentioned on that occasion. I was accused of other things, which were just as untrue. I continued to be detained until September 5, 1946 and forced to do heavy physical labor, with very poor rations. In August of last year my wife and daughter had also been arrested and confined to the concentration camp in Kaplitz. Later we were conscripted for hard agricultural labor. We lost all our possessions during our imprisonment. Our resettlement luggage did not amount to the permitted weight and consisted only of things that acquaintances gave us.

Hohenfurth, Report No. 3
Arrested for no reason, sent to deportation camp, luggage for deportation denied
Reported by Karl Leuchtenmüller - Report of November 2, 1946

I was a member of the Social Democratic Party for 27 years, and the Czech authorities were well aware of this fact. Nonetheless I was arrested on August 23, 1945 and committed to the District Court of Budweis, where I was dreadfully maltreated. I was detained there until February 12, 1946 and then transferred to the Budweis concentration camp. There inmates were treated badly there as well. My wife had also been arrested on August 29 and was imprisoned in the Kaplitz concentration camp for 14 months. After my wife's arrest our home was looted down to the bare walls, so that now we no longer have anything at all. We had neither clothes nor linen for the expulsion, and our luggage for 4 persons amounted only to 120 kg. My daughter's efforts to obtain some supplies from the *Národní výbor* in Hohenfurth were totally in vain.

Holleischen-Staab

Treatment of prisoners in May 1945
Reported by Robert Zürchauer - Report of June 3, 1946

I was arrested by Czech partisans on May 8 of last year and kept imprisoned until May 17 this year. In all that time I was never told why I had been arrested. On my release the Czechs asked me why I had been arrested, but neither they nor I knew that.

During my imprisonment I and my fellow prisoners were horribly maltreated with rifle butts, steel canes, wooden cudgels and rubber truncheons.

During the first three weeks we were chased around the prison yard in circles for half an hour every day, and beaten until we bled or collapsed. I myself collapsed twice under this abuse and had to be carried from the yard back into the prison cell.

Rations were so insufficient that in three months I lost 31 kilos [68 pounds] - I am 182 cm [6'] tall and my weight dropped to 45 kilos [99 pounds].

There was no medication for us at all, and sick people were left to die a wretched death. Among these were my acquaintances Janka and Kosler from Holleischen. Rudel from Staab was beaten to death in a cemetery near Klatten.

In November an inmate escaped, and another one in February. Each time the entire camp was subjected to corporal punishment.

I can take this testimony on my oath.

Hostau

Luggage inspection
Reported by Franz Stadtherr - Report of June 8, 1946

During the luggage inspection by the gendarmerie in Hostau near Bischofteinitz I was robbed of all the luggage belonging to my daughter who was being resettled [expelled] with me, all of my tools which I need for my profession as carpenter, the bricklayer tools belonging to my father, the bedding and blankets for my father and my mother, who were also being resettled [expelled] along with me, a baby bath, a laundry basket also containing dishes, a carrier with laundry tubs, and many smaller items. The other families who were being resettled were also robbed of many things, especially clothing, linen and tools. Objections were in vain.

I can take this testimony on my oath.

Jauernig and Wichstadtl

Jauernig, Report No. 1
Maltreatment, murders
Reported by Elisabeth Böse - Report of January 9, 1950

On May 8, 1945 we experienced the German surrender in Zöllnei near Wichstadl, District Grulich, whereto we - women, children and old people - had been evacuated by the Party leadership in Jauernig, East Sudetengau, as the Russians had approached to within 15 km of our town and a break-through was to be expected at any moment. My elderly parents and I were quartered in a more than primitive shack, which from outside looked more like a stable than a human habitation. But this was actually what we had to thank for the fact that we would later be spared the otherwise standard visits by Russians and other gangs. In fact, our lodgings, with the hayloft above, served the women of the town as night-time hiding-place from the Russians that were out to rape them. We had come to the town on March 23. On one single day 12 men were brutally murdered in Wichstadtl, where we had to do our shopping; they were hanged from the trees surrounding the church after the Czechs had first cut off their noses and ears, beaten them up and shoved them into the water. Among the victims there was also a Czech who had made weapons for the *"Volkssturm"*. The town's inhabitants were forbidden to leave their houses while this tragedy was happening. One neighbor (a farmer) had to dig his own grave before he was shot, allegedly because a military gun and ammunition had been discovered in his manure pile. Probably the murderers had put these things there themselves. That was done in many cases, to fabricate a reason for the murders. Some of the German Wehrmacht had fled into the nearby woods, and anyone who was discovered in the woods was shot as partisan. Real manhunts were staged, and the wild shooting went on for days. The people could venture into the streets only at risk to their lives.

On May 20 we had to leave the town, and started on our trip home together with several families of our acquaintance. As the train tracks had been destroyed, we traveled by horse-and-buggy, changing frequently in the various towns since the farmers were not allowed to go far beyond their town lines. After enduring many a danger and looting, we reached our home town three days later. But a new shock awaited us - our home had been totally looted. Beds, linen, clothing, all was gone. Good neighbors helped us set up a makeshift home. We had to report our presence immediately to the Communist authorities, some of which were still "German" at the time, and to register our civilian occupation. And so I was "black-listed" from the start, and conscripted to forced labor together with many other women from the NS Women's Auxiliary and the NS People's Welfare Association. I had been active in the latter organization for six years, as *Zellenwalterin* [a kind of low-ranking organizer].

On June 21, 1945 three gendarmes "tricked" me out of the house; I was supposed to come to an "interrogation". Otherwise I would probably never have left the house alive again, like my very aged parents whom I was never to see again in this world. And so I went along with them, unsuspecting, trusting in the assurances given publicly on garish posters, that no harm was to come to the insignificant little Party ranks. But my path led straight into prison, without any interrogation. Once my eyes had adjusted to the dark, I recognized my fellow-sufferers. For 14 days we nine women sat on three straw sacks. Meals consisted of black coffee, one slice of bread, and a watery soup at noon. In the mornings we were permitted to dip our hands into a bucket of water and to wipe our faces. The facilities consisted of a bucket that was only taken out once a day.

One day we were moved out. When the bus stopped we found ourselves in "Bieberteich" (District Freiwaldau). Later this *"Koncentracní tábor"*, as it was called, was transferred to the Regenhard factory. We had been interrogated briefly, once, in the prison. But the main hearing did not take place until three-quarters of a year later. The charges were read to me, it was the assertion of one Mrs. Dobisch. I was accused of having been a "leading member of the SdP" and of having engaged in Nazi propaganda, which was untrue. After about a year I and 70 other women were released from the camp.

We were approximately 300 women in the camp. We ranged in age from 14 to 70 years and served as labor slaves. Shoveling coal, felling trees in the woods, sweeping streets, cleaning up paint and brickwork etc. Rations consisted of bitter black coffee in the morning, first 160 and later 200 g bread daily, which for a time had sand baked into it. Potato soup at noon, and also in the evening. Once in all the time I was there we got some horse-meat stew. Many came down with dropsy, with swollen feet and faces, me too - and once I almost died of dysentery. However, I was not beaten. At times we were treated brutally, but sometimes our tormentors developed "human" feelings. The female camp leader was Anna Eret, the male camp leader was a gendarme, her brother, but I don't know if his name was Eret as well. During the last time in the camp we were given a little white bread and sugar weekly.

On June 6, 1945 Cardinal prince-bishop Dr. Adolf Bertram, our provider, passed away in Castle Johannesberg; a few days later he was laid to rest in the Jauernig cemetery. The day after, several hundred people, among them also my unhappy parents, were driven from their homes and rounded up on Ring Square like a herd of cattle. My father was the retired archiepiscopal accounts councillor Bruno König, 80 years old, and my mother Emma König, née Clement, was 77. (After an entire year in the concentration camp I found out from eyewitnesses that they had been involved in this action.) The men were taken into the concentration camp (a former labor camp) and the women to Castle Johannesberg. They were probably lured away with the same lie I had been told, i.e. that they would be back in their homes very soon, for they did not take any warm clothing or even a coat with them. A few days later they were transported off to Setzdorf, where they had to sleep in the lime works, on the bare ground in the lime dust. The German population in the area supplied these poor people with food, often incurring harsh punishment for their trouble. Two and a half thousand people were herded together from all the towns in the area, and one day they were loaded into open cattle cars. In pouring rain, after several days on the road, they reached Bodenbach on the Elbe, i.e. Herrnskretschen, where they were herded across the Saxon border in the dead of night after first being "assessed" one more time and relieved of anything of value they might still have had left. Probably on foot and half-starved (eyewitnesses report that for days they lived on grass), my parents reached Chemnitz in Saxony, where they were quartered in a school. My mother died there on October 1, 1945, and my father followed her on October 6. They were buried in a mass grave.

In May 1946 I was released from the concentration camp, and found myself homeless and on the streets. Our house, Johannesberg No. 38, had been damaged by bombs and was totally looted. My parents' house, Johannesberg No. 15, was occupied by Czechs. Relatives took me in, but I was conscripted into harvest labor right away, and until I was resettled [expelled] I worked on a dairy farm - this time I was paid. I used the money to buy shoes and clothes, as I only had rags left to wear.

On September 18 we were resettled [expelled]. For 12 more days we had to remain in the re-settlement camp of Niklasdorf. In the course of another strict "assessment" we were relieved of our remaining best things; the "assessors" even stole two cans of food from me, which I had saved up with food stamps and at the cost of increased hunger in order to have something in an emergency.

We were allowed to take 70 kg luggage, but mine only consisted of mostly old and worthless things that acquaintances had given me.

In conclusion I wish to list the casualties my family suffered through the expulsion:

Bruno König, retired archiepiscopal accounts councillor, age 80; Emma König, his wife, née Clement, age 77; engineer Hubert Leischner, my cousin, last resident in Trautenau, where he was beaten to death by Czechs (reported by eyewitnesses); Maria Weiser, merchant's wife, one of my father's sisters, died in Erfurt of the consequences of the expulsion; Maria Weiser's grandchild, 2 months old, died during the transport; Josef Rainold, mill owner in Jauernig, one of my father's cousins, died in a concentration camp; Lotte Brieter, my cousin's wife, died in Vienna in the camp, of typhus; Maria Hannich, née Clement (mother of 2 children), my cousin, died in Bonn/Rh., of malnutrition and nerve paralysis; Lydia Chmel, née König, my cousin, wife of Dr. Chmel, chief administrator in Wagstadt/East Sudetengau; Dr. Hans Chmel, chief administrator, his mother and his child, a girl aged about 7 years. It is doubtful that this family died of natural causes.

Addendum: people who brought charges against us Sudeten Germans are said to have been paid 200 Kc. per charge and person. The concentration camp guard N. N. sometimes bought bread and margarine from us, out of his own funds, when we had to work in the woods. On the other hand, according to eyewitnesses he is said to have participated in the murder of 10 men while posted as guard in the men's camp Adelsdorf (three quarters of an hour away from our camp). Among the victims were Dr. Franke, lawyer in Freiwaldau and Mr. Hauke, Rothwasser. Their wives were confined in our camp and did not learn of their husbands' deaths until after their release.

I received a few old items of underwear and clothes from the Czech community administration in Jauernig shortly before I was resettled [expelled].

On the whole, the regular Russian troops behaved far more decently than the Czech partisans.

I affirm that my report tells the truth in every regard.

Jauernig, Report No. 2
Torture in the camp
Reported by Heinz Girsig - Report of September 7, 1946

From June 1945 until March 1946 I was detained in the Jauernig concentration camp. While there, I was badly maltreated several times, and lost two teeth as a result. I also witnessed the severe maltreatment of other prisoners, and saw how several inmates were tortured and shot. In July of last year, the two Hauke brothers, 16 and 18 years old, were shot by the deputy camp leader Katiorek, one day after the latter had used a knife to carve a swastika into one of the boys' buttocks. They had also been shot at with cartridge blanks. Often we were chased out of our sleeping quarters at night and maltreated. Meissner from Krosse, a plumber from Zuckmantel, and Hauke from Jauernig were beaten to death in this camp. I endured my last maltreatment there in mid-February.

Jauernig, Report No. 3

Concentration camp Jauernig, maltreatment

Reported by Alfred Lorenz - Report of September 15, 1946

From June 22 until October 8 last year I was in the Jauernig concentration camp. Terrible maltreatment took place there. Some prisoners died of the consequences of how badly they were abused.

I recall two days in particular:

On July 9, 1945, we 70 prisoners were awakened by rifle and machine gun fire. Allegedly there had been a rescue attempt from outside the camp. At 10:30 at night we had to line up in the yard, wearing only our night shirts. Half of us were to be shot on the Jauernig market square.

Then that order was changed. Instead, we had to crawl around for an hour on our belly on the stony camp roads while being kicked and beaten on our buttocks and head with rifle butts. I received a kick in my right side that cracked two of my ribs. A blow from a rifle butt to my left upper thigh tore the flesh off the bone. A particularly sharp stone injured my heel, and I could not walk for 14 days. My elbows and knees were badly skinned and took two months to heal. After this torture we were chased with whips into the wash room, crowded closely together under the showers, doused with cold water, and constantly whipped throughout it all. Then we were chased into the barracks, accompanied by more beating.

On August 20 last year, after the first mass that was ever held for us in the camp - by chance it happened to include the parable of the Good Samaritan who had fallen into the hands of robbers - we had to spend the rest of the day, from 9 o'clock in the morning until 10:30 at night, barefoot and bare-chested in the prison yard, doing calisthenics non-stop and with nothing to eat or drink. Older prisoners collapsed from this.

Josefstadt

Maltreatment of free laborers

Reported by Johann Seidler - Report of September 21, 1946

After I was released from Russian captivity and was on my way home, Czechs imprisoned me in the concentration camp Josefstadt and then sent me to work in the coal mine of Klein-Schwadowitz near Trautenau. The works militia there indulged in undescribable orgies of beating the prisoners. These beatings took place several times a week throughout the year, right to the end. Even when we were designated "free laborers" on August 10 this year the beatings did not stop. As late as August this year, for example, Adolf Hanisch from Neu-Ermelsdorf was beaten so badly that he lost consciousness several times. All of the camp's prisoners always had to attend and watch such beatings.

Jungferndorf

Luggage inspection

Reported by Anna Nitschek - Report of August 15, 1946

My husband was a member of a Social Democratic organization, and therefore my ID papers stated that I was an anti-Fascist. During the luggage inspection in the resettlement [expulsion] camp I was nonetheless robbed of a suitcase and a chest of clothes, underwear and dishes. When I begged them to let me keep my things, I was rudely shouted at, and shoved out the door. I am 74 years old.

Kaaden

Detainment of German skilled workers

Reported by Dr. Julius Geppert - Report of January 8, 1946

Up until the revolution I was a notary in Kaaden but was expelled from my post by the Czechs. I had to leave my apartment as well as my house and lost the whole of my fortune and my property. After I had been temporarily employed as a coachman and gardener, I obtained a post at the kaolin works of Petzold & Döll, where I was employed as a clerk in the joiner's department. On December 18, 1945, I left Kaaden and emigrated to Bavaria.

I am in the position to make the following statements concerning the situation at the kaolin works: the works were nationalized, that is taken over by the State, and were then under the direction of the firm's former agent by the name of Schreier, who treated the Germans very well. Of the 300 workers, 10% were Czechs, and 25% of the office staff. The works were terribly short of coal. Only five of twenty furnaces were in operation.

Almost all of the skilled workers were Germans; among the Czech workmen were many who were not familiar with the techniques. Thus, for instance, there was a Czech porcelain worker who had been put in the company's form-casting section, of which he understood nothing. He did not even show the necessary interest to make himself acquainted with the subject. It was the same with almost all of the Czechs, who had formerly been employed as workers. They criticized the Czech management all day long, accusing them among other things of embezzling brandy and cigarettes destined for the workers. A petition referring to this and submitted to the Labour Office at Prague was nullified by the managers themselves, who displayed the articles in question.

The Czech management made every attempt to retain the German skilled workers. Applications for voluntary transfers, which had to be approved by the factory manager, were rejected on the grounds that the presence of the German workers in the factory was absolutely necessary for its operation. The factory managers even went to central Bohemia for the sole purpose of setting free the wives of the German skilled workers who were being held in deportation camps. They also petitioned the Ministries in Prague, pointing out that it would be better for German women to keep house for their husbands employed in the factory, rather than to vegetate unprofitably in mass agricultural employment.

Most of the workers in our factory were asked to opt for Czechoslovakia as their home country. This also applied to workers who had been members of the NSDAP. Nevertheless all German workers, including the anti-fascists, constantly applied for permission to be transferred. The majority had been forced to vacate their apartments and had lost most of their personal belongings as a result of looting. Although the German workers received special food allowances for heavy labourers, their position was still worse than that of the Czech workmen, as the German ration cards allowed for much less food (for instance, no butter and no meat).

The coal mines could not fill the quotas required, as most of the Czech miners were now employed in factories, formerly entirely German, in which the work and the techniques were completely strange to them.- Tens of thousands of Germans were seized for the work in the mines before Christmas. In consequence of the fact that these Germans were not familiar with the work there and also that they were treated like slaves, the output was extremely small, not least of all due to the workers' sheer physical incapacity.

Dr. N., a Czech notary who was my successor at Kaaden, advised me to opt for Czechoslovakia so that I could take over the office again. He himself would prefer to go back to Pardubitz, his former place of employment. I answered him that after my recent experiences I would sooner do the most menial labour in Germany than be a notary in Czechoslovakia.

Karlsthal

Maltreatment of a pregnant woman
Reported by Ida Tauber - Report of July 12, 1946

In November 1945, while the contents of my house and flat were being listed prior to their being taken over by a Czech, a paper showing that we had opted for Austrian citizenship was found. The Czechs tore up this paper and threw the pieces contemptuously at my feet. Afterwards the gendarme punched my head, face and ribs. I was at that time seven months pregnant. We then had to clear out of the house.

Karlsstadt

Maltreatment of an old woman
Reported by Anna Czasch - Report of July 12, 1946

In October 1945 I asked the *Národní výbor* (National Committee) for permission to go from Karlsstadt to Hermannstadt in order to obtain a copy of my birth certificate. I got the permission, but I was told also to go with the certificate to the gendarmerie, where it was to be endorsed.

At the gendarmerie I was dreadfully beaten by three men. I received several blows in the face, so that it was all swollen up and the sight of my left eye is still bad. I also received a blow in the abdomen, the consequences of which I am still suffering from. I am now 66 years old.

Karthaus

Report on the convict camp
Reported by Franz Lehmann - Report of August 11, 1950

On May 25, 1945, about 30 minutes past 1 o'clock in the afternoon, a car stopped in front of our house, 15 Oberhennersdorfer Strasse, Warnsdorf; two partisans got out of the car, carrying automatic pistols at the ready, and told me that I was under arrest. I was only half-dressed, but I was forced to get in the car at once and we left for Rumburg; there I was brought before the interrogator, a commissar, who had been appointed by the Revolutionary Committee. The interrogation took place in the former servants quarters of the district administration building. There were also other arrested persons assembled. I was told to face the wall. Rudolf Keil, the mayor of Oberhennersdorf, was interrogated before it was my turn. A number of gendarmes stood in the room, ready for action. Now my interrogation began.

The proceedings were under the direction of the elder son of one Wagner from Oberhennersdorf. In a voice filled with hatred this man accused me of all kinds of misdeeds. The main accusation consisted of the following points: You are a member of the NSDAP, you are an enemy of Czechoslovakia and of the Jews, you denounced a number of Communists in 1938 so that they were taken to concentration camps. You were also a member of the SA. I rejected these accusations, but they did not listen to me and I was forced to sign the protocol of the interrogation, otherwise they would have beaten me until I did so.

After the interrogation I was put into Cell 1 of the local jail at Rumburg. There were already five other men in the same room. As a result of the interrogation I was quite confused and sank down on the plank-bed, paying no attention to the other inmates. All of a sudden one of them said to me: "Franz, don't you know us?" Now I looked up and recognized the following men present:

Eduard Grohmann from Rumburg, Mehnert, a railroad-man, Ritt, who worked in the Rinco Motor Works, Hesse, an engineer from Rumburg, Töpfergasse, and Schubert from Rumburg, Zittauergasse. The appearance of the men was dreadful. Their faces and hands were covered with black and blue marks. Richard Ritt was writhing in pain. Shortly before I had entered the cell, the Czechs had pulled his feet between the seat and the back of a chair and had caned them on the soles, giving him 25 strokes.

May 25th was a Friday. At evening on the same day all inmates of the local jail had to line up in Rudolfstrasse; we were then locked up under heavy guard in the prison of the court building at Rumburg. In our cell there were some 20 persons, people from Rumburg, Oberhennersdorf and Niederehrenberg. We could hear the screaming of the inmates of the adjoining cells. At night we made ourselves as comfortable as possible on the bare floor. Again and again, all night long, the guards fired off their pistols in the yard of the prison. Saturday morning brought all sorts of new abuses. Inmates of the prison who had been members of the SS were forced by order of a partisan to spit at each other, to slap themselves, to pull each other's hair and to kick themselves. The men in our cell were ordered to do one hundred squats. Then they had to stand facing the wall with their faces a few inches from it; after they complied, one of the monsters approached and struck us violently on the back of the head so that our faces bumped against the wall. Blood was running down the walls, noses were broken, eyes and foreheads swollen up.

On Sunday morning we were told that we would be transported to Kosmanos. We washed the blood and dirt from our faces at a big water barrel. Shortly after noon we were to be loaded on a bus, parked in the Georgswalder Strasse. But before we were allowed to get in, we had to undress and everything was searched, afterwards one after the other of us was forced to run the gauntlet between partisans, gendarmes, and uniformed Czech civilians until we reached the bus. We were beaten with rubber truncheons, whips and so on. A howling Czech crowd awaited us at the bus. Many of us received from them something more as a memento, some of the crowd even aimed blows into the curtained windows of the bus. The interrogator, commissar Wagner, had devised a special reception for us at the convict prison: he had enclosed two rubber truncheons with the case records, which were sent with us, with the instruction that those German swine whose names were marked with a red pencil in the list attached should be received in a special way with these rubber truncheons.

After the martyrdom at Rumburg was ended, we drove under heavily armed gendarmerie escort into the interior of Czechoslovakia. We could not look outside, since the windows were covered with tent cloth. We stopped at Kosmanos. But the convict prison there did not accept us. We therefore drove to Jungbunzlau. But there was also no room for us. Finally we reached the convict prison of Karthaus in Waldice near Jitschin. We were turned over to this notorious prison. The reception was rough but correct. A gendarme from Rumburg, who had accompanied us, could not resist shouting at us: "Well, you won't come out of this place alive!" We were once more searched by the warders and then 26 of us were put in a cell. The whole transport consisted of about 40 persons. We received no food. We had to relieve nature in the cell and the vessels were only emptied into the cesspool in the morning.

On the first day of our imprisonment we were officially catalogued in the reception office, in which the director of the prison and two warders were working. We were lined up in front of the office, along the wall, and the nearer we came the more penetrating were the screams of those who were being tortured inside. All of these men had been in our transport. They left the office, one after the other, with tears in their eyes and faces distorted with pain. I stood next to the mayor of Oberhennersdorf, Rudolf Keil. We were not allowed to move. One of our comrades was beaten so badly that he lost control over his bowels and excrement ran out of his trousers. He had then to go back to the office with a rag to wipe up the mess. Arriving there, he was again dreadfully beaten. Now it was Rudolf Keil's turn, he left the room unmolested, and then I had to enter the torture chamber. The record of admission was made out by the director himself. Opposite him sat a burly warder, the rubber truncheons from Rumburg in his hand. My answers to the questions asked were correct. When I was asked why I would not acknowledge the protocol of my interrogation at Rumburg, I answered that I had signed it under duress. It was an advantage that I spoke Czech. On this occasion I was able to take a glance at the list of our transport and noticed that various names were marked with a prominent red tick. They were the names of those whom Wagner had chosen for the reception with the rubber truncheons.

My admission being over, I was locked up in a cell in which there were already four other men. These men were two Czech collaborators and two Germans from the Riesengebirge (Sudeten Mountains). For the present I was separated from my companions-in-misfortune from Rumburg. Routine prison life began. At eleven o'clock I received the first meal in a broken pot. No spoon; I had to use my fingers to pick the bigger pieces of cabbage out of the soup, but hunger is the best sauce and I emptied the pot, although with disgust. In the afternoon we received a cup of coffee. The diet consisted of 100 g of bread per day, a cup of coffee at 7 in the morning, at half past ten a pint of cabbage or potato soup and at 4 o'clock another cup of coffee. That was all we received to still our hunger, thin soups. Compared to this, the regular prisoners in the penitentiary at Karthaus lived in quite a lordly way; several times a week they received dumplings, fried potatoes, coffee with milk, enough bread, marmelade - in a word, they could appease their hunger. Moreover, their relation to the warders was almost comradely. The prisoners there were common convicts: murderers, sexual criminals, assassins etc., most of them sentenced to penal servitudes for 5, 15 or 25 years or for Life. The two prisoners who were detailed to shave us once a week were, one, a man guilty of manslaughter, and the other a murderer. In the eyes of the personnel of the convict prison we were evidently criminals more dangerous than the permanent inmates. Whenever a warden entered the cell, the eldest in the cell had to call in Czech: "Attention!" and after this to report: "Mr. Commandant, the cell has so many inmates, all present, nothing to report!" If one of the inmates did not stand at proper attention, he was promptly slapped.

Several days after our arrival at Karthaus, the inmates of the different cells were exchanged and I was put in another cell together with men from Rumburg. 25 men were packed into a cell, the sleeping accomodation consisted of six palliasses but no blankets. We were troubled more and more by hunger.

The assembling of labour columns began. Trucks and tractors took us to the immense sweet-turnip fields, where we worked on our knees the whole day long, in the scorching heat and without food. The slave-driving overseers and foremen on the farms were especially brutal, and some of us who did not make progress with their work as expected were struck on the back with a hatchet handle. The diet normally consisted of boiled potatoes or a vegetable soup with potatoes in it. We were driven like slaves. Places of work which were dreaded were the "hunger farm" at Detenitz, the farm at Popovic, the tree nursery Mazanek at Jitschin and the bridge building at Železnice. Those who were lucky enough to work for Czech farmers on smaller estates could for once appease their hunger. I may mention here that the Czech smallholders were for the most part humane and treated us well.

One month after another passed, again and again rumours were intentionally spread about, sometimes it was good news, which was always followed by bad; hunger broke us down, we were terribly afflicted with lice, our clothing went to rack and ruin, our shirts literally rotted on our backs and we could already register the first cases of death as a result of complete exhaustion. We were said to be prisoners awaiting trial, but there was never an interrogation at Karthaus. The noticeboard indicated that in August 1945 there were 1,200 prisoners awaiting trial, and there was really no room for more people at Kathaus, as there were also several hundred other prisoners and juvenile delinquents in the convict prison. The need for workers for various sorts of labour increased.

One morning, when we had lined up in the prison yard in order to be distributed for work, a column of men marched out from a wing of the building, which startled us very much. These men were prisoners who were specially marked off, and who had to live for six whole weeks in the case-mates. We had opportunity to talk to them. They lived in cells where water dripped continuously. Four or five to a one-man cell. At night they could only sleep by turns in brief snatches, moreover the cell doors were liable to open at any time, day or night, and brutal warders to enter and deal out blows in all directions. These conditions were ended only when a Russian commission made an investigation. By order of this commission the prisoners had to be put into normal cells. From the same moment the torturing of inmates also ceased. The men were reduced to skeletons and showed black and blue marks on their bodies and faces. A number of them died, but by reason of their greater vitality some survived. The physician in the convict prison showed no interest in us. He was said to have been an inmate of a German concentration camp for many years. According to the talk of the Czechs almost all of them had been in concentration camp, but they all looked strangely well-fed.

We were completely cut off from the outside world and had no contact whatsoever with our relatives. Every day some more of us were buried in shallow graves in the prison graveyard. Once I happened to witness such a burial of one of our comrades; he had been from Warnsdorf. I and another fellow-sufferer had some chores to do in the graveyard; two inmates accompanied by the prison inspector brought a coffin on a cart and carried it to a freshly-dug grave. The coffin lid was lifted, the coffin was tipped over, and the body dropped into the grave. The corpse was dressed only in a torn shirt, since the institution even kept any clothing that was even remotely re-usable.

As far as I know the following persons from Rumburg and its environs died at Karthaus: Hans Keil, municipal inspector, Mehnert, a railroad worker, Klier, bank employee, Anderle, salesman, Reindl, employee of the employment office; as a consequence of the imprisonment at Karthaus there died at Böhmisch Leipa: Otto Münzberg, salesman from Rumburg, Oskar Günther, porter from Rumburg, Möcke from Oberhennersdorf, head clerk of the firm of Schierz, Rus & Co. at Rumburg, Richard Walter from Oberhennersdorf, and many others whom I cannot remember. I believe that I do not exaggerate if I estimate the number of those who died as a result of the tortures endured at 20%. The prisoners came from the following districts: Rumburg, Warnsdorf, Hohenelbe, Niemes and Arnau. The most dreadful days at Karthaus were the holidays and Sundays. At half past ten a.m. we received lunch and dinner together, which was our last meal until Monday morning. A fellow-sufferer, one Aurich from Rumburg, an employee of the *"Deutsche Arbeitsfront"* [German Workmen's Association], had received such injuries that we doubted he would recover. His whole back was, as a result of the beatings, one festering wound. This man had endured a great deal, but thanks to his strong physique his condition improved at Böhmisch Leipa.

During the first days of our imprisonment at Karthaus, we were used for gardening. One of our comrades had probably not yet realized the situation in the convict prison. In the evening, when we were formed up for the roll call, he was missing. The entire garden was searched and the unfortunate man was found hidden behind a berry bush. Together with five cellmates I witnessed his ill-treatment from our window. The man was beaten by four warders and collapsed, then water was poured over him, he regained consciousness and the warders continued the beating. Finally they carried the pitiable man on a stretcher to the sick-room, where he eventually recovered.

There is another case: Tschapsky, a teacher from St. Georgenthal near Warnsdorf, worked for the military department at Jitschin. He received blows and kicks. Tschapsky gave way to the following remark: "Well, our time will come again!" He was beaten up at once and in such a manner that he had to be taken to Karthaus on a wheeled stretcher. But that was not the end of his suffering. He was taken to a special room where he was tortured and abused so badly that he died the following day. He was buried in the prison cemetery. Everybody in the prison behaved brutally towards us, we received blows on the slightest excuse. A warder by the name of Rosenbaum, whom we called "Watschenpeppi" (Peppi the Beater) was extraordinarily brutal. After our work was finished outside the prison, which was always before dusk, we marched in columns in the direction of the prison. In the yard we lined up once more and the warders inspected us for forbidden articles. On this occasion "Watschenpeppi" showed himself a great hero: anyone he disliked was simply punched in the face. One of his slogans was: "You German swine, I like you best two meters under ground."

During our absence they very often visited our cells. What seemed useful to them was stolen. We were not allowed to possess any needle, pencil, knife or similar article.

In September 1945 we were finally permitted to get in touch with our relatives. Later on we received the first parcels from home. What joy when one of the cell inmates received a parcel! Everything was divided up as exactly as possible. But the contents were not enough for a single person, let alone for all the comrades in the cell. However, it was encouraging to have contact with our homes again. Unfortunately there were many among us who could not expect to get anything, since by this time their relatives had already been expelled and we did not know their whereabouts. We were told that in October we would be sent home. And in fact at the end of October and in November, the men from Warnsdorf, Hohenelbe and Arnau were taken away, and finally on December 13, 1945 the happy day had come for those of us from Rumburg and Niemes. We were to be sent to the internment camp at Böhmisch Leipa. We were ordered to line up at 5 o'clock in the morning. Everybody who was at all able to walk got ready. The first one prepared was Otto Münzberg from Rumburg. I myself had about 10 abscesses and was unable to move my head. Münzberg was transported by us in a cart to the station and dragged into a railway carriage. The SNB, who escorted us, consisted of nothing but riffraff. They immediately looked for members of the SS. Our number included several. What these people had to endure from these demons during the transport is unbelievable. Their swollen-up faces and broken ribs showed the result of this maltreatment. Among those who suffered most severely was the son-in-law of the former mayor Herbrich from Niederehrenberg. In the meantime Otto Münzberg had become so exhausted that when we arrived at Böhmisch Leipa our comrade Richard Ritt had to carry him through the town. We reached the internment camp at noontime; Münzberg was immediately admitted to the hospital, but by 2 o'clock in the afternoon he was dead.

Karthaus is a complex of buildings, designed for the Carthusian friars and built by order of General Wallenstein between 1647 and 1654; the penitentiary cells have walls which are 2 to 3 meters thick (7 to 10 ft) and windows far from the floor, which could only be opened with sticks 4 meters long (13 ft). The church of the monastery still exists. We were not allowed to enter the church, because we had lice. The whole complex of buildings was surrounded by walls 4 to 5 meters high (13 to 17 ft). We were also not allowed to go into the courtyard even with our heads covered. Two big statues, representing St. Peter with the key and St. Paul, flanked the main entrance. The sight of prisoners with heavy chains of about 30 kilos (more than 60 pounds) riveted to their legs, who lived in special casemates, was terribly depressing. These men were those criminals who had again and again attempted to escape.

As mentioned above, we reached Böhmisch Leipa on December 13th. There we met our fellow-sufferers from Warnsdorf again and we soon learned that our release was still out of the question. After we had been sufficiently rid of lice, we were lodged. We found that we received a little more food there than at Karthaus, for we had 180 g of bread, more coffee and a better lunch. But for our exhausted bodies it was still not enough. We were unable to recover very much. There was not much work to do and we had the opportunity of getting better medical attendance, since the doctors were imprisoned Sudeten Germans who were familiar with our diseases. Quite a few of us were saved by means of this attendance and I myself cannot adequately express my gratitude for the doctor's sacrifices. However, the Czech camp commander Vebr (Weber), a staff sergeant, will also remain in our memories for ever. This man was always drunken, brutal and inhuman, hated everything German, a slavedriver without scruples, in a word he was downright subhuman. After a while former Czech gendarmerie officials were appointed to the internment camp and began to try and interrogate the inmates. The moment came when many of those imprisoned were released, but many also were severely punished. The hour for my freedom struck on September 6, 1946, since it became clear that no basis for the accusation existed, but all my suffering could have been avoided if a Sudeten German by the name of Johann Kantuzzi, living at Oberhennersdorf in the district of Rumburg, had not caused my imprisonment by completely false allegations.

Karwin

Karwin, Report No. 1
Forced labor in the coal mines
Reported by Dr. Paul Schmolik - Report of August 21, 1946

From early September 1945 until March 10, 1946 I was a prisoner-of-war posted to the labor camp of the L. M. colliery in Karwin. I had to do heavy labor in the coke refinery of the Johann shaft and had to work the entire time in three shifts. There was not a single day of rest. The rations were good but not nearly enough, and as a result I developed fluid in my feet. By the time I was released as invalid, my weight had dropped to 127 pounds (and I am an even 6'0" tall). After I had been released from Russian captivity I was sent directly to Karwin. Therefore I did not have enough clothes or underwear. The camp administration "rented" us pants, camouflage jackets and other items of clothing, and we had to buy wooden shoes. The amount of "rent" charged for letting us use the clothing is still unknown to us, but it was deducted time and again from our monthly pay. The wooden clogs were also charged for, but nonetheless taken from us again on our release. Our shift pay of Kcs 52 - later it was raised to 72 - was noted down, but we never received the accumulated wages in cash, or even their value in camp scrip, and so there was a credit on the books for me on my release, which I have not received to this day.

Our treatment in the camp was very bad. There was no real medical care. The doctor's assessment of our fitness for work was irrelevant, the only opinion that mattered was that of the camp administrator. Frequently, very ill prisoners still had to go to work, and the mortality rate rose. Prisoners of war were mixed indiscriminately with the civilians required to do hard labor. Restrictions imposed on correspondence with our relatives were the order of the day. Writing letters in German was forbidden. After about three months of this rule, we were permitted to send a postcard with a pre-printed message in Czech. In addition to eight-hour night shifts we also had to do unpaid, heavy labor, up to four hours of it at first, particularly unloading wood for the mines, and construction materials. All laborers from all three shifts were quartered in one and the same room, so there was no peace and quite after work. The entire arrangement was like a penal camp, not a labor camp. Corporal punishment with a rubber truncheon, being held under the jet of water from the hydrant in winter, withholding rations and food stamps were common punishments, as was being forced to run laps around the camp. During the time I was in the camp, there was one opportunity to transfer money to one's relatives. The amount that could be transferred was fixed by the administrator. Even though we had money owing to us in the form of a wage credit as described above, neither the prisoners nor their relatives received any money, and so our families were left to go hungry even though their providers performed heavy labor.

As leader of the transport that left Troppau on August 17, 1946 I am in a position to state that the transport commandant and escort units were above reproach. The treatment we received at their hands ranged from proper to accommodating. Also, there were generally no protests regarding the inspection at the customs checkpoint. Regarding the luggage, the members of the transport were quite unequally provided for. Former prisoners of war in particular, who depended on being issued absolutely everything, usually received their clothes and linen from other Germans; these things were old and used, though clean. The majority of the travelers probably exceeded the official 70-kilo limit, but as for the rest, that had neither possessions nor money and was dependent on charity, their luggage did not nearly approach this weight of 70 kg. Like many others, I had 25 kg at most. These people are in no position to make it through the winter safely.

In Troppau the rations provided to the transport were remarkably good. During the trip - particularly in Böhmisch Trübau - the soup, which was all we got, was insufficient. After our arrival at the provisions station in Prague the 60-year-old women Emma Wolf, from Wagon 24, and Olga Simon, from Wagon 15, went into a nearby turnip field to answer the call of nature. For that, one of the guards slapped them about the head. I reported this to the transport commandant, who noted it and promised to report it to his superiors. The duty corporal's conduct towards the women was abusive. The toilet facilities provided for the transport at the way stations must be described as inadequate, and there was also not enough drinking water.

Karwin, Report No. 2
Labor in the mines, abuse
Reported by cert. engineer Brancik - Report of November 4, 1946

On September 2 of last year I was released from Russian captivity, but rearrested by the Czechs and put to forced labor in the coal mine in Karwin. For half a year I had to work night shifts underground in the mine and was then transferred to the construction department. Working conditions in the underground mine were horrible. The German prisoners-of-war were supervised by three Czechs, who constantly went around with their rubber truncheons and mercilessly beat anyone who even so much as straightened his back for a moment. Rations were completely insufficient, even though the camp was being issued hard-labor ration cards for us. Any illness was regarded as a refusal to work, and treated with beatings. One elderly man who was already totally debilitated was measured alive for his coffin, and then shot at with blank cartridges in the basement just to terrorize him. But he was already so apathetic that even this no longer made much of an impression on him. Articles of clothing and shoes were sold to us prisoners, then confiscated from us a short time later and sold to us all over again.

Klattau, Report No. 1

Deportation camp

Reported by Ferdinand Bruxdorfer - Report of 7. 12. 1945

I am a day laborer, was never a member of the Nazi Party or its formations, and was also never a soldier because my eyesight is insufficient. On October 10, 1944 I was drafted into the *Volkssturm* [the German people's last-ditch defense effort, comprised mostly of young boys, old men, invalids etc.], was sent to the Hungarian front, and after the war was over I was released from American captivity in Linz. I had my regular discharge papers. On May 2, 1945 I arrived in Eisenstein, where my parents lived and where I had used to work in Regenhütte in the glass factory. On June 19 the Czechs arrested me for having been a member of the *Volkssturm*. After three days' incarceration in the Eisenstein prison I was transferred to the barracks camp Klattau.

We were housed in barracks, in military bunks, and had to do agricultural labor. Everyone was shorn bald. A big swastika was affixed to the back of my coat, and everyone also had to wear a yellow armband with the letter "N" printed on it. ["N" = *"Nemec"* = "German".]

Already on my arrival in Klattau I was slapped and punched to no end by the Czech guards. I was taken to the so-called "Correction", into a cellar, where they stripped me naked and poured cold water all over me, and then four to five men beat me with bullwhips. I fell unconscious into the water standing 10 cm high on the floor, and when I came to, I was beaten all over again. My hands were fettered with iron chains throughout all this. This procedure was repeated day and night, and was also inflicted on 10- to 12-year-old boys because weapons had allegedly been discovered in their possession.

Even women (among them my acquaintance Luise Jungbeck from Eisenstein) had to strip naked in this chamber. They were shorn bald, and then Czech legionaries also beat them up. However, they were not raped.

Many men could not endure the tortures, and died. Among those personally known to me were the merchant Karl Fuchs and the architect Passauer, both from Eisenstein. They were killed in Klattau in the "Black Tower".

Rations in the camp consisted of 2 kg bread daily for 8 men, plus potato soup twice. We had to work from 5 o'clock in the morning until it was dark again, but we were not allowed to lie down until 10:00 p.m.

A fellow named Schubek who had been with the Gestapo in Vienna was also imprisoned by the Czechs at first, but then he was made a warder and put in charge of the other Germans. He beat us too.

On November 29, 1945 I was released from this camp in which I had never even been interrogated, and, robbed of all my worldly possessions, I went to Germany.

Klattau, Report No. 2
"Correction-cell" at the prison
Reported by Rudolf Payer - Report of June 28, 1946

From May 8th, 1945 to June 6th, 1946 I was imprisoned in the court prison at Klattau. Besides the severe maltreatment, which I had to endure just like all the other prisoners, a special torture was inflicted upon me three times - once in June and twice in July 1945: the so-called "correction".

I was stripped naked, fettered at the wrists and ankles, and thrashed with steel rods covered with leather until I was bleeding all over. If one fainted, one was doused with water and the beating was continued until the men themselves were exhausted. Once they put a pile of wood shavings, soaked with gasoline, between my feet and set fire to it, so that my genitals were singed. I myself helped to carry corpses out of the jail in June and July, among them one Muckenschnabel from Teschenitz, who was said to have committed suicide in the "correction-cell", but in my opinion he had been tortured to death there. Among the bodies was that of the former delegate Zierhut, who died in the prison. The other bodies I was unable to identify. I saw with my own eyes how two young soldiers of 16 and 17 years were shot in the neck by a uniformed Czech, after they had been barbarously ill-used.

Klattau, Report No. 3
Prisoner-of-war camp, maltreatment and murders
Reported by Franz Neumayer - Report of June 28, 1946

While I was a patient in the Annaberg field hospital I fell into Russian captivity, and was released on June 6, 1945. My wound, a grenade shrapnel injury on my left foot, had not yet healed, and is still oozing to this day. In Kladno [Klattau?] the Czechs arrested me and put me into the prisoner-of-war camp there, where I had to stay for 6 weeks, after which time I was sent to work for a farmer. In the prisoner-of-war camp I and my comrades were beaten every day. One of the POWs could only stand hunched over and on two days was repeatedly beaten for that so badly that he died soon afterwards. Another one had dared express doubts about the truthfulness of a speech by President Beneš, which had been broadcast on the radio, and he too was maltreated so badly for it that he died.

Klein-Herrlitz

Shooting of a German farmer's wife on September 1st, 1945
Reported by Martha Kral - Report of June 24, 1946

After having been evacuated I lived with my sister at Klein-Herrlitz, in the district of Freudenthal. At the beginning of July a certain Heinrich Eschig was appointed to my sister's farm as manager. About 10 o'clock in the evening of September 1st somebody knocked at our door. We asked who was there; receiving no answer, we women became frightened and, escaping through the window, took refuge with our neighbour. We could hear the door being broken down; the seamstress, who lived in our house, cried out that she was being beaten. Our children were awakened by the noise and started to cry. We then decided to return to our house. When we entered the door, a shot was fired and my sister dropped down dead. The bullet had pierced her heart. It was the Czech commissar of Klein-Herrlitz, Franz Schimek, who had shot her. He was accompanied by his wife and by Mr. Eschig. When we women cried, he yelled at us. At 1 o'clock in the morning the commissar came back with the gendarmerie and the doctor. Everybody was questioned and our neighbour, Mrs. Güttler, was struck twice in the face. Since that time I have heard nothing more of the matter. Schimek and Eschig are still at Klein-Herrlitz. Several days after these events, the commissar began to spread the rumor that our neighbor's husband, Mr. Rudolf Güttler, had shot my sister. But Rudolf Güttler was only released on September 2nd at Auschwitz from Russian captivity.

Kleinbocken

Looting, murder, rape
Reported by Franz Limpächer - Report of May 11, 1946

I come from the village of Kleinbocken in the district of Tetschen/Elbe. I am a retailer and I owned a store in the place of my birth, dealing in groceries, merceries, corn, coal and building materials, moreover I possessed a farm of 6.55 hectares (16 acres), which I managed myself.

On May 10, 1945 at 9 o'clock in the morning the Polish army marched into our village and with that moment our period of suffering began. The looting, murders and fires lasted for five long days. Women and girls were raped. They stole my valuables, garments, 16,000 kilos of oats, 3,000 kilos of barley, 1,100 kilos of sugar and other goods to the value of 15,000 Marks as well as my Skoda 2½ ton truck. My wife and my daughter, who during this time were both hidden in our neighbour's pig sty, were deprived of all their clothes except the ones they were wearing. On May 14, 1945, at half past ten in the evening, Poles once more broke into my bedroom, put rifle cartridges into the pocket of my shirt, took them out again and maintained that I was a partisan. After that I was hustled downstairs; with my hands up, dressed only in my underwear and subjected to frequent blows with rifle butts, I had to watch for an hour while my own property was looted.

Afterwards the Poles dragged me to a water-tower outside the village, placed me against it and fired at me three times, but missed me; however, a Pole who had been in my employ came up and said that I had always treated him well; this saved my life.

The following days brought forth sporadic robberies and looting by Russians and Poles, accompanied by the raping of defenceless women and girls. In the meantime the only Czech who lived in our village returned home. He was one Stanislaus Mikesch, who in 1938 had married the daughter of my neighbour and who, being a fervent follower of Hitler, had moved to our village in 1939, saying that he could no longer live among Czechs. This man was wearing the ordinary uniform of the German "Todt Organization", but with two Communist stars on the collar of his blouse as well as five tricolor ribbons on uniform and cap. The first thing he said was: "I am now the commissar of the villages of Kleinbocken, Grossbocken and Karlsthal," and everybody had to obey him. He immediately requisitioned all my property, consisting of 2 houses, farm buildings, stores, 2 garages for the cars, a weekend house in the woods and a shed for bees with nine bee hives, furthermore 8 head of cattle and 1 calf, 2 pigs, 15 hens, 32 rabbits and 12 pigeons. The value of the goods in stock at the store - according to the inventory - was fixed at 50,000 Marks, which was only 50% of the real figure. The farm was fully equipped with all sorts of machinery. My wife, my daughter and I were forced to continue to work on the property, without being paid and without enough to eat, and only the circumstance that we had hidden food during the breakdown prevented us from starving. Bands of Czechs from the districts of Prague, Pardubitz and Tabor came into our area and occupied all properties whose owners had either been driven over the border to Saxony or had been put into a camp. Some of the Germans had been sent to the interior parts of Bohemia for employment and had, like me, to work together with their families as slaves, without any wages. Now the Czechs lived riotously on our possessions and we had to do the work. It should be mentioned here that each one of them maintained that he had been in a concentration camp. As it turned out later on, all of them had been previously convicted of theft or other delinquencies, none for political reasons. One had 27 previous convictions for theft. Once a commission came from Prague which stayed overnight at our house; the head of the commission said to me: "It is disgusting to see how these Czechs are behaving."

Also on Sundays we had to work all day long for the community's administration, for example demolishing houses the owners of which had already left and which were not good enough for the Czechs. These things happened under the control of the gendarmerie armed with clubs. On November 24, 1945, those of us who bad been allowed to stay on their property were expelled with only 30 kilos (66 pounds) of luggage within half an hour and checked by the gendarmerie; whatever articles the latter fancied, they took away.

My brother Richard, who had the degree of Doctor of Chemistry and had formerly been the Director of the G. Schicht Works A.G. at Aussig-Schreckenstein, had been in the concentration camp at Aussig since July 1945, without being told why or what for, and his wife, who had studied at the Academy of Fine Arts in Paris, was forced to clean the latrines. Their son of 11 was not permitted to attend school; and his father-in-law, 70 years old, who had formerly been the director of the weaving-mill of Regenhart and Reimann, was also an inmate of the camp at Jauernig.

A cousin of mine, official at the iron-works at Sandau, was in the Czech concentration camp at Böhmisch-Leipa, his wife and their two small children were expelled across the border into Saxony.

I saw with my own eyes how the woman who had been in charge of the local "Frauenschaft" [National Socialist Women's Association] was torn away from her four-year-old child and her hands were fettered, although she had never in her life committed a crime or done anything wrong. Thousands of Sudeten German soldiers who had been released by the Allies on account of illness were sent to the coal mines by the Czechs without even having the opportunity to see their relatives.

Kleinmohrau

Maltreatment of war-disabled ex-servicemen
Reported by Rudolf Klamert - Report of June 24, 1946

I am a war-invalid, and on August 14, 1945 I was arrested in Kleinmohrau and maltreated at the police station for 4 days. The Czechs Chalupa and Kopecký beat me with bullwhips on the bare soles of my feet until I lost consciousness. Then they poured water over me, and beat me all over again. When I said that I had a head injury from the war, one of the Czechs punched me in the head and knocked my head into the wall. After 4 days I was put into the concentration camp Freudenthal, into solitary confinement. On my arrival, a certain Jarosch gave me 25 lashes with a bullwhip. My friend Rudolf Beck was so badly beaten in this camp that he had open wounds on his back, and then needles were shoved under his fingernails and his fingertips were burned with lit cigarettes. He too was a war-invalid, who had been shot through the lung. On September 10 of last year we were transferred to the Olmütz prison, where we were also beaten daily. I spent 8 weeks there. Until November 23 I was still in the Olmütz labor camp, where I was put to hard physical labor until a medical exam certified me unfit for work, at which time I was released.

Klösterle and Kaaden

Maltreatment of young people
Reported by Josef Jugl, forestry official

On the evening before Whitsun 1945 a friend warned me that my arrest was imminent. To avoid it, I fled the same day to relatives living nearby in the *Erzgebirge* [Ore Mountains]. But already the next day, on Whitsun, my mother came to see me and told me that my father had been arrested by the Czechs, as hostage, and that he would be shot if I did not surrender myself voluntarily. With that trick they got me into their power. On the way home Mother told me how it had all happened. Since the Czechs didn't find me, they took Father instead. He had just been doing gardening chores when the Czechs arrived. Since he was only wearing a shirt and trousers he wanted to quickly put on a jacket, but he wasn't allowed to do even that. Amid crude curses they yanked the radio from its place and shoved it at my father to carry. My grandparents, who begged for mercy for my father, were pushed around and threatened that they too would be arrested. After the Czechs had once more threatened that my father would be shot if I did not turn myself in, they left the house. I arrived at home on Whitsun evening. Since curfew had arrived by that time, I decided to report the next day. I did so on Monday morning. At the *"Národní Výbor,"* where I reported, I was briefly searched by Czechs who had been employed as civilian workers in my home town during the war. They took various items from me, such as my wallet, ID papers etc. Then they took me into the basement of City Hall, where I was locked into a cell. One of the guards admonished me not to commit suicide, since that would be cowardly, as he put it. The cell was small and contained only a few things. Off to one side there lay an old straw pallet, and a few benches were piled up opposite it. In the corner behind the door stood a bucket that still contained my predecessor's excrements.

The time passed incredibly slowly, and minutes turned to hours. Since I could hear the City Hall clock strike I always knew what time it was. After about two hours, keys rattled outside the door and the bolts were pushed back. Two men in green uniforms entered, making a great deal of noise. Since they spoke not a word of German I couldn't make any sense of their yelling. In the assumption that they had come to take me to an interrogation, I headed for the door. That very instant they yanked me back, dragged my hands up and began beating me with leather belts. They also feigned that they would shoot me; barely had they left, when renewed stomping and rattling announced more visitors. This time it was an entire group of men, who regarded me hatefully. One tall, broad-shouldered man was particularly conspicuous in this group. He was the one who began the following interrogation. I had to answer his questions with lightning speed; as soon as I hesitated even for a second he swung his leather whip. I was not allowed to give explanations of any kind, so that I could mostly say only yes or no. I was accused of having been a werewolf, even though not a single shot had been fired by civilians anywhere in our entire region. With horrible threats he tried to force me to make a confession, but as yet I still had the strength to resist these accusations.

This is the only way that, for example, instructors from the Hitler Youth Organization's *Bann* Education Camp in Kaaden could have been made to testify that they had actually trained the students in their educational programs to be werewolves. This resulted in many totally innocent boys being arrested and put to great suffering. One method that the Czechs favored was to play one prisoner against the other. If they were willing to make accusations against each other, they got off more easily, but woe to any of them who dared deny the Czech allegations. For example, Mr. Otto Hammerschmidt from the Zuflucht suburb of Klösterle was badly maltreated because he had declared that I was innocent.

But now back into the cell. After the interrogation had failed to bring the desired result despite all attempts at intimidation, they broke it off, after telling me that I would be taken to the main prison in Kaaden. Again, hours passed. In the evening the Czechs even gave me a bag with food and a blanket that my parents had sent. Hardly had I finished eating before the guards returned to pick up the bag. They rummaged through it and noted that there was no knife among the cutlery. I tried to make them understand that my parents had not included a knife, but they wouldn't believe it and so they searched the entire cell. Since they absolutely could not find anything, I was searched again. They took almost everything I had, even my little pocket comb. When I asked them to at least let me keep the comb, they gave it back to me with the remark that I'd better not use it to scratch through my carotid artery. Before they left the cell they urged me to simply confess to everything when I was interrogated again. When I told them that I had nothing to confess, they took on a threatening demeanor. When this made me so upset that I had to throw up, the Czechs finally left.

I was left in peace during the night, and was also not harassed very much the following forenoon. But there was no food or drink to be had. I wasn't hungry anyway, but all the more thirsty. Around noon they got me from my cell. I had to keep my hands raised as they herded me, with blows from cudgels, to the market square, where I had to get on a vehicle loaded with loot. Aside from myself and many Czech soldiers there was also another German on this vehicle. Since it seemed that not everything was ready yet, we had some time to take a last look at our town. Suddenly, in the distance, I saw my sister approaching to bring me some food. But the Czechs did not let her near the vehicle, so that she had to make her way home again, mission unaccomplished. Later she told me that the Czechs had turned her away with the words, "he's not getting any slop for a while." Hours passed before the vehicle drove off. In Meretitz the ride was again interrupted, and we two Germans were taken into the former "Sumag" where we were again interrogated. My compatriot was fortunate - he was let go. As for me, they tried again to intimidate me with threats, but when that did not succeed I was put back onto the vehicle, which now drove on in the direction of Kaaden. But this had by no means been the last stop; we stopped outside almost every house along the road. The soldiers rushed in and looted to their hearts' content. They were especially eager to appropriate any alcohol they could lay their hands on. The result was that soon they were in the midst of a great booze fest. The soldier sitting to my right kept dropping a box containing some items he had looted, and since I helped him pick it up he grew increasingly friendly towards me. He asked me how old I was and why I had been arrested. Half way between Klösterle and Kaaden he advised me to jump off the truck and run for it. I hesitated, suspecting a trap. But he said to me: "Kaaden prison bad, you still young". Now I was convinced of his honest intent, and there was no stopping me; in only a few minutes the sheltering forest had taken me in. In Kaaden they waited for me in vain. Later I found out from acquaintances that my name had repeatedly been read out at roll call in the Kaaden prison, of course without anyone answering.

It would have been extremely dangerous to hide out at home, and so I decided to seek shelter with some acquaintances. Then, when house searches became more and more frequent, I could not hide there any longer either. So I went into the woods. One day the Czechs observed my 15-year-old cousin carrying food into the woods. This resulted in his being arrested, right along with my uncle. Since my cousin remained steadfast despite all abuse and stuck to his story of just having taken some food to a man who was returning home from abroad, they were ultimately released again, but from that time on they had to report to the *Národní výbor* every day. With that, the time of suffering had come for them as well, since beatings were the order of the day there. So now I could no longer stay in my homeland without endangering all those who helped me. On July 10, 1945 I managed to cross the border, after having been shot at by a Czech patrol only the day before.

Kohling, Schindelwald and Schönlind

Maltreatment, executions
Reported by Karl Sandner - Report of December 5, 1945

In Kohling and Schindelwald, two towns in Neudek District of the Sudetengau, ten men were shot after the unconditional surrender of the German Reich. These men were arrested by the Czechs, and maltreated. They were beaten bloody. In one case a picture of Hitler had been found in a closet when the man in question was arrested, and the Czechs forced him to eat it [the photo]. The ten men were arrested on a Monday (I no longer recall the exact date) in Schönlind, Neudek District, and were to be taken to Neudek on Tuesday. In the truck, which was manned all round by Czechs, they had to lie on their stomachs so that the townspeople wouldn't see how they were being maltreated. On the way to Neudek a Czech motorcyclist came towards us and issued different orders. They drove back to Schönlind again, and that same evening they had to dig their own graves. Wednesday morning, around 5 or 6 o'clock, they were shot after all. Their kin were forbidden to visit the grave, and were chased away by the Czechs standing guard there.

Kojetitz

Slave labor on farm
Reported by: Erna Zicha - Report of June 26, 1946

My son and I were arrested in Prague on May 9, 1945 and imprisoned first in a movie theater and then in a school. On June 4 - a day on which my son was so badly beaten that his back was bleeding - we were sent to Kojetitz, near Prague, to work on the estate of one Mr. Vávra. 104 Germans, primarily women and children, were forced to work there.

Our treatment was very bad. Even though many people fell ill, there was no medical care for us. In the beginning, an average of two people died each week of debilitation or due to the lack of medical care. Children died of diphtheria, and there was no care for them either.

We had only those clothes that we had worn at our arrest, and due to the hard work to which we were put they quickly wore out, and were not replaced. The poorly-dressed people had to work on the estate even in sub-zero temperatures. I had to load manure onto a cart and spread it on the field in -26° C [-15° F] weather, without gloves and in shoes so torn that my toes stuck out. At work many were beaten with a stick by the administrator. Miss Elfriede Schulz from Berlin, who had been raped and was now pregnant, was beaten on the lower back with a pitch fork. Mr. and Mrs.

Diehl were beaten so badly by the farmer Melwal that they turned to the police for help, which they were denied.

I have a severe heart condition, but nonetheless I had to do hard labor for 10 hours every day. Despite the hard work our rations consisted only of two cups of unsweetened black coffee, some watery soup, and 125 g [4½ oz.] bread per day. By October our number had been reduced to about 90 - the others had died. We were housed in a shed, and later in small rooms of 9 sq.m. [97 sq.ft.] for groups of 8 of us. Even in winter we received no blankets, nor was there any heating. We barely had the means to wash. All winter long, men and women alike had to wash at the outdoor pump in the square. There was also no warm water or tubs for doing laundry. As a result everyone had lice, and many got scabies, abscesses etc. There were people who were literally being eaten alive by worms and lice.

One almost 70-year-old woman who was totally debilitated and could no longer even get up was taken by the Czechs and laid onto an open cart in the yard, where she died miserably.

My husband had been in Russian captivity and had lost three fingers on his right hand in an accident in the mill where he had to work, and as a result the Russians had released him, but the Czechs imprisoned him in Brünn-Zidenice, Malá klaidovka, and refused all requests for his release even when I was being resettled [expelled].

Kolin

Kolin, Report No. 1
Labor camp Kolin, maltreatment
Reported by Ernst Hahn - Report of August 29, 1946

In June 1945 I and another 200 or so people from Neudek District, all between the ages of 13 and 80 years, were assigned by the Neudek Employment Office to a 3-week harvesting job in Kolin. From Neudek we were transported off in railway carriages, with normal occupancy. The train also included a carriage with Czech guard personnel. When we passed the American zone checkpoint in Chodau the transport was stopped by the Americans. The guards had vanished. In Komotau the guards, who had by then reappeared, chased us out of the carriages and penned us into two freight cars secured with barbed wire. That's where the maltreatment began. Clothes, linen and watches were all taken from us. When we were unloaded in Kolin the civilian population threw stones at us, spat at us, cursed and kicked us, and the guards not only tolerated this but even joined in. Systematic torture began in the internment camp Kolin. Confessions were to be extorted from us. Especially the children were threatened with pistols and with red-hot nails until they gave the desired statements. They were forced to write farewell letters to their parents and were totally worn down in every respect. One man was hung overnight from the eaves trough by his hands, which were tied behind his back, and then beaten to death the following day. Another man, Flasche by name, who was from West Germany and had been evacuated to Neudek, died a similarly horrible death. His genitals were kicked to a pulp.

Rations were so poor that everyone had dropsy, and legs bursting open was a common occurrence. There were several deaths each day, the consequence of malnutrition and maltreatment. Nonetheless we were forced with rifle butts and rubber truncheons, steel cables, whips etc. to do hard labor. Many collapsed and died while at work. After a temporary and barely noticeable improvement in late fall, the unbearable conditions resumed even worse at Christmas and went on for months. In May I was suddenly declared to be a prisoner of war, and was transferred to a different camp. I can take this statement on my oath.

Kolin, Report No. 2
Internment camp, maltreatment
Reported by Anton Kragl - Report of June 27, 1946

I was ordered to compulsory labour service for a whole year in the camp at Kolin. At first the camp had almost 700 inmates, among them juveniles aged 13 and up. The food was so bad that many developed swollen legs and open sores. Nevertheless they had to work and were often struck with fists or rifle butts. About ten men died of malnutrition. No wages were paid. Among the inmates were men with five children, who had been taken away from their families. They could not send money home, as they earned nothing. Everything, including clothing, was taken away from us on our arrival. Our work clothes had to be sent from home. When we were released we did not get back the things which had been taken from us. About 140 men were still in the camp when I was released on June 9th, 1946.

Komoschau

Inhuman brutality of a Czech farmer in February 1946
Reported by Antonia Stanek - Report of June 26, 1946

I was employed as agricultural laborer with a Czech innkeeper and farmer in Komoschau near Prague. One evening in February of this year, while listening to the Czech news on the radio, I commented that one need not believe everything one hears. At that, my employer's wife jumped up and said that I had no say in anything at all, that they had seen just by looking at my son that he had a large fortune on him and that he had surely stolen it. I asked her what she knew of my son. She replied that my son was buried on this farm and that her husband had wanted to tell me from the start. I asked her why they had killed him. I was told: "Because he was a German, and we have the right to kill any German we want to." The next morning the farmer said to me: "If we had known how indispensable you would become to us, we would have kept him to work for us as well." His mother then told me that a German had been beaten to death in the farmyard last August.

Königinhof

Maltreatment and murder in 1945
Reported by Julius Herrmann - Report of June 28, 1950

At the time of the German surrender I was in Königinhof a. E. with my life partner, Ernestine Merthen, and on Whit Sunday evening we were both arrested there for no reason whatsoever. To start, I want to stress that we were never Party members. We had barely entered the prison before the abuse began. We were sent in groups to work, and the very next day I and several comrades were sent to the cemetery where we had to dig graves for the murdered victims. Our work was made very much harder by the stony soil. The rabble all around us howled and cheered and we were not allowed to rest for even a second, since otherwise the people would immediately call the guard, who came with his submachine gun and beat the prisoners down. Comrade Hetfleisch, accountant with the company Staffa, was working on the grave next to mine. I saw how he was beaten to the ground with a rifle butt. His murderer screamed in Czech: "You German swine, get up!" When he gave no signs of life, water was dumped on him, but since even that did not help he was simply thrown into one of the finished graves, where other victims already lay.

In the evening, after we had returned to prison from this hard labor, we got some black coffee. By that time the morsel of bread which we were given had usually been eaten long ago, for all we got for the entire day was 200 g bread. At noon there was only a bowl of soup. Barely had we finished our coffee in the evening when we were ordered to "Line up!" Standing facing the wall in the hallway outside our cell, we awaited the things to come. Now we were ordered into the yard. We had to run until we could not go on, and then we were beaten senseless.

One day we had to carry logs, 36 to 43 feet long and about a foot in diameter, across the Elbe bridge. There were two of us per log, one in front and one behind. My shoulders were bleeding, but next day we had to do the same work again. Despite my objections, that I could not possibly do this kind of work, I was punched and hit. The flesh on my shoulders was crushed and hung off my bones, but it was not until the next day that I was freed from this painful labor and was assigned an easier task. Once, I and one of my comrades-in-suffering also had to carry a heavy trunk down two flights of stairs. The thug ordered us to "Run!" But since this was impossible, the monster screamed at us and beat us with his riding crop until we had loaded the trunk into the car. Bruises suffused with blood all over our bodies attested to the maltreatment.

Ernestine Merthen was accused of having brought food to SS men. Since this was only a pretext for tormenting and harassing her, she was chased into the yard on Whitsun morning, where seven thugs put their revolvers to her head and demanded that she confess. But since she declared that she was innocent, they said, well, then we'll go into the cellar. Once there, she was threatened that if she did not admit the charge, Russians would arrive within five minutes. But none came, and after a short time she was let out again. About 14 days afterwards, the thugs entered her cell around midnight to fetch her and her companion, Mrs. Lukas, and locked both of them into the cellar. Mrs. Lukas was put into the second cellar, where she received 25 lashes with a five-sectioned leather belt. Ernestine herself got away with three lashes. Then they were threatened that if they did not keep quiet about what had been done to them, they would have breathed their last.

A short time after that she was once again fetched around midnight. This time she had to strip naked in the cellar. Despite much begging and pleading she was hosed down from top to bottom with cold water, and a few days later this was repeated again. After the doctor diagnosed a severe heart condition and bronchitis, she was freed from these tortures. Many of her female comrades suffered the same fate. She had been completely healthy before all this, but thanks to the maltreatment the Czechs inflicted on her she is now an invalid at age 50, since the bronchitis gave rise to a severe asthma.

I also want to mention that we were freed from these torments after 10 weeks, and were sent to the camp from where we were transported off [expelled] after two days. At the border crossing to Bad Schandau the Czech financial inspectors searched us thoroughly once more, and with very few exceptions everything we still had was taken from us.

Königshof

Iron-works at Königshof, labour groups
Reported by engineer Ernst Deinl - Report of August 25, 1946

On October 5th, along with about 100 other persons from the district of Mies, I was employed at the ironworks in Königshof via the employment bureau. When we arrived at Königshof, the armed militia attached to the works took us over and kept us like prisoners behind barbed wire. We spent ten months there. 200 to 225 men were lodged in a single room of 20 x 10 x 3.5 meters (about 65 x 32 x 11 ft.). The food ration was so small that we would have been unable to do the hard work without the additional supplies sent by our families. In spite of this the camp drew the ration cards for heavy workers. There was practically no medical attendance, for, by order of the camp commander, no doctor was admitted to the camp; and even if a certificate of incapacity for work had been issued, the commandant would not have accepted it. Correspondence was reduced to such an extent that over a period of ten months only two post cards from my relatives were delivered to me. Packages containing food were looted regularly. We worked 8 hours per day and had to fulfil a certain quota of work; in addition we were worked up to a further 8 hours (unloading of coals, shipping of ore etc.). Although we were not considered to be internees, we received only two "Kronen" as our daily wage. We were paid neither for working on Sundays and holidays nor for our overtime. 14-year-old juveniles were employed on the same terms. They also worked in the night shift every third week. Corporal punishment was officially introduced and became customary. The same conditions obtained for the prisoners of war, who shared our quarters and worked together with us. On our arrival we had to hand over knives, razors and razor blades, money etc., and most of these things have never been returned. American discharge papers as well as identity cards were also never returned.

Krautenwalde

Severe maltreatment of a Social Democrat by the gendarmerie
Reported by Richard Stanke - Report of October 6, 1946

I have always belonged to the Socialist Labour Party and have never been a member of the NSDAP. In May 1945 I received a card proving my membership of the Social Democrats, issued by the party headquarters. In July 1945 a gendarme stopped me on the street, demanding my party membership card. I refused to show it, as in my opinion he had no right to demand it. He then took me to the gendarmerie and maltreated me severely. He struck me repeatedly, 6 to 8 times, on the head with great violence, pulled the membership card out of my pocket and tore it to pieces. I had a swollen head and swollen eyes for 14 days.

Kremsier

Rapes
Reported by M. S. - Report of August 26, 1950

In 1939 I took the children who were under my care (I am a kindergarten teacher) on a field trip, and on this trip we sang German songs. An adolescent Czech who happened to pass by objected to this, cursed us, and deliberately tripped the children. I told the young Czech that I would tell his mother about his behavior. Another Czech was watching these events. In 1945 this second fellow reported me to the police. From 1942 until 1945 I had been assigned as Red Cross nurse to the train station service in Kremsier. On May 5, 1945 Czechs arrested me there and threw me into a cell in the Kremsier Court.

In this cell there were 30 other people, including women and their children. Every night we were awakened five times, and the first few times we were also looted and robbed of our possessions. Every morning at 6 o'clock a Czech gendarme showed up and led us all out into the prison square, where the women and children had to line up on the left, the men on the right. After a despicable ritual of beatings we were herded off, despite the pain, to forced labor. Our rations consisted of 50 grams [1¾ oz.] bread per day, a cup of black coffee in the mornings and evenings, and at noon some watery soup that was distributed from pig-slop buckets. First we women had to clean the barracks and carry the furniture out of the upper stories. While I was working on this, a Russian led me away, saying "Your last hour has come," and presented me to a Czech officer. The two of them argued over me with the Czech prison commandant, and I was then handed over to the *Národní výbor*. On that day I was imprisoned again, and they shaved me bald and painted a large swastika on my bare back with oil paint. Then I and other imprisoned women were sent out to work on the fields, every day and regardless of how hot it was (we were forbidden to cover our heads or to receive water to drink while working). We were called "German sow", German whore" etc. In the cell we had to sleep on the hard floor. After the harvest and field work were finished I had to do hard labor for an entire year, first as a mason, then in a brickworks.

When my strength gave out and I repeatedly fainted while at work, I was assigned to clean a school instead. Then I was taken to the People's Tribunal in Hungarian Hradisch, where I was sentenced to five years imprisonment as per §3 (having sung German songs in 1939, etc.). The Czech judge's defense, namely that I had only tried to protect the children under my care from being attacked, was rejected by the People's Tribunal - with the reason that Germans have no right to defense.

I fell ill, with pleurisy and constant heart spasms. For these reasons I was put to lighter manual work, like sewing.

I did these lighter jobs for three years, and I would like to mention that even in winter I had to do them in an unheated room, so that I sustained frostbite on both my hands. Then I was ordered to work in a laundry storage room. We women were raped at all times of the day, our shirts simply torn off our bodies. We had to comply immediately, as the slightest hesitation was physically helped along, to the words, "How long are you going to take?" I would rather not go into detail about what kinds of bestial sex offenses took place, which the German women had to submit to with silent revulsion (it was no exception for the men to force their privates into our mouths etc.).

While I was working in this laundry storage room I was informed that I was to appear in a Prague court as witness. I was taken to Prague, and there to Pankratz to be interrogated, and I had to testify to the rations and treatment of the inmates in the prisons. 14 days after this interrogation I was transferred to Reichenberg, from there to Jitschin into the prison, and from there to Semil for forced labor. In Semil I had to work for a year in a spinning mill, side by side with hardened criminals.

A dispatch arrived from Reichenberg: "convicted in error" - and so I was released from Semil on May 5, 1950, but only two hours later members of the SNB arrested me again and kept me in "preventive detention" until May 27, 1950. On May 27, 1950 I was released, and found myself on the street without any civil rights and with only the clothes on my back. The International Red Cross took me in as a living corpse, emaciated and exhausted, and placed me in a recovery home in Teplitz-Schönau, from where I was able to set out on August 5, 1950 to go to my stepmother in Bavaria. My brother had to raise 2,000 Kc for me for the trip.

I also want to mention that the imprisoned women (in the Kremsier prison) had to line up every evening in the prison square, where the Russians looked them over, chose "you, and you, and you", etc., and dragged them off into the cellar to rape them. Afterwards these victims were thrown back into the cell, and always the same ones were taken back again after every three days for the same purpose. My friend T. was raped 30 times in a single night.

In the mornings the imprisoned German women, men and children had to line up and shout in unison: "We are reporting for work and request payment in advance." This payment consisted in the most horrible abuse and maltreatment. Then the tormented victims had to call out, "Thank you for our payment!" There was one 80-year-old man who had been so maltreated that he could no longer sit. He begged on his knees, with clasped hands, for a rope with which to hang himself, and we were not allowed so much as to give him a drink of water.

In 1945 children who had been in the Hitler Youth had to go out at night and dig up the bodies of Russians who had fallen in battle and been buried in the vicinity, and then had to rebury them in a cemetery.

Kunzendorf

Administrator Matonoha of Boskowitz, looting
Reported by Josef Zeche - Report of September 26, 1946

Since November 1945 my farming estate in Kunzendorf near Moravian Trübau had been in the charge of the Czech administrator Franz Matonoha from Boskowitz. He not only tormented my family in the most inhumane manner, but also harassed the entire village. My wife was paralyzed due to a spinal injury, but he showed her no consideration at all. He badly maltreated my daughter when my son had escaped from the Moravian Trübau concentration camp. He raged at us for every little thing, and held us responsible for everything he felt went wrong. He conducted inspections and searches of all the houses and stole everything he liked in the process. When we were to be resettled [expelled] he kept back our best things and made us make do with old and worthless items.

Kurim

Kurim, Report No. 1
Prisoner-of-war camp
Reported by Dr. Kurt Zamsch - Report of June 23, 1946

On October 6, 1945 I returned to my home in Moravian Schönberg from Russian captivity, where I had been released for health reasons (permanent unfitness for work due to malnutrition, body weight of 54 kg [119 lbs] even though I am 184 cm [6'] tall, and fluid in both legs). On my arrival in Brünn on November 4 I was detained by the Czechs and taken to the Czech prisoner-of-war camp Kurim. There, too, I was declared unfit for work, but nonetheless I repeatedly had to help bring in firewood. That meant a day's march of 24 km [15 miles] while carrying heavy loads. It surpassed my strength, and once (on January 14) I collapsed while doing this work. I was then urged on with blows from canes and had to march the rest of the way to our destination, albeit without being loaded down.

In the camp, beatings were the official mode of punishment, and every minor thing was punished with beatings so that the prisoners were totally bullied. Our rations were comparatively generous (800 ccm/3 cups thin barley soup and 500 g/1 lb bread per day), but entirely without salt or fat.

The Kurim camp had been opened in early October 1945 and by the time I left it in February 1946 there had been 750 recorded deaths, at an average camp population of 2,500. In February I was sent to the recuperation camp Kutiny. The rations were the same, but the treatment we got was considerably better. There was no corporal punishment there, and we were not obliged to do hard labor. Within three months, 75 of the 1,000 men there had died. Most of the inmates had contracted their disabilities in the coal mines or in the Batta factories in Zlin.

Kurim, Report No. 2
Camp, report of the camp physician
Reported by Dr. Alfred Schenk - Report of August 18, 1946

I was released from Russian captivity at the end of October; on my return I was arrested by the Czechs at Brünn and appointed as surgeon to the "recreation camp" at Kurim. In this capacity I had the opportunity to observe the hygienic and sanitary conditions particularly in this camp from November 1945 to March 1946. 600 inmates of the camp died of malnutrition during this period. Germans who had been sent from Zlin to Kurim were physically nothing but wrecks, of whom 50% died. During winter there was such a small quantity of fuel at the camp's disposal that not even the rooms for medical attendance could be heated. Soap for cleaning the bodies of the sick or for laundry purposes was not available. Tuberculosis broke out in the camp and 200 of my patients were affected. In spite of their weak condition the inmates of the labour barrack were forced to work and were often ill-treated by the guards when they could not accomplish their quota as a result of their physical state. While under arrest, numerous prisoners contracted frozen limbs which necessitated amputation. Corporal punishment was officially introduced; as a result of this I had cases of bruising which required attention for weeks. As to prisoners arriving from Zlin, the medical treatment given was so improper that it quite often resulted in complications (amputation of fingers, cases of blood-poisoning, thromboses, gangrene). Even for the sick the food consisted almost only of barley without meat, prepared without fat or salt, so that a recovery of those dangerously ill was rendered impossible.

Landskron

The Massacre on May 17, 1945
Reported by Julius Friedel - Report of February 22, 1951

On May 9, 1945 the last combat on the hills above the valley at Landskron began.

The invading Russians did not pay much attention to the frightened German population during the first days. They looked for alcohol, they plundered and they organized regular hunts for women at night. All night long one could hear the cries of the hunted victims.

At first the few Czech residents did not know themselves what to do, they were also worried about their possessions.

The German male inhabitants of the town, who had had to work at clearing the streets, were suddenly sent home, without reason, in the morning hours of May 17th.

About 11 o'clock of the very same day hundreds of armed Czechs, so-called partisans, arrived in trucks. They gathered in the market-place for a demonstration; a Russian officer made a fervent speech, which was greeted with roars of approval. As if by previous agreement, the Czechs then dispersed in all directions. It was not long before we knew what was going on.

The German men, and with them many women and children, were driven in larger or smaller groups to the market-place, the houses were thoroughly searched to insure that all men were present, old and young, also invalids and those seriously ill. The individual groups of Germans were escorted by yelling Czechs, heavily armed, who shot blindly in all directions and knocked down anyone who came in their way. Meanwhile other troops of Czechs drove to the surrounding villages and brought the men back to the town. More than a thousand German men were rounded up in the market place in the early hours of the afternoon. They were ordered to fall in and they stood there with their hands above their head, waiting for what would happen next.

There followed the most horrifying scenes that human beings ever conceived of. The men were forced to lie down on the pavement, to stand up quickly und then to get in line again. The Czechs passed down the lines and kicked the men, preferably on the shins or in the genitals. They hit them with whatever lay convenient to their hands; they spit at them and fired wildly with their rifles.

Many men were too badly wounded to get up again and lay in great pain. But this was still not enough. There was a large water tank for air raids in front of the town hall. Into this the victims of this terrible madness were finally thrown one after the other. As they came to the surface, they were struck at with sticks and poles and kept under water. The Czechs even shot into the mass and the water slowly reddened. Whenever anyone tried to scramble out of the tank, they stamped on his fingers; some of the men were fished out of the water, but they were already dead. Others, who were prostrate on the ground, were blasted with the fire hose, which had been fetched in the meantime, or were tortured in indescribable ways. While all these atrocities were taking place, the so-called People's Court established itself on the sidewalk in front of the district council building. Behind the tables which had been set up the Czechs seated themselves; among them were the following persons:

Hrabaček, owner of a sawmill at Weipertsdorf,

Wilhelm **Pfitzner,** clerk to the workmen's sick-fund, Landskron,

Franz **Matschat,** weaver in the firm of Thoma, Magdalenen St., Landskron,

Bernard **Wanitschek,** shoemaker, Karl St., Landskron,

Stefan **Matschat,** weaver in the firm of Thoma, Landskron,

Friedrich **Bednař,** carpenter for the tobacco-factory, Landskron,

Polak, officer of the gendarmerie, and a woman, probably

Mrs. **Lossner** of Landskron.

Around the table stood a number of Czechs, who functioned as prosecutors and who selected the individual Germans out of the rows. One behind the other, with their hands above the head, the Germans had to appear before the tribunal. The first man in each row had to carry a picture of Hitler; the picture was covered with excrement, which the man beside him had to lick off. The last 20 or 30 paces up to the tribunal had to be covered in a creeping position. Arriving there, each one of them received his sentence, which was written on his back with a piece of chalk. About 50 to 60 meters (165 to 200 ft) distant from the tribunal, on the opposite side, was a gate; up to this the victims had literally to run the gauntlet. Many of them collapsed on their way, even before the sentence could be carried out. The brutality which took place there is impossible to write down.

One of the first victims was Karl Piffl, a master joiner. After he had been selected, driven into the water and dragged out of it again half dead, he was beaten to death and trampled to pulp.

He was followed by the overseer of the firm of Pam at Landskron, a man by the name of Reichstädter, who had already been so badly beaten up that he was unrecognizable. Nevertheless he was stood against the wall of the town hall and shot to death by the Czechs with their automatic pistols. Josef Neugebauer, an engineer from Landskron, came running out of the little street which led to the prison. He was covered with blood. He, too, had to stand against the wall with his hands raised, and fell without a word before the bullets of his executioners. Another engineer, Otto Dietrich from Landskron, met his death in a similar manner. Viktor Benesch, a farmer, ended his life at the same place, with the top of his head shot off.

The cries of the bleeding victims soon downed out all other sounds; many of the living sat or lay with the indifference of despair beside the bodies of the dead. At 7 o'clock in the evening the majority of the men who had been rounded up were taken into custody; only a few were sent home.

On May 18th the victims were again driven together in the market place and the tortures and the brutal mistreatment were continued. Josef Jurenka from Angerstrasse, Landskron, a plumber, was sentenced to death by hanging. He was strung up on a street lamp after he himself had had to place the noose around his neck.

Robert Schwab from Ober-Johnsdorf, an employee of the district administration, died in the same manner. The Germans were forced to keep the bodies of the hanged men constantly swinging.

One Mr. Köhler from Landskron, an engineer of Reichs-German origin, was dragged in, dressed only in his leather shorts; these were like a red flag to the howling mob, who impaled him on their metal-pointed sticks.

On the same day dreadful scenes, even worse than on the day before, took place. A number of Germans were ordered to undress, to put on a show of prize fighting and beat each other up.

Terrible screams sounded all day long across the usually quiet marketplace. About 5 o'clock in the afternoon the excesses suddenly came to an end as a result of the sacrifice of Mrs. Auguste Heider. Her place of business was immediately behind the 'People's Court' which had been set up, and probably she had been watching from her attic the atrocities taking place close by. She decided to make a desperate end of it all by setting her house on fire and hanging herself in the flames. The conflagration caused a sudden panic and set an unexpectedly early end to the Czechs' amusements.

In front of the town hall, at the place where the executions ordered by the People's Court had taken place, the Germans lay in a great pool of blood, some shot down, some felled and literally trampled beyond recognition. The victims included the following:

1. Viktor **Benesch,** farmer and deputy *Ortsbauernführer* (Chairman of the local farmers' association), leader of the Association of Veterans of the First World War,
2. Josef **Neugebauer,** engineer and architect,
3. Otto **Dieterich,** engineer and architect,
4. Köhler, engineer and works-manager,
5. Leo **Janisch,** director of the employment office,
6. Karl **Langer,** clerk of the employment office,
7. Josef **Langer,** clerk of the employment office,
8. Karl **Kowarsch,** butcher, shot by his assistant,
9. Theodor **Benesch,** Director of the Forestry Administration, retired,
10. Rudolf **Gerth,** sergeant,
11. Hubert **Lug,** farmer from Lukau,
12. Johann **Klement,** electrician,
13. Reinhold **Schwab,** manufacturer of cement products,
14. Karl **Schmidt,** tinsmith,
15. Josef **Jurenka,** locksmith,
16. Robert **Schwab,** official of the district administration,
17. Richard **Antl,** farmer from Rudelsdorf,
18. Marek, railway man,
19. Josef **Koblischke,** teacher, retired,
20. Karl **Piffl,** master joiner,
21. Leopold **Hafler,** workman,
22. Julius **Reichstätter,** clerk,

23. Josef **Linhart,** farmer from Lukau,
24. Zandler, farmer from Rudelsdorf.

The bodies of these victims of mob justice remained lying there until May 19th. On the late afternoon of that day Eduard Neugebauer, a farmer from Anger Strasse, Landskron, was ordered to take them to the cemetery. The doctor who inspected the corpses - a German, but one whose behaviour placed him beyond the pale for the rest of the Germans from Landskron - reported that he had been unable to identify the men tortured to death. They were dumped without any ceremony into a mass grave.

Small wonder that many Germans committed suicide in consequence of these horrors.

Among the suicides the following can be named with certainty:

Auguste **Heider,** widow of a salesman, market-place,

Eduard **Maresch,** draper, together with his wife, Magdalenen St.,

Hubert **Richter,** shoemaker, together with his wife, Magdalenen St.,

Wenzel **Riedel,** retired gendarmerie-sergeant, Magdalenen St.,

Hans **Waschitschek,** popular lecturer, together with his wife, Badgasse,

Killer, farmer, Anger St.,

Karl **Janisch,** gardener, Friedhof St.,

Josef **Jandejsek,** tax-collector, retired, together with his wife, H. Knirsch-St.,

Otto **Portele,** shoemaker, market-place,

Wenzel **Kusebauch,** retired major, together with his wife, Anger St.,

Gerlinde **Knapek,** née Ringl, market-place,

Anna **Piffl,** née Schreiber, widow, together with her daughter Ingunde **Ilgner** and her little baby, Knirsch St.,

Dr. Franz **Pelzl** and his wife, Mathilde Pelzl, née Nagl, Johannesgasse,

Richard **Rotter** and one of his children,

Karl **Langer,** official of the municipal council, Schulplatz,

Viktor **Schromm,** road surveyor,

all of Landskron.

In most of the villages these days passed in the same way. Further cases of suicide are known of from the following villages:

Hilbetten: more than 60 persons, among them the doctor of the village, in whose house many sought death;

Türpes: the wife of the mayor, one Mrs. Schmidt, shot her children and then herself;

Ziegenfuss: the hereditary judge by the name of Franz Hübl shot his family of eight persons, only his father, who was 80 years of age, remained alive;

Rudelsdorf: a large number of people committed suicide;

Abtsdorf: the owner of an estate, Heinz Peschke, committed suicide together with his wife and his son, as did Max Wilder, the mayor, together with his wife and their three children.

A number of murders also took place. In the village of **Triebitz** Julius Klaschka, a farmer, and at **Sichelsdorf** Franz Kaupe, another farmer, were both shot down, and in **Tschenkowitz** there were also several persons shot.

Dr. Franz Nagl, who had been mayor successively of Landskron and Leitmeritz, was murdered at **Königgrätz.** The Czech shoemaker by the name of Janeček from **Hermanitz** showed special brutality. Later, when in jail, he boasted of having killed 18 German soldiers, who were walking through the woods unarmed, by shooting them from ambush.

At the same time Germans who were capable of working were formed into groups and handed over to the Russians, who shipped them off to the Soviet Union. Many of them never lived to return home after months or even years of hardship.

Other Czechs of the administration, who took part in the outrages against Germans, in robberies and looting, criminals definitely responsible for what took place, are the following: The two mayors of the town, Losser and Heil, as well as Zidlik, Vaguer, Dr. Řehák, Wanitschek, Kudlaček and Pfitzner, who were town councillors, and Dr. Skala, the Chairman, and a certain Vodička. I should like to stress especially the names of Hrabaček, the owner of the saw-mill, and Polak, an officer of the gendarmerie. Hrabaček later fled from Gottwald's Czechoslovakia via Germany to France, where he is today working as an agricultural labourer. Polak's destiny was also not a glorious one.

I affirm in lieu of oath that the foregoing statements are in correspondence with the truth.

Langenlutsch

Murder of a war invalid
Reported by Aloisia Ille - Report of September 26, 1946

My son had been badly injured in the war, his leg was amputated, and he was blind on one eye. His injury occurred in October 1943. As an invalid he was employed as clerk in the office for registration of the army at Zwittau and later on he trained the *"Volkssturm"* [sort of last reserve, comprising all men capable of bearing arms] at Türnau. On June 2, 1945 he was arrested by the Czechs, and on June 3, 1945 he was already dead, according to a notice from the mortuary, stating that he had been buried on June 4. I myself heard of his death only 4 weeks later and I still have no death certificate. An eyewitness, one Hlawatsch from Langenlutsch, told me that he had seen my son being dreadfully knocked about. He had also seen him lying in the mortuary.

Woman maltreated
Reported by Herta Kaiser - Report of November 4, 1946

I was supervisor at a Mothers' Rest Home in Liblin near Pilsen. On May 5th of last year the *Národní Výbor* informed me that the guests of the Rest Home would be transported off by the International Red Cross. On May 8 I and another woman and two men were arrested and tied by our hands to a car that drove to Kralowitz, fast enough that we had to run to keep up. A Czech bicyclist drove alongside us and spurred us on with a whip. On the Kralowitz market square we were handed over to the civilians there for maltreatment. We were punched in the face and about the head, and spat on. After eight days I was sent to work in a coal mine, and had to stay there for seven months, sleeping in a hay shed on the bare earth floor. I was the only woman there, and had to transport materials with a wheelbarrow, and later I had to do the cooking. On January 3rd of this year I was sentenced to 8 years imprisonment for having been the supervisor at the abovementioned rest home. The indictment did not specify any particular transgression on my part. For five months I was detained in the Women's Prison Repy, where we were treated very maliciously. Then I was sent to the labor camp of an artificial silk factory in Theresienthal, where I was suddenly the only one to be resettled [expelled], quite contrary to my expectations. I have none of my possessions left at all. In Jitschin, before being resettled [expelled], I was issued some old clothes and underthings that are barely usable.

75-year-old man abused, July 12, 1945
Reported by Josef, Adele und Elfriede Pomps

[Josef Pomps:] First of all I want to state that I, the undersigned, was not a member of either the National Socialist Party nor of any of its branches. My home town is Libochowan on the Elbe, District Leitmeritz, in the Sudetengau.

When I had to endure the maltreatment in question, I was 75 years old. On July 12, 1945 I was ordered by the Czech teacher Schwarz to report to the Czech school, where he confronted me with the community chronicle, which I had had to record until 1938. One passage discussing the teacher Schwarz's public incitement provided the excuse for three Czechs who were present to rain slaps and punches on me from all sides, to the point where my glasses shattered. As a consequence of the blows, I stumbled and fell, and came to lie on the floor; here all three men had at me with their boot heels, then yanked me back to my feet by my hair and ears, and beat me over and over again until

I was bloody. Then the Czech teacher wiped the blood from my face, and I staggered to the door, where I encountered my two daughters.

[Adele Pomps:] I, Adele Pomps, born on February 17, 1907, and my sister Elfriede, born on September 8, 1911, both of us resident in Libochowan, were also lured into the kindergarten of the former Czech school by the henchman Franz Dorant. We didn't suspect a thing, but when we entered the anteroom, our 75-year-old father was just being let out. Blood was running down his face. I asked what had been done to him - he was wiping the blood from his face - but he wasn't allowed to answer me.

He was permitted to go home. The doors closed behind us, and my sister and I were taken into the kindergarten room. The Czech teacher Schwarz said: "I'm going to read you what that old man wrote in the community chronicle." (The Czech teacher Karl Schwarz had often been a rabble-rouser.) One sentence stated: "The warriors' memorial was to be torn down, because the inscription on it read, 'Remember the brave ones, even if they fought in vain'." I had to return to the anteroom, while they dealt with my sister Elfriede first. I heard her screaming horribly, and my fear grew and grew. Then Schwarz came out. That monster no doubt thought that I would be trying to escape. But it wasn't possible. I begged Schwarz to shoot me rather than beat me like that, but he said: "No, you've still got to work!"

Now it was my turn. Just then they were trying to force my sister's mouth open. She was screaming like an animal with pain. With kicks and punches to my face, the same gangster who had maltreated my sister now greeted me as well. They only ever called us "whores and swine". In front of a bench about a foot long, Karl Dorant and Ladio beat me with a rubber truncheon and a rubber whip with many little straps to the point where I collapsed. Now I lay on the bench, and some fellows 20 to 22 years of age pulled my pants down and beat me until I fell off the bench. This was done repeatedly; and when those two criminals had grown tired, they were relieved by one Rudolf and a man who had taken over Breitfelder's grocery store. It was dreadful to have to endure all this. Schwarz only walked up and down laughing at the spectacle.

Now I stood beside my sister. The Czech street guard punched us in the face. Our hair was totally disheveled. The fellow who had taken Breitfelder's business gave us his comb, and we had to neaten ourselves. The people were not to see what these criminal had done to us. Everyone roared at us like lions. Karl Dorant stood in front of us holding a rifle, and pounded us on the feet with it, with the comment that if we told anyone outside what they had done to us we would get a bullet through the head.

Now we could go. At his words I made the mistake of placing my hand over my heart and shaking my head very slightly. At that, we had to go back and got the same beating all over again. This time the street guard held our heads between his legs. We got the comb again and had to neaten ourselves again. Once more we were threatened with the rifle. Now we were allowed to leave.

The people on the street looked at us as though they had turned to stone; they knew what had happened, for even in the street they had heard us scream. From our lower back to halfway down our legs we looked like a dark blue sheet, the color of blueberries. I'd be lying if I said there was a white spot even the size of a pin head to be seen on us there. I showed it all to Dr. Schmidt in Praskowitz. He called his wife to look, and both of them were speechless. He took down my statement, and I had to let him treat me.

My sister showed her injuries to Dr. Gintner from Schreckenstein. He too called his wife in. They wrung their hands and said that they had never seen anything like it, ever. I showed my injuries to many acquaintances, as I wanted to have witnesses for this atrocity. I also showed them to Czechs, and told my story over and over again. Mr. Husak from Raudnitz said, "it makes one ashamed to be Czech."

Mr. Swoboda from Libochowan called us to come to his neighbor, Mrs. Marie Finger, where we had to tell and show him everything. When he had seen the state we were in, he tore off his armband from the *Národní výbor,* threw it on my friend's manure pile and said, "I don't want to work with such criminals any more."

The one thing we don't understand is why we were beaten like that, since neither of us had written a word in the community chronicle. When they beat their other victims, they had turned the radio up to maximum volume to drown out the screams.

This is the whole truth and nothing but the truth, and I, my sister and my father are willing to swear to it at any time.

Liebenau

Execution threatened, handed over to the Russians
Reported by Oskar Tiel - Report of March 5, 1951

I was to be executed in Liebenau. I stood against the wall without a blindfold, and ten feet from me stood a firing squad from the Czech militia. They were waiting for the command to "fire". But they did not shoot, as instead two men beat me until I almost lost consciousness. Then I had to take my shirt off, and when they failed to find an SS tattoo they announced that they would beat me green, blue and bloody and get rid of me in the woods. But on the way there, the Czechs began to quarrel amongst themselves. Then their leader said that I should be handed over to the Russians, to be sent to work in Siberia. And that is what happened.

Liebesdorf

German shot at on the street
Reported by Grüner - Report of July 24, 1946

I am a railroadman. On November 27, 1945 I travelled from Liebesdorf to Oberhaid to look for work there. I had a permit to do so. On the way I was challenged just outside the town of Zartlersdorf. When I stopped, several shots rang out. One of them hit me in the knee. At the edge of the woods about 30 paces away, 12 Czech soldiers lay and shot at me. When I fell to the ground, they came over and kicked and cursed me. Then they left me lying there. The next passer-by found me unconscious, took me to Zartlersdorf and notified my family. I then had to spend two months in the care of Dr. Fuchs of Rosenberg, who treated me. I had to pay the cost of the treatment myself. A report made to the Czech authorities and the gendarmerie was totally useless. To this day I have not regained full use of my leg.

Liebeznice

Murder of 318 German soldiers on May 9, 1945

Reported by Ludwig Breyer - Report of January 29, 1951

For the "Schwere-Granatwerfer-Abteilung No 534" (Division No 534, heavy grenade-throwers), which was on garrison in the area of Zittau/Saxony, as well as for all German soldiers, the hostilities were over when the armistice was announced. On May 1945, about 11 o'clock at night - the division lay at Wetzwalde near Zittau - we heard the news of the capitulation. The division received the last command: to march off in the direction of Brüx-Karlsbad. At midnight, led by a young master-sergeant, 375 men marched in a truck column via Deutsch-Gabel and Böhmisch Leipa to the bridge of Melnik. The heavy guns and the ammunition had been destroyed and the troop was only in possession of small-arms for self-defense.

We only intended to get in touch with the Americans, and stood on the left side of the Elbe River, opposite to Melnik; there we met with the first Czechs.

Among them was also a Czech major, who talked like a soldier to soldiers, a comrade to comrades. He urged the Germans to lay down the arms which they were still carrying. The young master-sergeant accepted the major's word. He decided that the arms should be surrendered and these were assembled in a nearby barn.

This master-sergeant, who has since returned from Russian imprisonment, declared: "Had I ever suspected what would follow, we should never have laid down our arms and the tragedy of Liebeznice would never have happened."

What then happened was the following: the defenceless soldiers were ordered to group themselves in lines of five and to link arms with one another, and between 2 and 4 o'clock in the afternoon the soldiers marched along the main road from Melnik in the direction of Prague, escorted by partisans. 200 or 300 meters before they reached Liebeznice the entire platoon was ordered to halt.

In the meantime the partisans from Melnik had been relieved by others during the march and the major was no longer mentioned. Everything which the German soldiers still had in their possession was now thrown into the ditch, their last belongings, their last personal possessions. All they had was the uniform they stood up in. The order was given: "Hands-up! On the double through the village!"

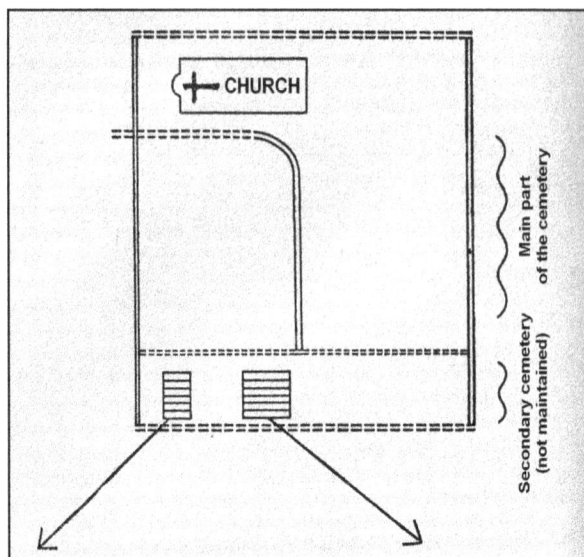

Grave of German forced labourers from Prague, who had died of hunger or had been tortured to death and who had been interned at the village of Bast, 2 kilometers distant from Liebeznice.

Mass grave with a flat surface, overgrown by woods, in which 318 German soldiers of the Division No. 534, garrisoned at Zwickau/Saxony, had been buried. On May 9, 1945, that is already after armistice, these soldiers were treacherously murdered by the inhabitants of the village of Liebeznice.

The master-sergeant has also reported what followed: "We had scarcely approached the first houses when shooting started from the doors and windows with all kinds of weapons. Everybody tried to save himself and to escape. Unfortunately only a few were able to do so. After all was over, our dead and wounded comrades lay about the street. The wounded were then shot through the neck. I was one of the 57 men who escaped from death, but we were soon recaptured by the Czechs. We were then transported to Prague."

318 German soldiers met their death. It was a Czech major who helped to capture the 57 survivors and who confirmed the suspicion of the German master-sergeant that not all of the 318 men had been killed immediately, but that a number of the wounded had been murdered by shots through the neck.

This statement also shows that Czech troops had been present at the massacre in Liebeznice. "I heard the revolver shots myself," added the German master-sergeant.

Germans from Prague, who later on were sent to Liebeznice as forced labourers, found the bloody uniforms of the German soldiers in the barns. These victims had not only been treacherously shot down, they had been buried naked in the cemetery of Liebeznice.

Littau

Maltreatment in the camp

Reported by Franz Mauder - Report of August 26, 1950

In March 1945, as the German Wehrmacht retreated, the Waffen-SS burned the town of Javoricka. The Czech partisans who followed on the Wehrmacht's heels herded the German inhabitants of the area together and penned them into the forester's lodge and Castle Busau, where they were murdered. The children were driven into the cellars of the rental houses there, and shot in those rooms. The murderers then dumped the jam that was being stored there, over the corpses of the children.

In the German linguistic enclaves of Wachtel and Brodek the German inhabitants were herded into the malt factory of Littau, which had been converted into an internment camp, where they were subjected to dreadful brutalities.

Everyone who was taken there first received the so-called baptism. They were beaten on their bare upper body and feet until they passed out. After they came to again, the victims were compelled to do forced labor, regardless of the injuries they had suffered.

Every morning at 6 o'clock, 36 Germans had to stand in the factory square, facing the wall, and then these people were beaten until they were bloody. Among these victims was the old former Austrian first lieutenant Fiedler, who was in so much pain that he lost control over his bowels. With incredibly brutal maltreatment, the Czech Commandants Vycidal and Nakladal forced the German prisoner standing next to Fiedler to eat the excrement, and made sure that he took big mouthfuls. Among the victims, of which I was one, it was common to be spat at, or that the Czech guards would spit on the ground before us. We Germans would then have to lick the spit off the ground.

Every night the partisans demanded women and girls from the Women's Section, and the Czech constable Grulich would select and deliver them. These victims had to stay two or three days, some of them as long as eight days, and were raped up to fifteen times per night by these hordes. The majority of these women were later diagnosed with venereal diseases.

Lyssa

Women severely maltreated

Reported by Hermine Henkel - Report of October 6, 1946

On October 16 of last year, my sister and I were taken from our home by the Commissar and a gendarme in order to do forced labor in the Czech region, for allegedly 4 to 6 weeks. We had to leave the house within 15 minutes and were allowed to take only the barest necessities. I begged the

Commissar to leave us at home, as we had enough work at home with the cultivation of our 4,000 square meter garden, and also went out to work. At that, both of us - aged 57 and 60 years - were badly maltreated by the Czechs. They punched us in the face and kicked us in the abdomen.

I sustained internal injuries from this abuse. For months my right side was swollen, and I threw up blood. After beating us they dragged us from the house by our hair, and herded us to the train station. Soon thereafter, a gendarme totally looted our house.

For nine months we had to work in a tree nursery in Lyssa, near Prag, and we were constantly threatened with pistols and whips.

Mährisch Rothwasser

Maltreatment
Reported by Oskar Minarsch - Report of October 13, 1946

On May 19, I and many of my comrades were herded together in Moravian Rothwasser, and taken to the barracks for punishment. I simply cannot describe how the Czech partisans carried on here. Several of my comrades were beaten to death. Where I myself am concerned, I was punched in the face many times, and forced to eat part of a portrait of Hitler. But on my arraignment the *Výbor* (chairman Kopa) released me as being innocent.

Ever since then I have lived in constant fear of more persecution. My entire house was looted, so that my family was left with nothing but the clothes on their backs. I had to beg for the barest necessities.

On August 21, 1945 I was taken from field work to the concentration camp in Moravian Schildberg. From there, I was sent to the camp in Hohenstadt (the Old Castle). After a three-days' stay there, I and several of my comrades were sent to the penal institution in Mürau.

In late September I was assigned to the paper factory of Lukawetz for hard labor. I had to work here until January 6, 1946, for very poor rations. I was not beaten here. From January 6 until mid-April I was in the concentration camp Heilendorf, near Hohenstadt. There was little work to be done there, but in return the rations were also very poor, especially at first. I was not beaten here, as I had not belonged to any NS organization.

After that I was in the labor camp of Hohenstadt until early May. Discipline was very strict here. One time, when I had smoked without permission, I was beaten so badly that I collapsed. I was not personally maltreated any more beyond that. But I did contract severe rheumatism in my shoulder joints, and I suffer from it to this day. On July 4, 1946 my family and I were resettled [expelled].

Mährisch Trübau

Maltreatment in the internment camp
Reported by Franz Wolf - Report of June 14, 1946

I was arrested in October 1945 and sent to the internment camp of Moravian Trübau. On my arrest I was boxed about the head. After three days I was released on my employer's request.

On February 2, 1946 I was again arrested, and again sent to the internment camp of Moravian Trübau. I and the other inmates were badly maltreated in this camp. At various times throughout the night, drunken gendarmes came and made us line up in front of our pallets, and interrogated us as to what NS organization we had belonged to. With every question they would punch us in the head, the face and all over our body, so that soon we were all disfigured. Everyone who was bleeding or bruised was then locked into the cellar so that no-one would see it.

In his despair at this maltreatment, my comrade Knorre from Kunzendorf hung himself in the washroom. Many of my comrades lost their hearing.

I had to spend 3 months in this camp in Moravian Trübau. These beatings extended over period of about 8 weeks. Then (in early April), after an interned Czech also hanged himself in despair, the abuse stopped. In early May I was transferred to the labor camp in Moravan Trübau, where conditions were better.

Rations in the internment camp were totally inadequate. Per day we only got one bowl of watery soup and two thin slices of bread. In early June I was transferred to the resettlement [expulsion] camp.

Malschin

Presbytery broken into
Reported by Johann Hutter - Report of November 2, 1946

Between the 12th and 18th [of August] this year the presbytery of Malschin was broken into and a large sum of money, 18,230 Czech crowns, was stolen. Being an anti-Fascist, I was permitted to frequent the public inn, where on August 14 I met the Czech Commissar Hoschek who came running in great excitement from the presbytery over to the inn and sat down beside me. When I asked him why he was so excited he declared that he had made a good catch in the presbytery. Four hundred-crown-bills fell out of his pants pockets, which were stuffed full of money, as were both his jacket pockets.

Next Sunday in church I found out about the break-in from the curate's public announcement, and I told him that I probably knew who had done it, and told him of my encounter with the

Commissar. He said that he had already suspected that the Commissar was the thief, since nobody else had access to the presbytery, but that it couldn't be proved and therefore nothing could be done. He would have preferred if I hadn't said anything about it. I did not try to do anything about it myself, as I know that a German's report is worthless and that the gendarmerie and the Commissar are in cahoots. The Commissar knew that I knew all about the incident, and was repeatedly heard to declare that the only one he was afraid of was Hutter. In early October he confiscated my anti-Fascist ID card, with the comment that the Kaplitz office had demanded it. But he did not give me a receipt for it when I asked for one.

Maschau

4 family members murdered
Reported by Rosa König - Report of June 10, 194[6]

In 1945 alone four members of my family lost their lives to the Czechs. In June 1945 [my husband's?] parents, Bruno König, retired senior audit counselor, born in 1865 and resident in Jauernig in the eastern Sudetenland, and his wife Emma König, born in 1867, were evicted from their home without any of their possessions at all and herded all the way to Chemnitz in Saxony, where they both died within 8 days of each other and were buried in a mass grave. A sister, Anna Fieber, born in 1887, was taken from her home in Kaaden/Eger by partisans in June 1945 and was dead by the very next day. [My?] brother Anton Totzauer, born in 1896, a farmer in Webeschau near Teplitz-Schönau, was tortured to death in May 1945 and dumped into a shallow grave on a depot site. As for ourselves, within half an hour on June 29, 1945 we were totally looted and evicted from our home in Maschau, Podersam District, and driven out along with other townspeople (including the Dean and a paralyzed woman), treated like criminals, and herded together in barns until our entire wretched group was expelled across the border, under military escort.

Meierhöfen

Luggage inspection in deportation camp
Reported by Hans Feigl - Report of August 29, 1946

As internee of the concentration camp Neurohlau I was posted to the resettlement [expulsion] camp Meierhöfen, near Karlsbad, from January 25 until August 20, 1946 and during this time I attended all of the luggage inspections that took place there for resettlement transports. The inspectors were usually drunk, and carried out their inspections in an entirely arbitrary, rough and brutal manner. They distributed the expellees' better-quality possessions amongst themselves. They took any valuable linen and clothing from the expellees, even if the latter had not even attained the luggage weight that was officially permitted. With rough treatment the expellees were so intimidated that they usually did not dare object, and if the occasional one did protest to the camp commandant he usually did nothing about it. Several young inspectors targeted especially older people standing off to the side, inspected their luggage and usually looted it. Also, the inspections were carried out so roughly that many things were damaged. Watches, even if they were not gold, were without exception taken from their rightful owners. No assistance was given to the expellees in loading their luggage onto the vehicles for transport [expulsion], so that old people and women with children had to stow away their own baggage.

Melnik

German post-war prisoners put to work as farm laborers
Reported by Elfriede Mattausch - Report of June 7, 1946

To this day more than 5,000 Germans from District Melnik are still being detained as agricultural laborers, as "German post-war prisoners". Work times are usually 16 hours a day, including Sundays. The Germans have to see to their own rations with their food stamp cards, that provide for only 290 g [9¼ oz.] fat [per month] and no meat at all. Only in summer were they given an additional 560 g [18 oz.] meat per month. Most farmers do not pay at all for the work they receive. The Germans lived in wretched holes, in old shacks, without water, light, toilet or anywhere to cook. The treatment they received was inhuman. Obscene curses and horrible threats serve to destroy the people psychologically. The children are neglected since their mothers are left no time to take care of them. There was no medical care in cases of illness. There was a public health service, but thanks to the inhumane treatment the Germans were so intimidated that no-one dared go to see a doctor, as the farmers for whom they must work threaten to send anyone who falls ill to a concentration camp. In the neighboring town of Straschnitz, one farmer beat all the Germans, even women and girls, with his riding crop because they had not reported for work exactly at 6 o'clock in the morning.

I myself lived under these conditions for ten months in Simorsch, District Melnik on the Elbe. The circumstance that my father was put on a resettlement [expulsion] transport in Asch is what I have to thank for the fact that I and my two little children, my mother and sister got away from there at all.

My family and I had to spend five days in the resettlement camp. The rations were unfit for human consumption. 500 people were quartered in one room and there was no place for the children to sleep.

During luggage inspection the inspectors simply took anything and everything they liked, and kept it for themselves.

Mies, Report No. 1

Forced labor in Tschaslau, Knezice/East Bohemia, Stoky (Stecken) near Havlickuv Brod 1945-1947

Reported by Dr. Wilhelm Weschta - Report of August 2, 1950

I was a professor at the *Obergymnasium* [High School] in Mies since 1922. I wish to report that I and my family, my wife and three children, were imprisoned for fully three years and forced to do hard labor. Despite repeated requests we were not informed why we had been arrested or why we had to do forced labor.

In early June 1945 all teachers, professors and students of the educational institutions of Mies - everyone aged 12 to 60 - were conscripted into forced labor for ten days on the Malesice estate near Pilsen. On my return I was not personally harmed, but the *poroucik* (lieutenant) Hala had moved into my house. On June 24, in the course of a general house search carried out from house to house jointly with American occupation forces, my house was searched as well.

On June 27, in other words three days after the house search, the younger of the two gendarmes came to my home and asked me to report to the gendarmerie in order to sign a statement confirming that nothing incriminating had been found on my premises. I immediately complied with this request, and after I had left the house I noticed that two other gendarmes armed with rubber truncheons and carbines were following us. In the Egergasse [Street] I made to turn off in the direction of the gendarmerie, but the gendarme accompanying me ordered me to keep going. At the entrance to Ring Square we turned towards City Hall, and I saw that the other two gendarmes were close behind us. When we had arrived outside City Hall the gendarme walking beside me hit me in the right shoulder.

Meanwhile the other two gendarmes had unlocked the front door. Then I was beaten so badly with rubber truncheons and blows from rifle butts that I was unable to even get up for a while. When they began kicking me I managed to get to my feet, and since the prison guard was absent I was handed over to the military guard standing outside the cell block. After the prison guard returned I was locked into Cell 2 on the left-hand side of the square. Many farmers from Lingau, Leiter and Oschelin were already locked up there. In the evening of the same day the retired teacher Steinbach from Mies and I were taken by a military guard to the forced labor camp (so-called internment camp) at the train station in Mies. Both of us were driven forward with incessant kicks and blows with cudgels. Between 7 and 8 o'clock in the evening we arrived in the camp, utterly exhausted. We had to report for registration in the building behind the camp entrance. The director of the camp, F. M. from Mies, and the camp administrator Kristofovec, who previously had been a baker's assistant in Mies, sat there. After I had been interrogated, M. turned to administrator Kristofovec and said: "That's the scoundrel who defiled the Czech colors." (M., laborer in Mies, could not speak Czech at all.) Kristofovec jumped up, seized his rubber truncheon, leaped at Steinbach, and there was a cracking sound. The first blow had hit Steinbach full-force across the neck and right on the back of his head. Steinbach sagged down. I had to pick him up, as Kristofovec kept beating him. After a while, when he had recovered a little, I had to lead him out. I informed the camp "Kapo" briefly of what had happened, and we were assigned to Barrack 4. We were refused any blankets for the night. The fellow prisoners of Barrack 4 helped both of us as best they could. The barracks were locked at night. If anyone needed to go outside, the *"straz"* (guards) had to be called first. Then the barracks were unlocked and a few men were let out. On one such occasion the teacher Steinbach, who had suffered brain damage from his beating and was totally confused, got out unnoticed. But he could not find his way back, was picked up by a guard, beaten again and locked into an empty goat shed. The next morning the old man was dragged out, carried into the Sick Room and handed over to the orderly there. He did not regain consciousness. A few days later his son came with a cart to take him home to die.

I had to remain in the concentration camp Mies until August 27, 1945. We had to go to work every day. Once, I and my former classmate Karl Haala, recently a teacher in Gibian, had to go to work in the High School that was now occupied my the military. Since they knew that I had taught at that same institution, and that Haala was a teacher in Gibian, they forced us to clean out the cesspit. To the crowd's amusement I was shoved into the cesspit, and Karl Haala had to collect snot and phlegm from the onlookers. Then he was hit on the back of his hands, so that the entire mess ran over his face and jacket.

We also had to work in the former Naschau Factory, where I had to clean toilets. I recognized my radio standing beside one of the toilets. In the evenings the guards always made their rounds and meted out punishment. This was usually done while we had to stand facing the "Wailing Wall". Often the older people collapsed, and then the torments were ended a little earlier. Or we had to leap around the square like frogs. One day a transport of mostly young men arrived from Wiesengrund-Dobrzan. These fellows had been beaten so badly that their welts had filled with pus and had to be lanced by the physician, Dr. Moravan. These men could not sleep at all for the first several days.

On August 27, 1945, at 4 o'clock in the morning, 60 men including myself were led off to the train station. A train already stood there holding our family members, more than 1,000 people in all, old, invalid, frail people etc. The train moved out and drove towards Prague, via Pilsen. At the zone border the transport was stopped by the Americans because ill and frail old people were among the passengers. The train was switched, and we were left to stand in the marshaling yard in Chrast near Pilsen for two days. Despite the oppressive August heat we were forbidden to fetch water. The little children cried because they got neither milk nor water. And then we were sent back again to Tuschkau. Some people were taken off the transport there by the Americans, and then our trip went on, via Prague to Tschaslau in Eastern Bohemia, where we arrived after four days without food or water, and were put to work on farms.

Knezice near Ronov, 18 km east of Tschaslau

My family - my wife, our six-year-old daughter, two boys aged 10 and 14, and I - were assigned to work for the *statkar* (estate owner) Josef Sedivý in Knezice No. 21. I was used as horse groom, my wife as maid for 48 head of cattle, and my 14-year-old son as stableboy for the oxen. We were not paid anything at all for our labor until November 1, 1945, after that 2 Kc. per day until June 1, and then the minimum wage for unskilled laborers, with total disregard for all the overtime and Sundays. In return, we had to pay out 20% of our so-called wages to the Resettlement Fund, 10% to the Town Council *(místní národní výbor)*, as well as all social welfare contributions. We were quartered in a miserable, vermin-infested barrack that contained neither a heating system nor even one piece of furniture. We were denied any pots or pans, and any washing facilities at all. All we got was a bit of straw to lie on. We had to see to our own rations. We only got what was provided for by the food-stamp cards for Germans, and a few potatoes from the feed cellar.

Under these conditions we had to perform the hardest kinds of work from sunrise until late at night. Neither Sundays nor holidays were time off for us, and we were beaten for even the slightest reason. At noon we had at most an hour to ourselves, and during that time we also had to buy and prepare our meal since we got off work so late at night that all the stores were long closed. My 14-year-old son had to carry the heaviest sacks, 70 kilos and even more. He was beaten just like all the other men and women. At first we were not allowed to see a physician for anything at all.

We were not resettled [expelled], but instead were sent right back to forced labor in the concentration camp Stecken. Two of the guards were constantly drunk. They were the farmer Slanina and the *dratenik* (wire binder[?]) Lanka. Both of them liked to beat the inmates when they were drunk.

It also happened that drunk men came into the camp and abused the women. For months we got nothing to eat but bitter, black coffee and some potato soup at noon, weekdays and Sundays alike. During the entire winter we lived in the barracks that consisted of nothing but bare walls, but we did not get the least bit of fuel to heat with.

The farmer for whom I had to work told me specifically that he had had to give Slanina 200 Kcs and a bottle of rum so that he could have me. It goes without saying that we were used for the meanest, dirtiest jobs. There was an unbelievable number of bedbugs in the barracks. Entire braids of them hung in the wooden bed frames or from the cracks in the boards. When the weather was warmer most men slept outside the barrack, in a meadow, or on the table or the floor. The camp physician's and our requests for disinfectants and insecticides were in vain.

On March 10, 1947 I was sent to the farmer Ferdinand Palan in Spinohy, near Vetrné Jenikov. Treatment there was very bad. I was beaten for asking to see a doctor, after I had had a high fever for several days. From the moment I could no longer work, I got nothing more to eat. Chickens and a young pig were let into the room where I slept.

Mies, Report No. 2
Shootings in the camp
Reported by Helmut Kommer - Report of December 27, 1945

On November 27th, 1945, I was taken to the camp at Mies together with my parents Karl and Lina Kommer; my father was a butcher in the town of Mies. On the same day about 1500 persons were brought to this camp. After three days, during which we received almost no food, 25 inmates were shot on November 30, 1945 at 4 o'clock in the afternoon, only about a hundred yards away from the camp. I was myself able to observe these shootings. The reasons for them are unknown to me. Among the persons shot were my parents and also two other persons, who were known to me as customers of our store, one by the name of Hans Sturba, about 50 years of age, a pensioner, who had been living in Mies, and a certain Frau Morger, about 20 years old, also residing in Mies. The other persons were not known to me.

The shootings were carried out by Czech soldiers. Afterwards 10 persons from the camp, including myself, were commanded to bury the corpses. I was thus able to determine that among the persons shot were 18 men and 7 women.

On December 1st, 1945, I fled from the camp during the night and reached Bayreuth via Marienbad-Asch-Rehau-Kulmbach.

I herewith declare that the statements made are in accordance with the truth.

Mies, Report No. 3
Starvation-related typhus at Bory
Reported by Irmgard Görner - Report of December 6, 1945

I had finished high school and lived in Mies, where I was employed by the Americans. My father, director of the glass works, was imprisoned by the Czechs at the beginning of June and taken to the convict prison in Bory near Pilsen.

We ascertained almost nothing of his fate. Only later we succeeded in sending small packages to him, for we knew that he must be in great need of food. We sent him 16 parcels in all. When he finally was able to send us a letter on August 15th, he acknowledged the receipt of only four parcels. The others had not been delivered to him.

On October 26th, one of the parcels we had sent was returned to us, marked "zemřel" (deceased). Thereupon I left for Bory on November 7th, in order to secure information as to my father's fate. The doorkeeper of the convict prison shouted at me and declared that nobody could enter or leave the prison, as illness had broken out. It was an epidemic of starvation-related typhus, the victims of which included almost all of the German inmates. Czechs residing in the neighbourhood of the prison told me (I myself speak Czech fluently) that in the course of a single day about 350 corpses had been transported out of the prison.

The Czechs entered our apartment at 4 o'clock in the morning on November 30th and ordered me and my 63-year-old mother to dress ourselves and to follow them, taking only hand luggage. We had to march to the railway station of Mies, which caused my mother great suffering since she has a serious heart condition. At the station of Mies many tables had been set up, at which typists sat. The German men, women and children were chosen by Czech farmers according to their physique, and recruited as labourers. Families were separated ruthlessly, the children crying for their mothers. My own mother was not wanted by anybody, because she was too old and not sufficiently robust.

She therefore was permitted to go home again. I myself was able to escape in an unwatched moment and to reach Germany with the assistance of American soldiers who took pity on me.

Mies, Report No. 4

Mies and Horní Počernice: Denial of medical assistance to a child

Reported by Margarethe Singhartl - Report of June 26, 1946

I was picked up together with my 3-year-old child at my apartment at Wasseraujesd in the district of Mies on October 3rd, 1945 and sent to labour to the Koschtir estate near Prague, at Horní Počernice. First I lived together with fourteen other people, then alone with my baby in a damp room, the windows of which were without glass. I scarcely had the opportunity to take care of the child. I was often forced to take the child with me into the fields and there, in the fog, to leave it on the bare ground. The baby became ill. First it got scabies. As a former nurse I was able to treat the child myself. Afterwards the child got exanthema on the head and finally diphteria.

I had to walk for half an hour to the doctor on icy roads with the feverish child in my arms; the doctor sent us to the hospital in Prague. In the Karlov Hospital the child received an injection. From there they sent me to the Bulowka Hospital. When I reached this hospital, medical assistance was denied to me, since the doctors were forbidden to attend German patients. They let me stand there with the child in my arms for 2½ hours until the child died. The dead child remained in the hospital.

Mies, Report No. 5

Internment camp, luggage inspection in deportation camp Mies

Reported by Heinrich Hornung - Report of August 25, 1946

As a prisoner of the internment camp Mies I worked with other comrades in the resettlement [expulsion] camp of Mies from early March until April 16 of this year, and during that time I was involved in the luggage inspections of 7 resettlement [expulsion] transports. In the course of these I observed that all expellees who still had any good-quality articles of clothing, linen or shoes were robbed of these. The best of the confiscated items were taken by the inspectors and stashed in their residence. Especially the chief constable Breier took entire suitcases of confiscated items home on his motorcycle every week, as did the camp's administrator, Kristofovec.

I can take this statement on my oath.

Modrany

Prague - Karls Square, luggage allowance for the Modrany transport, abuse
Reported by engineer A. Lendl - Report of October 14, 1946

I was the transport leader of the resettlement train that left Modrany on October 9 and arrived in Augsburg on October 10, 1946. The transport was comprised mainly of former soldiers and prisoners-of-war, of people who had spent a year or more on labor details, in internment camps or in prisons (police detention) and who had been deprived of all their possessions at the time of their initial arrest. For that reason the transport was in very bad shape where the luggage allowance was concerned, and this inadequacy was noted and objected to by the American transfer commission. The Czechs then sent some things, especially clothing, to remedy the situation; it didn't do much to improve the average luggage weight of only 35 kg, but at least the poorest of the poor, who had nothing at all, could be outfitted with the minimum that had been set contractually by the Americans. In general the state of clothing of the transport members was deplorable. Rations were very scarce due to the unexpected 3-day delay at the border. Especially the children and elderly people suffered from the cold weather. Where clothing and underthings are concerned, the supplementation of the expellees' luggage in the resettlement [expulsion] camp of Modrany was in no relation at all to what the expellees really needed. The clothing and linen that was distributed was totally unusable, and the Americans also rejected these items. Complaints made in Modrany were brutally refused, and the expellees' treatment in Modrany was also very crude and harsh in general.

In November 1946 my wife and I myself had come to Prague from English captivity, on the summons of the Czech government, but in Prague I was immediately arrested, led off in chains, and detained in several prisons for 11 months. In these prisons I witnessed terrible maltreatment of German prisoners, especially in the District Court in Prague-Karlsplatz.

Motol

Maltreatment, inadequate luggage allowance for deportation
Reported by Alois Zwatschek - Report of August 18, 1946

I had been with the German Wehrmacht, and in February 1946 I was released from Russian captivity in Odessa because I had been ill with diphtheria, which left me with paralysis of both my hands and feet, unable to speak, and almost totally deaf and blind. When the train crossed the Czech border, Czech soldiers came and looted the homecomers of their possessions. They yanked my wedding ring off my finger and a watch out of my pocket. Despite my helpless condition I was detained in the concentration camp Motol near Prague on such poor rations that after a month I even volunteered for farm labor, but rations were also very bad there. In May 1945 my mother, a 70-year-old lady, had been so badly maltreated in Moravian Neustadt by the Czechs that she lost consciousness, and all my things that I had deposited at her home for safekeeping were confiscated. When I was released from the Motol camp on August 1 I went to my wife, who lived with her parents in Lautsch. She too had lost all her better possessions to the Czech administrator who had taken over her parents' estate. Our resettlement [expulsion] luggage consists mostly of things given to us by my in-laws. I myself have no clothes beyond what I am wearing.

Mühlbach

House searches
Reported by Alois Mannl - Report of September 13, 1946

On the pretext of allegedly having stolen a motorcycle, my uncle and cousin and I were arrested on March 4, 1946 in Mühlbach near Eger and committed to the District Court of Eger, where we were detained until August 14. During the arrest in Mühlbach, and then in the District Court of Eger, we were badly maltreated. My uncle sustained a kidney injury and was ailing after that, but since he nonetheless had to work his condition worsened until he died two days before he was to be resettled [expelled]. I myself have suffered from kidney and stomach pain ever since the maltreatment. While in Eger I also saw how even 15- and 16-year-old youths were maltreated so badly that their faces were disfigured beyond recognition. Among the youths abused like that were Anton Lattisch and Alois Witwitzki.

In June the questioning of witnesses established our innocence. Nonetheless we were kept imprisoned until our parents were resettled [expelled]. In the course of house searches carried out on our arrest, all our clothing and linen was confiscated, so that we had nothing at all for our resettlement. To compensate for my lack of luggage, my parents were permitted to take their sewing machine.

Münchengrätz

Cases of ill-treatment
Reported by Otto Skrbeck - Report of June 26, 1950

On May 5th, 1945 the revolution began. On May 8th, 1945 we had to leave the Protectorate in the direction of Weisswasser [Protectorate = Czechoslovakia between 1939 and 1945, excluding Sudeten German areas]. I had put on civilian clothes and walked in the direction of Münchengrätz in order to join my family. A Czech surgeon who drove by gave me a ride to the town of Bakow on the Iser. When we drove down Kosmanos Hill we saw a dreadful sight. There were partisans all over the place, firing on Red Cross nurses and forcing them to turn back.

In Münchengrätz the Czechs came for me during the night, at 1:30 in the morning; they surrounded my house and dragged me through the dark to the Headquarters of the Revolutionary National Committee; arriving there they placed me against the wall and explained to me that if I moved I would be shot. Men with pistols were standing around. Suddenly something struck my head and I was lying on the floor with blood all over me. This went on until I collapsed. All I had with me had been stolen while I was standing with my face to the wall. Afterwards I was taken to the prison.

The man who followed me was an innkeeper from Reichenberg, who had been a member of the *Volkssturm* [last reserve]. They had smashed his head in. A few days later he died in horrible pain. It went on like this all the time, they took people out and shot them either outside the town or in the prison yard in Münchengrätz. Shots were always to be heard in the yard. The rattle of shooting lasted until the Russians came, it was said then that no more Germans were to be shot.

I was in Czech captivity from May 8, 1945 to July 12, 1945. We were beaten daily. We had to remove tank barricades. There was very little to eat and the food was bad. The bread was stored close to the gasoline so that it became inedible.

During our captivity we constantly received stretchers, pick-axes and shovels, and had to dig graves near the municipal bathing establishment at Münchengrätz, to salvage the bodies of dead comrades out of the Iser and to bury them. We refugees had not only been robbed of everything, but were also used for compulsory labour. Our conditions were very bad in the Haskov factory, the Czech military barracks, where our work was extremely hard; Czech soldiers drove us on with hatchets and axes while we were carrying heavy loads.

We three - my wife, my daughter and I - were expelled on July 12, 1945 at 1 o'clock at night with 25 kilos (55 pounds) of luggage and 100 RM; even our wedding-rings were taken from us. They told us that we were going to work and would come back soon.

Neudek

Severe abuse of a man with a heart condition
Reported by Anna Grimm - Report of August 29, 1946

My husband suffered from a heart condition, and was arrested on his sick-bed on June 17, 1945 and imprisoned in Neudek for three days, with dreadful maltreatment, and then transferred to the concentration camp of Neurohlau. There too he was badly maltreated, as he himself told me. I saw that his back was entirely black and blue. As a result of the bad rations he developed dropsy, with fluid in his legs all the way to his hips, so that he could no longer put on his shoes or close his trousers. On September 10 he collapsed at his place of work and had to be taken to hospital. On December 6 he was brought back to the concentration camp in Neurohlau even though the doctor had declared him totally unfit for imprisonment. On December 11 he suffered a stroke and could no longer speak. When I wanted to visit him, I was forbidden to do so. When I returned to the camp on Christmas Day he was led into the visiting room. He was the picture of misery. He had terrible trouble breathing, could not speak, and was all swollen. I tried time and again with personal and written petitions to have him released into home care, but he was not discharged from the concentration camp until February 8, 1946. He did not recover, and died on August 5, 1946.

Neuhof

Maltreatment
Reported by Eduard Geitler

Because I had insulted a Czech person in 1939, this Czech reported me to the gendarmerie in 1945. On July 3, 1945 I was arrested, and locked into a coal cellar in the police prison together with four other Germans. On the third day after my committal all four of us were led, singly, into a room on the second floor, where we were inhumanly beaten. I was punched in the face 15 times, then I had to lie down on a chair and was beaten with a leather whip. Then my tormentor turned the whip around and beat me with the handle. The doctor who later examined my injuries described them as serious physical damage.

After 10 days I was transferred to Sternberg into a collection camp. The rations we got there were very poor. We had to do sports [exercises] before going to work in the morning, and after we returned from work in the evening. Anyone who couldn't keep up got plenty of beatings. During work we were supervised by guards, and if someone didn't work to their satisfaction he had a beating to look forward to in the evening. Around 9 o'clock in the evening, when we were about to retire for the night, we were beaten for no reason at all. They wrapped blankets around our heads on this occasion to muffle our screams.

On January 9, 1946 I was sent to Neuhodolein, near Olmütz. We were kept in a constant state of starvation here. When we tried to pass the time in the long evenings by giving and attending lectures on educational subjects such as sugar production, beer brewing, fruit growing etc., we were reported for it, deprived of our straw pallets and forced to run the gauntlet. We were also inhumanly beaten. Our punishment, therefore, consisted of having to sleep in unheated rooms and without straw pallets, in *January* - as well as of two fasting days per week and the withholding of mail and parcel privileges. The beatings were easier to endure than the constant hunger. I had to continue working even though I was gravely ill. The slogan was, "there are only two kinds of people in the camp, the healthy and the dead!" In late June 1946 I was released, since there were no charges against me.

Neurohlau

Neurohlau, Report No. 1

Maltreatment of invalids

Reported by parish priest Oskar F. K. Hahn - Report of July 22, 1946

I am an invalid, but on October 20, 1945 I was put into the concentration camp of Neurohlau. As Catholic clergyman I had been parish priest, and was suspected of having massacred Russian soldiers in a butcher shop, with the assistance of the kitchen staff. The charge had been brought by a woman who was in an insane asylum three times already.

I am a war-disabled ex-serviceman myself, but nonetheless I was repeatedly badly maltreated, like all other prisoners as well. The worst time came in the night of November 2-3, when all inmates who had been members of the SS, the SA or the Party, including foot amputees, were forced to run laps around the square. In the process we were beaten so badly with rifle butts, steel canes and slats that many collapsed. As the result of maltreatment, the last of which to my knowledge took place in March 1946, an opera singer, Karl Tretsch from Prague, suffered seven broken ribs, and kidney and head injuries. This kind of maltreatment was also repeatedly inflicted on other prisoners. Among the prisoners in Neurohlau there were numerous 70- and 80-year-old men and women, some of whom suffered from severe injuries such as hernias. I shared my room with about 48 invalids (amputees). Even these were badly maltreated. The student Günther from Gottesgab was beaten with rubber truncheons on both his leg stumps until the blood shot out. One Mrs. B. from Lubenz, 68 years old, was recently sentenced by the People's Court to 20 years' imprisonment for allegedly being to blame for two girls committing suicide in 1936/37. Her husband had been beaten to death in the camp while she was forced to watch.

Neurohlau, Report No. 2

Cases of ill-treatment in the concentration camp at Neurohlau

Reported by Johann Schmelzer - Report of June 1, 1946

I was imprisoned at Elbogen on June 9, 1945. On June 26, I was transported to the concentration camp at Neurohlau together with other prisoners. On the same day all inmates - more than 100 men - were called to the office and knocked about in such a manner that the cries of pain could be heard in the street, even though the windows had been closed. The very moment I entered the office I myself was attacked by four men, who struck me in the face and on the head. After that I had to bend over the back of a chair and was then beaten with sticks and clubs by those four men until blood dripped from my nose. Afterwards they forced me to lick the blood off the chair. All prisoners were treated the same way. I was interrogated three times during my imprisonment of eleven months and released on May 11, 1946 without having been tried or sentenced.

For many weeks the food was not only completely insufficient, but also inedible. Many prisoners became ill and died from exhaustion. Among them were one Konhäuser, functionary at Altsattel, and Karl Wohlrab, formerly a pattern-maker at Dallwitz.

Once, in July, I saw a prisoner, who was standing in line for the roll call, shot down by a commissar with his pistol without warning. I remember a further case: a prisoner who, suffering from hunger, took some potato peels out of the dust-bin near the kitchen was warned by the commander and threatened with shooting. When the same prisoner ate potato peels again, several days later, he was killed by the commandant himself with a pistol-shot. When one of the SS-men escaped from the camp in August, all the SS-men there were beaten and SS-man Lippert from Elbogen was shot. I am prepared to swear to this statement and I am also able to name witnesses.

Neurohlau, Report No. 3
Permanent physical disability as result of maltreatment
Reported by Adolf Trägner - Report of July 22, 1946

On July 23, 1945 I was ordered to report the next day at the Altrohlau school, for work assignments. At the school I met 31 other men who had received the same order. From there, we were committed to the Neurohlau concentration camp, where we were all dreadfully maltreated. I was kicked in the genitals both from the front and from behind until I collapsed unconscious. When I came to again, I was laid on a bench and beaten unconscious all over again. When I regained consciousness this time, one man beat me over the head with a steel cane until I collapsed yet again. I sustained a severe head injury from this abuse. Ever since then I have suffered from constant headaches, which sometimes become so severe that I pass out from them. The camp physician in Kladno-Dubi diagnosed my head injury. A heart defect from which I also suffer now is related to this maltreatment as well.

Neurohlau, Report No. 4
Maltreatment and death
Reported by Marie Georgi - Report of September 2, 1946

Director Pohl of the paper factory at Neudek was picked up by the gendarmerie in September 1945. He was taken to the camp at Neurohlau and shot there. One Czech by the name of Kalupa afterwards bragged of having shot Pohl in Neurohlau.

Wenzel Siegert, a post-office employee, whose apartment had been requisitioned during his absence, was mistreated when he returned to his apartment; he was then taken to the local jail, where in September he was beaten to death.

Josef Schönecker, born on October 26, 1893, was arrested in November 1945 on his way to withdraw money from the savings bank, although he was already in possession of his transfer documents. Since that time he has been kept in Neurohlau, even though he is a sick man and unfit for work.

Anna G., the wife of a baker in Neudek, was taken prisoner in June 1945, severely ill-treated and brought to the court-prison at Karlsbad. I saw myself at Christmas the scars on her legs, originating from metal-studded scourges. During the night they would take her out of the cell several times, then she had to undress and they would pour cold water over her. Later she was sentenced by the "Volksgericht" [People's Court], often presided over by men without legal qualifications, to twelve years imprisonment.

Neurohlau, Report No. 5
Shooting of an old German man in the Neurohlau camp, 1945/46
Reported by Josef Heller - Report of June 22, 1946

I had to spend the time from December 28, 1945 until May 29, 1946 in the concentration camp in Neurohlau. Even before that time I had been in the camp a couple of times a week for several months, on deliveries I had to make for the camp.

On those occasions I witnessed many instances of maltreatment. Once I saw how an old man, who was in his sixties, walked across the camp square around noon and was suddenly gunned down by a Czech guard, without there even having been so much as an exchange of words between the old man and the guard. Then, when I became an inmate in the camp myself, I witnessed how the guards sought every opportunity to maltreat the prisoners.

During the night of April 30, 1946 we heard several shots being fired. On May 1 nobody was allowed to leave the camp. We were told that someone had shot at a guard from outside the camp. Allegedly the bullet had gone through a guard's cap. This incident was taken as an excuse to conduct house searches in the surrounding villages, ostensibly for weapons, and in the course of these searches the people were robbed of even their last poor possessions of clothes, linen, money etc. No weapons were found. A Czech investigative commission then determined that a guard had fallen asleep and when his hand had slipped down his gun it had triggered the shot that went through his cap. Another guard had responded to this shot by firing several times more.

During the luggage inspection in Neurohlau the inspectors, who were drunk, helped themselves to most of the expellees' possessions. My 79-year-old mother was robbed of her feather bedding, my wife of all our clothes and linen, and I myself of my best clothes and shoes. As compensation we were given 500 Marks each.

Neutitschein

Neutitschein, Report No. 1

Expropriation of anti-Fascists

Reported by retired public school director Josef Schramm - Report of May 14, 1950

Neutitschein was occupied by German troops on October 10, 1938. On November 22, 1938 the new authorities dismissed me from my post. I was dismissed with the comment that I could not expect to enter service in the Reich.

Prompted by a written denunciation, I had to justify myself to the new authorities because in April 1937 I had required the teachers on my staff to prove that they had adequately informed their students about the difference between democracy and dictatorship in a state, as per Decree 81/n issued by the District School Board on January 11, 1934.

And finally, in 1937, I had put my wife's landholdings[?] at the disposal of the Czech military administration, to use as a military magazine. This was done under contract, to avoid the risk of confiscateion.

On May 5, 1945 Neutitschein was occupied by the Russians. I had to submit to the first looting. Already the very next day it seemed that I would be granted protection, due to my early efforts to preserve the Czechoslovak state. On the basis of my written documentation, the local Czech výbor issued me a voucher with the Soviet stamp, that was to protect me from further looting. Nonetheless I had to surrender my radio.

In the night of July 4-5, 1945, 4,000 to 5,000 German inhabitants of the city Neutitschein were suddenly deported without prior notice to the city of Pirna on the Elbe. I was also still held exempt from that. The evening before, I was given a "white card" for myself and my family, for this purpose. But this card and my written documentation did not keep my wife from having to perform forced labor for Czechs. I mysef had to spend a Sunday from 7 o'clock in the morning until 6 in the evening performing public clearing work.

On August 21, 1945 a public announcement was posted in many places in the city Neutitschein. I myself had to keep such a poster, 85x60cm in size, displayed in my window for 14 days. I still have this poster today. The text on it stated, in Czech: "*Národní výbor* Neutitschein, No. 4735, August 4, 1945. Re.: trustworthiness of Germans. Announcement. The following persons living in Marxova Street have been exempted from the restrictions placed on persons of German nationality." Then there follow 7 names, including mine. "Because the *výbor* wishes to base its favorable decision on a fair and legal foundation, all persons of Czech nationality are requested to submit any objections to this decision in writing within 14 days. The *výbor* is certain that the Czech citizens of Neutitschein, who have lived here throughout the time of the German occupation, will be guided in their submissions only by the interests of the people and the state. Any and all intervention in the affairs of Germans are admissible. Jan Oplustil, Chairman of the *Národní výbor*." Nobody submitted any objections.

Soon after these posters were first put up, a vast number of red placards from the Communist Party appeared in every corner of the city. They declared that all Germans without difference would have to be expelled. Other posters obligated even the "so-called anti-Fascists" to display the 15-cm-tall "N" on the left side of their chest.

On December 18, 1945 I had to vacate my own home in favor of the Czech Major Dlouhý. As compensation I was assigned one room and kitchen, where 23 of the 36 window panes were missing. An appeal to the Mayor and Public School Director Bechný, with whom I was personally acquainted, was to no avail. Allegedly the government permitted a German to have one room at most.

I applied to the security consultant at the local Czech *výbor* in Neutitschein for a certificate attesting to my anti-Fascist activities. On the basis of my documentation I received a very detailed one. With this certificate I applied for resettlement as anti-Fascist, which was specially organized by the Social Democrats. Even though I had never belonged to a political party, I was accepted. Nonetheless, on March 19, 1946, I received the order to comply with regular resettlement [expulsion], with only 50 kg of luggage. When I showed my anti-Fascist certificate, it was taken from me. It bore the original signatures of the security consultant and the Chairman of the *výbor*, along with an official seal. My complaint to the Chairman resulted in him reissuing me the confiscated certificate, but he too could not exempt me from the imminent expulsion. Late in the evening before the scheduled expulsion, an order arrived from Prague, stating that the anti-Fascists should still be exempted for the time being.

I had to apply all over again for resettlement as anti-Fascist. It was again granted.

I had the Communist Chairman of the district *výbor* issue me written confirmation that due to my being resettled as anti-Fascist I was exempt from confiscation of my possessions. I was issued this confirmation politely and without problems. Armed with this document, and within the specified time frame, I reported to the national *výbor*, Moravian Ostrau branch office, to protest against the confiscation of my possessions. This office notified me that due to an October 18, 1946 decision of the Moravian-Silesian national *výbor*, Moravian Ostrau branch office, my protest was denied.

On November 26, 1946 my family and I had to report for resettlement [expulsion] to Bavaria.

Neutitschein, Report No. 2
Gross maltreatment and torture
Reported by Franz Bordirsky - Report of July 11, 1946

I was arrested on June 26, 1945 by Czech policemen, who took me right off the field where I was working and to the community office. There I was shown a gun which had allegedly been found in my house, and I was asked where it had come from.

I didn't know the first thing about this gun and was therefore unable to give them any information. Then they downright tortured me to extort a confession. First they beat me bloody with rubber truncheons. Two days later I was questioned again, and they accompanied the interrogation by whipping me on my legs and the soles of my feet. I was stabbed in the side with a knife so that the blood ran down. Then I was choked unconscious with a belt. After that they burned my face and ears with a red-hot iron and singed my hair, and then they forced me to press a shovel up against the wall with my nose while holding up a brick in each hand. Whenever my arms sagged or the shovel dropped, I was beaten again, so that I collapsed several times.

They concluded their treatment by beating me over my legs and feet with wooden sticks. This produced open wounds, one of which has still not scarred over to this day, a year later.

In the state I was in, they then kept me imprisoned for ten days in the basement of the school. Then I was taken by car to Neutitschein and again imprisoned.

The next day I was walked to the concentration camp. Not until the next day was I admitted to the hospital, but discharged again two weeks later on the order of the Czech doctor because the hospital had to be cleared of all Germans. I was returned to my prison cell, and on December 7 I was transferred to the concentration camp, where I remained until June 7 this year.

On that day a hearing was finally held, and I was acquitted of the charge of unlawful possession of a firearm, but nonetheless I was sentenced to ten months in prison for allegedly having pulled a bayonet out of a Czech policeman's boot and threatening him with it.

Nieder-Mohrau and Olmütz

Abuse of young people
Reported by Johann Stanzl - Report of July 3, 1946

On September 13, 1945 I was arrested in Nieder-Mohrau, even thought the police was aware that I had already been diabetic for a year and a half. I was 16 years old at the time and was accused of having been a "werewolf".

There had been no werewolf organizations in the entire surrounding region. 52 young people and adult men were arrested along with me. All food we had with us was confiscated. We were transferred to Olmütz and penned into a school there.

We were all dreadfully maltreated by the guards there every day. Rations were very scant, and frequently inedible. In six weeks at least ten people starved to death. In early November we were transferred to the Hodolein concentration camp, where I was released about three weeks later, for health reasons.

On April 7 of this year I and 15 other youths from Nieder-Mohrau were again imprisoned after a barn in Nieder-Mohrau had burned down. As it turned out later, a Czech had set it on fire. I was arrested even though at the time of the arson I had been bedridden for three days, as I'd been repeatedly since my release from the concentration camp.

After 24 hours I was again released for health reasons. The other boys were detained longer.

Women severely abused

Reported by Elfriede Brockelt - Report of October 15, 1946

After my father passed away, my son and I took care of my mother's agricultural estate in Niemes. On June 1st of last year the *Národní výbor* in Denis ordered me to move back to Denis to my own home. I complied with this order immediately. On June 6 my husband and I were suddenly arrested, with no reason being given, and incarcerated in the prison in Grottau. In Grottau I was badly maltreated. We had to work on the railroad, and every morning before work as well as after our return to the camp in the evening we were beaten with fists and rubber truncheons. My husband and I were separated, and I have not seen him again since. On June 13 of last year, we - approximately 30 people - were committed to the District Court of Reichenberg. On our arrival the men had to strip naked in the hallway and were beaten with rubber truncheons and whips. We five women were led to the Women's Section and badly maltreated there. Each of us had to strip completely naked and bend over a bed, and four soldiers would then beat us with rubber truncheons and whips. When it was my turn as the last of the five of us, I refused to undress, as it was that time of month for me. A sergeant checked to see if it was true, and then declared, "That doesn't matter." Since I still refused to undress, a sergeant pulled my top up and another one my pants down, and then four men beat me on my back, buttocks, legs and feet with rubber truncheons and whips. It must have been 25 to 30 blows. I was black and blue from this maltreatment. When I was supposed to return to my cell, I collapsed. I dragged myself into the cell with the last of my strength of will. An hour later we were fetched to report to the admissions office, where I was again threatened with the whip for having crossed the border with my children in 1938. When I returned to the cell one of the sergeants boxed me about the head and dragged me into the cell by my hair, because I "also" had children, as he put it. On September 5 this year I was sentenced to five years' imprisonment with forced labor. I had to do janitorial work. On October 10 I was released, without having tried to effect my release, and without being told a reason for it. My husband was also sentenced to five years' imprisonment and is still being detained in Karthaus.

Nikolsburg, Report No. 1

Maltreatment, torture to extort a confession

Reported by Johann Gerlinger - Report of June 17, 1946

On September 21, 1945, four Czechs came at night, knocked on the door of my house and asked me where I kept my pistol. I have never in my life owned a weapon, and said so. At that, they thrashed me with their rifle barrels, and beat me black and blue all over. To this day I have not regained the use of my left arm. Then I was ordered to report to the community office, where I was given water to wash up, as I was covered in blood. Then they led me into the basement and hung me up by my hands, which were tied behind my back, and left me hanging like that for half an hour. After they had untied me, I tried to drink from a water tub as we passed it on the street. One of the guards shoved my head under the water. Then I was locked up. The following night I was released without any further interrogation, and threatened that I would get more beatings if I told anyone how I had been maltreated. Meanwhile my family had been thrown out of our house. They had only been able to secretly take a few minor possessions with them. We stayed with my sister for three weeks. Then I and my wife were imprisoned in the Nikolsburg concentration camp, where I had to stay for nine months. My wife was released after two months because she was ailing.

Nikolsburg, Report No. 2
Severe maltreatment in the Nikolsburg concentration camp to extort a confession
Reported by M. Krebs - Report of June 17, 1946

I was arrested on May 26, 1945 and taken to the court-building of Nikolsburg on the following day. There I was asked for my NSFK-uniform [NSFK = organization affiliated to the NSDAP] and for my shot-gun. I declared that I had never possessed a uniform and that I had delivered the gun to a Czech trustee. This they refused to believe. In order to extort a confession from me I was then subjected to severe ill-treatment. On two occasions I was placed over a chair and received 25 strokes with a rubber hose, which they obliged me to count myself. Afterwards I was forced to undress completely and then I had to run the gauntlet in a secluded yard between 12 to 15 men, who were armed with rubber-truncheons, tubes, rods, cables etc. On this occasion I received blows especially in the epigastric region and the genitals. I broke down several times and while on the ground I was trampled under foot. Then I was left standing in the yard at dusk. Three Czechs returned and I was beaten for the second time; they placed me over a chair, one man pressing my head and the other my feet towards the floor. How many strokes I received I do not know, but in any case they were enough to cause me to faint. After they had poured water over me the beating was continued.

On May 28, in spite of my wounds, I was again maltreated. 14 days later the wounds on my buttocks burst open and for four weeks were in a festering condition. I stayed in the sick-room for the whole of this period. As a result of a blow which I had received on the spine from an automatic pistol I also suffered from neuralgia, followed by atrophy of the right hand which still persists. I myself saw many other prisoners being tortured and ill-treated in the same way. The beatings were carried out by the following Czechs: Malicek, Medek, Tyrsch, Trha, Blaha and Schick, the last of whom with his automatic pistol shot down Mrs. Mischensky from Weiss-Stätten in front of the other prisoners.

During the first six weeks no bread at all was distributed. The daily ration consisted of two cold potatoes and two slices of beet-root. Later on we received 250 g (½ pound) of bread daily and a potato-soup; for six weeks there was no salt in the soup. There was no heating even during the winter. The windows had been lime-washed and barbed wire stretched over them. A wagon full of clothes, linen and undergarments, a gift from UNRRA to the camp inmates, was shared out among the guards.

I am prepared to swear to this statement.

Ober-Lipka

Dreadful atrocities, murder, maltreatment
Reported by Johann Peschka, Dean - Report of August 3, 1946

Hardly any village suffered as much under the Czechs as Oberlipka. The 23-year-old commissar, a Czech Communist, immediately altered the War-Memorial into a Czech-Russian monument in commemoration of the victory, decorated it with Stalin's picture and with hammer and sickle. The kolkhoze-system was introduced. At 6 o'clock in the morning the inhabitants of the village had to fall in, in order to be distributed for work. Women who came late because they had had to attend their children were struck with a whip or punched in the face by this same commissar. Mrs. Hermine Fischer, wife of a mason, whose husband had not yet returned from the army, showed me her bleeding wounds and her broken nose. Miss Hedwig Seifert, who was supposed to have made an offensive remark concerning the Czechs, although this denunciation by the *Správce* (manager) was a false one, had to undress completely in the office of the commissar; she was then lashed, her hair cropped and she had to press a piece of paper against the wall [with her nose] for two hours. Whenever it slipped down, she received lashes with the whip. She was also not allowed to relieve nature, so that she defiled herself. At last she was confined to her room for a whole month, probably with the intention of preventing her from filing a protest.

This commissar also gave orders for the shooting of eight innocent persons, as for example Josef Kretschmer, a farmer, in whose field a weapon was found in a heap of stones and also Konrad Neutzler, who was a tenant of another farmer by the name of Pretschmer. It is reported by the neighbours that both these men were completely undressed, tied up and so terribly beaten that their cries of pain were audible far off, before they were actually executed.

One Winkler, a shoemaker and his wife, who had already crossed the German border, returned at night in order to fetch more clothes for themselves. They were both picked up and dreadfully tormented so that their cries could be heard at a great distance. Afterwards they were driven to Grulich, where they were locked up in the cellar of the Schiller printing-works and again cruelly maltreated. People from Grulich who saw these victims noticed their bloodshot eyes, swollen-up faces and the almost mad look in their eyes. Later on they were all shot, together with Berthold Seifert, a bricklayer's foreman, and Richard Hentschel, the leader of the local farmers' association. All the inhabitants of the village, including the children over eight, had to witness the execution, their hands above their heads. Everyone was forced to take with them their watches and jewellery.

The Czech woman secretary ordered the singing of the German anthem. The drunken soldiers could not aim right, and the woman among the condemned received shots in the abdomen. Some of those who had been shot were still living when they collapsed into the hole which they themselves had been forced to dig. From above, the Czechs gave a number of mercy-shots. Many of the spectators fainted. Johann Müller, a smallholder, on returning to his house hanged himself in a panic. Before the execution the enforced spectators were searched and all their valuables were taken from them.

A soldier who had many war-injuries and had recently returned home was shot without any trial or interrogation. My servant, Miss Maria Neutzler, who had to renew the eternal light in the church at Oberlipka, was interrogated and tormented for a considerable time, since she was accused of having given light signals to the enemies from the church. She died as a consequence of this maltreatment in the hospital at Mährisch-Rothwasser.

By order of the commissar five women between 40 and 60 years of age had to thrash corn in the barn of a farmer by the name of Johann Rotter. One of the women was Mrs. Prause, the mother of Berthold Winige's wife. Since it was very cold, the five women went to a neighbour's house in order to eat their dry bread there and to warm themselves up. When the commissar passed the barn and did not see the women, he furiously fetched them from the room and ordered them to follow him to the barn. There they had to undress partially. After this the enraged brute kicked them with his riding-boots and beat them with a [bullwhip] in an atrocious manner. Even after several weeks had passed, the doctor could still see the weals and wounds. This deed of the commissar was too much even for the decent persons among the Czechs and since our constant reports and representations were in vain, the Czechs helped so that finally a commissar from Prague arrived and put a stop to this commissar's activities.

It is also well known in what a barbarian way the owners were expelled from their farms and houses. Ferdinand Jäckel, for instance, a farmer and innkeeper, was working in the fields near Freudenberg, when the new Czech owners arrived at the farm. He had to leave his property there and then, still in his working clothes. He was a seriously wounded war veteran.

Grulich had 4,200 inhabitants, the majority of whom were catholics, with about 500 persons of protestant faith.

The population was peaceful and had lived on good terms with the Czechs during the period of the Czechoslovak Republic. When the Czechs had left the area after the annexation, no one had hurt a hair of their heads or taken anything from them. The Czechs who remained had been treated well during the war and the Czech labourers had also had good pay and working conditions. They were independent and free to move about just like the Germans and to visit movie theatres and restaurants. It was for this reason that the inhabitants of Grulich calmly looked forward to the return of the Czechs after the collapse of Germany. They were willing to work with them.

On May 22nd, at 7 o'clock in the morning, buses arrived at the market place and heavily armed partisans got out of them. They surrounded the town and searched every single house. They threatened the people with death if a single man would be found hidden. All of the men were assembled in the market-place, with their hands above their heads; later they were taken to the district administration building, a former Czech school. A Czech commission under the leadership of one Fiala, a gardener, and one Urban, a butcher, decided the number of strokes to be given - 50 to 200 - carried out with steel rods, whips, sticks etc. Only very few got away without corporal punishment. Many of the men were half maddened with pain and were bleeding so heavily that it took them hours to get home. Among those killed were Adolf Pospischil, a youth leader, and Ernst Pabel, a young soldier from Niederlipka, whom the Czechs had seized on the road. I lifted the tent-cloth from the corpses at the consecration and saw that [their] heads and the upper parts of the bodies had been beaten into a bloody mass. Pospischil had finally received a shot of mercy. Doctor Burek is able to testify to the above. Further persons beaten to death were: Amber, a tailor, also Schrutek, the owner of a printing-house and district forester, because he had altered his Czech name into a German one.

Political prisoners, functionaries of the NSDAP and other persons towards whom the Czechs bore ill-will were especially maltreated. In the evening after they returned from their daily labour, they were led to the school-yard, adjoining the parsonage, for the so-called "evening-gymnastics", which were supervised by Czech soldiers, allegedly former concentration camp inmates. We heard the cries of the tortured men and could overlook the whole school-yard through knot-holes and cracks in the boarding. First of all there were calisthenics, accompanied by lashing and face-slapping, after this the prisoners had to run the gauntlet. At the beginning and at the end of each row stood Czech soldiers, who kicked the running men in the abdomen and struck them on the back with their rifle butts. I saw Dr. Fanckel, a lawyer, who was suffering from a nervous ailment. He was running desperately, while the laughing soldiers kicked and beat him until he fell to the ground and with clasped hands pleaded for mercy. As an answer he received so many blows in the face that blood dripped from his mouth and nose. He died in the hospital at Mährisch-Rothwasser as a result of this treatment. The same happened to one Hugo Grund, a butcher

Another man was laid over a box and was beaten by two soldiers with their whips and steel-rods until he collapsed. Afterwards cold water was poured over him and as soon as he came-to he was beaten again.

A Russian major, who witnessed the proceedings from a window of the school, stopped the "evening gymnastics", so that these terrible beatings came to an end.

Returning soldiers in uniform were shot down by the Czechs and buried in the open fields or in the woods. One day in May 1945 two soldiers from Austria entered my house at noontime. I advised them to make their way only at night and to hide themselves during the day. They probably did not take my advice, for when I arrived at the cemetery in the evening in order to perform a consecration, both of them had meanwhile been placed against the wall and shot.

The Germans were not allowed to use the railways; nor could they walk on the pavement or visit each other's houses. Women who did use the pavement were attacked even by the children, who smacked them or struck at them with sticks. *"Nemecká kurva"* (German whore) was the Czech epithet for all German women. One day at Hermsdorf some men met in an apartment for a game of cards, when unexpectedly a Czech search-party entered the room. The card-players, among them Hugo Koschinger, Hugo Fischer and Josef Vogel, were terribly beaten and were imprisoned for a long time. Hugo Fischer, who was a war-invalid, had to have immediate medical attention after this incident.

One Sunday Miss Gertrud Wagner went to the cemetery. On her way she was stopped by Czech soldiers and asked if she did not know that every soldier had to be greeted by the Germans. She was then violently slapped and forced to walk up and down in front of the soldiers, greeting them constantly.

At Eichstädt, as I was told by a man from there, 10 or 12 persons were hanged on the lime-trees near the church, after they had endured indescribable tortures. Among them were Pischel, a teacher, Hentschel, the mayor and local party-leader, and Safar, a master joiner, the last because he had taken a German name. Pischel had his mustache burnt off, his ears and nose were severed and his tongue torn out. He was forced to roll on the ground and was then dreadfully beaten.

At Böhmisch-Petersdorf also about 15 persons were tortured to death. I can guarantee all reports concerning my parish and I am prepared to take an oath on these statements at any time.

Oberpaulowitz

Harassment of German farmer by Czech administrator
Reported by Max Pohl - Report of July 4, 1946

On the day in November 1945 when a Czech administrator took over my farm, I and my family were robbed of every piece of clothing, linen, shoes and food we owned. When I remarked, "it would be best to take a rope and hang oneself," the Commissar beat me to the ground. Then they took me to the gendarmerie, on a cart since I could not walk. There, the gendarmes again beat me up, and locked me into the court prison for three weeks. When I returned from the prison, I and my family had to vacate our farm.

Oderfurt

Internment camp Oderfurt near Moravian, May 1945
Reported by Steffi Lejsek - Report of June 10, 1945

I was committed to the concentration camp Oderfurt near Moravian Ostrau on May 22, 1945. Everything I had was taken from me.

For the first week in the camp we got no food at all, and everyone came down with starvation-related dysentery. Every day someone died. During the second and third weeks there, we received one ladle of watery soup of no nutritional value at all each afternoon. There was no bread to be had. At the same time, however, everyone had to work very hard (shoveling coal, etc.).

The men got beatings every day, and many were totally disfigured by them. Already on the second day I saw how men, boys and girls aged 14 and up were whipped and chased bare-chested in circles around the camp square.

In order to get away from the dreadful conditions in the camp, 40 women volunteered for agricultural labor. Before we left the camp, all 40 of us were shorn bald.

I heard nothing from my husband. On May 22 some acquaintances told me that on May 18 they had found my husband dead in our home, and had buried him. I am prepared to take this statement on my oath.

Pardubitz - Königgrätz

Pardubitz - Königgrätz, Report No. 1

Maltreatment in the prisoner-of-war camp

Reported by Josef Fuchs - Report of July 4, 1946

I was released from Russian imprisonment on August 28, 1945 and crossed the Czech border on October 2 last year, passing through the Customs Office of Wittau-Grottau as per regulations. I had been assured that I could immigrate without hindrance. Nonetheless I was arrested in Grottau and then taken via Reichenberg into the concentration camp on the Pardubitz airfield. Beatings were the order of the day there for months on end. Anyone who so much as straightened up for a moment at work was beaten with rifle butts, cudgels or whips. I really have no idea how many times I myself was beaten there; it was at least twice or three times every week. One Czech legionnaire was the terror of the entire camp. One day in early April I and an old man were cutting wood, when this legionnaire spoke to us in Czech. Since despite our best efforts we could not understand what he wanted, he beat us so badly that the old man needed a doctor. Thanks to the rebuke that the legionnaire now received from the doctor, he maltreated the old man all over again by forcing him to pull a hand cart laden with 300 kilos [660 pounds] of wood at a run from Pardubitz to the airfield, beating him all the while with a cudgel so that he arrived at the airfield totally exhausted. Two days later he beat me with a shovel handle to the point where I had blood-suffused welts across my back.

On April 17, 1946 I was transferred to the concentration camp on the airfield of Königgrätz. Similar beatings also took place there. While I was working I was supervised by a guard who frequently bragged that he had shot 15 German soldiers and chopped off the hands of two. The worst beatings took place there between May 5 and 9, 1946. I myself was beaten bloody on that occasion as well. I was released on June 1, 1946, but even during my last days there I still witnessed how an old man was beaten unconscious for being unable to pull a wooden post out of the ground.

I was not paid for any of my work the entire time. Rations were very meager. The money that had been taken from us on our imprisonment in Pardubitz was not returned to us. Even the few things we had managed to retain through our imprisonment were taken away from us in Pardubitz. The parcels which relatives sent us were always looted before we received them.

Pardubitz - Königgrätz, Report No. 2
Abuse, treatment of prisoners-of-war
Reported by Franz Bieberle - Report of June 15, 1946

On August 20, 1945 I was transported off to Moravian Ostrau for clearing work, and in early September I and about 200 other men were sent on from there to Pardubitz to do clearing work. On our arrival in Pardubitz we were beaten up by guards with rifle butts, rubber truncheons and sticks, and herded with constant beatings from the train station to the camp, a stretch of half an hour. In the camp we were beaten daily before, during and after work for months on end. Everyone was beaten, and many died of the consequences of this abuse. Despite the hard work we had to do, our rations consisted only of black coffee, watery soup and one slice of bread per day.

In early September a transport of German prisoners-of-war who had been released from Russia arrived and was taken to the concentration camp of Pardubitz. They too had to work in the Fanto Works, an hour's distance from the camp. On September 15 an explosive went off among the prisoners-of-war during their march to work. The explosion resulted in 4 dead and 25 badly injured prisoners.

The Czechs now claimed that the prisoners had wanted to take this explosive into the Fanto Works in order to detonate them. As punishment, the entire camp was placed under a mail, parcel and visiting ban for six weeks around Christmas; therefore, thousands of parcels and many envelopes with money that arrived for the camp inmates around Christmas were not handed out.

On Christmas Day we got no food at all. The maltreatment in the camp around this time was even worse than usual.

On January 21, the coldest day, all camp inmates from the military, the gendarmerie etc. were herded out of their barracks at 8 o'clock in the evening, most of them not fully dressed as the move-out had to proceed very quickly. Then we had to stand lined up in the square with our hands raised over our heads until 1 o'clock at night, while the barracks were searched.

The barracks were unheated the entire winter long. Most inmates had only a blanket. There were no washing facilities at all in the camp. No-one dared report sick, since then he would only be maltreated all the more. The people went to work literally until they dropped. Anyone who collapsed from exhaustion during the march was beaten with rifle butts until he continued. I spent nine months in this camp.

Parschnitz

Treatment of Jews
Reported by Dr. Rudolf Fernegg - Report of June 21, 1951

The son and former owner (now about 55 years old) of the factory of Josef Pfefferkorn at Parschnitz had already lived in the United States for some time, but came back after the collapse in 1945 in order to take over the factory, which was his before. In the meantime he had acted as representative of this factory in the United States. On his return home he was told that neither repossession of the factory nor the sale of the factory would be possible, since the Czechs had refused to transfer the purchase-money to America.

Pattersdorf

Conditions in the collection camp
Reported by Prof. Rudolf Pohl - Report of September 6, 1946

I shared my villa in Frauental No. 113 near Deutschbrod with my 86-year-old aunt and foster mother, Johanna Niewelt, a retired teacher who had taught in this town for more than 30 years. On June 23, 1945, during the days of the revolution, this old lady was committed to the collection camp at Pattersdorf, even though she was feeble and very sickly.

The collection camp consisted of a row of wooden barracks, where the women of the Labor Service had used to be quartered. Attached to the barracks was a pig pen dating from the same time, and that was the housing where my elderly aunt was put. She had to lie there on the concrete floor with just some straw as bedding, with no care or medical attention at all. Since she was no longer able to wash herself or even to move around, the inevitable results were not long in coming: covered in filth and lice, she lay helpless on her straw, which was soaked with her excrements. It was not until September 6, 1945 that death released her from this inhuman treatment.

This outrage was perpetrated by the retired Czech staff captain J. Losenicky, of Frauental (Pohled) near Deutschbrod, the Chairman of the *Národní výbor*. During the occupation Losenicky had cooperated closely with the National Socialists, and served as air raid commandant. He ordered the arrest of the priest, dean and episcopal vicar August Krpalek of the District Pfarrkirchen/Niederbayern, and had him brought before the People's Tribunal in Deutschbrod, where, however, he was acquitted and had to leave his homeland with only 50 kg of luggage. The leader of the Pattersdorf collection camp was a certain Pavlicek, who carried out the orders of Hlavac, the Chairman of the *Národní výbor* of Deutschbrod.

The truth of my statements can be corroborated by the German priest of Schlappenz, Franz Fitz, who is now the curate in Berching, District Beilngries, Upper Palatinate.

Hlavac ordered the imprisonment and dreadful maltreatment of not only German women and innocent children but also of members of his own people (the so-called collaborators). One of my former students, H., 17 years old, daughter of a Czech engineer, was taken to a prison in Deutschbrod for having attended a German school. In the prison she was raped 20 times in a single night, and then released - with a sexually transmitted disease.

Lieutenant Colonel of the Reserves R. J. Heger's 18-year-old son, who was of mixed blood and had therefore been put to forced labor by the Nazis, was a student at the German Commercial Academy in Prague and was forced to leave the school in 1944. In May 1945 he was taken to the prison in Pankratz, where he and his father were both horrifically maltreated. His father the Lieutenant Colonel was beaten to death in that prison.

Georg Theml, age 20, formerly a student at the German Commercial Academy in Prague, and an Austrian citizen, was also of mixed blood and had been sent to the labor camp Bistritz; his mother, a Jewess, was imprisoned in Theresienstadt. In May 1945 the Czechs imprisoned Theml in the Pankratz prison in Prague where he too was inhumanly maltreated by the Czechs for fully two months.

Pisek and Brünn

A German woman's ordeal
Reported by Friedrich Sinzig - Report of September 30, 1946

My wife Hildegard Sinzig, born on October 31, 1910, fled from Pisek in May 1945 but the Americans turned her back [at the border] as being a Czech citizen, and sent her back to Brünn on a transport. Once expelled from Brünn, she and 12 other German women had to return home on foot, and all of them were picked up by the authorities in Nezamyslic and put to work on an estate. After 6 weeks, when the work was finished, she was transferred to the concentration camp in Kojetein near Prerau. In this camp she was sent out each day to work somewhere. Beginning in August the men and women were terribly maltreated in this camp both before and after work. From 4 to 6 o'clock in the morning they had to do exercises in the camp yard - hopping and running up to the second story and back down. Three guards were posted as supervisors and beat each person with a bullwhip as he or she ran past. These blows were aimed randomly at the victim's head, face, shoulders, back, lower back and legs. Once my wife received a blow to the face that was so bad that she could not see for 14 days. My wife's Czech employer reported this maltreatment to the gendarmerie, which ordered that the maltreatment in the camp be stopped. The camp administration then informed the inmates that if anything was ever reported again, they would be made to pay for it in other ways.

When the prisoners returned to the camp in the evening after having worked all day, they were tormented for hours just like they were in the morning. These tortures took place on a daily basis, for months. In November my wife received such a severe blow to the kidney area that she fell gravely ill, could not work any more, and had to be admitted to the Kremsier hospital on November 26, 1945. She was diagnosed with severe chronic inflammation of the kidneys, which failed to improve. On my request I was permitted to bring my wife home to the Jägerndorf hospital in March. There, an x-ray found that both her kidneys had been severed and had begun to atrophy, and that therefore her condition was terminal.

On July 26, 1946, after much pain and suffering, my wife succumbed to the consequences of the severe abuse she had suffered in Kojetein. She had personally told me all about her ordeal. I can take this statement on my oath and can also bring written documentation to prove it.

Plan

Maltreatment during inspection of identification papers, February 15, 1946
Reported by Ignaz Böhm - Report of June 6, 1946

On February 15 of this year I left my home in order to fetch sauerkraut from my uncle who lived in the same street of Plan as I. On the way I was stopped by two Czech soldiers who ordered me to produce my ID. I showed them my citizenship paper, with my photograph and fingerprints. Two officers examined the document. They gave it back to me, and I was allowed to go on.

Only a few minutes later, when I was on my way back home from my uncle's, three Czech soldiers entered the house behind me. They again demanded to see my ID. I showed them the same paper as before, and they arrested me. I was led into the barracks, where several young Germans were already being detained.

Hardly had I entered the office before several Czech soldiers began punching me, until I fell to the floor. Then I was kicked in the head, and then they ordered me to get up. They asked repeatedly, "you German?", and with every question they beat me some more.

Then a member of the secret police showed up in civilian dress, threw my ID paper torn up at my feet and declared that it was a fake. I replied that the exact same ID paper had been examined only a brief time before by two Czech officers, and acknowledged as valid. At that, the sergeant who had led the beating ordered water brought in so that I could wash up.

In the meantime my boss, a Czech, called and had me released.

I am ready to take this statement on my oath.

Podmoky

Mail withheld from agricultural slave laborers
Reported by Franz Seidel - Report of July 15, 1946

My wife and I had to do agricultural forced labor in Podmoky, Caslau District, since October 7, 1945, and we had to work there under the worst imaginable conditions. In light of the hard labor, the rations were entirely insufficient. My wife's weight dropped by 66 pounds while we were there.

Physical violence and crude invectives were frequent. There were 12 of us Germans there, and 10 are still there today. I am 65 years old, and I had to carry 39 large feed bins 100 to 300 m each day. I was barely able to carry the bins, but I was constantly urged to work faster.

During the time I was there, most of the mail intended for me - including very important letters, some registered, from and to the Austrian Consulate in Prague - were withheld from me, which I can prove with the few letters I did later receive in the concentration camp Stecken.

Pohorsch and Karwin

Slave labor, maltreatment, death
Reported by Ferdinand Münster - Report of July 11, 1946

In Pohorsch in May of 1945 all the men of the town were brutally beaten and tortured in the town school by Czech partisans, daily for an entire month. Two men were tortured to death. After having been tortured and beaten for a day, I myself was released to go back home. In June a Czech administrator was assigned to my farm, and in late August he arranged via the Employment Office to have me shipped off to forced labor, as was done with all the men of the town between the ages of 14 and 50. At the same time my wife was driven from our home and robbed of all linen, shoes, clothing etc. I myself was sent to Karwin, where I had to work in the Franz Mine until June 26 of this year, underground at first and then later above-ground at haulage level. Conditions in the camps there were unbearable. Rations were totally inadequate, and there was no medical care whatsoever. The most horrible maltreatment and tortures were the order of the day, and continued until the very end. For example, after work two of us would be called into the guard room and asked to report who had not worked hard enough. If we refused to answer, we had to beat each other with rubber truncheons. That went on until May and June 1946. At the time of my resettlement [expulsion] I did not have the full weight allowance of luggage, since my administrator had already robbed me of everything I owned. I reported this in the resettlement [expulsion] camp, but my luggage was not supplemented even though the camp leader had promised to order the administrator by telephone to augment my luggage.

Maltreatment

Reported by Franz Richter - Report of Christmas 1948

I had returned home to Polepp one rainy night shortly after Whitsun 1945. There was not a soul to be found at home. Terrible things had already taken place in my home town during my absence. On May 30, 1945 around 9 o'clock in the evening two young Czech civilians suddenly showed up. They were armed to the teeth. There was a woman with them as well. They shoved their submachine guns in my face and took me by car to the gendarmerie in Leitmeritz, where the first maltreatment began. I had to stand facing the wall, was boxed about the head and worked over with their boots. Then my personal data was recorded, and I was again maltreated. Still that same night I was committed to the District Court. Registration, confiscation of valuables etc., blows to my head with the key ring. The guard was a puny fellow, with a yellowish-grey face and terribly dirty hands. His eyes were bloodshot. He did not speak a word the entire time, his maltreatment was absolutely impersonal, almost objective. The prison cell was opened, and I had to bend my upper body horizontally forward so that he could beat me all over with a rubber truncheon from my buttocks to my neck. Then he mumbled that my real treatment would not take place until tomorrow.

There was a straw sack in the cell, but no blanket. The next morning and noon I got beatings instead of something to eat. In the evening there was neither food nor a beating. Suddenly, in the night, keys rattled. The next day I was put into a cell on the first floor, where two fellow-sufferers already sat. One of them had to punch me in the face as a welcome. Both had already been here a while. They assured me that we had gotten off easily, since these welcoming scenes did not normally entail anything less than 40 to 50 blows. In Theresienstadt I came to know this method well, which was intended to keep the guards blameless. Heller from Prosmik, who had to beat me, reassured me by saying that maltreatment was not as frequent here on the first floor. The first days after committal, he said, were the worst. Both of them were surprised that I had been brought up from "Correction" (the penal section in the basement) so soon. As we found out later, the reason for this was the colossal increase in the number of arrests. The next morning we got some black coffee, but as yet there was no bread for me.

It was probably around 7:30 when I was taken from the cell. This time there were three guards, who scrutinized me carefully. One more joined us on the way. They had their fun with me, tripped me up, kicked me in the back, shoved and punched me. From their conversation I gathered that I was being taken to an interrogation. They spoke Czech. Once we had arrived in the bathroom, two of them took the safety off their guns. Suddenly they yelled at me. Even though nobody told me intelligibly what to do, I did know that they wanted me to undress. Another one or two fellows had joined us in the meantime. All of them carried cables as thick as a finger. They landed some very painful blows on me. Then I had to lie down in the empty bathtub, and cold water hit me. As yet there were a few moments of relative peace. But then I had to place my feet on the edge of the tub and was given the "bastinado". I couldn't endure it for very long, then I jerked one of my feet back. It was inevitable that I splashed some water in the process. And now all hell broke loose. I was choked and shoved under water for minutes on end. Then I had to get out of the tub, and now they rained blows and kicks on me from every direction. The smallness of the room hindered them, and they got out of breath. Again I was shoved into the icy-cold water, and now the torture continued systematically, with repeated bastinados while my groans were muffled by holding me under the water. When I reacted more slowly to their new idea of scorching my feet with burning strips of paper, they finally left me in peace. I could barely drag myself back to the cell, while being given another "back massage", as they called it, with a pendreck.

It is impossible to describe the terrible pain in my feet. Soon they came to fetch me again. For a long time I and many other German men had to stand facing the wall in the anteroom of the police station in Neutor Street. Every now and then one of us fainted, and one or the other received a beating. We were forbidden to speak a word. A good friend of mine stood about 25 feet away from me. I made use of the commotion resulting from the beatings and fainting fits to move closer to him. Cautiously we exchanged our opinions and tried to encourage each other a little. He later died while trying to escape.

My name was called, and I was taken to be interrogated. A pistol and a pendreck lay on the table. I was instructed to tell them everything they wanted to know, else - a threatening gesture. The interrogation was brief and relatively calm. I could not gather that I had been charged with anything specific. The questions were very general, regarding Party membership and my professional and private activities. The stereotypical questions that came up everywhere and in every interrogation, "How many did you send into the concentration camp? How many did you kill?" etc. were accompanied by accounts of how badly the Czechs had allegedly had it since 1938.

I was sent back to the District Court prison, into a cell with 10 other men. Beatings were less frequent here, and I recovered fairly quickly. After a few days I was well enough to go out on various work details. In mid-June - I don't recall the exact date - some of us were forbidden to go out to work. I was among these, and we were made to stand in the hallway. More and ever more prison guards showed up. Each of us was given a little packet that allegedly contained our valuables, but we were sharply forbidden to open it. A drunken guard gave a speech full of crude curses and accusations. From this speech we gathered that we were to die, but that we would have to earn the mercy of death by first working very hard.

I was sent to the Little Fortress in Theresienstadt. Together with many others, I spent a long time standing just a few centimeters before the gray wall. Anyone who moved got a terrible beating, and then had to press a sheet of paper against the wall with his chin or nose. Woe to anyone whose paper dropped. Finally the so-called Kapos took charge of us. All of the Kapos were criminal convicts. Well, to be perfectly objective, there was the occasional exception. The Kapos led us into a large cell where we had to strip completely naked. In front of each of us there was a basket into which we had to lay first our clothes, then our underwear, and then, on top of it all, the packet with our valuables.

We were gagged with an old stocking or rag and had to bend over. One henchman would squeeze our head between his knees while two others each held our wrists. Another stood to one side of us and beat us on our buttocks and back with a metal-fitted pick-axe handle. Or else the torture was performed without assistants - in which case we had to kneel to be beaten. Initially the Fortress Commandant, one Staff Captain Prusa and his two daughters (about 18 to 25 years of age), the camp Commandant Alfred Klink and the Administrator Otto performed this procedure personally. One of Prusa's daughters bragged that she had beaten at least 18 German men to death. These bestial murders were mostly performed with brutal blows to the back, and to the back of the head. Torn kidneys, fractured skulls and spinal injuries were often the result. Those of us who survived urinated blood for weeks.

After we were registered, we were thrown some old clothes and underwear, and I was assigned to Cell 43. Our own possessions were taken away, and we never saw them again. I can only give snapshots of life in Theresienstadt between the summer and fall of 1945. I don't know how many people - men, women and children alike - were beaten to death here, or starved, or died of dysentery, typhus and other illnesses for which the responsibility rests squarely on the Czech government. But there were definitely more than 1,000 of them, and I had to carry many of their corpses out. I saw their abused, maltreated bodies, emaciated like skeletons.

In those days a favorite form of entertainment for the Czechs were "sports". We were herded out of our cells, usually in the evening and at night, and had to run brisk laps around the yard. "Exercises" had to be performed. Guards, Czech civilians and several Kapos armed with whips, bullwhips and sticks stood off to the side and urged the gasping people on until they were totally exhausted. Shattered arms and especially elbows (raised to protect the head) were common. The Czech spectators in the bleachers expressed their delight at this spectacle with howls of glee.

In the evenings the women and girls had to strip naked, to be inspected by the Czech guards and the Russians for the nightly orgies.

I want to mention that these brutal, sadistic persecutions went through several high points alternating with somewhat calmer periods. This was partly due to the epidemics of dysentery and typhus, when the Czechs avoided entering the Fortress for fear of being infected, and partly to a change in the camp administration and the guards. Kling and Prusa with his two daughters had been arrested. I later saw them again in the District Court of Leitmeritz, as prisoners.

The arrival of the SNB *(Sbor Národní Bezpecnosti)* marked the beginning of a new time of suffering. This was also the time of the Aussig-Nestomitz explosion, which was simply laid to the Germans' charge. What happened there at that time was terrible. A small group of innocent, unhappy youths aged 13 to 17 who had been rounded up in Aussig were brought into the Little Fortress. Night after night they were taken out of the Special Cells, hounded with police dogs and beaten and tortured until there was not much left of any of them.

Normally every man had one blanket. If you were lucky you could find a spot somewhere in the four-story plank beds, which were a makeshift construction of uneven boards. If you were less lucky you slept on the concrete floor.

In August a few prisoners were interrogated - I was among them. My examining magistrate was one Dr. Ocadlík. He showed a particular interest in me. Among other things he claimed to have known my family "long enough", and made veiled threats to try to extort a confession from me. Sometimes a big Black man was also present. Ocadlík was visibly dissatisfied and tried time and again to prove that I had committed a crime of some kind. The third interrogation took place in the District Court of Leitmeritz, whence I was taken in shackles. At that time I had been frequently put to agricultural labor tasks in Kopitz. For example, I was accused of having caused the deaths of Anton Kaiser and Tyle. Both of them had committed suicide, for reasons unknown to me. I hadn't even know Tyle very well. Since I denied all the accusations being laid to my charge, and requested the opportunity for an appropriate defense, O. said mockingly, "At the next interrogation you'll see what's up."

So I was surprised when I was taken from Theresienstadt and back to Kopitz again. From a friend who had connections to the office I found out that strict measures had been ordered against me. I should not have been allowed to work outside the Fortress at all. The plan to notify my wife had been successful; I knew that she would come. But the evening before, I learned by chance that I was to be interrogated again the next day. In the morning I was taken back to Leitmeritz in chains.

In Leitmeritz I waited several days to be taken to the decisive interrogation. I was in a solitary-confinement cell on the first floor. As per regulations I was not allowed to leave the court building to go to work. Line-up for labor detail was in the morning, after coffee had been distributed. Since the prisoners in my cell block did not receive their coffee until those from the other blocks were already leaving for work, I calmly reported to the guard who was newly appointed to our section, *"Do práce!"* - off to work - and walked out into the long corridor. It happened to be one of the quieter periods again just then. Once more I was lucky; a few more people were needed for one of the work teams, I was entered into the list and was again able to leave the gray building regularly. There was no sign of an interrogation.

As far as I know, the following people from Polepp were arrested: Trojan Wenzel and Hermine Schafferbinder, Langer and his wife, young Mrs. Sipetzky, the teacher Welser (sentenced to 8 years), Weithofer, Munzig Albin, Franz Schwabge and I.

We frequently worked for the Russian occupation forces, and sometimes we were able to contact our relatives and to see or even talk to them every now and then. They knew, of course, what was happening, and put up with the hardship, harassment and abuse in order to see us when they could.

The arrests continued, and the prison was overcrowded. Here and there, People's Courts began to convene. None of the accused were given any opportunity to defend themselves properly. Often the verdicts were read without any preceding trial. Sometimes a longer show trial was staged, attended by many sensation-seeking spectators - and this usually resulted in a death sentence. The sentences were consistently severe. 10 years' imprisonment, imprisonment for life, and death. 5 to 10 years was considered a mild sentence, and these were relatively rare. Sentences under 5 years were the exception. To make room in the prisons, transports of prisoners were sent to Theresienstadt and the coal mines, but there was always a new, bloody and frightened face in the cell, to fill the space that had been cleared.

Christmas and New Year had passed. On March 7 they came to fetch me. I was only read the indictment, and was allowed to name only three witnesses. The indictment contained 7 charges.

Recently we had finally been able to have our laundry done every other week. Every second Thursday our relatives were allowed to come pick it up, and bring it back again the following week. Laundry distribution was supervised by the guard on duty. A so-called *chodbar* (hall worker) searched everything thoroughly and with considerable skill. Once I asked the supervisor to please let me have the bread that my loved ones had gone hungry to be able to send me. But he trampled on the slices of roasted bread and yelled scornfully that I should go ahead and eat my garbage, that it would soon be my last anyway. It was a welcome occasion to beat me up again.

In April we were allowed to receive food parcels, 2 kilos every two weeks. Regulations were unclear. At first we only received the bread that was in the parcels. Any butter, meat and meat dishes as well as sugar and fruit were confiscated by the guards for their own enjoyment.

On April 30, 1946, after our morning coffee, I was fetched from my cell. I was issued a better uniform, and was shaved. Zásvorka, one of the dumbest and most brutal of the guards, came to get me. For about 20 minutes I was able to speak to my defense counsel. The postcard that I had been allowed to write on March 7 had been withheld, he had not received it. But he was able to name witnesses for my defense (about 20 of them). He urged me to stay firm and straightforward, hinted that I was indeed in grave danger, but expressed hope that he could avert the worst if only I did not lose my nerve. This defense counsel also gave me to understand that my trial was being staged as a big deal.

Time was up, and I was led into the court building. The hallways were crowded with people, and at the entrance to the courtroom there stood the hangman in full uniform, black and red. My answers were brief and concise. The presiding judge seemed to be objective, and I grew more confident. The witnesses worked out wonderfully as well, but the witnesses for the prosecution were the tools of the examining magistrate Ocadlík. And so it went on until evening, with a short break for lunch. When O. realized in the course of the trial that I had managed to thoroughly unsettle the prosecution, he tried to induce the public prosecutor to bring new charges. The presiding judge commented that from the course of the trial it seemed to him that I had already disproved the new charge, but he left it up to the prosecutor to file a petition for the new charge. The prosecutor chose not to do so. At the end of the trial I was certain that we had won. Deliberations took a long time. A large part of the spectators had left; the case had lost its appeal for them. I knew that the Court would pronounce me guilty despite the facts - but still I had not expected to have to serve 15 years in prison, as forced laborer, with three months in a harsh penal camp.

For the time being, aside from my transfer to the third floor, not much changed. The third floor was for convicted prisoners who had been sentenced to more than 10 years. The room I was in had been designed for 6 prisoners, but now housed 14.

The greatest improvement that came about after my conviction was the right to write a short letter every six weeks, to receive a similar letter, and to have a visitor. In this way I managed to see my wife and children a few times before they were resettled [expelled] in July 1946. As of August 1, 1946 I again went to work regularly for the NWB, to Tschischkowitz into the cement factory, to Theresienstadt into the barracks, etc. We were kept under extremely close guard and had to work very hard. But we were rarely beaten. As of mid-September I was again forbidden to work, since I and a larger number of comrades were to be taken via Prague to Pilsen, to the prison of Bory, on September 24, 1946.

After our unpleasant and painful initiation into the customs of the Bory prison was over, I was assigned to a labor detail. The work was at times very hard, but the rations we received from the company we worked for were adequate.

Medical care in the prison varied. Frequently, the guard on duty in the sick-bay simply canceled the physician's orders.

After about 9 months our labor detail was changed, and instead of the iron foundry I now worked in a quarry outside Pilsen. The work was extremely hard, and some of my comrades could not hold up under it. We only had to work from 7 a.m. until 2 o'clock in the afternoon, and then we were left in peace, but what I liked about this job was something quite different. It seemed possible to attempt an escape from here. But by the time I was sufficiently familiar with my surroundings to begin preparations for an escape, I was reassigned to the agricultural labor detail Luhov, with new fellow-workers I did not know at all. But I quickly got used to the new work and the new environs. I cautiously began to get my bearings. I studied my new surroundings carefully, and found out where the rivers went and where the train crossings and street intersections were. It was impossible to obtain civilian clothes, maps and a compass. But I saved up some bread and dried some fruit as travel rations. For some time now I had been in charge of driving a team of horses, and systematically got my supervisors and fellow prisoners used to my not finishing my work until late in the evening. Then: a foggy night, dry weather had already held for some time, no rain was to be expected for the next days either, a waxing moon on the 13th - and we vanished into the dark. After three days and four nights we had done it.

Pössigkau and Taus

Maltreatment of women in May 1945
Reported by Anna Zitzmann - Report of June 8, 1946

On May 2 [1945] my husband and 16-year-old son were arrested by partisans and locked up for eight days in an ice cellar in Possigau [Pössigkau]. They were hung from a tree by their hands, which were tied behind their backs, and beaten with iron chains. From Possigau [Pössigkau] they were transferred to Taus. On the way there they were again beaten so badly that their entire bodies were black and blue.

On May 8 I too was arrested for no reason. I was detained in the ice cellar in Possigau [Pössigkau] as well, for two days without food. I too was beaten there. I had to bend over the back of a chair, and my skirts were lifted over my back. Two men then beat me with rubber truncheons. I was also hit in the face, and almost all my teeth were knocked out in the process. For 10 days I was beaten up like this several times each day. When I urinated I passed blood. From Possigau [Pössigkau] I was taken to the District Court in Taus. I was beaten there as well. For three weeks I was detained in the prison, with completely insufficient rations. There were approximately another 150 women there, and they were beaten just as badly as I was. My husband and my son were being held in the same prison. On June 17 my husband and son were transported off. I never heard from them again. A Czech woman later told me that 1,200 German men were said to be buried in a mass grave behind the Taus train station.

In late June I was sent from Taus to go to work for a farmer, where conditions were relatively good. In August I was brought back to the camp in Taus, and had to go to work in the milk hall, where things were also bearable. Then I was sent to work as housekeeper for a widower with 10 children. The widower proposed to me several times, but I turned him down. To escape his constant molestations, I fled across the border in April 1946.

I am prepared to take this statement on my oath.

Pribrans and Prague

Maltreatment
Reported by engineer Ing. Kurt Schmidt

On May 5, 1945 my family and I were imprisoned by Czech partisans. My wife had our three children with her, all of them under the age of three years, and we all were imprisoned in Pribram (Pribrans) in Bohemia, 75 km south of Prague, together with 300 other Germans, mostly women and children, primarily evacuees from Silesia. We were kept in a former orphanage.

We were quartered in groups of 15-20 per each small, totally unfurnished room. The few straw sacks that were there were hardly enough for the children to sleep on. We got nothing to eat for the first three days, and after that only a little soup once a day. There was no bread at all for eight days. We were allowed to open the windows only once a day for barely half an hour. The children were permitted to go out into the yard once a day, only for a very short time, and had to keep walking in circles.

Everyone was put to forced labor. The men had to dig mass graves and bury the corpses of the executed SS men. For example, my colleague from the office, engineer Leinweber, and a young girl had to work at a pit where the SS men that had fallen into the hands of Czech partisans had been executed. With their bare hands they had to dig up the bodies that had been torn apart by machine gun fire and hand grenades and were in some cases already partly decomposed, and had to load them onto a truck that took the corpse pieces to the mass graves.

The women were also put to this kind of work. For example, my two sisters-in-law Else Hübner and Marie Prutky had to work in the hospital morgue where they had to wash the bloody furnishings and floors. Other women had to sweep the streets, and they were maltreated by Czechs. In one case I myself witnessed how a group of women were attacked. They were shorn bald, their faces were painted with oil paint and the last clothes they had were smeared with oil paint, rendering them useless. The women were also robbed of their shoes and beaten and spat on.

After May 9, 1945, when the Russians marched in, the maltreatment grew even worse. Especially the women were in great danger after nightfall. The rooms in the internment camp could no longer be locked. The Russians, aided and abetted by the Czechs, came and got whomever they liked, and they did not hesitate to use force. For example, in a neighboring camp set up in a former community college a woman who would not submit to the Russians was plunged to her death from the third story into the square below. In the same camp another woman was raped repeatedly until she was dead. Of the women whom the Russians fetched from the camp, four never came back at all.

On May 12 partisans came, led by Czech gendarmes. There were women among them too, and they demanded at gunpoint that we surrender all our jewelry, watches, valuables, all cash down to the last penny, savings bank books and papers. We were not even allowed to keep our wedding rings. We were left with one set of cutlery each, but sharp knives and scissors were also confiscated.

That same day around 8 o'clock in the evening it was announced that the next day, Sunday, May 13, we would be marched off to Prague or Pilsen. We were allowed to take some hand luggage, but everything else was to remain behind. That night another group of prisoners arrived but because the camp was so overcrowded they had to spend the night on the staircase and outside in the square.

In the morning we were ordered to march out. A few carts were available to carry the old and ill prisoners as well as toddlers, but they were not enough to hold everyone who had need of them. And so we set out in the direction of Prague. It was scorchingly hot. Every now and then some old and sick people remained sitting by the side of the road because they could not go on, and in that way many died in the ditches, partly of exhaustion, partly at the hands of the Czech Revolutionary Guardsmen that accompanied us. We had not received any food for several days. In the towns we passed through, many were attacked and robbed of their last few possessions. The women and children were dragged off the carts and relieved of their luggage, and then they had to continue on foot as the cart waited for no-one. We reached Doberschisch in the evening after a 16-km march, and we camped in a meadow. The townspeople came in droves, rifled through any luggage they found, and whatever they liked, they kept. We were instructed to leave everything lying on the ground, since we would be relieved of our things anyway, one way or another. That evening my wife and our three children found a place in a car full of German soldiers being driven to Prague into captivity. Our march continued until 2 o'clock in the morning. The Russians came and took what they liked: suitcases, bags etc., and preferably women. From 2 to 5 o'clock we rested in the ditch. Then we were marched on to Königssaal (Zbraslav), where we were herded together in a large meadow. A Polish member of the Red Cross was holding a two or three month old infant that he had taken from its mother, who had died in the ditch. We got nothing to eat during this rest stop either. Even though it was oppressively hot, we were allowed to fetch only small quantities of water from the town, and only under close guard. In the course of the day several corpses were put on display in the camp near the entrance, and the camp inmates were forced to view them. They were the bodies of women with children who had chosen to commit suicide to escape further tortures.

On May 15 the order was given to move out, but all men between the ages of 16 and 60 were held back in the camp. These men were closely examined by the Czech Revolutionary Guard and the Russian military, and anyone who was suspected of having belonged to the Wehrmacht or the SS was detained. I was among the lucky ones who were allowed to return to their families. As our group left the camp we saw a young man standing in front of a pit ready to hold the bodies of executed prisoners. Four other men were digging more pits. As we crossed the street, we heard the sounds of shots from the camp square we had just left.

And so our march went on. Anyone who still had any luggage at all soon threw one piece after the other into the ditch just to be able to keep moving at all. In this way I too lost my last worldly possessions. In every town we were met with curses and thrown rocks, and beatings as well. Guards stood beside some of the wells and refused our requests for water with the words, "this water is for horses, not for Germans." The heat became ever more unbearable, and it was our third day with not even a bite to eat. At dusk we arrived in the suburb of Motol. Here we were allowed to rest in the ditch until 2 o'clock a.m., and then we were marched through Prague in the dark at high speed to Strahover Stadium, where we arrived at 6 o'clock in the morning of May 16, totally exhausted.

Some 9,000 to 10,000 people were confined in Strahover Stadium, under the open sky and on the bare ground. Most of the prisoners were members of the Wehrmacht, war-disabled ex-servicemen and sick people whom the Czechs had thrown out of their hospital beds. After 8 to 10 days the Wehrmacht members were sent to a different camp. Their vacated places were filled with new civilians, mostly women and children. According to the camp cook the population consistently remained between 9,000 and 10,000 people even though approximately 1,200 were sent off every second day to labor camps. The new arrivals were mostly taken from trains. I know of two cases personally (Mrs. Schlegel from L. and the engineer E. from Stauden in Bremen). The aforementioned had been interned in Winterberg and Budweis, respectively, then released again as they were citizens of the Reich proper, and furnished with train tickets and official release papers from both Russian and American authorities. On their trip home, as they passed through Prague, they were detained by the Czechs, taken from their trains by Revolutionary Guardsmen, and dragged into Strahover Stadium. The Czechs paid no heed to American or Russian papers.

The rations we received in the Stadium were quite inadequate. We got nothing at all for the first three days, and then, in irregular intervals of about 36 hours at first and a little more regularly once a day later on, we were given a cup of black coffee, some watery soup, and 100g bread - once a day, as I said. When the mortality rate began to rise, a little barley soup was cooked for the children and the sick people. The food was distributed to groups, not individually, and the buckets - insofar as there were any at all, since the inmates themselves had to provide them - were generally used for other purposes at night. Otherwise there were only open latrines in the middle of the stadium, with no segregation of women, men and children, healthy or ill. The latrines were crawling with vermin. It was mostly the great shortage of food that resulted in an outbreak of dysentery. The Czechs did not provide the German doctors (who were themselves prisoners) with any medications whatsoever. The Wehrmacht physician from the Red Cross station told me that children under two years of age and the elderly would not be able to cope with this situation, and would not leave the camp alive. I too lost my 15-month-old boy to starvation there, and the paper which the medical post issued me in this regard gave malnutrition as the cause of death (signed by Vogt, NCO). The bodies of 12 to 20 persons daily were taken out of the stadium on a manure cart.

Executions were done in full view of the entire camp. One day 6 young fellows were beaten until they remained where they fell, then water was poured on them (which the German women had to fetch) and then they were beaten some more, until they no longer gave any signs of life. The horribly mangled corpses were put on display beside the latrines, and were left there for days. One 14-year-old boy was shot, together with his parents, for allegedly having taken a stab a a Red Guardsman with a pair of scissors. Beyond that there was also the standard corporal punishment, which was usually carried out in the staff room. Even the women had to strip naked and were then whipped.

Both men and women were urged along on their forced labor duties with blows from rifle butts. This work consisted mostly of tearing down barricades, and the working people were mocked and jeered and spat at, and stoned as well. There were cases where some women, and sometimes even some infirm men, did not return from this work. At some work sites, however, the laborers received somewhat better rations (in Russian barracks, hospitals etc.).

The women were fair game for anyone. Everyone could come and choose whomever he liked, and if the children screamed for their mothers they were forcibly silenced. The Russians and Czechs often did not even bother to lead the women off, but raped them right then and there, between the children and in full view of all the other prisoners.

The transports into labor camps began in late May. On June 3, 1945 I and my family were sent to Kojetitz, outside Prague, for farm work. There were 63 of us in all. On June 5 another group of 54 civilians arrived in Prague from another camp. This group worked on the estate, while our own group had to hoe sugar beets for two large farms. We were quartered in a horse stable on wet straw, while the second group was put into an open shed. We were locked into our stable right away on our arrival, and the stable was then locked. In one of the corners, a tub served as makeshift toilet.

These conditions continued until early August, when members of both groups - specifically, those unfit for work, and families with many children - were culled and sent away. My wife's father and two sisters were among these, and we were unable to learn anything of their whereabouts despite our best efforts. The rest of us who remained in Kojetitz, a total of 79 persons, were divided up among a few farms on the one hand, and four damp, dark, dingy little rooms on the other, where we first had to sleep on straw sacks that were rotting from below. Later we got some Wehrmacht pallets. Our room, 12x15' in size, was home to 13 people, 6 of them children.

In summer our work day lasted 10 to 12 hours, in winter 8½ to 9½ hours, even on Sundays, and we were expected to do the hardest kinds of field work. We didn't receive a penny in wages.

Among the area's inhabitants there were a few that felt some pity for us, but they didn't dare help us since any attempt to do so resulted in the others denouncing them as being "friendly to Germans" and depriving them of their livelihood. At Christmas the town council even passed a special order, forbidding the locals to give us any assistance whatsoever or letting the children have any baked goods. On Christmas Eve we got black coffee like on every other evening, and that was that. For the first 8 weeks the Red Guards kept us under very strict supervision and even accompanied us into the fields with submachine guns. Later, a Czech named Vales was assigned to guard us. He would urge us to greater speed when we worked, and when it was time to distribute the already meager rations he would keep part of them back for himself. The treatment we got at the hands of the foreman Vysinský was very rough. He never called a German woman anything other than "German whore", and the men "bloodhound". Administrator Marek preferred to beat us, and he would whip the women across the face with his riding crop. He also beat a camp inmate with his whip until the man was unconscious on the ground. This administrator was the only Czech officer in town and was a member of the Czech National-Socialists (Beneš Party). He liked to play the big man, and instigated various torments against the internees. Another man who bore a major part of the responsibility for the conditions in the camp was the Chairman of the *Národní Výbor,* the Communist Suchý.

The children could not dare set foot outside the door to our poor hovel without immediately being cursed at and stoned, and by teenaged Czechs, no less. The grown-ups were also tormented by these youths. Some of them, approximately 14 or 15 years old, even tried to attack and rape our women in broad daylight.

In the very first days of our stay in Kojetitz, a child not even two years old died of the repercussions of measles. We were forbidden to bury this child in the cemetery, instead we had to bury it outside the town behind a straw shed, without a coffin of course. The farmer Tuma (Kojetitz No. 10) shot a 16-year-old boy after locking him up and starving him for two days in the pigsty. He paid no heed to the boy's cries for his mother, and after shooting him he had him thrown into a shallow pit in the farmhouse garden. A German named Pelz had to carry out this burial. After about 14 days Mrs. Anderson, about 67 years old, died in our camp of starvation and infirmity, and two days later the Silesian woman Mrs. Wittkopp succumbed to the same. These two women had been Protestants, and we managed to notify the minister from the Czech Protestant church. He came to the camp and saw to it that the bodies were put into wooden coffins and were given a proper burial in the Protestant cemetery in Libis. Mrs. Treske from Neisse, who died of heart failure a little later, was given the same care.

The Catholic priest of Kojetitz behaved quite differently. At first he would not permit the Germans to enter the church. Later he allowed them to attend a service on Sunday afternoons, but continued to forbid that any German should receive the sacrament. He also refused any other assistance whatsoever for the Germans. The Catholics who died are buried without coffins in mass graves in the Criminals' Corner of the Catholic cemetery. The flowers placed on these mass graves on All Saints' Day and Christmas were removed and destroyed by Czechs.

Among those buried in the Catholic cemetery are: the men Hollmann (who committed suicide on his arrest), Wieck (from Prague, age 46, probably of the consequences of a liver and stomach condition), E. von Stauden (furunculosis combined with a weak heart, age 52, from Bremen), the women Marie Prutky (my wife's mother, she died of heart failure and malnutrition, age 72, from Brünn), Mrs. Grosse (infirmity, gangrene and malnutrition, age 70, from Weisswasser, Silesia). The child Baduschek (4 years old, probably of diptheria, from Brünn), and an infant, Enders, of malnutrition. All these deaths took place within the first three months.

The doctor, who visited the camp only twice, refused to enter the stable for fear of all the vermin. He did not even examine the sick people, but just stood in the doorway and said that he couldn't help them. To the Czech guards he commented that it would be fine with him if all the Germans "croaked". This doctor was from Neratowitz, near Prague. Both my children caught the measles, and the younger of them, my little girl, also contracted pneumonia and inflammation of the middle ear. With a raging fever she had to lie on the straw in the drafty barn. Even while the children were so ill my wife nonetheless had to go to work from morning till night, and was forbidden to stay with the sick children on pain of being executed.

On April 6 we were sent to the Prague camp of Hagibor, where we were received in a halfway humane manner. Our treatment and rations (especially for toddlers) were somewhat better. On the work details we were usually treated well and received adequate rations. There was a labor shortage in Prague at the time.

On April 24, 1946, families with children and people unfit for work were sent from the Hagibor camp (with a population of 200) to the expulsion camp Modrany, where the housing and rations were again bad. 350 men were crowded into a small wooden barrack meant for about 100 people.

On May 1, 1946, 1,200 internees were loaded into 40 cattle cars and sent off to Bavaria as "Transport D". As travel rations we were given a little watery soup, one-eighth of a loaf of bread, and a slice of cake. On two rest stops along the way we got a bit more watery soup, and then, on May 2, 1946, we crossed the Czech border at Wiesau, and were taken in and cared for in exemplary fashion by the Bavarian Red Cross.

Qualisch

Treatment of Jews
Reported by Dr. Rudolf Fernegg - Report of June 21, 1951

The son of the owner of the firm of Bendix at Qualisch near Trautenau lived in the United States of America during the period of the "Third Reich". Even though he was an American citizen he was not permitted to take over the factory [after his return].

Radl

Husband was murdered; maltreatment, May 1945 to November 1946

Reported by Margarete Kaulfersch - Report of June 16, 1950

On Sunday, May 13, 1945, Czech partisans entered our home, rummaged through chests and closets, threatened my husband and me and held pistols against our necks, ready to fire. Two communists who had probably been alerted by all the noise arrived, and managed to make the partisans leave. My husband was a coach builder by profession, and he worked from morning till night. The next day another horde of looters came into our home, and one of them ordered my husband to go from house to house and see to it that all German-language signs and inscriptions on the houses and streets were removed. They left our house, not without first indulging in some nasty threats. On Tuesday I saw how a gang of partisans surrounded our house, and since it was locked, they broke the door down. My husband wasn't there with me. On the assumption that this horde perhaps wanted to ask me something, an acquaintance offered to go into the house with me. I had to sign a paper stating that my husband had to report to the Mayor's Office, and that if he failed to do so, I would be arrested. But they took me along with them right then and there, just to make sure. My husband was informed of the order by an acquaintance, and we met again at the community office *(Národní výbor).* We were not even questioned, but he had to get into a truck along with Emil Scheffel, who had also been ordered to report there, and that was the last I ever saw of my husband. 14 days later some acquaintances told me that he and four fellow sufferers, among them Scheffel, had been beaten and tortured to death, after they had first had to dig their own grave. I later had an opportunity to speak to the doctor who had issued the death certificate. I asked him to tell me more - he refused, and said, "Remember your husband the way you knew him when he was alive."

Our house was totally looted. I stayed with some neighbors until I had to join a transport that took me to forced labor in the Czech regions. At first the cattle car dropped us off at an estate near Turnau. The entire transport was housed in a large barn. During the day the Czech farmers came to choose the most promising workers. We were put on display like livestock at the market. After three days I and 11 other women were the only ones left. After the first night two girls had to be taken to the hospital after being severely raped. A guard gave his word that "nothing like that would happen again."

I was glad when we were taken away on the fourth day. We were taken to Sychrov into a beautiful building that had served as a youth shelter during the war. This shelter was now a gathering point for the Czech partisans. We had no opportunity to notify our relatives, nor to receive news from outside. The food we got was very bad, and not nearly enough. Our first work assignment was washing toilets, all day long. I had to throw up, and began to have diarrhea. A young doctor who realized that I had contracted stomach typhus and feared that I would infect the others asked an older doctor, his superior, to send me away. But this angel of mercy only said, "The Germans have to work." Finally they let me go home. One of the partisans barely took me as far as the Employment Office in Turnau. It was a well-known regulation that Germans were only permitted to use the train under Czech escort, but I was sent off alone. I had been gone for four weeks. When I got home I was allowed to move into the smallest room in what had been our own house.

Four weeks later, when I was still utterly exhausted, a Ukrainian informed me that I had been ordered to resettle [be expelled]. I collapsed; when I came to again, I found myself lying in bed, and he was sitting by my feet. He wrung his hands and said, "I beg you, I don't want to be a murderer!" He left to fetch my neighbors, and ordered them not to leave me alone. Then he returned with officials from the *národní výbor*. Dr. Köhler was called, and he diagnosed a nervous breakdown.

In November 1946 I was resettled [expelled].

Radonitz

Report on the events of May 1946
Reported by Friedrich Merten

The little, remote town in Northwestern Bohemia in which I had worked as teacher at the local elementary school for more than 20 years lay between the two military fronts: about an hour away in one direction were American troops and at about the same distance in the other direction were Russian divisions. Instead of the Americans, whom we expected, the Russians arrived first.

These Russians were armed civilians, who drove through our little town in smaller or larger vehicles of Russian construction. They were led by Russian officers on horseback and showed good discipline. No deeds of violence were committed during their first passage. Those who began the plundering were Polish and Ukrainian drivers and servants, who had fled together with the people from Silesia. These men took the weapons which German soldiers had thrown away on their march through the town some days before and, under a leader of their own, they began a reign of terror. The first Russian division had scarcely left the town when the first lootings began. The looters committed their excesses mostly at night. During the day - remembering the various proclamations over the radio - everybody went about his work, but everyone feared the nights. Unexpectedly, assistance was rendered by a Russian officer, who drove through our town on an official trip. One of our fellow-citizens, who was of Czech descent, laid before the Russian officer the request of the population for protection. The officer disarmed the commander of the plundering gang and shot him with his own hand. On the proposal of my fellow-citizens this officer installed me as mayor in the town hall ("You are mayor!"). I was later confirmed as such by the Russian command.

First of all I saw to the establishment of peace and order in the little town. The example which the Russian officer had made still had its after-effect. The French PoWs (Prisoners of War), who had worked with us since the end of the war with France and who were on good terms with the population, offered to establish a police corps, which was later on also joined by British PoWs.

These former PoWs armed themselves with weapons and put a stop to the plundering. I would like to stress my appreciation of the attitude of these former prisoners of war. The little town became an island of peace, everybody was able to do his work unmolested. The population recognized the former prisoners of war as their protectors.

I succeeded also in getting going the supply of the most necessary foods, so that nobody had to starve.

Meanwhile a Czech National Committee *("Národní výbor")* was established by the few Czech residents, who permitted me to perform my duties as mayor under their patronage. Even when in June 1945 a Czech commissar was installed, I still remained as mayor - although it was merely a title without any powers and my functions were limited to keeping the routine work going. The commissar was a decent and honest man. Since he was a stranger in this place, he quite often consulted me and paid attention to my suggestions. He was ordered to carry out the cruel measures against the Germans, decided on by the Prague Government, but he did so in a very considerate way. I remember quite well when one day this man brought the first transfer-order from the district town and directed me to make up a list of the so-called intelligentsia of the town. From the first moment I was clear about the meaning of this order. The commissar, whose name I prefer to pass over in silence, was of the opinion that various unpleasant things were to be expected. "Whether these measures will be for the best," he said, "I really don't know, but nothing can be done about them."

Although the measures were supposed to be kept secret, I was unable to conceal them from my friends. At the same time proclamations were posted up, saying that the Germans had lost their Czech citizenship and that their entire property would be confiscated on behalf of the Czech State without compensation.

In the meantime refugees from the neighbourhood had arrived at the homes of their acquaintances and relatives or had come to our peaceful valley on their flight. They brought with them the first alarming news concerning the expulsion of Germans from their apartments, the shootings and the hunting of German women and girls.

A Czech military division was quartered in our town. For each of the soldiers a bed with white sheets had to be made up in the Turnhalle (gymnasium). On June 22, 1945, shortly after lunch, the soldiers, led on by an officer, marched from one apartment to another, belonging to those persons who were on the expulsion-list. The officer handed over the order for expulsion and demanded first of all the surrender of all valuables. A guard remained in each house. In the evening the first column of expellees was formed; to begin with they were taken to a camp in the neighbouring town and, after they had been robbed of everything by the inspecting officials, they had to march to the border.

In spring 1946, after a quiet interval during which many of my fellow-citizens dared to hope for a change for the better, expropriations and expulsions began again.

Radwanitz, Report No. 1

Abduction of an American citizen

Reported by Josef Horbas - Report of October 6, 1946

I am 15 years old and an American citizen. My mother has resided at Pittsburgh in the United States of America since 1937 and has been an American citizen since 1944. I myself lived with my aunt at Setzdorf. In August 1945 I was summoned to appear before the municipal council; when I made known my American citizenship I was imprisoned in the local detention camp and was transferred to the coal-mine of Radwanitz the very next day. Only when a letter from Washington arrived at Radwanitz was I released. The months in the coal-mine were a time of unbearable suffering for us all. Notwithstanding our youth we were forced to work as hard as the adults, namely 8 hours underground in the mine and then several hours above ground. We had to get up at 3:30 in the morning and never got [back] before 8 o'clock in the evening or even later. For several months the food consisted exclusively of chopped turnips. Many of the workers died. Usually three to four a week. There were cases of cruel torturing every day. On our way to as well as from the coal mine we were forced on the way to perform strenuous exercises. Often we were so exhausted that we could hardly stand. In the evening we frequently had to [run on the] double several times around the barracks.

Radwanitz, Report No. 2

Coal-pit, maltreatment, murders

Reported by Josef Langenickel - Report of July 1, 194[7?]

I was in the internment camp at Radwanitz near Mährisch-Ostrau from August 27th, 1945 to August 13th, 1946. The inmates of the camp worked underground in the "Hedwig" and "Progress" pits. After a shift of 8 hours underground one had to work an additional 4-5 hours above ground. Our first holiday was Easter.

Treatment and food were bad. Corporal punishment was introduced officially. Even while working underground we were beaten by the Czech miners. On account of malnutrition production was going down. Everyone who failed to accomplish his full quota was beaten by the guards. The beatings took place in the cellar with the doors locked and was carried out by a special corporal punishment squad of 6-8 men. Many failed to survive the malnutrition and ill-treatment. In November Josef Kremer collapsed and died while marching from the pit to the camp. When anyone reported sick, he would be beaten. Johann Weinert died of malnutrition on March 7th, 1946; he was forced to work up to his last breath. On November 11, 1945 I myself received a severe thrashing in the manner known as the "Dreischlag" (characterized by blows in a triple rhythm, delivered by several persons), because I was quite unable to work by the reason of complete exhaustion and swollen legs.

It was not until February 1st, 1946 that I was given some easier work above ground. In the camp letter-writing was forbidden. The possession of a pencil was not allowed and was punished with cruel maltreatment.

Reichenau

Women severely maltreated
Reported by Franziska Hübl - Report of June 15, 1946

In July 1945 my daughter-in-law and I were in our barn and we happened to find two pieces of leather from a drive belt, about 12 inches long. We assumed that these two strips of leather had been left behind by a trek that had spent more than two months with us, and had left behind many other things as well, such as irons, neckties, slippers etc. In January 1946 we had to get some shoes re-soled at the cobbler's, but he had no soles. I remembered the two pieces of leather, and took them to the cobbler. But the cobbler didn't fix our shoes right away, as he was very busy.

In March my daughter-in-law and I were taken to the community office. Commissar Petr showed us the two pieces of leather and asked us where we had got them. Before we could even begin to explain, the Commissar beat us. First I was led into a separate room, where he hit me in the face and about the head with his hand, a belt and a dog whip until I was suffused with blood. Then my daughter-in-law was beaten in the same way. This was repeated three times.

As the consequence of this maltreatment my daughter-in-law suffered a miscarriage.

Reinowitz (concentration camp near Gablonz)

Imprisonment in this camp, confiscation of money
Reported by Alfred Porsche - Report of June 20, 1950

On March 26, 1946, after members of the Local Committee of Grünwald on the Neisse had looted my luggage, my family and I were imprisoned in the concentration camp Reinowitz. As the very first thing, even before the delousing, everyone had to report to the camp administrator Václav Vosträk's office and hand over their savings bank books and all German and Czech cash.

In early April, transports to the Reichenau camp were being assembled. We were told that from Reichenau we would be sent to Germany. The members of the individual transports were called out by name in the yard.

My turn came on April 10, 1946. On that day or the day before - I don't recall exactly - the members of these transports were called into the office opposite that of the camp administrator, to sign something. Everyone wanted to get away from there and so they hastened to comply with the order. I took a closer look at what was pre-printed there in Czech for us to sign. Most of my fellow prisoners did not understand Czech, and signed without knowing what the paper said. It was a statement to the effect that we had received our confiscated funds (savings bank books and cash) back. It goes without saying that these valuables were never actually returned to us.

Riegersdorf

Report of an anti-Fascist, Social Democratic representative
Reported by Josef Willkomm

The eviction of the Germans from their dwellings in 1945 was carried out irrespective of their political background. Even persons who were known as anti-fascists and who were in possession of anti-fascist certificates, issued by Czech authorities, did not get back their property.

In those first days after the 8th of May 1945, a Czech who had always resided at Riegersdorf took over provisionally the management of public affairs. By the time it was our turn to be transferred [expelled], the tenth provisional mayor within the year was already in office. He was the first honest and competent one of the lot.

In all cases where Czech families had not moved in at once [into the German homes], the apartments had been looted on the same night on which we had been expelled and the contents had been sent by truck into the inner part of Czechoslovakia.

Simultaneously, bad times also began for the anti-fascists. When I in my capacity as the Czech-speaking confidant of the Antifa (anti-fascist organization) went to Czech offices to discuss the problems of our members, I was first of all shown a picture of five Germans who had been hanged as an intimidation that the same would happen to me, if I asked too [many questions] or if I should help Nazis. My wife and I had also been driven out of our little house and had been put into a miserable flat, where what clothes and linen we had left were gnawed by rats, which also crept over our beds at night.

When I finally obtained an ANTIFA-certificate from the Czech officials and attempted to get back some of our household furniture, they simply laid a pistol onto the table and maintained that it had been found in my house - although in fact I had never owned one. They then told me that if I did not give up all claims to my property, they would immediately arrest me.

The very moment that we Social Democrats of North Bohemia had signed an agreement for our transfer [expulsion] to Thuringia and I had received the necessary papers for 69 families of our community so that we were ready to leave, the Czech commissar blocked all the roads out of our village and - going from one house to the other - began to weigh the 30 kilos of luggage allowed per head. This went on for several days. Beatings occurred, in consequence of which one young man died. He had attempted to protect his wife from insult. Some of the women had to undress completely and were molested by drunken Czechs. All this was done to German workers by Czech Communists!

Since the transfer to Thuringia had been frustrated, we had to look for another territory to which to be transferred. This was Hesse. We went through a hard time. Although we were acknowledged anti-fascists, we were treated in just the same way as the Nazis. Our wives had to work for Czech families or on farms, either for nothing or for a piece of bread. The men had to do heavy labour in the woods or elsewhere for 50 Hellers per hour [approximately 5 Pfennigs or 1 Cent].

There was always some special work to do on Sundays, for instance cleaning the latrines, clearing the little stream or collecting scrap iron etc. Every third Sunday, which was supposed to be free, all persons of more than 14 years of age had to report to the town-council, stand in a long row, in order to be taken to the movie theatre under police escort. There we had to pay an entrance-fee, three times as high as the normal one, but all they showed us on the screen were Hitler's atrocities.

German workers were sent into the inner part of Bohemia in open coal carts, in order to work on farms or in industry.

When we were about to be transferred to Hesse in July 1946 we had reason to be glad that this tenth provisional mayor for the first time was a man of sense. I was able to save various things for a number of families as well as clothes from the house of my parents-in-law, who had died in the meantime, for my wife and myself.

Before I was transferred to Germany I visited Prague five times, in order to get the exit and luggage permits from the Ministry of the Interior and the Ministry of Finance, so that several persons should be allowed to take along their bicycles, sewing-machines, radios and similar articles.

My sister and her husband with their two daughters and [our] 84-year-old mother could leave Czechoslovakia for Germany only in April 1950. My brother-in-law worked in the mines for two years. After this they all had to work on farms. They were lucky in that the owner of the estate was a good and honest man. When they took leave of him, he wept and said: "You are leaving us now, but what will become of us?"

I was the local representative of the Social Democratic Party at Riegersdorf, in the district of Tetschen, for 14 years till 1938.

Riesengebirge (the Sudeten Mountains)

Overview of murders 1945. Excerpts from the publication "Riesengebirgsheimat".

Hermannseifen: June 29, 1945, shot while the entire community had to watch: Andreas Pohl, master butcher; Franz Pohl, his son; Josef Gaber, master baker; Josef Stransky, barber; Alois Struchlik, laborer; by the verdict of the Commandant of Arnau. Frau Pohl committed suicide by hanging.

Mastig: June 1945, shot in front of the entire community: Nittner (from Hohenelbe); Stephan Rzehak, mayor; Josef Gall, master spinner; Josef Tauchmann, company representative of the Mandl factory; Anton Jochmann, railwayman; shot by Czech soldiers from Arnau and the *Národní výbor*.

Vordermastig: May 1945: Josef Schröfel, innkeeper, committed suicide by hanging, his wife took poison when their estate was looted and occupied.

Grossaupa: Hugo, tortured and shot in the cemetery (details unknown).

Keilbaude: Braun, innkeeper, killed.

Schüsselbauden: Raimund Kraus and Johann Hollmann shot by partisans.

Hütten-Witkowitz: the merchant Herbert Schier's father-in-law [executed?], while Rudolf Schier died in the Jitschin prison.

Harta: June 1945. Five people were horribly beaten.

Theresiental: June 1945. Alois Baruschka maltreated and shot.

Jablonetz: September 8, 1945. Schimmer died in Karthaus-Jitschin after severe maltreatment (arrested on May 9, 1945).

Mastig: May 1946. Alfred Kuhn, beaten to death in Jitschin.

Spindelmühle: Alfred Fischer, senior teacher, murdered in May 1945. Hans Buchberger and his mother, shot in Trautenau in May 1945, his father Vinzenz (innkeeper of St. Peter's) is a prisoner in the uranium mine of St. Joachimsthal.

Arnau: Josef Rumler and his wife Marie, née Petrik, were brutally maltreated on June 18, 1945, and then shot. Heinz Soukup, Eichmann's attorney, executed on June 10, 1945. Erich Kowarsch, brewery employee, shot or beaten to death in early June 1945. Many committed suicide by taking poison (Iwonsky, the family Schenk, Melichar etc.).

Klein-Borowitz: June 18, miller Linhart and his wife arrested in Arnau, beaten and tortured in Eichmann Cellar, then taken to Mastig on June 21 and shot in the presence and on the orders of the Czech Commandant of Arnau, Wurm, from Horschitz.

Ponikla: May 9, 1945, herdsman [shepherd?] Anton Wenzel arrested, taken to Hochstadt, maltreated. Knappe, Mayor, executed in Starkenbach (town square).

Jablonetz: engineer Schirmer and others, taken to Semil; Hirte, who had also been taken there on May 11, slashed his wrists.

Rochlitz: Fritz Seidel from Oberrochlitz arrested in May 1945, taken to Starkenbach in January 1946, then to the Hrabatschow camp, has been missing ever since.

Zittau - Neuhammer: on this stretch of road some 60-80 prisoners of war were killed by the Poles because they were unable to keep up the pace set for this death march. Many Sudeten Germans from Lauban were among the victims. The march led via Sagan to the Jaworczno camp near Auschwitz, where they all had to work in the mine and where (by August 1947) 18 had died, 1 had committed suicide and 1 had been shot while trying to escape. Many of the victims were from the Riesengebirge [Sudeten Mountains].

Kukus: mid-May 1945. Ginzkey, educator from Reichenberg, brutally beaten, died of the consequences. Petrak, senior educator from Seidenschwanz, and Karl Schneider, senior gardener from Graslitz, beaten and then shot behind the railway yard. Alois Slaboch, civil servant; Eusebius

Areyczuk, Ukrainian greengrocer; both beaten and then shot in the Stangendorf quarry. Frau Slaboch cut her throat.

Gutsmuts-Arnau: Wilhelm Pradler, construction supervisor, and his wife Maria, shot on June 23, 1945 in Proschwitz in front of the Elbemühl [mill]. Slanderously denounced by: Amler, Nossek and Schiefert, as well as a Czech from Proschwitz.

Schwarzenthal: Julius Gall, senior teacher, and Franz Baier, senior forester, arrested in June 1946, missing ever since. Hubert Wawra, administrator in Mencik, murdered in Hohenelbe. In total, 17 inhabitants of the town have been reported missing; the other 14 are: Franz Munser, master dyer; Franz Kröhn, from Mencik; Franz Kröhn, farmer; Josef Ettrich, coachman; Franz Seidel, carpenter; Wenzel Seidel, mailman; Maiwald, master saddler; Johann Kraus, master dyer; Josef Kraus, in Mencik; Oswald Renner, telephonist; Wonka, farmer; Josef Schneider, quarry laborer; Josef Langer, office employee; Edi Klust, master weaver.

Lauterwasser: January 24, 1946. Johann Zirm, policeman, hung in Jitschin.

Polkendorf: Johann Sagasser, 1946, suicide. Franz Erben, suicide.

Rokitnitz

Maltreatment and murders
Reported by Director Pischel - Report of July 31, 1950

When individual units and formations of the Silesian army passed through our little town on May 7 and 8, 1945, we knew that the catastrophe could only be a few days away at best. Alarming news abounded. The inhabitants stood outside their houses, and fleeing was impossible. Already Czech partisans had occupied all the streets, and disarmed our soldiers. Anyone who made even the slightest attempt to resist was shot. And in fact the Russians followed hard on the heels of the German troops, and thousands of artillery, tanks and motorized troops poured across the crest of the Adler Mountains, filled the mountain towns and, rushing towards Prague, overran the German troops.

But when the Czech partisans occupied our home town we had to witness horrible misdeeds. Anything that wasn't nailed down was stolen, and almost all men, regardless of their age, were arrested and maltreated terribly and dragged into the prison. The one-man cells were soon filled to bursting, and so the subsequent prisoners were taken to the barracks. It is simply impossible to describe what took place there. Many Germans sought to escape the dreadful maltreatment by committing suicide. May 19, 1945, the Saturday before Pentecost, was a particularly black day. The already half-starved prisoners, I among them, were herded to the barracks to work. For example, pairs of two each had to carry heavy wall units down the stairs, across the large barracks square, into other buildings and back up the stairs there. Partisans stood everywhere and beat the unhappy people with sticks, iron bars, rubber truncheons, bicycle inner tubes and rifle butts, with no regard for where they hit us. Blood ran from my many head wounds into my eyes and across my neck and down my back.

Many collapsed under the blows and were beaten and kicked while they were down. I myself once had more than 20 lumps on my head and two deep cuts on my arms. Since we got almost nothing to eat, we were soon totally debilitated. Even our town priest was arrested repeatedly and severely maltreated. Church services were banned and the Church locked. Finally he was committed to the state prison in Königgrätz.

More and ever more people - women, too - were still being brought to the prison from the surrounding towns. Interrogations began, accompanied by constant maltreatment. The architect Hermann was gunned down by partisans just a few steps away from me. Hitler Youths 10 to 14 years of age who were among the prisoners, and who had already been beaten green and blue, had to bury him behind the barracks in a shallow grave. I myself was led behind the barracks twice, and was to be shot there. But since I showed no fear, they beat me dreadfully with their truncheons instead and herded me back to the other prisoners. A cell in the barrack had been set up as torture chamber. Every evening inmates were dragged from their cells and tortured to death there in the most cruel and brutal ways imaginable. Often they were given up to 50 blows with heavy sticks. The well-known city physician Dr. Rudolf Wanitschke suffered a terrible fate; after several unsuccessful attempts to commit suicide, he was literally beaten to death here. The unconscious victims were regularly doused with a pitcher of cold water and thrown back into the cell, where the cold brought them back to consciousness. The torture was repeated for several days, until the unfortunate souls eventually died from blood loss or were shot. In the evening the murdered were buried in shallow graves in the vicinity of the town. Their next-of-kin were not notified of their loved ones' deaths.

Other than Dr. Wanitschke and the architect Hermann, men of my acquaintance who were brutishly murdered here include Franz Gregor, the head of the Municipal Savings Bank, my brother Wilhelm, Alois Kubitschke, watchmaker, Gottwald, the lessee of the *Schwarze Adler,* Spanel and Leichter, both staff members of the Employment Office, senior teacher Jörka from Gross-Stiebnitz, the teacher Spanel from Ober-Riebnei, Heinrich Letzel from Himml.-Riebnei, and many others.

The merchant Finger, master butcher Willi Pöter, and Fritz Habenicht (sawmill owner of the former Frosch Mill) were abducted to Senftenberg where they were first brutally tortured and then hanged. Those men who escaped death were taken by the Czechs to the hastily-set-up concentration camps, 51 of them, where they had to do heavy labor, for example down in the mines, while receiving only lousy rations and constant maltreatment. Many died in these camps, or suffered permanent damage to their health. Many died on or after their return, for example the forestry administrator Scherz and old man Kotisa's son-in law, Mr. Cernoch.

The misery of those who had remained behind reached its highest point thanks to the unexpected expulsion from their homeland, which began like a bolt out of the blue with no advance notice on June 5, 1945, as Rokitnitz was the first city in the Sudetengau where the German population was expelled.

Those poor people were going about their business unsuspectingly that morning, when the partisans invaded their homes and forced them to leave all they possessed behind, with the exception of only a few minor things they could carry.

Painfully, old and sick people dragged themselves to the collection point, urged along by curses and roars from the partisans. At the collection point everyone was closely searched, in other words robbed of anything and everything that had even the slightest value - small keepsakes, what little cash they had, children's clothes, and bedding.

Around 3 o'clock in the afternoon this pathetic procession moved across Ring Square, accompanied by the jeering gibes of the Czechs who watched the heart-rending spectacle with laughing enjoyment. Many Czechs stood by the wayside with their cameras to snap a photographic record of the event. At Herrenfeld and Batzdorf the heavily armed partisans herded the expellees across the border bridge and left them to their fate. On the second day our procession reached the Silesian city of Habelschwerdt, where the Red Cross took over our care and housed us in barracks. Habelschwerdt as well as the entire region of Glatz was under Polish occupation. The same conditions as we had experienced during the last few weeks in our homeland, also reigned here. In March 1946 the expellees and the Silesians of the region were jointly resettled [expelled] by the Poles.

Römerstadt

Römerstadt, Report No. 1
Daughter raped by Czech officer on October 14, 1945
Reported by Ottokar Montag - Report of June 21, 1950

On October 14th, 1950, my daughter Mrs. K., who was in charge of a Czech machine-weaving mill, an expropriated former German firm, was visiting a lady-friend.

At 6 o'clock, on her way home, she passed the former German College, which had been turned into Czech soldiers' barracks. Suddenly, in the dark, she was confronted by an officer, who spoke to her in Russian. Thinking him to be a Russian, she tried to run away. Immediately the officer signalled with his whistle; 6 soldiers ran out from the nearby barracks and a wild chase after her began. The officer was a Czech lieutenant by the name of Bischof, a former member of the Legion. Although man-handled on the street by all 7 men, my daughter managed to escape several times. She appealed to passers-by for help, without success; Germans dared not to help her for fear the same would happen to them, while Czechs laughed and enjoyed the show.

My daughter came within 50 metres (110 ft) of her flat, but then her strength deserted her. She was hit and kicked in the back and kidneys, was dragged to the barracks, taken into one of the rooms there and ill-treated by the officer in the most horrible way. He forced her to the ground several times and dragged her round by her hair, asking: "Are you going to do my bidding?" She received several blows in the face, so that blood kept streaming down, besmearing the officer's uniform from head to foot. The floor showed smears of blood where my daughter had been dragged about. In between she was forced to stand at attention and to shout: Long live Adolf Hitler! She received more blows because she did not shout it loud enough to be heard all through the barracks. As a result of one blow in the stomach she fainted. She does not know what happened to her while she was unconscious. When she came to, lying on the floor, the officer kicked her in the breast. Two Czech soldiers had to watch her ordeal. One of them put his hands before his eyes because he could not watch the horrible scene. It was with the help of this soldier that she finally managed to escape. She collapsed as soon as she reached her home. Her face was covered with blood and quite unrecognisable. The Czech landlord looked after her. Later he took her to the police and reported the incident. He was reprimanded for having helped a German. The case was recorded, but the victim was not allowed to sign. She was sent to hospital for a medical report, but no action was taken against the officer. We lived with this landlord and his wife, who were humane in mind and in their actions, on the best of terms until our expulsion. We were allowed to keep several rooms, all fully furnished. Every effort to take them away from us was frustrated by him.

Römerstadt, Report No. 2

Objections about the transport to First Lt. Lambert, American border official for Furth im Walde

Reported by Wank, border commissar for the refugees from Furth im Walde - Report of April 10, 1946

The following complaints regarding the transport of expelled persons have been received:

a.) from Römerstadt.

Many refugees could be found in every one of the railway coaches of our transport who were no longer in possession of their passports or identity cards, as these had been taken away from them in the camps where they had assembled, also all documents, commercial papers, employment certificates, social insurance papers and especially policies of insurance companies.

The babies did not receive warm milk on the trip, the milk provided was for the most part unboiled.

Mrs. Trampisch of Römerstadt was attacked in her own apartment by a member of the R. G. (Revolutionary Guards) and received a black eye, because she refused to allow this man to search her luggage, which he was not entitled to do. He, however, broke into the flat and appropriated the most valuable articles out of the luggage.

b.) from Iglau.

Identity cards, passports etc. of most of the participating persons were missing, also marriage certificates, documents of inheritance, business licenses, policies of insurance companies etc. These documents were taken away from the people in the camps with the assurance that they would be given back before they left the camp. But this promise was not kept, although the people asked for their property. Even wedding-rings were taken away. The luggage of this transport was the poorest so far. Some of the people possessed only what they stood up in.

In some cases they were able to take along two sets of underclothes or perhaps one suit when they left their homes; others were carrying their entire property in a rucksack, not more than 10 kilos (22 pounds) in weight. A few of those in the transport were in possession of luggage weighing 30 kilos (66 pounds) at the most.

All this misery was caused by the fact that the refugees had been expelled from their houses in the country by the Czech Agents without being given time to pack and to get together the 50 kilos (110 pounds) of luggage permitted.

Some of the men who had been prisoners of war or had been in jail had not even been allowed to return home in order to fetch their luggage, but were taken directly to the camps where they were assembled for transport. Some of the women were sent away without their husbands who were kept back in labour camps or in jail. So many of the women had serious complaints that there was not enough time to record them all.

The following is the case of a child who is reported as having been expelled without his parents:

Franz Zaboj, born on January 19, 1938, was transferred without his parents, who were held in the district prison of Iglau.

Rosshaupt

District Court Tachau - Pilsen 1945
Reported by Franz Voit - Report of June 5, 1946

I was arrested in Rosshaupt on June 20, 1945. In the Czech school there, I and four others were punched, kicked and beaten with rifle butts. Then we were committed to the Tachau District Court. That same day, in the time from 2 o'clock p.m. until 11 o'clock p.m., I and all the others there were beaten nine times with rubber truncheons and bull whips. We were maltreated naked, and to the point of unconsciousness each time. They always forced me to lie belly-down on the floor, and then four men beat me, beginning with my head and moving all the way down to my feet. Whenever I came to again, I found myself lying on my back, and my front was also covered in welts. The next day I and the others were maltreated yet again seven more times between 5 o'clock a.m. and 1 o'clock p.m. Then we were handcuffed and shipped off to Pilsen. In Bory Prison, we - 19 men and two women - were asked who had been planning to blow up the barracks in Tachau. When none of us answered, we were again beaten up, this time by Czech convicts. This was repeated three more times. Then we 19 men were locked into a joint cell, where we were once again beaten by guards. The next day we were beaten three more times in the cell. I sustained four broken and two cracked ribs. I was bleeding from an open head wound, and my nasal bone was injured. After eight days, we were locked in groups of two into one-man cells, with only a straw sack and a blanket.

The food we got was insufficient, and mostly inedible. At least there was opportunity to wash. In September a fifth man was locked into our cell with us. He was a Czech, about 60 years old, and had scabies and lice. After 5 days he died without having received any medical care. We too came down with scabies and had picked up the lice, and had to lie 6 weeks in our cell without medical attention, so that finally our arms and legs were covered with festering sores. Only then were we treated by a German physician, and the scabies disappeared in about a week. On September 24 my cellmate Johann Blei, 46 years old, succumbed to sepsis and died while I was holding him.

On December 21, I and 50 other men were transferred to the Karlov labor camp. From there I was sent out to go to work, until I was released to go home on April 17, 1946.

Sankt Joachimsthal

Sankt Joachimsthal, Report No. 1
Eyewitness account (the Kroupa case) of an execution
Reported by Rudolf Berthold - Report of August 26, 1949

I am from St. Joachimsthal, and was personally acquainted with Kroupa. At my expulsion on August 20, 1945, Kroupa turned up at my house "Sonnenblick" No. 924 in the company of four armed men and two women, and demanded that I hand over to him all my money, jewelry etc. and then vacate my house within 20 minutes. To my question whether he had any written authorization or order for this act of violence he replied with vicious threats. Kroupa gave himself such airs that I could not help but think that he was the city commissar, which was also public opinion, and so I had to succumb to force and was robbed of all I owned. Like the rest of the inhabitants, I was forced, on pain of being shot, to attend the execution of M. Steinfelsner, to which I am therefore an eyewitness. I can take these facts in my oath, as can the housekeeper Frau A. Martinez who is presently staying with me.

Sankt Joachimsthal, Report No. 2
House searches, brutal ill-treatment, public executions
Reported by Otto Patek - Report of August 25, 1949

The revolution began in May 1945 in the Sudeten area. That was the signal for the persecution of the German population to start. One Franz Kroupa, formerly a worker in the tobacco factory of St. Joachimsthal, was appointed as Chairman of the National Committee. Kroupa was one of the greatest enemies of Germans and Jews. He personally took part in visits to German apartments, houses, etc. It was he who decided who was to be arrested or liquidated.

My house was searched twice. The first house search was carried out by Czech military, who behaved very decently. The second search was carried out by the gendarmerie by order of Kroupa and under his personal leadership, pistol in hand. All my wardrobes and cupboards as well as all other storage places were broken into and looted. The guests who stayed at my house were rounded up and robbed.

Although they could find no grounds for prosecuting me, I was taken to the police station, supposedly in order to sign a protocol. All my jewellery, watches, gold and silverware as well as gold and coins from my shop and some boxes of valuables which had been stored in the cellar during the air raids, furthermore some luggage belonging to the patients at the health resort, were all carried off in two waiting cars. I was brought from the police station to the well-known camp at Schlackenwerth, a matter which was decided by Kroupa.

In this camp I was together with 37 other Germans and all of us were brutally mistreated. The same day as I arrived at the camp, I was led to the ball-room of the former restaurant *"Zum Franzosen"*; there the prisoners were stood against the wall and had already been so badly beaten that they were bleeding.

I was told to stand in line with the others. The Czechs then closed all the doors and placed two sentries with automatic pistols, trained on us. We were ordered to strip to the waist and then the Czechs started to beat us with rubber truncheons, leather and steel whips as well as sticks, until strips of flesh were hanging from our bodies and we were covered with blood. Whenever one of us collapsed, buckets of cold water were poured over him until he regained consciousness; they then continued the beating.

In this manner we were ill-treated three times a day and three times during the nights. In the night between June 5th and June 6th, 1945, at about 10 o'clock, eleven or twelve Czechs entered the ballroom and brought a bench as well as blankets with which they covered the windows. The first one they seized was Johann Müller, a watchmaker from St. Joachimsthal; they laid him on the bench, slashed off both his ears with a knife, put out his eyes, thrust a bayonet into his mouth and smashed his teeth in. They also broke his arms across their knees and his legs over the bench. Since he was still alive, they wound a cable twice around his neck and dragged him through the room until his neck was dislocated and the body showed no further sign of life. While the body was being dragged around, a Czech stood on it so as to increase the load. The corpse, which was nothing but a mass of bloody flesh, was then wrapped in my coat and laid in the middle of the room. In the same manner six other men were killed that night, among them three German soldiers. After the death of each man they continued to beat us with rubber truncheons.

Since I speak some Czech, I was forced to witness the killings while the others had to face the wall. The murdered men screamed terribly, for they were fully conscious at the time of their death. In consequence of what they were forced to witness three prisoners went out of their minds and I myself was close to madness. Among the victims of that night there were, besides the aforementioned Müller, the watchmaker Kraus, a forester, and Zechel, a master joiner from Joachimsthal, as well as a Sudeten German unknown to me. All arrests and imprisonments at St. Joachimsthal were carried out on the orders of Kroupa. The killing was to continue the next day, but as a military commission arrived, the murdering was stopped. From there I came to another camp at Karlsbad and to Neurohlau; I was imprisoned for a total of 17 months. I could not be released earlier, since Kroupa at Joachimsthal prevented it.

On June 4th, 1945, on the day of my arrest, Mr. Steinfelsner, owner of the sawmill at Joachimsthal, was publicly hanged in front of the town hall without any proper legal proceedings. Every German inhabitant of St. Joachimsthal was "invited" under pain of death to attend the execution. The taking down of the body is supposed to have taken place by order of American officers, who drove through Joachimsthal. My family had themselves seen American troops driving through the town. My wife did everything she could to secure my release by showing documents to the camp commander, but she was expelled by the gendarmerie at the instigation of Kroupa with only 20 minutes notice, without even a coat and with only 7 Marks in cash, so that she was unable to take any further steps. I herewith declare that my statements are in accordance with the truth and that I am also prepared to take them on my oath.

Schankau

Blinded in the camp
Reported by Josef Dörfl - Report of September 29, 1946

I was arrested in Schankau on August 27, 1945 and on my committal to the Karlsbad District Court I was boxed so badly about the head that I staggered. I also received a punch in my right eye. In January I suddenly went blind on my right eye. I immediately reported to an ophthalmologist, but I was not examined until three weeks later, when I had also developed numerous abscesses on my head and upper body and had to be treated in the hospital. For a time I had to visit the eye specialist every day, and he gave me injections. Due to my transfer to the Eger District Court the treatment was interrupted for two months. It was not until July 1940 that I was again able to consult an ophthalmologist in Eger, who told me that there was nothing left to be done for me.

Schildberg

Murder
Reported by Ottilie Smrtschka

I boarded with Mr. Wilhelm Bartosch, master plumber, in Schildberg No. 346. We were seven families there, among us the master cooper Josef Assmann, a family man and the father of five children. One day in mid-May, around 10 or 10:30 in the morning, I was looking out my kitchen window and saw a number of men, 14 or 15, rushing towards our house with cudgels and guns. They were Czechs, most of them partisans.

They forced their way into Josef Assmann's home from two directions. He tried to flee, but unfortunately failed. They beat him with cudgels and rifle butts. The shirt hung in tatters from his upper body, which was blue with bruises and suffused all over with blood. Screaming, he collapsed several times. Several of the men kept yanking him back to his feet and beating him anew. Suddenly he gave a piercing, loud scream, and I saw how a heavy blow from a rifle butt split his head literally in half. He collapsed and did not get up again. The blood simply poured over his body. His clothes had been torn entirely off his body, and in this state they dragged him into his neighbor's yard, where they shot him. His own children, 10, 7, 5 and 3 years old, witnessed this murder. They screamed and cried loudly for their father. He was left lying naked and mutilated in the middle of the yard for more than an hour, and children and grown-ups alike could go and look at him. One man from the crowd went to fetch a sack, and covered the dead man. Germans who had been unjustly imprisoned then had to carry him to the cemetery and bury him in a shallow grave there.

Schlackenwerth, Karlsbad, Kaschlitz and Spickengrün

Maltreatment to extort statements

Reported by Josef Czech - port of September 18, 1946

I served as gendarme in Czechoslovakia until 1938 and then, after the Sudetenland joined Germany proper, I entered service as gendarme in the Reich. On May 18, 1945 I transferred my position as gendarme in Schlackenwerth to Czech control.

On June 13, 1945 I was arrested by partisans, severely maltreated, and then taken to a military counter-espionage division. This division was quartered in the Fasolt villa in Karlsbad. There, I was repeatedly grossly maltreated because the authorities hoped to extort statements from me, about hidden weapons, Nazi leaders etc. An SA man from Kaschlitz near Karlsbad, whose name unfortunately I do not know, was beaten to death before my very eyes during the same kind of maltreatment.

On June 14 in Spickengrün, where I had been taken by car, I also witnessed how five of seven farmers who had been arrested were shot after first having been severely maltreated. Two were taken to Karlsbad, and beaten to death there the same day. I myself had to load the two corpses onto a truck. On June 15, 1945 I was released.

The Reichenau concentration camp, maltreatment
Reported by A. Heinl - port of October 14, 1946

I was an active member of the Social Democratic Party until 1937 and - for some time - even the Social Democratic representative of the community of Schlag. On May 28, 1945 I was arrested at Schlag and cruelly ill-treated. This ill-treatment was resumed at the camp at Reichenau a few days later; many were literally beaten to death there. Many lost their teeth or had their noses broken. One lost his right eye as a result of the ill-treatment. Each one of us was disfigured past recognition. At the end of June 1945, suffering from malnutrition, I was taken to the hospital at Gablonz, where little attention was given to the German patients. After my recovery in September I was returned to the camp at Reichenau; from there I was sent to work as a printer. My first interrogation took place on December 29th, but no reason for my detention could be given. My release was authorized on June 29, 1946, but the notice was only given to me on October 4, 1946. My wife, although seriously ill, was driven out of our apartment and expelled from the country on July 8, 1946. All she could take was small hand-luggage.

Schlaggenwald, Report No. 1
Looting during luggage inspection
Reported by Josefine Otto - port of June 1, 1946

During the luggage inspection in Schlaggenwald my expulsion luggage, which was for two people, was looted, and almost all my linen, tablecloths, hand and dish towels, one suit, one coat, two blankets and a pillow were stolen. The inspection took place while I was being strip-searched, that's why I couldn't tell until later what all was missing.

Schlaggenwald, Report No. 2
Maltreatment
Reported by Helmut Nordmann - Report of September 13, 1946

I was arrested on July 10, 1945 in Schlaggenwald near Elbogen and imprisoned first in Elbogen Castle and later in Neurohlau. In Elbogen and in Neurohlau I was severely maltreated. Once, in Neurohlau, I was beaten so badly that I lay unconscious in the infirmary barrack for 48 hours. The Commandant himself was the one who had beaten me unconscious. I sustained severe head injuries, with meningeal bleeding and nerve damage. Nonetheless I had to do hard physical labor, with almost nonexistent rations, for months. My physical weakness made me the target for further maltreatment. It was not until April 9, 1946 that I was committed to the Karlsbad Hospital, to the neurological ward, but my condition improved only marginally by the time I was to be resettled. On my resettlement [expulsion] I had only a little luggage, which comrades had given me. I had almost no clothing, and so I turned to the camp office for help; I was given a pair of torn pants and a smoking jacket.

Schönbach

Severe abuse of a German in September 1945
Reported by Antonia Honsek - Report of June 22, 1950

I, Antonia Honsek, née Pietsch, born on October 2, 1875 in Schönbach, District Deutsch-Gabel (Sudetenland), having been resident at Schönbach No. 168, District Deutsch-Gabel, from my birth until the expulsion in 1946, wish to submit the following account of my experiences. My statement tells the truth and nothing but the truth, and I am ready and willing to take this on my oath at any time. Names and dates may be published in their entirety, and I can bring witnesses for corroboration.

In 1945 the Czech Commissar Kvaz who had been posted to our home community arrived together with a 21-year-old Czech fellow from the interior of Bohemia and a 17-year-old Czech girl in order to inspect and confiscate our house and property.

My husband was 75 years old and frail, and had lain down for a rest, therefore he did not immediately hear the Czech's knocking at the door. The Czech Commissar then smashed several window panes on our house. When my husband opened the door then, he did not even get the chance to say a single word before Kvaz punched him in the face over and over again until he collapsed, covered in blood. When my husband regained consciousness quite a long time afterwards, his lips were so badly swollen that they burst in a few places. His hearing had also been severely damaged. What is more, my husband was mentally disturbed from that time on. My husband had been a blue-collar worker. All his life he had been in a labor union, and for decades he had been a member of the Social Democratic Party.

In June 1946 I, my husband who was broken in body and spirit, and our granddaughter were chased out of our home town, and found emergency shelter in Schönow, District Niederbarnim, in the Soviet Occupation Zone of Germany. On October 13, 1947 my husband died in Schönow of the consequences of the maltreatment he had received at the hands of that Czech Commissar Kvaz, consequences which had been intensified further by starvation.

Schönhengst

German miner murdered
Reported by Emma Prudl - Report of June 15, 1946

The Czechs conscripted my husband for labour in the mines at Schönhengst. He had already worked there before. During the night of September 9th, 1945, four partisans came and asked for my husband. I told them that he was not at home, as he had gone to Klein-Heringsdorf to see his parents.

At 5:30 in the morning a partisan came back and asked for my husband again, who was not home yet. At 6 o'clock my husband returned. I told him that they had been looking for him. My husband washed himself and went to see our neighbour. 10 minutes later the partisans came again. When they were standing in the yard, my husband stepped out of the neighbour's house. The moment the partisans caught sight of him, they made a dash for him. As my husband turned round, several shots were fired and he dropped dead. Two men, Leo Mrkwec and his father, had shot him. I am prepared to swear to this statement.

Schönlinde

Young people murdered, deportation camp, rape
Reported by N. N. - Report of July 3, 1950

Our home town Schönlinde is 6 km away from the Saxon border. It was a totally German town, with all of 17 Czech inhabitants. In June 1945 the first expulsion took place, of 1,500 German businessmen, teachers and officials. Each family was allowed to take as much clothing and linen as they could carry, but everything that was new and nice was confiscated during the body search conducted at the outskirts of the town. Then they were driven out in long, pitiful treks, urged on with whip lashes and blows from rifle butts, to the border via the longest possible detour, 25 km via Dittersbach. Naturally most of the expellees had to leave the rest of their possessions lying by the wayside when they became too exhausted to carry them further. All the prominent male inhabitants were arrested, including Dr. Petzold the chief surgeon from the hospital, and were brutally beaten every day and forced to do the most demeaning work. Water and bread was all they got to eat. The Mayor and his family, a doctor, and many others put an end to their torment by committing suicide. Weeks later, the prisoners were taken to the infamous concentration camp Rabstein near Bohemian Kamnitz. I want to mention one case in particular, namely the Köhler family. The father and his two 17-year-old sons (twins) were arrested. The two boys were inhumanly beaten, and trampled with boots, until they showed no more signs of life; their father was forced to watch the torture until his sons were dead. A short time later he too was finished off.

In July a second wave of expulsions from Schönlinde was carried out, accompanied by the same maltreatment. In the meantime a similar kind of trek, 2,400 people, arrived from Warnsdorf, which was located right by the border; nonetheless the people were herded via Schönlinde to Hermsdorf, a distance of 27 km. On three-wheeled handcarts, wheelbarrows and the like, they carted their ill and elderly family members to their wretched fate. So that we would not get in their way, we were removed to the Czech interior, as labor slaves. We were taken to the limestone quarry of Biskup near Prague. We were actually treated and housed very decently there. But after six months, orders arrived from the government to send us to the Modrany camp, and from there to the infamous concentration camp Lesany, known as "the Green Hell", where we were exploited as camp laborers for 9 months. Families were torn apart, and anyone who was unable to work almost starved to death. Fleeing from the Russians, many Silesians passed through parts of the Sudeten region on their way to West Germany. 15,000 of them were separated from their treks, brought here and robbed of their last few possessions, and then left to perish from starvation-related typhus. The huge camp cemetery with its thousand crosses speaks volumes.

In spring 1947 we were sold to the farmers as work slaves, the price was some bacon and butter. A government decree stipulated that all Germans had to work from 5 o'clock in the morning until 10 p.m., for regular prison rations. We were sent to the farmer Jirsa in Pelec, District Kamenice. We had to work 16 hours a day under constant guard, as did my school-aged children. Black coffee and dry bread was all we got. In the winter we had to chop wood in the forest while the children stripped feathers. They were not allowed to go to school.

In May 1945, 7 members of the Wehrmacht had been nailed to the farmer's gate and tortured to death. His neighbors testified to it. Two Silesian girls, sisters aged 18 and 20, were left to the Russians' tender mercies every day after they returned from their field work.

After 11 months of heavy labor I managed to be transferred to a brickworks, where we were treated quite a bit better. In autumn 1948 we were brought back to Lesany, where we were robbed of our hard-earned bit of cash and then expelled to Saxony.

Schwarzental and Hohenelbe

Maltreatment
Reported by N. N. - Report of June 19, 1950

On July 18, 1945, around 10 o'clock, a truck full of Czech soldiers arrived on the market square of Schwarzental. The truck was carrying a considerable number of Czech soldiers, all of them armed to the teeth. They got off the truck outside the Hotel "Erben", and went in. One or two platoons of Czech soldiers had been quartered in this hotel for some time already, but their presence or demeanor had not given rise to any complaints. Only the new arrivals turned out to be criminals shortly after their arrival. After a brief stay at the Hotel "Erben" they rushed off to the upper section of Schwarzental. The first German man to be brought out was the master dyer Franz Munssner, the father of two underaged children. Like all those who followed, he had been forcibly taken from his home and family. He was followed by the coachman Josef Ettrich, the father of one underaged child; master dyer Josef Krauss, father of three underaged children; and master dyer Johann Krauss, brother of the previous. To loud curses all these men were dragged to the Hotel "Erben", while kicks and blows from rifle butts and rubber truncheons rained down on them. Further, the Czechs also invaded the homes of the farmer Wonka, Franz Kröhn, father of four underaged children, Josef Schneider, also father of four underaged children, a quarry worker in the limestone works, master saddler Möhwald, Oswald Renner, father of two underaged children, a telegraph worker, and then it was my turn as well. I too was dragged away from my wife and my four underaged children. In my case these bandits invaded my shoemaking shop and demanded, with violent threats, that I should come with them right away. In the hallway they beat me to the floor with several blows from their rifle butts. I had to cover the short distance to the Hotel "Erben" almost at a run, while they cursed me in the most insulting and crude manner. Since I understand the Czech language perfectly, I understood all their slurs, such as "German pig", "German bastard" etc. In the hallway of the Hotel "Erben" all the German men who had been brought in, including myself, had to stand side by side facing the wall. We were strictly forbidden to move. Some of the Czechs apparently got their pleasure from hitting us severely on the back of the head, so that our faces crashed into the wall. This was repeated at short intervals, and soon we were all bleeding badly from our noses and the wall was also blood-spattered. Then the Czechs brought on the German man Kröhn, a cobbler; he had been taken from his place of employment in the Mencik factory. This poor man could hardly walk any more, and so he was dragged in across the floor. He had been beaten horribly on the way here, so that he was already totally exhausted. His clothes were smeared with blood. He had to stand up across from us and with his back to the wall, and then his clothes were searched. One of the Czechs found a sports badge in one of his pockets. Kröhn stood fairly close to my position, and so I saw clearly how they hit him in the face and even on his glasses with a rubber truncheon. His glasses shattered. His tormentors also tried to pin the sports badge on him, pushing the pin (meant for fixing it to one's shirt) into his skin and into the flesh of his forehead. Since such a pin is about 3 mm thick and relatively blunt, these attempts failed. But the victim sustained considerable injuries to his forehead, which was bleeding badly. He then had to turn and face the wall also, and he and Seff Ettrich, who stood beside him, had to raise their arms and lean against the wall with the palms of their hands, and then both were beaten with rubber truncheons on the backs of their hands and fingers as well as on their head and back until they both collapsed. They were then still treated to vicious kicks, mostly in the stomach area.

A few hours later - it may have been around 5 o'clock p.m. - we were all ordered to get into the truck that was standing at the ready. As I was getting in, my wife, who had approached the truck along with some children, tried to hand me a jacket, but she was turned away with the words, "He doesn't need a jacket any more, he's going to get one over the head and then a stone to mark his place." Once we were on the truck, we had to squat on the floor in the middle. The walls were lined with benches, on which the Czechs sat. Squatting with our knees drawn up, and holding our knees with our hands, we had to huddle in the middle of that truck. Some of the ruffians hit us on the knees and elbows with the butts of their pistols. The truck moved out, and we drove towards Lauterwasser-Forstbad. The farmer Wonka and the master saddler Möhwald each had a large mustache. Some of the Czechs made a game of it and passed the time by ripping the moustache hairs of these two unfortunate men out one by one, until there was not a single hair left to pull out. The poor men then asked to be allowed to smoke. They were permitted to; but the Czechs first removed the mouthpieces from their pipes and stuffed the pipes with horse manure, and the two men then had to take the pipes in their mouths without the mouthpieces. Then they were given a light, and they actually had to smoke the horse manure. After a brief time, for which they had been forced to continue smoking, the pipe heads were simply knocked out of their mouths, along with some of their teeth. The Czechs then stuffed their mouths full of hay. But finally this trip was over, and when we were ordered to get out of the truck we found ourselves in the courtyard of the welfare home in Hohenelbe.

We were told to get off as quickly as we could, and had to stand up along the wall of the welfare home, facing the wall. Shortly afterwards we were allowed to turn around, and were then called one by one to the steps that led down to the basement. Two Czechs had taken up position there, and hit each arrival ruthlessly over his head and torso with their rubber truncheons and then kicked him brutally down the steps. Once all of us had arrived down there in the dark, unlit basement hallway, all of us except for two - one of which was myself - were to be roped together into one big pile. In the hallway there was also a large number of dirty and blood-soaked shirts from the former Hitler Youth. The two of us who had been sent off to one side were ordered to rip the sleeves off these uniform shirts, and were then ordered to put them on our fellow-prisoners as gags. We were told to tie these gags tightly at the neck so that our comrades-in-suffering would be completely unable to speak. We were also to take such torn-out sleeves and tie our fellow-prisoners' hands firmly behind their backs. Since we did not carry out these orders quite to the liking of the soldateska, we were shoved aside, and now these criminals did it themselves and the two of us were also gagged and tied up.

Before this tying-up and gagging was even complete, some of the ruffians led some other Germans in from one of the basement rooms. They had probably been brought here a few days earlier. They were the mailman Wenzel Seidel, the father of two underaged children, and the carpenter Franz Seidel, also father of two underaged children. These two men were totally disfigured. They had been shaved bald, and their faces were suffused with blood. Their heads were grossly swollen. They were almost unrecognizable and could barely keep upright. During an unguarded moment they whispered to us that during the interrogations that were no doubt about to begin for us, we should simply admit to everything we would be asked, and confess to everything. These two men had been told that they could save their lives only by a full confession. The criminals now ordered them to check and make sure that we new arrivals were properly gagged and that our hands were tied tightly enough. In the course of this examination I had to take a step backward in the dark basement hallway, and I stumbled over something lying on the ground there. A cold sensation suddenly ran over me, for I felt that I had bumped against a stiff human body. I whispered, as best I could, "What's that?" Wenzel Seidel replied, also in a whisper: "That's first lieutenant Langer, he was beaten to death about an hour ago." I shuddered.

Now we were distributed amongst the basement rooms. Together with five others, I was put into a very dark room. It was a larger room containing a large number of old bicycles and bicycle parts. Franz Munssner, the farmer Wonka, master saddler Möhwald and Seff Ettrick were imprisoned in a smaller room, about 9 meters square, windowless and with a fairly large table and an iron door. The four comrades-in-suffering were tied together in a standing position, which made it impossible for them to sit or lie down. The brothers Seidel were locked back into their basement room in which they had already spent several days prior to our arrival. I had taken up position by the door, and through said door I could hear how the soldateska were divided up into guard teams and how these guards were instructed to check the various basement rooms at least once an hour to make sure that none of us were sitting down. Seff Ettrich was beaten especially badly, until he was quite mangled. I too was beaten about my head and back every time the guards inspected our cell; to protect myself a little I had turned my face to the wall at one spot where there was a small depression that just fit my nose, so that when they shoved and hit me there was a bit of a safeguard for me when my face hit the wall. - The master weaver Edi Klust had been in the same cell as I for several days already. He had snapped and gone insane, but whenever the guards entered he was again brutally beaten like the rest of us.

In these prison cells it was impossible for us to tell whether it was day or night. We got nothing to eat, nor to drink, at least not for the first three or four days. After that we got a few mouthfuls of water, and then - it may have been the day after - a little black coffee and a bit of dry bread. For the first days we had to answer the call of nature while still tied up. Due to the severe blows we also received to our stomachs, some comrades had had to throw up, and they were not helped in any way. The air in the basement rooms had taken on a dreadful stench, and when the guards entered they always had to let the room air out for a few minutes. It was not until the third day that we were given a pot to serve as toilet, and when the guards arrived one of us would have to carry it out. I was virtually unable to open one of my eyes, which was suffused with blood and totally swollen shut. I had only partial vision left in my other eye, which had also been injured by the brutal blows. One day the guards again came by on their rounds - I have to add that the guards were different Czechs almost every day - and they had brought small flat pliers with them and used them to shove wood splinters under our fingernails. We had no choice but to endure this helplessly as well. One particularly brutal torture technique that deserves mention here was their practice of hanging us head-down, by our feet from the ceiling, and beating us savagely with their rubber truncheons.

While all these brutalities were going on in the basement rooms, individual interrogations were also being performed. The men were taken from the rooms one at a time to be interrogated. Screams of pain were also to be heard from this interrogation room, which was not far from the basement room in which I was imprisoned. After the interrogation the Czechs dragged the prisoners back as a misshapen bloody mass, which they threw into the room and left there. These people were no longer able to speak. As the days passed I was able to ascertain, by looking through the keyhole of the locked door that connected our cellar room with the adjoining one, that aside from the two Seidel brothers the chief forester Franz Bayer, the administrator Hubert Wawra and senior teacher Gall were also locked into that adjoining cell. Hubert Wawra was lying on a large table, totally exhausted and almost as though dead. At certain intervals, as I heard, the guards made him drink considerable quantities of iodine. I also happen to know that the Seidel brothers, Wenzel and Franz, as well as comrade Wawra were taken from the cellar one night by a severely drunk Czech, were tormented and tortured horribly, and then simply shot. Senior teacher Gall was transferred to the Hohenelbe District Prison, where he was subjected to long and agonizing interrogations in Ober-Hohenelbe-Steinwag and then shot.

Then it was my turn to be taken to be interrogated. My manacles and gag were removed in the basement hallway. The manacles had been too tight, and had bitten deeply into my flesh. I was in a great deal of pain. The laundry room of the house we were in served as the interrogation room. Once there, I was allowed to sit down on a chair. The room contained a long table, on which my comrades who had been 'interrogated' before me had to lie down and were then beaten dreadfully with rubber truncheons in order to force them to make confessions. A laundry mangle and a clothes press were also in the room. The concrete floor, the walls and especially the ceiling were spattered all over with blood. In one corner I saw not only blood that had been swept together there, but also a large amount of hair and even some human fingers.

My interrogation was relatively brief, and I was not even beaten. A verdict, which was first read to me and then given to me to sign, stated that I was to be sent to a penal camp, that my wife would be deported to Germany and my children taken into the Czech interior. I was also informed that the money that had been taken from me on my arrest would not be returned to me. Then I was asked whether I had shoes, for I had come to the interrogation room barefoot. I had also lost my suspenders in the cellar room and had to hold my pants up with my hands.

One of the Czechs was sent to the cellar room to get my shoes and suspenders. He returned just a few seconds later and said that he had been unable to find anything. Then I heard the Czechs debate which of them was to escort me to the gate. The chief interrogator saw fit to accompany me personally. As we walked through the large garden, he insisted most forcefully that I was not to tell anyone about anything I had seen and experienced here. At the gate he ordered the guard to let me pass.

I went as best I could, and as quickly as possible, to the house where my father lived in Hohenelbe. On my way there, Czech soldiers stopped me several times and laughed and made fun of me because of the dreadful state I was in. My father hardly recognized me. After something to eat, and several hours' rest, I left to go home. At home my children did not recognize me either. My comrades which I have mentioned in this report were tortured to death and died in the most horrible agonies.

Schwarzwasser and Freiwaldau, Report No. 1

Maltreatment of an apprentice boy

Reported by Karl Volkmar - Report of September 7, 1946

I was an apprentice in my father's blacksmith forge in Schwarzwasser. On April 4, 1946 two gendarmes came and criticized the format of our Czech business sign. We told them that we would have a larger one made. Then they went and inspected the crane standing outside the smithy. When I saw them there, I pointed out the window at them and said to the second apprentice, "they're standing over there." The two gendarmes came into the workshop and wanted to know what I had said. When I told them, they took me with them to the gendarmerie, where I was terribly maltreated. They beat me with rubber truncheons to the point where I had to vomit.

Schwarzwasser and Freiwaldau, Report No. 2

Freiwaldau: severe maltreatment of young people

Reported by Lothar Latzel - Report of September 7, 1946

One Sunday in early February this year, a drive belt and some carpenter's tools allegedly went missing from an abandoned quarry. To this day I don't know any of the details. The following Tuesday five boys were taken to the gendarmerie. I was one of them. I am 13 years old, the others were 14. Several gendarmes asked us if we knew anything about the theft. None of us knew anything. Now we were dreadfully boxed about the head, and then we had to stand facing a wall for several hours. Then we were locked up, separately. I was locked into the washroom. Around 1:30 in the afternoon they fetched us out again, and proceeded to beat us alternately all afternoon long. We also had to beat each other, and to do 100 squats until we were totally exhausted. In the end I was thrown head-first against the wall by one of the gendarmes. Around 6:30 we were sent home, after first being threatened that we would be sent into the concentration camp if we failed to find the thief within two days. I was totally disfigured by all the abuse and had to stay in bed for four days.

Schwarzwasser and Freiwaldau, Report No. 3

Freiwaldau: maltreatment prior to expulsion

Reported by Max Ehrlich - Report of August 23, 1946

At about 9:30 p.m. on August 16, 1946, the last evening before I had to report to the resettlement [expulsion] camp, I heard some whistled signals in the street, followed quickly by the sounds of violent blows, and cries for help. 67-year-old Franz Gärtner, who was also to go to the resettlement camp the next day, had been on his way to say farewell to a friend, and had been attacked and severely maltreated by a Czech. The next day Gärtner's face was totally suffused with blood and covered in bandages. His body also bore bruises where the Czech had kicked him. Consequently, Gärtner was detained in the resettlement camp until the abuse he had suffered was no longer visible.

Setzdorf

Maltreatment of agricultural laborers
Reported by Emma Latzel - Report of August 23, 1946

I was put to agricultural labor for the Czech farmer Folter in Setzdorf from approximately July 15, 1946 until August 15, and while I was there I was badly maltreated. As consequence of a past compound fracture of the forearm I have no strength in my left hand. Therefore I could not milk with my left hand. For this reason the farmer beat me five times, with his fist, with bull whips and with a rake. When my sister and my brother-in-law came to the farm to take me to the doctor, because I have stomach trouble, they were stoned and chased from the farm, and I was beaten. 16-year-old Rudolf Geier, who worked there as stableboy, was also repeatedly beaten, which I witnessed. He was beaten with a whip and an iron chain, and once he was hit on the chest with an iron hammer. I received no pay for my work.

Sörgsdorf

Concentration camp Jauernig, maltreatment during an interrogation
Reported by Gustav Keller - Report of August 15, 1946

During the night of August 11th, 1945, I was arrested and taken to the office of the parish council in Sörgsdorf. There I was asked for information about German anti-tank weapons. I was unable to give any information. I had also not been a member of the *"Volkssturm"* [last reserve, see previous reports]. Then I had to lie naked on the floor while a Czech by the name of Mischka threw 10 or 15 knives at me, which stuck in the floor to the right and left of me. As I was still unable to give information about the anti-tank weapons, they put a wire around my head and twisted it until it cut deeply into my skin and I lost consciousness. After this I was released. But 14 days later I was again arrested and held in the camp at Jauernig for nine months. Like all the others I was severely maltreated during my stay in the camp.

Spillendorf

Harassment by the Employment Office
Reported by Maria Kühnel - Report of August 2, 1946

From August [1945] until April [1946] I was forced to do farm labor for a Czech administrator. As a consequence of tonsilitis I have had a chronic kidney infection and abnormally high blood pressure for five years. In time the farm work became too hard for me. So I went to the doctor, and the Czech district physician gave me a paper certifying that I am totally unfit for hard work. I took this document to the Employment Office and asked them to assign me to lighter work. The Employment Office refused to admit the document, and five employees of the Employment Office proceeded to beat me until I passed out. Only then was my unfitness for work acknowledged.

Stecken (concentration camp near Iglau)

Slave auction
Reported by Hermine Kunzer - Report of July 14, 1946

After we had been assigned to farmers in the district of Tschaslau for a period of one year with extremely heavy work and the small amount of food obtainable on German ration cards, we returned to the camp at Stecken near Iglau on June 7, 1946 in a state of complete exhaustion. On June 18th we were ordered on parade; Czech farmers from the neighbourhood came and examined us to find out if we were fit for work. Hundreds of those chosen by the farmers had to return to agricultural work.

Anyone who complained of illness or other disability was answered with a blow or an insult of the lowest kind. Women fainted or suffered heart attacks and had to be carried away. Many of them had been diagnosed by Czech surgeons of the district of Tschaslau as needing an operation. Nevertheless they had to go to agricultural work. Certificates from Czech doctors that they were incapable of working were torn up. I myself, 53 years of age, had both ankles dislocated and a contused heel-bone, as a result of jumping out of the window to avoid being raped. I limped along with a stick, but none the less had to perform heavy agricultural labour. A wooden shed without windows was our apartment. All this took place at Markowitz near Tschaslau. My husband, 73 years of age, who was also working there, contracted pneumonia.

Stefanau

Severe injuries inflicted
Reported by Karl Ottahal - Report of June 28, 1946

I was imprisoned in the Stefanau concentration camp since May 25, 1945. The prisoners there were beaten every evening. On June 17 we 20 prisoners from Sternberg were given a day's so-called home leave in order to get some clothes and linen. When we reported to the *Národní Dum* at 7 o'clock that evening to return under guard escort to the camp, members of the Employment Office that was quartered there took us into a basement room and maltreated us. I was eighteenth, and they kicked me down approximately 20 steps into the dark basement room. Due to the fall I suffered a broken pelvis, and bruised my right hand and broke my arm in landing on a box in the basement. In this condition I was given 10 more blows to my face with a rubber truncheon. Then they led me to my home, which was quite close by. The doctor who was called ordered me taken to the hospital, where I had to be treated for 4½ months. The treatment cost 4,700 Kc, which I had to pay out of my own pocket.

Sternberg

Sternberg, Report No. 1
Gross abuse of women, 1945
Reported by Marie Mittmann - Report of June 13, 1946

I was arrested in Sternberg on May 28, 1945 in Sternberg. The day before, in my absence, my home had been searched by partisans. On August 25 I received a written summons to report to the secret state police, where I was shown the photograph of a Romanian who had worked with my daughter in Berlin in a cannery. I was asked who the man in the photograph was. I told them, and added truthfully that the man had since died in a bombing raid on Berlin. Then I was sent into a cell. About 16 other women were already there. All of them had also been arrested without being given any reason for it. Two days later I was transferred from the court prison into the internment camp. During the night of August 27/28 I was called up, as Number 890, and led off to the guards. They put a mask on my head and draped a blanket over it. I had to lie down on two chairs. One man held the blanket closed behind my head and pushed my head into the chair. Another man took my clothes off. Then four men beat me on my naked body with rubber truncheons. I received about 35-40 blows. Then I was supposed to stand up. But I couldn't, and dropped from the chair to the floor instead, and since I could not get up I crawled to the door on my hands and knees. I was kicked several times all over my body before I made it to the door. They cursed me obscenely. Then I was threatened that I would have to come back for another beating if I didn't send them other women. I dragged myself back to my barrack and told the others there that if the women didn't go voluntarily to be maltreated, they would be fetched. Four women went to the guard room, where they were beaten the same way I had been. One Mrs. Berger died of the consequences of this beating. Then we were put to heavy labor. We had to load scrap metal, bricks, sand etc. onto wagons, and had to pull the loaded wagons ourselves. I was detained for 5 months in this camp. Often we had to spend half a day "exercising", until the women collapsed. We had to do up to 100 squats, push-ups and other strenuous exercises, even in winter in snow and ice. Our rations consisted only of 200 g of bread and some watery soup daily. There was only one well as source of water for about 100 people. There were no basins to wash in. We were permitted to receive food parcels from our families, but any bread spreads, sugar, baked goods etc. they contained were regularly looted.

On January 9, 1946 I was transferred to Hodolein near Olmütz. The treatment we women received was a little better there, as were the rations after a commission from Brünn had inspected the camps. We were forced to work here as well, but the work was more suited to a woman's physical strength. On June 5 I was transferred from Hodolein back to the Sternberg camp. In the few days I still had to spend there prior to my resettlement [expulsion] I again had to do hard labor.

Sternberg, Report No. 2
Severe maltreatment in the Sternberg-Olmütz camp
Reported by Rudolf Pauler, engineer - Report of June 13, 1946

Until May 5th, 1945, I was mayor of the town of Sternberg-Olmütz. On this day there took place an attempt on the Kreisleiter's life. Standing next to him, I myself took two bullets in my right arm. I had used all my influence to secure that the town should be surrendered without any resistance and had negotiated to this end with the Wehrmacht and with the *"Volkssturm"* (comprising all men capable of bearing arms, a kind of last reserve). The surrender took place as I had proposed and almost no lives were lost. On May 5 I was sent to the hospital at Mährisch-Schönberg in order to be operated on. The hospitals of Mährisch-Schönberg were however evacuated on May 6. I was sent on an ambulance train to Tannwald, where, although a civilian, I was arrested at the station by the Russians. This took place on May 13th. I was together with 5,000 soldiers and civilians, and the Russians marched us in the direction of Lauban.

On May 19 I was released at Lauban and - in spite of my injuries - made my way back to Sternberg on foot (a distance of about 500 kilometers = more than 300 miles). On my way I stayed for three weeks in the hospital at Jauernig, where my wounds healed almost completely. On June 30, 1945, I reported to the Czech police at Sternberg. They sent me home and ordered me to report again on July 2nd.

On this day they interrogated me for eight hours in the presence of German Communists. Both the interrogation and the treatment were conducted decently. Following this I was taken to the district court, just an hour after my wife had been handed over to the internment camp. I was detained in the building of the court until December 1945 and was well treated. The same month I was transferred together with 80 other men and women to the camp in Sternberg.

On December 15th a staff-sergeant called me to the guard-room. Arriving there I was ordered to go to barrack I. Four or five men were waiting for me there; the moment I entered the room they ordered me to raise my arm and give the Hitler Salute. When I refused to do so, I was punched 15 times in the face until I fell to the ground. The order to give the Hitler Salute was then repeated. When I refused for the second time I was laid over three chairs and, while one of the guards gripped my head between his knees and another held my legs, I was thrashed with rubber-truncheons. I fainted for a moment. When I was picked up I noticed that the windows and doors were open; I was kicked outside and landed in the snow. After this I was ordered to clean the blood off myself. On December 23rd in barrack II, which was next to the sick-rooms, I was again tortured by the same persons and in the same manner. On the following day I was ordered to do the heaviest type of work. In view of the maltreatment to which I had been subjected in the camp I welcomed the news that I was to be brought before the "Volksgericht" in Olmütz. I left Sternberg on January 9, 1946 along with 300 other prisoners.

Because of my injuries, I was admitted to the sickroom at Olmütz. The conditions in the camp at Olmütz were, if possible, even worse than at Sternberg. The diet was quite insufficient, barrack 10 for example had 4 fast-days within 14 days so that the prisoners became completely enfeebled. Many prisoners were driven by hunger to forage for rotten potato-peels among the garbage. The camp-prison was an unheated structure, formerly an air-raid shelter, in which people were sometimes confined for as long as 14 days; many suffered serious frost-bites, which led to amputations. Prisoners were lashed with whips, hoses etc. for the most trivial reasons. The inmates grew vegetables of various kinds in the camp, which were then sold in the town. Not a single vegetable made it to the camp kitchen. When we had to break up the soil between the camp and the barracks of the Ulan Regiment, we were ordered not to dig deeper than 30-35 cm (approx. 1 ft.) because of the corpses of the slaughtered Germans, alleged to be buried there.

I remained in the camp until June 5, 1946. I was not questioned during this time.

Sternberg, Report No. 3
Woman abused
Reported by Marie Wilhelm - Report of June 13, 1946

Even though my husband was very ill - he suffered from angina pectoris and paralysis - I was arrested on August 21, 1945 on the pretext that we had weapons in our home. I was detained for six weeks in the court prison in Sternberg and then transferred to the concentration camp. I repeatedly asked that I be released so that I could care for my husband, but this was refused. The first morning in the camp I was slapped about the head for having greeted [a guard] with "good morning".

On November 1, 1945 my husband died. After I was given the news, I immediately had to report for "exercises" (even though I am 58 years old) and to participate for fully three hours, under guard by a watchman who kept a particularly close eye on me. Then I was given two hours off in order to see my husband one last time before the coffin was closed. I was not allowed to attend the cremation, and none of my husband's kin were either.

Then I was constantly maltreated, harassed and rudely cursed in the camp. Once, when I rested for ten minutes after shoveling sand for six hours straight, I was locked into the punishment cell for the night, and choked, slapped and kicked while I was there. One of the guards wanted my wedding ring, but since it would not come off due to chronic arthritis the guard shoved me against a red-hot furnace so that my coat was burned. I spent 9 months in the Sternberg camp. While I was still in the camp, I was given one hour off to bury the urn with my husband's ashes. A guard accompanied me. When I returned to the camp I was taunted dreadfully, ridiculed, and I and my dead husband were cursed most obscenely.

Sternberg, Report No. 4

Maltreatment in the camp

Reported by Ludwig Englisch - Report of June 13, 1946

I was arrested on June 21, 1945 without being given a reason, and transferred to the newly opened Sternberg camp on June 23, along with another 14 men. The next day all prisoners were punched and beaten with rubber truncheons etc. in an empty barrack until they bled; in the evening the beatings were repeated. During the night we had to get up several times at all hours and line up in front of our cots for "exercises", during which we were once again beaten. One of the prisoners, Professor Kittel, was beaten more than anyone else. He died of the consequences of this maltreatment.

As of September I had to work in the Krockersdorf mine. Beatings were common there too. Later on, the mine administration forbade the beatings in the interests of safeguarding production.

Stimmersdorf

Inhumanity towards old women

Reported by Hugo Kleinpeter - Report of January 7, 1950

On October 7, 1945 three Czechs conducted a house search of my home, even though I was an anti-Fascist. On this occasion they stole 600 RM in bank notes and 300 RM in five-mark pieces from me and a great deal of linen, clothing and other things from my two married daughters and my son. In the course of their search they also found the Eastern Medal that my son had received for the winter campaign against Russia. For this a young Czech beat me for about 45 minutes so severely about the head that I collapsed. My ears were swollen and I had constant headaches for two full weeks. When my wife begged him to stop beating me, he threw her against the kitchen door, and a second Czech held his rifle aimed at her, ready to fire.

I was threatened with a pistol and told that if they were to find even the smallest military artifact or a photograph of a soldier during a second house search, they would shoot my entire family.

The people who had been expelled first had not received any food stamps from the Saxon authorities for months, and prompted by the great distress that this caused, a woman who had already been evacuated risked returning across the border in order to beg for some food for herself and her children. On her way back in the dark, around midnight, this woman had wandered off the path for a few steps, fell off a 10-meter [30-ft.] cliff and lay unconscious where she fell. Even though a Czech soldier was standing guard nearby at the bridge crossing and had observed the entire accident, he did not bother about her. Not until the next morning at about 10 o'clock was the woman fetched by some inhabitants of the town, and put into a garage on the orders of the Czechs. She had to stay there without any help at all until a Czech car required the garage space in the evening. And so we had to carry the unfortunate woman, who was still alive, to the cemetery and into the morgue where we had to put her directly on the bare concrete floor. On the orders of the Czech commissar, a grave had to be dug for the still-living woman at the edge of the cemetery. It was the next day before a Slovak shot her and ended her suffering.

One Saturday afternoon in late May 1946 I was driving home from work. It was cold and rained heavily. On the way, still half an hour from my home, I suddenly heard someone whimper in the ditch beside the road. To my horror I saw an old woman lying in the water there. She was soaked to the skin, could not move, and shook with the cold.

After I had puller her out of the water I quickly drove home and reported the incident immediately to the Czech Commissar and to the guards. I was told that there was nothing they could do for her and that she'd surely get up by herself again.

When I drove back to work again on Monday morning, I found her five steps farther downhill, lying dead in the water. I again reported this to the gendarmerie. The woman was buried in the woods.

In September 1945 my wife and daughter were in the woods looking for mushrooms. They found a woman lying under a tree. She was already half dead from starvation and could no longer speak. She had been among the early evacuees [expellees] and had taken the risk of coming back across the border again to get a bit of food. A car came to pick her up, and we anti-Fascists took her in to care for her. Ten days later, when she was more or less able to walk again, we were ordered to take her back to the border again immediately. So now she was taken half an hour's drive back into the mountains across the border and left to her fate once again. Some time later we heard that this woman had been found dead on the road in the mountains.

I personally know of eight cases where German privates, already dressed in civilian clothes, crossed the border from the Protectorate in order to get to their homes. Many were shot, usually right on the spot. My comrades and I had to bury one of them in the town.

Concentration camp Klaidovka: Sadistic punishment of an invalid
Reported by Johann Böhm - Report of August 31, 1946

For 6½ months, from November 5, 1945 until May 11, 1946, I was detained in the court prisons in Strakonitz and Brünn. I was never even questioned, nor was I told why I had been arrested. In Brünn I was boxed about the head and maltreated, as were all the prisoners. As a result of the inadequate rations I developed dropsy and phlegmone. Since I was unable to put on my boots due to the swelling in my legs, I and a fellow prisoner traded our footwear, my boots for his shoes. I was punished for this with 16 days of solitary confinement, worsened by four days of fasting, in total darkness and without bedding to soften the floor. The cell was unheated, and the temperature was at the freezing mark. On May 11, 1946, when I was at death's door, weighing all of 42 kg (I am 1.63 m tall) and with a raging fever, I was transferred to the concentration camp Klaidovka.

Tabor, Report No. 1
Robbery, maltreatment
Reported by Marie Kuhn - Report of May 15, 1950

From 1940 until 1945 I lived in Tabor, at Riegerplatz 1886. In late April 1945 I left the city and moved into a temporary home in the small town of Stepanice in the District of Bergreichenstein. I shared this home with several other German families and my apartment with the wife of the senior army doctor of the police, Dr. Bön. One day after the German collapse some 18-20 heavily armed partisans appeared in our house, accompanied by an official from the Czech gendarmerie. These partisans maltreated us so badly, with punches to the face and head and kicks to the abdomen, that the blood shot from my mouth and nose. They also used a hay fork to beat us. The partisans demanded jewelry from me. Since I no longer had any, these bandits stood me up against a tree, pressed a pistol to my chest and kept repeating their demands that I should surrender my valuables. Later on, in the same context, they threw a rope around my neck, literally dragged me down the attic stairs and hauled me to a tree to hang me. It was not until a Czech gendarmerie official intervened that they stopped maltreating me like that. On the official's orders one of the partisans flung a towel into my face so that I should wipe off the blood. In the meantime our luggage had been loaded onto a truck and taken away. We were allowed to keep only the barest necessities. For the next 10 days we were not permitted to leave our quarters. Two guards stood in front of and behind the door.

After 10 days, three Czechs armed to the teeth picked us up and drove us to Schüttenhofen to the court prison, under the pretext that we were to be interrogated. Along with 15 other people of both sexes I was squeezed into a small, cold and damp cell whose only ventilation consisted of a small hole at the top of the ceiling, which also allowed only a little bit of daylight to penetrate the cell. Our stay in this cell - about 10 days - was largely spent standing up. Only two old understuffed straw sacks were thrown into the cell, and these were not enough for the prisoners to sit, much less lie on. There was also a reeking bucket in the cell, which served as toilet and had to be emptied once a day. Our rations during these 10 days consisted only of a morsel of bread and a little water each day, and a few cold potatoes.

Several times each day the guards came by and called to one or the other of us: "Tomorrow morning you're going to be strung up!", in other words, tomorrow morning you're going to be hanged.

One evening around 10 o'clock, after a 10-day stay in this hell, we were loaded onto an open truck and driven through the pouring rain, with no protection from the elements whatsoever, about 120 km from Schüttenhofen to Tabor, where we arrived in the early dawn. After a thorough physical exam, which was performed by a female prison guard, we received a plentiful and tasty meal, contrary to all our expectations. In the afternoon of that same day we were transferred yet again. Along with 9 other women and 14 children, including infants, I was taken to the farm belonging to the widow Maria Kremencová in Ceské-Zahori, No. 10, Post Milicin, District of Tabor. Here we were to be put to agricultural labor.

We were quartered in a totally filthy and run-down, medium-sized room, and one smaller one that had served as a coop for about 80 chickens until our arrival. There were no cots or bunks, and no dishes at all, neither knives nor forks, and no pots. There was only one wash bowl for all of us nine women and 14 children. The same vessel served as salad bowl and wash bowl alike, and on the occasion of a birth it was used to hold the placenta etc.

In 12- to 14-hour shifts we women had to perform the hardest jobs, under constant guard by armed overseers. Aside from the farm work we were also put to road construction, loading and unloading entire wagons of fruit and coal, reshingling roofs, weeks of shoveling snow in the winter, whitewashing stables and store rooms, etc. Very often we were still working in the fields even by moonlight, picking potatoes and turnips.

There was no break time except at noon. Insofar as we even had any bread, we had to choke it down dry while constantly continuing to work. When we went home for the noon break, we had two hours to prepare the meal, which was no small feat considering that anything we got to eat we first had to sneak and steal from the surrounding fields, and often it was not possible to do so.

Our rations were distributed by the widow who owned the estate. She bought the food for us on ration cards and then distributed it among us according to her own judgement and discretion. Our food allowances were very scanty.

The treatment we received at the hands of our boss and her two sons was very bad. Even though we were not subjected to physical abuse, we were forever chased around and urged to work faster and treated to vile curses, so that we hardly knew what was what. We were also constantly threatened that they would hand us over to the Russians who were billeted very close by. Very often it happened that when the Russians had gone to the distillery that was part of the estate, and had become badly drunk, they came by to molest us. Thanks to the Czech still master, who was a reasonable man, we were always warned of their intentions in time so that we could hide in the nearby corn fields until dawn.

Once we had to put new shingles on a stable roof, and I was at the roof ridge where I had to catch the shingles as they were thrown to me, and pass them on. Some of the roof boards were rotten, and I broke through and fell to the floor below. I suffered a very bad bruise and was forced to seek medical help.

The saddest chapter of this life was our clothing. We had been looted down to the last rag, and almost without exception we had no change of clothes. Incidentally, we were also not issued any clothing, linen or shoes at all from 1945 to 1947. Nonetheless we had to do the hardest kinds of physical labor day in, day out, summer and winter alike, in snow and rain, and even in the winter cold of up to -34°C. As a result it was necessary for us to keep our wet clothes on at night, since otherwise they would not be dry by morning. We could not undress for the night anyway since there were no blankets. One consequence of all this was that we were inundated with all kinds of colds, pests and vermin, boils, scabies and skin rashes (there was no soap either). The skin conditions were very much worsened by the fact that we nonetheless had to go to work on the fields and spread chemical fertilizers, such as potash etc.

To supplement our clothing we eventually began to undress the scarecrows that were set out in the fields. In the winter we had to wrap old burlap bags around our legs and feet.

Three times I went to see the Czech Major who was responsible for the treatment of prisoners in Tabor, to try and find out what our legal situation was, specifically, whether we were considered to be prisoners-of-war, civilian internees, or specialty laborers. This would have determined what other conditions we could have expected, such as the duration of our work shifts, supervision by the guards, pay, rations etc. The Czech Major was of the opinion that we were civilian internees. He promised me that he would arrange for the dispatch of a control commission that would see to the appropriate changes. The delegation came, but conditions remained the same. It was not until the last few months, when there were only three of us left, that some improvements were made.

I would also like to mention that in 1945 I was already 50 years old and had undergone no less than three serious abdominal operations. Nonetheless I was forced to work with the labor gang in the fields without any sort of supporting bandage.

But I would also like to gratefully recall those who always treated us humanely during this time of imprisonment, with no regard for the danger that doing so meant for themselves. They were: **1.** Dr. N. N. from the General Public Hospital in Tabor. **2.** The still master of the estate. **3.** Dr. N., general practitioner. **4.** The businesspeople of M. **5.** The gendarmerie officials serving in M. at that time. All of these people sought to alleviate our difficult fate as best they could, and in doing so especially the two doctors went far beyond the bounds of what was permitted them, by helping us not only with medication and bandages but financially as well.

The gendarmerie officials proved to be decent and kind insofar as they never "found" anything in their searches for stolen small food animals, for example rabbits - even though they would have had every opportunity to do so.

What I have said in this statement is the truth, and nothing but the truth.

Tabor, Report No. 2
Maltreatment in prison
Reported by Ernst Mahl - Report of August 3, 1946

On August 28, 1945 I was released from Russian captivity in Tabor, and the Czech Employment Office immediately assigned me to work for a farmer near Tabor. I was treated relatively well there. On January 8, 1946, as I was having my lunch, I was suddenly arrested for no reason at all, and was then detained in the Tabor prison until May 18, 1946. I hadn't even been allowed to take any of my clothes. Treatment and rations were very bad in Tabor. About 100 soldiers were kept under arrest there, and they were constantly being beaten with rubber truncheons. Many of them were beaten unconscious and had festering wounds. At the same time, however, we had to do hard labor. Two days each week we got nothing at all to eat. From Tabor I was transferred to the Troppau prison. When I had been committed to Tabor they had taken my money from me - the wages I had earned from the farmer I had worked for - and I now had to sign a receipt confirming that I had received this money back, even though it had not been returned to me.

Tachau

Tachau, Report No. 1
Conditions in the expulsion camp Tachau, May 1945
Reported by Anton Fleissner - Report of June 5, 1946

On May 29 and 30, 1946, approximately 1,200 people from Tachau District were rounded up in the Tachau resettlement camp, a former tobacco factory, in order to be resettled [expelled] from there. At that time the camp already housed some 500 people, who had been left behind as exceeding the quota of previous transports or who were waiting in the camp for family members who were still imprisoned in the concentration camp. This district concentration camp is located on the same factory grounds. Some of these people have been waiting for 4 to 6 weeks, some even longer.

Rations in the camp consisted of a cup of coffee in the morning and evening and some watery soup at noon. Those people who had to endure an extended stay in the camp depended on the charity of new arrivals who had brought a few supplies with them and shared them with acquaintances.

Whenever people outside tried to bring their relatives in the resettlement [expulsion] camp some food, they were turned away, frequently also severely maltreated and fined.

Sanitary conditions in the camp were bad. For approximately 1,700 people there were only 40 water taps and 40 toilets. The toilets were mostly plugged The people to be resettled were treated like convicts. When they arrived, their hand luggage was checked; any and all documents relating to employment, real estate holdings, bank savings, valuables etc. were mercilessly confiscated, as were ID papers and even everyday items such as better-quality razors, cigarettes etc. The slightest objection was cut off with threats of imprisonment in the concentration camp.

During the inspection of the larger luggage, sewing machines (even if they were accompanied by official export permits), all objects of art, rugs, mattresses (even if damaged), jewelry, linen and crafts items were ruthlessly expropriated. Confiscation was entirely arbitrary and depended on the controlling officer's personal tastes.

Shortly before departure, every expellee was issued RM 500 as compensation, even though official regulations provided for RM 1,000. Our objections were cut off with the claim that the remaining RM 500 would be given to us at the Wiesau border crossing.

The space allotted for the transport was totally insufficient, and most of the people had to make the trip standing up. It took 20 hours from Tachau to Eger.

Tachau, Report No. 2
Negligent use of firearms, November 9, 1945
Reported by Franz Voit - Report of June 5, 1946

I was arrested on September 7, 1945 and committed to the Tachau internment camp without being told why I had been arrested or what crime I was supposed to have committed. As I am a carpenter by profession, I was posted to a labor team on a chicken farm, a 1½-hour walk from the camp, to make windows.

We were led to our work site and back every day by two guard soldiers. The guards repeatedly fired their rifles for no reason other than that they felt like it. On November 9, as I was walking back to the camp at the end of our marching column, I heard the guard soldier behind me fire a shot. I guess he had fired into the air. After another 10 steps or so a second shot rang out, and this one hit me in the right calf and shattered my fibula. I had to spend 6 weeks in the hospital. When the wound closed up I was carried into a sick-room in the camp where I remained for another 9 weeks. I did not receive any more medical care there.

The doctor's request for my release into home care was refused. To this day I haven't regained the full use of my leg.

Maltreatment in order to extort a confession
Reported by Arthur Januschek - Report of November 4, 1946

I was arrested in Tannwald on June 11 last year. To extort a confession from me, I was severely maltreated seven times, twice in Tannwald by the SNB and five times in the prison of Eisenbrod. Each time I was stripped naked and beaten with rubber truncheons until I was half unconscious, and then I was shoved into a tub of cold water and my head was held underwater. My nasal bone and both my eardrums were damaged in the process. Ever since then I also suffer from lung trouble. I was released to be resettled [expelled].

Tepl, Report No. 1
Concentration camp Tepl, maltreatment
Reported by Engelbert Haber - Report of July 14, 1946

I was interned in the camp at Tepl on January 15th, 1946; the inmates of the camp were severely maltreated all the time. On June 25, 1946, I myself was terribly beaten. I was felling trees in the woods together with 20 other men. We were watched by four guards. These were all of them drunk on this day and while we were working they knocked us about. This lasted from 2 to 5 o'clock in the afternoon without interruption. Me they struck with rifle butts and with their fists and they also kicked me. In the course of this maltreatment I had two teeth knocked out and suffered a cracked rib.

The camp diet was so insufficient that everybody depended on what their relatives brought in.

Tepl, Report No. 2
Severe maltreatment in the internment camp
Reported by Josef Mayer - Report of July 14, 1946

On November 28 last year I was interned in the Tepl concentration camp because my 2 sons, who had been released to Bavaria from American captivity, had come home, had each fetched a suit and then returned to Bavaria again to where they had been released, where they now worked. 8 days later my wife was also interned. My wife and I were both beaten in the camp. My right ear was injured in the process. The worst maltreatment took place in the night of December 23-24. Many were beaten unconscious. One man sustained a broken arm, several others suffered broken ribs. I was released on May 28, my wife on June 4, 1946. On our release we were both given a discharge paper stating that we had spent 2 months in the camp, even though we had actually been imprisoned for 6 months. The first and only interrogation was held 8 days before we were released.

Totzau

Maltreatment, murders
Reported by H. K. W. - Report of May 1, 1951

On May 25, 1945, two Communist members of the criminal police entered the office of the mayor at Totzau in order to look for the Ortsleiter and the Kreisleiter (functionaries of the local NSDAP), who both were alleged to have hidden themselves in the last house of the village. The policemen then went to house No. 85, which had been pointed out to them; arriving there, they were told that the men they were looking for were not there. Nevertheless they forced their way into all the rooms; they found the nephew of the house-owner, one Josef Kutt, from the neighbouring village of Saar near Duppau. They declared him to be under arrest. Suddenly Kutt fired several shots, killing one of the Communists and injuring the second. He then jumped out of the window and fled. The injured policeman ran bleeding through the village. When he met the mayor, Alfred Schmidt, the Communist shouted: "Why didn't you tell us?" and shot the mayor through the chest. (On the same evening, after Miss Christl Müller, a student of medicine, had bandaged him, he was transported to the hospital in Karlsbad. He recovered, but died later on, shortly after he had been expelled to Saxony.) The Communist reached the post office and reported the incident to the nearest Czech gendarmerie-station.

The following day at 7 o'clock in the morning all the inhabitants of the village were ordered to fall in in the square near the church. In the meantime the Czechs searched the houses; the men were beaten and articles of use were stolen; all this was carried out with much tumult and shouting.

On June 2, 1945, about 7 o'clock in the evening, two trucks with 20 soldiers of the Czech Revolutionary Guard, dressed in parts of German uniforms and with red scarves, drove through the village and stopped in front of the church. Shortly afterwards the order was given that everybody was to gather in the square near the church. A little fearful, men, women and children assembled. The men were told to strip to the waist. After this they had to line up, with the children and women behind them, in rows of three. The commander stood in front of them, holding a pistol, while the others went up and down, equipped with sub-machine guns. The commander, after he had taken several deep draughts from a bottle which he had stolen shortly before in the church, made a speech in broken German, shouting repeatedly: "All of you will be shot to-day! All the Sudeten Germans must die like vermin! I am not afraid, I can endure the sight of blood! All of you will be shot, I say!"

Meanwhile the women were chased around, the men tormented. The children were crying loudly. Again and again one could hear the words: "All of you will be shot to-day!"

In order to emphasize this threat, those assembled had to parade again and were then led to the last house of the village. In the meantime terrible things had happened there. In this little house there lived a family by the name of Bartl - Johann and Marie and their children Marie, Willi and Fritz, 17, 15 and 12 years old. These five residents of the house lay dead in the entrance-hall, killed by many shots. Since it was already growing dark, the commander ordered that the corpses should be illuminated with candles, after which men, women and children had to file past and to look at the dreadful sight. Afterwards the corpses were buried without ceremony outside the cemetery.

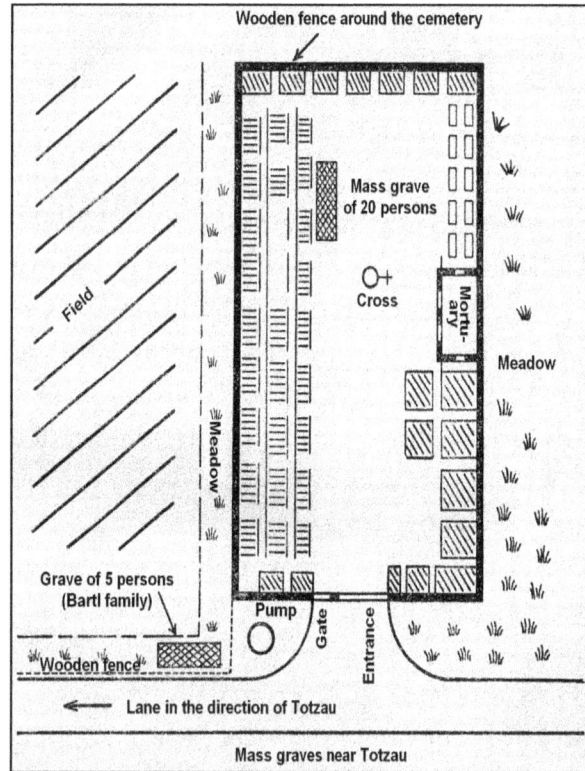

Mass graves near Totzau

Between June 2 and 3, 1945, a similar tragedy took place at Kottershof No. 80, a place 20 minutes distant from the village. This was the home of a family by the name of Sacher and also one Mr. Klotz, an innkeeper, who lived there with his daughter Anna Bernt, née Klotz. The Czechs shot down Oswald and Therese Sacher - still under the pretext that the Kreisleiter was hidden there - then followed Oswald's brother, one Konrad Sacher, and the owner of the neighbouring house and his brother; their names were Josef and Ludwig Tobisch. The child of the Sacher family, only a few months old, was found a year later in the nearby cesspool. Details of the murder became known only after some time, for the survivors had been threatened with death if they talked about it. In this very night Mrs. Anna Bernt, née Klotz, Mrs. G. H. from Chemnitz, who was an air-raid evacuee and lived in the same house, and Mrs. Tobisch, the wife of the murdered man, had to wipe up the blood-stains and to bury the corpses in the garden.

On June 5, 1945 carloads of Czech militia arrived in the early morning. They surrounded the village so that nobody was able to leave it; then they roamed through the fields and forests, breaking into the houses, maltreating the inhabitants and plundering. Before noontime the Czech militia dragged along Mr. Klotz, who had lost his mind as a result of the past days of terror, maintaining that they had found a revolver in his house. The commanding officer shouted: "Weapons have been found, twenty of you will be shot! If other weapons are found, the same thing will happen to the whole village." In front of the church there stood a car and by noontime it had been piled full of plundered property by the Revolutionary Guard.

At three o'clock in the afternoon the order was given for the entire population to form up near the inn. On their way the inhabitants were beaten, women who were unable to run fast enough were shouted at: "You German bastards, will you get a move on!" Not only members of the Revolutionary Guard maltreated the people, there were also Czech civilians, equipped with riding-whips, who had come to the Sudeten territories in order to appropriate German property. In the middle of all this chaos in the streets Czech gendarmerie marched up, armed with their automatic pistols. Lashes and kicks rained down on the helpless women: "Hurry up, you German bastards."

A Captain of the gendarmerie read out the names of six former members of the NSDAP, who were forced to place themselves on the other side of the street, facing an old wooden shed. The leader of the troop, a Czech commissar, then went through the lines of the German men, picking first one and then another, until the number of twenty was reached. He often uttered remarks like: "That's it for this German swine," or "You'll have to die too, you blond German," and he selected only tall, blond men and boys. After this, everything the men had on them was taken away; their boots or shoes were removed. They were lashed, beaten with rifle butts and so on, enduring the severest maltreatment. A boy of 17 collapsed. He was revived with a bucket of cold water and the brutes dragged him to his feet again. After these men had been ill-used and tortured for two whole hours, the commandant ordered them to line up in two rows. Then the Czechs faced us and showed us a new, but damaged revolver, which allegedly had been found. The commandant held a short speech, declaring that these men would be shot in the name of the Czechoslovak Republic.

Machine gun fire stuttered, single pistol shots rang out.... and there followed despairing and confused screaming of the women and children.

Gisela Hanl, Totzau No. 59, later wrote to the reporter: "My husband, Otto Hanl, was among those who had to stand against the wall; he was only 30 years old and the father of two children. They took his shoes and valuables and then he was ill-treated for two hours in the most dreadful manner. We could hardly bear to watch it but we were forced to keep our eyes fixed on what was taking place. When they had been beaten half to death, one of their torturers ordered that they should be shot. There they lay in their blood on the ground and we had to bid them farewell in our thoughts. If that had been all that had happened to me, it would have been enough, but I had also to leave my home, just like all the other inhabitants, together with my two children. I left my house and my homeland, which is today isolated and deserted."

Mrs. Rosa Schmidt, living at Totzau No. 60, who was at that time pregnant, reported: "My husband, Ernst Schmidt, had returned from the hospital as a healthy man, but we enjoyed his presence for only four weeks. He himself was also happy to be reunited with his family, especially with his little son Günther, our three-year-old boy. My husband and my little son were among those who waited in the assembled crowd. Then the dreadful moment came. A Czech went through the rows and examined the men with his piercing, hateful eyes; he chose one after the other. I stood paralyzed and the blood in my veins seemed no longer to circulate when he turned his eyes on my husband and tore him away from his family, driving him with lashes and blows from a rifle butt... I cannot describe my grief and anguish on leaving, with my boy, the place where my husband met his death. And when I had to quit my homeland, my last visit was dedicated to his grave."

Mrs. Rosa Schmidt is today an invalid. She was never able to recover her health after her physical and nervous collapse. In consequence of the heavy agricultural work she was forced to do while pregnant, the twins she bore both died; the boy immediately after birth, the girl at six months.

The list of the dead:

1. Paul Heinze
2. Josef Otto Hanl
3. Ernst Schmidt
4. Erich Leger
5. Josef Kauer
6. Wenzel Leger
7. Willibald Zörkler
8. Josef Kräupel
9. Johann Bärtl
10. Emil Meinlschmidt I
11. Emil Meinlschmidt II
12. Friedrich Schulz
13. Erich Pagelkopf
14. Josef Endisch
15. Josef Zörkler
16. Willi Klotz
17. Josef Zengler
18. Franz Schmidt
19. Rudolf Klotz
20. Erich Schmidt

Those killed in house No. 85:

1. Johann Bartl
2. Marie Bartl [mother]
3. Marie Bartl [daughter]
4. Willi Bartl
5. Fritz Bartl

Those killed at the farm "Kotterhof":

1. Oswald Sacher
2. Konrad Sacher
3. Resi Sacher
4. the little girl Elfriede
5. Josef Tobisch
6. Ludwig Tobisch

After many requests it was permitted to bury the bodies of the 20 executed victims in the local cemetery. They were put on three carts to be taken to the cemetery and a trail of blood showed for some time afterwards the way they had gone. A mass-grave was dug and the dead were laid in it. No mound was to mark the place, everything had to be levelled and the squares of turf had to be placed over it just as they had been cut out.

Trautenau

Concentration camp, execution of 20-30 people in June 1945

Reported by N. N. - Report of August 1950

My wife and I lived in our own house in Trautenau and since 1926 I had managed an agency and commission business. I never took an active part in politics.

On May 8, 1945, 26 men of a Russian guard unit were quartered on the ground floor of my house. They behaved relatively well and left in the early morning of the following day.

A few days later, Czech SNB-partisans made themselves noticed in a very unpleasant way. These men were mostly students and "intellectuals" from the region of Neupaka and from Prague; they soon began with the searching of houses and interrogations, quite often several times a day. I speak Czech very well, so I could easily answer their questions. As a result of a serious intestinal complaint from which I had already suffered for several months, I had to stay in bed most of the time. Although I showed a medical certificate written in Czech, I was dragged out of my bed one day in the middle of May and forced by blows from rifle butts to work on the demolition of the German barricades. On one of the following days, by order of the superintending SNB-man, I had to strike with a pickaxe a picture of Hitler, which was fastened on a truck, and with each time I had to shout "Heil Hitler". After this I received a violent kick in the back that threw me to the ground. I was bleeding heavily from my anus, but further blows with rifle butts forced me to continue my work. Only after several big barricades had been removed and other similar tasks were finished, were my comrades and I released.

All sorts of riffraff and also Bolshevist soldiers were hanging around, especially at night, so the *Národní výbor* itself (National Committee) told us to appoint night-watchmen. Those selected received a certificate and a badge. Moreover, we - that is, German men and women - had to carry or drag heavy loads for the Russians.

June 19th, 1945 came. I received an official communication informing me that my 83-year-old mother was to be transferred to Trautenau from one of the neighbouring towns of the former Protectorate (i.e. Czechoslovakia between 1939 and 1945). I was very happy at the news, but I never actually saw her again. She died 18 months later, miserable and in want, in a town near the Baltic Sea.

At noontime three men, who identified themselves as secret-police men Žižka, Doležal and another, entered our house and demanded to inspect it. They left it after a very superficial inspection. Scarcely an hour later several SNB-men forced their way into the house and ordered my wife and me to be ready within a quarter of an hour for some outside work which would last 2 or 3 days. With threats and blows from rifle butts were urged to hurry up. We put on our oldest clothes, packed a few necessities in a rucksack, and SNB-men pushed us out of the door. They then took us to a truck waiting nearby and thrust us into it. A number of acquaintances, women and children between 2 and 15 years, already stood in the truck. Soon the overcrowded truck was shut and we all drove to the little town of Eipel, about 13 kilometers (8 miles) distant. After our arrival there, we were lodged in an old, dilapidated and neglected theatre-hall with dirty and inadequate palliasses. Many persons from Trautenau who had arrived here in the same way only the day before, were already assembled there. About 200 or 250 persons had been rounded up in this way. Very few of us had blankets and food. We spent the first night and the following nights fully dressed and always 2 or 3 persons to a palliasse. There was no tap or water-supply at our disposal and also no latrines. For two days we received no food, but we were allowed to fetch water from the houses in the neighbourhood. Only from the third day onwards did we receive three "meals" a day, consisting of black coffee, a thin soup and a thin piece of dry bread. In exchange for the food the men had to do heavy work in the town from the very first morning, while the women had to clean the streets, latrines and buildings. On the third day of our stay in the Czech concentration camp all of the men were ordered to dig the foundations of barracks destined for us; meanwhile, in our absence, most of the women were handed over as servants to Czech farmers in the neighbourhood of Eipel or were distributed as servants or labourers for the Czech population. The people at Eipel often indulged in mean insults towards us. Jabs and blows from the SNB-partisans who guarded us and even more often from Czech civilians had to be endured. At 6 o'clock in the morning we were taken to our place of work where we remained until late in the evening. The only break was 30 minutes for lunch (hot water, which they called soup, and a tiny piece of bread). But Czech civilians, who felt pity for us, secretly gave us food when they could do so unobserved. On June 21, 1945 - it was a Thursday - we accidentally learned that our wives had been assigned to farmers as menials. I asked the Czech surveyor, one Mr. Hlášek, who was about 60 years old, very politely if this was true, since my wife had my necessities in her bag. Hlášek answered gruffly that this was no business of mine. He called another SNB-man and asserted that I had told him that what was happening here was barbarous. He asked him accordingly to book me for a whipping for next Saturday. This he did, although I politely pointed out that Hlášek's statement was untrue.

Thinking of the whipping which was to take place on Saturday and was to be executed by the notorious Podzimek, I was unable to sleep at night, and thought of escape. Friday afternoon, a radio was playing in front of the open windows of the SNB-barracks. Suddenly the broadcast was interrupted and the speaker of Radio Prague said: *"Pozor, pozor, pozor!"* (Attention,...) and then something to the effect of: "The Government requests the population to suspend the persecutions of Germans." This was repeated three tunes. Later on the radio was shut off. Two SNB-men stepped out of the barracks and joined Hlášek to whom they remarked on the broadcast, adding that such orders were intended only for foreign countries. They, the SNB, had other directives. Soon afterwards a long-lasting and violent downpour of rain flooded everything, but nevertheless we had to continue our work. We were standing in water up to our knees and were soaked completely through. Mr. Effenberger, an engineer, tried to find shelter from the rain under the jutting roof. Inspector Hlášek drove him back and had him too booked for a whipping the next day.

In the course of the night Effenberger and I discussed how we could escape the whipping and agreed that at the reveille we would immediately report to the doctor, since only a limited number were admitted every day for examination. We succeeded in being booked. When inspector Hlášek called up our names for the whipping, we told him of this. Hlášek threatened us with more severe punishment on our return. A guard took us to the doctor; this was the local health officer by the name of Dr. P.; after we had waited for four hours, he examined the seven or eight of us very thoroughly. We learned that we were all ill and could only be used for light labour. The young manager of the employment exchange then told us that he had enough people for light labour and that he would suggest our being discharged and sent home to Trautenau. We begged him to do so. Here we also obtained the addresses of our wives, who were working for the farmers. They then told us to go to another section of the camp where we received our discharge papers. The wife of my comrade Amler and my own wife were working in the same village (Libnatov), which was situated about 4 kilometers (2½ miles) away.

Together with this man, who had been released at the same time, I escaped without delay in the direction of Libnatov, going by side-roads to avoid running into Hlášek. We found our wives in despair. I talked to my wife and urged her to see the health officer as soon as possible. (As a result she was also released two days later.) The farmer for whom my wife worked even went so far as to point out to me the shortest way to Trautenau, and together with Amler and his wife I hurried home to Trautenau.

The first thing I heard from an acquaintance I met was that our house had been looted on June 19, 1945, immediately after we had left it, and that on the same day a secret-police agent by the name of Žižala had moved in. He was still living there with his whole family and was using my furniture. I found shelter in the house of my former clerk, who gave me a small room. There my wife rejoined me two days later. With the assistance of friends, who helped us with food and clothes, we spent three months there. When this house was also requisitioned, we lived for three further months in an attic and the last 2½ months, until we were finally transferred, we stayed with an old man.

It was the end of July or the beginning of August when I asked Mr. Morawek, my former tobacconist, if he could get me something to smoke. Mr. Morawek lived not far away in a little house near the Jewish cemetery. During the day he was away from home, but returned in the late afternoon. It was for this reason that he asked me to see him at 7 p. m. in his apartment. I was there on time, but Mr. Morawek was late and did not arrive until 8. But no German was allowed on the streets after 8. The day was rainy and it was dark and I intended to make my way by the "Schützenhausgarten" (a garden around the shooting range) so that I might reach my room unseen. - I only waited until the violent shower of rain was over. I had almost reached the exit of the Schützenhausgarten and only a few steps separated me from my house, when suddenly I heard the sound of an engine. I hesitated for a moment by the shrubbery, but was terribly frightened when I noticed that a covered truck was turning towards the gate. I pressed myself quickly into the wet bushes. The truck stopped in front of the terrace of the ruined Schützenhaus, which lay in my view. Soon 5 to 7 SNB-men stepped from the truck, lifted the back tilt and dragged something out which I recognized as fettered and half-naked human bodies. Almost without words, one after another of these unfortunate men was quickly and roughly dragged out; the bodies writhed, but the men were bound and gagged. After they had been thrown on the ground, the SNB-men, exclaiming *"rychle, rychle"* (quick, quick), dragged them behind the Schützenhaus to the former shooting grounds. There were from 21 to 23 bodies and, as I was able to see, all were men. Soon two bursts of machine gun fire followed, also a number of single shots. The next moment the SNB-men re-appeared, running and carrying the corpses; they threw them into the truck without uttering a word. The driver had remained at the wheel and after they had closed up the car with the tilt as before, they drove at high speed towards the centre of the town. Only when it had grown very dark did I dare to run home.

It was extremely dangerous at that time to mention anything to anybody about such things. A few days later Helene Demuth, a Red Cross nurse, said that she had heard that 15 to 20 Germans had been shot in the Schützenhaus. It became known that hundreds of suicides had taken place. Whole families committed suicide. Every German feared for his own and his family's lives.

Letter from a family from Trautenau that committed suicide:

(Gisi Seidlová)
Pan Jan Celba, rolník
Libnatov 38

Friday, June 15 / 45

Dear Gisi!

We have just received your letter of Wednesday. Pech, Müller and Schinkmann and their wives, and many others as well, had to vacate their homes today. Perhaps our turn will come as well, and there will not be enough time to fetch you. The situation is hopeless, and there is nothing left for us but to put an end to it. (NB: rest of letter is in a different handwriting.)

Dear Giserl! Today 72 officials and their wives and children were taken from our village. Their homes and property were immediately confiscated. The members of the National Socialist Women's Auxiliary are next. Papa and I are old and ill, and we can no longer earn our living abroad. Therefore, take heart and follow us. Then we will all be reunited with our Walter.

May God forgive us this terrible sin. There is no other way out for us. If there is enough time I will go to confession one last time on Sunday.

We love you beyond measure, and only ever wanted the best for you. May God grant that we shall meet again in the Hereafter.

Forgive us this unholy act.

Your parents.

Tremošna (Concentration camp near Pilsen)

Concentration camp Tremošna, maltreatment of sick Germans
Reported by Dr. Brandl - Report of December 9, 1945

I was practising as a doctor in the American PW-Hospital 712e in which civilians working for the US Forces were cared for. The camp was situated in Pilsen and Colonel Bost was in charge.

In the middle of November seven Germans were also assigned to us, who had come from the internment camp at Třemošna and were residents of villages in the Erzgebirge. The Germans were in a deplorable physical and medical condition. Their bodies were like skeletons, revealing every bone. Their backs showed signs of severe beating. There were numerous scars which originated from weals left by whips or rods.

All of them reported that their rations had been totally insufficient. For weeks they had only received soup and one quarter of a loaf twice a day. Three of them were suffering from heart-ailments, but had received no medical treatment, since medicaments were lacking. Any medicaments would have had to be bought by the German inmates of the camp, and this was impossible since they had been deprived of all their money.

Mr. Weidlich from Graslitz, an editor, reported that many of the camp-inmates had been transferred to the house of correction in Bory, where they had died of hunger-typhus.

The seven Germans were taken before the American Colonel Bost, who expressed his indignation at their condition.

Triebendorf

Woman robbed
Reported by Erna Mildner - Report of June 15, 1946

I was employed by the Raiffeisen bank for 15 years and have boarded with the farmer Heger since July 20, 1945. When Heger was assigned a Czech administrator, I worked for him for four months without any pay.

On December 5 the Czech administrator Urbanek from Nemcic, District Prerau, ordered me to move out of the house, and I was forbidden to take any clothes or linen for myself or my children, even though these things belonged to me, not to the farm estate, since I had only lived and worked there. Finally he gave me a few old rags, and forced me to sign a list written in Czech which I couldn't read. He also took all the groceries I had on hand. When I went back to him the next day to ask for a few more of my things, he shoved me out the door and threatened to have me sent to the concentration camp. I did not dare report him to the gendarmerie.

At Christmas my daughter went to him to fetch our Christmas decorations and nativity scene, but he threatened the child as well with sending her to the concentration camp, and smashed the Christmas decorations and nativity scene on the floor before her very eyes.

Urbanek was a bricklayer by profession and had no clue of agricultural matters, but I saw him beat the farmer Heger in the field with his whip and shove him to the ground, even though Heger was an invalid.

I am prepared to take this statement on my oath.

Tschachwitz

Multiple murders of Sudeten Germans in June 1945
Reported by Josef Fassl - Report of June 27, 1950

On June 6th, there occurred the murder of a miller, Wenzel Ment, 42 years old; following this a group of drunken partisans drove in a car through our village. They dragged my sister, then 42 years old and mother of five children, out of her house, threw her into the car and drove away for about a kilometer; they then pushed her into a ditch and killed her with a burst of fire from automatic pistols. They left cheering and singing.

On June 13, my brother, 40 years old, was decoyed under a pretext to Tuschmitz to see the commissar, officiating as station-master at the Tuschmitz railway-station. On his arrival there he was seized and was tortured all night long, so that his screams could be heard even at the next village, 2 kilometers [1.3 miles] distant. He was finally taken into the country next morning, shot, and buried without ceremony.

The criminal who was responsible for this and other crimes, most of them committed in this area, boasted in public that he had already killed 36 Germans and hoped to increase the number to 50; the same man murdered also the farmer of the name of Josef Baier from Liebisch some days later. At the end of June the licensee of the casino, one Mr. Bechine, Edmund Miser, a workman, Josef Strohwasser, a farmer, the two brothers Karl and Walter Merker and Hermann Peinelt, a shoe-maker, were all shot close by the cemetery wall of Tschachwitz. Their next of kin were forced to watch the executions and to pretend to laugh.

The following persons may be named as witnesses: the children of Mrs. Franziska Müller, my murdered sister, Mrs. Emilie Gläser as well as the former mayor of the community of Liebisch, Mr. Franz Löbling.

Two Germans hanged
Reported by Erna Peschke - Report of June 21, 1946

My husband came home from the army on April 19, 1945. On May 9th the population of Tschenkowitz was summoned to an assembly. We were on our way to this assembly, when my husband was sent for from the municipal council. I went with him to the office. He was detained there and, after some hours, he was taken to the town of Gabel on the Adler, together with several other men from Tschenkowitz. When I made inquiries from the mayor, Mr. Burian, I received the information that the Germans were only under protective custody and would probably be released within a few days. On May 14, at 9 o'clock in the morning, about 30 men, among them my husband, were brought back from Gabel. They were disfigured past recognition. I heard that my husband was to be hanged. I took my child, aged three months, and hurried to the municipal council, in order to appeal for mercy. My father-in-law also begged for clemency. Two men were hanged on that day, my husband and also a man by the name of Spiller. The mayor told me: "It serves him right, he is a German!"

Daughter murdered, June 17, 1945
Reported by Franz Schreier - Report of June 9, 1950

In Tschirm No. 84, Troppau District, on Sunday, July 17th, 1945 at 11 o'clock at night, four Czech partisans (two of them civilians, one man in Czech and one man in Russian uniform) broke into the bedroom of my daughter, Angela Schreier, 25 years old, in order to rape her. She resisted. Furious at this, one of the partisans leveled an army pistol at her and fired. She died after a few minutes.

Dr. Baier from Wigstadtl, who was called immediately, certified the cause of death as a shot through the lungs.

The Reverend H. Alfred Possel performed the consecration and officiated at the funeral.

In the same bed with my daughter when she was murdered was her child, Ingrid, born on March 15, 1943, who was also hit by a shot in the spine and has been paralyzed since that time. The child was afterwards in the children's hospital at Munich for 9 months.

Shortly after the murder the Czech community official Jan Bayger from Tschirm arrived at the scene of the crime. When he left, he took with him all the shoes that he could find, the new clothes, and all underwear and linen.

Tüppelsgrün

Death as result of maltreatment, Altrohlau
Reported by Emma Eigler - Report of September 18, 1946

My husband worked as cemetery gardener and sexton in Tüppelsgrün. On June 21 he was arrested and severely maltreated all night long. When he returned home the next day he was disfigured beyond recognition. After that he was always ill. During the maltreatment he had sustained an injury to his spleen, which suppurated. In June 1946 he died of this. The Czech physician of Altrohlau confirmed that my husband had died of the consequences of the maltreatment he had been subjected to.

Tuschkau

Tuschkau, Report No. 1
Death by starvation in Bory Prison, August 20, 1945
Reported by Eleonore Hochberger - Report of June 18, 1950

On May 18, 1945 the Czechs arrested my husband Adalbert Hochberger, teacher in Tuschkau, resident at Kosolup 123 near Pilsen, District of Mies. As of May 7 the Czechs had made him and other Germans tear down tank barricades and then clear rubble, since our town had sustained several direct hits during air raids. At first the Czechs were still somewhat restrained since they were afraid to incur the Americans' displeasure. But that changed when they realized that they had nothing to fear from the Americans and could do whatever they liked to us Sudeten Germans.

When my husband did not return from work on May 18, my daughter told me that many men had been arrested. I immediately ran to the *výbor*, and there I saw about 20 men standing, lying or huddling around. I saw my husband standing, he was as yet uninjured. Many local Czechs as well as gendarmes who had arrived from Pilsen by bus were at the *výbor*. I went to them and cried: "What has my husband done, whom has he harmed? I was with the Party too, so take me as well." One of the Czechs approached me and said, *"Tak pojdte."* [Come along.] One of the gendarmes took my arm and pulled me into the community office. He took down my particulars, and then accompanied me and four Czechs to my home. Everything, the entire house and even the yard and garden, was searched. One of the Czechs said, "where is revolver?" I told him that we had never had one. He said, "your husband said he has revolver." When they were finally finished with the house search two hours later without having found anything, they left. As he was leaving, the gendarme, who had behaved with relative restraint and had only confiscated the radio, said to my daughter, in Czech: "Tell your mother not to be so upset. Her husband will come back soon." He never came back.

When I dared go back out again some time later, the bus with the prisoners was gone. It was not until four weeks later that I found out, via a preprinted postcard with my husband's signature, that he had been taken to Pilsen to the Bory prison. The card stated that relatives were permitted to bring the prisoners fresh clothes every week. Once I tried to obtain a permit from the Czechs to take the train to Pilsen. "You criminals want to ride the train? You can walk," said the Czech, but then he did give me a permit. The Americans, on the other hand, did not give me one, and before entering Pilsen we were warned that it was very dangerous for us Germans there. Twice I managed to send clean laundry to Bory, that is, somebody took it from me but I don't know if my husband ever actually received it. I took various steps to help my husband and to try to save him, but it was all in vain. I wrote a petition but they just laughed at me at the *výbor*.

I tried time and again to see the Commandant to appeal to him for help. It was simply impossible to get to him. Two Czech legionnaires stood guard at the gate and admitted only those who had a permit from the *výbor*. Once I managed to speak with the American interpreter. He told me curtly: "We Americans haven't come to help the Germans, we've come to liberate the Czechs from you. We don't care what they do to you. Only the Reich German refugees are under our protection, nothing must happen to them."

One day a Czech whom I had never met before brought me a letter from my husband in which he told me that he was suffering terribly from hunger and that I should send him some food. The Czech left no address, and I had been away from home when he had arrived. This was about the same time that the Czechs ordered me to vacate our house. My daughter told an American soldier of our plight, and he came the next day with two friends and carried our heavy furniture into the quarters we had been assigned to. The soldiers only thought it was strange that we were moving out of our beautiful home and into this old inferior one and they could not understand why we obeyed the Czechs.

My daughter had to work on the local estate without receiving any meals or pay for her work.

When we had vacated the house, I found out that my husband had died. It was on August 20, 1945. I was trying to take the first food parcel to him, which was finally permitted since the great dying had already begun among the prisoners. Three small potatoes in two cups of hot water was all they got per day. I was just trying to pass the barricade when once again something was not in order with my papers. I gave the parcel to an acquaintance who was also going to Bory. In the afternoon she brought it back, and told me that my husband had died that morning. For two days I went from one office in Pilsen to the next. I ignored all the rules and prohibitions for the Germans. Without our armbands we went around, my daughter and I, took the streetcars even though it was forbidden on penalty of heavy fines, but I didn't care about any of it. We were sent from one office to the next, and I hoped to at least be able to recover the body of my poor husband, who had starved to death. But when we had finally come to the right place, the Czech official just said to me, in Czech: "You are Germans? No, do you think we were able to have the bodies of our dead transferred home from the German concentration camps?"

On the fourth day we left our homeland. An American helped us, so that we were able to take at least a few necessities with us.

Tuschkau, Report No. 2
Discharged soldiers forced into camp in autumn 1945
Reported by Franz Zitterbart - Report of June 8, 1950

After being discharged from the army I came home to the town of Tuschkau on May 5, 1945. I worked for the Czechs as a tailor and also pressed uniforms for the Americans. On July 19, 1945 the American Military Police sent me an order via the Czech mayor, one J. Reiser, to report to the town-hall. After a short interrogation I was sent in a truck to the PoW-camp at Hammelburg in Bavaria. The American guards at this camp were extremely friendly. When I was released on September 20, 1945, the Americans brought me to Tirschenreuth, near the Bavarian border. I was now a free man, but my family was still living in our house in Tuschkau. Following orders I reported to the American border officer at Altmugl, showing my American discharge papers. Together with 29 other comrades I crossed the Czech border and came to Promenhof (Proumov) on September 22, 1945. In front of the custom-house the Czechs took away our discharge papers and our money, from myself 186 Marks and 100 Kčs, giving us receipts for it. We had also to deliver up all blankets, underclothes, knives, watches, canned food and tobacco. Then - after we had waited for an hour - gendarmes and partisans arrived on bicycles and, led by the Czech platoon commander Šnaidr, we all marched to the town of Plan, while the people shouted at us, slapped and kicked us. In an old wooden barrack at the station, which was full of bugs, we then had to sleep on old palliasses, always two men to a bed, and without blankets. In this wretched camp we were exposed to slapping, whipping and kicking and were forced to sing Czech marching songs in addition to having to work extremely hard. Very often they searched the palliasses, sometimes even at night, looking for newspapers, letters and weapons.

On October 12, 1945 twenty of us had to dig up bodies in a forest near Raketendörflas. We stood at attention in front of a Czech judicial commission (gendarmes, railroad workers, partisans) for almost an hour, while the partisans struck us, insulted and slapped us. After that we marched into the forest, where the graves were. Mr. Bittner, a teacher, Mr. Kanzler, a mechanic, Mr. Ernst, a tailor, and I myself reached an isolated grave. We dug hurriedly. Then the half-decomposed body appeared. Now two Czech civilians began to strike us unmercifully with rubber-truncheons. I was already exhausted, when a Czech captain of the gendarmerie yelled: "What is your profession?" I answered: "Tailor, wounded in the war". The gendarme shouted: "Use your fingers then and dig him up neatly!" So I dug with my fingers in the dirt and the stinking ooze that had once been a human being. All of a sudden I received such blows on my head, neck, back and legs that I lost consciousness and rolled over beside the grave. Later on we were drawn up in a meadow and ordered at the double to tear up grass for the purpose of cleaning off the corpses. A Czech grave-digger took me along with him to the car, so that I was able to rest. This Czech was unable to bear watching our ill-treatment. At eight o'clock in the evening we marched back to the barracks of our camp; there some of us were slapped in the face by the Czech camp commander Ulma. On November 2, 1945, 150 men (including myself) were sent to the labour camp at Třemošna near Pilsen. To begin with there was also ill-treatment here of which several persons from Graslitz died. But later on the Czech commandant of the camp, K., prohibited the excesses. On February 2, 1946 we (150 men) returned in closed cattle-vans to the miserable camp at Plan. There, under the leadership of the drunken commandant of the camp, Šnaidr, the beatings and the stay in the camp-prison were a regular custom. I was lucky in that I was able to work as a kind of home-tailor in the apartments of higher Czech officials. These Czechs treated me very well. I also worked for three Czech Communists to whom I had to tell all the atrocities we had endured. Suddenly, in the beginning of May 1946, the brutal commandant Šnaidr was dismissed and the conditions in the internment camp at Plan became more bearable.

Only a few Germans were sent to the district prison of Eger. At last, on July 27, 1946, I was released, equipped with some necessities by the Czechs, and sent home by train.

The *"Národní výbor"* (Czech National Committee) and the Czech Communist mayor S. had been humane and considerate to my wife and my children. The American soldiers at Tuschkau (the 16th division, I assume) had also helped my family. On August 2nd we were transferred to Bavaria.

Czechs even gave us food for our transfer. All this I must honestly admit.

Udritsch (Estate near Lubenz)

Estate Udritsch near Lubenz, Luditz, conditions along the linguistic border
Reported by Max Hilscher - Report of December 12, 1945

I am the owner of the Udritsch estate near Lubenz and I was still on the estate when the Russians arrived. I then left temporarily in order to escape the Czech partisans, but returned to the estate on May 17th, 1945. I had been neither an active member of the NSDAP nor had I ever held any prominent position. I had therefore no reason to fear anything.

On June 6, 20 year old František Sedláček was appointed as manager *(Národní správce)* of the estate. He was certainly no expert, indeed, he had no idea whatsoever about the problems of an agricultural undertaking. This young man was accompanied by 40 men of the so-called "Svoboda Troop". These men searched the farm and found remnants of equipment of German units who, in the course of their retreat, had sought lodging there. The Czechs made me responsible for the existence of the remnants, undressed me and struck me with clubs, ropes and [bullwhips], without giving me the chance to speak in my defence. After this I was taken to the cellar of the Czech school at Luditz, which had been equipped as a jail. The conditions in this jail were very bad. Previous to my arrival one Melchner, a salesman, Frank, a shoemaker, and Mr. Victor Hutterer, all from Luditz and none of whom had been a party-activist, had all been shot without prior interrogation. Mr.

Liehm, the former mayor, had been reduced to complete physical prostration. In spite of his age - he was 65 years old - he had been incessantly beaten ever since his arrival. Among those in the jail, there was also a certain Mrs. Maria Brehm, 74 years old, an aunt of the author and poet Bruno Brehm. She showed clear signs of mental disturbance and constantly asked for chicken-food for her poultry. One day she got away from the camp; every tenth man of us was to be shot in reprisal. But in the evening the old woman was brought back by a Czech soldier, bruised all over and with her clothing torn. I had to stay in this prison at forced labour for four months and was finally released in October, because I could not be convicted of any crime.

During the first days of May the Czechs from the neighbourhood broke into German villages and farms, possessed themselves of the goods and chattels without any official authorization. At Lubenz 18 Germans were shot without any reason being given, among them also one Mrs. v. Brechler, the widow of the former district governor of Marienbad.

The Czech managers and the new settlers were mostly unskilled and ruined the farms in a short time. There are cases known where these people sowed oats in autumn or plowed up clover. Czechs who took over industrial undertakings had no professional training and the industries broke down in a short time. Eight Czech managers, who had been imprisoned because of unfair management, sat together with me in the cellar at Luditz. A certain Prokopoc from Nebosedl, who, although a simple miner, had acted as manager of the estate there, had been already imprisoned for the second time.

Unterparsching

Harassment of a farmer's family
Reported by M. Sch.

On August 6, 1945 Miloslav Kubitschek, a tailor from Prague, was assigned to our farm as harvest commissar. He sold the entire harvest. On November 11 he took over our farm as administrator. We had to work for him for an entire year, for no pay and only so-called German ration stamps. We got only 700 g [24½ oz.] meat for the entire year. We five persons had to do all the hard farm labor in the stable and on the fields, and we received only 1,100 Kr. compensation for the entire year. For the entire time until our resettlement [expulsion], we were severely maltreated several times each week. He repeatedly raped my daughter. 14 days before our expulsion he punched her, kicked her in the legs and stomach, and even stabbed her in the leg with a knife. She got pregnant from his repeated rapes. Reporting him to the gendarmerie was totally useless. He searched my married daughter's house five times and took anything and everything he liked. He often fired shots in the house, terrifying the entire family. Several doors have bullet holes.

I can take this statement on my oath at any time, and the entire town can verify what I have said.

Attack on a village in the Bohemian Forest

Reported by B. Zeisel, ex-locum tenens of Vollmau - Report of March 6, 1946

It was Sunday, May 13th, 1945. The German population of Vollmau was preparing to go to church.

In spite of the armistice and of the good neighbourly relations between Germans and Czechs, uniformed Czech bands, heavily armed, suddenly broke into the village. They murdered, looted and finally drove the peaceable, defenceless German population out of their homes, to face an unknown future. Most of those affected were old people, women and children, the young men being with the army or in captivity.

Their misery reached its climax when the American border control did not allow them to cross the border of Bavaria. They were unable to return to their home village nor were they allowed to cross the border. They lay down in the nearby meadows - robbed of all their personal possessions, without food, not knowing what was going to become of them. The children were famished, but the horror they had been through closed their mouths; they did not even ask for bread. An old woman actually died there on the meadow as a result of all she had endured. Others collapsed. Women, far advanced in pregnancy, had to be hurried to the hospital at Furth in view of the danger of premature births. The first victims were J. and A., a married couple, almost 70 years old. J. M. and his wife were shot before the eyes of their five young children. The children's grandmother also received a shot in the thigh. The children themselves reported the murder. F. K. was also shot. K. S., who in his first fright tried to defend himself with an axe, was slain with the very same tool. His wife found him lying with his head split open. A refugee from Heidelberg was shot while in bed.

An eyewitness told me of six refugees on their way from Böhm.-Kubitzen to Bavaria, whom the horde caught up with at Vollmau and massacred. He himself was only able to save his life by taking refuge in a barn. Dr. Sladký, a detective, later spoke of 47 persons who had been shot at Vollmau on this day. A later victim was St. W., a girl of 16 years, who was shot down by the Czechs. All victims, save the last, were buried on the spot.

After all the inhabitants of the village had been expelled, the lootings started. On the first day of the looting, cabinets, wardrobes and chests were broken open. Their contents were thrown on the floor and whatever the plunderers liked, was taken away. Later on the Czechs also took clothes, food, cattle, agricultural implements and furniture, in a word, everything which was of any value. This looting at Vollmau took place even before the Czech Government had decided on the expropriation of German property. The raids were carried out on May 13, 14 and 15, 1945. On May 25, by Edict of the President of the Republic, the draft of a bill of the Czechoslovak Government, dated May 19, 1945, concerning the transfer of private and public property, movable or immovable possessions of Germans, Hungarians and traitors to the National Administration, was announced.

Some days later the local Czech Representative of the Prague Government, one Čhák, said: "We still don't know who ordered the raids or for what reason."

Hundreds of inhabitants of Vollmau can swear to the truth of this report.

Vorderheuraffel

Maltreatment in the internment camp
Reported by Franz Moherndl - Report of November 2, 1946

For the last 7 months of the war I was deputy Mayor of Vorderheuraffel, District Kaplitz, and because of that, I was arrested on September 3, 1945 and detained in the internment camp Kaplitz for 14 months, on no grounds at all. An interrogation in October 1945 had shown that I was not guilty of anything. The camp was the scene of many a dreadful maltreatment. One Josef Schuster of Friedberg had a hand chopped off, and one Eduard Prischl of Deutsch-Reichenau had three of his ribs kicked in. Three times I saw Rudolf Wagner of Vorderheuraffel beaten so badly that he remained lying unconscious on the ground. I myself was also beaten so badly several times that I was swollen beyond recognition. These maltreatments were especially bad and frequent until Christmas, so that even the Russians intervened to put a stop to the inhumanities. The systematic maltreatment stopped after that, but did continue sporadically until my release in October of this year. The prisoners were totally at the mercy of the guards. The Germans had no right to complain, and no German had the opportunity to defend himself against any accusation that was made against him. When I was released from the internment camp I was transferred directly to the resettlement [expulsion] camp and was not permitted to set foot in my house again.

Waldau

German war invalid murdered
Reported by Josef Sonnberger - Report of November 2, 1946

My son, 21 years old, was wounded 16 times during the war. One of his arms had been amputated, and he was classed as severely war-disabled. On July 19 of last year, at around 9:30 p.m., my son was shot near the residential area of Waldau, and bled to death within a few hours. Due to his injuries he had been unable to work, and so had been tending livestock. On the evening in question I had sent him to our neighbor, who lived some 500 steps distant from my house. The likely perpetrators are two Czech soldiers, who had been out hunting at that time and who also gave themselves away after the shooting by their excited behavior. Two shots had been fired, and the soldiers also admitted that they had fired two shots. But aside from taking a report, the gendarmerie did nothing; no investigation was even begun.

Wallern

Maltreatment
Reported by Emil Havlik - Report of July 19, 1946

During the last year, Germans in Wallern and vicinity were maltreated by Czech public servants during interrogations on a daily basis. They were beaten with whips or rubber truncheons, and often they were kicked as well. Destructive house searches were carried out, during the course of which looting was a free-for-all. The Germans had no right to object, and besides, they were so intimidated by the intolerable treatment they received at the hands of the authorities that they would not have dared to register a complaint anyway. In most cases German laborers were not paid wages, or were paid only in part. Those who were put to forest work, loggers and the like, were generally paid only about 65% of the wages they were entitled to. No accounting or compensation payment ever came about.

In most cases, notice of imminent expulsion was given while the people were at their place of work, so that often the one or two hours that were granted for packing hardly sufficed for them to gather up even the barest necessities. Many people didn't even have enough time to buy the travel provisions that their ration coupons entitled them to.

I can bring witnesses to support my statements at any time.

Warnsdorf

Warnsdorf, Report No. 1
Maltreatment of a blind man
Reported by Otto Müller - Report of June 20, 1950

I was a soldier. In 1942 I was discharged from active service as totally blind. I have always been well known and respected in my native town. In November 1945 a group of armed SNB-men entered the office of the firm of Johann Liebisch & Co, Warnsdorf, where I worked. They fetched me away, but without giving any reason.

After keeping me waiting for hours in an office, they took down evidence. They insulted me and accused me of having in 1938 threatened a Czech citizen of Warnsdorf with a stick. This accusation was untrue and the incident entirely fictitious. Indeed, it was only during the war that I had used a stick at all, for a short time following an injury to my leg. This was known all over the town. When the officials had finished their hearing, they left me under the "protection" of the SNB-men, who treated me like a criminal. They vented their anger on me in the following ways: after they had emptied my pockets and also taken away my boot-laces, waistbelt etc., they pushed me onto a camp-bed. Then they covered me with a blanket and, yelling ferociously, they struck me with sticks and straps with such force that I rolled from the bed to the floor and lay there, unconscious. After some time I came to. I heard their brutal laughter and noticed that they had defiled me. Gathering all my strength I attempted to protect my face and to regain my feet.

All of a sudden with a friendly impulse one of the policemen offered me a cigarette. I replied that I did not smoke. After this I was offered a candy. I refused it. Thereupon I received a blow in the face which knocked me down again. After some time had passed two policemen took me between them. They took me to a flight of steps which led to the cellar of the house. It was the former Kunert Villa which I knew well. I was pushed downstairs, but I must have made a successful attempt to recover myself, for as though by a miracle I suffered no broken bones. I regained consciousness and found myself lying on the floor of the cellar. I stretched out my hands and felt the walls, but there was nowhere to sit down. Only two little cans which were supposed to be used in order to relieve nature. The cellar was not opened for three days and three nights. It was winter weather and I suffered terribly from cold and also from extreme hunger and thirst.

By the time the cellar-door was unbolted I was in a state of complete exhaustion. My clothing was restored to order and I received a dry roll, which I could not swallow in spite of my hunger. Although I made repeated attempts to do so, they grew impatient and brought me some overly sweet coffee. I was taken to the doctor, who assured me repeatedly that the Czechs are not sadists like the followers of Hitler and that in view of my condition I should be taken out of the cellar at once. My case, however, would be an exception.

Thereupon they took me back to the office of the SNB, in a villa which had belonged to the dentist Jungnickel. There, for the second time, they made an official record, which was quite meaningless. My hand trembled so much that I was unable to sign it. I could also, of course, not read what was written on the paper.

The cell of the district prison at Warnsdorf, in which I was put, was overcrowded. I was together with Czechs who were nothing but common criminals. There was also a German in the cell. During the time I spent in the district jail I had several collapses as a consequence of my treatment at the hands of the SNB. Naturally the only witnesses were my Czech tormentors themselves. The physician at Warnsdorf, Dr. Laupelt, examined me after my release in the middle of January. Although I tried to conceal them, the doctor noticed the marks on my body even after such a long time. I explained to him that those marks were scars, caused by scratching as there had been vermin in my cell.

When I was released - temporarily, as they said - in the middle of January 1946, the jailer insisted on hearing from my own mouth that I had been treated with consideration. I shall never forget the screams of those being flogged in the jail. Doctor Weber of our neighbourhood was also among the victims.

Warnsdorf, Report No. 2

Nachod, Blood bath in the prisoner-of-war camp, June-July 1945

Reported by Adam Ehrenhard - Report of June 24, 1946

I was released from American captivity on June 12, 1945 and, equipped with an American border-crossing permit, I went to Czechoslovakia to find my family. When I crossed the border the Czech border guards took from me all the food and provisions I had been given on my release, as well as my discharge money, blankets and my coat.

In Warnsdorf I was arrested, my discharge papers notwithstanding, and committed to the prisoner-of-war camp, where I was detained from July 24, 1945 until May 28, 1946. Approximately 2,000 German prisoners-of-war, most of them citizens of the Reich, were imprisoned in this camp even though they had been released earlier from American or Russian captivity. They lived under the worst imaginable conditions, were all malnourished, and are being forced to do unpaid labor in the mines.

Approximately 200 members of the SS were taken to the brewery house in Nachod and handed over to the civilian population to be maltreated. I myself was an eyewitness to the brutal murder of all 200 of them by the civilians. Czech women particularly distinguished themselves in this butchery - for example Mrs. Zinke, of Nachod, Komenského 233, who repeatedly bragged that she would kill even more if only she could.

I know many other Czech women personally, though I cannot name their names here.

The SS men were stabbed by the women with knives and daggers, and bludgeoned with truncheons and rifle butts. Bodies that still showed signs of life were doused with gasoline and set on fire. I myself had to help load the corpses onto trucks and to bury them in three mass graves on the Nachod Castle grounds.

The prisoners-of-war were beaten daily. Several suffered broken jaws, or were stabbed. Some also had an eye punched out. On May 8, 1946, around 5 o'clock in the afternoon, the market square of Nachod - decorated with Allied flags - was the site of gross maltreatment of the Germans by the civilian inhabitants. The Germans were individually driven about 500 meters through an echelon of Czech civilians, and men, women and children alike were beaten with sticks and canes. When they fell they were kicked while they were down. With loudspeakers the German victims were called up by name to be thus maltreated. The Czech police was there to witness this spectacle. One man, aged 54, suffered a broken jaw, a broken ankle, and was blinded on one eye.

Weidenau

Weidenau, Report No. 1

Maltreatment of an old woman

Reported by Josefine Titz - Report of October 9, 1946

In March of 1946 Czech gendarmes searched my home. In the course of this house search they boxed me, a 69-year-old woman, about the head so badly that I fell down unconscious. One of the gendarmes then kicked me until I came to again and got up. Since then I have lost all hearing on my left ear.

Weidenau, Report No. 2

Pastoral activities curtailed, camps Jauernig, Adelsdorf, deaths

Reported by Dr. Adolf Schreiber - Report of October 9, 1946

In my capacity as parish priest of Weidenau I was personally not molested by the Czechs, but my pastoral activities were restricted. All religious instruction for Germans was forbidden, also instruction in religious knowledge for children as well as the so-called hours for spiritual counsel. Czech priests were not active at Weidenau before the beginning of September 1946. Divine services for Germans were allowed, including sermon, but not processions. German funerals were permitted at Weidenau, but at other places forbidden, as well as divine services and sermons. At Schwarzwasser, for example, German sermons, funerals and the delivery of funeral orations etc. were prohibited. There was no internment camp at Weidenau itself, but parishioners of Weidenau were interned in the camps of Jauernig and Adelsdorf, where four of them died. The pastorate received notice of their death only 4-5 months later, without details of place and causes of death or the location of their graves. Numerous juveniles were conscripted for labour in the mines of Ostrau, whence deaths from typhoid fever have been reported. These youths truly underwent great suffering.

Weidsiefen (concentration camp near Thomasdorf)

Concentration camp Weidsiefen, maltreatment

Reported by Hans Tautz - Report of August 15, 1946

On June 19, 1945 I was arrested, and was taken to the Weidsiefen concentration camp on June 24 along with 48 other men. In this camp I witnessed many cases of severe maltreatment, which recurred on a daily basis. On July 8 Kuchartsch from Zuckmantel was severely maltreated and then shipped to Moravian Ostrau for forced labor; on July 9 the lumber merchant Raschke from Thomasdorf was so badly abused that he hanged himself during the night. On August 3, Böhm, the community farmers' leader from Oberlindewiese, was found dead on his pallet after he had been beaten unconscious the evening before. On July 26, Vater from Hermannstadt escaped from his place of work after having been badly maltreated two days before. As reprisal for his escape, the other 10 laborers from his work unit were so badly abused that some of them had to be admitted to the hospital. On July 29, 1945 18 prisoners were brought from their place of work into the camp and horribly beaten before being transferred to the resettlement [expulsion] camp. On August 14 Dr. Pavlowski succumbed to severe injuries which he had sustained from maltreatment. On August 15 it was alleged that the camp had been raided at night, and six comrades - Dr. Franke, Seifert, Klimesch, Hanke, Buchmann and Reinhold - were shot. That same day the Weidsiefen camp was closed down and the inmates transferred to Adelsdorf, where the maltreatment continued. On August 16 Schiebel from Niklasdorf was so badly maltreated that he died during the following night. On August 17 the lumber merchant Schubert received a blow to the face, fell down unconscious and died half an hour later. The same day the 15-year-old lad Knoblich from Würbenthal was severely abused. The next morning he was dead. I myself saw two bullet holes in his throat. On August 21 the gendarmerie took over the camp. After that, maltreatment became the exception rather than the norm. Our rations also improved, and there was medical care for the prisoners.

Wekelsdorf

Wekelsdorf, Report No. 1
List of persons executed
Reported by Ch. S. - Report of February 4, 1950

In May of 1945 I was alone in my home in Reichenberg-Alt-Paulsdorf 282, Weinergasse 16. My husband was still on soldier duty.

Our house was spared from Russian occupation. On September 1, 1945 I had to "voluntarily" vacate our home. On November 9, 1945 I left Czechslovakia with a "propustka". I was able to take some bedding, linen, clothes and the most necessary dishes with me after paying duty on them, but my luggage was looted on the road from Grossenhain/Saxony to Leipzig.

My father, born on April 17, 1873, had already been taken away by the Czechs in May 1945 and was sent from camp to camp, and finally to Theresienstadt. According to his fellow prisoners he starved to death there, in Theresienstadt, on or about October 7, 1945.

Regarding the events in Wekelsdorf near Braunau, I wish to report:

The following citizens of Wekelsdorf, who were personally known to me, were expelled by the Czechs and herded off towards Friedland in Silesia. At the border the Poles did not want to admit them, so they were simply shot "on the bridge": Josef Kudernatsch, mailman, approx. 65-70 years old, and his wife; Josef Wrabetz, music teacher, approx. 70-75 years old, and his wife; Paul Süssner and his wife, details unknown; railroadman Maul and his wife, details unknown; District forester Lindner and his family, details unknown; Herr Unger and his wife and daughter, details unknown; Director Jüptner from the Community Office of Wekelsdorf, approx 50 years old, with his parents-in-law.

Wekelsdorf, Report No. 2
Execution of 26 persons, June 28-29,1945
Reported by N. N. - Report of June 13, 1950

We, the two undersigned, wish to report an incident which took place during the night from June 28th to 29th, 1945, at Wekelsdorf, district Braunau, Sudetenland.

At the end of May 1945, the notorious Captain Svoboda and his troop marched into our village. Arrests were made every day. The victims were put in the local jail, where they were maltreated, being whipped in the most atrocious way. Witnesses reported that in the room in which the trial took place, bloodstains and whole pieces of skin were afterwards to be seen. It was Captain Svoboda's habit, when drunk, to enter the jail at a time when everybody might be supposed to be asleep, between 11 at night and 3 o'clock in the morning, and to order that the persons be whipped or otherwise maltreated. Those in the neighbourhood of the court building were unable to sleep on account of the cries of pain. Captain Svoboda's conduct reached its high point on June 28th, 1945. On that day 26 persons, of whom the youngest was a child of 8 months while the others were for the most part old people, were driven to the Silesian border by the accomplices of Captain Svoboda. The Poles refused to take over the transport and all were taken back again and lodged in the jail. At 3 o'clock in the morning the men were led to the so-called "Buche" (beech), a remote place on the outskirts of the village, driven together and shot down by machine-gun fire. The horrible screams of these poor people caused the farmer Friedrich Bittner and his sister, whose farm was the last one of the village, to hang themselves in panic at these terrible events. The Czech militia demanded spades from the farmers residing in the neighbourhood, and buried the corpses without ceremony. The farmers were ordered not to go into the fields before 11 o'clock in the morning. Among the victims of the massacre was a woman who had been of Czech nationality but had married a Sudeten German. New crimes were committed every day.

The commissar of the místní správní komise at Wekelsdorf was a certain Josef Černý. This man had quite a sensational past. He was sentenced to penal servitude in 1917 for safe-breaking, for the same reason in 1924 and also in 1942. I have myself seen copies of all the sentences passed, attested by the district-court of Königgrätz. And to this man we were delivered over unconditionally. In the course of his and Captain Svoboda's administration the number of crimes increased to an appalling extent. The transfers were carried out in the most atrocious and inhuman manner.

There were also many decent Czechs whom we had known well for many years - they were ashamed of the brutal actions of their countrymen and utterly despised their behaviour.

Welpet

Gross maltreatment in May 1945
Reported by Josef Grössl - Report of June 26, 1946

On May 28, 1945 I was arrested on my father-in-law's estate in Welhenitz, Bilin District. I was handcuffed and beaten and taken by car to Welpet where, shackled hand and foot, I was beaten unconscious three times in a row and then thrown into a one-man bunker.

On May 22 eleven men from the farming community had already been executed there by a squad led by lieutenant Anton Cerný. By a lucky coincidence I escaped the same fate, and had to remain in this camp for 14 days as the lieutenant's batman. Every day I saw people being maltreated, shot, or beaten to death with a hammer. The lieutenant carried out the executions himself. I witnessed them personally in about 20 cases. Among other things, I then had to lick the lieutenant's blood-spattered boots clean. After about 14 days I was taken to Prague to be shot. But once there, it was found that there were no grounds for my execution. I was taken to the Rusin camp, where I again witnessed gross maltreatment. Later I had to work on the Rusin airfield, where life was somewhat bearable.

Willens

Treatment of a sick woman and victim of political persecution in June 1945
Reported by Emma Trägner - Report of June 1, 1946

Even though I had been politically persecuted, which I can document, the Czechs threw me out of my house as early as June 5, 1945, and robbed me of all my possessions. My request for supplementary food ration coupons due to my medically attested illness (a liver condition) was refused. I can take this statement on my oath.

Witeschau

The murder of the German men of Witeschau

Reported by: Martha Kramer - Report of June 28, 1946

At Witeschau near Hohenstadt all German men were murdered between May 8th and May 10th, 1945. Sixteen of them lie in a pit which they themselves were forced to dig in advance. Among them were several soldiers, who had recently returned home.

My husband returned from the hospital at Hohenstadt as an invalid on May 6th, 1945. He was afraid of being killed like all the others and therefore fled on his bicycle in the direction of Olmütz, in order to take shelter with his Czech sister. On his way he was shot down by the Czechs at Lukavic. On the same day (May 13th, 1945) soldiers of the militia notified me on a piece of paper, written in pencil, the exact time of my husband's shooting (11:45 a.m.).

Witkowitz and Auschwitz

Sudeten Germans shipped off to forced labor in Poland

Reported by Rudolf Heinisch - Report of September 30, 1946

I had been committed to so-called voluntary labor service, and had to work for seven months in Witkowitz and five months in Auschwitz. In Witkowitz I and more than 100 other men had to work on the slagheap.

We were badly maltreated each and every day, through all the months. I had to endure the worst abuse on March 1st this year, when two Czechs beat me with rubber truncheons and kicked me for half an hour straight, so that I urinated blood for two months and still suffer from occasional kidney pain and dizziness to this day.

On March 15 I and ten other men were sent to Auschwitz to load ore. The Sudeten German laborers were gradually smuggled in small groups across the Polish border to Auschwitz, where the Czechs announced them as Reich-German SS men, even though they were actually without exception civilians and had not been members of any formation.

The barracks in Auschwitz were so crawling with lice and bedbugs that we could only sleep out of doors. Our rations were only bread and potatoes, with no meat or fat. Yet we had to do hard labor for 14 to 16 hours each day.

Wockendorf

Maltreatment
Reported by Anna Seichter - Report of September 9, 1946

In June of last year several SA men from Wockendorf were arrested, imprisoned in my house, and dreadfully maltreated. They were beaten so badly with whips, sticks, rubber truncheons etc. that their screams rang through the entire house. The foremost thug was Machaletz, who is still in Wockendorf and torments the German population there to this day. He routinely robs and loots the German inhabitants' belongings, and intimidates women and children with beatings and threats. He grossly curses the Germans in the street and always carries a whip. I can take this statement on my oath.

Zittau

Expatriate German severely maltreated
Reported by Josef Schickling - Report of June 19, 1946

I had to flee from my home town of Zittau, in the Jägerndorf District, on October 1, 1938 after the Sudetengau was annexed, and I have documents to prove it. My house was expropriated, and I was stripped of my citizenship by a decree of the Jägerndorf District Council and had to go live in the Protectorate. My wife was not allowed to return to the Sudetengau until she could prove that she had divorced me. The Party persecuted me in the Protectorate as well.

I returned to my home town Zittau on May 17, 1945 after the German Wehrmacht had withdrawn. In late July I was arrested there by the Czechs, but was released again the next day after an interrogation. On August 1 I was arrested a second time, and sent to Olmütz. Even though five Czechs attended my interrogation and testified that I had saved them from being executed or sent to a concentration camp, I was locked up, with the comment: "Should we perhaps reward him? A German is a German. Off to the camp with the crook!" In the camp I was brutally maltreated. I was forced onto a table and then beaten so badly by policemen with rubber truncheons and bullwhips that my entire body was black and blue. At least six times each night, partisans entered the barracks where up to 48 of us lay on the floor without so much as blankets or straw, and arbitrarily maltreated the prisoners until they collapsed. Many inmates were beaten to death on these occasions. Hundreds whose names were never recorded were beaten to death in the Olmütz camp. I myself had to clean up the blood of one such victim (the pharmacist Ziegenfuss from Olmütz).

After the fire in the Hajkorn factory, which was proven to have been caused by a short-circuit (and reported as such in the newspaper) but was blamed on the Germans as an act of sabotage, the camp inmates were so badly maltreated for three hours that many of them died of their injuries.

With one slice of bread and some black coffee as breakfast ration, we had to work all day long. Not until the evening did we get some watery soup and another slice of bread. Due to the insufficient rations and the constant maltreatment, many prisoners collapsed even during the night, and they were beaten some more for it. Many inmates went deaf from the blows to the head.

In the camp I had been looted of everything I possessed, and did not receive any pay for my work.

On March 7, 1946 I was arrested for the third time and put behind bars in Jägerndorf. Since I was ill, my daughter succeeded in having me released for resettlement [expulsion].

There are many children and teenagers in the Olmütz camp as well. They are totally emaciated and some suffer from dropsy. I myself saw how several children fought over some old, moldy bread entirely unfit for human consumption. When I pointed out to them that they could die from eating that bread, they replied: "We're going to die one way or another."

Punishment in the camp was brutal. People being punished were locked up in air raid shelters for up to 21 days and received only one slice of bread and water per day. I saw girls returning from these punishment cells bloated beyond recognition.

Zlin

Maltreatment during forced labor
Reported by: Rudolf Kunert - Report of October 9, 1946

I was arrested for no reason at all on September 24 of last year, and was detained until mid-August this year without so much as a questioning. From October last year until my release I had to work in Zlin. The rations we got were very bad. Food was cooked without salt. When my wife sent me salt, onions and garlic, everything was confiscated. The camp personnel used a large part of the food supplies for their own purposes, as I can prove. 10% of the German prisoners died of malnutrition. Even sick people were beaten to make them go to work. One man who suffered from lung disease had to go on working until he died, even though he had already collapsed several times at work. During the luggage inspection in the resettlement [expulsion] camp my children's mattresses were confiscated by the Czechs.

Znaim

Maltreatment in the prisoner-of-war camp
Reported by Franz Hausenbigl - Report of June 17, 1946

I was released from French captivity on June 6, 1945 and on June 13 I returned to my home town of Nikolsburg where I worked until December 15, 1945.

On December 15 at 6 o'clock in the morning the police fetched me from my home. I was handed over to the gendarmerie and committed to the prisoner-of-war camp in Znaim. My French release papers, which I had already shown to the police on June 13, were taken from me. In the camp I was assigned the number 1380. By June 10, 1946 the camp's population had risen to more than 3,000. The rations we received in this camp were very bad. We had to do hard labor at the train station and on the roads. Many people collapsed at work due to debilitation. There were also many war-disabled ex-servicemen in the camp, who also had to do hard work due to the labor shortage. Anyone who so much as straightened up at work to catch his breath, or whomever the guards didn't like, was noted down and beaten after our return to the camp. In this way an average of about ten people were beaten each evening. They had to lie down across a chair and received 25 blows with a rubber truncheon or bull whip. At first the beatings were handed out by Czech soldiers. In March of this year a German camp police was set up, and they then had to administer the beatings. At first they refused, and were themselves beaten for it, so that they were finally forced to do this dirty work.

Former members of the SS, SA and the Party were beaten especially severely. For months on end they were all beaten three times each day. There were youths 16 and 17 years of age among them. On May 1st of this year one 19-year-old ex-soldier was beaten and kicked so badly that he fell unconscious, and died the next day in the hospital of Znaim without ever having regained consciousness. It was the chief guard Hansa who had beaten the lad.

Zwittau

Captivity, maltreatment
Reported by Ullrich Reinhold - Report of June 15, 1946

When I returned from Russian captivity to my home town of Brüsau near Zwittau, I was arrested all over again only three weeks later by the Czechs and sent to the POW camp Brünn-Slatina. We had to sleep on the bare floor without even a blanket. Several times each week the prisoners were called out at night, had to line up in the yard, barefoot and dressed only in their underwear even in winter, and were beaten with rifle butts, bullwhips etc., arbitrarily and for no reason whatsoever. Every Sudeten German prisoner was questioned about his membership in various organizations. I had a paper from the *národní výbor* of Brüsau, confirming that I had not belonged to any organization. Nonetheless I was accused of having belonged to the SdP and the SA, and since I denied it I was beaten until I collapsed. The paper from the *národní výbor* was torn up before my eyes. For a time I was sent to work outside the camp, as truck driver in Rotowitz. I was treated fairly well there.

On June 2, 1946 I was released to Zwittau to be resettled [expelled]. In the resettlement camp there, Frau Wirschich gave me a nickel wrist watch which was very precious to her, as it was a keepsake from her son who had fallen in the war. During the luggage inspection she was asked about this watch. I admitted that I had it, and laid it on the table. A partisan then showed up and took me away. In the guard room I was punched twice in the face so that the blood ran from my nose. Then I received about eight blows with a lead cable on the bare soles of my feet, and then I was punched and kicked all over until I collapsed. I was locked up until the following day. The next day I had to sign a paper stating that the watch had been confiscated from me and that I was not asking for it back.

Appendix 1 - Chapter 6 of Mémoire III of the Czech Delegation to the Paris Peace Conference of 1919. Memorandum No. 3. The Problem of the Germans in Bohemia. VI. The Position of the Germans in the Czechoslovak Republic

Appendix 2 - The Germans in Bohemia: Les Allemands de Bohême (Addendum to Memorandum No. 3, Appendix 1)

Appendix 3 - Linguistic map of the Sudeten Germans

Appendix 4 - Letter from Jan Masaryk to research director Max Weinreich, dated May 5, 1942

Appendix 5 - Expulsion Order of the Military Commandant of Bohemian Leipa, June 14, 1945

Appendix 6 - Food ration card for the Germans in Czechoslovakia, ration period from May 28 to June 24, 1945

Appendix 7 - Proclamation of the Národní výbor (National Committee) in Saaz from 1945

Appendix 8 - Letter from Mr. R. R. Stokes, a British Member of Parliament and Minister, to the Manchester Guardian, October 1945, about the Czech concentration camps

Appendix 9 - Chapters VIII and IX of the "Statute issued in Košice" [Kaschau], Slovakia, April 5, 1945 (Program of the new Czechoslovak Government, the National Front of Czechs and Slovaks, adopted by the cabinet council on April 5, 1945)

Appendix 10 - Edict of the President of the Republic, dated May 19, 1945 concerning the Invalidity of Transactions Involving Property Rights from the Time of the Oppression and Concerning the National Administration of Property Assets of Germans, Magyars, Traitors and Collaborators and of Certain Organizations and Associations (Decree No. 5)

Appendix 11 - Edict of the President of the Republic, dated June 21, 1945 concerning the confiscation and early re-allotment of agricultural property of Germans, Magyars, as well as of traitors and enemies of the Czech and Slovak people (Decree No. 12)

Appendix 12 - Decree of President Dr. Beneš of June 19, 1945 concerning the punishment of Nazi criminals, traitors and their accomplices, and concerning the Special People's Courts (Decree No. 16)

Appendix 13 - Decree of President Dr. Beneš of August 2, 1945 concerning the right to Czechoslovak citizenship of persons of German and Magyar nationality (Decree No. 33)

Appendix 14 - The instructions of the German (Hungarian) occupation forces according to which the nationality of Czechoslovak citizens of Czechoslovakia was regulated

Appendix 15 - Decree of President Dr. Beneš of October 25, 1945 concerning the confiscation of enemy property and the Funds of National Renovation (Decree No. 42)

Appendix 16 - Estimate of the value of German national property within the Czechoslovak Republic

Appendix 17 - The Atlantic Charter of August 14, 1941

Appendix 18 - Text of the United Nations Convention on the Prevention and Punishment of the Crime of Genocide

Appendix 19 - Agreement signed on August 4, 1950 between General Lev Prchala, representing the Czech National Committee in London, and the Joint Committee for the Protection of Sudeten German Interests in Munich, represented by Dr. Rudolph Lodgman, Mr. R. Reitzner and Mr. H. Schuetz

Chapter 6 of Mémoire III of the Czech Delegation to the Paris Peace Conference of 1919

Memorandum No. 3. The Problem of the Germans in Bohemia

VI.
The Position of the Germans in the Czechoslovak Republic

"It is absolutely necessary to know how the German population will be dealt with in the Czechoslovak State. The Czechoslovak Republic is not only willing to accept - if occasion arises - any international legal regulation laid down by the Peace Conference in favour of the minorities, but is moreover willing to go beyond such regulation and to grant the Germans all the rights due to them.

The Czechoslovak Republic will be an absolutely democratic State; all elections will be by universal and direct suffrage; all offices will be open to all citizens; the right to their own schools, judges and courts will never be denied to any minority. It must be added here that the Czechs, although conscious of the fact that the Germans were specially favoured by the previous regime, have no intentions of suppressing, for example, the German schools, universities, schools of technicology, notwithstanding the fact that these have not recently been well attended.

To sum up: the Germans in Bohemia would possess the same rights as the Czechoslovaks. The German language would be the second language of the country and measures of oppression would under no circumstances be used against the German part of the population. The constitution would be similar to the constitution of Switzerland.

This constitution will be established not only because the Czechs have always had a profound feeling for democracy, right and justice and would justly admit those rights even to their enemies, but also because the Czechs are of the opinion that the aforesaid arrangement, favourable to the Germans, would also be advantageous to the political interests of their own country.

They (the Czechs) proved during the 19th century that they had a practical, but above all a political sense. They are much too "realistic" and have too much commonsense not to see that violence and injustice were the causes of the decline of Austro-Hungary and that any similar policy would harm their own country. These historical facts are admitted by the Germans themselves. The German press was filled with descriptions of the revolution which took place in Prague in November 1918. The reports state unanimously that the Czechs guaranteed freedom to all Germans and respected their personal security and property as well as their rights as free citizens.

Résumé:

1. The traditions of Czechoslovakia guarantee that the new Republic will in no way oppress the Germans, on the contrary, they will have the benefit of a regime of freedom and justice.

2. In the course of the recent revolution in Bohemia the Czechs demonstrated this by guaranteeing to the Germans complete security."

LES ALLEMANDS DE BOHÊME.

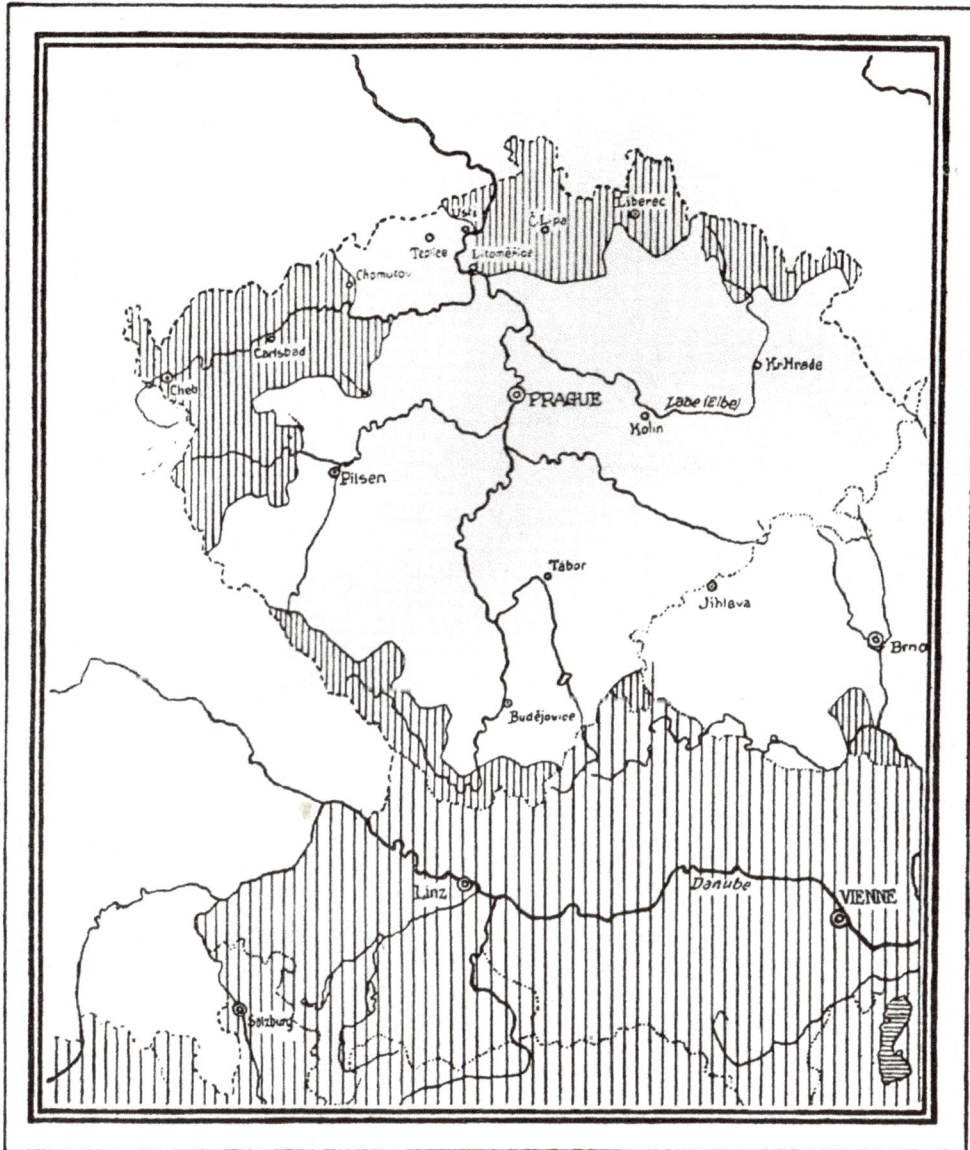

Les Allemands dans les Pays Tchécoslovacues.

Les Allemands d'Autriche.

Linguistic map of the Sudeten Germans
based on the official census of December 1, 1930
Scale 1:1.500.000.

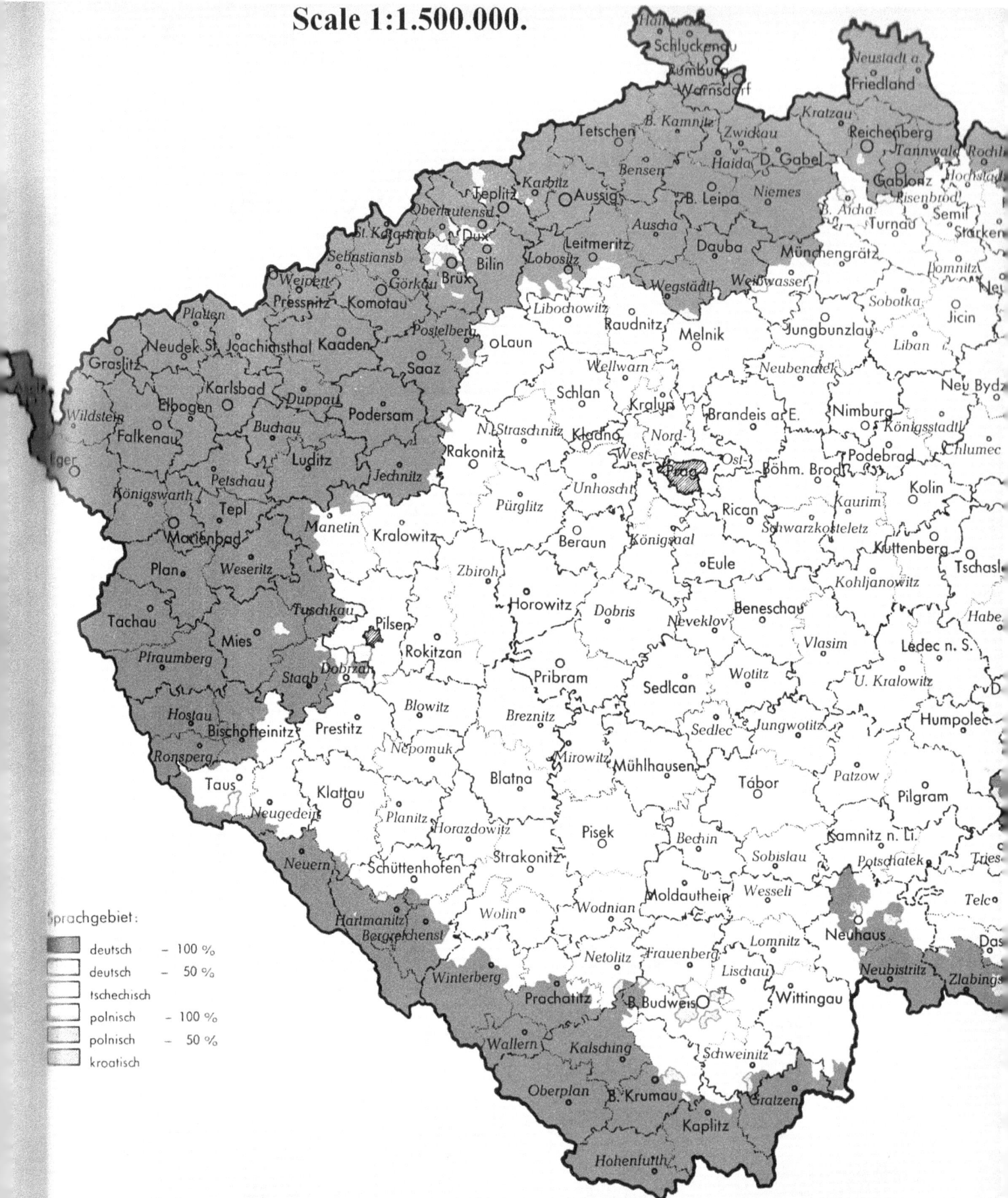

Sprachgebiet:

deutsch	– 100 %
deutsch	– 50 %
tschechisch	
polnisch	– 100 %
polnisch	– 50 %
kroatisch	

Schluckenau
Rumburg
Warnsdorf
Neustadt a.
Friedland
Tetschen
B. Kamnitz
Zwickau
Kratzau
Reichenberg
Bensen
Haida
D. Gabel
Tannwald
Rochl
Karbitz
B. Leipa
Niemes
Gablonz
Hochsta
Teplitz
Aussig
B. Aicha
Risenbrod
Oberleutensd.
Dux
Auscha
Turnau
Semil
Starken
Bilin
Leitmeritz
Dauba
Münchengrätz
St. Katharab
Lobositz
Lomnitz
Sebastiansb
Weisswasser
Görkau
Brüx
Wegstädtl
Ne
Weipert
Libochowitz
Sobotka
Pressnitz
Komotau
Raudnitz
Jungbunzlau
Jicin
Platten
Postelberg
Melnik
Liban
Neudek St. Joachimsthal Kaaden
Laun
Neu Bydz
Graslitz
Saaz
Wellwarn
Neubenatek
Karlsbad
Duppau
Schlan
Kralup
Nimburg
Königsstadtl
Elbogen
Podersam
N. Straschnitz
Kladno
Brandeis ar. E.
Chlumec
Wildstein
Buchau
Nord-
Podebrad
Falkenau
Luditz
Rakonitz
West-
Prag
Böhm. Brod
Ost-
Kolin
Eger
Jechnitz
Unhoscht
Kaurim
Königswarth
Petschau
Pürglitz
Beraun
Rican
Kuttenberg
Tepl
Kralowitz
Königsaal
Eule
Kohljanowitz
Tschasl
Marienbad
Zbiroh
Schwarzkosteletz
Manetin
Horowitz
Dobris
Neveklov
U. Kralowitz
Habe
Plan
Weseritz
Tachau
Tuschkau
Pilsen
Rokitzan
Breznitz
Sedlcan
Wotitz
Vlasim
Ledec n. S.
Pfraumberg
Mies
Staab
Dobrza
Pribram
Sedlec
Jungwotitz
Hostau
Blowitz
Mühlhausen
Humpole
Bischofteinitz
Prestitz
Nepomuk
Mirowitz
Tábor
Patzow
Pilgram
Ronsperg
Taus
Klattau
Blatna
Pisek
Bechin
Kamnitz n. Li.
Neugedein
Planitz
Horazdowitz
Sobislau
Potschatek
Tries
Strakonitz
Wesseli
Telc
Neuern
Schüttenhofen
Wolin
Wodnian
Moldautheir
Neuhaus
Das
Hartmanitz
Bergreichenst
Netolitz
Lomnitz
Neubistritz
Zlabings
Winterberg
Frauenberg
Lischau
Wittingau
Prachatitz
B. Budweis
Wallern
Kalsching
Schweinitz
Oberplan
B. Krumau
Gratzen
Kaplitz
Hohenfurth

Sprachenkarte der Sudetenländer

Nach den amtlichen Volkszählungsergebnissen vom 1. 12. 1930

Maßstab 1 : 1 500 000

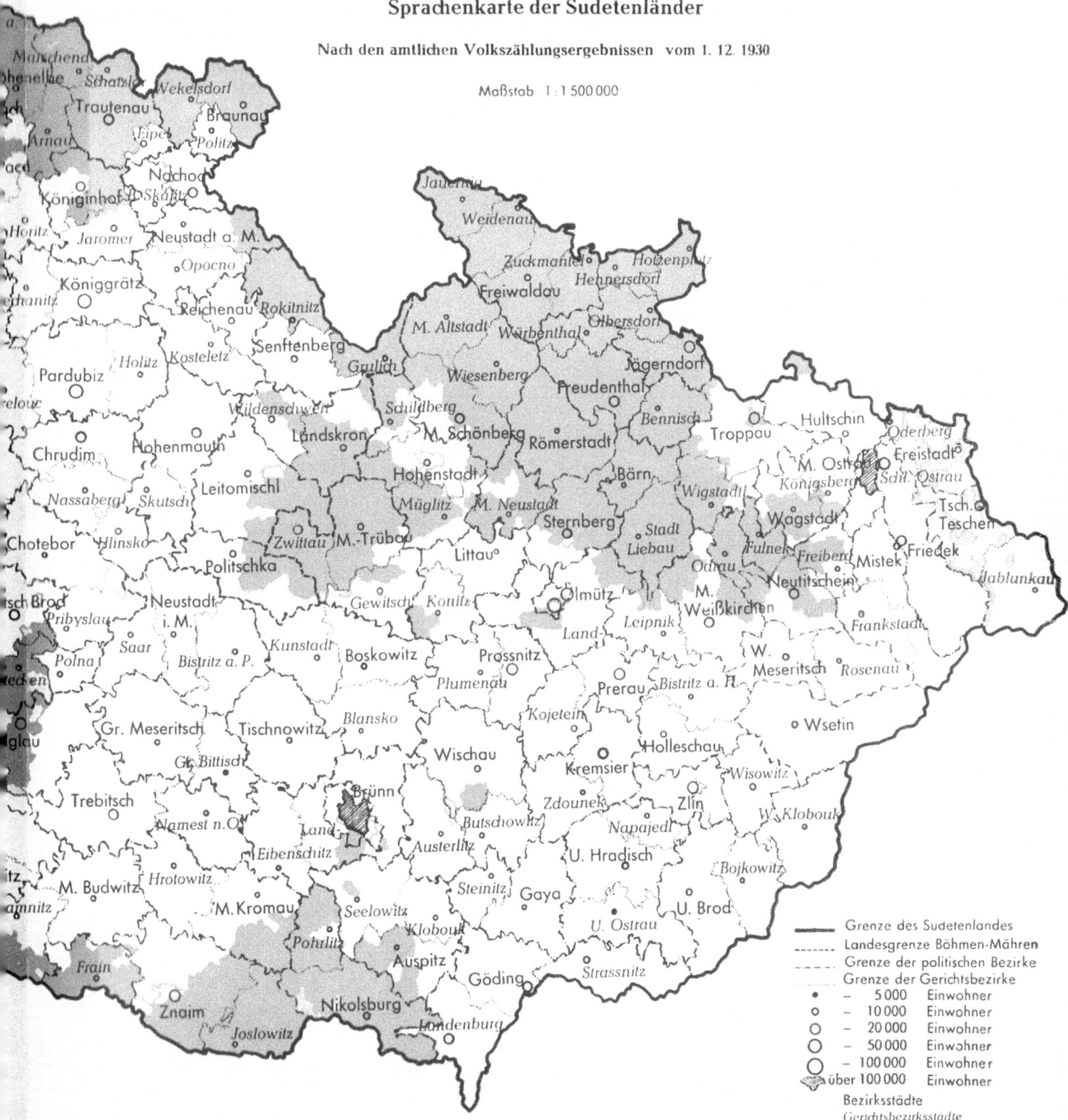

———		Grenze des Sudetenlandes
········		Landesgrenze Böhmen-Mähren
— — —		Grenze der politischen Bezirke
– – –		Grenze der Gerichtsbezirke
•	– 5 000	Einwohner
○	– 10 000	Einwohner
○	– 20 000	Einwohner
○	– 50 000	Einwohner
○	– 100 000	Einwohner
◈	über 100 000	Einwohner
		Bezirksstädte
		Gerichtsbezirksstädte

Letter from Jan Masaryk
to research director Max Weinreich,
dated May 5, 1942

JAN MASARYK

May 5,1942.

My dear Mr. Weinreich:

Pray forgive my delay to your
interesting letter of April 14th. I was away from
New York, hence only to-day I am settling down to
my correspondence.

I can understand that under
the unprecedently tragic circumstances that the
heroic and sorely tried Jewish people find themselves
in to-day, Dr. Beneš's mentioning the possibility of
exchanging populations could give rise to worry.

It has been my honor and plea-
sure to work for Beneš for the last twenty-five years
and I know that when he speaks of "exchange of populations" he means that within the realms of possibilities we must - after this war - try to get rid of
some of the Germans around the frontiers of Germany
who have never been much good to us and I do not
think they will be a great addition to Germany. Naturally - there are some decent people among them.
We will find who is who when the war is over.

I would like to go on record,
and you have my approval to use this letter in any
way you want to,in stating that Jews are certainly
not included in these as yet very hazy plans. And I
have Dr. Beneš's authority in emphasizing this point.

I am off to a sanatorium to do
a bit of a cure after seven vacationless years. When
I return to New York, I would like to discuss this
question in order to dispel any possible misgivings
you and yours may still have after reading this letter.

With cordial greetings,

Sincerely yours,

Max Weinreich, Esq.
Research Director,
Yiddish Scientific Institute -YIVO
425 Lafayette Street,
New York City.

Anlage IV

Překlad: Befehl des Militärortskommandanten.

Die Einwohner deutscher Volkszugehörigkeit der Stadtgemeinden Böhmisch-Leipa, Alt-Leipa und Niemes, ohne Unterschied des Alters und des Geschlechtes, verlassen am 15. Juni 1945 um 5 Uhr früh ihre Wohnungen und marschieren durch die Kreuz- und Bräuhausgasse auf den Sammelplatz beim Bräuhaus in Česke Lípé. In Niemes versammeln sie sich im Raum Kreuzung 200 Meter westlich der Eisenbahnbrücke (Straße in der Richtung Reichstadt).

Diese Anordnung betrifft nicht die nachstehend angeführten Personen und die Familien derselben:

I. 1. Aerzte, Tierärzte, Apotheker, Pflegepersonal und Feuerwehr. 2. Gewerbetreibende und Angestellte der im Gange befindlichen Versorgungsunternehmungen. 3. Schmiede, Schlosser- Kraftfahrzeug-Reparaturwerkstätten, Schneider und Schuhmacher, die ihr Gewerbe betreiben. 4. Angestellte der im Gange befindlichen Fabriken und Unternehmungen. 5. Angestellte der Eisenbahn, der Post sowie der Verkehrsunternehmungen.

Die unter Nr. 1—5 angeführten Pesonen haben sich mit einer Bestätigung über die Beschäftigung auszuweisen. Falls sie sich entfernen, werden sie zurückgeführt und entsprechend bestraft.

II. Die Ausweisung findet keine Anwendung auf Angehörige der kommunistischen und der sozialdemokratischen Partei, die sich mit eines Legitimation der Partei legitimieren und nachweisen können, daß sie wegen ihrer Gesinnung und der bejahenden Einstellung zur ČSR. verfolgt d. h. inhaftiert oder ihres Postens enthoben wurden.

Jeder Einzelperson, auf die sich die Ausweisung bezieht, ist es gestattet, mitzunehmen: a) Lebensmittel auf 7 Tage und b) die allernotwendigsten Sachen für ihren persönlichen Bedarf in einer Menge, die sie selbst tragen kann; c) Personalbelege und alle Lebensmittelkarten samt der Haushalts-Stammkarte.

Wertsachen: Gold, Silber und alle aus diesen Metallen hergestellten Gegenstände (Ringe, Broschen usw.), Gold- und Silbermünzen, Einlagebücher, Versicherungen, Bargeld, mit Ausnahme von 100 RM. pro Kopf sowie Photoapparate sind in ein Säckchen einzulegen oder in verschnürte Papierpäckchen einzupacken, unter Reiseschließung eines genauen Verzeichnisses dieser Wertsachen und unter Anführung der genauen Anschrift des bisherigen Wohnortes, der Wohnung und der Hausnummer. Diese Wertsachen in Säckchen werden an der Versammlungsstelle abgegeben.

Ich mache aufmerksam, daß jede Einzelperson einer strengen Leibesvisite unterzogen wird. Auch der Inhalt der Gepäckstücke wird genau überprüft werden. Es ist daher jede Verheimlichung der angeführten Gegenstände bei sich, sowohl in der Kleidung, als auch in den Schuhen und anderen Stellen, so z. B. im Handgepäck, zwecklos und wird bestraft werden.

Haustiere bleiben an Ort und Stelle, das Verzeichnis der Tiere ist unter Angabe der Hausnummer und der Straße gleichzeitig mit den Schlüsseln an der Versammlungsstelle abzugeben. Unbewegliches Eigentum und Einrichtung, wie verschiedene Maschinen, landwirtschaftliche Maschinen und Geräte, ist am Ort und Stelle zu belassen. Jede absichtliche Beschädigung dieses Eigentums oder Einrichtung wird streng bestraft werden. Desgleichen wird die Uebergabe der angeführten Gegenstände und Einrichtungen an andere Personen zwecks Aufbewahrung bestraft werden. Schlüssel: Beim Abgang sind alle Haus- und Wohzimmereingänge sowie die Eingänge der Hofgebäude bzw. der Werks- und Betriebsstätten zu verschließen, die Schlüssel von diesen Gebäuden von allen einzelnen Räumen sind mit Schnur zusammenzubinden und mit der genauen Anschrift der bisherigen Wohnstelle oder der Wohnung auf starkem Papier zu versehen, die an den Schlüsseln mittels Schnur zu befestigen ist. Vor dem Verlassen der Wohnzimmer und der Gebäude muß jede Eingangstür versdmlossen und mit einem starken Papier so versiehlt werden, daß dieser beide Türflügel verbindet und das Schlüsselloch überdeckt. In Häusern, in denen einige Mieter weiter verbleichen, werden bloß alle Eingänge der verlassenen Wohnräume abgesperrt und die Türen mit Papierstreifen überklebt. Nach Uebernahme der Schlüssel werden alle Gebäude sofort von Militär- und Gendarmeriorganen durchsucht werden. Personen welche unberechtigt und absichtlich die Gebäude nicht verlassen haben, haben eine strenge Bestrafung zu erwarten. Kranke, jedoch des Transports in einem Beförderungsmittel fähige Personen, werden von den Angehörigen ihres Haushalts zur Versammlungsstelle gebracht, von wo sie gemeinsam mit Transport durch das Rote Kreuz weiter befördert werden.

Böhmisch-Leipa, den 14. Juni 1945.

Der Militärortskommandant: **pplk. Voves e. h.**

hl des Militärkommandanten von Böhm.-Leipa vom 14. Juni 1945

r Befehl wurde am 14. Juni um 22.00 Uhr, also nach der offiziellen Sperrstunde Deutsche veröffentlicht, sodaß die deutschen Bewohner von Böhmisch-Leipa erst am Morgen des 15. Juni, unmittelbar vor der Ausweisung zur Kenntnis men.

**Expulsion Order of the Military Commandant
of Bohemian Leipa, June 14, 1945.
Translation:**

The inhabitants of German nationality, residing in the municipalities of Bohemian Leipa, Alt-Leipa and Niemes, irrespective of their age or sex, will leave their apartments on June 15th, 1945 at 5 o'clock in the morning and march to the rallying-point at the "Bräuhaus" of Ceske Lipe, via Kreuz- and Bräuhaus-Strasse.

At Niemes they will gather at the junction, 200 metres to the West of the railway bridge (street leading in the direction of Reichstadt).

This order does not concern the following persons and their families:

I. 1. doctors, veterinarians, apothecaries, nursing personnel and the members of the fire-brigade. 2. manufacturers and employees of the public supply undertakings in operation. 3. black smiths, mechanics, employees of repairing shops, tailors and shoemakers, still in business. 4. employees of factories and enterprises in operation. 5. employees of the railway, post and other public communications.

The persons quoted under 1-5 are to identify themselves by means of a certificate stating their employment or business. Those absenting themselves will be brought back and punished accordingly.

II. The transfer does not concern members of the Communist or Socialdemocratic Parties who may prove their membership by means of a membership-card of the Party in question and who should also prove that they have been persecuted, that is, imprisoned or dismissed from their offices by reason of their political opinions and loyal attitude towards Czechoslovakia.

Each individual to be transferred is permitted to take the following: **a)** food for 7 days and **b)** the most necessary articles but only such as he is able to carry himself; **c)** identity-cards, passports, all ration cards together with the household-"Stammkarte" (basic ration card).

Valuables: Gold, silver and all articles made of these metals (rings, brooches etc.), gold and silver coins, savings-bank deposit-books, insurance-policies, currency with the exception of 100 RM per head and also cameras are to be tied up in small bags or paper-packages with an exact list enclosed of the valuables in question and giving the owner's address. **These are to be delivered at the rallying-points.**

All are warned that they will be required to undergo a thorough bodily examination (strip search). The contents of the luggage will also be thoroughly examined. Any concealment of the articles mentioned above whether in clothes, shoes or other places, such as in the hand luggage, will therefore be useless and such conduct will be punished.

Domestic animals (pets) will be left at home, a list of the animals together with the address and the keys will be delivered at the rallying-points.

Immovables and furniture, such as industrial machines, agricultural machines and tools will remain where they are. Any intentional damaging of immovables or furniture will be severely punished. The delivery of immovables and furniture to other persons for the purpose of preserving them will likewise be punished. Keys: All doors to houses or rooms as well as to outbuildings, to workshops or factories are to be locked on departure, the keys of the buildings and individual rooms must be tied together and, furnished with the exact address written on thick paper, attached to the keys by means of a string. **Before the rooms and buildings are left, each front-door is to be locked and a slip of paper pasted on them in such a way that it connects the two leaves of the door and covers the key-hole. In houses in which some of the lodgers are permitted to remain, only the doors of those dwellings evacuated are to be locked and the slips of paper pasted on the doors.** After the keys have been delivered all buildings will immediately be searched by military or gendarmerie personnel. Persons not entitled to stay, who deliberately failed to leave the buildings, must anticipate severe punishment. Sick persons able to use public conveyances will be taken by relatives or members of the household to the rallying-point, whence the Red Cross will provide further transport.

Bohemian Leipa, June 14th, 1945.
The military commander: **pplk. Voves e.h.**

This order was posted on June 14 at 10 o'clock p.m.,
i.e. after the official curfew for Germans,
so that the German inhabitants of Bohemian Leipa
did not even become aware of it until the morning of June 15th,
immediately before their expulsion.

Food ration card for the Germans in Czechoslovakia
Ration period from May 28 to June 24, 1945

Proclamation of the Národní výbor
(National Committee) in Saaz from 1945

Vyhláška.

Nařizuji, aby dnes všechny osoby ženského pohlaví, česke a německé národnosti, bez rozdílu stáří a děti hlásily se ihned po vyhlášení tohoto rozkazu v bývalých „SS" Kasárnách na Trnovanske silnici.

Osoby německé národnosti vezmou s sebou:

1.) zavazadla s nejnutnějšími cestovními potřebami ve váze 25 kg na osobu včetně přikrývky a jídelních potřeb.

2.) potraviny na 3 dny.

3.) Všechny osobní průkazy.

4.) Klíče bytů a domů svázané ve svazku a označené číslem domu a bytu.

5.) Všechny cenné věci, peníze, vkladní knížky, cenné papíry a drahé skvosty s připojeným seznamem

Toto opatření se provádí pro přesnou evidenci osob německé národ nosti a jejich rozdělení do pracovního nasazení. Zatajení jakýchkoliv uvedených hodnot nebo neuposlechnuti tohoto rozkazu se trestá smrti.

Národní Výbor.

Kundmachung.

Es wird angeordnet, daß sich heute alle Personen weiblichen Geschlechtes, čechischer und deutscher Nationalität ohne Unterschied des Alters und Kinder sofort nach Veröffentlichung dieser Kundmachung in der ehemaligen „SS" Kaserne in der Trnovanerstraße in Saaz zu melden haben.

Personen, deutscher Nationalität haben mitzubringen:

1.) Gepäck mit dem allernotwendigsten Reisebedarf im Höchsgewichte von 25 kg je Person einschließlich Decken und Eßbedarf.

2.) Lebensmittel für 3 Tage.

3.) Alle Personalausweise.

4.) Wohnungsschlüßel in einen Bund, der mit der Hausnummer und der Wohnung bezeichnet ist.

5.) Alle Wertsachen, Geld Einlagebücher, Wertpapiere und kostbaren Schmuck mit einem genauen Verzeichnis dieser Gegenstände.

Diese Vorkehrungen werden zur Durchführung einer genauen Evidenz aller Personen deutscher Nationalität und ihrer Einteilung zum Arbeitseinsatz durchgeführt.

Die Verheimlichung irgend einer der angeführten Wertsachen oder die Nichtbefolgung dieser Anordnung wird mit dem Tode bestraft.

Národní Výbor.

Proclamation of the Národní výbor (National Committee) in Saaz from 1945
Translation:

Proclamation.

We hereby order that all individuals of female sex and also all children, of Czech and German nationality, irrespective of their age, will report to the former SS-barracks at Saaz, Trnovaner Strasse, immediately following publication of this proclamation.

Individuals of German nationality will bring with them the following:

1.) Luggage containing personal necessities for travel, maximum weight 25 kilos per head (55 pounds), including blankets and food.

2.) Food for 3 days.

3.) Identity cards, passports etc.

4.) The keys of all apartments and houses, which are to be tied together and labelled, giving the exact address.

5.) Valuables, currency, savings-bank deposit-books, bonds and jewellery, together with an exact list of the individual items.

These arrangements will be carried out in order to obtain accurate statistics of persons of German nationality and their further distribution to places of work.

Any concealment of the valuables mentioned above or non-observance of this order will be punished by the death sentence.

Národní Výbor

Letter from Mr. R. R. Stokes, a British Member of Parliament and Minister, to the Manchester Guardian, October 1945, about the Czech concentration camps

(Retranslated from the German in the absence of the original)

Some months ago I heard of the Czech practice of assembling young men, who according to the Potsdam Agreement were to be transferred on account of their nationality, and of putting them in concentration camps. And in fact, many Sudeten German Social Democrats, who as anti-Nazis had been in German concentration camps, have now been put in Czech labour camps simply on the ground that they are German. I therefore attempted to find one of the so-called political internment camps and had the luck to come on one at Hagibor near Prague. The main part of the camp consisted of ten big huts, in [each of] which 70 to 80 persons were lodged. At the time of my first visit, on September 12, at 9 o'clock in the morning, most of the inmates were absent at work. The huts were typical concentration camp barracks with three tiers of beds, lacking the most primitive conveniences and with the most horrible sanitary arrangements. I met all kinds of people in the camp, some of them had only been there a few days and others for months. None of those to whom I spoke had the slightest idea why he had been arrested. An old lady of 72 had already been two weeks in the camp and no reason for her internment would be given other than that she was an Austrian. She had lived near Prague for 55 years, where her late husband had been the well-to-do owner of a sugar refinery. I found her in a corner of the sick-bay reading a copy of Cronin's book "The Stars Look Down".

A 70-year-old professor of dramatic art from Belgrade and his wife were also there. The old man was almost blind in both eyes. He had left Russia in 1911 and had lived in Yugoslavia since that time. While he was in Vienna to consult a specialist about his eyes, he was interned by the Nazis as a Yugoslav; on the day of liberation he was imprisoned by the Czechs, probably because he was a White Russian.

I also saw a 75-year-old lady, the widow of a Russian admiral of the First World War, whose only wish was to reach her daughter in Tyrol. She had already been there several months and was kept on bread and water.

I should like to know what these people, who were typical of many whom I saw, may have done to deserve such treatment. I at any rate was unable to find out.

When I brought this matter to the attention of the Ministry of the Interior, they promised me to look into it.

There are 51 such camps in Czechoslovakia, in which famished people are vegetating. And when I say famished, I mean it literally. In front of me lies the menu of this camp, the same for every day:

Breakfast - black coffee and bread

Lunch - vegetable soup

Supper - black coffee and bread.

The bread ration is distributed every morning and amounts to 250 grams a day per person, and what is left over from supper may be eaten next morning. The camp kitchen consists of a small room 9 by 9 ft in the cellar of the building. Two old women peeling carrots for the mid-day soup and two buckets [of water] made up the whole equipment and personnel.

On September 3, there were 912 persons in the camp and the total amount of food distributed on this day consisted of:

550 lbs of bread

750 lbs of potatoes

80 lbs of sugar

30 lbs of coffee

18 lbs of mixed butter and margarine

70 lbs of vegetables.

Reckoning bread and potatoes together, each man received 1.5 pounds, 25 grams of sugar and vegetables and 5 grams butter or margarine [1 gram = 0.035 oz]. It is therefore no wonder that the camp inmates were glad of the slave labour outside the camp, since the employers had to provide food in order to obtain workers. This also explains why at the time of my first visit the camp was almost empty. Everybody except the old people and the so-called "dangerous persons", who were lodged in another part of the camp, were out at work.

I was able to observe the methods by which the slaves were selected when, two days later, to the astonishment of the camp authorities, I appeared in the camp at half past five in the morning. At 6 o'clock the first employers arrived in the camp with cars and lorries to choose and to take away the slaves. They were taken into a big hut which had been empty at the time of my previous visit. 300-400 slaves were then let in from the camp and the visitors made their choice and gave written receipts for those whom they took away and would bring back at the end of the day. I moved freely among employers and slaves; and I was told that anyone who showed the slightest sign of unwillingness to go to work would receive a severe beating. In honor of my visit this practice was discontinued on this morning. The slaves receive no payment of any kind.

On my previous visit to the special section of the camp, to which I have referred, I noticed that during the whole three hours of my stay on a fine sunny day hardly anyone was to be seen outside the huts. This time I demanded to see the huts themselves and found them crowded. All inmates, with few exceptions, lay rolled up on their palliasses. These were the "dangerous" men. As such they were not allowed to go out to work; and since they did not work, they received only camp rations. A half pound of bread per day and black coffee cannot keep body and soul together, still less allow any physical effort. According to my estimate their rations amounted to 750 calories per day, that is to say less than in Belsen. The only men I saw outside were a dozen young Jews and Poles, who had been brought in a couple of days before because they had not kept to the prescribed route from Russia and Poland to the Mediterranean.

I can only assume that the conditions in other camps are similar.

The officials who gave me the information as to the number of camps, did so without shame; and I should be interested to know whether Dr. Beneš knows that these disgraceful things are going on. As he was absent from Prague, I was unfortunately unable to see him, but I left reports at the Ministry of the Interior and the Ministry of Foreign Affairs.

R. R. Stokes, m.p.

Chapters VIII and IX of the "Statute issued in Košice" [Kaschau],
Slovakia, April 5, 1945
(Program of the new Czechoslovak Government,
the National Front of Czechs and Slovaks,
adopted by the cabinet council on April 5, 1945)

Collection of Documents, issued by the Ministry of Information, Publication No. 2/45

Chapter VIII

The bitter experiences of the Czechs and Slovaks with the German and Hungarian minorities - who, for the most part, became compliant instruments of a policy of conquest against the Republic and of whom the Germans especially led a war of extermination against the Czech and Slovak nation - compel the restored Czechoslovakia to take a definitive action against those guilty. Loyal German and Hungarian citizens and above all those who proved their faithfulness to the Republic in the difficult times will not be affected, but the culprits will be severely and pitilessly punished as the conscience of our people demands, remembering our unnumbered martyrs and for the peace and security of the generations to come. The Government, therefore, will be guided in its decisions by these principles.

As to the Czechoslovak citizens of German and Hungarian nationality, who were Czechoslovak citizens prior to the Munich Pact in 1938, their citizenship will be confirmed and their eventual return to the Republic may be permitted only in the following categories: for anti-Nazis and anti-Fascists who fought against Henlein and Hungarian irredentism, who fought for Czechoslovakia, and who after the Munich Pact and after March 15 were persecuted for their loyalty to Czechoslovakia and imprisoned in jails and concentration camps or those who fled abroad, where they participated in the struggle for the restoration of Czechoslovakia.

The Czechoslovak citizenship of the other Czechoslovak German and Hungarian citizens will be cancelled. Although they may again express a choice for Czechoslovakia, public authorities will retain the right of individual decision. Those German and Hungarian transgressors who are under indictment for crimes against the Republic and the Czech and Slovak nations and who are condemned, will lose their citizenship and will be expelled from the Republic for ever - if not under sentence of death.

Germans and Hungarians who immigrated into Czechoslovak territories after the Munich Pact in 1938 will, if not sentenced to capital punishment, be expelled from the Republic at once, except those persons who worked on behalf of Czechoslovakia.

Chapter IX.

The government considers it its highest moral duty to turn over to the courts and to punish all war criminals, traitors and active helpers of the German and Hungarian oppressors. The Government will carry out its task without delay and will spare no one.

As to the German and Hungarian War Criminals, the Government will see to their immediate removal, arrest and delivery to Special People's Courts. Those [German and Hungarian] persons guilty of war crimes will be tried and punished not only for crimes committed against the [peoples] of Czechoslovakia or Czechoslovak territory, but also for crimes committed against other [peoples], especially against the allied Soviet Union. The German and Hungarian culprits convicted will be handed over to Soviet organs. Camps for the detention of German and Hungarian individuals who were connected with Nazi or Fascist organizations will be established.

The Government will take special steps to secure the punishment of traitors, collaborators and fascist elements of Czech and Slovak nationality. In connection with the National Committees, Special People's Courts will be set up whose [jurisdiction] will be limited to the localities and to the prosecution of the minor offenders. A National Court will be established in the Bohemian territories and one in Slovakia for the cases of notorious offenders and those responsible for major crimes. The regulations of the edict concerning the punishment of war criminals, issued by the President of the Republic, will be considered as a general basis for criminal proceedings against traitors and collaborators.

Persons guilty of high treason, like Hácha, all members of the Beran Government who confirmed Hácha's so-called Berlin Pact of March 15, 1939, and those who welcomed Hitler when he arrived in Prague, will be brought before the National Court. The Government will take care that all members of the "Protectorate" Government of March 16, 1939, [as well as] Tiso and the members of the so-called Slovak Government of March 14, 1939 and members of the so-called Slovak Parliament, shall be brought before the National Court. And furthermore all of Hácha's political and official helpers, and the responsible leading authorities and officials of the Protectorate Administration. The country will also be cleared of treacherous journalists, who sold themselves to the Germans and served them. Legal proceedings will be instituted against the following organizations, their functionaries and members etc.: the functionaries of the "Curatorship for the education of Czech youth," against the members of the "Vlajka," the members of the Committee and the functionaries of the "National Association of Employees" *(Nationale Fachzentrale der Angestellten)*, of the "Union of Agriculture and Forestry" and other organizations which helped the Germans; in addition, functionaries who handed over Czechs and Slovaks to the Gestapo, who participated actively in the displacement of Slovaks and Czechs in order to send them to Germany as slave labourers and who rendered assistance in the evacuation of the Czechoslovak population. In Slovakia, the helpers of Tiso and his treacherous regime, the spies of the "Hlinka-Garde", that is the Slovak Gestapo, the tools of Gašpar's Nazi propaganda, will be tried, but especially those who were active against the Slovak uprising and who participated in the atrocities and bestialities of the Germans against the Slovaks.

Bankers, industrialists and big land owners who [used their positions in banking, industry, agriculture, and other economic organisations to] help the Germans to plunder the land and wage war will also be punished without mercy.

However, even if an employment with the administration of the former treacherous and occupational regime is not considered as punishable, a thorough examination of the activities of every single individual will be carried out under democratic conditions; a number of steps will be taken by the Government so that the new administration of the State shall be cleared of all elements who sinned against the Republic and the nation - of the fascist and pro-fascist elements who showed disloyalty, unreliability and cowardice towards the [people] and the state during the critical years of 1938 and 1939 and during the period of the German and Hungarian occupation. The conduct of all those Czechoslovak citizens abroad who became disloyal to the Republic and who helped the enemy by their undermining activities, as well as that of persons who failed to remain loyal citizens even though they were not under the pressure of Nazi terror, will also be examined and prosecuted by the court.

Being resolved to root out fascism politically and morally, the Government herewith declares that all fascist parties and organizations will be banned and that a renewal of those political parties which worked against the interests of the nation and the Republic (the Agrarian party and its branches, the *Gewerbepartei* [Trade party], the National Union and those parties which in 1938 fused with the Slovak Hlinka party) will not be permitted. No harm will come to former members of the parties mentioned above as concerns their moral or political honour - if they remained loyal to the Republic. Any political activity or participation in organizations of democratic parties, however, will be forbidden to the politically responsible functionaries of the parties aforementioned, who compromised themselves and whose activities were damaging to the interests of the [people] and the Republic.

Signed by the members of the cabinet as given in the edict mentioned:

Zdenék Fierlinger

Josef David, Klement Gottwald, Viliam Siroký, Dr. Jan Sramek, Jan Ursiny, Jan Masaryk, Ludwig Svoboda, Dr. Hubert Ripka, Václav Nosek, Dr. Vávro Srobár, Dr. Zdenek Nejedlý, Dr. Jaroslav Stránský, Václav Kopecký, Bohumil Lausman, Julius Duris, Dr. Jan Pietor, Antonín Hasal, Frantisek Hala, Dr. Josef Soltész, Dr. Adolf Prochaska, Václav Majer, Dr. Vladimir Clementis, Dr. Mikulas Ferencik, Jan Lichner.

Edict of the President of the Republic, dated May 19, 1945
Concerning the Invalidity of Transactions Involving Property Rights from the Time of the
Oppression and Concerning the National Administration of Property Assets of Germans,
Magyars, Traitors and Collaborators and of Certain Organizations and Associations
(Decree No. 5)

Upon proposition of the Government I decree:

§1

1. All transfers and transactions involving property rights, regardless of whether they involve movable or immovable, public or private property, are invalid provided that they have been made under the pressure of the occupation or under the national, racial or political persecution after October 29, 1938.

2. The manner in which claims arising by virtue of the provision of Subsection 1 shall be raised will be prescribed in a particular edict of the President of the Republic, provided that it has not been prescribed in this edict.

§2

1. The property of persons upon whom the country cannot place reliance, being within the territory of the Czech Republic, will be placed under national administration in accordance with the further provisions of this edict.

2. Property transferred by such persons after October 29, 1938 shall also be deemed to be property of persons upon whom the country cannot rely, unless the person acquiring such property had no knowledge of the fact that property of such nature was involved.

§3

All enterprises and all property assets shall be taken under national administration wherever this is required in the interests of continuous production and economic life. This applies especially to production plants and other enterprises which have been deserted and to property assets relinquished or to such facilities or such property assets which are in the possession of, or administered by, or leased to persons upon whom the country cannot rely.

§4

The following shall be considered to be persons upon whom the country cannot rely:

a) Persons of German or Magyar nationality,

b) Persons whose activities have been directed against the governmental authority, independence, integrity, democratic-republican system, security and strength of the Czechoslovak Republic, who instigated such activities or tended to induce other persons to take such actions, and intentionally supported the German and Magyar occupiers in any manner whatsoever. As such supporters shall be considered, for example: The members of Vlajka Rodobrana, the Advance Battalions of the Hlinka-Guard, the leading officers of the Association for the Cooperation with the Germans, of the Czech League against Bolshevism, of the Curatory for Education of the Czech Youth, of the national Central Association of Employees, of the Association for Agriculture and Forestry, of the German-Slovak Association, and of other fascist organizations of similar nature.

§5

Those juristic persons shall be deemed persons upon whom the country cannot rely, whose administration has intentionally and knowingly served the Germans or Magyars in carrying on the war, or has served fascist or Nazi purposes.

§6

As persons of German and Magyar nationality shall be considered those who on the occasion of any census since 1929 acknowledged their German or Magyar nationality or who became members of national groups or organizations or political parties in which persons of German or Magyar nationality were united.

§7

1. Competent to take property under national administration are:

a) in the case of financial institutions and enterprises, the Zemský národní výbor (Provincial National Committee), in Slovakia the Slowenská národní rada (Slovak National Council),

b) with respect to mining enterprises in the districts, the competent Okresní národní výbor (District National Committee), with respect to central organs of the mining corporations the competent Zemský národní výbor (Provincial National Committee), in Slovakia the Slowenská národní rada (Slovak National Council).

c) with respect to industrial, commercial and other business enterprises:

 aa) up to 20 employees, the Místní národní výbor (Local National Committee),

 bb) from 21 up to 300 employees, the Okresní národní výbor (District National Committee),

 cc) in case of a higher number of employees, the Zemský národní výbor (Provincial National Committee), in Slovakia the Slowenská národní rada (Slovak National Council).

The normal business situation in the year 1943 shall be taken as basis for the determination of the number of employees.

d) with respect to estates with agricultural an forest land:

aa) up to 50 hectares [123.6 acres], the Místní národní výbor (Local National Committee),

bb) from 50 hectares to 100 hectares [247 acres], the Okresní národní výbor (District National Committee), in Slovakia the Slowenská národní rada (Slovak National Council).

e) with respect to dwelling houses and sites, the Místní národní výbor (Local National Committee), and in the case that the value thereof exceeds the sum of 5 million Kčs, the Okresní národní výbor (District National Committee).

f) with respect to any other estate:

aa) in the case the value thereof is less than 500,000 Kčs, the Místní národní výbor (Local National Committee),

bb) in the case that the value thereof exceeds the sum of 500,000 Kčs but is less than 5 million Kčs, the Okresní národní výbor (District National Committee),

cc) if the value exceeds the sum of 5 million Kčs, the Zemský národní výbor (Provincial National Committee), in Slovakia the Slowenská národní rada (Slovak National Council).

g) In the event that the scope of activity of the enterprises and estates as listed under a) to f) covers the whole territory of the country, then such enterprises and estates shall be taken under administration by the competent ministry.

2. In the event that the estimated value of the property listed under e) and f) is in dispute once it is placed under national administration, then said value shall be determined finally by a higher authority.

3. In communities and districts in which an administrative commission or an administrative officer has been appointed in place of the národní výbor (National Committee), the former are competent to establish the national administration.

§8

1. A decision within the meaning of §7 which relates to enterprises listed in §7 a), b), c), d), shall be rendered upon consent of the works-council or of other representatives of the employees of the enterprises. In the event that an agreement cannot be reached, then a higher authority shall have the power of decision.

2. The decision concerning agricultural and forested estates of more than 50 hectares shall be rendered upon hearing of the competent National Committee.

§9

In emergency cases, especially if a deserted estate is involved or if persons the country cannot rely on control the estate or the enterprise, the Okresní národní výbor (District National Committee) is authorized to appoint a temporary national custodian for the time until the decision of the authority competent according to §7 has been rendered, even if it would not otherwise be competent to do so.

§10

1. The competent Zemský národní výbor (Provincial National Committee), in Slovakia the Slovenská národní rada (Slovak National Council), upon hearing the works-council, may modify ex officio the decision of the Okresní národní výbor (District National Committee) or of the Místní národní výbor (Local National Committee) concerning the establishment of the administration or the appointment of national custodians and take other measures, if the public interest requires it.

2. The competent Zemský národní výbor (Provincial National Committee), in Slovakia the Slovenská národní rada (Slovak National Council), shall also take measures to establish the national administration in cases where the Okresní or Místní výbor (District or Local National Committee) has been unable to do so.

§11

The national administration shall be terminated as soon as the reasons for its establishment cease to exist. It shall be terminated by the authority by which it was established.

§12

1. All co-operative enterprises and organizations (agricultural, consumers and banking co-operatives etc.) shall be under temporary national administration. Such temporary national administration shall secure the election of a new leading organ within 4 weeks in addition to the proper operation of the enterprise.

2. Those competent to place cooperatives under national administration are: the Místní národní výbor (Local National Committee) if the scope of their operation does not go beyond the local area, the Okresní národní výbor (District National Committee) if the scope of their operations goes beyond the local area but does not exceed the district area, and the Zemský národní výbor (Provincial National Committee) - in Slovakia the Slovenská národní rada (Slovak National Council) - with respect to any other cooperatives.

3. Before the cooperatives are placed under temporary national administration, their members shall be heard, if possible.

4. The temporary national administration shall be terminated as soon as the members of the cooperative have elected a new administrative organ.

§13

The competent Zemský národní výbor (Provincial National Committee) - in Slovakia the Slovenská národní rada (Slovak National Council) - may also place business institutions, economic, cultural and interested organisations and institutions under national administration, for good reasons shown.

§14

1. The decision concerning the imposition and release from national administration, and the appointment of the national custodian and the cancellation thereof, shall be announced in writing.

2. A copy of the decision shall be forwarded to the Zemský národní výbor (Provincial National Committee), in Slovakia to the Slovenská národní rada (Slovak National Council).

§15

The decision according to §14 is carried out ex officio:

a) with respect to immovable property, by the competent court, which has to make the entries in the land register evidencing the placing under national administration,

b) with respect to mining rights, by the competent court or office, which shall make the entries in the mineral land registers or records evidencing the placing under national administration,

c) with respect to enterprises (business institutions) registered in the commercial register, or in Slovakia by the firms register, by the competent court, which shall make the entries evidencing their placing under national administration.

§16

1. A national custodian can only be a person who is possessed of high moral standards, upon whom the country can rely, and who has the necessary training and practical knowledge.

2. As a rule persons shall not be appointed national custodians who are debtors or creditors of the enterprise (business institution) or property unless the authority competent according to §7 decides otherwise, for good reason given.

3. As a rule the national administration shall consist of competent employees of the business institution concerned.

4. A member of the Národní výbor (National Committee) competent according to §7 shall not be appointed national custodian.

§17

1. In cases of smaller properties, small enterprises, small factories and similar objects a single national custodian may be appointed for several enterprises or properties.

2. If the extent of the national administration requires it, the authority competent according to §7 may appoint a five-man commission national custodian which shall manage the administration in accordance with the majority principle.

§18

Upon their assumption of office the national custodians shall take an oath before the authority competent according to §7 that they will perform their duties accurately and with the diligence of a prudent manager in accordance with economic, national and other interests.

§19

In the performance of their functions the national custodians have the position of public authorities within the meaning of §68 of the Criminal Code of May 27, 1852, No. 117 R.G.Bl., §461 of the Law, Article V/1878 and §5 of the Law, Article XI/1914.

§20

1. Legal transactions of the owners, possessors and managers of properties subject to national administration, which affect the substance of such properties and have been carried out after this Edict had become effective, are invalid.

2. It is the duty of the owners, possessors and managers of properties placed under national administration, not to interfere with the transactions of the national custodians.

§21

The national custodian administers the property placed under national administration and has the right and the duty to engage in all transactions necessary for its normal conduct of business. It is his duty to act with the diligence and care of a prudent manager and he shall be liable for damage resulting from negligence in the performance of his duties.

§22

1. The national custodian has the duty to give account to the authority competent according to §7 with respect to his management, at such times as determined by such authority, and to provide necessary information or explanations requested at any time.

2. Transactions of the national custodian which are not incidental to the normal conduct of business, as well as transactions of particular importance, leases, negotiation of loans, mortgages, liquidations and similar transactions require approval in advance by the authority competent according to §7.

3. The authority competent according to §7 supervises the management of the national custodian.

4. It is the duty of the national custodian to follow the rules which have been established for him by the authority competent according to §7 or by the superior of the Zemský národní výbor (Provincial National Committee), or by the Slovenská národní rada (Slovak National Council) in Slovakia, or by the competent Ministry in cases where the activities of the enterprise (business institution) extend to the whole country.

§23

The national custodian is entitled to be reimbursed for expenses incurred and to a compensation the amount of which shall be fixed by the authority competent according to §7. These expenditures shall be charged against the property placed under administration.

§24

1. Property placed under national administration which was owned by workers, farmers, tradesmen, owners of small and medium-sized enterprises, officials, by persons who have a liberal profession and persons in a similar social position and which property has been lost by them in consequence of national, political or racial persecution shall be released from the national administration and be returned immediately to the former owners or their heirs provided that they are not persons referred to under §4.

2. Persons referred to under §4 Subsection a), provided that they are workers, farmers, tradesmen, owners of small or medium-sized enterprises, officials or have a liberal profession, and persons in a similar social position, or their heirs, may also request the release of their property from the national administration and the return thereof to them, provided that they offer sufficient proof that they have been victims of political or racial persecution and that they have adhered faithfully to the democratic-republican system of the Czechoslovak Republic.

3. Decisions on such requests are rendered by the authority competent according to §7.

4. Any other property confiscated remains under national administration pending the enactment of new laws.

§25

1. Appeal against the decision of the Místní národní výbor (Local National Committee) may be filed with the Okresní národní výbor (District National Committee) which renders the final decision.

2. Appeal against the decision of the Okresní národní výbor (District National Committee) rendered by the latter as first instance may be filed with the Zemský národní výbor (Provincial National Committee), or with the Slovenská národní rada (Slovak National Council) in Slovakia.

3. An appeal shall have no dilatory effect.

§26

a) Whoever violates or evades the provisions of this edict, especially anyone who interferes with or makes impossible the authorized transactions of a national custodian, or

b) a national custodian who intentionally or by reason of gross negligence violates any of the duties imposed upon him under the aforegoing provisions,

shall be punished by imprisonment not to exceed 5 years and by a fine not to exceed 10 million Kčs, and his property shall be ordered confiscated in whole or in part if the circumstances call for it, provided that the act does not constitute an offense subject to more severe punishment.

§27

The Government shall be authorized to allot the financial means required for the operation of the enterprises (business institutions) placed under national administration provided that such operation is necessary and in the interests of the economy.

§28

1. This edict shall become effective on the day of its publication.

2. It will be carried out by the Government.

[signed:]

Dr. Eduard Beneš   Zd. Fierlinger

Gottwald, Srámek, David, Ján Ursíny, Siroký, Václ. Nosek, Dr. V. Srobár, Pietor, Dr. H. Ripka, J.
Duris, Dr. Soltész, A. Procházka, Svoboda, Nejedlý, gen. Hasal, Frant. Hála, J. Stránský, V. Majer,
B. Lausman, Dr. V. Clementis, téz za min. J. Masaryka, gen. Dr. Ferjencik, J. Lichner

Edict of the President of the Republic, dated June 21, 1945
concerning the confiscation and early re-allotment of agricultural property of Germans, Magyars,
as well as of traitors and enemies of the Czech and Slovak people
(Decree No. 12)

Following the demand of the Czech and Slovak people without land for an effective implementation of the land reform, and led by the desire once and for all to take Czech and Slovak soil out of the hands of the foreign - German and Magyar - landowners as well as out of the hands of the traitors to the Republic and to give it into the hands of the Czech and Slovak farmers and persons without land, I decree upon proposition of the government as follows:

§1

1. With immediate effect and without compensation and for the purpose of the land reform such rural property shall be confiscated as is owned by:

a) all persons of German or Magyar nationality, without regard to their citizenship,

b) traitors and enemies of the Republic without regard to their nationality and citizenship, especially those who demonstrated their hostility during the crisis and during the war in the years 1938 to 1945,

c) corporations, partnerships and other associations, the management of which knowingly and intentionally supported the Germans in carrying on the war or which served fascist or Nazi aims.

2. The agricultural property of persons of German or Magyar nationality who participated in the combat for the protection of the integrity and for the liberation of the Czechoslovak Republic shall not be confiscated under the provisions of Subsection 1.

3. The District National Committee is competent to decide upon application of the competent farmers committee whether an exception according to Subsection 2 shall be made. Doubtful cases shall be submitted by the District National Committee to the Provincial National Committee which shall forward them with an opinion to the Ministry of Agriculture for final decision. The latter shall decide by agreement with the Ministry of the Interior.

§2

1. Those persons shall be considered as of German and Magyar nationality who on the occasion of any census since 1929 acknowledged their German or Magyar nationality or who became members of national groups, organizations or political parties in which persons of German or Magyar nationality were united.

2. Exemptions from the provisions of Subsection 1 will be laid down in a special Edict.

§3

1. Those persons shall be considered as traitors and enemies of the Czechoslovak Republic:

a) whose activities were jointly or separately directed against the sovereignty, the independence, the integrity, the democratic-republican system, the security and the defensive power of the Czechoslovak Republic, who instigated such activities or seduced other persons thereto, and, in any manner, intentionally and actively supported the German and Magyar occupiers;

b) such juristic persons whose activities intentionally and actively served the Germans in carrying on the war or served fascist or Nazi purposes.

2. The authorities competent to decide whether or not a natural or juristic person is subject to the provisions of Subsection 1 a), b), are: the Provincial National Committee in the area of which the rural estate concerned is located, upon application of the competent District National Committee. Doubtful cases shall be submitted by the Provincial National Committee to the Ministry of Agriculture for final decision. The latter shall decide by agreement with the Ministry of the Interior.

§4

Rural property within the meaning of §1 Subsection 1 shall include the land used for agricultural and forestry purposes, the buildings and equipment relating thereto, the facilities serving the agricultural and forestry management thereof as well as all movable accessories (livestock, tools etc.), and all rights connected with the possession of the property confiscated and the parts thereof.

§5

1. If the rural property confiscated by virtue of §1 has been leased, all lease contracts shall become null and void. In the event, however, that the lessee is a person having a claim for the allotment of land (§7 Subsection 1), then he may be permitted to utilize the land in his possession until the end of the economic year. In the event that the rural property leased should not be allotted to such person for any reason whatsoever, then the lessee shall pay rent to the National Land Fund (§6 subsection 1). In the event that natural or juristic persons not subject to §3 are affected by the confiscation, the National Land Fund, upon application by the Local National Committee, shall grant them a compensation for the current expenses and investments.

2. Patronage rights and duties connected with the agricultural property confiscated by virtue of §1 cease on the date of confiscation. In cases with special merit, the National Land Fund will grant compensation.

3. Questions relating to debts and claims connected with the property confiscated by virtue of §1 shall be clarified by a government ordinance. Wages, pensions, taxes and charges as well as other current expenses shall be reimbursed temporarily by the national custodian.

§6

1. Rural property confiscated by virtue of §1 shall be administered by the National Land Fund (which is established hereby) jointly with the Ministry of Agriculture until such property is turned over to the Receiver. The government is authorized to issue the charter for this Fund.

2. Continuous forest areas of more than 50 hectares confiscated by virtue of §1 will be taken over by the government. In the event that the forest areas cannot be consolidated with government owned forest areas into one continuous area, and in the event that they do not exceed an area of 100 hectares, the National Land Fund shall transfer such areas to the competent National Committee.

§7

1. Out of the rural property administered by the National Land Fund, land shall be allotted to persons of Slav nationality as follows:

a) to farm workers normally compensated for their work by agricultural products and to other farm workers, up to 8 hectares of fields or up to 12 hectares of agricultural land according to its productiveness;

b) to smallholders, such amount of land as shall bring their total holdings up to not more than 8 hectares of fields or not more than 12 hectares of agricultural land according to its productiveness;

c) to farmers with large families, such amount of land as shall bring their total holdings up to not more than 10 hectares of fields or not more than 13 hectares of agricultural land according to its productiveness;

d) to localities and districts for public purposes;

e) to building, agricultural and other co-operatives of which the members are applicants privileged according to Subsections a), b), c) and f);

f) to workers, employees in public and private services, merchants with small businesses for the purpose only of building private dwellings and laying out gardens up to 0.5 hectares.

2. In districts in which the population of German nationality is in the majority the land shall remain under the administration of the National Land Fund for the purposes of interior colonization if enough applicants of Czech and Slovak nationality who are qualified according to subsection 1 a) to f) are not available.

3. Forest land up to 50 hectares, or up to 100 hectares (§6 Subsection 2), may be allotted to localities and forestry co-operatives. Such land is subject to supervision by the government.

4. Confiscated buildings, facilities serving the agricultural and forestry management, institutions of the agricultural industry, parks, memorial institutions and objects, archives and other objects of similar nature as well as all rural estates confiscated, unless they are allotted to juristic persons created under the public law, may be allotted as property to:

a) co-operatives founded by privileged applicants for the purposes of joint utilization,

b) in exceptional cases to individuals (allotment receivers) who are listed under Subsection 1 a) to c).

5. The decision whether property confiscated shall be allotted to co-operatives or to individual persons shall be rendered in accordance with §9.

6. Those persons have a preferential right to receive an allotment who have distinguished themselves in the national combat for liberation, especially soldiers and partisans, former political prisoners and deportees, as well as their relatives and legal heirs, and farmers injured by reason of the war. The right to preferential treatment must be established according to the above provisions.

§8

The property allotted according to §7 may be disposed of, leased or encumbered only upon approval in advance by the National Land Fund.

§9

1. The applicants privileged according to §7 Subsections 1 a), b), c), d) and f) shall elect a local commission of farmers consisting of not more than 10 members. This commission shall sit at the place which is the seat of the Local National Committee in the area of which the property confiscated is located.

2. In a subsequent meeting representatives of the local farmers commission shall elect a district farmers commission which shall consist of not more than 10 members.

3. The local farmers commission shall set up an allotment plan with a valuation (§10) for the property to be allotted and shall submit such plan to the district farmers commission for approval.

4. The district farmers commission shall examine the allotment plans and valuation and shall use them in setting up an allotment plan and a valuation estimate for the entire district. If there is no divergence between the allotment plans and valuations submitted by the individual local farmers commission or if such divergence is removed, the district allotment plan and valuations shall become final upon approval in accordance with Subsection 5.

5. The allotment plan of the district farmers commission and the valuation estimate shall be submitted to the Provincial National Committee without delay. The latter shall forward the same with its opinion to the Ministry of Agriculture which may modify the allotment plan and the valuation estimates, if important public or national interests are imperilled or the provisions of §7 Subsection 1 a) to f) have not been complied with. In the event that agricultural industrial plants are concerned (§7 Subsection 4), the Ministry of Agriculture, upon consent of the Ministry of Food, shall decide if the decision relates to an allotment according to §7 Subsection 4 b).

6. If the district farmers commission is unable to remove the divergences between the allotment plan and the valuations submitted by the local farmers commission and if a settlement cannot be reached, or if it provokes a conflict between district farmers commissions of adjacent districts, then the district farmers commission shall submit the matter to the Provincial National Committee which shall forward the same with its opinion to the Ministry of Agriculture for final decision.

7. The Ministry of Agriculture and the Provincial National Committee shall delegate assistants to the district farmers commission who shall assist in technical matters relating to the allotment.

§10

1. The compensation shall be assessed according to the productivity, the location, the distance, the present condition of the land (fertilization, cultivation and planting) as well as according to the financial position of the allotment receiver and his family conditions, as follows:

a) at least in the amount equivalent to the value of an annual average crop gathered from the land, the allotment of which has been applied for;

b) at the maximum in the amount equivalent t the value of 2 average annual crops gathered from the land, the allotment of which has been applied for;

c) the compensation to be assessed for the buildings allotted shall be the equivalent of 1-2 annual rents to be paid for the buildings allotted. In any case the rent can be expressed in natural products.

2. The compensation for livestock and equipment allotted shall be assessed in accordance with regulations which will be set up by the Provincial National Committees and approved by the Ministry of Agriculture.

§11

1. The compensation assessed shall be paid as follows:

(1) in one sum either in cash or in agricultural products not later than 12 months after the property allotted has been taken into possession, or

(2) in cash or in agricultural products as follows:

a) 10% of the compensation to be paid for the land and the equipment shall be paid at the time the property allotted is taken over. Upon application of the local farmers commission, which must be submitted together with the allotment plan (§9), the National Land Fund may grant a postponement of the payment of the first installment for a period not exceeding three years;

b) the remaining payment in respect of the allotment shall fall due in accordance with the payment plan set up by the National Land Fund, in any case, however, not later than 15 years from the date the property allotted has been taken over.

2. In cases deserving particular consideration, or which are socially justified, the National Land Fund, upon application of the farmers commission, may relieve the allotment receiver from his obligation to pay the amount due and may allot the particular agricultural property without payment especially to persons who have a right to preferential treatment in the allotment (§7 Subsection 6).

§12

The compensation shall be paid by the allotment receivers to the National Land Fund in accordance with a plan set up by the latter. It shall be used for the payments of debts and obligations in respect of the property confiscated, provided that such debts and obligations have been acknowledged. It shall further be used for the compensation of war damage and such damage which was caused to property of persons who during the time of occupation were persecuted for national, political or racial reasons and for increasing the agricultural production and for purposes of interior colonization. Remaining funds of the National Land Fund shall accrue to the National Treasury.

§13

1. The assessment according to §10 includes all expense charges which are connected with the confiscation (§1), the allotment (§7) and with the registration of the property transfer in the land registers.

2. The registration of the allotments in the land registers shall be made by the National Land Fund at its own expense.

3. The transfer of property in accordance with the provisions of this edict shall not be subject to charges or fees.

§14

This edict shall become effective in the lands of Bohemia and Moravia-Silesia on the day of its publication; the Ministers of Agriculture, Finance, Justice, the Interior and for Food are responsible for carrying out this Edict.

[sgd.:]

Dr. Eduard Beneš   Fierlinger

Nosek, Dr. Srobár, Dr. Stránský, Duris, Majer

Decree of President Dr. Beneš of June 19, 1945
concerning the punishment of Nazi criminals, traitors and their accomplices, and concerning the
Special People's Courts
(Decree No. 16)

The appalling crimes committed by the Nazis and their treacherous associates against Czechoslovakia call for strict justice. The oppression of the fatherland, the murder, enslavement, robbery
and humiliation of which the Czechoslovak people has been the victim, and all the ferocious bestialities of the Germans unfortunately contributed to by unfaithful Czechoslovak citizens (among
whom there were certain persons who abused their high offices or positions) all call for the speedy
execution of well-deserved punishment in order to eradicate the evil of National Socialism and
Fascism. Upon application of the Government I therefore decree:

Chapter I
Crimes Against the State

§1
Whoever, within the territory of the Republic or abroad, and during the time of the increased
threat to the Republic (§18), committed any of the following offences in violation of the Law
for the Protection of the Republic of March 19, 1923, No. 50, will be punished. An attack on
the Republic (§1) will be punished by death, the preparation of attacks (§2), the endangering of
the security of the Republic (§3), treason (§4, No. 1), the disclosure of a state secret (§5, No. 1),
military treason (§6, Nos. 1, 2 and 3) or violence against constitutional institutions (§10, No. 1),
will be punished by confinement in a penitentiary for a period from 20 years to Life, and in case of
particularly aggravating circumstances by death.

§2
Whoever, during the time of the increased threat to the Republic (§18), was a member of
the Schutzstaffeln of the N.S.D.A.P. (SS), or of the Voluntary Schutzstaffeln (F.S.), or of the
Rodobrana, or of the Szabadcsapatok, or of any other organization of similar nature not mentioned
herein, shall be punished as for a crime by confinement in a penitentiary for a period from five to
20 years and, in case of particularly aggravating circumstances, by confinement in a penitentiary

for a period from 20 years to Life, provided that the person in question is not guilty of an offense carrying more severe punishment.

§3

1. Whoever, during the time of the increased threat to the Republic (§18), propagated or supported the fascist or Nazi movement, or who, during the said period, consented to, or defended the enemy government in the territory of the Republic or approved individual unlawful acts of the occupational military posts and authorities or organs subordinated by using press, radio, motion picture or theatre facilities or in public meetings shall be punished as for a crime by confinement in a penitentiary for a period from five to 20 years, provided that the person in question is not guilty of an offence carrying more severe punishment. In the case that he has committed such crime with the intention of destroying the moral and national consciousness of the Czechoslovak people, in particular of the Czechoslovak Youth, he shall be punished by confinement in a penitentiary for a period from ten to 20 years, and in case of particularly aggravating circumstances by confinement for a period from 20 years to Life, or by death.

2. Any person who was officer or leader in the N.S.D.A.P., in the Sudetendeutsche Partei (SdP), or in the Vlajka, Hlinková or Svatopluková Garda, or in any other fascist organization of similar nature during this time, shall be punished as for a crime by confinement in a penitentiary for a period from five to 20 years, provided that he is not guilty of an offense carrying more severe punishment.

§4

A Czechoslovak citizen who, during the time of the increased threat to the Republic (§18), attempted to corrupt the liberation movement abroad which was endeavoring to regain for the Republic the status it had had prior to Munich, or who knowingly impaired the interests of the Czechoslovak Republic in any other manner, in particular one who endangered the security of citizens working at home for the liberation of the Republic, shall be punished by confinement in a penitentiary for a period from five to 20 years, provided that he is not guilty of an offense carrying more severe punishment.

Crimes Against the Individual

§5

1. Whoever, during the time of the increased threat to the Republic (§18), in the service of or in the interest of Germany or of her associates, or in the service of a movement hostile to the Republic or the organizations of such a movement, or who as a member thereof committed any of the following crimes:

a) in violation of the Criminal Code of 27 May 1852 No. 117 R. G. Bl., the crime of open violence by kidnapping (§90), the crime of open violence by treating a human being as a slave (§95), the crime of murder (§§134 to 137), of manslaughter (§§140 and 141) or of inflicting serious bodily injury (§156);

b) in violation of the Criminal Code Stat. Art. V/1878, the crime of murder (§278), of intentional manslaughter (§279), of inflicting serious bodily injury resulting in death (§§306 and 307), or of kidnapping of a child (§317), shall be punished by death.

2. Whoever, during the same period, under the same circumstances, and for the same purposes, committed any of the following crimes:

a) in violation of the Criminal Code of 27 May 1852 No. 117 R. G. Bl., the crime of open violence by an unauthorized restriction of the personal liberty of a human being (§93), the crime of open violence by extortion (§98), of public violence by threats (§99) or of inflicting serious bodily injury (§§152 and 155);

b) in violation of the Criminal Code Stat. Art. V/1878, the crime of unlawful violation of the personal liberty of a human being (§§323, 324 and 325), of inflicting serious bodily injury (§301) and of extortion (§§350 and 353), shall be punished by confinement in a penitentiary for a period from ten to 20 years.

§6

1. Whoever, during the time of the increased threat to the Republic (§18), ordered the performance of compulsory or obligatory work favourable to the endeavours by Germany or one of her associates to carry on the war, and who participated in the issuance or the execution of such order, shall be punished as for a crime by confinement in a penitentiary for a period from five to ten years, provided that he is not guilty of an offense carrying more severe punishment.

2. If by virtue of such order an inhabitant of the Republic was compelled to work abroad or under such circumstances or at such places that may have endangered his life or impaired his health, the guilty person shall be punished by confinement in a penitentiary for a period from ten to 20 years without regard to the purpose of the work in question.

§7

1. Whoever, alone or in cooperation with others, during the time of the increased threat to the Republic (§18), in the services of or in the interest of Germany or of her associates, or of a movement hostile to the Republic, its organizations, or as a member thereof, has been responsible for the loss of liberty of an inhabitant of the Republic without further consequences, shall be punished as for a crime by confinement in a penitentiary for a period from five to 20 years. If the guilty person has been responsible for a larger number of inhabitants of the Republic losing their liberty, the court may impose confinement in a penitentiary for a period from 20 years to Life, and in case of particularly aggravating circumstances, the death penalty.

2. Whoever, during the same period, under the same circumstances, for the same purposes, and in the same manner, has inflicted upon an inhabitant of the Republic a serious bodily injury without more serious consequences (Subsection 3), shall be punished as for a crime by confinement in a penitentiary for a period from ten to 20 years and in case of particularly aggravating circumstances,

by confinement in a penitentiary for a period from 20 years to Life. If his actions affected a larger number of persons, the court may impose the death penalty.

3. Whoever, during the same period, and under the same circumstances, for the same purpose, and in the same manner, has caused the death of an inhabitant of the Republic, or a serious bodily injury to an inhabitant of the Republic, or his deportation in execution of a court order, a judgment, or any other court decision, or in execution of an administrative decision of any kind, or in execution of a judgment or of another court decision, or of an administrative decision, or in any other manner, shall be punished as for a crime by death in accordance with §156 of the Criminal Code No. 117/1852 R. G. Bl., and in accordance with §§306, 307 of the Criminal Code Stat. Art V/1878.

Crimes Against Property

§8

1. Whoever, during the time of the increased threat to the Republic (§18), in the service of or in the interest of Germany or of her associates, or of a movement hostile to the Republic or of its organizations, or as a member thereof, committed any of the following crimes:

a) in violation of the Criminal Code of 27 May 1852 No. 117 R. G. Bl., the crime of open violence by wilful damage to the property of another person (§85) with the consequences according to §86 Subsection 2, or arson (§166) under the circumstances and with the consequences according to §167 a), of robbery (§190) under the circumstances and with the consequences according to §195;

b) in violation of the Criminal Code Stat. Art. V/1878, the crime of arson (§424), of robbery (§§344 and 345), under the circumstances and with the consequences according to §349 Subsection 1, No. 2, and Subsection 2, shall be punished by death.

2. Whoever, during the same period, and under the same circumstances, for the same purpose, and in the same manner, has committed any of the following offenses:

a) in violation of the Criminal Code of 27 May 1852 No. 117 R. G. Bl., the crime of open violence by invading by force the immovable property of another person (§83), of open violence by wilful damage to the property of another person (§§85, 86 Subsection. 1), of arson (§166) under the circumstances and with the consequences according to §167 b) to g), of larceny (§§171 to 180), of embezzlement (§§181 to 183), of participating in larceny or embezzlement (§§181 to 183), of robbery (§190) under the circumstances and with the consequences according to §§191 to 194, of participating in robbery (§196), of fraud (§§197 to 201, 203);

b) in violation of the Criminal Code Stat. Art. V/1878, the crime of trespass committed by non-official persons (§§330 and 331), the offense of damage to the property of another person (§§418 and 420) which shall be considered a crime under the circumstances of Subsection 1 of this Article, of arson (§§422 and 423), of larceny (§§333 to 341) provided that the offense is not punishable by virtue of Subsection 1 b) of this Article, of receiving stolen goods (§370), of fraud (§379, as amended by §50 of the Law Amending the Criminal Code, or §383 Subsection 2 with the exception of §382), shall be punished by confinement in a penitentiary for a term from ten to 20 years, and, in case of particularly aggravating circumstances, by confinement in a penitentiary for a period from 20 years to Life.

§9

Whoever, alone or in cooperation with others, during the time of the increased threat to the Republic (§18), in the services of or in the interest of Germany or of her associates or of a movement hostile to the Republic, has caused in execution of a court order, a judgment, or another court decision, or administrative decision of any kind, in execution of a judgment, or another court decision, or of an administrative decision, that the Czechoslovak Government or a juristic or natural person be deprived of their property in whole or in part contrary to the law of the Republic, shall be punished as for a crime by confinement in a penitentiary for a period from ten to 20 years, and in case of particularly aggravating circumstances, by confinement in a penitentiary for a period from 20 years to Life, provided that he is not guilty of an offense carrying more severe punishment.

§10

Whoever, during the time of the increased threat to the Republic (§18), used the distress which had been caused by the national, political or racial persecution to enrich himself at the expense of the government, of juristic or of natural persons, shall be punished as for a crime by confinement in a penitentiary for a period from five to ten years, provided that he is not guilty of an offense carrying more severe punishment.

Denunciation

§11

Whoever, during the time of the increased threat to the Republic, in the services of or in the interest of the enemy, or by taking advantage of the situation resulting from the occupation by the enemy, has accused another person of an actual or invented activity, shall be punished as for a crime by confinement in a penitentiary for a period from five to ten years. If, however, the person who has made the denunciation has caused the loss of liberty of a Czechoslovak citizen by reason of his accusation, he shall be punished by confinement in a penitentiary for a period from ten to 20 years. If such an accusation resulted directly or indirectly in the loss to a greater number of persons of their personal liberty or in serious impairment of health, he shall be punished by confinement in a penitentiary for Life, and if it resulted in the loss of life of any person, he shall be punished by death.

General Provisions

§12

A foreigner who has committed the crime referred to under §1 or who has committed abroad any of the offenses listed in §§4 to 9, if such offense was directed against a Czechoslovak citizen or against public or private Czechoslovak property, is liable to punishment in accordance with the provisions of this Edict.

§13

1. It shall not be a justification of an act punishable under this Edict that its performance was ordered or that it was permitted by regulations other than that of Czechoslovak law or by organs appointed by a governmental authority other than that of the Czechoslovak Government, nor shall it be a valid excuse that the perpetrator believed such invalid regulations to be justified.

2. It shall also not constitute a valid excuse of the perpetrator that he fulfilled his duties, if he acted with particular zeal and exceeded the normal scope of such duties, or if he acted with the intention of supporting the endeavors of the Germans (or their Allies) to carry on the war, or to impede or to ruin the endeavors of Czechoslovakia (or her Allies) to carry on the war, or if he acted for any other obviously base motive.

3. Irresistible compulsion by reason of the order of a superior shall not constitute an excuse in respect of a person who voluntarily became a member of an organization, membership in which imposed the carrying out of any order, even if such order was unlawful.

§14

A court convicting a person of a crime under this Edict and not abstaining from the pronouncement of a sentence (§16 Abs. 2) simultaneously decrees:

a) that the person convicted loses his civic rights, for a certain period or permanently (§15);

b) that the person convicted shall serve his sentence in whole or in part in one of the particular camps for compulsory labor which shall be established by virtue of a special law;

c) that the property of such person shall be forfeit, in whole or in part, for the benefit of the Government.

§15

Loss of civic rights (§14 a) shall imply:

1. the permanent loss of decorations, medals and certificates of merit, public offices, rights and functions, academic degrees, as well as the loss of pensions and retirement allowances;

2. in case of non-commissioned officers, demotion; in case of commissioned officers, cashiering;

3. the loss of the capacity to acquire, to exercise and to reacquire rights listed under No. 1 and 2, or of rights connected with the position lost;

4. the loss of the right to vote in an election and of the right to be nominated as a candidate, and of the right to hold public office or to vote on public issues;

5. the loss of the capacity to hold a position in societies (associations and similar organizations);

6. the loss of the capacity to be the owner, the publisher or the editor of a periodical or to participate in the publication or edition in any manner, as well as to edit or to publish non-periodical printed matter;

7. the loss of the capacity to hold public lectures or meetings;

8. the loss of the capacity to work in institutions of education or art or in other organizations of similar nature;

9. the loss of the capacity to be an employer or a partner;

10. the loss of the capacity to engage in a liberal profession;

11. the loss of the capacity to be a member of a board of directors (administrative council) of corporations and of co-operatives;

12. the loss of the capacity to hold a leading position in a private enterprise.

The violation of any of the prohibitions laid down in this article shall be punished by imprisonment for a period from 1 week to 3 months.

§16

1. Punishment by incarceration cannot be reduced beyond the minimum term provided by law, nor can its nature be modified into a punishment of a milder type.

2. The court can reduce the punishment below the minimum term provided by law and convert the same into a punishment more lenient in its nature, and, in cases deserving particular consideration, abstain from the imposition of punishment, if it is generally known or can immediately be proved that the accused acted with the intention of furthering the interests of the Czech and Slovak nation or of the Czechoslovak Republic or of its Allies or of some other general purpose, or if he deserves reward because of his later activities relating to the liberation of the Republic from the occupation power or to the restitution or diminution of the damage caused by the enemy, and if he after his conversion has followed the path of duty. This provision cannot be applied if the damage caused by the perpetrator is disproportionately great if compared with the profit resulting from his activities.

§17

Neither prosecution nor the serving of sentences in respect of any of the crimes punishable by virtue of this Edict shall be nullified by lapse of time.

§18

The period of the increased threat to the Republic shall be considered as the period from 21 May 1938 to a date which shall be determined by a government ordinance.

§19

The crimes punishable under this Edict shall always be considered to be crimes of a particularly despicable nature within the meaning of §1 Subsection 1 of the Law concerning the State Prison of 16 July 1931 No. 123 Comp.

§20

Aid in connection with a crime punishable under this Edict shall be prosecuted in accordance with the criminal statutes in force, subject to the following modifications:

1. in the case of a crime against the State, the aid shall be punished equally with the crime;

2. in the case of a crime of the same nature, the aid by the harboring of intimate persons [i.e. family members, friends] (§39 No. 4 of the Law No. 50/1923 Comp. for the Protection of the Republic) shall constitute a crime and shall be punished by confinement in a penitentiary for a period from one to ten years, and, if the Edict provides the death penalty for the crime itself, by confinement in a penitentiary for a period from five to 20 years;

3. in the case of any other crime the aid shall be punished by confinement in a penitentiary

a) for a period from ten to 20 years, if this Edict provides for the crime itself punishment by death or confinement in a penitentiary for a period of more than 20 years,

b) for a period from one to ten years, if under this Edict the crime itself is punishable by a lesser penalty.

Chapter II
The Special People's Courts

§21

1. The Special People's Courts are competent to adjudge all crimes punishable under this Edict, if the persons listed in §§2 and 3, Subsection 2 are criminally responsible for them as perpetrators, co-actors, conspirators, participants or accessories; in the event that other persons are criminally responsible for them, the Special People's Courts shall be competent to adjudge them if the public prosecutor (§24) moves for leave to institute proceedings against them in the Special People's Courts.

2. The venue of the Special People's Courts shall be prescribed by the provisions of the Codes of Criminal Procedure in force within the territory of the Republic.

The Composition and the Seat of the Special People's Courts

§22

1. The Special People's Courts are composed of a five-member senate which consists of the presiding judge who must be a professional judge (judge from the usual law courts or of courts-martial) and of four laymen (the People's Judges).

2. The presidents of the Special People's Courts, their deputies and the professional judges (Subsection 1) shall be appointed by the President of the Republic who will select them from among the persons whose names have been entered in a roll made out by the District National Committees (okresní národní výbor) for this purpose. The non-professional judges are appointed and selected by reason of another roll made out by the District National Committees.

3. The president of the Special People's Court or his deputy has the duty of setting up the necessary senates and of appointing the substitutes from among the persons listed in Subsection 2.

4. The Special People's Court shall be established at the seat of the District Courts; each senate of a Special People's Court may also convene, if necessary, at any place within the judicial district.

The Local National Committee (místní národní výbor) appoints the persons to execute the death penalties, and their assistants, in the place where the District Court has its seat.

5. A government ordinance shall prescribe the oath to be sworn by the non-professional judges and the amount chargeable by them in respect of expenses and sacrifices of income.

§23

In reaching a decision the non-professional judges shall vote first, and in descending order of age.

The Public Prosecutor

§24

1. The public prosecutor of the Special People's Courts shall be appointed by the government or upon its application by the Minister of Justice for a certain time, for particular cases, or for the entire period of the operation of the court. He shall hold a Doctor's degree in the field of law or shall have passed the three State examinations in law, or as a minimum, the examination in Jurisprudence and shall be among those listed in the roll made out by the District National Committees for this purpose.

2. The public prosecutors for the Special People's Courts are subordinated to the Minister of Justice.

The Procedure Before the Special People's Courts

§25

1. The procedure before the Special People's Courts shall be governed by the principles of procedure before courts-martial in the version laid down in §§26 to 31 of this Edict. In cases where this Edict refers to the provisions of the ordinary procedure such provisions shall be those of the Code of Criminal Procedure in force.

2. An acquittal by a Special People's Courts shall not exclude prosecution before a competent ordinary court, or before the State Court according to the Law No. 68/1935 Comp., or before the competent district court in respect of military treason under Law No. 130/1936 Comp. and to governmental ordinance No. 238/1937 Comp. Such a court proceeds in the matter de novo and the provisions of this Edict which contain substantive law (§§1 to 20) shall apply with the same force as if the guilty person had been brought before the ordinary court in the first instance (§21). The motion to proceed against the accused in the aforesaid manner must be made within three months from the date of his acquittal.

§26

1. The proceedings before the Special People's Court shall commence upon motion of the public prosecutor (§24). Pregnant women shall not be brought before the Special People's Court during the period of their pregnancy.

2. The entire proceedings against a single accused shall be carried on, if possible without interruption, before the Special People's Court. The proceedings against a single accused shall not consume more than three days. This period shall commence at the moment when the accused is brought before the court.

3. If the Special People's Court has not reached a decision within the three-day period it shall forward the case to the competent ordinary court (§23 Subsection 2). In such case it shall also decide whether or not the accused shall remain in pre-trial custody.

4. If the accused fails to appear before the court for any reason whatsoever or is unable to appear, then the public prosecutor may move to try the accused in absentia. In such case the court must appoint a counsel for the accused.

§27

The proceedings before the Special People's Court are oral and public. The accused has the right to appoint a counsel or to request the court to do so for him, if he is without means. If the accused fails to avail himself of this right, the court will appoint a counsel on his behalf. The accused as well as the court may also appoint as counsel a person whose name is not entered in the list of attorneys, provided that he has the degree of a doctor of law or has passed the three State examinations of law or, as a minimum, the examination of Jurisprudence.

§28

1. The trial before the Special People's Court is to commence after the case has been called and the data necessary have been recorded with a statement by the public prosecutor, setting forth the charges and particulars being brought against the accused. The interrogation of the accused and the evidence shall in general be governed by the provisions of the Code of Criminal Procedure. The records of the interrogation of co-actors and of witnesses and the opinions of expert witnesses may be read, provided that the President of the Senate deems such reading to be appropriate.

2. The proceedings shall only relate to the act or the acts in respect of which the accused has been brought before the Special People's Court. Acts not punishable under this Edict shall not be in issue. If such acts are prosecuted at a later date before the Special People's Court or before the ordinary court, or before the State Court or the District Court which is competent for the adjudication of military treason, the punishment imposed by the Special People's Court shall be taken into consideration in determining the measure of punishment to be imposed.

3. The proceedings before the Special People's Court shall not be delayed by the assessment of damages which have been caused by the criminal act.

4. The discovery of co-actors shall not be neglected but it shall not be allowed to result in delaying the judgment and the execution thereof.

5. After all of the evidence has been introduced, the public prosecutor shall evaluate its weight and shall make his final motion. Thereupon the presiding judge shall give the accused and his counsel occasion to argue the case of the defense. If the public prosecutor responds, the accused and his counsel shall have the last word.

§29

1. Thereafter the court will consider in camera the judgment to be rendered, whereby it will follow the appropriate provisions of the ordinary procedure to the extent that this Edict does not provide otherwise.

2. If the conviction of a crime which is punishable by death under this Edict is based on three votes only, or if the court is convinced that there are circumstances in view of which the death penalty would be disproportionately grave, the court may impose confinement in a penitentiary for a period from 20 years to Life and, in the presence of the prerequisites laid down in §16 Subsection 2, may also apply that provision.

3. The judgment shall be announced in open court immediately following its decision.

§30

The proceedings before the Special People's Court shall be recorded in accordance with the ordinary procedure. Such record shall be signed by all members of the Senate and by the clerk of the court.

§31

1. There shall be no appeal against the judgment of the Special People's Court. An application for pardon shall be without dilatory effect regardless of the person filing such application.

2. In principle the death penalty shall be executed within two hours after judgment has been given. Upon express request of the person convicted, such period may be extended for one hour. If the accused was tried in absentia the death penalty shall be executed within 24 hours after his apprehension.

3. The Special People's Court may also decide that the death penalty shall be executed in public. Such decision shall be rendered in particular if the base manner in which the crime was committed, or the despicable character of the perpetrator, the number of the crimes committed by him, or his position call for such public execution of the judgment. In such case the court may extend the period of two hours but not beyond 24 hours in order to secure the publicity of the penal execution.

Intermediary and Final Provisions

§32

1. The provisions of the Law of 3 May 1934 No. 91 Comp. concerning the imposition of the death penalty and of life term penalties shall not apply to crimes punishable under this Edict.

2. The provisions of the Law of 11 March 1931 No. 48 Comp. concerning criminal jurisdiction over youthful offenders shall remain in force.

§33

The Edict shall become effective on the date of its publication and shall remain in force for a period of one year unless it be modified or amended or the period of its effectiveness be reduced or extended by the competent legislative authorities.

§34

This Edict will be carried out by all members of the Government.

[sgd.:]

Dr. Beneš

David, Gottwald, Siroký, Dr. Srámek, Ursíny, gen. Svoboda, Dr. Ripka, Nosek, Dr. Srobár, Dr. Nejedlý, Dr. Stránský, Kopeckýy, Lausman, Duris, Dr. Pietor, gen. Hasal, Hála, Dr. Soltéesz, Dr. Procházka, Majer, Dr. Clementis (auch für Min. Masaryk), gen. Dr. Ferjencik, Lichner

Decree of President Dr. Beneš of August 2, 1945
concerning the right to Czechoslovak citizenship of persons of German and Magyar nationality
(Decree No. 33)

With regard to the proposal of the Government and in accordance with the Agreement with the Slovak National Council, I decree:

§1

1. Czechoslovak citizens of German or Magyar nationality who acquired German or Magyar citizenship under the regulations of the foreign occupational forces shall have lost their Czechoslovak citizenship by so doing.

2. The other Czechoslovak citizens of German or Magyar nationality shall lose their Czechoslovak citizenship on the day this edict comes into force.

3. This edict does not apply to Germans or Magyars who, during the time of increased threat to the Republic (§18 of the Edict of the President of the Republic, dated June 19, 1945, concerning the punishment of National Socialist criminals, traitors and their accomplices and concerning the Special People's Courts), registered as Czechs or Slovaks during the official census.

4. Czechs, Slovaks and persons of other Slav nationalities who during that time professed themselves Germans or Magyars under pressure or under extenuating circumstances shall not be adjudged Germans or Magyars insofar as the Ministry of the Interior, after a thorough examination of the facts quoted, approves the attestation of national reliability as issued by the appropriate District National Committee.

§2

1. Persons to whom the provisions of §1 are applicable, and who prove that they remained loyal to the Czechoslovak Republic, that they never committed any offence against the Czech and Slovak people, and that they either participated actively in the fight for liberation or suffered under the National Socialist or fascist terror, shall retain Czechoslovak citizenship.

2. The application for a certificate stating that Czech citizenship may be retained can be submitted to the appropriate District National Committee within 6 months of the day this Edict comes into force and, if the applicant resides abroad, can be submitted to the appropriate consular authorities. The result of the application shall be decided by the Ministry of the Interior after considering the recommendation of the Provincial National Committee and, in Slovakia, the proposal of the National Council. The persons in question shall be considered as Czechoslovak citizens until a final decision is made, provided that the District National Committee or the authorities representing it issue a certificate stating the circumstances mentioned above.

3. The retention of Czechoslovak citizenship in the case of Czechoslovak military persons of German or Magyar nationality shall be decided on ex officio in the shortest possible time by the Ministry of the Interior after considering the recommendation of the Ministry of National Defence. Until the official decision is made they shall be considered as Czechoslovak citizens.

§3

Persons who have lost their Czechoslovak citizenship under §1 may apply to the appropriate District National Committee or the authorities representing it for restitution within 6 months of the date which will be appointed in the promulgation of the Ministry of the Interior and published in the Compilation of Statutes and Enactments. The Ministry of the Interior, after considering the recommendation of the Provincial National Committee - in Slovakia, after considering the recommendation of the Slovak National Council - shall decide the result of such an application after an objective consideration of the case; it shall not approve an application, however, if the applicant has violated his duties as a Czechoslovak citizen. Provided that no Government Decrees stipulate otherwise, the general regulations concerning the acquisition of Czechoslovak citizenship shall apply also to these cases.

§4

1. For the purposes of this Edict, married women and juveniles shall be judged separately.

2. Applications under §3 submitted by the wives and underage children of Czechoslovak citizens are to be judged with lenience; until a final decision is made the applicants are to be considered as Czechoslovak citizens.

§5

Czechs, Slovaks and members of other nations, who applied for German or Magyar citizenship during the time of the increased threat to the Republic (§18 of the Edict of the President of the Republic No. 16/1945, Compilation of Statutes and Enactments) without being forced to do so by reason of pressure or special circumstances, shall lose their Czechoslovak citizenship as of the day on which this Edict comes into force.

§6

This Edict shall become effective as of the date of its publication. It will be carried out by the Minister of the Interior conjointly with the Secretary of State for Foreign Affairs and the Minister of National Defence.

[sgd.:]

Dr. Beneš   Fierlinger

Masaryk   Nosek   General Svoboda

The instructions of the German (Hungarian) occupation forces
according to which the nationality
of Czechoslovak citizens of Czechoslovakia was regulated

1. The treaty between Czechoslovakia and Germany of November 20th, 1938, No. 300, Compilation of Statutes and Enactments concerning the problems of nationality and option (the so-called Berlin Treaty).

2. The edict of March 16th, 1939, concerning the establishment of the Protectorate Bohemia and Moravia and the regulation of April 20th, 1939, RGBl. I, pg. 815, concerning the acquisition of citizenship by former Czechoslovak citizens of German nationality.

3. The regulation of July 6th, 1941, RGBl. I, pg. 308, deciding citizenship in connection with the Protectorate Bohemia-Moravia.

4. The regulation of March 4th, 1941, RGBl. I, pg. 118, concerning the German population statistics and the nationality in the Eastern territories annexed (valid for Czechs).

5. Regulation of October 3rd, 1939, RGBl. I, pg. 1997, concerning the recognition of citizenship of the Protectorate Bohemia-Moravia.

6. The treaty between the Czechoslovak Republic and Hungary of February 18th, 1939, No. 43, Compilation of Statutes and Enactments I-i 1939, concerning the problems of nationality and option.

7. Article VI/1939 of the law of June 23rd, 1939, concerning the annexation of Carpatho-Ukraine to the territories of Hungary.

See also:
a) RGBl. II 1939, page 895 (German-Czechoslovak treaty concerning problems of nationality and option);
b) RGBl. I 1938, page 1641 (Law concerning reunion of Sudeten German territories with Germany);
c) RGBl. I 1939, page 205 (Regulation concerning citizenship in Sudeten German territories).

Decree of President Dr. Beneš of October 25, 1945
concerning the confiscation of enemy property
and the Funds of National Renovation
(Decree No. 42)

With regard to the proposal of the Government and in accordance with the Agreement with the Slovak National Council, I decree:

Part I
Confiscation of Enemy Property

§1
Extent of the Property Confiscated

1. Any immovable and movable property shall be confiscated without any compensation, to the benefit of the Czechoslovak Republic, and to the extent that this has not been effectuated until now, in particular property rights (as claims, securities, immaterial rights) which on the day of the factual termination of the German and Hungarian occupation was owned or which is still owned:

(1) by the German Reich, the Kingdom of Hungary, by juristic persons incorporated under the public laws of Germany or Hungary, by the German National Socialist Party, by the Magyar political parties and other groups, organizations, enterprises, institutions, associations, funds and property of these regimes or connected therewith, as well as of other German or Magyar juristic persons, or

(2) by natural persons of German or Magyar nationality with the exception of persons who prove that they adhered faithfully to the Czechoslovak Republic, that they never committed any offense against the Czech and Slovak people and that they either participated actively in the combat for their liberation, or suffered under the National Socialist or fascist terror, or

(3) by natural persons who have displayed activities directed against the sovereignty, the independence, the integrity, the democratic-republican system, the security and defense of the Czechoslovak Republic, who have instigated such activities or have solicited other persons to carry on such activities, who, by any manner, have intentionally supported the German or Magyar occupants or during the period of the increased threat to the Republic (§18 of the Edict of the President of the Republic, dated June 19, 1945, Compilation of Statutes and Enactments No. 16, Concerning the

Punishment of National Socialist Criminals, Traitors and Their Accomplices, and Concerning the Special People's Courts) have favored the Germanization or Magyarization within the territory of the Czechoslovak Republic or who have taken a hostile position against the Czechoslovak Republic or against the Czech or Slovak people, as well as by persons who have tolerated such activities by persons who have administered their property or enterprises.

2. The provisions of Subsection 1, No. 3 apply also to juristic persons to the extent that natural persons who are members thereof or share in the property or the enterprise (shareholders) are responsible for the steps taken by the board representing the juristic person or that these persons have failed to use the appropriate diligence in the selection and supervision of the board.

3. Likewise subject to confiscation is any property which during the period subsequent to September 29, 1938 has been owned by persons mentioned in Subsections 1 and 2 and which during the time set forth in Subsection 1 Sentence 1 has been owned or is still owned by persons in the possession of whom it would not be subject to confiscation unless the inclusion of such property in the confiscation would not comply with the principles of equity.

4. The competent District National Committee shall determine whether or not the prerequisites of the confiscation under this Edict exist. The decision can be served by publication, even if the prerequisites of §33 of the Government Ordinance dated January 13, 1928, Comp. No. 8, concerning the procedure in matters which do not fall within the competence of political authorities (administrative procedures), are not complied with. An appeal can be filed against the decision of the District National Committee with the Provincial Committee, in Slovakia with the competent authority of the Slovak National Council. The Provincial National Committee (in Slovakia the competent authority of the Slovak National Council) may - even in the course of the proceeding - assume the carrying out of the procedure and decide the matter as the first instance. If the Provincial National Committee (in Slovakia the competent authority of the Slovak National Council) decides in this manner as first instance, an appeal may be filed against its decision with the Ministry of the Interior. The Minister of the Interior is authorized to prescribe the manner in which a decision shall be rendered in accordance with this subsection.

§2
Exemptions from Confiscation
and the Granting of Compensation

1. That part of the movable property owned by persons listed in §1 Subsection 1, Nos. 2 and 3 which is indispensably necessary to cover the livelihood or to carry on the occupation of such persons and the members of the family thereof, as clothing, featherbeds, linen, household furniture, food, and tools is exempted from the confiscation. Particulars concerning the extent of such property shall be prescribed by the Government by ordinance.

2. The Government may prescribe by ordinance that the property of a particular category of persons falling under the provisions of §1 shall be exempted in whole or in part from the confiscation.

3. Property which has been lost by persons not covered by the provisions of §1 during the time after September 29, 1938 by reason of the pressure of the occupation or in consequence of the national, racial or political persecution is not subject to confiscation.

4. In the case of confiscation of property owned by a juristic person, persons who hold shares of stock shall be entitled to a proportional compensation, provided that they are not subject to the provisions of §1 Subsections 1 and 2. Particulars shall be prescribed by the Government by ordinance.

5. If persons whose property is subject to confiscation share in the ownership with persons who are not subject to the provisions of §1, and their share should exceed one half of the total, then the entire property is subject to confiscation. Persons who are not subject to §1 are entitled to be compensated by delivery of items of the same kind and the same value as their share, and if this should not be possible they shall be compensated in money.

Part II
Fund of National Regeneration

§3
Establishment and Organization of
the Funds of National Regeneration

1. To facilitate the temporary administration of the property confiscated and the tasks connected with its disposition, a Fund of National Regeneration (hereafter referred to only as "Fund") shall be established with every settlement office. This Fund shall be an independent legal entity. To the extent that the charter of the Fund (Subsection 7) does not provide otherwise, it is represented by the Procuratory for Finances.

2. The Fund is controlled by a president who shall be appointed by the government with regard to the proposal of the Minister of the Interior after hearing the president of the settlement office. The president represents the Fund. In his absence he shall be substituted by the vice principal of the Fund, who will be appointed by the Government by proposition of the president of the Fund and after hearing the president of the settlement office.

3. The Fund of National Regeneration is controlled by the settlement office with which it has been established. The president of the settlement office and his deputy together with the president and the vice president of the Fund shall form a council which shall determine the manner in which the respective settlement office and the Fund attached thereto shall operate. Decisions of the council require a majority of more than one half of the votes. In case that the votes are equal, the Central Commission for Interior Colonisation shall decide.

4. The agenda are taken care of by the employees of the respective settlement offices who insofar are subject to the directions of the president of the Fund.

5. The money upon which the Funds are based shall consist of advance payments out of governmental means, further of deposits and claims due confiscated by virtue of this Edict, and of the compensations eventually received for the properties allotted.

6. The Funds shall not be required to make any payments for the performance of official acts.

7. The charters of the Funds and the standing orders governing them shall be prescribed by the Government by ordinance upon application of the Central Commission for Interior Colonisation.

§4
The Permanent Advisory Board and Economic Control

1. A Permanent Advisory Board shall be established with every Fund. Representatives shall be delegated to the Permanent Advisory Board which shall be established with the Fund in the settlement office in Prague by the Ministries of the Interior, of Finance, for National Defense, for Education and Culture, of Justice, for Industry, for Agriculture, for Interior Trade, for Traffic, for Labor Protection and Social Welfare, for Health and Food, as well as by the Economic Council. The representatives of the delegate of the Slovak National Council as well as a representative of the Economic Council are members of the Permanent Advisory Board which shall be established with the Fund in the settlement office at Pressburg (Bratislava). The Central Commission for Interior Colonisation shall determine the functions of the Permanent Advisory Board and shall enact the bylaws for it.

2. The economic administration of the Funds is subject to the control of the Ministry of Finance and of the highest comptroller's office. Any disposition of means belonging to the Funds, to which the representative of the Ministry of Finance (in Slovakia, the delegate for finances of the Slovak National Council) objects, shall not be effected before the conflict has been settled in negotiations among the respective ministries and, in case this should prove to be unsuccessful, has been terminated by a decision of the Government.

§5
Operational Scope of the Funds

1. In particular, the Funds are competent:

(1) to record the property confiscated by virtue of this Edict. The District National Committees must record any property confiscated by virtue of this Edict within their districts and must submit such records to the competent district office of the settlement office as well as to the competent Fund. The evidence necessary for such recording shall be submitted by the Local National Committees. Everyone who possesses, administers, or retains property confiscated must declare such

property for recording upon request of the District National Committee and must take proper care of such property as long as the Funds entrusted therewith or the public authority does not dispose otherwise;

(2) in agreement with the competent National Committees and the Ministries and through them to take such actions as are necessary for the taking under control, assumption, deposition, preservation and administration of this property, if that has not been done already. The regulations governing such actions shall be enacted by the settlement office upon consent of the Funds. Upon request of the Fund the competent court will order entries to be made in the public files and registers indicating the confiscation;

(3) to record and to satisfy claims against property confiscated in compliance with the regulations which will be enacted by the Government by ordinance; the Government shall not be liable for any claim which has not been satisfied hereunder;

(4) to effectuate the transfer of the property confiscated by reason of the basic plans (§6 Subsection 1) and of the final allotment decree (§8 Subsection 6);

(5) to negotiate loans for the receivers of allotments in accordance with regulations enacted by the Central Commission for Interior Colonization.

2. The Fund has the right to supervise the economic management of the national custodians and to request the competent authorities to cancel their appointment and to apply for their appointment.

Part III
Distribution of the Property Confiscated

Section 1
Basic Plans and Allotment Decrees

§6

1. The settlement office, with the consent of the competent ministries and of the Economic Council (in Slovakia with the consent of the competent delegate of the Slovak National Council) and after hearing the competent economic associations (in Slovakia the competent economic organisations) and the Central Council of Business Associations (in Slovakia the Center of Business Associations) shall establish basic plans in which it shall be defined in particular:

a) how many small properties shall be allotted at the particular localities and how the remainder shall be disposed of;

b) what properties of medium size shall be allotted and how the remainder shall be disposed of,

c) how industrial property and other large properties shall be disposed of.

2. In the manner set forth in the foregoing subsection, the settlement offices prepare propositions for particular allotment decrees according to the nature of the property confiscated which is subject to distribution, and determine therein the characteristics to be followed in order to distinguish properties of small, medium and large size, the qualifications to be possessed by persons to whom property of the aforementioned category is allotted, the rules to be followed in determining the amount of the compensation and payment thereof by the person to whom property has been allotted, the terms and conditions upon which an allotment can be secured or the property allotted can be taken away, and how the property shall be disposed of. Upon these factors the Government will render the particular allotment decrees. Competent for the carrying out of these decrees is the settlement office, which may carry them out gradually according to the extent and the nature of the property allotted.

3. On the basis of the basic plans (Subsection 1) and the allotment decrees (Subsection 2), the allotment and compensation plans (§§10 to 12) shall be drawn up. It shall be the object of the settlement office to examine whether the allotment and compensation plans comply with these prerequisites, in which case they will approve them. Allotments which are contrary to the basic plans or the allotment decrees will be eliminated from the allotment and compensation plans by the settlement office. As long as the plans have not been approved by the settlement office from this perspective, the final approval or correction of the allotment and compensation plan cannot be effectuated by the competent authority.

4. An allotment which is contrary to the basic plan, to the particular allotment decree, or to the allotment and compensation plans approved or corrected in the appropriate manner (§10 Subsection 3), shall be invalid. The Fund may cause the reversal of the invalid allotment decree by the superior authorities and, if it is an allotment decree by the Ministry, by the Central Commission for Interior Colonisation within a period of 6 months as from the time of the delivery of the final allotment decree (§8 Subsection 6).

Section 2
Allotment Procedure

§7
Qualifications of Applicant

1. Individual assets will be allotted (§8) against compensation to qualified applicants, who shall acquire ownership thereby, from the property confiscated by virtue of this Edict.

2. Assets may be allotted to provinces, districts, communities, and other public corporations, in particular to corporations (§6 Subsection 2).

3. In allotting property confiscated, the following persons shall be given particular consideration: participants in the national resistance and their surviving relatives, persons who suffered damage by reason of the war and by reason of the national, racial or political persecution, persons who returned to the territory near the border which they had had to leave or who returned to their homeland from abroad and persons who took residence in the remaining territory of the Czechoslovak

Republic as consequence of the annexation. The prerequisites of this privileged status must be properly proved.

§8
Allotment Decree

1. By view of the final allotment plans (§§10 to 12) the small properties are allotted by the District National Committee, the medium-sized properties by the Provincial National Committee (in Slovakia, by the competent authority of the Slovak National Council), industrial property and the large properties by the competent Ministry (in Slovakia, with the consent of the competent delegate of the Slovak National Council).

2. The allotment decree shall show:

a) the items comprising the property allotted,

b) the rights and privileges connected with the allotment,

c) the obligations to be assumed by the allotment receiver,

d) the date on which the property allotted is transferred,

e) the amount of compensation (the price of acquisition) and the manner of payment thereof,

f) possible restrictions imposed upon the allotment receiver or other conditions imposed upon him.

3. The allotment receiver shall not be liable for obligations accrued to the property allotted to him, provided that they have not been assumed by him after receiving the allotment decree.

4. An applicant who deems himself damaged by virtue of the District National Committee's allotment decree has the right to file an appeal with the Provincial National Committee (in Slovakia, with the competent authority of the Slovak National Council). The final decision on appeal is rendered by the Provincial National Committee (in Slovakia, by the competent authority of the Slovak National Council).

5. An applicant who deems himself damaged by virtue of the allotment decree of the Provincial National Committee (or of the competent authority of the Slovak National Council) has the right to file an appeal with the competent Ministry.

6. The authority which has decided on the allotment forwards the allotment decree which has become res judicata to the competent Fund which carries out the transfer of the property allotted.

§9
Allotment Commission

1. Upon request of the settlement office the Local National Committee in the district of which the property confiscated is located, calls by publication in the manner usual in the locality and by publication in the Official Gazette of the settlement office, for persons interested in allotments to file applications. The applications shall be filed with the Local National Committee. From these applicants who comply with the conditions for allotment (§6 Subsection 2) as well as from the members of the Local National Committee who are not applicants, the Local National Committee appoints the local allotment commission which shall consist of at least 3 and not more than 10 members of whom the applicants shall not have the majority. Membership in such local allotment commissions is a honorary position. The Local National Committee may cancel the appointment of the members of the commission at any time. The president of the local allotment commission is elected by the Local National Committee from among its members. In communities with a population not exceeding 10,000 persons, the Local National Committee also appoints representatives of the economic associations (in Slovakia of the appropriate economic organisations) and of the Central Council of Business Associations (in Slovakia of the Center of Business Associations) as members of the local allotment commission. If the appointment of a member is rescinded or his membership ceases for another reason, a new member shall be elected from the same group from which the member to be replaced came. In the case of gradual carrying-out of the allotment decree (§6 Subsection 2, last sentence) different allotment commissions may be appointed for the individual kinds of property.

2. Upon request of the settlement office the District National Committee in the district of which the property confiscated is located, calls by publication in the manner usual in the district and by publication in the Official Gazette of the settlement office, for persons interested to file applications. The applications shall be filed with the District National Committee. From the applicants complying with the conditions for allotment (§6 Subsection 2) and from the representatives of the District National Committee, from the economic associations (in Slovakia, from the appropriate economic organizations) and from the Central Council of Business Associations (in Slovakia, the Center of Business Associations) the District National Committee appoints an allotment commission which shall consist of not more than 10 members among whom applicants for allotment shall not have the majority. To the members of the district allotment commission the provisions concerning the members of local allotment commissions apply *mutatis mutandis*. The president of the district allotment commission is elected by the District National Committee from amongst its members.

3. The appointment of members of the local allotment commission shall be checked and approved by the District National Committee, the appointment of members of the district allotment commission shall be checked and approved by the Provincial National Committee (in Slovakia by the competent authority of the Slovak National Council).

4. The settlement office prescribes the rules governing the structure, the organization and the activities of the local and district allotment commissions and prescribes the bylaws for them.

§10

1. The local allotment commission sets up an allotment plan for the small properties designated for allotment within the district of the Local National Committee together with an estimate of the compensation to be claimed for the property allotted. It shall make available the plan for public inspection in the premises of the Local National Committee for a period of 15 days and at the same

time shall call attention to the opportunity for such public inspection by notice which shall appear on the official board of the Local National Committee as well as in the Official Gazette of the settlement office on the first day of its exhibition, together with an instruction concerning the objections which may be raised thereto. Any Czechoslovak citizen more than 18 years old has the right to raise objections to such allotment plan and to the compensation proposed with the local allotment commission within a period of 16 days, such period commencing on the last day the plan is exhibited. After expiration of the period for objections the local allotment commission submits the allotment plan together with the proposed compensation and the objections filed with its statements thereto to the district allotment commission for examination. At the same time it forwards a copy of the allotment plan and of the compensation proposed to the settlement office (§6 Subsection 3), to the tax administration and to the District National Committee (Subsection 2).

2. The district allotment commission examines the allotment plans and compensation proposals with due regard to the objections raised. It will request statements by the tax administration, by the technical authorities and by the price stabilization authorities of the competent District National Committee to the question whether the compensations proposed in the plans are appropriate and will notify them of the time that hearings on the individual allotment plan will be held in order to enable them to participate in such hearings.

3. The allotment and compensation plan for the small properties shall be the basis for the allotment, as soon as it has been approved or adjusted, if necessary, by the district allotment commission upon consideration of the position taken by the settlement office (§6 Subsection 3).

§11
The Allotment Plans for Medium-Sized Properties

1. The district allotment commission sets up an allotment plan for the medium-sized properties designated for allotment within the area of the District National Committee together with a proposition concerning the compensation to be claimed for the property allotted. It shall make available the plan for public inspection in the premises of the District National Committee for a period of 15 days and at the same time shall call attention to the opportunity of such public inspection by notice which shall appear on the official board of the District National Committee as well as in the Official Gazette of the settlement office on the first day of its exhibition, together with an instruction concerning the objections which may be raised thereto. Any Czechoslovak citizen more than 18 years old has the right to raise objections to such allotment plan and compensation proposition with the district allotment commission within a period of 15 days, such period commencing on the last day the plan is exhibited. After expiration of the period for objections the district allotment commission submits the allotment plan together with the compensation proposal and the objections filed with its statement thereto, to the Provincial National Committee (in Slovakia, to the competent authority of the Slovak National Council) for examination. At the same time it forwards a copy of

the allotment plan and of the compensation proposal to the settlement office (§6 Subsection 3), to the tax administration and to the District National Committee (Subsection 2).

2. The Provincial National Committee (in Slovakia, the competent authority of the Slovak National Council) requests statements by the tax administration and by the technical as well as price stabilization authorities of the competent District National Committee on the question whether such compensations are appropriate, and notifies them of the time the hearing on the individual allotment plan will be held in order to enable them to participate in such hearings. It examines the allotment plans and compensation proposals submitted with due regard to the objections raised and to the statements of the tax administration and of the technical authorities of the District National Committees, having the power to modify such plans if important public, particularly national interests require it.

3. The allotment and compensation plan for the medium-sized properties shall be the basis for the allotment after it has been approved or adjusted, if necessary, by the Provincial National Committee (in Slovakia, by the competent authority of the Slovak National Council) upon consideration of the position taken by the settlement office (§6 Subsection 3).

§12
The Allotment Plans for Industrial and Large Properties

1. The Provincial National Committee (in Slovakia, the competent authority of the Slovak National Council) sets up an allotment plan for the industrial property and the large properties designated for allotment within its area together with a proposition of the compensation to be claimed for the property allotted. The plans shall be published in the Official Gazette of the settlement office. Any Czechoslovak citizen more than 18 years old has the right to raise objections to such allotment plan and compensation proposal with the Provincial National Committee (in Slovakia, with the competent authority of the Slovak National Council) within a period of 15 days, such period commencing on the date of the publication of the plan. After expiration of the period for objections the Provincial National Committee (in Slovakia, the competent authority of the Slovak National Council) submits the allotment plan together with the compensation proposal, the objections filed and its own statements thereto to the competent Ministry for examination. At the same time it forwards a copy of the allotment plan and of the compensation proposal to the settlement office (§6 Subsection 3), to the Ministry of Finance, the Ministry for Traffic (Subsection 2) and to the highest price stabilization authority.

2. The Ministry (in Slovakia, with the agreement of the competent delegate of the Slovak National Council) examines the allotment plan and compensation proposal submitted with due regard to the objections and to the statements of the Ministry of Finances and the Ministry of Traffic (public technical administration) as well as to the statements of the highest price stabilization authority which have been requested for the compensation proposal.

3. The allotment and compensation plan for industrial and large properties shall be the basis for the allotment after it has been approved and adjusted, if necessary, by the Ministry (in Slovakia, with the agreement of the competent delegate of the Slovak National Council) upon consideration of the position taken by the settlement office (§6 Subsection 3).

§13
Disposition of the Property Allotted

The property allotted in accordance with §8 may be disposed of, leased or mortgaged only after expiration of the period fixed in the individual allotment decrees. During this period this may be done only with the permission of the Fund.

§14
Payment and its Appropriation

1. The compensation (allotment price) shall be paid by the allotment receivers to the competent Fund in accordance with the allotment decree. On the basis of a certificate issued by the Fund concerning arrears in payment of the compensation, action may be taken either through administrative channels or by a court order.

2. These compensations shall be used for the payment of the obligations resting upon the property confiscated, if these have been acknowledged when the balance was made (§5 Subsection 1 No. 3) and if they have not been assumed by the allotment receiver; the remaining amount shall accrue to the treasury of the Government for the purposes designated.

Part IV
General and Final Provisions

§15
Procedure before the Funds

Government Ordinance Comp. No. 6/1928 shall apply *mutatis mutandis* to the procedure before the Funds.

§16
Transfer of Real Property and of Registered Rights to the Government

The transfer to the Czechoslovak Government of real property and of registered rights which have not been allotted to other persons shall be registered in the public registers by the courts administering the public land registers upon application of the competent Fund and, if property listed in §18 is involved, upon application of the Health Ministry with reference to this Edict.

§17
Scope of this Edict with Respect to Rural Property

This Edict does not refer to such rural property as confiscated in accordance with the Edict of the President of the Republic, dated June 21, 1945, Comp. No. 12, concerning the confiscation and expedited allotment of rural property of Germans, Magyars, as well as of traitors and enemies of the Czech and Slovak people, and confiscated in accordance with the corresponding provisions applicable in Slovakia.

§18
Scope of this Edict with Respect to Property of Health Resorts and of Cure and Treatment Institutions

1. The provisions of parts II and III shall not apply to:

1. cure and treatment institutions,

2. to the following property of health resorts:

a) real estate with springs of natural health or mineral waters, cure gases and emanations, or with deposits of medicinal mud, moor, peat, or other kinds of soil,

b) real estate, enterprises and institutions which serve or are necessary to utilize the natural health springs or mineral waters,

c) the equipment of health resorts,

d) cure lodging enterprises which are primarily used by patients or are designated to be used by them or which are part of the equipment of the health resort,

e) auxiliary institutions of the facilities and enterprises listed under b) to d),

f) all accessories of the enterprises and the equipment listed under b) to d) as well as all property used in their operation.

2. The Minister for Public Health (in Slovakia, the competent authority in the Slovak National Council) will determine the property which shall be covered by the provisions of Subsection 1.

3. The manner in which the property referred to in Subsection 2 shall be disposed of shall be determined by special provisions.

§19
Penalties

1. Who knowingly violates any provisions of this Edict or of the ordinances enacted thereunder, or who participates in activities which tend to interfere with the confiscation or the proper allotment of the property confiscated shall - notwithstanding a criminal court procedure - be punished by the District National Committee by a fine not to exceed 100,000 Kcs or by imprisonment in a prison for a period not to exceed one year, or by both of these penalties. In default of payment of the fine imposed, the convicted persons shall undergo a prison term not exceeding one year which shall be determined according to the nature of the wrong done by him.

2. The prosecution of the offenses listed above shall be barred after the expiration of a period of 3 years.

§20
Cooperation of Public Organs and Authorities

All public authorities have the duty to co-operate upon request with the Funds of the National Renovation and to support them actively in the carrying out of their functions.

§21

This Edict shall become effective on the date of its publication. It will be carried out by all members of the Government.

[sgd.:]
Dr. Beneš Fierlinger

David, Gottwald, Siroký, Dr. Srámek, Ursíny, Masaryk, General Svoboda, Dr. Ripka, Nosek, Dr. Srobár, Dr. Nejedlý, Dr. Stránský, Kopecký, Lausman, Duris, Dr. Pietor, General Hasal, Hála, Dr. Soltész, Dr. Procházka, Majer, Dr. Clementis, General Dr. Ferjencik, Lichner

(The Edict was promulgated on October 30, 1945.)

Estimate of the value of German national property
within the Czechoslovak Republic

A Memorandum concerning the national property left behind by the Sudeten Germans was submitted to the Bavarian Prime Minister Dr. Ehard by the Association for the Protection of Sudeten German Interests in 1947. This Memorandum was assembled by experts at the request of the Bavarian State Chancellery, of the State Refugee Organization and of the German Office for Peace Problems in Stuttgart.

This Memorandum is mainly based on Czechoslovak sources (*Statistical Annual Chronicle of the Czechoslovak Republic*, Prague, 1938) and on the statistical data contained in German and Czech economic publications, as well as on balances and bases for a valuation, calculated by experts from the various economic branches.

Two different dates have been taken as basis for its elaboration, namely September 30th, 1938, that is one day before the transfer of Sudeten German territories to the German Reich, and May 8th, 1945, the day of Germany's capitulation. The increase in national property value occurring between these two dates may be traced back in the first place to the higher valuation of landed property in Germany, in the second place to the intensification of production and increased output as a result of higher wages.

It was calculated for both dates as follows:
on September 30th, 1938: $13.44 billion ($13,440,000,000)
on May 8th, 1945: $19.44 billion ($19,440,000,000)
(The dollar values are based on the exchange value of the Reichsmark in 1938.)

These figures are rendered all the more significant by the comparison of the Sudeten German population with the total population of the Czechoslovak Republic.

According to the census of 1930 there were 3.23 million Sudeten Germans among the 14,729,586 residents in Czechoslovakia (=22.3%). They were therefore not a "minority", but an integral part of the population in Czechoslovakia. In the provinces Bohemia, Moravia and Silesia, which were the only ones of economic importance, there were 3.08 million Germans to 7.59 million Czechs, the Germans thus representing more than one third of the entire population of these provinces. It is also of vital significance that in the Czechoslovak economy the Sudeten Germans had a higher percentage of persons active in industry. Of every 100 Germans practicing a profession, 54 persons were active in industry and commerce. This is a higher percentage than in any other country in the world (the comparative figures are: 49 in Scotland, 48 in England and Wales, 54 in Switzerland, 48 in Belgium and 40 in Germany proper). According to the figures given by the Czech economist Hajda, published in the journal *Pritomnost* in 1927, the Germans controlled 66% of the Czechoslovak coal-mining, 80% of the lignite-mining, 70% of the foundries and steel works, 90% of the textile-machinery factories, 80% of the cement works, 90% of the industry of musical instruments, 80% of the artificial silk industry, 100% of the silk factories, 100% of the trimmings industry, 70% of the chemical industry, 90% of the porcelain factories, 85% of the glass works and 89% of the entire textile industry.

In land, the losses of the Sudeten Germans amounted to 1,150,000 hectares of forest (1 hectare = 2.47 acres) and 1,650,000 hectares of farm land. The amount of the social product for which the Sudeten Germans were responsible may be deduced from these figures.

A closer examination of the basic figures of Sudeten German national property gives the following detailed valuations in the various branches of the economy.

	Value in millions of dollars	
	30. 9. 1938	**8. 5. 1945**
Agriculture and Forestry	3,220.73	4,822.00
Industry	2,393.38	3,824.10
Commerce	308.58	308.58
Handicrafts	600.00	600.00
Hotels, inns, restaurants, health resorts and spas	642.84	734.00
Banks	640.00	3,600.00
Insurance companies	297.64	3,323.00
Cinemas	16.00	16.00
Free professions	6.76	8.80
Private property (real estate)	3,956.00	3,956.00
Property of the public Provincial Government and the State	3,363.60	1,243.20

This break-down does not take into consideration the following:

- a considerable part of the German share of the property of the Czechoslovak Government and the provincial administrations;

- a considerable part of the mineral wealth which, for want of adequate statistical data, could only be estimated in part;

- collections of works of art, libraries and other cultural assets;

- the paper currency in circulation;

- the value of the metal currency and also the cover of the bank-notes, consisting of gold and foreign currency;

- the labor output of those Sudeten Germans who had been forced to work without payment in pits, internment camps, for Czech contractors and Czech farmers, likely amounting to several billion Czech crowns.

The figures given above therefore represent a minimum and not a maximum value. They are a mere inventory of the properties available and do not take into account incalculable values of tradition, of a culture which is hundreds of years old, of education, of foreign relations, of the world-wide reputation of firms or business branches (e.g. the spas of Karlsbad, Franzensbad, Marienbad), of the so-called "free property" and all those creative powers which set in motion the production of the goods listed above. They do not take into account the great loss of those expellees who, unable to practice their professions, will be subjected to a diminution of their productive capacity.

The Memorandum is of importance for the purposes of Germany's *"Lastenausgleich"* (a partial compensation for the German refugees forcibly expelled from the Eastern countries, as laid down in the Potsdam Agreement) as well as in relation to the coming negotiations for a peace treaty. The third law concerning the new order of monetary matters (finances) No. 63, §29 expressly refers to the necessity that the *"Lastenausgleich"*, carried out by German authorities, should take into consideration "especially losses which had been caused by Law No. 5 of the Allied Control Commission and by drawings on behalf of reparations". Undoubtedly this interpretation would include the national property of those Germans who had been expelled from their former homeland, and who have paid in advance a considerable part of the German war reparations by surrendering their entire property.

The Atlantic Charter of August 14, 1941

The President of the United States of America and the Prime Minister, Mr. Churchill, representing His Majesty's Government in the United Kingdom, being met together, deem it right to make known certain common principles in the national policies of their respective countries on which they base their hopes for a better future for the world.

1. First, their countries seek no aggrandizement, territorial or other;

2. Second, they desire to see no territorial changes that do not accord with the freely expressed wishes of the peoples concerned;

3. Third, they respect the right of all peoples to choose the form of government under which they will live; and they wish to see sovereign rights and self government restored to those who have been forcibly deprived of them;

4. Fourth, they will endeavor, with due respect for their existing obligations, to further the enjoyment by all States, great or small, victor or vanquished, of access, on equal terms, to the trade and to the raw materials of the world which are needed for their economic prosperity;

5. Fifth, they desire to bring about the fullest collaboration between all nations in the economic field with the object of securing, for all, improved labor standards, economic advancement and social security;

6. Sixth, after the final destruction of the Nazi tyranny, they hope to see established a peace which will afford to all nations the means of dwelling in safety within their own boundaries, and which will afford assurance that all the men in all the lands may live out their lives in freedom from fear and want;

7. Seventh, such a peace should enable all men to traverse the high seas and oceans without hindrance;

8. Eighth, they believe that all of the nations of the world, for realistic as well as spiritual reasons must come to the abandonment of the use of force. Since no future peace can be maintained if land, sea or air armaments continue to be employed by nations which threaten, or may threaten, aggression outside of their frontiers, they believe, pending the establishment of a wider and permanent system of general security, that the disarmament of such nations is essential. They will likewise aid and encourage all other practicable measures which will lighten for peace-loving peoples the crushing burden of armaments.

[sgd.] Franklin D. Roosevelt   [sgd.] Winston S. Churchill

Text of the United Nations Convention
on the Prevention and Punishment of the Crime of Genocide

[Adopted by Resolution 260 (III) A of the United Nations General Assembly on 9 December 1948.]

The contracting parties having considered the declaration made by the General Assembly of the United Nations in its Resolution 96 (I) dated December 11, 1946, that genocide is a crime under international law, contrary to the spirit and the aims of the United Nations and condemned by the civilized world,

recognizing that at all periods of history genocide has inflicted great losses on humanity, and

being convinced that in order to liberate mankind from such an odious scourge, international co-operation is required,

hereby agree as hereinafter provided.

Article 1. The Contracting Parties confirm that genocide, whether committed in time of peace or in time of war, is a crime under international law which they undertake to prevent and to punish.

Article 2. In the present Convention, genocide means any of the following acts committed with intent to destroy, in whole or in part, a national, ethnical, racial or religious group, as such:
a) Killing members of the group;
b) Causing serious bodily or mental harm to members of the group;
c) Deliberately inflicting on the group conditions of life calculated to bring about its physical destruction in whole or in part;
d) Imposing measures intended to prevent births within the group;
e) Forcibly transferring children of the group to another group.

Article 3. The following acts shall be punishable::
a) Genocide;
b) Conspiracy to commit genocide;
c) Direct and public incitement to commit genocide;
d) Attempt to commit genocide;
e) Complicity in genocide.

Article 4. Persons committing genocide or any of the other acts enumerated in Article 3 shall be punished, whether they are constitutionally responsible rulers, public officials or private individuals.

Article 5. The Contracting Parties undertake to enact, in accordance with their respective Constitutions, the necessary legislation to give effect to the provisions of the present Convention and, in particular, to provide effective penalties for persons guilty of genocide or any of the other acts enumerated in Article 3.

Article 6. Persons charged with genocide or any of the other acts enumerated in Article 3 shall be tried by a competent tribunal of the State in the territory of which the act was committed, or by such international penal tribunal as may have jurisdiction with respect to those Contracting Parties which shall have accepted its jurisdiction.

Article 7. Genocide and the other acts enumerated in Article 3 shall not be considered as political crimes for the purpose of extradition.

The Contracting Parties pledge themselves in such cases to grant extradition in accordance with their laws and treaties in force.

Article 8. Any Contracting Party may call upon the competent organs of the United Nations to take such action under the Charter of the United Nations as they consider appropriate for the prevention and suppression of acts of genocide or any of the other acts enumerated in Article 3.

Article 9. Disputes between the Contracting Parties relating to the interpretation, application or fulfilment of the present Convention, including those relating to the responsibility of a State for genocide or any of the other acts enumerated in Article 3, shall be submitted to the International Court of Justice at the request of any of the parties to the dispute.

Article 10. The present Convention, of which the Chinese, English, French, Russian and Spanish texts are equally authentic, shall bear the date of 9 December 1948.

Article 11. The present Convention shall be open until 31 December 1949 for signature on behalf of any Member of the United Nations and of any non-member State to which an invitation to sign has been addressed by the General Assembly.

The present Convention shall be ratified, and the instruments of ratification shall be deposited with the Secretary-General of the United Nations.
After 1 January 1950, the present Convention may be acceded to on behalf of any Member of the United Nations and of any non-member State which has received an invitation as aforesaid.

Instruments of accession shall be deposited with the Secretary-General of the United Nations.

Article 12. Any Contracting Party may at any time, by notification addressed to the Secretary-General of the United Nations, extend the application of the present Convention to all or any of the territories for the conduct of whose foreign relations that Contracting Party is responsible.

Article 13. On the day when the first twenty instruments of ratification or accession have been deposited, the Secretary-General shall draw up a proces-verbal and transmit a copy of it to each Member of the United Nations and to each of the non-member States contemplated in Article 11. The present Convention shall come into force on the ninetieth day following the date of deposit of the twentieth instrument of ratification or accession. Any ratification or accession effected subsequent to the latter date shall become effective on the ninetieth day following the deposit of the instrument of ratification or accession.

Article 14. The present Convention shall remain in effect for a period of ten years as from the date of its coming into force.

It shall thereafter remain in force for successive periods of five years for such Contracting Parties as have not denounced it at least six months before the expiration of the current period.

Denunciation shall be effected by a written notification addressed to the Secretary-General of the United Nations.

Article 15. If, as a result of denunciations, the number of Parties to the present Convention should become less than sixteen, the Convention shall cease to be in force as from the date on which the last of these denunciations shall become effective.

Article 16. A request for the revision of the present Convention may be made at any time by any Contracting Party by means of a notification in writing addressed to the Secretary-General.

The General Assembly shall decide upon the steps, if any, to be taken in respect of such request.

Article 17. The Secretary-General of the United Nations shall notify all Members of the United Nations and the non-member States contemplated in Article 11 of the following:
a) Signatures, ratifications and accessions received in accordance with Article 11;
b) Notifications received in accordance with Article 12;
c) The date upon which the present Convention comes into force in accordance with Article 13;
d) Denunciations received in accordance with Article 14;
e) The abrogation of the Convention in accordance with Article 15;
f) Notifications received in accordance with Article 16.

Article 18. The original of the present Convention shall be deposited in the archives of the United Nations. A certified copy of the Convention shall be transmitted to all Members of the United Nations and to the non-member States contemplated in Article 11.

Article 19. The present Convention shall be registered by the Secretary-General of the United Nations on the date of its coming into force.

Agreement

signed on the Fourth day of August in the year One Thousand Nine Hundred and Fifty between General LEV PRCHALA, representing the Czech National Committee in London for the one part, and the Joint Committee for the Protection of Sudeten German Interests in Munich, represented by Dr. Rudolph LODGMAN, Mr. R. Reitzner and Mr. H. Schuetz for the other part.

Whereby it is mutually agreed as follows,

1. THAT both parties confirm their belief and support of the ideology of Democracy and reject any and all totalitarian regimes. Both parties consider that the achievement of democratic order in Bohemia, Moravia and Silesia is part of the struggle for a unified Europe. In their opinion, this democratic order can be achieved only if their respective peoples come freely together and employ their right to self-determination.

2. THAT both parties acknowledge the principle that no body of exiles is empowered to enter into agreements deemed to be binding upon their nations and that they are cognizant of the fact that the nation only is competent to decide its own fate and must itself decide freely in which way it wishes to proceed, the final decision being made by the vote of the people.

3. THAT both parties consider that the return to their homes of the expelled Sudeten Germans is right and proper. Being cognizant of the fact that such return can take place only when the Czech people are liberated, both parties are willing to do all within their power to bring about this liberation.

4. THAT both parties reject the theory of collective guilt and ensuing vengeance but hereby establish a claim for the compensation of all damages inflicted upon the Czech and Sudeten German peoples and furthermore demand the punishment of the authors and perpetrators of the crimes which have been committed against the Czech and Sudeten German peoples. Both parties consider these measures to be necessary because the events of the last decades would render it impossible for these two nations to live in harmony together while the present generation still lives unless their worthy sections dissociate themselves from those which are criminal, for the present generation is and was directly affected by the committing of crimes against lives and property, in some cases as authors and perpetrators of crimes and in others as the victims of crime, so that the memory of past events cannot be obliterated even if the will to forget were present until the criminal element is segregated. It is further the opinion of both parties that the execution of the measures outlined above should be in the hands of the respective nationals, for crimes have been committed not only by members of one nation against members of the other nation but also by members of one nation against fellow nationals, to the extent that the good repute and respect in which these nations have been held have been diminished in the eyes of all decent people.

5. THAT in accordance with Clause 2 above the peoples of the two nations shall decide upon their state and political organization as soon as the Czech people are liberated and the Sudeten German people have returned to their homes, and as the pre-requisite for a neighbourly settlement cannot be anticipated today, both parties hereby decide to establish a Federative Committee, which will work to create the required conditions, for the two nations are going to live together in the future, having so lived in Bohemia, Moravia and Silesia during the last thousand years. The two nations shall be equally represented upon their Federative Committee.

6. THAT the draft of this Agreement is subject to ratification by both the Czech National Committee in London and the Joint Committee for the Protection of Sudeten German Interests in Munich, and that after the act of ratification, this Agreement - up to that time treated as confidential - shall be published.

7. THAT this Agreement be recorded in the Czech and German languages, both texts to be treated as authentic, and that both texts be signed by the Presidium of the Joint Committee for the Protection of Sudeten German Interests in Munich and by General Lev Prchala on behalf of the Czech National Committee in London.

AS WITNESS TO THE HANDS OF THE PARTIES HERETO

For the Czech National Committee in London:
PRCHALA
PEKELSKY

For the Joint Committee for the Protection of Sudeten German Interests in Munich: The Presidium:
LODGMAN
REITZNER
SCHUETZ

Munich, 4th August 1950.

RATIFIED by the Joint Committee for the Protection of Sudeten German Interests in Munich, 4th August 1950.
RATIFIED by the Czech National Committee in London, 5th August 1950.

For more books on this subject and many other little-known aspects of German history, please visit us at VersandbuchhandelScriptorium.com and our sister site wintersonnenwende.com !

Featured publications include:

the German original of the present volume:
• *Dokumente zur Austreibung der Sudetendeutschen: Überlebende kommen zu Wort.* Selbstverlag der Arbeitsgemeinschaft zur Wahrung Sudetendeutscher Interessen, 1951. Reprint: Scriptorium, Canada 1999, 2024, print ISBN 9781998785124, ebook ISBN 9781998785131.

• Bertram de Colonna, *Czecho-Slovakia Within,* Thornton Butterworth, London, 1938. Reprint: Scriptorium, Canada 2006, 2022, print ISBN 9781778144523, eBook ISBN 9781778144530.

• Edwin Erich Dwinger: *Death in Poland. The Fate of the Ethnic Germans in September 1939.* Scriptorium, Canada 2004, 2021, print ISBN 9781777543600, eBook ISBN 9781777543617,
as well as the German original:
• Edwin Erich Dwinger: *Der Tod in Polen. Die volksdeutsche Passion.* Eugen Diederichs Verlag, Jena, 1940. Nachdruck: Scriptorium, Canada 2000, 2024, ISBN 9781998785087, eBook ISBN 9781998785094.

• Erhard Wittek: *Long Night's Journey Into Day. The Death March of Lowicz.* Scriptorium, Canada 2015, 2023, print ISBN 9781998785049, eBook ISBN 9781998785056,
as well as the German original:
• Erhard Wittek: *Der Marsch nach Lowitsch.* Zentralverlag der NSDAP., Franz Eher Nachf. G.m.b.H., Berlin 1940. Reprint: Scriptorium, Canada 2010, 2024, print ISBN 9781998785063, eBook ISBN 9781998785070.

More titles are being added regularly in German and English.